A Writer's Reader

Read John
McPhee for
Thursday 6th

"The Language Instinct"

A WRITER'S READER

EIGHTH EDITION

Donald Hall

D. L. Emblen
Santa Rosa Junior College

 LONGMAN

An imprint of Addison Wesley Longman, Inc.

New York • Reading, Massachusetts • Menlo Park, California • Harlow, England
Don Mills, Ontario • Sydney • Mexico City • Madrid • Amsterdam

Executive Editor: Anne Elizabeth Smith
Developmental Editor: Lynne Cattafi
Project Coordination and Text Design: Ruttle, Shaw & Wetherill, Inc.
Cover Designer: Kay Petronio
Electronic Production Manager: Angel Gonzalez Jr.
Manufacturing Manager: Willie Lane
Electronic Page Makeup: Ruttle, Shaw & Wetherill, Inc.
Printer and Binder: R. R. Donnelley & Sons Company
Cover Printer: The Lehigh Press, Inc.

Library of Congress Cataloging-in-Publication Data

A writer's reader / [edited by] Donald Hall, D.L. Emblen. —8th ed.
    p. cm.
  Includes indexes.
  ISBN 0–673–52505–8 (student's ed.). —ISBN 0–673–52333–0
(instructor's ed.)
    1. College readers. 2. English language—Rhetoric. I. Hall,
Donald, [date] . II. Emblen, D. L. (Donald Lewis), [date] .
PE1417.W67 1997
808'.0427—dc20   96–33814
                                               CIP

Student Edition ISBN 0-673-52505-8
Instructor's Edition ISBN 0-673-52333-0

  345678910—DOC—9998

For William R. Booth

Contents

Preface

Reading well precedes writing well. Of all the ancestors claimed by a fine piece of prose, the most important is the prose from which the writer learned his craft. Writers learn craft, not by memorizing rules about restrictive clauses, but by striving to equal a standard formed from reading.

A composition course, then, must be two courses: one in reading, another in writing. If students lack practice in writing, they are usually unpracticed readers as well. Most students lack quality of reading as well as quantity; and if we assert that good models help us, we admit that bad models hurt us. People who read bad prose twelve hours a week—newspapers, popular fiction, textbooks—are as ill served as people who read nothing at all. Surely most textbooks, from freshman handbooks through the text for Psych 101, encourage the illusion that words merely stand in for ideas, or carry information on their backs—that words exist for the convenience of thinking much as turnpikes exist for the sake of automobiles.

This barbarism underlies the vogue of speed reading, which urges us to scan lines for comprehension, ignoring syntax and metaphor, ignoring image and feeling and sound. If we are to grow and to learn—and surely if we are to write well—we must learn to read slowly and intimately, and to read good writing. We must learn to read actively, even aggressively, without the passivity derived from watching television. The active reader questions as he reads, subjects each author's ideas to skeptical scrutiny, and engages the writer in dialogue as part of the reading process.

For language embodies the human psyche. Learning to read—that privilege so recently extended to the ancestors of most of us—allows us to enter human history. In books we perceive the gesture, the pulse, the heartbeat, the pallor, the eye movement, the pitch, and the tone of people who lived before us, or who live now in other places, in other skins, in other habits, customs, beliefs, and ideas.

Language *embodies* the human psyche, which includes ideas and the feelings that properly accompany ideas. There is no sleight-of-mind by which the idea may be separated from its body and remain alive. The body of good writing is rhythm and image, metaphor and syntax, order of phrase and order of paragraph.

A NOTE TO LATER EDITIONS

Many teachers have helped us prepare the many editions of *A Writer's Reader*—in letters, in conversations at colleges all over the country, in responses to the publisher's survey of users. We thank more people than we can list.

We have added considerable material, and we are pleased with the result. We believe that we have made a representative sampling of good prose. We like some pieces more than others, heaven knows, but we believe that all of them provide something to learn from. We have included a wide variety of prose, mostly contemporary but also historical. We hope that young Americans will attach themselves to the body of our history by immersion in its significant utterances.

We have numbered paragraphs for ease of reference. Although *A Writer's Reader* is a collection of essays, we have again violated coherence by including fiction, feeling that the contrast afforded by a few short stories among the essays was useful and refreshing. We have also included several poems, for the same reason. Perhaps we should make an argument for including poems—but let us just say that we enjoy them, and we hope you do too. To satisfy students' curiosity, we have included headnotes to the poems; but we have stopped short of suggesting questions after them, lest we seem to surround a landscape garden with a hundred-foot-high concrete wall.

We have chosen to arrange our essays, stories, and poems alphabetically by author. This arrangement makes for random juxtaposition, irrational sequence, and no sense at all—which is why we chose it. We expect no one to teach these pieces in alphabetical order. We expect teachers to find their own order—which they would do whatever order we attempted to impose. In our first edition we struggled to make a stylistic organization, listing some essays as examples of "Sentences," others as examples of "Paragraphs." For the editors themselves, a year after deciding on our organization, it was no longer clear why essay X was to be studied for its sentences, essay Y for its paragraphs. With a rhetorical organization, one runs into another sort of problem. Although an essay may contain Division, or Process Analysis, or an example of Example, the same essay is likely to use three or four other patterns as well. No piece of real prose is ever so pure as our systems of classification. Thematic organizations, which have their attractions, have similar flaws; is E. B. White's theme in "Once More to the Lake" Mortality? Aging? Youth and Age? or, How I Spent My Summer Vacation?

Our arrangement is more arbitrary than an arrangement by style or rhetoric or theme, and presents itself only to be ignored. At the same time, there are dozens of ways in which these essays (and poems and stories) can be used together. Our Instructor's Manual suggests several combinations. Our Rhetorical Index, printed as an appendix to the text itself, lists single-paragraph examples of rhetorical patterns as well as longer units. We hope that students will find the Rhetorical Index useful. Freshmen who return to their rooms from class, set to write a paper using Comparison and Contrast, sometimes find themselves in need of a concrete example of the assigned pattern to imitate. We have also added a Thematic Index.

Thus, we have tried to supply some useful maps to go with our arbitrary arrangement. Following suggestions from several teachers, we have chosen to represent a few authors by small clusters of their work. We have expanded our representation of writing by scientists. In response to many suggestions, we have looked for short, complete essays in exposition and argument on a variety of topics.

If you miss essays or authors that we eliminated in this edition, please let us know. If there are authors we overlook, whom you would recommend, we solicit your help. Although we intend to remain alert to good prose and to the needs of the classroom, we need help from the outside.

In this eighth edition, we have added a little poetry—in response to the suggestion of several long-time users.

ACKNOWLEDGMENTS

We thank the following users of the first, second, third, fourth, and fifth editions for their helpful comments: Louise Ackley, Maureen Andrews, Tony Ardizzone, Jo Ann Asbury, Ann Avery, Tom Barnwell, Conrad S. Bayley, Jane Berk, Meredith Berman, Dennis Berthold, Barbara Blaha, C. Bogarad, Linda Schafer Emblen, Charles E. Bolton, Charles Bressler, Patrick Broderick, Otis Bronson, Laurel Broughton, Ingrid Brunner, Ed Buckley, Sandra Burns, Jon Burton, Ann Cameron, Marti Carpenter, Richard Cloyed, Edythe Colello, Randy Conine, Steven Connelly, Roger Conner, Rebecca Coogan, Charles L. Cornwell, Valecia Crisafulli, Garber Davidson, Virginia de Araujo, Loretta Denner, Robert Duxbury, Ida Egli, Cirre Emblen, Clovis Emblen, Lee Engdahl, Elizabeth Failla, Ralph Farve, Gala Fitzgerald, Jerome T. Ford, Frances B. Foreman, Susan Forrest, David S. Gadziola, Peggy Gledhill, Ronald Gurney, Barbara Hamilton, Bill Harby, Walter Harrison, Lowell Hawk, Carol T. Hayes, Peter Heitkamp, Allan Hirsh, Samuel G. Hornsby, Jr., Nancy Hunt, John Huntington, C. S. Joyce, Donald Kansch, Gregory Keeler, Jeff Kluewer, Deborah Lambert, John Larner, Karen LeFerre, Kennedy P. Leisch, Richard H. Lerner, Opal A. Lovett, Neillie McCrory, Sherry McGuire, Andrew Makarushka, Steven J. Masello, Richard Maxwell, Kenneth Maue, Deanne Milan, Molly Moore-Kehler, Harriet Napierkowski, John Necker, Wayne

Neel, Jean O'Donnell, Barbara Olive, Stephen O'Neil, Beverly Palmer, John V. Pastoor, Ray Peterson, Roscoe Poland, Muriel Rada, Martha Rainbolt, Shari Rambo, Dennison G. Rice, James Rosen, Harriet Susskind Rosenblum, Robert Schwegler, Terry Shelton, Marvin and Helen Sherak, James Shokoff, Donald K. Skiles, Thomas Skmetzo, Marilyn Smith, Arnold Solkov, Andrew Solomon, Richard Speakes, David A. Spurr, Helen Stauffer, Art Suchoki, Bernard Sugarman, Kathleen Sullivan, Ron Taylor, Jane Bamblin Thomas, Richard Tubbs, E. Guy Turcotte, Darlene Unrue, Peter Valenti, Sara Varhus, Craig Watson, Richard Webster, Joyce Welch, Richard Welin, Dorothy Wells, Joseph F. Whelan, Roberta White, Shirley and Russell White, Edith Wiard, Richard A. Widmayer, Gary Williams, J. J. Wilson, Suzanne Wilson, George Wymer, B. Yu, and Robert Lee Zimmerman.

We would like to thank the following people for their help in preparing the eighth edition: Peter Balbert, Trinity University; Rebecca Brittenham, Rutgers University; Patsy Callaghan, Central Washington University; Vincent Casaregola, Saint Louis University; Frank R. Cunnigham, University of South Dakota; Charles Harrison, San Jacinto College South; Maura Ives, Texas A&M University; Rodney Keller, Ricks College; Deborah K. Richey, Owens Community College.

Donald Hall
D. L. Emblen

A Writer's Reader

Shirley Abbott (b. 1934) was born in Hot Springs, Arkansas. After she graduated from Texas State College for Women, she won a Fulbright to study in France. She has worked as an editor, written essays for magazines, and published her first book, The Art of Food, *in 1977. In 1983 she produced* Womenfolk: Growing Up Down South, *which appeared in 1985. "The Importance of Dissimulation" is her fifth chapter.*

1

SHIRLEY ABBOTT

The Importance of Dissimulation

A Footnote on Southern Belles

Of all the skills a Southern woman is supposed to master, manag- 1
ing men is the most important. She can dispense with all others if necessary. The unified field theory of the science, briefly stated, is that the
first step in managing men is to be a belle. Having captured and married the man of her choice, the belle then turns into a lady. The difference between a lady and a belle is that the former has a multitude of re-
sponsibilities and hence a more solid power base, while the belle
thinks only of herself. Some women become ladies without ever having been belles; some remain belles all their lives, though not always
successfully. A belle, unlike a lady, however, can operate part time.

The ground rules for playing the belle were invented, or at least 2
elaborated, in the drawing rooms and on the verandas of the old plantation South, but the belle's role, like the lady's, received a particularly thick coat of lacquer in the last part of the nineteenth century.
About that time reinventing the Old South took on the status of a pagan ritual, and everybody's grandmother, no matter how plain and shy

she may actually have been, was declared to have been "the belle of three counties." Thomas Nelson Page, whose *Social Life in Old Virginia* set out the qualifications for Southern lady, did not forget to describe the old-time belle: "She was exquisite, fine, beautiful; a creature of peach blossom and snow; languid; delicate, saucy; now imperious, now melting, always bewitching. She was not versed in the ways of the world, but she had no need to be; she was better than that; she was well bred. She had not to learn to be a lady, because she was born one . . . She lived in an atmosphere created for her—the pure, clean, sweet atmosphere of her country home . . . Truly she was a strange being. In her muslin and lawn; with her delicious, low, slow musical speech; accustomed to be waited on at every turn, with servants to do her every bidding; unhabituated often even to putting on her dainty slippers or combing her soft hair, she possessed a reserve force which was astounding. She was accustomed to have her wishes obeyed as commands."

3   Venus on Olympus could hardly have outdone her, at least as Mr. Page described her. Even the daughters of the Czar or the King of France knew how to put on their own shoes. I wonder whether Thomas Nelson Page ever saw such a person or whether he was just trying to play a little joke on his gullible Yankee readers. In any case, he got some of the paraphernalia right, even if he completely missed the point. As a period creation, the belle should by all logic have died out by now: not many young women still lurk around the Corinthian columns flirting their fans and waiting for their beaus to call or lounging at their dressing tables waiting for Mammy to do up the buttons on their kidskin boots. And yet the Southern belle has survived. Not because Southern society is unchanging but because the managerial techniques devised by the belle have proved sound. One of the inexplicable peculiarities of the human species is that females usually outnumber males and must chase them down, whereas among most other animals males invariably outnumber females and must therefore exert themselves to find a mate, usually against rough and even deadly competition.

4   And thus even now, all over the South, belles thrive. They turn out in the hundreds to be presented at debutante balls and grand assemblies and cotillions as authorized, anointed belles. Anointed or not, they inhabit every college campus and sorority house and the corridors of every high school. They roam up and down in their pretty little dresses or maybe their neatly ironed jeans. They look shy. They pull mirrors out of their purses and pat their hair. They do whatever else they can do to attract attention without seeming forward. They speak softly, do not express any but admiring opinions about any given subject, smile. Money and social position are the least of the qualifications for being a belle. It requires instead a natural theatricality, a talent for taking on a special role in a comedy of manners that

will apparently run forever, no matter how transparent its characters and aims.

Belles are not hard to recognize, though it is more than the accent that gives them away. Young women from Michigan and Idaho can be just as beautiful and studiedly feminized when they want to, but they don't go about things in quite the same way as a Southerner—or if they do, that makes them Southern belles. Southern girls invariably, at an early age, catch on to the idea that being honest with men is a basic tactical error. You cannot judge a Southern belle by what you see. She is likely to be ostentatiously charming, polite, enthusiastic, sincere, and soft-headed. That's the standard model, but there are all styles: wisecracking, predatory, corruptible. It takes a keen eye to know what the performance conceals. Sometimes, of course, it is merely vapidity masking vapidity. 5

What the belle is after is not love but power—using the prettiest possible weapons, she is fighting a guerrilla war. Beauty is a valuable asset in the game but not a necessity. Brains also help, although any form of intellectuality will have to be muted or even totally concealed, depending on the situation. As in any underground operation, guile is helpful, as are a cool head and a tough hide. But it is most essential that she remember she is engaged in a covert activity, and the penalty for tipping one's hand is losing the game. This is why Scarlett O'Hara, who is so often cited as the model of the Southern belle, was not a very successful practitioner of the art. Her creator never even intended her to be. From the start, Margaret Mitchell tells us that Scarlett was incapable of keeping her feelings under wraps: "But for all the modesty of her spreading skirts, the demureness of hair netted smoothly into a chignon and the quietness of small white hands, her true self was poorly concealed. The green eyes in the carefully sweet face were turbulent, willful, lusty with life, distinctly at variance with her decorous demeanor." Scarlett is too terrifying to be a belle. I have seen sixteen-year-old amateurs in east Texas in 1979 who could out-belle Scarlett. 6

Being a belle has its risks, the worst of which is that she may be permanently seduced by her own propaganda. She may end up believing that she really is helpless and dumb and dependent, in which case she will cease to be a belle and become a victim. The literature of the South is piled high with the battered corpses of belles, for their strategic and evasive game has tragic potential. Of all the women Tennessee Williams has created, his failed belles are the most vivid. There is Amanda, the mother of Laura and Tom in *The Glass Menagerie*. In her Chicago tenement she is pathetic and crazy and broke; her son hates her, her daughter is lame and shy. Amanda lives on her recollection of an afternoon in Blue Mountain, her probably fictitious Southern manse, when seventeen gentlemen callers arrived all at once, and 7

there weren't enough chairs to sit them down in. She keens their wonderful Mississippi names, "Young Champ Laughlin, Hadley Stevenson
who was drowned in Moon Lake, the Cutrere brothers Wesley and
Blake, that beautiful young Fitzhugh boy from Green County, that
wild Wainwright boy."

8   Blanche du Bois from *Streetcar Named Desire* is the archetype of
all failed beauties, dreaming of lost and supposedly better days, recol-
lecting which fraternity pin it was that she wore in her senior year at
the university, mourning over her lost manor house. Her delusions
and evasions, like Amanda's, are too feeble to serve against the misery
of her life. Like the South, she nourishes herself on false memories.
But she is one of the most touching madwomen ever invented, and
even as she is led offstage to the madhouse, she takes the arm of the
doctor and remarks, "I have always depended upon the kindness of
strangers."

9   Zelda Sayre Fitzgerald was another belle who ended her days in a
madhouse. As F. Scott Fitzgerald's wife, she has turned up in so many
memoirs of the 1920's as to have taken on the identity of a fictional
heroine. In her photographs with her husband, she might have been
some Jazz Age movie queen or a character out of one of his novels. But
she was no work of fiction. She came from Montgomery, Alabama, an
authentic belle by all accounts, in the wild and reckless mode. If there
had been no such thing as a belle, she would have invented it, and she
captured a talented, handsome Northerner who could be counted on
to provide one thing that all belles crave—glamour.

10   But in Nancy Milford's splendid biography of Zelda, another
woman emerges besides the Alabama flapper and the chic young wife
in her fur coat, posing with her husband on some Paris sidewalk. Scott
and Zelda, two perfectly matched people—as Nancy Milford observes,
they even looked alike—were to unhinge one another. They got married in 1920, and in ten years Scott had become an alcoholic, and
Zelda had begun to go incurably insane. There is, of course, no simple
explanation for her madness, but one thread of it was surely her
Southern origins. She was playing an ancient female role perfectly,
and was an even greater success in New York and Paris than she had
been in Montgomery. But along the way she discovered that she had
ambitions of her own. She was a writer herself, and she showed real
promise as a ballet dancer. She began to realize, apparently, that she
could not exist as the adjunct of even the most successful writer in
America. Glamour suddenly ceased to suffice. For a Southern belle,
this must have been the most self-destructive of insights. And so she
lost her mind, dying at last in a fire in a mental hospital in 1948. Not a
dancer, not a writer, not a wife, not a belle.

11   Most belles don't come to a tragic end. In an article in *Playboy* in
1972, Marshall Frady described some of his own skirmishes, as he
called them, with the ladies of the magnolia, by which he clearly

meant not ladies but belles. He was out to sink the notion that belles were either adorable or desirable. Having encountered a number of them, he had observed that the greater their beauty, the greater their stupidity, self-centeredness, and manipulative tendencies. Moreover, he learned that their skills were passed on like some invidious, hemophiliac gene from mother to daughter: among their other tenacious qualities, belles are intent on replicating themselves, and they usually do. What astonished Mr. Frady most was that the classic Southern belle, in all her silky allure, believes that men exist only to serve her purposes. It is hard to believe this came as news to a reporter so perceptive as he or to the editors of *Playboy*, however accustomed they may be to marketing the reverse idea.

Belles can indeed be lethal. Not only to the men they attract or 12 to themselves but to other women. A teacher I know in an integrated Arkansas high school described the teenaged white belle as the most seriously disruptive force in a student body that had barely managed, over the past eight years, to maintain an uneasy peace. This is a newly consolidated high school of about 1,000 students, equipped with every kind of sports facility, gymnasium, and athletic coach imaginable for the boys and the expectable number of pep squads, bands, and cheerleading teams for the nonathletes, including the girls.

As often happens, the black boys were stronger, taller, more 13 skillful than their white teammates, and soon every varsity squad and track team was filled with black players. This, according to the teacher, had worked out splendidly. The black kids had an instant path to achievement, and the white boys had been able to take the competition in a gentlemanly way. In fact, to everyone's delight, the football team began winning championships. The blacks' edge in sports also gave them a political weapon. One year the football players brought an entire season to a halt by striking for better black representation in student government. They won, too.

But, my informant continued, for girls of either race high school 14 is the time to forget other kinds of achievements and start competing for boys. What matters is getting elected homecoming queen or being invited to parties, buying pretty clothes. Obviously, in all such endeavors, the white girls were ahead of the blacks. They were more likely to be categorized as pretty, to have money for clothes and jewelry and hairdos, to have pleasant homes and parents who could afford to give them cars, more likely to have their families behind them with the effort it takes to get elected homecoming queen or chief cheerleader and to have the money for uniforms and long dresses and out-of-town trips. Furthermore—just as their granddaddies had feared—the white girls were, in an unadmitted way, attracting the black boys. Why not? The white girls were all well-dressed and comparatively rich and smooth. There had been no interracial dating, needless to say, but the thought had crossed a few minds. The black girls, though the

teacher didn't say so, were simply being outgunned in the belle department. Hence racial animosities among the girls had become an in-
tractable problem, with both camps attacking and retaliating and even
occasionally growing violent. In an incident last winter, she said, a
black girl had literally jumped on a white one in the corridor and
pulled out a handful of her well-coiffed blond hair. I tried to look appropriately shocked, but I understood too well how the attacker felt.

15   I never made any attempt at becoming a belle, having realized in
early adolescence that I had almost none of the qualifications. But I
grew up watching some virtuosos. In a corner of the South as remote
as Arkansas, with no particular connection to any Tidewater *beau
idéal*, and in a little town such as I came from, which hardly even existed before 1880, it is a miracle that anybody had ever heard of the
idea anyway. There are, after all, plenty of other ways to find a man.
And yet the old notions hung as heavy in the air as the fume of Blue
Waltz cologne around the cosmetic counters at the Kress store. No
matter how lowly your origins or plain your person, you were expected to be a belle.

16   There was a nucleus of girls who scarcely needed any training,
among them a natural talent named Margaret Anne. She was a glorious gold-hued redhead, tending to rotundity at the bottom unless she
kept to a strict diet, but brown-eyed and agreeably diminutive.
Brought up in a rather splendid home (or so it seemed to her friends),
an only child with indulgent and adoring parents, she had already begun to plot by the age of thirteen how to capture a husband and remove herself from this paradise. Her mother, Lula, had been married
at fifteen, and Margaret Anne had come along, as they put it, before
Lula's sixteenth birthday, so the two of them enjoyed their adolescence together, scheming about bridal gowns and whom to pick as
bridesmaids, though the prospective bridegrooms had barely begun to
shave. What Margaret Anne wanted was not so much a husband, however, or even a lot of dance dresses and corsages or a sexual partner—
though she did want all those—but independence. Some control over
her own affairs. Marriage may seem an odd means to that end, but not
the way Margaret Anne figured it. She knew who the boss of her house
was going to be and who was going to have the fun of spending the
money.

17   As she set out, she had the first necessity of her trade well in
hand—not her beauty, which was marginal, but the understanding
that her first job in life was to attract boys. Second, although she was
not stupid, neither was she excessively troubled by her own intelligence or cultural yearnings, which were nil, and she knew better than
to display the slightest proficiency at anything. Third, she had the
quality of being unattainable, of coming from that "pure, clean, sweet
atmosphere" described by Mr. Page. Fourth, she had something Page
completely forgot to mention: she was pious, or appeared to be. That

is the herbal bouquet for the sauce and an excellent mask for all the calculated moves that a belle has to make.

Margaret Anne never missed a Sunday at the Baptist church and 18 following her mother's advice, she sang in the choir. It was a good way to cultivate an otherworldly image as well as to display oneself and to flirt a little tiny bit with the boys in the pews. (In addition to all these benefits, Margaret Anne naturally expected a gold star to be stuck down in the Books Above.) Her silky hair looked very nice against the navy-blue choir robe with its starched white collar. During the preaching, she kept her great serious brown eyes mostly upon the swirling locks and the flapping coattails of the preacher. When the invitation came, and the piano played "Just as I Am," and the stray lambs walked up the aisle to Jesus, her face would glow like an archangel's, and tears would gleam in her eyes. It was worth sitting through church for.

On Saturdays she used to drive around town, ostensibly doing er- 19 rands with her mama, but in fact making herself visible, as she did later by herself, when she had her own car. She always knew where to find the boys, recognized every one of their old Pontiacs and Fords, knew exactly who was at basketball practice or football scrimmage and when, could have told the whereabouts of any one of fifteen boys at any time you asked her, as well as the name of every girl any particular boy had dated over the past year and where they had all gone on the date. She herself was usually going steady, but now and then she broke away. She could hug and kiss and loll and fondle in the back seat of a car for hours, but she had no difficulty controlling herself, and she only fondled the steadies. Her mother had directed her to go to her marriage bed intact, and she did.

Approaching eighteen, she decided to go after the captain of the 20 football team, a massive, handsome, slow-witted blond named Billy Ray who liked to drink beer and go out with his buddies on weekends stealing hubcaps and drag racing. Margaret Anne naturally disapproved of his mischief-making, but she didn't frown too much. His mischief was her means of controlling him. She let him know just how much beer he could drink and how much devilment he could get into without actually provoking her to return his ponderous class ring, which was adjusted to her finger by means of a pad of adhesive tape. (She did return it, two or three times, just to teach her boy a lesson.) But though Jesus had saved her soul, she intended to save her football captain's soul only so far as she chose. What she wanted for a husband was a bad little boy—not too bad, of course—but flawed enough to be unable to do without her, someone with a dependable need to be forgiven. She understood, and gently caused him to understand, just what the trade-offs were going to be.

So they were married, and Billy Ray gave up beer for bourbon be- 21 fore switching to vodka. He quenched his passion for cars by taking over the local Mercury dealership, and he prospered as a salesman because he gave his customers the impression of being too simple-minded to be dishonest. For the same reason, he has made some profitable deals in real estate. He somehow got in on some Title One housing money and contracted to build a series of small-scale high-rises for poor tenants, all of them black and none with any wish to live in an apartment. He now sits on the boards of two banks and is working on a deal to develop some prime lake-shore property. In every respect, he behaves as a man of his station should—he is a grateful husband, a cheerful companion to his friends, a generous if not very interested father, and a heavy drinker who never quite goes over the edge.

22   Margaret Anne, now quite fat but still redheaded, has remained a belle in spite of the arrival of three children. In fact, I have seldom seen so perfect a belle as she has become in middle age. She is always "fixed up," goes twice a week to the hairdresser, and wears plenty of nail polish. (She has seventy-five pairs of shoes—and handbags to match—all lined up in a special closet which she showed me the last time I visited her. When the heels need new tips, she gives the shoes and the matching handbag to the maid.) Fat or not, she wears tight clothes, but her favorite outfits are a demure suit with a frothy blouse for day and a pastel chiffon gown for evening.

23   She gives elaborate, noisy parties (catered) where all the men get drunk. She claims to be a dedicated boozer, but she drinks very little in public or, I suspect, in private. She moves about these massive brawls like a queen at a garden party. I have never heard her discuss any abstract subject with anyone, except that occasionally she will talk politics with the men. When she does, she takes care to display irrationality and passion. In his position, Billy Ray has had to get quite close to local politics and sometimes even woo a congressman or senator. Margaret Anne's political acumen consists, therefore, in admiring the men whose favor her husband is currently courting. Her husband's friends, including the politicians, are all as wild about her as if she were still sixteen. Most of them have tried to "get friendly with her," as she calls it, but she tells me that she just gives them a little pat on the arm, tells them they are the sweetest, dearest, best of things, and then reminds them as gently as possible that she loves Billy Ray. She is not interested in middle-aged men, nor reckless enough to sin with her husband's colleagues.

24   Her fascination, whatever it is composed of, certainly does not consist of wit. But she is amusing—she has raised calculated silliness to the level of an art. She never misses a chance to tell you how scatterbrained she is or that she is taking lessons in disco dancing or that she still has all her pink angora sweaters from high school. She dislikes cooking, but when she does cook, she makes silly things: salads with canned fruit and miniature marshmallows and shredded coconut

in them; things consisting of canned beans and mushroom soup mixed together and topped off with another can of French-fried onions; green and purple jello in layers; unidentifiable mixtures baked in fish-shaped molds and decorated with pimento and green olives; pies concocted from cracker crumbs and frozen lemonade mixes and aerosol whipped cream. Her basic principle is that nothing should look like what it is, and the compliment she most wants to hear is that "it looks too pretty to eat." Billy Ray used to loathe this sort of stuff but was too intimidated to say so. Now he has grown used to it, and in any case they have a cook six days out of seven.

She appears to have gotten everything she wanted out of her mar- 25
riage: several furs (in a subtropical climate), white wall-to-wall carpet in every room, and a succession of casual daytime lovers not chosen from among her husband's acquaintances or his age group. One of these young men, she confided to me, was the father of her third child. She speaks of her love affairs with giggles of innocence, for she is as indestructible a virgin as she ever was, and I am sure she fantasizes that she and her "baby boys," as she calls them with a little smile and shiver, are merely hugging and kissing in the back seat. Her eldest child is a redheaded daughter who of course sings in the choir at the Baptist church and last autumn, though a mere sophomore, was chosen homecoming queen.

_____ CONSIDERATIONS _____

1. Point out a few specific words or phrases in Abbott's paragraph 1 that establish the tongue-in-cheek tone of her essay.

2. What is especially appropriate in Abbott's use of fictional characters, such as Scarlett O'Hara, from _Gone with the Wind,_ and Amanda and Blanche du Bois from Tennessee Williams' plays, to describe and explain the Southern belle?

3. How did the popularity of belles in an integrated high school contribute to racial strife?

4. Find an example of Abbott's use of irony and explain how it contributes to her effort to strip romanticism from her account of Margaret Anne.

5. In what way—see paragraph 22—did Margaret Anne fail to complete the process that Abbott describes in paragraph 1?

6. What is Abbott's point, if any, in closing her essay with a brief account of Margaret Anne's eldest child?

Diane Ackerman (b. 1948) was born in Waukegan, Illinois, attended Penn State, and did graduate work at Cornell University. Her many books of poems are represented in Jaguar of Sweet Laughter: New and Selected Poems *(1991). She has received grants from the National Endowment for the Arts and the Rockefeller Foundation, and has written many essays for the* New Yorker. *Her books of non-fiction include* On Extended Wings *(1985), her memoir of flying, and* A Natural History of the Senses *(1990), from which we take this sensuous essay.*

2

DIANE ACKERMAN
The Importance of Touch

1   Language is steeped in metaphors of touch. We call our emotions feelings, and we care most deeply when something "touches" us. Problems can be thorny, ticklish, sticky, or need to be handled with kid gloves. Touchy people, especially if they're coarse, really get on our nerves. *Noli me tangere,* legal Latin for "don't meddle or interfere," translates literally as "Don't touch me," and it was what Christ said to Mary Magdalen after the Resurrection. But it's also one term for the disease lupus, presumably because of the disfiguring skin ulcerations characteristic of that illness. A toccata in music is a composition for organ or other keyboard instrument in a free style. It was originally a piece intended to show touch technique, and the word comes from the feminine past participle of *toccare,* to touch. Music teachers often chide students for having "no sense of touch," by which they mean an indefinable delicacy of execution. In fencing, saying *touché* means that you have been touched by the foil and are conceding to your opponent, although, of course, we also say it when we think we have been foiled because someone's argumentative point is well made. A touchstone is a standard. Originally, touch-stones were hard black stones like jasper or basalt, used to test the quality of gold or silver by comparing the streaks they left on the stone with those of an alloy. "The touchstone of an art is its precision," Ezra Pound once said. D. H. Lawrence's use of the word touch isn't epidermal but a profound

From Diane Ackerman, *A Natural History of the Senses.* Reprinted by permission.

penetration into the core of someone's being. So much of twentieth-century popular dancing is simultaneous solo gyration that when people returned to dancing closely with partners again a couple of years ago, we had to call it something different—"touch dancing." "For a while there, it was touch and go," we say of a crisis or precarious situation, not realizing that the expression goes back to horse-and-carriage days, when the wheels of two coaches glanced off each other as they passed, but didn't snag; a modern version would be when two swerving cars brush fenders. What seems real we call "tangible," as if it were a fruit whose rind we could feel. When we die, loved ones swaddle us in heavily padded coffins, making us infants again, lying in our mother's arms before returning to the womb of the earth, ceremonially unborn. As Frederick Sachs writes in *The Sciences*, "The first sense to ignite, touch is often the last to burn out: long after our eyes betray us, our hands remain faithful to the world. . . . in describing such final departures, we often talk of losing touch."

Although I am not a portly middle-aged gentleman with nothing else to do, I am massaging a tiny baby in a hospital in Miami. Often male retirees volunteer to enter preemie wards late at night, when other people have families to tend or a nine-to-five job to sleep toward. The babies don't care about the gender of those who cosset and cuddle them. They soak it up like the manna it is in their wilderness of uncertainty. This baby's arms feel limp, like vinyl. Still too weak to roll over by itself, it can flail and fuss so well the nurses have laid soft bolsters on its bed, to keep it from accidentally wriggling into a corner. Its torso looks as small as a deck of cards. That this is a baby boy lying on his tummy, who will one day play basketball in the summer Olympics, or raise children of his own, or become a heliarc welder, or book passage on a low-orbital plane to Japan for a business meeting, is barely believable. The small life form with a big head, on which veins stand out like river systems, looks so fragile, feels so temporary. Lying in his incubator, or "Isolette," as it's called, emphasizing the isolation of his life, he wears a plumage of wires—electrodes to chart his progress and sound an alarm if need be. Reaching carefully scrubbed, disinfected, warmed hands through the portholes of the incubator with pangs of protectiveness, I touch him; it is like reaching into a chrysalis. First I stroke his head and face very slowly, six times for ten seconds each time, then his neck and shoulders six times. I slide my hands down his back and massage it in long sweeping motions six times, and caress his arms and legs six times. The touching can't be light, or it will tickle him, nor rough, or it will agitate him, but firm and steady, as if one were smoothing a crease from heavy fabric. On a nearby monitor, two turquoise EKG and breath waves flutter across a radiant screen, one of them short and saw-toothed, the other leaping high and dropping low in its own improvisatory dance. His heartbeat

2

reads 153, aerobic peak during a stiff workout for me, but calm for him, because babies have higher normal heart beats than adults. We turn him over on his back and, though asleep, he scrunches up his face in displeasure. In less than a minute, he runs a parade of expressions by us, all of them perfectly readable thanks to the semaphore of the eyebrows, the twisted code of the forehead, the eloquent India rubber of the mouth and chin: irritation, calm, puzzled, happy, mad. . . . Then his face goes slack and his eyelids twitch as he drifts into REM sleep, the blackboard of dreams. Some nurses refer to the tiny preemies, sleeping their sleep of the womb, as fetuses on the outside. What does a fetus dream? Gently, I move his limbs in a mini-exercise routine, stretching out an arm and bending the elbow tight, opening the legs and bending the knees to the chest. Peaceful but alert; he seems to be enjoying it. We turn him onto his tummy once more, and again I begin caressing his head and shoulders. This is the first of three daily touch sessions for him—it may seem a shame to interrupt his thick, druglike sleep, but just by stroking him I am performing a life-giving act.

3   Massaged babies gain weight as much as 50 percent faster than unmassaged babies. They're more active, alert, and responsive, more aware of their surroundings, better able to tolerate noise, and they orient themselves faster and are emotionally more in control. "Less likely to cry one minute, then fall asleep the next minute," as a psychologist, detailing the results of one experiment, explained in *Science News* in 1985, they're "better able to calm and console themselves." In a follow-up examination, eight months later, the massaged preemies were found to be bigger in general, with larger heads and fewer physical problems. Some doctors in California have even been putting preterms on small waterbeds that sway gently, and this experiment has produced infants who are less irritable, sleep better, and have fewer apneas. The touched infants, in these studies and in others, cried less, had better temperaments, and so were more appealing to their parents, which is important because the 7 percent of babies born prematurely figure disproportionately among those who are victims of child abuse. Children who are difficult to raise get abused more often. And people who aren't touched much as children don't touch much as adults, so the cycle continues.

4   A 1988 *New York Times* article on the critical role of touch in child development reported "psychological and physical stunting of infants deprived of physical contact, although otherwise fed and cared for . . .," which was revealed by one researcher working with primates and others working with World War II orphans. "Premature infants who were massaged for 15 minutes three times a day gained weight 47 percent faster than others who were left alone in their incubators . . . the massaged infants also showed signs that the nervous system was maturing more rapidly: they became more active . . . and more responsive to such things as a face or a rattle . . . infants who were massaged

were discharged from the hospital an average of six days earlier." Eight months later, the massaged infants did better in tests of mental and motor ability than the ones who were not.

At the University of Miami Medical School, Dr. Tiffany Field, a child psychologist, has been studying a group of babies admitted to the intensive care unit of its hospital for various reasons. With 13,000 to 15,000 births a year at the hospital, she never lacks for a steady supply of babies. Some are receiving caffeine for bradycardia and apnea problems, one is hydroencephalic, some are the children of diabetic mothers who must be carefully monitored. At one Isolette, a young mother sits on a black kitchen chair by her baby, reaches a hand in and gently strokes, whispering motherly nothings into its ear. Inside another Isolette, a baby girl wearing a white nightie with pink hearts bursts into a classic textbook wail that rises and pulses and sets off the alarm on her monitor. Across the room, a male doctor sits quietly beside a preemie, holding a two-pronged plastic stopper close to her nostrils, trying to teach her to breathe. Next to him, a nurse turns a baby girl onto her tummy and begins a "stim," as they call the massage, shorthand for stimulation. They use the word interchangeably as a verb or a noun. What old faces the preemies have! Changing expressions as they sleep, they seem to be rehearsing emotions. The nurse follows her massage schedule, stroking each part of the preemie six times for ten seconds. The stimulation hasn't changed the baby's sleep patterns, but she's been gaining thirty grams more a day and will soon be going home, almost a week ahead of what one would expect. "There's nothing extra going into the babies," Field explains, "yet they're more active, gain weight faster; and they become more efficient. It's amazing," she continues, "how much information is communicable in a touch. Every other sense has an organ you can focus on, but touch is everywhere."

Saul Schanberg, a neurologist who experiments with rats at Duke University, has found that licking and grooming by the mother rat actually produced chemical changes in the pup; when the pup was taken away from the mother, its growth hormones decreased. ODC (the "now" enzyme that signals it is time for certain chemical changes to begin) dropped in every cell in the body, and protein synthesis fell. Growth began again only when the pup was returned to the mother. When experimenters tried to reverse the bad effects without the mother, they discovered that gentle stroking wouldn't work, only very heavy stroking with a paintbrush that simulated the mother's tongue; after that the pup developed normally. Regardless of whether the deprived rats were returned to their mothers or stroked with paintbrushes by experimenters, they overreacted and required a great deal of touching, far more than they usually do, to respond normally.

Schanberg first began his rat experiments as a result of his work in pediatrics; he was especially interested in psychosocial dwarfism.

Some children who live in emotionally destructive homes just stop growing. Schanberg found that even growth-hormone injections couldn't prompt the stunted bodies of such children to grow again, but tender loving care did. The affection they received from the nurses when they were admitted to a hospital was often enough to get them back on the right track. What's amazing is that the process is reversible at all. When Schanberg's experiments with infant rats produced identical results, he began to think about human preemies, who are typically isolated and spend much of their early life without human contact. Animals depend on being close to their mothers for basic survival. If the mother's touch is removed (for as little as forty-five minutes in rats), the infant lowers its need for food to keep itself alive until the mother returns. This works out well if the mother is away only briefly, but if she never comes back, then the slower metabolism results in stunted growth. Touch reassures an infant that it's safe; it seems to give the body a go-ahead to develop normally. In many experiments conducted all over the country, babies who were held more became more alert and developed better cognitive abilities years later. It's a little like the strategy one adopts on a sinking ship: First you get into a life raft and call for help. Baby animals call their mothers with a high-pitched cry. Then you take stock of your water and food, and try to conserve energy by cutting down on high-energy activities—growth, for instance.

8   At the University of Colorado School of Medicine, researchers conducted a separation experiment with monkeys, in which they removed the mother. The infant showed signs of helplessness, confusion, and depression, and only the return of its mother and continuous holding for a few days would help it return to normal. During separation, changes occurred in the heart rate, body temperature, brain-wave patterns, sleep patterns, and immune system function. Electronic monitoring of deprived infants showed that touch deprivation caused physical and psychological disturbances. But when the mother was put back, only the psychological disturbances seemed to disappear; true, the infant's behavior reverted to normal, but the physical distresses—susceptibility to disease, and so on—persisted. Among this experiment's implications is that damage is not reversible, and that the lack of maternal contact may lead to possible long-term damage.

9   Another separation study with monkeys took place at the University of Wisconsin, where researchers separated an infant from its mother by a glass screen. They could still see, hear, and smell each other, only touch was missing, but that created a void so serious that the baby cried steadily and paced frantically. In another group, the dividing screen had holes, so the mother and baby could touch through it, which was apparently sufficient because the infants didn't develop serious behavior problems. Those infants who suffered short-term de-

privation became adolescents who clung to one another obsessively instead of developing into independent, confident individuals. When they suffered long-term deprivation, they avoided one another and became aggressive when they did come in contact, violent loners who didn't form good relationships.

In University of Illinois primate experiments, researchers found that a lack of touch produced brain damage. They posed three situations: (1) touch was not possible, but all other contact was, (2) for four hours out of twenty-four the glass divider was removed so the monkeys could interact, and (3) total isolation. Autopsies of the cerebellum showed that those monkeys who were totally isolated had brain damage; the same was true of the partially separated animals. The untampered-with natural colony remained undamaged. Shocking though it sounds, a relatively small amount of touch deprivation alone caused brain damage, which was often displayed in the monkeys as aberrant behavior. 10

As I rearrange the preemie in his glass home, I notice that on the walls a bright circus design shows clowns, a merry-go-round, tents, balloons, and a repeat banner that says "Wheel of Fortune." "Touch is far more essential than our other sense," I recall Saul Schanberg saying when we spoke, on Key Biscayne, at Johnson & Johnson's extraordinary conference on touch in spring, 1989, a three-day exchange of ideas that brought together neurophysiologists, pediatricians, anthropologists, sociologists, psychologists, and others interested in how touch and touch deprivation affect the mind and body. In many ways, touch is difficult to research. Every other sense has a key organ to study; for touch that organ is the skin, and it stretches over the whole body. Every sense has at least one key research center, except touch. Touch is a sensory system, the influence of which is hard to isolate or eliminate. Scientists can study people who are blind to learn more about vision, and people who are deaf or anosmic to learn more about hearing or smell, but this is virtually impossible to do with touch. They also can't experiment with people who are born without the sense, as they often do with the deaf or blind. Touch is a sense with unique functions and qualities, but it also frequently combines with other senses. Touch affects the whole organism, as well as its culture and the individuals it comes into contact with. "It's ten times stronger than verbal or emotional contact," Schanberg explained, "and it affects damn near everything we do. No other sense can arouse you like touch; we always knew that, but we never realized it had a biological basis." 11

"You mean how adaptive it is?" 12

"Yes. If touch didn't feel good, there'd be no species, parenthood, or survival. A mother wouldn't touch her baby in the right way unless the mother felt pleasure doing it. If we didn't like the feel of touching 13 and patting one another, we wouldn't have had sex. Those animals who did more touching instinctively produced offspring which survived, and their genes were passed on and the tendency to touch became even stronger. We forget that touch is not only basic to our species, but they key to it."

14   As a fetus grows in the womb, surrounded by amniotic fluid, it feels liquid warmth, the heartbeat, the inner surf of the mother, and floats in a wonderful hammock that rocks gently as she walks. Birth must be a rude shock after such serenity, and a mother re-creates the womb comfort in various ways (swaddling, cradling, pressing the baby against the left side of her body where her heart is). Right after birth, human (and monkey) mothers hold their babies very close to their bodies. In primitive cultures, a mother keeps her baby close day and night. A baby born to one of the Pygmies of Zaire is in physical contact with someone at least 50 percent of the time, and is constantly being stroked or played with by other members of the tribe. A Kung! mother carries her baby in a *curass*, a sling that holds it upright at her side so that it can nurse, play with her bead necklaces, or interact with others. Kung! infants are in touch with others about 90 percent of the time, whereas our culture believes in exiling babies to cribs, baby carriages, or travel seats, keeping them at arm's length and out of the way.

15   An odd feature of touch is that it doesn't always have to be performed by another person, or even by a living thing. Maternity Hospital in Cambridge, England, discovered that if a premature baby were just placed on a lamb's-wool blanket for a day it would gain an average of fifteen grams more than usual. This was not due to additional heat from the blanket, since the ward was kept warm, but more akin to the tradition of "swaddling" infants, which increases tactile stimulation, decreases stress, and makes them feel lightly cuddled. In other experiments, snug-fitting blankets or clothes reduced the infants' heart rate, relaxed them; they slept more often in their womblike bindings.

16   All animals respond to being touched, stroked, poked in some way, and, in any case, life itself could not have evolved at all without touch—that is, without chemicals touching one another and forming liaisons. In the absence of touching and being touched, people of all ages can sicken and grow touch-starved.* In fetuses, touch is the first sense to develop, and in newborns it's automatic before the eyes open

---

*What a curious and deprived life the Dionne quints lived. Born in Ontario, Canada, they were seized by the government and put in a kind of zoo. So they lived in a sterile room behind bars. At one point their mother, who wasn't allowed to touch them, stood in line with the other paying viewers. Only after a lawsuit was she able to get her children back. None of them grew up normally.

or the baby begins to make sense of the world. Soon after we're born, though we can't see or speak, we instinctively begin touching. Touch cells in the lips make nursing possible, clutch mechanisms in the hands begin to reach out for warmth. Among other things, touch teaches us the difference between *I* and *other*, that there can be someone outside of ourselves, the mother. Mothers and infants do an enormous amount of touching. The first emotional comfort, touching and being touched by our mother, remains the ultimate memory of selfless love, which stays with us life long.

The little three-pound universe named Geoffrey, which I am stroking in long gentle caresses, has idly twisted his mouth and just as quickly untwisted it again. In other incubators around the room, other lives are stirring, other volunteers continue reaching in through portholes to help the infants begin to make sense of the world. The head research nurse of the ward, a graduate student in neonatal care, gives the Brazelton sensory test to a baby boy, who responds to a bright-red egg-rattle. Picking the baby up, she swings it gently around and its eyes go in the direction of the spin, as they should, then return to the midline. Next she rings a small schoolbell for ten seconds at each side, and repeats this four times. It is a very Buddhist scene. In a nearby crib, a preemie who is having his hearing tested wears a headset that makes him look like a telegraph operator. The policy with premature babies used to be not to disturb them any more than necessary, and they lived in a kind of isolation booth, but now the evidence about touch is so plentiful and eloquent that many hospitals encourage touching. "Did you hug your child today?" asks the bumper sticker. As it turns out, this is more than a casual question. Touch seems to be as essential as sunlight.

_____ CONSIDERATIONS _____

1. Study the differences in Ackerman's style between paragraph 1 and paragraph 2. What are the prominent features of each?

2. Compare the length of Ackerman's paragraphs, especially 1, 2, 5, 7, and 11, with that of other writers in the text, and comment on your findings.

3. "Reaching. . .through the portholes of the incubator. . .is like reaching into a chrysalis," writes Ackerman in paragraph 2. Look up the word "chrysalis" to make sure you understand it. Do the same for the word "simile." Then explain why Abbott's use of a figure of speech here is more effective than a literal description would be. Identify other uses of figurative language by this writer.

4. Inevitably, in a report of this sort, Ackerman uses a number of technical terms, some of which she explains and some she doesn't: aerobic, apnea,

bradycardia, "stim," ODC, REM, EKG, anosmic, neonatal, preterms, "pree-mie." Which of these is explained, more or less, by the context?

5. In several places, but particularly in paragraph 11, Ackerman says, in effect, that touch is the most important of all the senses. If you doubt her, write an essay that shows the pre-eminence of a different sense. If you agree with her, build an essay around a specific experience of your own or of some-one you know.

6. How, in her conclusion, does Ackerman move her discussion from the isolated preemie ward to the streets of everyone's town?

Henry Adams (1838–1918) entertained notions of a
political career, in keeping with family traditions, but
never ran for office. For a time, he taught history at
Harvard and edited the North American Review. *He wrote*
political journalism and essays on geology, economics,
and history; he wrote two novels that he published
anonymously. In middle life he undertook and completed
the massive History of the United States During the
Administrations of Jefferson and Madison, *recently*
reissued in two volumes by the Library of America. Later
he wrote the books by which he is most remembered,
Mont St. Michel and Chartres *(1904) and his*
autobiography—written in the third person and called The
Education of Henry Adams *(1907)—from which we take*
this fragment of reminiscence.

Hundreds of American writers have recollected visits to
grandfather's house; none other was grandson to one
president and great-grandson to another. Adams's
contrasts of style—eighteenth century with nineteenth,
Boston with the small town of Quincy, the Brooks
grandfather with the Adams grandfather—culminate in an
anecdote that illuminates the fundamental contrast of
private and public.

3

HENRY ADAMS
Winter and Summer

Boys are wild animals, rich in the treasures of sense, but the New   1
England boy had a wider range of emotions than boys of more equable
climates. He felt his nature crudely, as it was meant. To the boy
Henry Adams, summer was drunken. Among senses, smell was the
strongest—smell of hot pine-woods and sweet-fern in the scorching
summer noon; of new-mown hay; of ploughed earth; of box hedges; of
peaches, lilacs, syringas; of stables, barns, cow-yards; of salt water and
low tide on the marshes; nothing came amiss. Next to smell came
taste, and the children knew the taste of everything they saw or

touched, from pennyroyal and flagroot to the shell of a pignut and the letters of a spelling book—the taste of A-B, AB, suddenly revived on the boy's tongue sixty years afterwards. Light, line, and color as sensual pleasures, came later and were as crude as the rest. The New England light is glare, and the atmosphere harshens color. The boy was a full man before he ever knew what was meant by atmosphere; his idea of pleasure in light was the blaze of a New England sun. His idea of color was a peony, with the dew of early morning on its petals. The intense blue of the sea, as he saw it a mile or two away, from the Quincy hills; the cumuli in a June afternoon sky; the strong reds and greens and purples of colored prints and children's picture-books, as the American colors then ran; these were ideals. The opposites or antipathies, were the cold grays of November evenings, and the thick, muddy thaws of Boston winter. With such standards, the Bostonian could not but develop a double nature. Life was a double thing. After a January blizzard, the boy who could look with pleasure into the violent snow-glare of the cold white sunshine, with its intense light and shade, scarcely knew what was meant by tone. He could reach it only by education.

2   Winter and summer, then, were two hostile lives, and bred two separate natures. Winter was always the effort to live; summer was tropical license. Whether the children rolled in the grass, or waded in the brook, or swam in the salt ocean, or sailed in the bay, or fished for smelts in the creeks, or netted minnows in the salt-marshes, or took to the pine-woods and the granite quarries, or chased muskrats and hunted snapping-turtles in the swamps, or mushrooms or nuts on the autumn hills, summer and country were always sensual living, while winter was always compulsory learning. Summer was the multiplicity of nature; winter was school.

3   The bearing of the two seasons on the education of Henry Adams was no fancy; it was the most decisive force he ever knew; it ran through life, and made the division between its perplexing, warring, irreconcilable problems, irreducible opposites, with growing emphasis to the last year of study. From earliest childhood the boy was accustomed to feel that, for him, life was double. Winter and summer, town and country, law and liberty, were hostile, and the man who pretended they were not, was in his eyes a schoolmaster—that is, a man employed to tell lies to little boys. Though Quincy was but two hours' walk from Beacon Hill, it belonged in a different world. For two hundred years, every Adams, from father to son, had lived within sight of State Street, and sometimes had lived in it, yet none had ever taken kindly to the town, or been taken kindly by it. The boy inherited his double nature. He knew as yet nothing about his great-grandfather, who had died a dozen years before his own birth: he took for granted that any great-grandfather of his must have always been good, and his

enemies wicked; but he divined his great-grandfather's character from his own. Never for a moment did he connect the two ideas of Boston and John Adams; they were separate and antagonistic; the idea of John Adams went with Quincy. He knew his grandfather John Quincy Adams only as an old man of seventy-five or eighty who was friendly and gentle with him, but except that he heard his grandfather always called "the President," and his grandmother "the Madam," he had no reason to suppose that his Adams grandfather differed in character from his Brooks grandfather who was equally kind and benevolent. He liked the Adams side best, but for no other reason than that it reminded him of the country, the summer, and the absence of restraint. Yet he felt also that Quincy was in a way inferior to Boston, and that socially Boston looked down on Quincy. The reason was clear enough even to a five-year-old child. Quincy had no Boston style. Little enough style had either; a simpler manner of life and thought could hardly exist, short of cave-dwelling. The flint-and-steel with which his grandfather Adams used to light his own fires in the early morning was still on the mantelpiece of his study. The idea of a livery or even a dress for servants, or of an evening toilette, was next to blasphemy. Bathrooms, water-supplies, lighting, heating, and the whole array of domestic comforts, were unknown at Quincy. Boston had already a bathroom, a water-supply, a furnace, and gas. The superiority of Boston was evident, but a child liked it no better for that.

The magnificence of his grandfather Brooks's house in Pearl 4 Street or South Street has long ago disappeared, but perhaps his country house at Medford may still remain to show what impressed the mind of a boy in 1845 with the idea of city splendor. The President's place at Quincy was the larger and older and far the more interesting of the two; but a boy felt at once its inferiority in fashion. It showed plainly enough its want of wealth. It smacked of colonial age, but not of Boston style or plush curtains. To the end of his life he never quite overcame the prejudice thus drawn in with his childish breath. He never could compel himself to care for nineteenth-century style. He was never able to adopt it, any more than his father or grandfather or great-grandfather had done. Not that he felt it as particularly hostile, for he reconciled himself to much that was worse; but because, for some remote reason, he was born an eighteenth-century child. The old house at Quincy was eighteenth-century. What style it had was in its Queen Anne mahogany panels and its Louis Seize chairs and sofas. The panels belonged to an old colonial vassal who built the house; the furniture had been brought back from Paris in 1789 or 1801 or 1817, along with porcelain and books and much else of old diplomatic remnants: and neither of the two eighteenth-century styles—neither English Queen Anne nor French Louis Seize—was comfortable for a boy, or for anyone else. The dark mahogany had been painted white to suit daily life in the winter gloom. Nothing seemed to favor, for a child's objects, the older forms. On the contrary, most boys, as well as grown-up people, preferred the new, with good reason, and the child felt himself distinctly at a disadvantage for the taste.

5   Nor had personal preference any share in his bias. The Brooks grandfather was as amiable and as sympathetic as the Adams grandfather. Both were born in 1767, and both died in 1848. Both were kind to children, and both belonged rather to the eighteenth than to the nineteenth centuries. The child knew no difference between them except that one was associated with winter and the other with summer; one with Boston, the other with Quincy. Even with Medford, the association was hardly easier. Once as a very young boy he was taken to pass a few days with his grandfather Brooks under charge of his aunt, but became so violently homesick that within twenty-four hours he was brought back in disgrace. Yet he could not remember ever being seriously homesick again.

6   The attachment to Quincy was not altogether sentimental or wholly sympathetic. Quincy was not a bed of thornless roses. Even there the curse of Cain set its mark. There as elsewhere a cruel universe combined to crush a child. As though three or four vigorous brothers and sisters, with the best will, were not enough to crush any child, everyone else conspired towards an education which he hated. From cradle to grave this problem of running order through chaos, direction through space, discipline through freedom, unity through multiplicity, has always been, and must always be, the task of education, as it is the moral of religion, philosophy, science, art, politics, and economy; but a boy's will is his life, and he dies when it is broken, as the colt dies in harness, taking a new nature in becoming tame. Rarely has the boy felt kindly towards his tamers. Between him and his master has always been war. Henry Adams never knew a boy of his generation to like a master, and the task of remaining on friendly terms with one's own family, in such a relation, was never easy.

7   All the more singular it seemed afterwards to him that his first serious contact with the President should have been a struggle of will, in which the old man almost necessarily defeated the boy, but instead of leaving, as usual in such defeats, a lifelong sting, left rather an impression of as fair treatment as could be expected from a natural enemy. The boy met seldom with such restraint. He could not have been much more than six years old at the time—seven at the utmost—and his mother had taken him to Quincy for a long stay with the President during the summer. What became of the rest of the family he quite forgot; but he distinctly remembered standing at the house door one summer morning in a passionate outburst of rebellion against going to school. Naturally his mother was the immediate victim of his rage; that is what mothers are for, and boys also; but in this case the boy had his mother at unfair disadvantage, for she was a guest, and had no

means of enforcing obedience. Henry showed a certain tactical ability by refusing to start, and he met all efforts at compulsion by successful, though too vehement protest. He was in fair way to win, and was holding his own, with sufficient energy, at the bottom of the long staircase which led up to the door of the President's library, when the door opened, and the old man slowly came down. Putting on his hat, he took the boy's hand without a word, and walked with him, paralyzed by awe, up the road to the town. After the first moments of consternation at this interference in a domestic dispute, the boy reflected that an old gentleman close on eighty would never trouble himself to walk near a mile on a hot summer morning over a shadeless road to take a boy to school, and that it would be strange if a lad imbued with the passion of freedom could not find a corner to dodge around, somewhere before reaching the school door. Then and always, the boy insisted that this reasoning justified his apparent submission; but the old man did not stop, and the boy saw all his strategical points turned, one after another, until he found himself seated inside the school, and obviously the centre of curious if not malevolent criticism. Not till then did the President release his hand and depart.

The point was that this act, contrary to the inalienable rights of   8 boys, and nullifying the social compact, ought to have made him dislike his grandfather for life. He could not recall that it had this effect even for a moment. With a certain maturity of mind, the child must have recognized that the President, though a tool of tyranny, had done his disreputable work with a certain intelligence. He had shown no temper, no irritation, no personal feeling, and had made no display of force. Above all, he had held his tongue. During their long walk he had said nothing; he had uttered no syllable of revolting cant about the duty of obedience and the wickedness of resistance to law; he had shown no concern in the matter; hardly even a consciousness of the boy's existence. Probably his mind at that moment was actually troubling itself little about his grandson's iniquities, and much about the iniquities of President Polk, but the boy could scarcely at that age feel the whole satisfaction of thinking that President Polk was to be the vicarious victim of his own sins, and he gave his grandfather credit for intelligent silence. For this forbearance he felt instinctive respect. He admitted force as a form of right; he admitted even temper, under protest; but the seeds of moral education would at that moment have fallen on the stoniest soil in Quincy, which is, as everyone knows, the stoniest glacial and tidal drift known in any Puritan land.

_____ **CONSIDERATIONS** _____

1. Earlier in his autobiography, Adams gives the reader some idea of how the young Henry, because of the peculiar nature of his family and its po-

sition, was burdened with expectations arising from the family's deep involvement in American history and politics. In the present excerpt, study his vocabulary and look for words that express his constant awareness of that involvement.

2. Adams chose an unusual point of view for an autobiography—the third person. Change a given paragraph to the first person point of view to see what difference the author's decision on that technical matter can make.

3. What illustrations does Adams use to help the reader understand what is meant by "He felt his nature crudely . . ."?

4. Adams's essay might fairly be said to be built on a system of opposites. List several of these opposites to understand how a series of contrasts can serve as an organizing principle of an essay.

5. In paragraph 6, Adams sets forth clearly and firmly his conviction about what education must be. Judging from your educational experience, to what extent can you agree with him?

6. What allowed the boy to respect his grandfather, even as the old man was disciplining him?

Maya Angelou (b. 1928) told an interviewer, "One would say of my life—born loser—had to be; from a broken family, raped at eight, unwed mother at sixteen . . . it's a fact, but it's not the truth."

When she grew up, Maya Angelou became an actress, a singer, a dancer, a songwriter, a teacher, an editor, and a poet. She sang and danced professionally in Porgy and Bess *with a company that traveled through twenty-two countries of Europe and Asia. She wrote for the* Ghana Times *and she taught modern dance in Rome and in Tel Aviv. After reading a poem at the inauguration of President Clinton, in 1993, she reached new audiences with all her work. In the same year, she published her most recent prose volume,* Wouldn't Take Nothing for My Journey Now. The Complete Collected Poems of Maya Angelou *appeared in 1994.*

In 1969 she began her autobiography, I Know Why the Caged Bird Sings, *which was an immediate success. As she says, "I speak to the black experience, but I am always talking about the human condition." The book recounts her early life, with realism and with joy. This section describes a masterful black con man, skillful at turning white bigotry into black profits.*

4

MAYA ANGELOU
Mr. Red Leg

Our house was a fourteen-room typical San Franciscan post-Earthquake affair. We had a succession of roomers, bringing and taking their different accents, and personalities and foods. Shipyard workers clanked up the stairs (we all slept on the second floor except Mother and Daddy Clidell) in their steel-tipped boots and metal hats, and gave way to much-powdered prostitutes, who giggled through their makeup and hung their wigs on the doorknobs. One couple (they were college graduates) held long adult conversations with me in the big kitchen downstairs, until the husband went off to war. Then the wife who had been so charming and ready to smile changed into a silent shadow that played infrequently along the walls. An older couple lived with us for a year or so. They owned a restaurant and had no personality to enchant or interest a teenager, except that the husband was called Uncle Jim, and the wife Aunt Boy. I never figured that out.

2   The quality of strength lined with tenderness is an unbeatable combination, as are intelligence and necessity when unblunted by formal education. I was prepared to accept Daddy Clidell as one more faceless name added to Mother's roster of conquests. I had trained myself so successfully through the years to display interest, or at least attention, while my mind skipped free on other subjects that I could have lived in his house without ever seeing him and without his becoming the wiser. But his character beckoned and elicited admiration. He was a simple man who had no inferiority complex about his lack of education and, even more amazing, no superiority complex because he had succeeded despite that lack. He would say often, "I had been to school three years in my life. In Slaten, Texas, times was hard, and I had to help my daddy on the farm."

3   No recriminations lay hidden under the plain statement, nor was there boasting when he said, "If I'm living a little better now, it's because I treats everybody right."

4   He owned apartment buildings and, later, pool halls, and was famous for being that rarity, "a man of honor." He didn't suffer, as many "honest men" do, from the detestable righteousness that diminishes their virtue. He knew cards and men's hearts. So during the age when Mother was exposing us to certain facts of life, like personal hygiene, proper posture, table manners, good restaurants and tipping practices, Daddy Clidell taught me to play poker, blackjack, tonk and high, low, Jick, Jack and the Game. He wore expensive tailored suits and a large yellow diamond stickpin. Except for the jewelry, he was a conservative dresser and carried himself with the unconscious pomp of a man of secure means. Unexpectedly, I resembled him, and when he, Mother and I walked down the street his friends often said, "Clidell, that's sure your daughter. Ain't no way you can deny her."

5   Proud laughter followed those declarations, for he had never had children. Because of his late-arriving but intense paternal sense, I was introduced to the most colorful characters in the Black underground. One afternoon, I was invited into our smoke-filled dining room to make the acquaintance of Stonewall Jimmy, Just Black, Cool Clyde, Tight Coat and Red Leg. Daddy Clidell explained to me that they were the most successful con men in the world, and they were going to tell me about some games so that I would never be "anybody's mark."

To begin, one man warned me, "There ain't never been a mark   6
yet that didn't want something for nothing." Then they took turns
showing me their tricks, how they chose their victims (marks) from
the wealthy bigoted whites and in every case how they used the victims' prejudice against them.

Some of the tales were funny, a few were pathetic, but all were   7
amusing or gratifying to me, for the Black man, the con man who
could act the most stupid, won out every time over the powerful, arrogant white.

I remember Mr. Red Leg's story like a favorite melody.   8

"Anything that works against you can also work for you once   9
you understand the Principle of Reverse.

"There was a cracker in Tulsa who bilked so many Negroes he   10
could set up a Negro Bilking Company. Naturally he got to thinking,
Black Skin means Damn Fool. Just Black and I went to Tulsa to check
him out. Come to find out, he's a perfect mark. His momma must
have been scared in an Indian massacre in Africa. He hated Negroes
only a little more than he despised Indians. And he was greedy.

"Black and I studied him and decided he was worth setting up   11
against the store. That means we were ready to put out a few thousand
dollars in preparation. We pulled in a white boy from New York, a
good con artist, and had him open an office in Tulsa. He was supposed
to be a Northern real estate agent trying to buy up valuable land in
Oklahoma. We investigated a piece of land near Tulsa that had a toll
bridge crossing it. It used to be part of an Indian reservation but had
been taken over by the state.

"Just Black was laid out as the decoy, and I was going to be the   12
fool. After our friend from New York hired a secretary and had his
cards printed, Black approached the mark with a proposition. He told
him that he had heard that our mark was the only white man colored
people could trust. He named some of the poor fools that had been
taken by that crook. It just goes to show you how white folks can be
deceived by their own deception. The mark believed Black.

"Black told him about his friend who was half Indian and half   13
colored and how some Northern white real estate agent had found out
that he was the sole owner of a piece of valuable land and the Northerner wanted to buy it. At first the man acted like he smelled a rat, but
from the way he gobbled up the proposition, turns out what he
thought he smelled was some nigger money on his top lip.

"He asked the whereabouts of the land but Black put him off. He   14
told this cracker that he just wanted to make sure that he would be interested. The mark allowed how he was being interested, so Black said
he would tell his friend and they'd get in touch with him. Black met
the mark for about three weeks in cars and in alleys and kept putting
him off until the white man was almost crazy with anxiety and greed

and then accidentally it seemed Black let drop the name of the Northern real estate agent who wanted the property. From that moment on we knew we had the big fish on the line and all we had to do was to pull him in.

15   "We expected him to try to contact our store, which he did. That cracker went to our setup and counted on his whiteness to ally him with Spots, our white boy, but Spots refused to talk about the deal except to say the land had been thoroughly investigated by the biggest real estate concern in the South and that if our mark did not go around raising dust he would make sure that there would be a nice piece of money in it for him. Any obvious inquiries as to the rightful ownership of the land could alert the state and they would surely push through a law prohibiting the sale. Spots told the mark he would keep in touch with him. The mark went back to the store three or four times but to no avail, then just before we knew he would crack, Black brought me to see him. That fool was as happy as a sissy in a C.C.C. camp. You would have thought my neck was in a noose and he was about to light the fire under my feet. I never enjoyed taking anybody so much.

16   "Anyhow, I played scary at first but Just Black told me that this was one white man that our people could trust. I said I did not trust no white man because all they wanted was a chance to kill a Black man legally and get his wife in the bed. (I'm sorry, Clidell.) The mark assured me that he was the only white man who did not feel like that. Some of his best friends were colored people. In fact, if I didn't know it, the woman who raised him was a colored woman and he still sees her to this day. I let myself be convinced and then the mark began to drag the Northern whites. He told me that they made Negroes sleep in the street in the North and that they had to clean out toilets with their hands in the North and even things worse than that. I was shocked and said, "Then I don't want to sell my land to that white man who offered seventy-five thousand dollars for it." Just Black said, 'I wouldn't know what to do with that kind of money,' and I said that all I wanted was to have enough money to buy a home for my old mom, to buy a business and to make one trip to Harlem. The mark asked how much would that cost and I said I reckoned I could do it on fifty thousand dollars.

17   "The mark told me no Negro was safe with that kind of money. That white folks would take it from him. I said I knew it but I had to have at least forty thousand dollars. He agreed. We shook hands. I said it would do my heart good to see the mean Yankee go down on some of 'our land.' We met the next morning and I signed the deed in his car and he gave me the cash.

18   "Black and I had kept most of our things in a hotel over in Hot Springs, Arkansas. When the deal was closed we walked to our car, drove across the state line and on to Hot Springs.

"That's all there was to it."   19

When he finished, more triumphant stories rainbowed around   20
the room riding the shoulders of laughter. By all accounts those story-
tellers, born Black and male before the turn of the twentieth century,
should have been ground into useless dust. Instead they used their intelligence to pry open the door of rejection and not only became
wealthy but got some revenge in the bargain.

It wasn't possible for me to regard them as criminals or be any-   21
thing but proud of their achievements.

The needs of a society determine its ethics, and in the Black   22
American ghettos the hero is that man who is offered only the crumbs
from his country's table but by ingenuity and courage is able to take
for himself a Lucullan feast. Hence the janitor who lives in one room
but sports a robin's-egg-blue Cadillac is not laughed at but admired,
and the domestic who buys forty-dollar shoes is not criticized but is
appreciated. We know that they have put to use their full mental and
physical powers. Each single gain feeds into the gains of the body collective.

Stories of law violations are weighed on a different set of scales   23
in the Black mind than in the white. Petty crimes embarrass the community and many people wistfully wonder why Negroes don't rob
more banks, embezzle more funds and employ graft in the unions.
"We are the victims of the world's most comprehensive robbery. Life
demands a balance. It's all right if we do a little robbing now." This
belief appeals particularly to one who is unable to compete legally
with his fellow citizens.

My education and that of my Black associates were quite differ-   24
ent from the education of our white schoolmates. In the classroom we
all learned past participles, but in the streets and in our homes the
Blacks learned to drop s's from plurals and suffixes from past-tense
verbs. We were alert to the gap separating the written word from the
colloquial. We learned to slide out of one language and into another
without being conscious of the effort. At school, in a given situation,
we might respond with "That's not unusual." But in the street, meeting the same situation, we easily said, "It be's like that sometimes."

———— CONSIDERATIONS ————————————————————

1. Most of Angelou's essay is devoted to Mr. Red Leg telling a story. Notice how close to pure narration that story is. Compare it with the selections
in this book by Carol Bly, George Orwell, or Richard Wright, and contrast the
amount of description and narration in Mr. Red Leg's story with that in one of
the others.

2. Compare Angelou's essay with that of Frank Conroy, who also emphasizes memorable characters. How do the two authors differ in their reasons

for devoting so much space to Mr. Red Leg and to Ramos and Ricardo, respectively?

3. At the end of her essay, Angelou sets out an important linguistic principle. Paraphrase that idea and provide examples from your own experience or research.

4. "Stories of law violations are weighed on a different set of scales in the Black mind than in the white." Does a similar difference occur in the minds of two generations? Discuss relative justice versus absolute law.

5. Angelou demonstrates her versatility as a writer throughout this essay by managing two voices. Find examples and discuss.

6. From what you learn of Angelou's upbringing in the essay, compile a *negative report* by a social worker on Angelou's childhood. Are there positive details in the essay that would allow you to refute a negative report?

Margaret Atwood (b. 1939) is a Canadian novelist and poet. Born in Ottawa, she now lives in Toronto with her daughter and husband. Her novels include The Edible Woman *(1969),* Surfacing *(1972),* Lady Oracle *(1976),* Life Before Man *(1979),* Bodily Harm *(1982),* The Handmaid's Tale *(1986),* Cat's Eye *(1989),* Wilderness Tips *(1992), and* Good Bones and Simple Murders *(1994). Her original* Selected Poems *came out in 1976, a second volume in 1987. In 1978 she issued a collection of short stories,* Dancing Girls, *and in 1986 published* Bluebeard's Egg and Other Stories.

Although she is largely known for her novels, Margaret Atwood has published much nonfiction, including literary criticism as well as topical essays such as this one.

5

MARGARET ATWOOD

Pornography

When I was in Finland a few years ago for an international writ- 1
ers' conference, I had occasion to say a few paragraphs in public on the subject of pornography. The context was a discussion of political repression, and I was suggesting the possibility of a link between the two. The immediate result was that a male journalist took several large bites out of me. Prudery and pornography are two halves of the same coin, said he, and I was clearly a prude. What could you expect from an Anglo-Canadian? Afterward, a couple of pleasant Scandinavian men asked me what I had been so worked up about. All 'pornography' means, they said, is graphic depictions of whores, and what was the harm in that?

Not until then did it strike me that the male journalist and I had 2
two entirely different things in mind. By "pornography," he meant naked bodies and sex. I, on the other hand, had recently been doing the research for my novel *Bodily Harm*, and was still in a state of shock from some of the material I had seen, including the Ontario Board of Film Censors' "outtakes." By "pornography," I meant women getting

their nipples snipped off with garden shears, having meat hooks stuck into their vaginas, being disemboweled; little girls being raped; men (yes, there are some men) being smashed to a pulp and forcibly sodomized. The cutting edge of pornography, as far as I could see, was no longer simple old copulation, hanging from the chandelier or otherwise; it was death, messy, explicit and highly sadistic. I explained this to the nice Scandinavian men. "Oh, but that's just the United States," they said. "Everyone knows they're sick." In their country, they said, violent "pornography" of that kind was not permitted on television or in movies; indeed, excessive violence of any kind was not permitted. They had drawn a clear line between erotica, which earlier studies had shown did not incite men to more aggressive and brutal behavior toward women, and violence, which later studies indicated did.

3   Some time after that I was in Saskatchewan, where, because of the scenes in *Bodily Harm*, I found myself on an open-line radio show answering questions about "pornography." Almost no one who phoned in was in favor of it, but again they weren't talking about the same stuff I was, because they hadn't seen it. Some of them were all set to stamp out bathing suits and negligees, and, if possible, any depictions of the female body whatsoever. God, it was implied, did not approve of female bodies, and sex of any kind, including that practised by bumblebees, should be shoved back into the dark, where it belonged. I had more than a suspicion that *Lady Chatterley's Lover*, Margaret Laurence's *The Diviners*, and indeed most books by most serious modern authors would have ended up as confetti if left in the hands of these callers.

4   For me, these two experiences illustrate the two poles of the emotionally heated debate that is now thundering around this issue. They also underline the desirability and even the necessity of defining the terms. "Pornography" is now one of those catchalls, like "Marxism" and "feminism," that have become so broad they can mean almost anything, ranging from certain verses in the Bible, ads for skin lotion and sex texts for children to the contents of *Penthouse*, Naughty '90s postcards and films with titles containing the word *Nazi* that show vicious scenes of torture and killing. It's easy to say that sensible people can tell the difference. Unfortunately, opinions on what constitutes a sensible person vary.

5   But even sensible people tend to lose their cool when they start talking about this subject. They soon stop talking and start yelling, and the name-calling begins. Those in favor of censorship (which may include groups not noticeably in agreement on other issues, such as some feminists and religious fundamentalists) accuse the others of exploiting women through the use of degrading images, contributing to the corruption of children, and adding to the general climate of violence and threat in which both women and children live in this society; or, though they may not give much of a hoot about actual women

and children, they invoke moral standards and God's supposed aversion to "filth," "smut" and deviated *preversion*, which may mean ankles.

The camp in favor of total "freedom of expression" often comes 6 out howling as loud as the Romans would have if told they could no longer have innocent fun watching the lions eat up Christians. It too may include segments of the population who are not natural bedfellows: those who proclaim their God-given right to freedom, including the freedom to tote guns, drive when drunk, drool over chicken porn and get off on videotapes of women being raped and beaten, may be waving the same anticensorship banner as responsible liberals who fear the return of Mrs. Grundy, or gay groups for whom sexual emancipation involves the concept of "sexual theater." *Whatever turns you on* is a handy motto, as is *A man's home is his castle* (and if it includes a dungeon with beautiful maidens strung up in chains and bleeding from every pore, that's his business).

Meanwhile, theoreticians theorize and speculators speculate. 7 Is today's pornography yet another indication of the hatred of the body, the deep mind—body split, which is supposed to pervade Western Christian society? Is it a backlash against the women's movement by men who are threatened by uppity female behavior in real life, so like to fantasize about women done up like outsize parcels, being turned into hamburger, kneeling at their feet in slavelike adoration or sucking off guns? Is it a sign of collective impotence, of a generation of men who can't relate to real women at all but have to make do with bits of celluloid and paper? Is the current flood just a result of smart marketing and aggressive promotion by the money men in what has now become a multibillion-dollar industry? If they were selling movies about men getting their testicles stuck full of knitting needles by women with swastikas on their sleeves, would they do as well, or is this penchant somehow peculiarly male? If so, why? Is pornography a power trip rather than a sex one? Some say that those ropes, chains, muzzles and other restraining devices are an argument for the immense power female sexuality still wields in the male imagination: you don't put these things on dogs unless you're afraid of them. Others, more literary, wonder about the shift from the 19th-century Magic Woman or Femme Fatale image to the lollipop-licker, airhead or turkey-carcass treatment of women in porn today. The proporners don't care much about theory: they merely demand product. The antiporners don't care about it in the final analysis either: there's dirt on the street, and they want it cleaned up, now.

It seems to me that this conversation, with its *You're-a-* 8 *prude/You're-a-pervert* dialect, will never get anywhere as long as we continue to think of this material as just "entertainment." Possibly we're deluded by the packaging, the format: magazine, book, movie, theatrical presentation. We're used to thinking of these things as part of the "entertainment industry," and we're used to thinking of ourselves as free adult people who ought to be able to see any kind of "entertainment" we want to. That was what the First Choice pay-TV debate was all about. After all, it's only entertainment, right? Entertainment means fun, and only a killjoy would be antifun. What's the harm?

9   This is obviously the central question: *What's the harm?* If there isn't any real harm to any real people, then the antiporners can tsk-tsk and/or throw up as much as they like, but they can't rightfully expect more legal controls or sanctions. However, the no-harm position is far from being proven.

10   (For instance, there's a clear-cut case for banning—as the federal government has proposed—movies, photos and videos that depict children engaging in sex with adults: real children are used to make the movies, and hardly anybody thinks this is ethical. The possibilities for coercion are too great.)

11   To shift the viewpoint, I'd like to suggest three other models for looking at "pornography"—and here I mean the violent kind.

12   Those who find the idea of regulating pornographic materials repugnant because they think it's Fascist or Communist or otherwise not in accordance with the principles of an open democratic society should consider that Canada has made it illegal to disseminate material that may lead to hatred toward any group because of race or religion. I suggest that if pornography of the violent kind depicted these acts being done predominantly to Chinese, to blacks, to Catholics, it would be off the market immediately, under the present laws. Why is hate literature illegal? Because whoever made the law thought that such material might incite real people to do real awful things to other real people. The human brain is to a certain extent a computer: garbage in, garbage out. We only hear about the extreme cases (like that of American multimurderer Ted Bundy) in which pornography has contributed to the death and/or mutilation of women and/or men. Although pornography is not the only factor involved in the creation of such deviance, it certainly has upped the ante by suggesting both a variety of techniques and the social acceptability of such actions. Nobody knows yet what effect this stuff is having on the less psychotic.

13   Studies have shown that a large part of the market for all kinds of porn, soft and hard, is drawn from the 16-to-21-year-old population of young men. Boys used to learn about sex on the street, or (in Italy, according to Fellini movies) from friendly whores, or, in more general surroundings, from girls, their parents, or, once upon a time, in school, more or less. Now porn has been added, and sex education in the schools is rapidly being phased out. The buck has been

passed, and boys are being taught that all women secretly like to be raped and that real men get high on scooping out women's digestive tracts.

Boys learn their concept of masculinity from other men: is this 14 what most men want them to be learning? If word gets around that rapists are "normal" and even admirable men, will boys feel that in order to be normal, admirable and masculine they will have to be rapists? Human beings are enormously flexible, and how they turn out depends a lot on how they're educated, by the society in which they're immersed as well as by their teachers. In a society that advertises and glorifies rape or even implicitly condones it, more women get raped. It becomes socially acceptable. And at a time when men and the traditional male role have taken a lot of flak and men are confused and casting around for an acceptable way of being male (and, in some cases, not getting much comfort from women on that score), this must be at times a pleasing thought.

It would be naïve to think of violent pornography as just harm- 15 less entertainment. It's also an educational tool and a powerful propaganda device. What happens when boy educated on porn meets girl brought up on Harlequin romances? The clash of expectations can be heard around the block. She wants him to get down on his knees with a ring, he wants her to get down on all fours with a ring in her nose. Can this marriage be saved?

Pornography has certain things in common with such addictive 16 substances as alcohol and drugs: for some, though by no means for all, it induces chemical changes in the body, which the user finds exciting and pleasurable. It also appears to attract a "hard core" of habitual users and a penumbra of those who use it occasionally but aren't dependent on it in any way. There are also significant numbers of men who aren't much interested in it, not because they're undersexed but because real life is satisfying their needs, which may not require as many appliances as those of users.

For the "hard core," pornography may function as alcohol does 17 for the alcoholic: tolerance develops, and a little is no longer enough. This may account for the short viewing time and fast turnover in porn theatres. Mary Brown, chairwoman of the Ontario Board of Film Censors, estimates that for every one mainstream movie requesting entrance to Ontario, there is one porno flick. Not only the quantity consumed but the quality of explicitness must escalate, which may account for the growing violence: once the big deal was breasts, then it was genitals, then copulation, then that was no longer enough and the hard users had to have more. The ultimate kick is death, and after that, as the Marquis de Sade so boringly demonstrated, multiple death.

The existence of alcoholism has not led us to ban social drinking. 18 On the other hand, we do have laws about drinking and driving, exces-

sive drunkenness and other abuses of alcohol that may result in injury
or death to others.

19   This leads us back to the key question: what's the harm? Nobody
knows, but this society should find out fast, before the saturation
point is reached. The Scandinavian studies that showed a connection
between depictions of sexual violence and increased impulse toward it
on the part of male viewers would be a starting point, but many more
questions remain to be raised as well as answered. What, for instance,
is the crucial difference between men who are users and men who are
not? Does using affect a man's relationship with actual women, and, if
so, adversely? Is there a clear line between erotica and violent pornography, or are they on an escalating continuum? Is this a "men versus
women" issue, with all men secretly siding with the proporners and
all women secretly siding against? (I think not; there are lots of men
who don't think that running their true love through the Cuisinart is
the best way they can think of to spend a Saturday night, and they're
just as nauseated by films of someone else doing it as women are.) Is
pornography merely an expression of the sexual confusion of this age
or an active contributor to it?

20   Nobody wants to go back to the age of official repression, when
even piano legs were referred to as "limbs" and had to wear pan-
taloons to be decent. Neither do we want to end up in George Orwell's
1984, in which pornography is turned out by the State to keep the
proles in a state of torpor, sex itself is considered dirty and the approved practice is only for reproduction. But Rome under the emperors
isn't such a good model either.

21   If all men and women respected each other, if sex were considered joyful and life-enhancing instead of a wallow in germ-filled glop,
if everyone were in love all the time, if, in other words, many people's
lives were more satisfactory for them than they appear to be now,
pornography might just go away on its own. But since this is obviously
not happening, we as a society are going to have to make some informed and responsible decisions about how to deal with it.

_____ CONSIDERATIONS _____

1. In explaining that "pornography" means different things to different
people, Atwood separates "erotica" from *her* definition of "pornography."
How does she make that distinction and, more important, why?

2. Paragraph 7 consists largely of questions. Are they real questions or
rhetorical questions? Explain the difference.

3. According to Atwood, what is the central question in the debate
about pornography?

4. What is Atwood's strategy as demonstrated in paragraph 11? What
does she hope to accomplish using it?

5. In paragraph 6, Atwood refers to "the return of Mrs. Grundy." Who was Mrs. Grundy, and why does her name pop up in many discussions of pornography, sexual values, and the like? You will find references to Mrs. Grundy in a literary handbook (e.g., *The Reader's Encyclopedia*, edited by William Rose Benet, or *The Oxford Companion to English Literature*, edited by Margaret Drabble).

6. Why do many people, including judges and lawyers, continue to disagree on a definition of "pornography"? Think of issues that pose the same problem. Note Atwood's wisdom in clarifying early in her essay what *she* means by the word. Discuss your own views of pornography.

In 1994, the Michigan Quarterly Review *published an issue devoted to the male body, to which Margaret Atwood contributed "Alien Territory." See page 584 for John Updike's "The Disposable Rocket," from the same issue of the same magazine.*

6

MARGARET ATWOOD
Alien Territory

1

1   He conceives himself in alien territory. Not his turf—alien! Listen! The rushing of the red rivers, the rustling of the fresh leaves in the dusk, always in the dusk, under the dark stars, and the wish-wash of the heavy soothing sea, which becomes—yes!—the drums of the natives, beating, beating, louder, faster, lower, slower. Are they hostile? Who knows, because they're invisible.

2   He sleeps and wakes, wakes and sleeps, and suddenly all is, movement and suffering and terror and he is shot out gasping for breath into blinding light and a place that's even more dangerous, where food is scarce and two enormous giants stand guard over his wooden prison. Shout as he might, rattle the bars, nobody comes to let him out. One of the giants is boisterous and hair-covered, with a big stick; the other walks more softly but has two enormous bulgy comforts which she selfishly refuses to detach and give away, to him. Neither of them looks anything like him, and their language is incomprehensible.

3   Aliens! What can he do? And to make it worse, they surround him with animals—bears, rabbits, cats, giraffes—each one of them

stuffed and, evidently, castrated, because although he looks and looks, all they have at best is a tail. Is this the fate the aliens have in store for him, as well?

Where did I come from? he asks, for what will not be the first 4 time. *Out of me,* the bulgy one says fondly, as if he should be pleased. Out of *where?* Out of *what?* He covers his ears, shutting out the untruth, the shame, the pulpy horror. It is not to be thought, it is not to be borne!

No wonder that at the first opportunity he climbs out of the win- 5 dow and joins a gang of other explorers, each one of them an exile, an immigrant, like himself. Together they set out on their solitary journeys.

What are they searching for? Their homeland. Their true coun- 6 try. The place they came from, which can't possibly be here.

2

All men are created equal, as someone said who was either very 7 hopeful or very mischievous. What a lot of anxiety could have been avoided if he'd only kept his mouth shut.

Sigmund was wrong about the primal scene: Mom and Dad, key- 8 hole version. That might be upsetting, true, but there's another one:

Five guys standing outside, pissing into a snowbank, a river, the 9 underbrush, pretending not to look down. Or maybe *not* looking down: gazing upward, at the stars, which gives us the origin of astronomy. Anything to avoid comparisons, which aren't so much odious as intimidating.

And not only astronomy: quantum physics, engineering, laser 10 technology, all numeration between zero and infinity. Something safely abstract, detached from you; a transfer of the obsession with size to anything at all. Lord, Lord, they measure everything: the height of the Great Pyramids, the rate of fingernail growth, the multiplication of viruses, the sands of the sea, the number of angels that can dance on the head of a pin. And then it's only a short step to proving that God is a mathematical equation. Not a person. Not a body, Heaven forbid. Not one like yours. Not an earthbound one, not one with size and therefore pain.

When you're feeling blue, just keep on whistling. Just keep on 11 measuring. Just don't look down.

3

The history of war is a history of killed bodies. That's what war 12 is: bodies killing other bodies, bodies being killed.

Some of the killed bodies are those of women and children, as a 13 side effect you might say. Fallout, shrapnel, napalm, rape and skewering, antipersonnel devices. But most of the killed bodies are men. So are most of those doing the killing.

14   Why do men want to kill the bodies of other men? Women don't want to kill the bodies of other women. By and large. As far as we know.

15   Here are some traditional reasons: Loot. Territory. Lust for power. Hormones. Arenaline high. Rage. God. Flag. Honor. Righteous anger. Revenge. Oppression. Slavery. Starvation. Defense of one's life. Love; or, a desire to protect the women and children. From what? From the bodies of other men.

16   What men are most afraid of is not lions, not snakes, not the dark, not women. Not any more. What men are most afraid of is the body of another man.

17   Men's bodies are the most dangerous things on earth.

4

18   On the other hand, it could be argued that men don't have any bodies at all. Look at the magazines! Magazines for women have women's bodies on the covers, magazines for men have women's bodies on the covers. When men appear on the covers of magazines, it's magazines about money, or about world news. Invasions, rocket launches, political coups, interest rates, elections, medical breakthroughs. *Reality.* Not *entertainment.* Such magazines show only the heads, the unsmiling heads, the talking heads, the decision-making heads, and maybe a little glimpse, a coy flash of suit. How do we know there's a body, under all that discreet pinstriped tailoring? We don't, and maybe there isn't.

19   What does this lead us to suppose? That women are bodies with heads attached, and men are heads with bodies attached? Or not, depending.

20   You can have a body, though, if you're a rock star, an athlete, or a gay model. As I said, *entertainment.* Having a body is not altogether serious.

5

21   Or else too serious for words.

22   The thing is: Men's bodies aren't dependable. Now it does, now it doesn't, and so much for the triumph of the will. A man is the puppet of his body, or vice versa. He and it make tomfools of each other: It lets him down. Or up, at the wrong moment. Just stare hard out the schoolroom window and recite the multiplication tables and pretend this isn't happening! Your face at least can be immobile. Easier to have a trained dog, which will do what you want it to, nine times out of ten.

The other thing is: Men's bodies are detachable. Consider the 23
history of statuary: The definitive bits get knocked off so easily,
through revolution or prudery or simple transportation, with leaves
stuck on for substitutes, fig or grape; or in more northern climates,
maple. A man and his body are soon parted.

In the old old days, you became a man through blood. Through 24
incisions, tattoos, splinters of wood; through an intimate wound, and
the refusal to flinch. Through being beaten by older boys, in the dormitory, with a wooden paddle you were forced to carve yourself. The
torments varied, but they were all torments. *It's a boy*, they cry with
joy. *Let's cut some off!*

Every morning I get down on my knees and thank God for not 25
creating me a man. A man so chained to unpredictability. A man so
much at the mercy of himself. A man so prone to sadness. A man who
has to take it like a man. A man, who can't fake it.

In the gap between desire and enactment, noun and verb, inten- 26
tion and infliction, *want* and *have,* compassion begins.

6

Bluebeard ran off with the third sister, intelligent though beauti- 27
ful, and shut her up in his palace. *Everything here is yours, my dear,*
he said to her. *Just don't open the small door. I will give you the key;*
however I expect you not to use it.

Believe it or not, this sister was in love with him, even though 28
she knew he was a serial killer. She roamed over the whole palace, ignoring the jewels and the silk dresses and the piles of gold. Instead she
went through the medicine cabinet and the kitchen drawers, looking
for clues to his uniqueness. Because she loved him, she wanted to understand him. She also wanted to cure him. She thought she had the
healing touch.

But she didn't find out a lot. In his closet there were suits and 29
ties and matching shoes and casual wear, some golf outfits and a tennis racquet, and some jeans for when he wanted to rake up the leaves.
Nothing unusual, nothing kinky, nothing sinister. She had to admit to
being a little disappointed.

She found his previous women quite easily. They were in the 30
linen closet, neatly cut up and ironed flat and folded, stored in mothballs and lavender. Bachelors acquire such domestic skills. The
women didn't make much of an impression on her, except the one
who looked like his mother. That one she took out with rubber gloves
on and slipped into the incinerator in the garden. *Maybe it was his*
mother, she thought. *If so, good riddance.*

She read through his large collection of cookbooks, and prepared 31
the dishes on the most-thumbed pages. At dinner he was politeness

itself, pulling out her chair and offering more wine and leading the conversation around to topics of the day. She said gently that she wished he would talk more about his feelings. He said that if she had his feelings, she wouldn't want to talk about them either. This intrigued her. She was now more in love with him and more curious than ever.

32   *Well,* she thought, *I've tried everything else; it's the small door or nothing. Anyway, he gave me the key.* She waited until he had gone to the office or wherever it was he went, and made straight for the small door. When she opened it, what should be inside but a dead child. A small dead child with its eyes wide open.

33   *It's mine,* he said, coming up behind her. *I gave birth to it. I warned you. Weren't you happy with me?*

34   *It looks like you,* she said, not turning around, not knowing what to say. She realized now that he was not sane in any known sense of the word, but she still hoped to talk her way out of it. She could feel the love seeping out of her. Her heart was dry ice.

35   *It is me,* he said sadly. *Don't be afraid.*

36   *Where are we going?* she said, because it was getting dark, and there was suddenly no floor.

37   *Deeper,* he said.

7

38   Those ones. Why do women like them? They have nothing to offer, none of the usual things. They have short attention spans, falling-apart clothes old beat-up cars, if any. The cars break down, and they try to fix them, and don't succeed, and give up. They go on long walks, from which they forget to return. They prefer weeds to flowers. They tell trivial fibs. They perform clumsy tricks with oranges and pieces of string, hoping desperately that someone will laugh. They don't put food on the table. They don't make money. Don't, can't, won't.

39   They offer nothing. They offer the great clean sweep of nothing, the unseen sky during a blizzard, the dark pause between moon and moon. They offer their poverty, an empty wooden bowl; the bowl of a beggar, whose gift is to ask. Look into it, look down deep, where potential coils like smoke, and you might hear anything. Nothing has yet been said.

40   They have bodies, however, Their bodies are unlike the bodies of other men. Their bodies are verbalized. *Mouth, eye, hand, foot,* they say. Their bodies have weight, and move over the ground, step by step, like yours. Like you they roll in the hot mud of the sunlight, like you they are amazed by morning, like you they can taste the wind, like you they sing. *Love,* they say, and at the time they always mean it, as you do also. They can say *lust* as well, and *disgust;* you wouldn't trust

them otherwise. They say the worst things you have ever dreamed. They open locked doors. All this is given to them for nothing.

They have their angers. They have their despair, which washes 41 over them like gray ink, blanking them out, leaving them immobile, in metal kitchen chairs, beside closed windows, looking out at the brick walls of deserted factories, for years and years. Yet nothing is with them; it keeps faith with them, and from it they bring back messages.

Hurt, they say and suddenly their bodies hurt again, like real 42 bodies. *Death,* they say, making the word sound like the backwash of a wave. Their bodies die, and waver, and turn to mist. And yet they can exist in two worlds at once: lost in earth or eaten by flames, and here. In this room, when you re-say them, in their own words.

But why do women like them? Not *like,* I mean to say: *adore.* 43 (Remember, that despite everything, despite all I have told you, the rusted cars, the greasy wardrobes, the lack of breakfasts, the hopelessness, remain the same.)

Because if they can say their own bodies, they could say yours 44 also. Because they could say *skin* as if it meant something, not only to them but to you. Because one night, when the snow is falling and the moon is blotted out, they could put their empty hands, their hands filled with poverty, their beggar's hands, on your body, and bless it, and tell you it is made of light.

_____ CONSIDERATIONS _____

1. Which of these authors in your text—Ackerman, Hegland, Dillard— might he helpful in understanding the first few paragraphs of Atwood's essay? Explain.

2. In paragraph 10, deploring our tendency to quantify whatever crosses our path, Atwood cries out, "Lord, Lord, they measure everything." In what way, as a student, are you all too familiar with that tendency to reduce reality to numbers?

3. The obvious companion piece in this text for Atwood's "Allen Territory" is Updike's "The Disposable Rocket," page 584. Point out and discuss some of the differences and/or similarities.

4. How do you account for the apparent disconnectedness of Atwood's essay—separate sentences or even fragments presented as though they were paragraphs?

5. Given the fact that much of Atwood's reputation derives from aggressive and unyielding feminist writings, are any of her statements in "Alien Territory" surprising?

6. Paragraph 23 ends with a statement that probably sounds familiar: A man and his body are soon parted. Something you've heard before? Atwood's use of it demonstrates a useful device for a writer. Explain.

W. H. Auden (1907–1973), born Wystan Hugh, was a leading poet of the twentieth century. An Englishman, he attended Oxford where he began to publish as an undergraduate in the 1920s. He was a poet of ideas who spoke for his generation, beginning as a Marxist imbued with the ideas of Freud. Before the Second World War, he moved to the United States, where he lived for much of the rest of his life. From the political and psychological fascinations of his youth, he turned to Christianity. Shortly before he died he returned to Oxford, to live in his old Christ Church College.

Auden was master of many styles, from lyrical to narrative to didactic, with a passion for varieties of poetic form. In this poem, we see him writing something like a folksong.

7

W. H. AUDEN
As I walked out one Evening

As I walked out one evening,
　Walking down Bristol Street,
The crowds upon the pavement
　Were fields of harvest wheat.

5　And down by the brimming river
　I heard a lover sing
Under an arch of the railway:
　'Love has no ending.

'I'll love you, dear, I'll love you
10　Till China and Africa meet,
And the river jumps over the mountain
　And the salmon sing in the street,

'I'll love you till the ocean
  Is folded and hung up to dry
And the seven stars go squawking   15
  Like geese about the sky.

The years shall run like rabbits,
  For in my arms I hold
The Flower of the Ages,
  And the first love of the world.'   20

But all the clocks in the city
  Began to whirr and chime:
'O let not Time deceive you,
  You cannot conquer Time.

'In the burrows of the Nightmare   25
  Where Justice naked is,
Time watches from the shadow
  And coughs when you would kiss.

'In headaches and in worry
  Vaguely life leaks away,   30
And Time will have his fancy
  To-morrow or to-day.

'Into many a green valley
  Drifts the appalling snow;
Time breaks the threaded dances   35
  And the diver's brilliant bow.

'O plunge your hands in water,
  Plunge them in up to the wrist;
Stare, stare in the basin
  And wonder what you've missed.   40

'The glacier knocks in the cupboard,
  The desert sighs in the bed,
And the crack in the tea-cup opens
  A lane to the land of the dead.

'Where the beggars raffle the banknotes   45
  And the Giant is enchanting to Jack,
And the Lily-white Boy is a Roarer,
  And Jill goes down on her back.

'O look, look in the mirror,
  O look in your distress;   50
Life remains a blessing
  Although you cannot bless.

'O stand, stand at the window
    As the tears scald and start;
55   You shall love your crooked neighbour
    With your crooked heart.'

It was late, late in the evening,
    The lovers they were gone;
The clocks had ceased their chiming,
60   And the deep river ran on.

Wendell Berry (b. 1934), essayist, novelist, and poet, was born and educated in Kentucky. He left home to teach in New York and California, and eventually returned to his "native hill." In 1986 his collection of short stories, The Wild Birds, *was published by the North Point Press, which had also reissued his earlier novels,* A Place on Earth *and* Nathan Coulter. *In 1992 he brought out a second story collection,* Fidelity. *Among his many volumes of poetry are* Collected Poems: 1957–1982 *and* Sabbaths *(1987). His essay collections include* Recollected Essays, The Gift of Good Land *(both 1982),* Standing By Words *(1984), and* Standing on Earth *(1991). While he continues to farm his Kentucky acreage, he harvests literature in three genres: In 1994 he cropped one book of poetry,* Entries, *and one of fiction,* Watch With Me; *in 1995 he collected new essays,* Another Turn of the Crank.

Wendell Berry writes an essay—or a novel or a short story or a poem—in the same spirit with which he plows a field.

8

WENDELL BERRY
A Native Hill

I start down from one of the heights of the upland, the town of Port Royal at my back. It is a winter day, overcast and still, and the town is closed in itself, humming and muttering a little, like a winter beehive.

The dog runs ahead, prancing and looking back, knowing the way we are about to go. This is a walk well established with us—a route in our minds as well as on the ground. There is a sort of mystery in the establishment of these ways. Any time one crosses a given stretch of country with some frequency, no matter how wanderingly one begins, the tendency is always toward habit. By the third or fourth trip, without realizing it, one is following a fixed path, going the way one went before. After that, one may still wander, but only by deliberation, and when there is reason to hurry, or when the mind wanders rather than the feet, one returns to the old route. Familiarity has begun. One has made a relationship with the landscape, and the form and the symbol and the enactment of the relationship is the path. These paths of mine are seldom worn on the ground. They are habits of mind, directions, and turns. They are as personal as old shoes. My feet are comfortable in them.

3   From the height I can see far out over the country, the long open ridges of the farmland, the wooded notches of the streams, the valley of the river opening beyond, and then more ridges and hollows of the same kind.

4   Underlying this country, nine hundred feet below the highest ridgetops, more than four hundred feet below the surface of the river, is sea level. We seldom think of it here; we are a long way from the coast and the sea is alien to us. And yet the attraction of sea level dwells in this country as an ideal dwells in a man's mind. All our rains go in search of it and, departing, they have carved the land in a shape that is fluent and falling. The streams branch like vines, and between the branches the land rises steeply and then rounds and gentles into the long narrowing fingers of ridgeland. Near the heads of the streams even the steepest land was not too long ago farmed and kept cleared. But now it has been given up and the woods is returning. The wild is flowing back like a tide. The arable ridgetops reach out above the gathered trees like headlands into the sea, bearing their human burdens of fences and houses and barns, crops and roads.

5   Looking out over the country, one gets a sense of the whole of it: the ridges and hollows, the clustered buildings of the farms, the open fields, the woods, the stock ponds set like coins into the slopes. But this is a surface sense, an exterior sense, such as you get from looking down on the roof of a house. The height is a threshold from which to step down into the wooded folds of the land, the interior, under the trees and along the branching streams.

6   I pass through a pasture gate on a deep-worn path that grows shallow a little way beyond and then disappears altogether into the grass. The gate has gathered thousands of passings to and fro, that have divided like the slats of a fan on either side of it. It is like a fist holding together the strands of a net.

7   Beyond the gate the land leans always more steeply toward the branch. I follow it down, and then bear left along the crease at the bottom of the slope. I have entered the downflow of the land. The way I am going is the way the water goes. There is something comfortable and fit-feeling in this, something free in this yielding to gravity and

taking the shortest way down. The mind moves through the watershed as the water moves.

As the hollow deepens into the hill, before it has yet entered the 8 woods, the grassy crease becomes a raw gulley, and along the steepening slopes on either side I can see the old scars of erosion, places where the earth is gone clear to the rock. My people's errors have become the features of my country.

It occurs to me that it is no longer possible to imagine how this 9 country looked in the beginning, before the white people drove their plows into it. It is not possible to know what was the shape of the land here in this hollow when it was first cleared. Too much of it is gone, loosened by the plows and washed away by the rain. I am walking the route of the departure of the virgin soil of the hill. I am not looking at the same land the first-comers saw. The original surface of the hill is as extinct as the passenger pigeon. The pristine America that the first white men saw is a lost continent, sunk like Atlantis in the sea. The thought of what was here once and is gone forever will not leave me as long as I live. It is as though I walk knee-deep in its absence.

The slopes along the hollow steepen still more and I go in under 10 the trees. I pass beneath the surface. I am enclosed, and my sense, my interior sense, of the country becomes intricate. There is no longer the possibility of seeing very far. The distances are closed off by the trees and the steepening walls of the hollow. One cannot grow familiar here by sitting and looking as one can up in the open on the ridge. Here the eyes become dependent on the feet. To see the woods from the inside one must look and move and look again. It is inexhaustible in its standpoints. A lifetime will not be enough to experience it all.

Not far from the beginning of the woods, and set deep in the 11 earth in the bottom of the hollow, is a rock-walled pool not a lot bigger than a bathtub. The wall is still nearly as straight and tight as when it was built. It makes a neatly turned narrow horseshoe, the open end downstream. This is a historical ruin, dug here either to catch and hold the water of the little branch, or to collect the water of a spring whose vein broke to the surface here—it is probably no longer possible to know which. The pool is filled with earth now, and grass grows in it. And the branch bends around it, cut down to the bare rock, a torrent after heavy rain, other times bone dry. All that is certain is that when the pool was dug and walled there was deep topsoil on the hill to gather and hold the water. And this high up, at least, the bottom of the hollow, instead of the present raw notch of the streambed, wore the same mantle of soil as the slopes, and the stream was a steady seep or trickle, running most or all of the year. This tiny pool no doubt once furnished water for a considerable number of stock through the hot summers. And now it is only a lost souvenir, archaic and useless, except for the bitter intelligence there is in it. It is one of the monuments to what is lost.

12   Like the pasture gates, the streams are great collectors of comings and goings. The streams go down, and paths always go down beside the streams. For a while I walk along an old wagon road that is buried in leaves—a fragment, beginningless and endless as the middle of a sentence on some scrap of papyrus. There is a cedar whose branches reach over this road, and under the branches I find the leavings of two kills of some bird of prey. The most recent is a pile of blue jay feathers. The other has been rained on and is not identifiable. How little we know. How little of this was intended or expected by any man. The road that has become the grave of men's passages has led to the life of the woods.

> And I say to myself: Here is your road
> without beginning or end, appearing
> out of the earth and ending in it, bearing
> no load but the hawk's kill, and the leaves
> building earth on it, something more
> to be borne. Tracks fill with earth
> and return to absence. The road was worn
> by men bearing earth along it. They have come
> to endlessness. In their passing
> they could not stay in, trees have risen
> and stand still. It is leading to the dark,
> to morning where you are not. Here
> is your road, beginningless and endless as God.

13   Now I have come down within the sound of the water. The winter has been rainy, and the hill is full of dark seeps and trickles, gathering finally, along these creases, into flowing streams. The sound of them is one of the elements, and defines a zone. When their voices return to the hill after their absence during summer and autumn, it is a better place to be. A thirst in the mind is quenched.

14   I have already passed the place where water began to flow in the little stream bed I am following. It broke into the light from beneath a rock ledge, a thin glittering stream. It lies beside me as I walk, overtaking me and going by, yet not moving, a thread of light and sound. And now from below comes the steady tumble and rush of the water of Camp Branch—whose nameless camp was it named for?—and gradually as I descend the sound of the smaller stream is lost in the sound of the larger.

15   The two hollows join, the line of the meeting of the two spaces obscured even in winter by the trees. But the two streams meet precisely as two roads. That is, the stream *beds* do; the one ends in the other. As for the meeting of the waters, there is no looking at that.

The one flow does not end in the other, but continues in it, one with it, two clarities merged without a shadow.

All waters are one. This is a reach of the sea, flung like a net over   16
the hill, and now drawn back to the sea. And as the sea is never raised in the earthly nets of fishermen, so the hill is never caught and pulled down by the watery net of the sea. But always a little of it is. Each of the gathering strands of the net carries back some of the hill melted in it. Sometimes, as now, it carries so little that the water seems to flow clear; sometimes it carries a lot and is brown and heavy with it. Whenever greedy or thoughtless men have lived on it, the hill has literally flowed out of their tracks into the bottom of the sea.

There appears to be a law that when creatures have reached the   17
level of consciousness, as men have, they must become conscious of the creation; they must learn how they fit into it and what its needs are and what it requires of them, or else pay a terrible penalty: the spirit of the creation will go out of them, and they will become destructive. The very earth will depart from them and go where they cannot follow.

My mind is never empty or idle at the joinings of streams. Here   18
is the work of the world going on. The creation is felt, alive, and intent on its materials, in such places. In the angle of the meeting of the two streams stands the steep wooded point of the ridge, like the prow of an upturned boat—finished, as it was a thousand years ago, as it will be in a thousand years. Its becoming is only incidental to its being. It will be because it is. It has no aim or end except to be. By being it is growing and wearing into what it will be. The fork of the stream lies at the foot of the slope like hammer and chisel laid down at the foot of a finished sculpture. But the stream is no dead tool; it is alive, it is still at its work. Put your hand to it to learn the health of this part of the world. It is the wrist of the hill.

Perhaps it is to prepare to hear some day the music of the spheres   19
that I am always turning my ears to the music of streams. There is indeed a music in streams, but it is not for the hurried. It has to be loitered by and imagined. Or imagined *toward,* for it is hardly for men at all. Nature has a patient ear. To her the slowest funeral march sounds like a jig. She is satisfied to have the notes drawn out to the lengths of days or weeks or months. Small variations are acceptable to her, modulations as leisurely as the opening of a flower.

The stream is full of stops and gates. Here it has piled up rocks in   20
its path, and pours over them into a tiny pool it has scooped at the foot of its fall. Here it has been dammed by a mat of leaves caught behind a fallen limb. Here it must force a narrow passage, here a wider one. Tomorrow the flow may increase or slacken, and the tone will shift. In an hour or a week that rock may give way, and the composition will advance by another note. Some idea of it may be got by walking

slowly along and noting the changes as one passes from one little fall or rapid to another. But this is a highly simplified and diluted version of the real thing, which is too complex and widespread ever to be actually heard by us. The ear must imagine an impossible patience in order to grasp even the unimaginableness of such music.

21   But the creation is musical, and this is a part of its music, as birdsong is, or the words of poets. The music of the streams is the music of the shaping of the earth, by which the rocks are pushed and shifted downward toward the level of the sea.

22   And now I find lying in the path an empty beer can. This is the track of the ubiquitous man Friday of all our woods. In my walks I never fail to discover some sign that he has preceded me. I find his empty shotgun shells, his empty cans and bottles, his sandwich wrappings. In wooded places along roadsides one is apt to find, as well, his overtravelled bedsprings, his outcast refrigerator, and heaps of the imperishable refuse of his modern kitchen. A year ago, almost in this same place where I have found his beer can, I found a possum that he had shot dead and left lying, in celebration of his manhood. He is the true American pioneer, perfectly at rest in his assumption that he is the first and the last whose inheritance and fate this place will ever be. Going forth, as he may think, to sow, he only broadcasts his effects.

23   As I go down the path alongside Camp Branch, I walk by the edge of croplands abandoned only within my own lifetime. On my left are south slopes where the woods are old, long undisturbed. On my right, the more fertile north slopes are covered with patches of briars and sumacs and a lot of young walnut trees. Tobacco of an extraordinary quality was once grown here, and then the soil wore thin, and these places were given up for the more accessible ridges that were not so steep, where row-cropping made better sense anyway. But now, under the thicket growth, a mat of bluegrass has grown to testify to the good nature of this ground. It was fine dirt that lay here once, and I am far from being able to say that I could have resisted the temptation to plow it. My understanding of what is best for it is the tragic understanding of hindsight, the awareness that I have been taught what was here to be lost by the loss of it.

24   We have lived by the assumption that what was good for us would be good for the world. And this has been based on the even flimsier assumption that we could know with any certainty what was good even for us. We have fulfilled the danger of this by making our personal pride and greed the standard of our behavior toward the world—to the incalculable disadvantage of the world and every living thing in it. And now, perhaps very close to too late, our great error has become clear. It is not only our own creativity—our own capacity for life—that is stifled by our arrogant assumption; the creation itself is stifled.

We have been wrong. We must change our lives, so that it will be   25
possible to live by the contrary assumption that what is good for the
world will be good for us. And that requires that we make the effort to
know the world and to learn what is good for it. We must learn to co-
operate in its processes, and to yield to its limits. But even more important, we must learn to acknowledge that the creation is full of mystery; we will never entirely understand it. We must abandon arrogance
and stand in awe. We must recover the sense of the majesty of creation, and the ability to be worshipful in its presence. For I do not
doubt that it is only on the condition of humility and reverence before
the world that our species will be able to remain in it.

Standing in the presence of these worn and abandoned fields,   26
where the creation has begun its healing without the hindrance or the
help of man, with the voice of the stream in the air and the woods
standing in silence on all the slopes around me, I am deep in the interior not only of my place in the world, but of my own life, its sources
and searches and concerns. I first came into these places following the
men to work when I was a child. I knew the men who took their lives
from such fields as these, and their lives to a considerable extent made
my life what it is. In what came to me from them there was both
wealth and poverty, and I have been a long time discovering which
was which.

It was in the woods here along Camp Branch that Bill White, my   27
grandfather's hired hand, taught me to hunt squirrels. Bill lived in a
little tin-roofed house on up nearer the head of the hollow. And this
was, I suppose more than any other place, his hunting ground. It was
the place of his freedom, where he could move without subservience,
without considering who he was or who anybody else was. On late
summer mornings, when it was too wet to work, I would follow him
into the woods. As soon as we stepped in under the trees he would become silent, and absolutely attentive to the life of the place. He was a
good teacher and an exacting one. The rule seemed to be that if I
wanted to stay with him, I had to make it possible for him to forget I
was there. I was to make no noise. If I did he would look back and
make a downward emphatic gesture with his hand, as explicit as writing: Be quiet, or go home. He would see a squirrel crouched in a fork or
lying along the top of a branch, and indicate with a grin and a small
jerk of his head where I should look; and then wait, while I, conscious
of being watched and demanded upon, searched it out for myself. He
taught me to look and to listen and to be quiet. I wonder if he knew
the value of such teaching or the rarity of such a teacher.

In the years that followed I hunted often here alone. And later in   28
these same woods I experienced my first obscure dissatisfactions with
hunting. Though I could not have put it into words then, the sense
had come to me that hunting as I knew it—the eagerness to kill some-

thing I did not need to eat—was an artificial relation to the place, when what I was beginning to need, just as inarticulately then, was a relation that would be deeply natural and meaningful. That was a time of great uneasiness and restlessness for me. It would be the fall of the year, the leaves would be turning, and ahead of me would be another year of school. There would be confusions about girls and ambitions, the wordless hurried feeling that time and events and my own nature were pushing me toward what I was going to be—and I had no notion what it was, or how to prepare.

29   And then there were years when I did not come here at all—when these places and their history were in my mind, and part of me, in places thousands of miles away. And now I am here again, changed from what I was, and still changing. The future is no more certain to me now than it ever was, though its risks are clearer, and so are my own desires. I am the father of two young children whose lives are hostages given to the future. Because of them and because of events in the world, life seems more fearful and difficult to me now than ever before; but it is also more inviting, and I am constantly aware of its nearness to joy. Much of the interest and excitement that I have in my life now has come from the deepening, in the years since my return here, of my relation to this countryside that is my native place. For in spite of all that has happened to me in other places, the great change and the great possibility of change in my life has been in my sense of this place. The major difference is perhaps only that I have grown able to be wholeheartedly present here. I am able to sit and be quiet at the foot of some tree here in this woods along Camp Branch, and feel a deep peace, both in the place and in my awareness of it, that not too long ago I was not conscious of the possibility of. This peace is partly in being free of the suspicion that pursued me for most of my life, no matter where I was, that there was perhaps another place I *should* be, or would be happier or better in; it is partly in the increasingly articulate consciousness of being here, and of the significance and importance of being here.

30   After more than thirty years I have at last arrived at the candor necessary to stand on this part of the earth that is so full of my own history and so much damaged by it, and ask: What *is* this place? What is in it? What is its nature? How should men live in it? What must I do?

31   I have not found the answers, though I believe that in partial and fragmentary ways they have begun to come to me. But the questions are more important than their answers. In the final sense they *have* no answers. They are like the questions—they are perhaps the same questions—that were the discipline of Job. They are part of the necessary enactment of humility, teaching a man what his importance is, what his responsibility is, and what his place is, both on the earth and in the

order of things. And though the answers must always come obscurely and in fragments, the questions must be persistently asked. They are fertile questions. In their implications and effects, they are moral and esthetic and, in the best and fullest sense, practical. They promise a relationship to the world that is decent and preserving.

They are also, both in origin and effect, religious. I am uneasy   32 with the term, for such religion as has been openly practiced in this part of the world has promoted and fed upon a destructive schism between body and soul, heaven and earth. It has encouraged people to believe that the world is of no importance, and that their only obligation in it is to submit to certain churchly formulas in order to get to heaven. And so the people who might have been expected to care most selflessly for the world have had their minds turned elsewhere—to a pursuit of "salvation" that was really only another form of gluttony and self-love, the desire to perpetuate their own small lives beyond the life of the world. The heaven-bent have abused the earth thoughtlessly, by inattention, and their negligence has permitted and encouraged others to abuse it deliberately. Once the creator was removed from the creation, divinity became only a remote abstraction, a social weapon in the hands of the religious institutions. This split in public values produced or was accompanied by, as it was bound to be, an equally artificial and ugly division in people's lives, so that a man, while pursuing heaven with the sublime appetite he thought of as his soul, could turn his heart against his neighbors and his hands against the world. For these reasons, though I know that my questions *are* religious, I dislike having to *say* that they are.

But when I ask them my aim is not primarily to get to heaven.   33 Though heaven is certainly more important than the earth if all they say about it is true, it is still morally incidental to it and dependent on it, and I can only imagine it and desire it in terms of which I know of the earth. And so my questions do no aspire beyond the earth. They aspire *toward* it and *into* it. Perhaps they aspire *through* it. They are religious because they are asked at the limit of what I know; they acknowledge mystery and honor its presence in the creation; they are spoken in reverence for the order and grace that I see, and that I trust beyond my power to see.

The stream has led me down to an old barn built deep in the hol-   34 low to house the tobacco once grown on those abandoned fields. Now it is surrounded by the trees that have come back on every side—a relic, a fragment of another time, strayed out of its meaning. This is the last of my historical landmarks. To here, my walk has had insistent overtones of memory and history. It has been a movement of consciousness through knowledge, eroding and shaping, adding and wearing away. I have descended like the water of the stream through what I know of myself, and now that I have there is a little more to know.

But here at the barn, the old roads and the cow paths—the formal connections with civilization—come to an end.

35   I stoop between the strands of a barbed wire fence, and in that movement I go out of time into timelessness. I come into a wild place. I walk along the foot of a slope that was once cut bare of trees, like all the slopes of this part of the country—but long ago; and now the woods is established again, the ground healed, the trees grown big, their trunks rising clean, free of undergrowth. The place has a serenity and dignity that one feels immediately; the creation is whole in it and unobstructed. It is free of the strivings and dissatisfactions, the partialities and imperfections of places under the mechanical dominance of men. Here, what to a housekeeper's eye might seem disorderly is nonetheless orderly and within order; what might seem arbitrary or accidental is included in the design of the whole as if by intention; what might seem evil or violent is a comfortable member of the household. Where the creation is whole nothing is extraneous. The presence of the creation here makes this a holy place, and it is as a pilgrim that I have come—to give the homage of awe and love, to submit to mystification. It is the creation that has attracted me, its perfect interfusion of life and design. I have made myself its follower and its apprentice.

36   One early morning last spring, I came and found the woods floor strewn with bluebells. In the cool sunlight and the lacy shadows of the spring woods the blueness of those flowers, their elegant shape, their delicate fresh scent kept me standing and looking. I found a rich delight in them that I cannot describe and that I will never forget. Though I had been familiar for years with most of the spring woods flowers, I had never seen these and had not known they grew here. Looking at them, I felt a strange feeling of loss and sorrow that I had never seen them before. But I was also exultant that I saw them now— that they were here.

37   For me, in the thought of them will always be the sense of the joyful surprise with which I found them—the sense that came suddenly to me then that the world is blessed beyond my understanding, more abundantly than I will ever know. What lives are still ahead of me here to be discovered and exulted in, tomorrow, or in twenty years? What wonder will be found here on the morning after my death? Though as a man I inherit great evils and the possibility of great loss and suffering, I know that my life is blessed and graced by the yearly flowering of the bluebells. How perfect they are! In their presence I am humble and joyful. If I were given all the learning and all the methods of my race I could not make one of them, or even imagine one. Solomon in all his glory was not arrayed like one of these. It is the privilege and the labor of the apprentice of creation to come with his imagination into the unimaginable, and with his speech into the unspeakable.

_____ CONSIDERATIONS _____

1. To think of habits as paths worn in the mind is no very original metaphor. How does Berry distinguish this image as he works it into the essay?

2. Berry's essay, like the walk he is reporting, is a leisurely experience that should be taken in an unhurried manner. Much of this easy pace is due to his style: he makes an observation, then pauses to reflect on it and related things, then moves along to another observation, and another reflective pause, and so on. The result is a pleasing, thoughtful mix of the factual and the insightful. Try writing a short, descriptive essay in this style.

3. "Nature has a patient ear," writes Berry in paragraph 19, using a literary technique called personification. Look for examples of personification in the works of other writers, or make up several yourself (e.g., "the blindness of the night," "the laughter of the wind," "the soul of the abandoned house"). Then explain the meaning of personification and its value to a writer like Berry.

4. Assuming paragraph 30 is an explicit pronouncement of his thesis, what varied means does Berry use to embody these ideas?

5. On his walk, Berry follows the downward course of streams and slopes and gulleys. In what way does his essay also follow downward, converging courses to lead you to his conclusion?

6. Throughout his essay, Berry works to evoke a sense of place—that hill where he grew up and to which he now returns. Yet he also thinks on a wider scale—the state of the nation, and even the world. Is he successful in fusing the various planes? If so, how does he manage it? If not, why not?

Ambrose Bierce (1842–1914?) was born in a log cabin on Horse Cave Creek in Ohio. He educated himself by reading the books in his father's small library, and as a young man served in the army during the Civil War. Starting as a journalist in California, he made himself an elegant writer of short stories, which were often supernatural or macabre in theme. Because he was writing in the primitive West, in a country still generally primitive, his serious work went largely unrecognized. Melancholy deepened into misanthropy. The definitions in The Devil's Dictionary *(1906) are funny indeed—but the humor is serious, and the wit is bitter.*

In 1913, Bierce put his affairs in order and went to Mexico, which was in the midst of a civil war. He wrote a friend as he left, ". . . if you hear of my being stood up against a Mexican stone wall and shot to rags please know that I think it a pretty good way to depart this life. It beats old age, disease, or falling down a flight of stairs." He was never heard from again.

9

AMBROSE BIERCE
Some Devil's Definitions

1   *Belladonna, n.* In Italian a beautiful lady; in English a deadly poison. A striking example of the essential identity of the two tongues.

2   *Bigot, n.* One who is obstinately and zealously attached to an opinion that you do not entertain.

3   *Bore, n.* A person who talks when you wish him to listen.

4   *Brute, n. See* HUSBAND.

5   *Cabbage, n.* A familiar kitchen-garden vegetable about as large and wise as a man's head.

6   *Calamity, n.* A more than commonly plain and unmistakable reminder that the affairs of this life are not of our own ordering. Calamities are of two kinds: misfortune to ourselves, and good fortune to others.

Cannibal, n. A gastronome of the old school who preserves the   7
simple tastes and adheres to the natural diet of the pre-pork period.

Cannon, n. An instrument employed in the rectification of na-   8
tional boundaries.

Cat, n. A soft, indestructible automaton provided by nature to be   9
kicked when things go wrong in the domestic circle.

Christian, n. One who believes that the New Testament is a di-   10
vinely inspired book admirably suited to the spiritual needs of his
neighbor. One who follows the teachings of Christ in so far as they are
not inconsistent with a life of sin.

Clairvoyant, n. A person, commonly a woman, who has the   11
power of seeing that which is invisible to her patron—namely, that he
is a blockhead.

Commerce, n. A kind of transaction in which A plunders from B   12
the goods of C, and for compensation B picks the pocket of D of
money belonging to E.

Compromise, n. Such an adjustment of conflicting interests as   13
gives each adversary the satisfaction of thinking he has got what he
ought not to have, and is deprived of nothing except what was justly
his due.

Compulsion, n. The eloquence of power.   14

Congratulation, n. The civility of envy.   15

Conservative, n. A statesman who is enamored of existing evils,   16
as distinguished from the Liberal, who wishes to replace them with
others.

Consul, n. In American politics, a person who having failed to se-   17
cure an office from the people is given one by the Administration on
condition that he leave the country.

Consult, v.t. To seek another's approval of a course already de-   18
cided on.

Corsair, n. A politician of the seas.   19

Coward, n. One who in a perilous emergency thinks with his   20
legs.

Curiosity, n. An objectionable quality of the female mind. The   21
desire to know whether or not a woman is cursed with curiosity is one
of the most active and insatiable passions of the masculine soul.

Cynic, n. A blackguard whose faulty vision sees things as they   22
are, not as they ought to be. Hence the custom among the Scythians of
plucking out a cynic's eyes to improve his vision.

Dance, v.i. To leap about to the sound of tittering music, prefer-   23
ably with arms about your neighbor's wife or daughter. There are
many kinds of dances, but all those requiring the participation of the
two sexes have two characteristics in common: they are conspicuously innocent, and warmly loved by the vicious.

24   *Debauchee, n.* One who has so earnestly pursued pleasure that he has had the misfortune to overtake it.

25   *Decalogue, n.* A series of commandments, ten in number—just enough to permit an intelligent selection for observance, but not enough to embarrass the choice.

26   *Defame, v.t.* To lie about another. To tell the truth about another.

27   *Dentist, n.* A prestidigitator who, putting metal in your mouth, pulls coins out of your pocket.

28   *Die, n.* The singular of "dice." We seldom hear the word, because there is a prohibitory proverb, "Never say die."

29   *Discussion, n.* A method of confirming others in their errors.

30   *Distance, n.* The only thing that the rich are willing for the poor to call theirs, and keep.

31   *Duel, n.* A formal ceremony preliminary to the reconciliation of two enemies. Great skill is necessary to its satisfactory observance; if awkwardly performed the most unexpected and deplorable consequences sometimes ensue. A long time ago a man lost his life in a duel.

32   *Eccentricity, n.* A method of distinction so cheap that fools employ it to accentuate their incapacity.

33   *Edible, adj.* Good to eat, and wholesome to digest, as a worm to a toad, a toad to a snake, a snake to a pig, a pig to a man, and a man to a worm.

34   *Education, n.* That which discloses to the wise and disguises from the foolish their lack of understanding.

35   *Effect, n.* The second of two phenomena which always occur together in the same order. The first, called a Cause, is said to generate the other—which is no more sensible than it would be for one who has never seen a dog except in pursuit of a rabbit to declare the rabbit the cause of the dog.

36   *Egotist, n.* A person of low taste, more interested in himself than in me.

37   *Erudition, n.* Dust shaken out of a book into an empty skull.

38   *Eulogy, n.* Praise of a person who has either the advantages of wealth and power, or the consideration to be dead.

39   *Female, n.* One of the opposing, or unfair, sex.

40   *Fib, n.* A lie that has not cut its teeth. A habitual liar's nearest approach to truth: the perigee of his eccentric orbit.

41   *Fiddle, n.* An instrument to tickle human ears by friction of a horse's tail on the entrails of a cat.

42   *Friendship, n.* A ship big enough to carry two in fair weather, but only one in foul.

Garter, n. An elastic band intended to keep a woman from com- 43
ing out of her stockings and desolating the country.

Ghost, n. The outward and visible sign of an inward fear.   44

Glutton, n. A person who escapes the evils of moderation by 45
committing dyspepsia.

Gout, n. A physician's name for the rheumatism of a rich pa- 46
tient.

Grammar, n. A system of pitfalls thoughtfully prepared for the 47
feet of the self-made man, along the path by which he advances to distinction.

Guillotine, n. A machine which makes a Frenchman shrug his 48
shoulders with good reason.

___ CONSIDERATIONS _____

1. To appreciate the humor in some of Bierce's definitions, you may
have to look up in your dictionary some of the words found here, such as
"gastronome," "zealously," "adversary," "civility," "insatiable," "prestidigitator," "perigee," "dyspepsia." How do you add words to your working
vocabulary?

2. *The Devil's Dictionary* was first published in 1906. Judging from the
definitions here, would you say that Bierce's book is dated? Which items
strike you as most relevant to our times? Which are least relevant? Why?

3. Do you find a consistent tone or attitude in Bierce's dictionary? Explain and provide ample evidence.

4. Who among these authors would most appreciate Bierce's brand of
humor: Frederick Douglass ("Plantation Life"), Molly Ivins ("As Thousands
Cheer"), Flannery O'Connor ("A Good Man Is Hard to Find"), or George Orwell ("A Hanging")? Explain, making comparisons.

5. Compose a page of definitions for your own Devil's Dictionary, perhaps concentrating on words currently popular.

Caroline Bird (b. 1915) was born in New York City, taught at Vassar, and now divides her time between Manhattan and Poughkeepsie. She has been an editor and a teacher and is the author of Born Female *(1968),* The Case Against College *(1975),* What Women Want *(1979),* The Two-Paycheck Marriage *(1982), and* The Good Years: Your Life in the 21st Century *(1983).* Lives of Our Own: Secrets of Salty Old Women *came out in 1995. Here she argues the case against college with a clear vigor and a committed pugnacity; only a skilled debater with a good college education could dispute her.*

10

CAROLINE BIRD
Where College Fails Us

1   The case *for* college has been accepted without question for more than a generation. All high school graduates ought to go, says Conventional Wisdom and statistical evidence, because college will help them earn more money, become "better" people, and learn to be more responsible citizens than those who don't go.

2   But college has never been able to work its magic for everyone. And now that close to half our high school graduates are attending, those who don't fit the pattern are becoming more numerous, and more obvious. College graduates are selling shoes and driving taxis; college students sabotage each other's experiments and forge letters of recommendation in the intense competition for admission to graduate school. Others find no stimulation in their studies, and drop out—often encouraged by college administrators.

3   Some observers say the fault is with the young people themselves—they are spoiled, stoned, overindulged, and expecting too much. But that's mass character assassination, and doesn't explain all campus unhappiness. Others blame the state of the world, and they

are partly right. We've been told that young people have to go to college because our economy can't absorb an army of untrained eighteen-year-olds. But disillusioned graduates are learning that it can no longer absorb an army of trained twenty-two-year-olds, either.

Some adventuresome educators and campus watchers have 4 openly begun to suggest that college may not be the best, the proper, the only place for every young person after the completion of high school. We may have been looking at all those surveys and statistics upside down, it seems, and through the rosy glow of our own remembered college experiences. Perhaps college doesn't make people intelligent, ambitious, happy, liberal, or quick to learn new things—maybe it's just the other way around, and intelligent, ambitious, happy, liberal, and quick-learning people are merely the ones who have been attracted to college in the first place. And perhaps all those successful college graduates would have been successful whether they had gone to college or not. This is heresy to those of us who have been brought up to believe that if a little schooling is good, more has to be much better. But contrary evidence is beginning to mount up.

The unhappiness and discontent of young people is nothing new, 5 and problems of adolescence are always painfully intense. But while traveling around the country, speaking at colleges, and interviewing students at all kinds of schools—large and small, public and private—I was overwhelmed by the prevailing sadness. It was as visible on campuses in California as in Nebraska and Massachusetts. Too many young people are in college reluctantly, because everyone told them they ought to go, and there didn't seem to be anything better to do. Their elders sell them college because it's good for them. Some never learn to like it, and talk about their time in school as if it were a sentence to be served.

Students tell us the same thing college counselors tell us—they 6 go because of pressure from parents and teachers, and stay because it seems to be an alternative to a far worse fate. It's "better" than the Army or a dead-end job, and it has to be pretty bad before it's any worse than staying at home.

College graduates say that they don't want to work "just" for the 7 money: They want work that matters. They want to help people and save the world. But the numbers are stacked against them. Not only are there not enough jobs in world-saving fields, but in the current slowdown it has become evident that there never were, and probably never will be, enough jobs requiring higher education to go around.*

---

*Editor's note: Ms. Bird's article appeared in 1975. According to Howard Fullerton at the Bureau of Labor Statistics, an average of 1.1 million new college graduates will enter the work force yearly between 1990 and 2005. Another 214,000 college graduates will reenter the work force yearly over the same period. These roughly 1.3 million college graduates will compete for an estimated 914,000 job openings per year between 1993 and 2005.

8   Students who tell their advisers they want to help people, for example, are often directed to psychology. This year the Department of Labor estimates that there will be 4,300 new jobs for psychologists, while colleges will award 58,430 bachelor's degrees in psychology.

9   Sociology has become a favorite major on socially conscious campuses, but graduates find that social reform is hardly a paying occupation. Male sociologists from the University of Wisconsin reported as gainfully employed a year after graduation included a legal assistant, sports editor, truck unloader, Peace Corps worker, publications director, and a stockboy—but no sociologist *per se.* The highest paid worked for the post office.

10   Publishing, writing, and journalism are presumably the vocational goal of a large proportion of the 104,000 majors in Communications and Letters expected to graduate in 1975. The outlook for them is grim. All of the daily newspapers in the country combined are expected to hire a total of 2,600 reporters this year. Radio and television stations may hire a total of 500 announcers, most of them in local radio stations. Nonpublishing organizations will need 1,100 technical writers, and public-relations activities another 4,400. Even if new graduates could get all these jobs (they can't, of course), over 90,000 of them will have to find something less glamorous to do.

11   Other fields most popular with college graduates are also pathetically small. Only 1,900 foresters a year will be needed during this decade, although schools of forestry are expected to continue graduating twice that many. Some will get sub-professional jobs as forestry aides. Schools of architecture are expected to turn out twice as many [architects] as will be needed, and while all sorts of people want to design things, the Department of Labor forecasts that there will be jobs for only 400 new industrial designers a year. As for anthropologists, only 400 will be needed every year in the 1970s to take care of all the college courses, public-health research, community surveys, museums, and all the archaeological digs on every continent. (For these jobs graduate work in anthropology is required.)

12   Many popular occupations may seem to be growing fast without necessarily offering employment to very many. "Recreation work" is always cited as an expanding field, but it will need relatively few workers who require more special training than life guards. "Urban planning" has exploded in the media, so the U.S. Department of Labor doubled its estimate of the number of jobs to be filled every year in the 1970s—to a big, fat 800. A mere 200 oceanographers a year will be able to do all the exploring of "inner space"—and all that exciting underwater diving you see demonstrated on television—for the entire decade of the 1970s.

13   Whatever college graduates *want* to do, most of them are going to wind up doing what *there is* to do. During the next few years, ac-

cording to the Labor Department, the biggest demand will be for stenographers and secretaries, followed by retail-trade salesworkers, hospital attendants, bookkeepers, building custodians, registered nurses, foremen, kindergarten and elementary-school teachers, receptionists, cooks, cosmetologists, private-household workers, manufacturing inspectors, and industrial machinery repairmen. These are the jobs that will eventually absorb the surplus archaeologists, urban planners, oceanographers, sociologists, editors, and college professors.

Vocationalism is the new look on campus because of the discouraging job market faced by the generalists. Students have been opting for medicine and law in droves. If all those who check "doctor" as their career goal succeed in getting their MDs, we'll immediately have ten times the target ratio of doctors for the population of the United States. Law schools are already graduating twice as many new lawyers every year as the Department of Labor thinks we will need, and the oversupply grows annually. 14

Specialists often find themselves at the mercy of shifts in demand, and the narrower the vocational training, the more risky the long-term prospects. Engineers are the classic example of the "Yo-Yo" effect in supply and demand. Today's shortage is apt to produce a big crop of engineering graduates after the need has crested, and teachers face the same squeeze. 15

Worse than that, when the specialists turn up for work, they often find that they have learned a lot of things in classrooms that they will never use, that they will have to learn a lot of things on the job that they were never taught, and that most of what they have learned is less likely to "come in handy later" than to fade from memory. One disillusioned architecture student, who had already designed and built houses, said, "It's the degree you need, not everything you learn getting it." 16

A diploma saves the employer the cost of screening candidates and gives him a predictable product: He can assume that those who have survived the four-year ordeal have learned how to manage themselves. They have learned how to budget their time, meet deadlines, set priorities, cope with impersonal authority, follow instructions, and stick with a task that may be tiresome without direct supervision. 17

The employer is also betting that it will be cheaper and easier to train the college graduate because he has demonstrated his ability to learn. But if the diploma serves only to identify those who are talented in the art of schoolwork, it becomes, in the words of Harvard's Christopher Jencks, "a hell of an expensive aptitude test." It is unfair to the candidates because they themselves must bear the cost of the screening—the cost of college. Candidates without the funds, the academic temperament, or the patience for the four-year obstacle race are ruled out, no matter how well they may perform on the job. But if 18 "everyone" has a diploma, employers will have to find another way to choose employees, and it will become an empty credential.

19   (Screening by diploma may in fact already be illegal. The 1971 ruling of the Supreme Court in *Griggs* v. *Duke Power Co.* contended that an employer cannot demand a qualification which systematically excludes an entire class of applicants, unless that qualification reliably predicts success on the job. The requiring of a high school diploma was outlawed in the *Griggs* case, and this could extend to a college diploma.)

20   The bill for four years at an Ivy League college is currently climbing toward $70,000; at a state university, a degree will cost the student and his family about $10,000 (with taxpayers making up the difference).

21   Not many families can afford these sums, and when they look for financial aid, they discover that someone else will decide how much they will actually have to pay. The College Scholarship Service, which establishes a family's degree of need for most colleges, is guided by noble principles: uniformity of sacrifice, need rather than merit. But families vary in their willingness to "sacrifice" as much as the bureaucracy of the CSS thinks they ought to. This is particularly true of middle-income parents, whose children account for the bulk of the country's college students. Some have begun to rebel against this attempt to enforce the same values and priorities on all. "In some families, a college education competes with a second car, a color television, or a trip to Europe—and it's possible that college may lose," one financial-aid officer recently told me.

22   Quite so. College is worth more to some middle-income families than to others. It is chilling to consider the undercurrent of resentment that families who "give up everything" must feel toward their college-age children, or the burden of guilt children must bear every time they goof off or receive less than top grades in their courses.

23   The decline in return for a college degree within the last generation has been substantial. In the 1950s, a Princeton student could pay his expenses for the school year—eating club and all—on less than $3,000. When he graduated, he entered a job market which provided a comfortable margin over the earnings of his age-mates who had not been to college. To be precise, a freshman entering Princeton in 1956, the earliest year for which the Census has attempted to project lifetime earnings, could expect to realize a 12.5 percent return on his investment. A freshman entering in 1972, with the cost nearing $6,000 annually, could expect to realize only 9.3 percent, less than might be available in the money market. This calculation was made with the help of a banker and his computer, comparing college as an investment in future earnings with other investments available in the booming money market of 1974, and concluded that in strictly finan-

cial terms, college is not always the best investment a young person can make.

I postulated a young man in 1974 (the figures are different with a 24 young woman, but the principle is the same) whose rich uncle would give him, in cash, the total cost of four years at Princeton—$34,181. (The total includes what the young man would earn if he went to work instead of to college right after high school.) If he did not spend the money on Princeton, but put it in the savings bank at 7.5 percent interest compounded daily, he would have, at retirement age sixty-four, more than five times as much as the $199,000 extra he could expect to earn between twenty-two and sixty as a college man rather than a mere high school graduate. And with all that money accumulating in the bank, he could invest in something with a higher return than a diploma. At age twenty-eight, when his nest egg had reached $73,113, he could buy a liquor store, which would return him well over 20 percent on his investment, as long as he was willing to mind the store. He might get a bit fidgety sitting there, but he'd have to be dim-witted to lose money on a liquor store, and right now we're talking only about dollars.

If the young man went to a public college rather than Princeton, 25 the investment would be lower, and the payoff higher, of course, because other people—the taxpayers—put up part of the capital for him. But the difference in return between an investment in public and private colleges is minimized because the biggest part of the investment in either case is the money a student might earn if he went to work, not to college—in economic terms, his "foregone income." That he bears himself.

Rates of return and dollar signs on education are a fascinating 26 brain teaser, and, obviously, there is a certain unreality to the game. But the same unreality extends to the traditional calculations that have always been used to convince taxpayers that college is a worthwhile investment.

The ultimate defense of college has always been that while it 27 may not teach you anything vocationally useful, it will somehow make you a better person, able to do anything better, and those who make it through the process are initiated into the "fellowship of educated men and women." In a study intended to probe what graduates seven years out of college thought their colleges should have done for them, the Carnegie Commission found that most alumni expected the "development of my abilities to think and express myself." But if such respected educational psychologists as Bruner and Piaget are right, specific learning skills have to be acquired very early in life, perhaps even before formal schooling begins.

So, when pressed, liberal-arts defenders speak instead about 28 something more encompassing, and more elusive. "College changed me inside," one graduate told us fervently. The authors of a Carnegie Commission report, who obviously struggled for a definition, concluded that one of the common threads in the perceptions of a liberal education is that it provides "an integrated view of the world which can serve as an inner guide." More simply, alumni say that college should have "helped me to formulate the values and goals of my life."

29   In theory, a student is taught to develop these values and goals himself, but in practice, it doesn't work quite that way. All but the wayward and the saintly take their sense of the good, the true, and the beautiful from the people around them. When we speak of students acquiring "values" in college, we often mean that they will acquire the values—and sometimes that means only the tastes—of their professors. The values of professors may be "higher" than many students will encounter elsewhere, but they may not be relevant to situations in which students find themselves in college and later.

30   Of all the forms in which ideas are disseminated, the college professor lecturing a class is the slowest and most expensive. You don't have to go to college to read the great books or learn about the great ideas of Western Man. Today you can find them everywhere—in paperbacks, in the public libraries, in museums, in public lectures, in adult-education courses, in abridged, summarized, or adapted form in magazines, films, and television. The problem is no longer one of access to broadening ideas; the problem is the other way around: how to choose among the many courses of action proposed to us, how to edit the stimulations that pour into our eyes and ears every waking hour. A college experience that piles option on option and stimulation on stimulation merely adds to the contemporary nightmare.

31   What students and graduates say that they did learn on campus comes under the heading of personal, rather than intellectual, development. Again and again I was told that the real value of college is learning to get along with others, to practice social skills, to "sort out my head," and these have nothing to do with curriculum.

32   For whatever impact the academic experience used to have on college students, the sheer size of many undergraduate classes in the 1970s dilutes faculty-student dialogue, and, more often than not, they are taught by teachers who were hired when colleges were faced with a shortage of qualified instructors, during their years of expansion and when the big rise in academic pay attracted the mediocre and the less than dedicated.

33   On the social side, colleges are withdrawing from responsibility for feeding, housing, policing, and protecting students at a time when the environment of college may be the most important service it could render. College officials are reluctant to "intervene" in the personal lives of the students. They no longer expect to take over from parents, but often insist that students—who have, most often, never

lived away from home before—take full adult responsibility for their plans, achievements, and behavior.

Most college students do not live in the plush, comfortable coun- 34 try-clublike surroundings their parents envisage, or, in some cases, remember. Open dorms, particularly when they are coeducational, are noisy, usually overcrowded, and often messy. Some students desert the institutional "zoos" (their own word for dorms) and move into rundown, overpriced apartments. Bulletin boards in student centers are littered with notices of apartments to share and the drift of conversation suggests that a lot of money is dissipated in scrounging for food and shelter.

Taxpayers now provide more than half of the astronomical sums 35 that are spent on higher education. But less than half of today's high school graduates go on, raising a new question of equity: Is it fair to make all the taxpayers pay for the minority who actually go to college? We decided long ago that it is fair for childless adults to pay school taxes because everyone, parents and nonparents alike, profits by a literate population. Does the same reasoning hold true for state-supported higher education? There is no conclusive evidence on either side.

Young people cannot be expected to go to college for the general 36 good of mankind. They may be more altruistic than their elders, but no great numbers are going to spend four years at hard intellectual labor, let alone tens of thousands of family dollars, for "the advancement of human capability in society at large," one of the many purposes invoked by the Carnegie Commission report. Nor do any considerable number of them want to go to college to beat the Russians to Jupiter, improve the national defense, increase the Gross National Product, lower the crime rate, improve automobile safety, or create a market for the arts—all of which have been suggested at one time or other as benefits taxpayers get for supporting higher education.

One sociologist said that you don't have to have a reason for go- 37 ing to college because it's an institution. His definition of an institution is something everyone subscribes to without question. The burden of proof is not on why you should go to college, but why anyone thinks there might be a reason for not going. The implication—and some educators express it quite frankly—is that an eighteen-year-old high school graduate is still too young and confused to know what he wants to do, let alone what is good for him.

Mother knows best, in other words. 38

It had always been comfortable for students to believe that au- 39 thorities, like Mother, or outside specialists, like educators, could determine what was best for them. However, specialists and authorities no longer enjoy the credibility former generations accorded them. Patients talk back to doctors and are not struck suddenly dead. Clients question the lawyer's bills and sometimes get them reduced. It is no longer self-evident that all adolescents must study a fixed curriculum that was constructed at a time when all educated men could agree on precisely what it was that made them educated.

40   The same with college. If high school graduates don't want to continue their education, or don't want to continue it right away, they may perceive more clearly than their elders that college is not for them.

41   College is an ideal place for those young adults who love learning for its own sake, who would rather read than eat, and who like nothing better than writing research papers. But they are a minority, even at the prestigious colleges, which recruit and attract the intellectually oriented.

42   The rest of our high school graduates need to look at college more closely and critically, to examine it as a consumer product, and decide if the cost in dollars, in time, in continued dependency, and in future returns, is worth the very large investment each student—and his family—must make.

_____ CONSIDERATIONS _____

1. To what extent is Bird's essay an attack on the conviction that universal education is the surest way to cure the ills and injustices of the world?

2. In her first paragraph, the author states three popular justifications for a college education. Examine her essay to see how closely it is organized around those three reasons.

3. In her final paragraph, Bird urges high school graduates to examine college "as a consumer product." Is this possible? Explain. Read about Richard Wright's struggle to educate himself ("The Library Card") and try to imagine him examining that experience as "a consumer product."

4. Bird makes extensive use of statistics to prove her first proposition: that college is a poor investment. Does she cite the sources of her figures? Does she use the figures fairly? How can you tell?

5. How many of your college friends have clear ideas of their vocational or educational goals? Do you? What about friends who are not in college?

6. Bird points out, rightly enough, that "you don't have to go to college to read the great books or learn about the great ideas of Western Man." Judging from your experience with self-directed reading programs, how effective is Bird's statement as an argument?

7. What would Richard Feynman, Nancy Mairs, and Bertrand Russell think of Bird's emphasis on college as a vocational prep school?

Sven Birkerts (b. 1951) was awarded the National Book Critics Circle Citation for Excellence in Reviewing in 1986, and in 1991 received a Lila Wallace–Reader's Digest Award. His four books of essays are An Artificial Wilderness *(1987),* The Electric Life *(1989),* American Energies *(1992), and* Gutenberg Elegies *(1994). Birkerts frequently reviews contemporary fiction and poetry, publishing in the* New Republic, Mirabella, *and the* Atlantic, *among other magazines. In addition he writes essays that observe American culture with an eye both critical and shrewd. Birkerts teaches in the Bennington College MFA Program and collaborates with Donald Hall on* Writing Well.

11

SVEN BIRKERTS

Objections Noted: Word Processing

People ask me why I refuse to use a word processor. I tell them 1 because it feels like a typewriter with a condom over it. The very sight of one of those sculpted plastic instruments with its pert ticket-counter "everything's under control" screen depresses me beyond measure. It makes me feel how close the final victory of technology over spirit really is. Hell, it *is* the victory of technology over spirit.

Neither can I bear the chirping good humor with which owners 2 talk about their disks and programs.

The word-processor argument. Most people, I'm sure, maintain 3 that there *is* no word-processor argument. Indeed, I hardly ever meet anyone who writes who isn't using one—a few poets, maybe . . . Louis Simpson . . .

4   Lemmings!

5   Literature has got lightweight and modular enough without writers all shifting their idly fluffed-together paragraphs around. If you can't organize it in your head, it's not ready to be organized.

6   The WP is a death-ray directed at the last remnants of the prophetic soul.

7   The word processor is just a tool, they say. Just a tool. Just a tool. Never mind that it's an ugly tool, utterly alien from anything relating to spirit. (Would you paint with a steel-handled brush?) Never mind that the machine you work on changes the compositional process, changes you. It's just a tool.

8   Like any tool, the WP came into being to meet a need. Writers were tired of wadding up sheets of paper, of playing cut and paste with paragraphs, of drawing lines to bridge one part of a text to another. The technology was there to bring the material/production side of writing in line with the rest of the twentieth century. The quasi-"intelligence" of the computer was put into the service of the infinitely complex intellectual/psychological operation of writing.

9   Given that so many writers profess themselves to be iconoclasts, sturdy individualists, etc., the rate of defection from paper and metal to plastic and electricity is nothing short of astonishing.

10   These are the same people who love the old game of baseball and scream at any move to modernize or streamline its immemorial rituals.

11   But the lemmings did line up to leap. Why?

12   They say it's because the user can *quickly* make changes, corrections, erasures, rearrangements. Because he can try things out and then get rid of them. Because he has more access to his text, more control, a sense of mastery. Because the WP vanquishes fear, eliminates the block-inducing threat that the white page seems to hold.

13   I've heard it said that now *everyone* can become a writer.

14   Hot dog.

15   I think the real reason for the rush to molded plastic, the deep-down unacknowledged reason, is that the apparatus confers a feeling of power, of being plugged in to something. For we all know, in that same deep-down place, that the writer, the thinker, the person who would speak up for spirit, has never had less power. Ever. Has never been such a zero. Why not a humming bright unit that allows the user to say, "I, too, belong to the modern world. You can see screens just like this at the airport, on Wall Street, in the offices on Madison Avenue."

The word processor has, among other things, made the word 16
more susceptible to the directives of the will. The ruling paradigm is
now one of change, of changeability. The writer says, with Valéry,
that the work is never finished. Clearly demarcated draft stages have
been superceded by a single stage—the unstable, open, "in-process"
stage. Writing is closer to becoming that unfixed play of signifiers celebrated by French literary theoreticians. Literary morticians. Indeed:
writing has been brought many steps closer to resembling the muta-
bility of thought itself—which never rests, except in the crystalliza-
tions of written language.

The stability of the word—epitomized by the independent, fixed, 17
printed sign—has been correspondingly undermined.

Writing on the word processor: It's like eating those force-fed 18
new chickens that have never seen sunlight. Like eating fish bred in
indoor pools.

Word "processing": In the sixties the word "processed" was a 19
term of fierce derision. Blacks called a brother "processed" when they
wanted to mark him as a "Tom."

The shift from manual writing to the typewriter to the word 20
processor roughly corresponds to the shift from walking to riding in a
carriage to riding in a car. In both cases, the progression is toward ease
and facilitation. But, we might ask, what has become of our ancient
relationship to land, to sky, to time itself?

A flat, opaque two-sided sheet of paper is replaced by an elec- 21
tronic screen of indeterminate depth. Where a black mark was conspicuously *imposed* upon the white surface, we now find a green mark
elicited from the humming green screen. The broken-up left-to-right
linearity is replaced, for the writer, by what *feels* like an unbroken
continuity (the apparatus does the lineation). The static character of
the typed sign gives way to the fluid, provisional character of the
processed sign. The composition blocks—sentences, paragraphs—are
no less fluid.

If the movement from speech to writing was, in part, an attempt 22
to impose fixity upon the fleeting, then might we not in some sense be
moving back toward the laxity of the impromptu—at least on the
level of conception, where everything exists under the aspect of re-
placeability?

Writing on a word processor: the principle of Don Juanism pro- 23
jected upon the sentence. The writer is more likely to be haunted by

the thought that there is a better word than this, a better sentence, a more interesting ordering of paragraphs.

24   Writing by hand, even typewriter, inevitably results in visible corrections, in drafts. These are, in effect, the record of the evolution of the thought and its expression. The WP handily eliminates every trace. The writer never has to look over his shoulder and see what a botch he's made of things. Less conscience, less sense of consequence.

25   As Louis Simpson wrote: "If I think I can easily change the next word and there's nothing final about what I'm writing, then the nature of my writing changes."

26   How would you live if you knew you could live forever?

27   The ideal of *le mot juste* is vaporized; the new ideals are of plurality and provisionality.

28   I've noticed that I read a word-processed page differently—more casually—than a typewritten page. Could the mode of writing significantly influence the mode of reading? Maybe. When everybody becomes a writer, no one will read.

29   The difference between seeing your words drawn forth from the depths of a screen versus seeing them planted on the page through the mechanical action of a key is enormous. The screen, with its electrical "live" humming and its impatiently pulsing cursor, represents (much like TV) a quasi-consciousness. Does the writer feel just the slightest bit less responsible?

30   Speaking for myself: writing is very much a matter of drafts, *distinct* written drafts. I believe that prose if produced as much by the body, the rhythmic sense, as it is by intellect and verbal imagination. It wants to build up a certain musculature on the page. The instant correctability afforded by the WP allows for cosmetic alterations that are often quite adequate. But *merely* adequate. My experience has shown me that the best writing comes when I am forced to type over something that I've already deemed to be finished. My impatience—not to mention the new rhythmic state I'm in—forces me to push the language further. In the process of retyping the text, I reach more deeply into it. Later, the words give me the impression of having been handled, worn smooth.

31   Even simple mistakes can be read as signs, parapraxias signaling the incompleteness of an expression. When a page of prose is done, I no longer make typos.

32   Already it's getting hard to find ribbons. The people who used to repair typewriters are retiring, dying off. The day will come—soon—when journals will accept only disk submissions.

There . . . I've succeeded in depressing myself. All of a sudden my   33
desk looks like a museum: the beautiful pencil, the sharpener, the
pens, the stack of paper like a street of dreams. The Olivetti clattering
as I type this: sad hoofbeats of a retreating army. . . .

_____ CONSIDERATIONS _____

1. Would you say that Birkerts presents a well-organized argument
against the writer's use of word processors? Explain.
2. Why, in paragraph 3, does Birkerts select Louis Simpson as his example of a poet who does not use a word processor?
3. Birkerts uses two methods of dividing his essay into units. One of
them is the conventional paragraph break. What is the other, and what effect
does it have on the whole essay?
4. With what kind of voice are we supposed to read paragraph 14, which
consists solely of "Hot dog"?
5. To understand the gist of Birkert's paragraphs 25, 26, and 27, one
must understand the French phrase he uses in 27. Explain.
6. See Michael Booth's essay, page 93, for additional comments on tech-
nological progress.

*Carol Bly (b. 1930) was born in Minnesota and
graduated from Wellesley College. Now living in
Minnesota, she lectures, writes, and teaches. Her short
stories from the* New Yorker *and the* American Review,
among other magazines, are collected in Backbone *(1985)
and* The Tomcat's Wife *(1991). This essay was originally
published in* Preview, *magazine of Minnesota Public
Radio, and collected in her 1981 book,* Letters from the
Country.

12

CAROL BLY
Getting Tired

1   The men have left a gigantic 6600 combine a few yards from our
grove, at the edge of the stubble. For days it was working around the
farm; we heard it on the east, later on the west, and finally we could
see it grinding back and forth over the windows on the south. But now
it has been simply squatting at the field's edge, huge, tremendously
still, very professional, slightly dangerous.

2   We all have the correct feelings about this new combine: this
isn't the good old farming where man and soil are dusted together all
day; this isn't farming a poor man can afford, either, and therefore it
further threatens his hold on the American "family farm" operation.
We have been sneering at this machine for days, as its transistor radio,
amplified well over the engine roar, has been grinding up our silence,
spreading a kind of shrill ghetto evening all over the farm.

3   But now it is parked, and after a while I walk over to it and climb
up its neat little John-Deere-green ladder on the left. Entering the big
cab up there is like coming up into a large ship's bridge on visitors'
day—heady stuff to see the inside workings of a huge operation like
the Queen Elizabeth II. On the other hand I feel left out, being only a
dumbfounded passenger. The combine cab has huge windows flaring

wider at the top; they lean forward over the ground, and the driver sits so high behind the glass in its rubber moldings, it is like a movie-set spaceship. He has obviously come to dominate the field, whether he farms it or not.

The value of the 66 is that it can do anything, and to change it   4
from a combine into a cornpicker takes one man about half an hour, whereas most machine conversions on farms take several men a half day. It frees its owner from a lot of monkeying.

Monkeying, in city life, is what little boys do to clocks so they   5
never run again. In farming it has two quite different meanings. The first is small side projects. You monkey with poultry, unless you're a major egg handler. Or you monkey with ducks or geese. If you have a very small milk herd, and finally decide that prices plus state regulations don't make your few Holsteins worthwhile, you "quit monkeying with them." There is a hidden dignity in this word: it precludes mention of money. It lets the wife of a very marginal farmer have a conversation with a woman who may be helping her husband run fifteen hundred acres. "How you coming with those geese?" "Oh, we've been real disgusted. We're thinking of quitting monkeying with them." It saves her having to say, "We lost our shirts on those darn geese."

The other meaning of monkeying is wrestling with and main-   6
taining machinery, such as changing heads from combining to cornpicking. Farmers who cornpick the old way, in which the corn isn't shelled automatically during picking in the field but must be elevated to the top of a pile by belt and then shelled, put up with some monkeying.

Still, cornpicking and plowing is a marvelous time of the year on   7
farms; one of the best autumns I've had recently had a few days of fieldwork in it. We were outside all day, from six in the morning to eight at night—coming in only for noon dinner. We ate our lunches on a messy truck flatbed. (For city people who don't know it: *lunch* isn't a noon meal; it is what you eat out of a black lunch pail at 9 A.M. and 3 P.M. If you offer a farmer a cup of coffee at 3:30 P.M., he or she is likely to say, "No thanks, I've already had lunch.") There were four of us hired to help—a couple to plow, Celia (a skilled farmhand who worked steady for our boss), and me. Lunch was always two sandwiches of white commercial bread with luncheon meat, and one very generous piece of cake-mix cake carefully wrapped in Saran Wrap. (I never found anyone around here self-conscious about using Saran Wrap when the Dow Chemical Company was also making napalm.)

It was very pleasant on the flatbed, squinting out over the yellow   8
picked cornstalks—each time we stopped for lunch, a larger part of the field had been plowed back. We fell into the easy psychic habit of farmworkers: admiration of the boss. "*Ja*, I see he's buying one of

those big 4010s," someone would say. We always perked up at inside information like that. Or *"Ja,"* as the woman hired steady told us, "he's going to plow the home fields first this time, instead of the other way round." We temporary help were impressed by that, too. Then, with real flair, she brushed a crumb of luncheon meat off her jeans, the way you would make sure to flick a gnat off spotless tennis whites. It is the true feminine touch to brush a crumb off pants that are encrusted with Minnesota Profile A heavy loam, many swipes of SAE 40 oil, and grain dust.

9   All those days, we never tired of exchanging information on how *he* was making out, what *he* was buying, whom *he* was going to let drive the new tractor, and so on. There is always something to talk about with the other hands, because farming is genuinely absorbing. It has the best quality of work: nothing else seems real. And everyone doing it, even the cheapest helpers like me, can see the layout of the whole—from spring work, to cultivating, to small grain harvest, to cornpicking, to fall plowing.

10   The second day I was promoted from elevating corncobs at the corn pile to actual plowing. Hour after hour I sat up there on the old Alice, as she was called (an Allis-Chalmers WC that looked rusted from the Flood). You have to sit twisted part way around, checking that the plowshares are scouring clean, turning over and dropping the dead crop and soil, not clogging. For the first two hours I was very political. I thought about what would be good for American farming—stronger marketing organizations, or maybe a law like the Norwegian Odal law, preventing the breaking up of small farms or selling them to business interests. Then the sun got high, and each time I reached the headlands area at the field's end I dumped off something else, now my cap, next my jacket, finally my sweater.

11   Since the headlands are the last to be plowed, they serve as a field road until the very end. There are usually things parked there—a pickup or a corn trailer—and things dumped—my warmer clothing, our afternoon lunch pails, a broken furrow wheel someone picked up.

12   By noon I'd dropped all political interest, and was thinking only: how unlike this all is to Keats's picture of autumn, a "season of mists and mellow fruitfulness." This gigantic expanse of horizon, with everywhere the easy growl of tractors, was simply teeming with extrovert energy. It wouldn't calm down for another week, when whoever was lowest on the totem pole would be sent out to check a field for dropped parts or to drive away the last machines left around.

13   The worst hours for all common labor are the hours after noon dinner. Nothing is inspiring then. That is when people wonder how they ever got stuck in the line of work they've chosen for life. Or they wonder where the cool Indian smoke of secrets and messages began to vanish from their marriage. Instead of plugging along like a cheerful

beast working for me, the Allis now smelled particularly gassy. To stay awake I froze my eyes onto an indented circle in the hood around the gas cap. Someone had apparently knocked the screw cap fitting down into the hood, so there was a moat around it. In this moat some overflow gas leapt in tiny waves. Sometimes the gas cap was a castle, this was the moat; sometimes it was a nuclear-fission plant, this was the horrible hot-water waste. Sometimes it was just the gas cap on the old Alice with the spilt gas bouncing on the hot metal.

Row after row. I was stupefied. But then around 2:30 the shadows 14 appeared again, and the light, which had been dazing and white, grew fragile. The whole prairie began to gather itself for the cool evening. All of a sudden it was wonderful to be plowing again, and when I came to the field end, the filthy jackets and the busted furrow wheel were just benign mistakes: that is, if it chose to, the jacket could be a church robe, and the old wheel could be something with some pride to it, like a helm. And I felt the same about myself: instead of being someone with a half interest in literature and a half interest in farming doing a half-decent job plowing, I could have been someone desperately needed in Washington or Zurich. I drank my three o'clock coffee joyously, and traded the other plowman a Super-Valu cake-mix lemon cake slice for a Holsum baloney sandwich because it had garlic in it.

By seven at night we had been plowing with headlights for an 15 hour. I tried to make up games to keep going, on my second wind, on my third wind, but labor is labor after the whole day of it; the mind refuses to think of ancestors. It refuses to pretend the stalks marching up to the right wheel in the spooky light are men-at-arms, or to imagine a new generation coming along. It doesn't care. Now the Republicans could have announced a local meeting in which they would propose a new farm program whereby every farmer owning less that five hundred acres must take half price for his crop, and every farmer owning more than a thousand acres shall receive triple price for his crop, and I was so tired I wouldn't have shown up to protest.

A million hours later we sit around in a daze at the dining-room 16 table, and nobody says anything. In low, courteous mutters we ask for the macaroni hotdish down this way, please. Then we get up in ones and twos and go home. Now the farm help are all so tired we *are* a little like the various things left out on the headlands—some tools, a jacket, someone's thermos top—used up for that day. Thoughts won't even stick to us any more.

Such tiredness must be part of farmers' wanting huge machinery 17 like the Deere 6600. That tiredness that feels so good to the occasional laborer and the athlete is disturbing to a man destined to it eight months of every year. But there is a more hidden psychology in the issue of enclosed combines versus open tractors. It is this: one gets too many impressions on the open tractor. A thousand impressions enter as you work up and down the rows: nature's beauty or nature's stubbornness, politics, exhaustion, but mainly the feeling that all this repetition—last year's cornpicking, this year's cornpicking, next year's cornpicking—is taking up your lifetime. The mere repetition reveals your eventual death.

18   When you sit inside a modern combine, on the other hand, you are so isolated from field, sky, all the real world, that the brain is dulled. You are not sensitized to your own mortality. You aren't sensitive to anything at all.

19   This must be a common choice of our mechanical era: to hide from life inside our machinery. If we can hide from life in there, some idiotic part of the psyche reasons, we can hide from death in there as well.

_____ CONSIDERATIONS _____

1. In paragraphs 5 and 6, Carol Bly clarifies the slang term "monkeying." Hers is not a conventional definition. Does she make the term understandable to someone who has never heard it before? What are the requirements of a definition? Have you read essays built as extended definitions? See Daniel Boorstin's "The Pseudo-Event" (page 86) and Consideration 6 following that essay.

2. Compare paragraphs 9 and 17 on the nature of work. How do you account for the positive view of paragraph 9 and the negative view of paragraph 17?

3. Why, in paragraph 12, does Bly allude to John Keats's famous ode, "To Autumn" (1819)? Can you appreciate what she is doing if you've never read the poem? How quickly can you find it in your college library? Aside from the collected poems of John Keats, what would be the surest source for the poem?

4. Notice when Bly changes suddenly from past to present tense. Why does she make the shift? Is something gained by the change?

5. Think about Bly's generalizations in her final paragraph. Selecting an appropriate piece of machinery—a car, a computer, a television set—respond to Bly's generalizations in a short essay.

Louise Bogan (1897–1970)—poet, and critic of poetry in her quarterly reviews of "Verse" for the New Yorker—*was born in Maine and spent her adult life in New York City. Her poetry, criticism, and letters have been collected in many volumes.* Journey Around My Room *(1980), from which we take "Miss Cooper and Me," is subtitled The* Autobiography of Louise Bogan. *It was edited by Ruth Limmer, after Bogan's death, from the poet's notebooks and private papers.*

13

LOUISE BOGAN
Miss Cooper and Me

Boston was a city that possessed a highly civilized nucleus composed of buildings built around a square. These buildings were copies of palaces in Italy, churches in England, and residences in Munich. The square's centre was occupied by a triangular plot of grass, garnished at its three corners by large palms growing in tubs. The streetcars rattled by these. Perhaps, too, a bed of begonias and coleuses pleased the eye with some simple horticultural pattern. I can't remember clearly. It was the architecture which warmed my heart. The sight of imitation true Gothic, imitation true Italian Renaissance, and imitation false Gothic revival often gave me that sensation in the pit of the stomach which heralds both love and an intense aesthetic experience. And to this day I have never been able to extirpate from my taste a thorough affection for potted palms.

Harold Street, on the other hand, had not emerged from the brain of an architect of any period. It was a street not only in a suburb but on the edge of a suburb, and it was a carpenter's dull skill with pine planks and millwork in general that could be thanked for the houses' general design. Our house, built to accommodate three families, one to a floor, was perhaps two years old. Carpenters hammered new

*From Journey Around My Room: The Autobiography of Louise Bogan ed. by Ruth Limmer. Copyright © 1980 by Ruth Limmer. Reprinted by permission of the author.

1

2

three-family houses together continually, on all sides of it. For several of my adolescent years, until the street was finally given up as completed, I watched and heard the construction of these houses. Even when finished, they had an extremely provisional look, as though a breath of wind could blow them away.

3   Sometimes I think that, between us, my mother and I must have invented Miss Cooper; this is impossible, however, because of our splendid ignorance of the materials of which Miss Cooper was composed. We both lighted upon her simultaneously through the commendation of the drawing teacher in my school, who thought I was Talented, and Should Have Further Instruction. I was, it is true, thrown into a high state of nervous tension at the sight of a drawing board. This state passed for talent at the time. It must have been something else, since nothing ever came of it.

4   Miss Cooper lived in the Hotel Oxford, and I lived on Harold Street, and a whole world, a whole civilization, or, if you will, the lack of a whole world, of a whole civilization, lay between.

5   The Hotel Oxford stood a few yards up one street leading to the remarkable square. A fair-sized section of quarry had gone into its manufacture. And within it was heavily weighted down with good, solid woodwork, mahogany in color; with statues, large and small, of bronze and of marble, representing draped winged creatures which, although caught in attitudes of listening or looking or touching, gave the impression of deafness, blindness, and insensibility. (I thought these quite pretty at the time.) It was weighted with plush draperies, with gilt picture frames half a foot broad, with a heavy, well-fed, well-mustached staff of clerks. The little elevator, manned by a decrepit old boy in a toupee, sighed up through floors heavily carpeted in discreet magenta. Miss Cooper's studio was at the top of the building. It had no skylight and it looked out onto the railway yards, but it was directly under the roof; it had that distinction.

6   The big room looked as though, at some time in the past, the great conflagration of art had passed over it, charring the walls, the floor, and the ceiling, together with the objects they contained. Everything looked burned and tarnished: the brown pongee curtains; the dull bronze, brass, and copper; the black, twisted wrought iron; the cracked and carved wood of the Spanish chairs. Or perhaps it was the wave of art that had once washed briefly against it, leaving pale casts of the human hand and foot, life and death masks, a little replica of the Leaning Tower of Pisa, a tiny marble bowl surmounted by alabaster doves (the litter of art-form bric-a-brac) in its wake. In any case, there it was, and I had never seen anything like it before, and had it been Michelangelo's own workroom, it could not have been more remarkable to me.

Against this sombre background, Miss Cooper stood out like 7
porcelain. She was smaller at sixty than myself at thirteen. Her white
hair, combed into a series of delicate loops over her forehead, resembled
the round feathers that sometimes seep out of pillows. Her white teeth,
solid and young, made her smile a delightful surprise. She dressed in the
loose Liberty silks which constituted a uniform for the artistic women
of the period; around her neck hung several chains of Florentine silver.
Personal distinction, in those days, to me meant undoubted nobility of
soul. Distinguished physical traits went right through to the back, as it
were, indelibly staining mind and spirit. And Miss Cooper, being
stamped all over with the color and designs of art as well as by the traits
of gentility, made double claims upon my respect and imagination.

It is difficult to put down coldly the terrific excitement engen- 8
dered in my breast by those Saturday afternoons. I would come in, un-
pin my hat, lay off my coat, and there was the still life, freshly fitted
into chalk marks, on the low table, and there was the leather stool on
which I sat, and there was the charcoal paper pinned to its board, and
the array of wonderful materials: sticks of charcoal, beautifully black,
slender, and brittle; pastels, running through shade after delicate
shade in a shallow wooden box; the fixative; the kneaded rubber. And
there was Miss Cooper, the adept at these mysteries. Sometimes in
the autumn evenings, after the lesson was finished, she lighted candles and made me tea. That is, she brought in from a kitchen as big as
a closet, off the hall, a tray on which sat two cups and two saucers of
Italian pottery, and a plate of what I called cookies and she called bis-
cuits. Many times, after a cup of this tea, I staggered out into a world
in which everything seemed suspended in the twilight, floating in
mid-air, as in a mirage. I waited for the trolley car which would take
me back to Harold Street in a daze, full of enough romantic nonsense
to poison ten lives at their root.

Sometimes I wondered about Miss Cooper's own work in the 9
field of graphic art. Pictures produced by her hand—pastels and water
colors, all very accurate and bright—hung on the walls. But there was
never anything on drawing board or easel. Every summer she disappeared into that fabulous region known as "abroad"; she did not bring
back portfolios full of sketches, but only another assortment of small
objects: carved wood from Oberammergau, Tanagra figurines, Florentine leather boxes, and strings of gold-flecked beads from Venice.
These joined the artistic litter in the studio.

The enchantment worked for two years. In the autumn of the 10
third, something had changed. In a pupil, the abstracted look in Miss
Cooper's eye could have been put down to loss of interest; in a
teacher, I could not account for it. Miss Cooper lived in my mind at a

continual point of perfection; she was like a picture: she existed, but not in any degree did she live or change. She existed beyond simple human needs, beyond hunger and thirst, beyond loneliness, weariness, below the heights of joy and despair. She could not quarrel and she could not sigh. I had assigned to her the words and the smile by which I first knew her, and I refused to believe her capable of any others. But now, behind my shoulder, those October afternoons, I often heard her sigh, and she spent more time in the closet-like kitchen, rattling china and spoons, than she spent in the studio itself. I knew that she was having a cup of tea alone, while I worked in the fading light. She was still gentle, still kind. But she was not wholly there. I had lost her.

11   It is always ourselves that we blame for such losses, when we are young. For weeks I went about inventing reasons for Miss Cooper's de-fection; I clung to some and rejected others. When we are young, we are proud; we say nothing; we are silent and we watch. My ears be-came sharpened to every tired tone in her voice, to every clink of china and spoon, to every long period of her silence. One afternoon she came out of the kitchen and stood behind me. She had something in her hand that crackled like paper, and when she spoke she mumbled as though her mouth were full. I turned and looked at her; she was standing with a greasy paper bag in one hand and a half-eaten dough-nut in the other. Her hair was still beautifully arranged; she still wore the silver and fire-opal ring on the little finger of her right hand. But in that moment she died for me. She died and the room died and the still life died a second death. She had betrayed me. She had betrayed the Hotel Oxford and the replica of the Leaning Tower of Pisa and the whole world of romantic notions built up around her. She had let me down; she had appeared as she was: a tired old woman who fed herself for comfort. With perfect ruthlessness I rejected her utterly. And for weeks, at night, in the bedroom of the frame house in Harold Street, I shed tears that rose from anger as much as disappointment, from disil-lusion and from dismay. I can't remember that for one moment I en-tertained pity for her. It was for myself that I kept that tender and cleansing emotion. Yes, it was for myself and for dignity and gentility soiled and broken that I shed those tears. At fifteen and for a long time thereafter, it is a monstrous thing, the heart.

_____ CONSIDERATIONS _____

1. Why, in this account of an individual, does Bogan open her essay with two paragraphs about architecture?

2. What's the point, in paragraph 3, of capitalizing "Talented" and "Should Have Further Instruction"?

3. What are some examples of the way Bogan re-creates her girlhood ex-perience as though we were seeing it through the girl's eyes?

4. What do you make of the curious phrase," . . . it is a monstrous thing, the heart"?

5. If you have had a disillusioning experience, build it into a personal essay, making use of "Miss Cooper and Me."

14

DANIEL J. BOORSTIN
The Pseudo-Event

Admiring Friend: "My, that's a beautiful baby you have there!"
Mother: "Oh, that's nothing—you should see his photograph!"

1   The simplest of our extravagant expectations concerns the amount of novelty in the world. There was a time when the reader of an unexciting newspaper would remark, "How dull is the world today!" Nowadays he says, "What a dull newspaper!" When the first American newspaper, Benjamin Harris' *Publick Occurrences Both Forreign and Domestick*, appeared in Boston on September 25, 1690, it promised to furnish news regularly once a month. But, the editor explained, it might appear oftener "if any Glut of Occurrences happen." The responsibility for making news was entirely God's—or the Devil's. The newsman's task was only to give "an Account of such considerable things as have arrived unto our Notice."

Although the theology behind this way of looking at events soon 2
dissolved, this view of the news lasted longer. "The skilled and faithful journalist," James Parton observed in 1866, "recording with exact-
ness and power the thing that has come to pass, is Providence address-
ing men." The story is told of a Southern Baptist clergyman before the
Civil War who used to say, when a newspaper was brought in the
room, "Be kind enough to let me have it a few minutes, till I see how
the Supreme Being is governing the world." Charles A. Dana, one of
the great American editors of the nineteenth century, once defended
his extensive reporting of crime in the New York *Sun* by saying, "I
have always felt that whatever the Divine Providence permitted to occur I was not too proud to report."

Of course, this is now a very old-fashioned way of thinking. Our 3
current point of view is better expressed in the definition by Arthur
MacEwen, whom William Randolph Hearst made his first editor of
the San Francisco *Examiner*: "News is anything that makes a reader
say, 'Gee whiz!'" Or, put more soberly, "News is whatever a good editor chooses to print."

We need not be theologians to see that we have shifted responsi- 4
bility for making the world interesting from God to the newspaperman. We used to believe there were only so many "events" in the
world. If there were not many intriguing or startling occurrences, it
was no fault of the reporter. He could not be expected to report what
did not exist.

Within the last hundred years, however, and especially in the 5
twentieth century, all this has changed. We expect the papers to be
full of news. If there is no news visible to the naked eye, or to the average citizen, we still expect it to be there for the enterprising newsman. The successful reporter is one who can find a story, even if there
is no earthquake or assassination or civil war. If he cannot find a story,
then he must make one—by the questions he asks of public figures, by
the surprising human interest he unfolds from some commonplace
event, or by "the news behind the news." If all this fails, then he must
give us a "think piece"—an embroidering of well-known facts, or a
speculation about startling things to come.

This change in our attitude toward "news" is not merely a basic 6
fact about the history of American newspapers. It is a symptom of a
revolutionary change in our attitude toward what happens in the
world, how much of it is new, and surprising, and important. Toward
how life can be enlivened, toward our power and the power of those
who inform and educate and guide us, to provide synthetic happenings
to make up for the lack of spontaneous events. Demanding more than
the world can give us, we require that something be fabricated to
make up for the world's deficiency. This is only one example of our
demand for illusions.

7   Many historical forces help explain how we have come to our present immoderate hopes. But there can be no doubt about what we now expect, nor that it is immoderate. Every American knows the anticipation with which he picks up his morning newspaper at breakfast or opens his evening paper before dinner, or listens to the newscasts every hour on the hour as he drives across country, or watches his favorite commentator on television interpret the events of the day. Many enterprising Americans are now at work to help us satisfy these expectations. Many might be put out of work if we should suddenly moderate our expectations. But it is we who keep them in business and demand that they fill our consciousness with novelties, that they play God for us.

8   The new kind of synthetic novelty which has flooded our experience I will call "pseudo-events." The common prefix "pseudo" comes from the Greek word meaning false, or intended to deceive. Before I recall the historical forces which have made these pseudo-events possible, have increased the supply of them and the demand for them, I will give a commonplace example.

9   The owners of a hotel, in an illustration offered by Edward L. Bernays in his pioneer *Crystallizing Public Opinion* (1923), consult a public relations counsel. They ask how to increase their hotel's prestige and so improve their business. In less sophisticated times, the answer might have been to hire a new chef, to improve the plumbing, to paint the rooms, or to install a crystal chandelier in the lobby. The public relations counsel's technique is more indirect. He proposes that the management stage a celebration of the hotel's thirtieth anniversary. A committee is formed, including a prominent banker, a leading society matron, a well-known lawyer, an influential preacher, and an "event" is planned (say a banquet) to call attention to the distinguished service the hotel has been rendering the community. The celebration is held, photographs are taken, the occasion is widely reported, and the object is accomplished. Now this occasion is a pseudo-event, and will illustrate all the essential features of pseudo-events.

10   This celebration, we can see at the outset, is somewhat—but not entirely—misleading. Presumably the public relations counsel would not have been able to form his committee of prominent citizens if the hotel had not actually been rendering service to the community. On the other hand, if the hotel's services had been all that important, instigation by public relations counsel might not have been necessary. Once the celebration has been held, the celebration itself becomes evidence that the hotel really is a distinguished institution. The occasion actually gives the hotel the prestige to which it is pretending.

11   It is obvious, too, that the value of such a celebration to the owners depends on its being photographed and reported in newspapers, magazines, newsreels, on radio, and over television. It is the report

that gives the event its force in the minds of potential customers. The power to make a reportable event is thus the power to make experience. One is reminded of Napoleon's apocryphal reply to his general, who objected that circumstances were unfavorable to a proposed campaign: "Bah, I make circumstances!" The modern public relations counsel—and he is, of course, only one of many twentieth-century creators of pseudo-events—has come close to fulfilling Napoleon's idle boast. "The counsel on public relations," Mr. Bernays explains, "not only knows what news value is, but knowing it, he is in a position to *make news happen*. He is a creator of events."

The intriguing feature of the modern situation, however, comes   12 precisely from the fact that the modern news makers are not God. The news they make happen, the events they create, are somehow not quite real. There remains a tantalizing difference between man-made and God-made events.

A pseudo-event, then, is a happening that possesses the following   13 characteristics:

1: It is not spontaneous, but comes about because someone has planned, planted, or incited it. Typically, it is not a train wreck or an earthquake, but an interview.

2: It is planted primarily (not always exclusively) for the immediate purpose of being reported or reproduced. Therefore, its occurrence is arranged for the convenience of the reporting or reproducing media. Its success is measured by how widely it is reported. Time relations in it are commonly fictitious or factitious; the announcement is given out in advance "for future release" and written as if the event had occurred in the past. The question, "Is it real?" is less important than, "Is it newsworthy?"

3: Its relation to the underlying reality of the situation is ambiguous. Its interest arises largely from this very ambiguity. Concerning a pseudo-event the question, "What does it mean?" has a new dimension. While the news interest in a train wreck is in *what* happened and in the real consequences, the interest in an interview is always, in a sense, in *whether* it really happened and in what might have been the motives. Did the statement really mean what it said? Without some of this ambiguity a pseudo-event cannot be very interesting.

4: Usually it is intended to be a self-fulfilling prophecy. The hotel's thirtieth-anniversary celebration, by saying that the hotel is a distinguished institution, actually makes it one.

A perfect example of how pseudo-events can dominate is the re-   14 cent popularity of the quiz show format. Its original appeal came less from the fact that such shows were tests of intelligence (or of dissimulation) than from the fact that the situations were elaborately contrived—with isolation booths, armed bank guards, and all the rest— and they purported to inform the public.

The application of the quiz show format to the so-called "Great   15 Debates" between Presidential candidates in the election of 1960 is only another example. These four campaign programs, pompously and self-righteously advertised by the broadcasting networks, were remarkably successful in reducing great national issues to trivial dimensions. With appropriate vulgarity, they might have been called the $400,000 Question (Prize: a $100,000-a-year job for four years). They were a clinical example of the pseudo-event, of how it is made, why it appeals, and of its consequences for democracy in America.

16   In origin the Great Debates were confusedly collaborative between politicians and news makers. Public interest centered around the pseudo-event itself: the lighting, make-up, ground rules, whether notes would be allowed, etc. Far more interest was shown in the performance than in what was said. The pseudo-events spawned in turn by the Great Debates were numberless. People who had seen the shows read about them the more avidly, and listened eagerly for interpretations by news commentators. Representatives of both parties made "statements" on the probable effects of the debates. Numerous interviews and discussion programs were broadcast exploring their meaning. Opinion polls kept us informed on the nuances of our own and other people's reactions. Topics of speculation multiplied. Even the question whether there should be a fifth debate became for a while a lively "issue."

17   The drama of the situation was mostly specious, or at least had an extremely ambiguous relevance to the main (but forgotten) issue: which participant was better qualified for the Presidency. Of course, a man's ability, while standing under klieg lights, without notes, to answer in two and a half minutes a question kept secret until that moment, had only the most dubious relevance—if any at all—to his real qualifications to make deliberate Presidential decisions on long-standing public questions after being instructed by a corps of advisers. The great Presidents in our history (with the possible exception of F.D.R.) would have done miserably; but our most notorious demagogues would have shone. A number of exciting pseudo-events were created—for example, the Quemoy-Matsu issue.* But that, too, was a good example of a pseudo-event: it was created to be reported, it concerned a then-quiescent problem, and it put into the most factitious and trivial terms the great and real issue of our relation to Communist China.

18   The television medium shapes this new kind of political quiz-show spectacular in many crucial ways. Theodore H. White has proven this with copious detail in his *The Making of the President: 1960* (1961). All the circumstances of this particular competition for

---

*Hotly debated by Kennedy and Nixon in 1960: should these islands off the Chinese mainland be defended by the United States as part of Nationalist China's territory?

votes were far more novel than the old word "debate" and the comparisons with the Lincoln-Douglas Debates suggested. Kennedy's great strength in the critical first debate, according to White, was that he was in fact not "debating" at all, but was seizing the opportunity to address the whole nation; while Nixon stuck close to the issues raised by his opponent, rebutting them one by one. Nixon, moreover, suffered a handicap that was serious only on television: he has a light, naturally transparent skin. On an ordinary camera that takes pictures by optical projection, this skin photographs well. But a television camera projects electronically, by an "image-orthicon tube" which has an x-ray effect. This camera penetrates Nixon's transparent skin and brings out (even just after a shave) the tiniest hair growing in the follicles beneath the surface. For the decisive first program Nixon wore a make-up called "Lazy Shave" which was ineffective under these conditions. He therefore looked haggard and heavy-bearded by contrast to Kennedy, who looked pert and clean-cut.

This greatest opportunity in American history to educate the 19 voters by debating the large issues of the campaign failed. The main reason, as White points out, was the compulsions of the medium. "The nature of both TV and radio is that they abhor silence and 'dead time.' All TV and radio discussion programs are compelled to snap question and answer back and forth as if the contestants were adversaries in an intellectual tennis match. Although every experienced newspaperman and inquirer knows that the most thoughtful and responsive answers to any difficult question come after long pause, and that the longer the pause the more illuminating the thought that follows it, nonetheless the electronic media cannot bear to suffer a pause of more than five seconds; a pause of thirty seconds of dead time on air seems interminable. Thus, snapping their two-and-a-half-minute answers back and forth, both candidates could only react for the cameras and the people, they could not think." Whenever either candidate found himself touching a thought too large for two-minute exploration, he quickly retreated. Finally the television-watching voter was left to judge, not on issues explored by thoughtful men, but on the relative capacity of the two candidates to perform under television stress.

Pseudo-events thus lead to emphasis on pseudo-qualifications. 20 Again the self-fulfilling prophecy. If we test Presidential candidates by their talents on TV quiz performances, we will, of course, choose presidents for precisely these qualifications. In a democracy, reality tends to conform to the pseudo-event. Nature imitates art.

We are frustrated by our very efforts publicly to unmask the 21 pseudo-event. Whenever we describe the lighting, the make-up, the studio setting, the rehearsals, etc., we simply arouse more interest. One newsman's interpretation makes us more eager to hear another's. One commentator's speculation that the debates may have little significance makes us curious to hear whether another commentator disagrees.

Pseudo-events do, of course, increase our illusion of grasp on the 22
world, what some have called the American illusion of omnipotence. Perhaps, we come to think, the world's problems can really be settled by "statements," by "Summit" meetings, by a competition of "prestige," by overshadowing images, and by political quiz shows.

Once we have tasted the charm of pseudo-events, we are tempted 23
to believe they are the only important events. Our progress poisons the sources of our experience. And the poison tastes so sweet that it spoils our appetite for plain fact. Our seeming ability to satisfy our exaggerated expectations makes us forget that they are exaggerated.

____ CONSIDERATIONS _____

1. "VIKING PROMOTION HITS TOWN THIS WEEK"—banner headline on page 1 of the *Park Rapids* (Minnesota) *Enterprise*, July 30, 1986. Hard news or pseudo-event? Explain. See also newspaper coverage of Microsoft's "Windows 95," on August 24, 1995. Which seemed to be more important: the new product itself or the publicity campaign promoting it?

2. Daniel J. Boorstin, a professor of history, distinguishes between spontaneous events and events that are staged to advance a position or to promote a person or an institution. He argues that there "remains a tantalizing difference between man-made and God-made events." In what sense is that difference "tantalizing"?

3. Use Boorstin's criteria to find an example of a pseudo-event in a newspaper or a newsmagazine. Analyze the piece to determine if it possesses the characteristics he lists. Does it, for example, contain ambiguities?

4. Why, according to Boorstin, are these pseudo-events harmful? Do you agree?

5. Through the first three paragraphs of his essay, Boorstin makes extensive use of short quotations carefully chosen to illustrate his point. Is there a limit to the number of questions a given essay can employ effectively? Explain. Where might you find several quotations on a particular subject?

6. Study Boorstin's essay as an example of argument. Which of his techniques reveal the argumentative nature of his writing? (Don't ignore the epigraph that precedes his first paragraph.)

Michael Booth (b. 1965) is a staff writer for the Denver
Post. *Since growing up in northern Minnesota and
attending Macalester College in St. Paul, he has worked
for the* Washington Post *Foreign Desk and as a freelance
writer. His articles and essays have appeared in the* New
York Times, *the* Minnesota Monthly, *and* Sojourners. *This
commentary on the information superhighway first
appeared in the* Sunday Perspective *of the* Denver Post.

15

MICHAEL BOOTH

Watch out for Traffic Jams on the Information Highway

Fifty-three years ago, essayist E. B. White, who tended to carry 1
the weight of the world's future on his shoulders, added a new worry
to his long list of forebodings. It was 1938, and he had recently seen
television for the first time.

"I believe television is going to be the test of the modern world, 2
and that in this new opportunity to see beyond the range of our vision
we shall discover either a new and unbearable disturbance of the general peace or a saving radiance in the sky," White wrote, in his column, "One Man's Meat."

"We shall stand or fall by television—of that I am quite sure." 3

White's words are not only remarkable because the past five 4
decades have proven them to be dead-on prophesy. They are stunning
because we may repeat them today and see that the next test of the
modern world is likely to be the hottest concept in popular culture:
"The Information Superhighway."

Last spring the news magazines and science writers couldn't say 5
enough about the glorious revolution that fiber optic cable would
bring into our homes. This fall, the business pages are full of specula-

tion about possible mergers among Paramount, Viacom and cable giant TCI Inc., with journalists buying wholesale the claims of financial analysts that such mega-combinations will create exciting synergies of programming, technology and marketing.

6   Put simply, the information superhighway means that every conceivable function of computers, telephones, stereos and video will be combined onto a television screen. We will be able to order any movie ever made, at any time. Or call the boss from the home computer, watch him pitch a new idea to the sales staff on our video screen, and fax him a summary. Or pick out a new coffee pot on the Sears Shopping Channel and charge it electronically.

7   Amid the pro-technology hype whipped up by a media frenzy, we hear over and over that the information superhighway will fundamentally transform our lives. The gurus of the information age, whether in the words of cable czar John Malone or of Vice President Al Gore, chant the mantra that the changes will free our minds. As with all new waves of technology, we assume the transformation will be for the better.

8   You would think we might have learned by now.

9   The simple point that seems to be lost, perhaps because it is so simple, is that what we are talking about here is television. Each of the wonderful new powers we will have, whatever their other value, will mean spending more time shackled before the television, the same box that brought us "Three's Company"; the same box that tries to sell Thighmasters to Americans and Greater Serbia to Yugoslavians; the same box that hails "Seinfeld," a shallow satire of such minutiae as frequent flyer miles and handicapped parking spaces, as its greatest triumph in recent years.

10   Why is it even necessary to point out the absurdity of television people, who tell us, "Yes, you're right, we can't create anything worth watching on 80 channels right now, but just watch what we can do on 500." The new programming will be different, they tell us, because it won't be the same old sitcoms and formula cop dramas; the new programs will be service-oriented. We will have the Macy's Channel, and the Hotel Channel, and channels that allow us to walk through the Library of Congress and pick out what we want without leaving the La-Z-Boy.

11   Again it's a simple question: Why do we want that? Even in-person shopping at Macy's is neither a happy nor uplifting experience. It means shopping at a mall, even the best of which are merely artificial catacombs of consumption. Then remove the experience to yet another level of artificiality, television, and you have eliminated the only remotely redeeming element of shopping: human contact.

12   Fine, the TV gurus will say, but how can you criticize the concept of the Library Channel? Imagine all that information at our fin-

gertips. Every written fact or opinion known to mankind will be contained in the television.

But what's wrong with getting into the car, or, god forbid, walking down to the local public library, asking someone at the counter for help (or better yet looking it up for ourselves), walking up the musty back stairway past the posters of upcoming author readings and paintings of ships at sea, and hunkering down at the end of a dimly lit row to browse through a hand-stitched clothbound copy of "The Caine Mutiny," and in the process discovering three other Herman Wouk novels that we'd like to read someday? 13

Not everyone can get to the library, they will say; to oppose change is elitist, a roadblock to progress for the masses of people who see television as their friend. In that case, the cable moguls should provide their electronic miracle free of charge to every disabled American, and also wire the homes of every single parent or elderly shut-in or high school dropout stuck in a blighted neighborhood, and tutor them in how to use it, and leave the rest of us alone to live our lives that are too busy, too complicated and too humane to settle for virtual reality. 14

E.B. White knew what trouble would come from man's preference for the artful copy over the original. Television, White wrote 53 years ago, "will insist that we forget the primary and the near in favor of the secondary and remote. . . . In sufficient accumulation, radio sounds and television sights may become more familiar to us than their originals." 15

Let's ask one more question that seems to concern so few who have jumped on the technology bullet train. Is it the primary intent of cable executives like John Malone or Ted Turner to provide for the spiritual enlightenment of the world? Or is their first goal to make as much money as humanly possible for themselves and their shareholders? Certainly there's nothing wrong with making money, but there is also nothing heroic about it. Remember that it is not Mahatma Gandhi, Albert Einstein and Martin Luther King, Jr. asking the world to welcome the information superhighway. It is Time-Warner, AT&T and the Cartoon Channel. 16

Forget the new programming we may or may not see, which may or may not change our lives. Think about how this new technology may change for the worse what we already have, as these things tend to do. The true genius of the superhighway may just be that the television folks will get us to pay for things in the future that we currently enjoy free. The executive mind looks at it this way: Broadcast TV channels are free. Public libraries, bottomless wells of information, all free. For a nominal, fixed charge, access to local phone service is unlimited. What a waste. 17

The solution? Run every TV program and information service through a fiber optic cable and a "smart box" in every home, an inno- 18 vation which, of course, is far too expensive and progressive to be offered free. Add a video picture to the telephone, so that callers can see each other and pay for the privilege. If people don't want to see each other, they may have to pay not to.

19   Perhaps that sounds too much like a conspiracy. Until we recall that our benevolent neighborhood phone company, the same one now forging billion-dollar alliances with cable TV firms, recently offered us a new service dubbed "Caller ID," allowing us to see the phone number and name of an incoming call before we pick up the phone. It soon followed that if we didn't want the new service, we would have to pay a "blocking fee."

20   That dispute was not a fluke, it was a wake-up call. The American psyche is not rooted in information and education; it is rooted in salesmanship. And the first tenet of salesmanship is to convince customers they can't live without your product; the second tenet is that if the first tenet fails, create a monopoly so that they have to buy it.

21   No doubt any hope for a massive popular resistance to all the new information technology is fleeting.

22   We demanded and got cable television reform and regulation long before we demanded health-care reform, and that fact alone offers insight into the state of our culture. But let us at least learn to question those who claim they will bring a revolution to our lives through the 20-inch screen.

23   We owe that to someone like E.B. White, who was worried about us and television long before we thought to worry for ourselves.

24   "When I was a child people simply looked about them and were moderately happy," White wrote in his closing thoughts on television. "Today they peer beyond the seven seas, bury themselves deep in tidings, and by and large what they see and hear makes them unutterably sad."

25   I hope that decades from now, I will stumble across White's words again as I scroll through the electronic library stored conveniently in my television set. And I hope that as the digitized letters float across the screen, I will reach for my remote control, and turn the television off.

_____ CONSIDERATIONS _____

1. Summarize Booth's objections to the heralding of the "information superhighway."

2. If you disagree with Booth's position on the "superhighway," what are some questions you might put to him?

3. In an essay, describe and evaluate your own present sources of information. That is, discuss the relative importance to you of teachers, books, magazines, newspapers, radio, TV.

4. "The changes will free our minds" is a claim often made by proponents of the new communication technology. Free them from what?

5. In paragraph 15, following E.B. White's lead, Booth envisions a future in which we value image over reality. Read the two-line dialog Daniel Boorstin uses as an epigraph for his essay, "The Pseudo-Event," page 000, written nearly two generations ago. Discuss your notions of the impact of electronic information on our perception of reality.

6. Consider Booth's use of the term "catacombs" in paragraph 11. Would "halls" or "palaces" work as well? Think about the nature of connotations as opposed to denotations.

Gwendolyn Brooks (b. 1917) grew up in Chicago. She lives there still, and has been Poet Laureate of Illinois since 1968. Her books of poems began with A Street in Brownsville *(1945);* Annie Allen *(1949) won the Pulitzer Prize. "The Bean Eaters" was the title poem of a volume published in 1960. She has written autobiography and work for children.*

16

GWENDOLYN BROOKS
The Bean Eaters

They eat beans mostly, this old yellow pair.
Dinner is a casual affair.
Plain chipware on a plain and creaking wood,
Tin flatware.

5   Two who are Mostly Good.
Two who have lived their day,
But keep on putting on their clothes
And putting things away.

And remembering . . .
10 Remembering, with twinklings and twinges,
As they lean over the beans in their rented back room
        that is full of beads and receipts and dolls and clothes,
        tobacco crumbs, vases and fringes.

Michelle Cliff (b. 1946) was born in Kingston, Jamaica, educated in New York and London, and lives in California. Her books include prose poems, Claiming an Identity They Taught Me to Despise *(1980), two novels—* Abeng *(1984) and* No Telephone to Heaven *(1987)—and a book of short stories,* Bodies of Water *(1990). In 1990 she won the James Baldwin Award of the Oakland Black Writers Guild and International Black Writers Association.*

17

MICHELLE CLIFF
If I Could Write This in Fire, I Would Write This in Fire

I

We were standing under the waterfall at the top of Orange River. 1
Our chests were just beginning to mound—slight hills on either side. In the center of each were our nipples, which were losing their sideways look and rounding into perceptible buttons of dark flesh. Too fast it seemed. We touched each other, then, quickly and almost simultaneously, raised our arms to examine the hairs growing underneath. Another sign. Mine was wispy and light-brown. My friend Zoe had dark hair curled up tight. In each little patch the riverwater caught the sun so we glistened.

The waterfall had come about when my uncles dammed up the 2
river to bring power to the sugar mill. Usually, when I say "sugar mill" to anyone not familiar with the Jamaican countryside or for that

matter my family, I can tell their minds cast an image of tall smoke-stacks, enormous copper cauldrons, a man in a broad-brimmed hat with a whip, and several dozens of slaves—that is, if they have any idea of how large sugar mills once operated. It's a grandiose expression—like plantation, verandah, out-building. (Try substituting farm, porch, outside toilet.) To some people it even sounds romantic.

3   Our sugar mill was little more than a round-roofed shed, which contained a wheel and woodfire. We paid an old man to run it, tend the fire, and then either bartered or gave the sugar away, after my grandmother had taken what she needed. Our canefield was about two acres of flat land next to the river. My grandmother had six acres in all—one donkey, a mule, two cows, some chickens, a few pigs, and stray dogs and cats who had taken up residence in the yard.

4   Her house had four rooms, no electricity, no running water. The kitchen was a shed in the back with a small pot-bellied stove. Across from the stove was a mahogany counter, which had a white enamel basin set into it. The only light source was a window, a small space covered partly by a wooden shutter. We washed our faces and hands in enamel bowls with cold water carried in kerosene tins from the river and poured from enamel pitchers. Our chamber pots were enamel also, and in the morning we carefully placed them on the steps at the side of the house where my grandmother collected them and disposed of their contents. The outhouse was about thirty yards from the back door—a "closet" as we called it—infested with lizards capable of changing color. When the door was shut it was totally dark, and the lizards made their presence known by the noise of their scurrying through the torn newspaper, or the soft shudder when they dropped from the walls. I remember most clearly the stench of the toilet, which seemed to hang in the air in that climate.

5   But because every little piece of reality exists in relation to an-other little piece, our situation was not that simple. It was to our yard that people came with news first. It was in my grandmother's parlor that the Disciples of Christ held their meetings. Zoe lived with her mother and sister on borrowed ground in a place called Breezy Hill. She and I saw each other almost every day on our school vacations over a period of three years. Each morning early—as I sat on the cement porch with my coffee cut with condensed milk—she appeared: in her straw hat, school tunic faded from blue to gray, white blouse, sneakers hanging around her neck. We had coffee together, and a piece of hard-dough bread with butter and cheese, waited a bit and headed for the river. At first we were shy with each other. We did not start from the same place.

There was land. My grandparents' farm. And there was color.   6

(My family was called *red*. A term which signified a degree of   7
whiteness. "We's just a flock of red people," a cousin of mine said
once.) In the hierarchy of shades I was considered among the lightest.
The countrywomen who visited my grandmother commented on my
"tall" hair—meaning long. Wavy, not curly.

I had spent the years from three to ten in New York and spoke—   8
at first—like an American. I wore American clothes: shorts, slacks,
bathing suit. Because of my American past I was looked upon as the
creator of games. Cowboys and Indians. Cops and Robbers. Peter Pan.

(While the primary colonial identification for Jamaicans was Eng-   9
lish, American colonialism was a strong force in my childhood—and
of course continues today. We were sent American movies and American music. American aluminum companies had already discovered
bauxite on the island and were shipping the ore to their mainland.
United Fruit bought our bananas. White Americans came to Montego
Bay, Ocho Rios, and Kingston for their vacations and their cruise ships
docked in Port Antonio and other places. In some ways America was
seen as a better place than England by many Jamaicans. The farm laborers sent to work in American agribusiness came home with dollars
and gifts and new clothes; there were few who mentioned American
racism. Many of the middle class who emigrated to Brooklyn or Staten
Island or Manhattan were able to pass into the white American
world—saving their blackness for other Jamaicans or for trips home; in
some cases, forgetting it altogether. Those middle-class Jamaicans
who could not pass for white managed differently—not unlike the Ba-
jans in Paule Marshall's *Brown Girl, Brownstones*—saving, working,
investing, buying property. Completely separate in most cases from
Black Americans.)

I was someone who had experience with the place that sent us   10
triple features of B-grade western and gangster movies. And I had tall
hair and light skin. And I was the granddaughter of my grandmother.
So I had power. I was the cowboy, Zoe was my sidekick, the boys we
knew were Indians. I was the detective, Zoe was my "girl," the boys
were the robbers. I was Peter Pan, Zoe was Wendy Darling, the boys
were the lost boys. And the terrain around the river—jungled and dark
green—was Tombstone, or Chicago, or Never-Never Land.

This place and my friendship with Zoe never touched my life in   11
Kingston. We did not correspond with each other when I left my
grandmother's home.

12   I never visited Zoe's home the entire time I knew her. It was a given: never suggested, never raised.

13   Zoe went to a state school held in a country church in Red Hills. It had been my mother's school. I went to a private all-girls school where I was taught by white Englishwomen and pale Jamaicans. In her school the students were caned as punishment. In mine the harshest punishment I remember was being sent to sit under the *lignum vitae* to "commune with nature." Some of the girls were out-and-out white (English and American), the rest of us were colored—only a few were dark. Our uniforms were blood-red gabardine, heavy and hot. Classes were held in buildings meant to recreate England: damp with stone floors, facing onto a cloister, or quad as they called it. We began each day with the headmistress leading us in English hymns. The entire school stood for an hour in the zinc-roofed gymnasium.

14   Occasionally a girl fainted, or threw up. Once, a girl had a grand mal seizure. To any such disturbance the response was always "keep singing." While she flailed on the stone floor, I wondered what the mistresses would do. We sang "Faith of Our Fathers," and watched our classmate as her eyes rolled back in her head. I thought of people swallowing their tongues. This student was dark—here on a scholarship—and the only woman who came forward to help her was the gamesmistress, the only dark teacher. She kneeled beside the girl and slid the white web belt from her tennis shorts, clamping it between the girl's teeth. When the seizure was over, she carried the girl to a tumbling mat in a corner of the gym and covered her so she wouldn't get chilled.

15   Were the other women unable to touch this girl because of her darkness? I think that now. Her darkness and her scholarship. She lived on Windward Road with her grandmother; her mother was a maid. But darkness is usually enough for women like those to hold back. Then, we usually excused that kind of behavior by saying they were "ladies." (We were constantly being told we should be ladies also. One teacher went so far as to tell us many people thought Jamaicans lived in trees and we had to show these people they were mistaken.) In short, we felt insufficient to judge the behavior of these women. The English ones (who had the corner on power in the school) had come all this way to teach us. Shouldn't we treat them as the missionaries they were certain they were? The creole Jamaicans had a different role: they were passing on to those of us who were light-skinned the creole heritage of collaboration, assimilation, loyalty to our betters. We were expected to be willing subjects in this outpost of civilization.

16   The girl left school that day and never returned.

After prayers we filed into our classrooms. After classes we had 17
games: tennis, field hockey, rounders (what the English call baseball),
netball (what the English call basketball). For games we were divided
into "houses"—groups named for Joan of Arc, Edith Cavell, Florence
Nightingale, Jane Austen. Four white heroines. Two martyrs. One
saint. Two nurses. (None of us knew then that there were Black
women with Nightingale at Scutari.) One novelist. Three involved
in white men's wars. Two dead in white men's wars. *Pride and
Prejudice.*

Those of us in Cavell wore red badges and recited her last words 18
before a firing squad in W. W. I: "Patriotism is not enough. I must
have no hatred or bitterness toward anyone."

Sorry to say I grew up to have exactly that. 19

Looking back: To try and see when the background changed 20
places with the foreground. To try and locate the vanishing point:
where the lines of perspective converge and disappear. Lines of color
and class. Lines of history and social context. Lines of denial and rejection. When did *we* (the light-skinned middle-class Jamaicans) take
over for *them* as oppressors? I need to see when and how this happened. When what should have been reality was overtaken by what
was surely unreality. When the house nigger became master.

"What's the matter with you? You think you're white or some- 21
thing?"
"Child, what you want to know 'bout Garvey for? The man was 22
nothing but a damn fool."
"They not our kind of people." 23
Why did we wear wide-brimmed hats and try to get into Oxford? 24
Why did we not return?

Great Expectations: a novel about origins and denial, about the 25
futility and tragedy of that denial, about attempting assimilation. We
learned this novel from a light-skinned Jamaican woman—she concentrated on what she called the "love affair" between Pip and Estella.

Looking back: Through the last page of *Sula*. "And the loss 26
pressed down on her chest and came up into her throat. 'We was girls
together,' she said as though explaining something." It was Zoe, and
Zoe alone, I thought of. She snapped into my mind and I remembered
no one else. Through the greens and blues of the riverbank. The flame
of red hibiscus in front of my grandmother's house. The cracked grave

of a former landowner. The fruit of the ackee which poisons those
who don't know how to prepare it.

27   *"What is to become of us?"*

28   We borrowed a baby from a woman and used her as our dolly.
Dressed and undressed her. Dipped her in the riverwater. Fed her with
the milk her mother had left with us: and giggled because we knew
where the milk had come from.

29   *A letter*: "I am desperate. I need to get away. I beg you one fifty-
dollar."

30   I send the money because this is what she asks for. I visit her on
a trip back home. Her front teeth are gone. Her husband beats her and
she suffers blackouts. I sit on her chair. She is given birth control pills
which aggravate her "condition." We boil up sorrel and ginger. She is
being taught by Peace Corps volunteers to embroider linen mats with
little lambs on them and gives me one as a keepsake. We cool off the
sorrel with a block of ice brought from the shop nearby. The shopkeeper immediately recognizes me as my grandmother's granddaughter and refuses to sell me cigarettes. (I am twenty-seven.) We sit in the
doorway of her house, pushing back the colored plastic strands which
form a curtain, and talk about Babylon and Dred. About Manley and
what he's doing for Jamaica. About how hard it is. We walk along the
railway tracks—no longer used—to Crooked River and the post office.
Her little daughter walks beside us and we recite a poem for her:
"Mornin' buddy/Me no buddy fe wunna/Who den, den I saw?" and on
and on.

31   I can come and go. And I leave. To complete my education in
London.

II

32   Their goddam kings and their goddam queens. Grandmotherly
Victoria spreading herself thin across the globe. Elizabeth II on our TV
screens. We stop what we are doing. We quiet down. We pay our respects.

33   1981: In Massachusetts I get up at 5 A.M. to watch the royal wedding. I tell myself maybe the IRA will intervene. It's got to be better
than starving themselves to death. Better to be a kamikaze in St.
Paul's Cathedral than a hostage in Ulster. And last week Black and

white people smashed storefronts all over the United Kingdom. But I really don't believe we'll see royal blood on TV. I watch because they once ruled us. In the back of the cathedral a Maori woman sings an aria from Handel, and I notice that she is surrounded by the colored subjects.

To those of us in the commonwealth the royal family was the 34 perfect symbol of hegemony. To those of us who were dark in the dark nations, the prime minister, the parliament barely existed. We believed in royalty—we were convinced in this belief. Maybe it played on some ancestral memories of West Africa—where other kings and queens had been. Altars and castles and magic.

The faces of our new rulers were everywhere in my childhood. 35 Calendars, newsreels, magazines. Their presences were often among us. Attending test matches between the West Indians and South Africans. They were our landlords. Not always absentee. And no matter what Black leader we might elect—were we to choose independence—we would be losing something almost holy in our impudence.

WE ARE HERE BECAUSE YOU WERE THERE BLACK PEOPLE 36 AGAINST STATE BRUTALITY BLACK WOMEN WILL NOT BE INTIMIDATED WELCOME TO BRITAIN . . . WELCOME TO SECOND-CLASS CITIZENSHIP (slogans of the Black movement in Britain)

Indian women cleaning the toilets in Heathrow airport. This is 37 the first thing I notice. Dark women in saris trudging buckets back and forth as other dark women in saris—some covered by loosefitting winter coats—form a line to have their passports stamped.

The triangle trade: molasses/rum/slaves. Robinson Crusoe was 38 on a slave-trading journey. Robert Browning was a mulatto. Holding pens. Jamaica was a seasoning station. Split tongues. Sliced ears. Whipped bodies. The constant pretense of civility against rape. Still. Iron collars. Tinplate masks. The latter a precaution: to stop the slaves from eating the sugar cane.

A pregnant woman is to be whipped—they dig a hole to accom- 39 modate her belly and place her face down on the ground. Many of us became light-skinned very fast. Traced ourselves through bastard lines to reach the duke of Devonshire. The earl of Cornwall. The lord of this and the lord of that. Our mothers' rapes were the things unspoken.

You say: But Britain freed her slaves in 1833. Yes.   40

41   Tea plantations in India and Ceylon. Mines in Africa. The Cape-to-Cairo Railroad. Rhodes scholars. Suez Crisis. The white man's bloody burden. Boer War. Bantustans. Sitting in a theatre in London in the seventies. A play called *West of Suez.* A lousy play about British colonials. The finale comes when several well-known white actors are machine-gunned by several lesser-known Black actors. (As Nina Simone says: "This is a show tune but the show hasn't been written for it yet.")

42   The red empire of geography classes. "The sun never sets on the British empire and you can't trust it in the dark." Or with the dark peoples. "Because of the Industrial Revolution European countries went in search of markets and raw materials." Another geography (or was it a history) lesson.

43   Their bloody kings and their bloody queens. Their bloody peers. Their bloody generals. Admirals. Explorers. Livingstone. Hillary. Kitchener. All the bwanas. And all their beaters, porters, sherpas. Who found the source of the Nile. Victoria Falls. The tops of mountains. Their so-called discoveries reek of untruth. How many dark people died so they could misname the physical features in their blasted gazetteer. A statistic we shall never know. Dr. Livingstone, I presume you are here to rape our land and enslave our people.

44   There are statues of these dead white men all over London.

45   An interesting fact: The swear word "bloody" is a contraction of "by my lady"—a reference to the Virgin Mary. They do tend to use their ladies. Name ages for them. Places for them. Use them as screens, inspirations, symbols. And many of the ladies comply. While the national martyr Edith Cavell was being executed by the Germans in 1915 in Belgium (called "poor little Belgium" by the allies in the war), the Belgians were engaged in the exploitation of the land and peoples of the Congo.

46   And will we ever know how many dark peoples were "imported" to fight in white men's wars. Probably not. Just as we will never know how many hearts were cut from African people so that the Christian doctor might be a success—i.e., extend a white man's life. Our Sister Killjoy observes this from her black-eyed squint.

47   Dr. Schweitzer—humanitarian, authority on Bach, winner of the Nobel Peace Prize—on the people of Africa: "The Negro is a child, and with children nothing can be done without the use of authority. We must, therefore, so arrange the circumstances of our daily life that my

authority can find expression. With regard to Negroes, then, I have coined the formula: 'I am your brother, it is true, but your elder brother.' " (*On the Edge of the Primeval Forest*, 1961)

They like to pretend we didn't fight back. We did: with obeah, 48 poison, revolution. It simply was not enough.

"Colonies...these places where 'niggers' are cheap and the earth 49 is rich." (W.E.B. DuBois, "The Souls of White Folk")

A cousin is visiting me from Cal Tech where he is getting a de- 50 gree in engineering. I am learning about the Italian Renaissance. My cousin is recognizably Black and speaks with an accent. I am not and do not—unless I am back home, where the "twang" comes upon me. We sit for some time in a bar in his hotel and are not served. A light-skinned Jamaican comes over to our table. He is an older man—a professor at the University of London. "Don't bother with it, you hear. They don't serve us in this bar." A run-of-the-mill incident for all recognizably Black people in this city. But for me it is not.

Henry's eyes fill up, but he refuses to believe our informant. 51 "No, man, the girl is just busy." (The girl is a fifty-year-old white woman, who may just be following orders. But I do not mention this. I have chosen sides.) All I can manage to say is, "Jesus Christ, I hate the fucking English." Henry looks at me. (In the family I am known as the "lady cousin." It has to do with how I look. And the fact that I am twenty-seven and unmarried—and for all they know, unattached. They do not know that I am really the lesbian cousin.) Our informant says—gently, but with a distinct tone of disappointment—"My dear, is that what you're studying at the university?"

You see—the whole business is very complicated. 52

Henry and I leave without drinks and go to meet some of his 53 white colleagues at a restaurant I know near Covent Garden Opera House. The restaurant caters to theatre types and so I hope there won't be a repeat of the bar scene—at least they know how to pretend. Besides, I tell myself, the owners are Italian *and* gay; they *must* be halfway decent. Henry and his colleagues work for an American company which is paying their way through Cal Tech. They mine bauxite from the hills in the middle of the island and send it to the United States. A turnaround occurs at dinner: Henry joins the white men in a sustained mockery of the waiters: their accents and the way they walk. He whispers to me: "Why you want to bring us to a battyman's den, lady?" (*Battyman* = *faggot* in Jamaican.) I keep quiet.

54   We put the white men in a taxi and Henry walks me to the underground station. He asks me to sleep with him. (It wouldn't be incest. His mother was a maid in the house of an uncle and Henry has not seen her since his birth. He was taken into the family. She was let go.) I say that I can't. I plead exams. I can't say that I don't want to. Because I remember what happened in the bar. But I can't say that I'm a lesbian either—even though I want to believe his alliance with the white men at dinner was forced: not really him. He doesn't buy my excuse. "Come on, lady, let's do it. What's the matter, you 'fraid?" I pretend I am back home and start patois to show him somehow I am not afraid, not English, not white. I tell him he's a married man and he tells me he's a ram goat. I take the train to where I am staying and try to forget the whole thing. But I don't. I remember our different skins and our different experiences within them. And I have a hard time realizing that I am angry with Henry. That to him—no use in pretending—a queer is a queer.

55   1981: I hear on the radio that Bob Marley is dead and I drive over the Mohawk Trail listening to a program of his music and I cry and cry and cry. Someone says: "It wasn't the ganja that killed him, it was poverty and working in a steel foundry when he was young."

56   I flash back to my childhood and a young man who worked for an aunt I lived with once. He taught me to smoke ganja behind the house. And to peel an orange with the tip of a machete without cutting through the skin—"Love" it was called: a necklace of orange rind the result. I think about him because I heard he had become a Rastaman. And then I think about Rastas.

57   We are sitting on the porch of an uncle's house in Kingston—the family and I—and a Rastaman comes to the gate. We have guns but they are locked behind a false closet. We have dogs but they are tied up. We are Jamaicans and know that Rastas mean no harm. We let him in and he sits on the side of the porch and shows us his brooms and brushes. We buy some to take back to New York. "Peace, missis."

58   There were many Rastas in my childhood. Walking the roadside with their goods. Sitting outside their shacks in the mountains. The outsides painted bright—sometimes with words. Gathering at Palisadoes Airport to greet the Conquering Lion of Judah. They were considered figures of fun by most middle-class Jamaicans. Harmless—like Marcus Garvey.

59   Later: white American hippies trying to create the effect of dred in their straight white hair. The ganja joint held between their straight

white teeth. "Man, the grass is good." Hanging out by the Sheraton pool. Light-skinned Jamaicans also dredlocked, also assuming the ganja. Both groups moving to the music but not the words. Harmless. "Peace, brother."

III

My grandmother: "Let us thank God for a fruitful place." 60
My grandfather: "Let us rescue the perishing world."

This evening on the road in western Massachusetts there are 61
pockets of fog. Then clear spaces. Across from a pond a dog staggers in front of my headlights. I look closer and see that his mouth is foaming. He stumbles to the side of the road—I go to call the police.

I drive back to the house, radio playing "difficult" piano pieces. 62
And I think about how I need to say all this. This is who I am. I am not what you allow me to be. Whatever you decide me to be. In a bookstore in London I show the woman at the counter my book and she stares at me for a minute, then says: "You're a Jamaican." "Yes." "You're not at all like our Jamaicans."

Encountering the void is nothing more nor less than understand- 63
ing invisibility. Of being fogbound.

Then: It was never a question of passing. It was a question of hid- 64
ing. Behind Black and white perceptions of who we were—who they thought we were. Tropics. Plantations. Calypso. Cricket. We were the people with the musical voices and the coronation mugs on our parlor tables. I would be whatever figure those foreign imaginations cared for me to be. It would be so simple to let others fill in for me. So easy to startle them with a flash of anger when their visions got out of hand— but never to sustain the anger for myself. It could become a life lived within myself. A life cut off. I know who I am but you will never know who I am. I may in fact lose touch with who I am.

I hid from my real sources. But my real sources were also hidden 65
from me.

Now: It is not a question of relinquishing privilege. It is a ques- 66
tion of grasping more of myself. I have found that in the real sources are concealed my survival. My speech. My voice. To be colonized is to be rendered insensitive. To have those parts necessary to sustain life numbed. And this is in some cases—in my case—perceived as privi-

lege. The test of a colonized person is to walk through a shantytown
in Kingston and not bat an eye. This I cannot do. Because part of me
lives there—and as I grasp more of this part I realize what needs to be
done with the rest of my life.

67   Sometimes I used to think we were like the Marranos—the
Sephardic Jews forced to pretend they were Christians. The name was
given to them by the Christians, and meant "pigs." But once out of
Spain and Portugal, they became Jews openly again. Some settled in
Jamaica. They knew who the enemy was and acted for their own sur-
vival. But they remained Jews always.

68   We also knew who the enemy was—I remember jokes about the
English. Saying they stank, saying they were stingy, that they drank
too much and couldn't hold their liquor, that they had bad teeth, were
dirty and dishonest, were limey bastards, and horse-faced bitches. We
said the men only wanted to sleep with Jamaican women. And that
the women made pigs of themselves with Jamaican men.

69   But of course this was seen by us—the light-skinned middle
class—with a double vision. We learned to cherish that part of us that
was them—and to deny the part that was not. Believing in some cases
that the latter part had ceased to exist.

70   None of this is as simple as it may sound. We were colorists and
we aspired to oppressor status. (Of course, almost any aspiration in-
stilled by Western civilization is to oppressor status: success, for example.) Color was the symbol of our potential: color taking in hair
"quality," skin tone, freckles, nose-width, eyes. We did not see that
color symbolism was a method of keeping us apart: in the society, in
the family, between friends. Those of us who were light-skinned,
straight-haired, etc., were given to believe that we could actually attain whiteness—or at least those qualities of the colonizer which
made him superior. We were convinced of white supremacy. If we
failed, we were not really responsible for our failures: we had all the
advantages—but it was that one persistent drop of blood, that single
rogue gene that made us unable to conceptualize abstract ideas, made
us love darkness rather than despise it, which was to be blamed for
our failure. Our dark part had taken over: an inherited imbalance in
which the doom of the creole was sealed.

71   I am trying to write this as clearly as possible, but as I write I
realize that what I say may sound fabulous, or even mythic. It is. It
is insane.

Under this system of colorism—the system which prevailed in   72
my childhood in Jamaica, and which has carried over to the present—
rarely will dark and light people co-mingle. Rarely will they achieve
between themselves an intimacy informed with identity. (I should say
here that I am using the categories light and dark both literally and
symbolically. There are dark Jamaicans who have achieved lightness
and the "advantages" which go with it by their successful pursuit of
oppressor status.)

Under this system light and dark people will meet in those ways   73
in which the light-skinned person imitates the oppressor. But imitation goes only so far: the light-skinned person becomes an oppressor in
fact. He/she will have a dark chauffeur, a dark nanny, a dark maid, and
a dark gardener. These employees will be paid badly. Because of the
slave past, because of their dark skin, the servants of the middle class
have been used according to the traditions of the slavocracy. They are
not seen as workers for their own sake, but for the sake of the family
who has employed them. It was not until Michael Manley became
prime minister that a minimum wage for houseworkers was en-
acted—and the indignation of the middle class was profound.

During Manley's leadership the middle class began to abandon   74
the island in droves. Toronto. Miami. New York. Leaving their houses
and businesses behind and sewing cash into the tops of suitcases. Today—with a new regime—they are returning: "Come back to the way
things used to be" the tourist advertisement on American TV says.
"Make it Jamaica again. Make it your own."

But let me return to the situation of houseservants as I remember   75
it: They will be paid badly, but they will be "given" room and board.
However, the key to the larder will be kept by the mistress in her
dresser drawer. They will spend Christmas with the family of their
employers and be given a length of English wool for trousers or a few
yards of cotton for dresses. They will see their children on their days
off: their extended family will care for the children the rest of the
time. When the employers visit their relations in the country, the servants may be asked along—oftentimes the servants of the middle class
come from the same part of the countryside their employers have
come from. But they will be expected to work while they are there.
Back in town, there are parts of the house they are allowed to move
freely around; other parts they are not allowed to enter. When the family watches the TV the servant is allowed to watch also, but only
while standing in a doorway. The servant may have a radio in his/her
room, also a dresser and a cot. Perhaps a mirror. There will usually be
one ceiling light. And one small square louvered window.

76   *A true story*: One middle-class Jamaican woman ordered a Persian rug from Harrod's in London. The day it arrived so did her new maid. She was going downtown to have her hair touched up, and told the maid to vacuum the rug. She told the maid she would find the vacuum cleaner in the same shed as the power mower. And when she returned she found that the fine nap of her new rug had been removed.

77   The reaction of the mistress was to tell her friends that the "girl" was backward. She did not fire her until she found that the maid had scrubbed the teflon from her new set of pots, saying she thought they were coated with "nastiness."

78   The houseworker/mistress relationship in which one Black woman is the oppressor of another Black woman is a cornerstone of the experience of many Jamaican women.

79   I remember another true story: In a middle-class family's home one Christmas, a relation was visiting from New York. This woman had brought gifts for everybody, including the housemaid. The maid had been released from a mental institution recently, where they had "treated" her for depression. This visiting light-skinned woman had brought the dark woman a bright red rayon blouse and presented it to her in the garden one afternoon, while the family was having tea. The maid thanked her softly, and the other woman moved toward her as if to embrace her. Then she stopped, her face suddenly covered with tears, and ran into the house, saying, "My God, I can't, I can't."

80   We are women who come from a place almost incredible in its beauty. It is a beauty which can mask a great deal and which has been used in that way. But that the beauty is there is a fact. I remember what I thought the freedom of my childhood, in which the fruitful place was something I took for granted. Just as I took for granted Zoe's appearance every morning on my school vacations—in the sense that I knew she would be there. That she would always be the one to visit me. The perishing world of my grandfather's graces at the table, if I ever seriously thought about it, was somewhere else.

81   Our souls were affected by the beauty of Jamaica, as much as they were affected by our fears of darkness.

82   There is no ending to this piece of writing. There is no way to end it. As I read back over it, I see that we/they/I may become confused in the mind of the reader: but these pronouns have always co-existed in my mind. The Rastas talk of the "I and I"—a pronoun in

which they combine themselves with Jah. Jah is a contraction of Jahweh and Jehova, but to me always sounds like the beginning of Jamaica. I and Jamaica is who I am. No matter how far I travel—how deep the ambivalence I feel about ever returning. And Jamaica is a place in which we/they/I connect and disconnect—change place.

____ CONSIDERATIONS _____

1. Why is it difficult for many to see this sample of Cliff's writing as an "essay"?

2. Which passages in Cliff seem to be carefully thought out? Which seem to be the most impulsively written?

3. "I and Jamaica is who I am," writes Cliff in paragraph 82. Is that what Wallace Stegner means by a "sense of place" (page 503)?

4. How does Cliff's childhood friendship with Zoe contribute to the general drift of the essay?

5. Paragraph 40 ends with the word "Yes," punctuated as though it were a sentence. What else does that sentence say besides "Yes"?

6. At the end of the little story Cliff tells in paragraph 79, why did the gift-bearing guest run away from the maid and cry, "My God, I can't, I can't." What has this to do with Cliff?

Frank Conroy (b. 1936) grew up in various towns along the eastern seaboard, and attended Haverford College in Pennsylvania. He plays jazz piano, was director of the literature program at the National Endowment for the Arts from 1982 to 1987, and now directs the writing program at the University of Iowa. He writes about his early life in Stop-Time, *from which we take this episode. His prose possesses the qualities that make the best reminiscence: details feel exact and bright, though miniature with distance, like the landscape crafted for background to model trains. In 1985 he published a collection of short stories called* Midair, *and his novel* Body and Soul *in 1993.*

18

FRANK CONROY

A Yo-Yo Going Down

1   The common yo-yo is crudely made, with a thick shank between two widely spaced wooden disks. The string is knotted or stapled to the shank. With such an instrument nothing can be done except the simple up-down movement. My yo-yo, on the other hand, was a perfectly balanced construction of hard wood, slightly weighted, flat, with only a sixteenth of an inch between the halves. The string was not attached to the shank, but looped over it in such a way as to allow the wooden part to spin freely on its own axis. The gyroscopic effect thus created kept the yo-yo stable in all attitudes.

2   I started at the beginning of the book and quickly mastered the novice, intermediate, and advanced stages, practicing all day every day in the woods across the street from my house. Hour after hour of practice, never moving to the next trick until the one at hand was mastered.

3   The string was tied to my middle finger, just behind the nail. As I threw—with your palm up, make a fist; throw down your hand, fin-

gers unfolding, as if you were casting grain—a short bit of string would tighten across the sensitive pad of flesh at the tip of my finger. That was the critical area. After a number of weeks I could interpret the condition of the string, the presence of any imperfections on the shank, but most importantly the exact amount of spin or inertial energy left in the yo-yo at any given moment—all from that bit of string on my fingertip. As the throwing motion became more and more natural I found I could make the yo-yo "sleep" for an astonishing length of time—fourteen or fifteen seconds—and still have enough spin left to bring it back to my hand. Gradually the basic moves became reflexes. Sleeping, twirling, swinging, and precise aim. Without thinking, without even looking, I could run through trick after trick involving various combinations of the elemental skills, switching from one to the other in a smooth continuous flow. On particularly good days I would hum a tune under my breath and do it all in time to the music.

Flicking the yo-yo expressed something. The sudden, potentially   4
comic extension of one's arm to twice its length. The precise neatness of it, intrinsically soothing, as if relieving an inner tension too slight to be noticeable, the way a man might hitch up his pants simply to enact a reassuring gesture. It felt good. The comfortable weight in one's hand, the smooth, rapid-descent down the string, ending with a barely audible snap as the yo-yo hung balanced, spinning, pregnant with force and the slave of one's fingertip. That it was vaguely masturbatory seems inescapable. I doubt that half the pubescent boys in America could have been captured by any other means, as, in the heat of the fad, half of them were. A single Loop-the-Loop might represent, in some mysterious way, the act of masturbation, but to break down the entire repertoire into the three stages of throw, trick, and return representing erection, climax, and detumescence seems immoderate.

The greatest pleasure in yo-yoing was an abstract pleasure—   5
watching the dramatization of simply physical laws, and realizing they would never fail if a trick was done correctly. The geometric purity of it! The string wasn't just a string, it was a tool in the enactment of theorems. It was a line, an idea. And the top was an entirely different sort of idea, a gyroscope, capable of storing energy and of interacting with the line. I remember the first time I did a particularly lovely trick, one in which the sleeping yo-yo is swung from right to left while the string is interrupted by an extended index finger. Momentum carries the yo-yo in a circular path around the finger, but instead of completing the arc the yo-yo falls on the taut string between the performer's hands, where it continues to spin in an upright position. My pleasure at that moment was as much from the beauty of the experiment as from pride. Snapping apart my hands I sent the yo-yo into the air above my head, bouncing it off nothing, back into my palm.

6   I practiced the yo-yo because it pleased me to do so, without the slightest application of will power. It wasn't ambition that drove me, but the nature of yo-yoing. The yo-yo represented my first organized attempt to control the outside world. It fascinated me because I could see my progress in clearly defined stages, and because the intimacy of it, the almost spooky closeness I began to feel with the instrument in my hand, seemed to ensure that nothing irrelevant would interfere. I was, in the language of jazz, "up tight" with my yo-yo, and finally free, in one small area at least, of the paralyzing sloppiness of life in general.

7   The first significant problem arose in the attempt to do fifty consecutive Loop-the-Loops. After ten or fifteen the yo-yo invariably started to lean and the throws became less clean, resulting in loss of control. I almost skipped the whole thing because fifty seemed excessive. Ten made the point. But there it was, written out in the book. To qualify as an expert you had to do fifty, so fifty I would do.

8   It took me two days, and I wouldn't have spent a moment more. All those Loop-the-Loops were hard on the strings. Time after time the shank cut them and the yo-yo went sailing off into the air. It was irritating, not only because of the expense (strings were a nickel each, and fabricating your own was unsatisfactory), but because a random element had been introduced. About the only unforeseeable disaster in yo-yoing was to have your string break, and here was a trick designed to do exactly that. Twenty-five would have been enough. If you could do twenty-five clean Loop-the-Loops you could do fifty or a hundred. I supposed they were simply trying to sell strings and went back to the more interesting tricks.

9   The witty nonsense of Eating Spaghetti, the surprise of The Twirl, the complex neatness of Cannonball, Backwards Round the World, or Halfway Round the World—I could do them all, without false starts or sloppy endings. I could do every trick in the book. Perfectly.

10   The day was marked on the kitchen calendar (God Gave Us Bluebell Natural Bottled Gas). I got on my bike and rode into town. Pedaling along the highway I worked out with the yo-yo to break in a new string. The twins were appearing at the dime store.

11   I could hear the crowd before I turned the corner. Kids were coming on bikes and on foot from every corner of town, rushing down the streets like madmen. Three or four policemen were busy keeping the street clear directly in front of the store, and in a small open space around the doors some of the more adept kids were running through their tricks, showing off to the general audience or stopping to compare notes with their peers. Standing at the edge with my yo-yo safe in my pocket, it didn't take me long to see I had them all covered. A boy

in a sailor hat could do some of the harder tricks, but he missed too often to be a serious threat. I went inside.

As Ramos and Ricardo performed I watched their hands carefully, noticing little differences in style, and technique. Ricardo was a shade classier, I thought, although Ramos held an edge in the showy two-handed stuff. When they were through we went outside for the contest. 12

"Everybody in the alley!" Ramos shouted, his head bobbing an inch or two above the others. "Contest starting now in the alley!" A hundred excited children followed the twins into an alley beside the dime store and lined up against the wall. 13

"Attention all kids!" Ramos yelled, facing us from the middle of the street like a drill sergeant. "To qualify for contest you got to Rock the Cradle. You got to rock yo-yo in cradle four time. Four time! Okay? Three time no good. Okay. Everybody happy?" There were murmurs of disappointment and some of the kids stepped out of line. The rest of us closed ranks. Yo-yos flicked nervously as we waited. "Winner receive grand prize. Special Black Beauty Prize Yo-Yo with Diamonds," said Ramos, gesturing to his brother who smiled and held up the prize, turning it in the air so we could see the four stones set on each side. ("The crowd gasped . . ." I want to write. Of course they didn't. They didn't make a sound, but the impact of the diamond yo-yo was obvious.) We'd never seen anything like it. One imagined how the stones would gleam as it revolved, and how much prettier the tricks would be. The ultimate yo-yo! The only one in town! Who knew what feats were possible with such an instrument? All around me a fierce, nervous resolve was settling into the contestants, suddenly skittish as race-horses. 14

"Ricardo will show trick with Grand Prize Yo-Yo. Rock the Cradle four time!" 15

"One!" cried Ramos. 16

"Two!" the kids joined in. 17

"Three!" It was really beautiful. He did it so slowly you would have thought he had all the time in the world. I counted seconds under my breath to see how long he made it sleep. 18

"Four!" said the crowd. 19

"Thirteen" I said to myself as the yo-yo snapped back into his hand. Thirteen seconds. Excellent time for that particular trick. 20

"Attention all kids!" Ramos announced. "Contest start now at head of line." 21

The first boy did a sloppy job of gathering his string but managed to rock the cradle quickly four times. 22

"Okay." Ramos tapped him on the shoulder and moved to the next boy, who fumbled. "Out." Ricardo followed, doing an occasional 23

Loop-the-Loop with the diamond yo-yo. "Out . . . out . . . okay," said Ramos as he worked down the line.

24   There was something about the man's inexorable advance that unnerved me. His decisions were fast, and there was no appeal. To my surprise I felt my palms begin to sweat. Closer and closer he came, his voice growing louder, and then suddenly he was standing in front of me. Amazed, I stared at him. It was as if he'd appeared out of thin air.

25   "What happen boy, you swarrow bubble gum?"

26   The laughter jolted me out of it. Blushing, I threw down my yo-yo and executed a slow Rock the Cradle, counting the four passes and hesitating a moment at the end so as not to appear rushed.

27   "Okay." He tapped my shoulder. "Good."

28   I wiped my hands on my blue jeans and watched him move down the line. "Out . . . out . . . out." He had a large mole on the back of his neck.

29   Seven boys qualified. Coming back, Ramos called out, "Next trick Backward Round the World! Okay? Go!"

30   The first two boys missed, but the third was the kid in the sailor hat. Glancing quickly to see that no one was behind him, he hunched up his shoulder, threw, and just barely made the catch. There was some loose string in his hand, but not enough to disqualify him.

31   Number four missed, as did number five, and it was my turn. I stepped forward, threw the yo-yo almost straight up over my head, and as it began to fall pulled very gently to add some speed. It zipped neatly behind my legs and there was nothing more to do. My head turned to one side, I stood absolutely still and watched the yo-yo come in over my shoulder and slap into my hand. I added a Loop-the-Loop just to show the tightness of the string.

32   "Did you see that?" I heard someone say.

33   Number seven missed, so it was between myself and the boy in the sailor hat. His hair was bleached by the sun and combed up over his forehead in a pompadour, held from behind by the white hat. He was a year or two older than me. Blinking his blue eyes nervously, he adjusted the tension of his string.

34   "Next trick Cannonball! Cannonball! You go first this time," Ramos said to me.

35   Kids had gathered in a circle around us, those in front quiet and attentive, those in back jumping up and down to get a view." "Move back for room," Ricardo said, pushing them back. "More room, please."

36   I stepped into the center and paused, looking down at the ground. It was a difficult trick. The yo-yo had to land exactly on the string and there was a chance I'd miss the first time. I knew I wouldn't miss twice. "Can I have one practice?"

Ramos and Ricardo consulted in their mother tongue, and then 37
Ramos held up his hands. "Attention all kids! Each boy have one practice before trick."

The crowd was then silent, watching me. I took a deep breath 38
and threw, following the fall of the yo-yo with my eyes, turning
slightly, matador-fashion, as it passed me. My finger caught the string,
the yo-yo came up and over, and missed. Without pausing I threw
again. "Second time," I yelled, so there would be no misunderstanding. The circle had been too big. This time I made it small, sacrificing
beauty for security. The yo-yo fell where it belonged and spun for a
moment. (A moment I don't rush, my arms widespread, my eyes
locked on the spinning toy. The Trick! There it is, brief and magic
right before your eyes! My hands are frozen in the middle of a deaf-
and-dumb sentence, holding the whole airy, tenuous statement aloft
for everyone to see.) With a quick snap I broke up the trick and made
my catch.

Ramos nodded. "Okay. Very good. Now next boy." 39

Sailor-hat stepped forward, wiping his nose with the back of his 40
hand. He threw once to clear the string.

"One practice," said Ramos. 41

He nodded. 42

"C'mon Bobby," someone said. "You can do it." 43

Bobby threw the yo-yo out to the side, made his move, and 44
missed. "Damn," he whispered. (He said "dahyum.") The second time
he got half-way through the trick before his yo-yo ran out of gas and
fell impotently off the string. He picked it up and walked away, winding slowly.

Ramos came over and held my hand in the air. "The winner!" he 45
yelled. "Grand prize Black Beauty Diamond Yo-Yo will now be
awarded."

Ricardo stood in front of me. "Take off old yo-yo." I loosened the 46
knot and slipped it off. "Put out hand." I held out my hand and he
looped the new string on my finger, just behind the nail, where the
mark was. "You like Black Beauty," he said, smiling as he stepped
back. "Diamond make pretty colors in the sun."

"Thank you," I said. 47

"Very good with yo-yo. Later we have contest for whole town. 48
Winner go to Miami for State Championship. Maybe you win. Okay?"

"Okay." I nodded. "Thank you." 49

A few kids came up to look at Black Beauty. I threw it once or 50
twice to get the feel. It seemed a bit heavier than my old one. Ramos
and Ricardo were surrounded as the kids called out their favorite
tricks.

"Do Pickpocket! Pickpocket!" 51

52   "Do the Double Cannonball!"

53   "Ramos! Ramos! Do the Turkish Army!"

54   Smiling, waving their hands to ward off the barrage of requests, the twins worked their way through the crowd toward the mouth of the alley. I watched them moving away and was immediately struck by a wave of fierce and irrational panic. "Wait," I yelled, pushing through after them. "Wait!"

55   I caught them on the street.

56   "No more today," Ricardo said, and then paused when he saw it was me. "Okay. The champ. What's wrong? Yo-yo no good?"

57   "No. It's fine."

58   "Good. You take care of it."

59   "I wanted to ask when the contest is. The one where you get to go to Miami."

60   "Later. After school begins." They began to move away. "We have to go home now."

61   "Just one more thing," I said, walking after them. "What is the hardest trick you know?"

62   Ricardo laughed. "Hardest trick is killing flies in air."

63   "No, no. I mean a real trick."

64   They stopped and looked at me. "There is a very hard trick," Ricardo said. "I don't do it, but Ramos does. Because you won the contest he will show you. But only once, so watch carefully."

65   We stepped into the lobby of the Sunset Theater. Ramos cleared his string. "Watch," he said, and threw. The trick started out like a Cannonball, and then unexpectedly folded up, opened again, and as I watched breathlessly the entire complex web spun around in the air, propelled by Ramos' two hands making slow circles like a swimmer. The end was like the end of a Cannonball.

66   "That's beautiful," I said, genuinely awed. "What's it called?"

67   "The Universe."

68   "The Universe," I repeated.

69   "Because it goes around and around," said Ramos, "like the planets."

_____ CONSIDERATIONS _____

1. List the ways in which Conroy says one can get pleasure from the yo-yo.

2. How much of performance is play? Would you use the word performance for the work of a painter, an opera singer, a tennis star, a poet? Are professional athletes paid to play? What is the difference between work and play?

3. One respected writer says that "play is the direct opposite of seriousness"; yet writers like Conroy are serious in recalling their childhood play. Can you resolve this apparent contradiction?

4. Conroy's essay might be divided into two major sections. Where would you draw the dividing line? Describe the two sections in terms of the author's intention. In the second section, the author makes constant use of dialogue; in the first, there is none. Why?

5. "I practiced the yo-yo because it pleased me to do so, without the slightest application of will power." Consider the relevance or irrelevance of will power to pleasure. Are they mutually exclusive?

6. In paragraph 14, Conroy interrupts his narrative with a parenthetical remark about himself as the writer: "('The crowd gasped...' I want to write. Of course they didn't. They didn't make a sound, but the impact of the diamond yo-yo was obvious.)" Are such glimpses of the writer useful or merely distracting? Discuss.

Charles Dickens (1812–1870) was the most popular English novelist of his time. Thriving in the mid-nineteenth century, he wrote among other fictions Pickwick Papers, Oliver Twist, David Copperfield, Bleak House, *"A Christmas Carol,"* Hard Times, A Tale of Two Cities, *and* Great Expectations.

In 1842, his transatlantic popularity extensive, he toured the United States lecturing and reading from his fiction. Later in the same year, Dickens published his American Notes; *the book was not popular in this country. Here are some of Charles Dickens's summary thoughts from* American Notes.

19

CHARLES DICKENS
Concluding Remarks

1   There are many passages in this book, where I have been at some pains to resist the temptation of troubling my readers with my own deductions and conclusions: preferring that they should judge for themselves, from such premises as I have laid before them. My only object in the outset, was, to carry them with me faithfully wheresoever I went, and that task I have discharged.

2   But I may be pardoned, if on such a theme as the general character of the American people, and the general character of their social system, as presented to a stranger's eyes, I desire to express my own opinions in a few words, before I bring this volume to a close.

3   They are, by nature, frank, brave, cordial, hospitable, and affectionate. Cultivation and refinement seem but to enhance their warmth of heart and ardent enthusiasm; and it is the possession of these latter qualities in a most remarkable degree, which renders an educated American one of the most endearing and most generous of friends. I never was so won upon, as by this class; never yielded up my full confidence and esteem so readily and pleasurably, as to them; never can make again, in half-a-year, so many friends for whom I seem to entertain the regard of half a life.

These qualities are natural, I implicitly believe, to the whole peo- 4
ple. That they are, however, sadly sapped and blighted in their growth
among the mass; and that there are influences at work which endan-
ger them still more, and give but little present promise of their
healthy restoration; is a truth that ought to be told.

It is an essential part of every national character to pique itself 5
mightily upon its faults, and to deduce tokens of its virtue or its wisdom from their very exaggeration. One great blemish in the popular
mind of America, and the prolific parent of an innumerable brood of
evils, is Universal Distrust. Yet, the American citizen plumes himself
upon this spirit, even when he is sufficiently dispassionate to perceive
the ruin it works; and will often adduce it, in spite of his own reason,
as an instance of the great sagacity and acuteness of the people, and
their superior shrewdness and independence.

"You carry," says the stranger, "this jealousy and distrust into 6
every transaction of public life. By repelling worthy men from your
legislative assemblies, it has bred up a class of candidates for the suf-
frage, who, in their every act, disgrace your Institutions and your people's choice. It has rendered you so fickle, and so given to change, that
your inconstancy has passed into a proverb, for you no sooner set up
an idol firmly, than you are sure to pull it down and dash it into fragments; and this, because directly you reward a benefactor, or a public
servant, you distrust him, merely because he *is* rewarded; and immediately apply yourselves to find out, either that you have been too
bountiful in your acknowledgments, or he remiss in his deserts. Any
man who attains a high place among you, from the President downwards, may date his downfall from that moment; for any printed lie
that any notorious villain pens, although it militate directly against
the character and conduct of a life, appeals at once to your distrust,
and is believed. You will strain at a gnat in the way of trustfulness and
confidence, however fairly won and well deserved; but you will swallow a whole caravan of camels, if they be laden with unworthy doubts
and mean suspicions. Is this well, think you, or likely to elevate the
character of the governors or the governed, among you?"

The answer is invariably the same: "There's freedom of opinion 7
here, you know. Every man thinks for himself, and we are not to be
easily overreached. That's how our people come to be suspicious."

Another prominent feature is the love of "smart" dealing, which 8
gilds over many a swindle and gross breach of trust; many a defalca-
tion, public and private; and enables many a knave to hold his head up
with the best, who well deserves a halter—though it has not been
without its retributive operation, for this smartness has done more in
a few years to impair the public credit, and to cripple the public resources, than dull honesty, however rash, could have effected in a century. The merits of a broken speculation, or a bankruptcy, or of a suc-

cessful scoundrel, are not gauged by its or his observance of the golden rule, "Do as you would be done by," but are considered with reference to their smartness. I recollect, on both occasions of our passing that ill-fated Cairo on the Mississippi, remarking on the bad effects such gross deceits must have when they exploded, in generating a want of confidence abroad, and discouraging foreign investment: but I was given to understand that this was a very smart scheme by which a deal of money had been made: and that its smartest feature was, that they forgot these things abroad, in a very short time, and speculated again, as freely as ever. The following dialogue I have held a hundred times:—"Is it not a very disgraceful circumstance that such a man as So and So should be acquiring a large property by the most infamous and odious means, and notwithstanding all the crimes of which he has been guilty, should be tolerated and abetted by your Citizens? He is a public nuisance, is he not?" "Yes, Sir." "A convicted liar?" "Yes, Sir." "He has been kicked, and cuffed, and caned?" "Yes, Sir." "And he is utterly dishonourable, debased, and profligate?" "Yes, Sir." "In the name of wonder, then, what is his merit?" "Well, Sir, he is a smart man."

9   In like manner, all kinds of deficient and impolitic usages are referred to the national love of trade; though, oddly enough, it would be a weighty charge against a foreigner that he regarded the Americans as a trading people. The love of trade is assigned as a reason for that comfortless custom, so very prevalent in country towns, of married persons living in hotels, having no fireside of their own, and seldom meeting from early morning until late at night, but at the hasty public meals. The love of trade is a reason why the literature of America is to remain for ever unprotected: "For we are a trading people, and don't care for poetry," though we *do*, by the way, profess to be very proud of our poets; while healthful amusements, cheerful means of recreation, and wholesome fancies, must fade before the stern utilitarian joys of trade.

10   These three characteristics are strongly presented at every turn, full in the stranger's view. But the foul growth of America has a more entangled root than this; and it strikes its fibres, deep in its licentious Press.

11   Schools may be erected, East, West, North, and South; pupils be taught, and masters reared, by scores upon scores of thousands; colleges may thrive, churches may be crammed, temperance may be diffused, and advancing knowledge in all other forms walk through the land with giant strides; but while the newspaper press of America is in, or near, its present abject state, high moral improvement in that country is hopeless. Year by year, it must and will go back; year by year, the tone of public feeling must sink lower down; year by year, the Congress and the Senate must become of less account before all

decent men; and year by year, the memory of the Great Fathers of the Revolution must be outraged more and more, in the bad life of their degenerate child.

Among the herd of journals which are published in the States, 12 there are some, the reader scarcely need be told, of character and credit. From personal intercourse with accomplished gentlemen, connected with publications of this class, I have derived both pleasure and profit. But the name of these is Few, and of the others Legion; and the influence of the good, is powerless to counteract the mortal poison of the bad.

Among the gentry of America; among the well-informed and 13 moderate; in the learned professions; at the Bar, and on the Bench; there is, as there can be, but one opinion, in reference to the vicious character of these infamous journals. It is sometimes contended—I will not say strangely, for it is natural to seek excuses for such a disgrace—that their influence is not so great as a visitor would suppose. I must be pardoned for saying that there is no warrant for this plea, and that every fact and circumstance tends directly to the opposite conclusion.

When any man, of any grade of desert in intellect or character, 14 can climb to any public distinction, no matter what, in America, without first grovelling down upon the earth, and bending the knee before this monster of depravity; when any private excellence is safe from its attacks; when any social confidence is left unbroken by it, or any tie of social decency and honour is held in the least regard; when any man in that Free Country has freedom of opinion, and presumes to think for himself, and speak for himself, without humble reference to a censorship which, for its rampant ignorance and base dishonesty, he utterly loathes and despises in his heart; when those who most acutely feel its infamy and the reproach it casts upon the nation, and who most denounce it to each other, dare to set their heels upon, and crush it openly, in the sight of all men; then, I will believe that its influence is lessening, and men are returning to their manly senses. But while that Press has its evil eye in every house, and its black hand in every appointment in the state, from a president to a postman; while, with ribald slander for its only stock in trade, it is the standard literature of an enormous class, who must find their reading in a newspaper, or they will not read at all; so long must its odium be upon the country's head, and so long must the evil it works, be plainly visible in the Republic.

To those who are accustomed to the leading English journals, or 15 to the respectable journals of the Continent of Europe; to those who are accustomed to anything else in print and paper; it would be impossible, without an amount of extract for which I have neither space nor inclination, to convey an adequate idea of this frightful engine in

America. But if any man desire confirmation of my statement on this head, let him repair to any place in this city of London, where scattered numbers of these publications are to be found; and there, let him form his own opinion.*

16   It would be well, there can be no doubt, for the American people as a whole, if they loved the Real less, and the Ideal somewhat more. It would be well, if there were greater encouragement to lightness of heart and gaiety, and a wider cultivation of what is beautiful, without being eminently and directly useful. But here, I think the general remonstrance, "we are a new country," which is so often advanced as an excuse for defects which are quite unjustifiable, as being, of right, only the slow growth of an old one, may be very reasonably urged: and I yet hope to hear of there being some other national amusement in the United States, besides newspaper politics.

17   They certainly are not a humorous people, and their temperament always impressed me as being of a dull and gloomy character. In shrewdness of remark, and a certain cast-iron quaintness, the Yankees, or people of New England, unquestionably take the lead; as they do in most other evidences of intelligence. But in travelling about, out of the large cities—as I have remarked in former parts of this volume—I was quite oppressed by the prevailing seriousness and melancholy air of business: which was so general and unvarying, that at every new town I came to, I seemed to meet the very same people whom I had left behind me, at the last. Such defeats as are perceptible in the national manners, seem, to me, to be referable, in a great degree, to this cause: which has generated a dull, sullen persistence in coarse usages, and rejected the graces of life as undeserving of attention. There is no doubt that Washington, who was always most scrupulous and exact on points of ceremony, perceived the tendency towards this mistake, even in his time, and did his utmost to correct it.

18   I cannot hold with other writers on these subjects that the prevalence of various forms of dissent in America, is in any way attributable to the non-existence there of an established church: indeed, I think the temper of the people, if it admitted of such an Institution being founded amongst them, would lead them to desert it, as a matter of course, merely because it *was* established. But, supposing it to exist, I doubt its probable efficacy in summoning the wandering sheep to one great fold, simply because of the immense amount of dissent which prevails at home; and because I do not find in America any one form of religion with which we in Europe, or even in England, are un-

---

*Or, let him refer to an able, and perfectly truthful article, in *The Foreign Quarterly Review*, published in the present month of October: to which my attention has been attracted, since these sheets have been passing through the press. He will find some specimens there, by no means remarkable to any man who has been in America, but sufficiently striking to one who has not.

acquainted. Dissenters resort thither in great numbers, as other people do, simply because it is a land of resort; and great settlements of them are founded, because ground can be purchased, and towns and villages reared, where there were none of the human creation before. But even the Shakers emigrated from England; our country is not unknown to Mr. Joseph Smith, the apostle of Mormonism, or to his benighted disciples; I have beheld religious scenes myself in some of our populous towns which can hardly be surpassed by an American camp-meeting; and I am not aware that any instance of superstitious imposture on the one hand, and superstitious credulity on the other, has had its origin in the United States, which we cannot more than parallel by the precedents of Mrs. Southcote, Mary Tofts the rabbit-breeder, or even Mr. Thom of Canterbury; which latter case arose, some time after the dark ages had passed away.

The Republican Institutions of America undoubtedly lead the 19 people to assert their self-respect and their equality; but a traveller is bound to bear those Institutions in his mind, and not hastily to resent the near approach of a class of strangers, who, at home, would keep aloof. This characteristic, when it was tinctured with no foolish pride, and stopped short of no honest service, never offended me; and I very seldom, if ever, experienced its rude or unbecoming display. Once or twice it was comically developed, as in the following case; but this was an amusing incident, and not the rule or near it.

I wanted a pair of boots at a certain town, for I had none to travel 20 in, but those with the memorable cork soles, which were much too hot for the fiery decks of a steamboat. I therefore sent a message to an artist in boots, importing, with my compliments, that I should be happy to see him, if he would do me the polite favour to call. He very kindly returned for answer, that he would "look round" at six o'clock that evening.

I was lying on the sofa, with a book and a wine-glass, at about 21 that time, when the door opened, and a gentleman in a stiff cravat, within a year or two on either side of thirty, entered, in his hat and gloves; walked up to the looking-glass; arranged his hair; took off his gloves; slowly produced a measure from the uttermost depths of his coat pocket; and requested me, in a languid tone, to "unfix" my straps. I complied, but looked with some curiosity at his hat, which was still upon his head. It might have been that, or it might have been the heat—but he took it off. Then, he sat himself down on a chair opposite to me; rested an arm on each knee; and, leaning forward very much, took from the ground, by a great effort, the specimen of metropolitan workmanship which I had just pulled off—whistling, pleasantly, as he did so. He turned it over and over; surveyed it with a contempt no language can express; and inquired if I wished him to fix me a boot like *that*? I courteously replied, that provided the boots were large enough, I would leave the rest to him; that if convenient and practicable, I should not object to their bearing some resemblance to the model then before him; but that I would be entirely guided by, and would beg to leave the whole subject to, his judgment and discretion. "You an't partickler, about this scoop in the heel, I suppose then?" says he: "we don't foller that, here." I repeated my last observation. He looked at himself in the glass again; went closer to it to dash a grain or two of dust out of the corner of his eye; and settled his cravat. All this time, my leg and foot were in the air. "Nearly ready, Sir?" I inquired. "Well, pretty nigh," he said; "keep steady." I kept as steady as I could, both in foot and face; and having by this time got the dust out, and found his pencil-case, he measured me, and made the necessary notes. When he had finished, he fell into his old attitude, and taking up the boot again, mused for some time. "And this," he said, at last, "is an English boot, is it! This is a London boot, eh?" "That, Sir," I replied, "is a London boot." He mused over it again, after the manner of Hamlet with Yorick's skull; nodded his head, as who should say, "I pity the Institutions that led to the production of this boot!"; rose, put up his pencil, notes, and paper—glancing at himself in the glass, all the time—put on his hat, drew on his gloves very slowly, and finally walked out. When he had been gone about a minute, the door reopened, and his hat and his head reappeared. He looked round the room, and at the boot again, which was still lying on the floor; appeared thoughtful for a minute; and then said, "Well, good afternoon." "Good afternoon, Sir," said I; and that was the end of the interview.

22   There is but one other head on which I wish to offer a remark; and that has reference to the public health. In so vast a country, where there are thousands of millions of acres of land yet unsettled and un-cleared, and on every rood of which, vegetable decomposition is annu-ally taking place; where there are so many great rivers, and such oppo-site varieties of climate; there cannot fail to be a great amount of sickness at certain seasons. But I may venture to say, after conversing with many members of the medical profession in America, that I am not singular in the opinion that much of the disease which does pre-vail, might be avoided, if a few common precautions were observed. Greater means of personal cleanliness, are indispensable to this end; the custom of hastily swallowing large quantities of animal food, three times a-day, and rushing back to sedentary pursuits after each meal, must be changed; the gentler sex must go more wisely clad, and take more healthful exercise; and in the latter clause, the males must be included also. Above all, in public institutions, and throughout the whole of every town and city, the system of ventilation, and drainage, and removal of impurities requires to be thoroughly revised. There is no local Legislature in America which may not study Mr. Chadwick's excellent Report upon the Sanitary Condition of our Labouring Classes, with immense advantage.

_____ CONSIDERATIONS _____

1. Dickens' _American Notes_ was published in 1842 upon his return to England from a lengthy visit to the United States. Some of his harshest criticism was leveled at land swindlers and unprincipled entrepreneurs who enticed the gullible into buying worthless land or investing in cities that did not exist. His reference to "ill-fated Cairo," in paragraph 8, identifies one such fiasco, which he made much use of in the American chapters of his novel, _Martin Chuzzlewit_. Look into the reports of one or more other foreign travelers in the United States and compare or contrast with Dickens' account.

2. What, according to Dickens, was the single most deplorable force in America that cancelled the efforts of schools, churches, temperance societies, and politicians to improve the morality of the population?

3. In contrast to his more readable style in his novels, Dickens' 19th Century rhetorical mannerisms often make "Concluding Remarks" difficult for students to read. Study the lengthy sentence that occupies most of paragraph 14 and comment on its structure. How might you simplify it?

4. Some students also complain about Dickens' choice of words. What is characteristic of his diction in this selection?

5. "These three characteristics. . . .," Dickens writes in paragraph 10. What three does he mean? Do you agree with him in all cases? In any of the three?

6. What is Dickens' chief complaint in paragraph 17? Before you answer, look into a dictionary to see how the meaning of "humorous" has changed.

Emily Dickinson (1830–1886) was little known as a poet in her lifetime, but now is acknowledged as among the greatest American poets. She lived her entire life in Amherst, Massachusetts, and spent her later years as a virtual recluse in the Dickinsons' brick homestead on Main Street. She always remained close to her family, and kept contact with the outside world through a vast correspondence.

She published little poetry in her lifetime. After her death, however, more than a thousand poems were discovered neatly arranged in the bureau of the upstairs bedroom where she wrote. In 1955, a definitive edition of The Poems of Emily Dickinson *was published, containing 1,775 poems and fragments.*

20

EMILY DICKINSON
He Preached Upon "Breadth"

He preached upon "Breadth" till it argued him narrow—
The Broad are too broad to define
And of "Truth" until it proclaimed him a Liar—
The Truth never flaunted a Sign—

5   Simplicity fled from his counterfeit presence
As Gold the Pyrites would shun—
What confusion would cover the innocent Jesus
To meet so enabled a Man!

From *The Complete Poems of Emily Dickinson* ed. by Thomas H. Johnson. Copyright © 1960. Boston: Little, Brown.

*Joan Didion (b. 1934) worked as an editor in New York
for some years, and then returned to her native California
where she supports herself by writing. She has
collaborated on screenplays (often with her husband, John
Gregory Dunne), including* Panic in Needle Park *(1971)
and* A Star Is Born *(1976). Best known for her novels—*Play
It As It Lays *appeared in 1971,* A Book of Common Prayer
in 1977, and Democracy *in 1984—she is also admired for
her essays, collected in* Slouching Towards Bethlehem
(1969), from which we take this piece, and The White
Album *(1979). Her long essay,* Salvador, *appeared as a
book in 1983 and* Miami *in 1987. In 1992,* After Henry
*collected recent short essays. Students who keep journals
or notebooks, or who practice daily writing, may learn a
thing or two from Joan Didion.*

21

JOAN DIDION
On Keeping a Notebook

" 'That woman Estelle,' " the note reads, " 'is partly the reason   1
why George Sharp and I are separated today.' *Dirty crêpe-de-Chine
wrapper, hotel bar, Wilmington RR, 9:45 A.M.* August Monday
morning."

Since the note is in my notebook, it presumably has some mean-   2
ing to me. I study it for a long while. At first I have only the most general notion of what I was doing on an August Monday morning in the
bar of the hotel across from the Pennsylvania Railroad station in
Wilmington, Delaware (waiting for a train? missing one? 1960? 1961?
why Wilmington?), but I do remember being there. The woman in the
dirty crêpe-de-Chine wrapper had come down from her room for a
beer, and the bartender had heard before the reason why George Sharp
and she were separated today. "Sure," he said, and went on mopping
the floor. "You told me." At the other end of the bar is a girl. She is

---

talking, pointedly, not to the man beside her but to a cat lying in the triangle of sunlight cast through the open door. She is wearing a plaid silk dress from Peck & Peck, and the hem is coming down.

3   Here is what it is: the girl has been on the Eastern Shore, and now she is going back to the city, leaving the man beside her, and all she can see ahead are the viscous summer sidewalks and the 3 A.M. long-distance calls that will make her lie awake and then sleep drugged through all the steaming mornings left in August (1960? 1961?). Because she must go directly from the train to lunch in New York, she wishes that she had a safety pin for the hem of the plaid silk dress, and she also wishes that she could forget about the hem and the lunch and stay in the cool bar that smells of disinfectant and malt and make friends with the woman in the crêpe-de-Chine wrapper. She is afflicted by a little self-pity, and she wants to compare Estelles. That is what that was all about.

4   Why did I write it down? In order to remember, of course, but exactly what was it I wanted to remember? How much of it actually happened? Did any of it? Why do I keep a notebook at all? It is easy to deceive oneself on all those scores. The impulse to write things down is a peculiarly compulsive one, inexplicable to those who do not share it, useful only accidentally, only secondarily, in the way that any compulsion tries to justify itself. I suppose that it begins or does not begin in the cradle. Although I have felt compelled to write things down since I was five years old, I doubt that my daughter ever will, for she is a singularly blessed and accepting child, delighted with life exactly as life presents itself to her, unafraid to go to sleep and unafraid to wake up. Keepers of private notebooks are a different breed altogether, lonely and resistant rearrangers of things, anxious malcontents, children afflicted apparently at birth with some presentiment of loss.

5   My first notebook was a Big Five tablet, given to me by my mother with the sensible suggestion that I stop whining and learn to amuse myself by writing down my thoughts. She returned the tablet to me a few years ago; the first entry is an account of a woman who believed herself to be freezing to death in the Arctic night, only to find when day broke, that she had stumbled onto the Sahara Desert, where she would die of the heat before lunch. I have no idea what turn of a five-year-old's mind could have prompted so insistently "ironic" and exotic a story, but it does reveal a certain predilection for the extreme which has dogged me into adult life; perhaps if I were analytically inclined I would find it a truer story than any I might have told about Donald Johnson's birthday party or the day my cousin Brenda put Kitty Litter in the aquarium.

6   So the point of my keeping a notebook has never been, nor is it now, to have an accurate factual record of what I have been doing or thinking. That would be a different impulse entirely, an instinct for

reality which I sometimes envy but do not possess. At no point have I ever been able successfully to keep a diary; my approach to daily life ranges from the grossly negligent to the merely absent, and on those few occasions when I have tried dutifully to record a day's events, boredom has so overcome me that the results are mysterious at best. What is this business about "shopping, typing piece, dinner with E, depressed"? Shopping for what? Typing what piece? Who is E? Was this "E" depressed, or was I depressed? Who cares?

In fact I have abandoned altogether that kind of pointless entry; instead I tell what some would call lies. "That's simply not true," the members of my family frequently tell me when they come up against my memory of a shared event. "The party was *not* for you, the spider was *not* a black widow, *it wasn't that way at all.*" Very likely they are right, for not only have I always had trouble distinguishing between what happened and what merely might have happened, but I remain unconvinced that the distinction, for my purposes, matters. The cracked crab that I recall having for lunch the day my father came home from Detroit in 1945 must certainly be embroidery, worked into the day's pattern to lend verisimilitude; I was ten years old and would not now remember the cracked crab. The day's events did not turn on cracked crab. And yet it is precisely that fictitious crab that makes me see the afternoon all over again, a home movie run all too often, the father bearing gifts, the child weeping, an exercise in family love and guilt. Or that is what it was to me. Similarly, perhaps it never did snow that August in Vermont; perhaps there never were flurries in the night wind, and maybe no one else felt the ground hardening and summer already dead even as we pretended to bask in it, but that was how it felt to me, and it might as well have snowed, could have snowed, did snow. 7

How it felt to me: that is getting closer to the truth about a notebook. I sometimes delude myself about why I keep a notebook, imagine that some thrifty virtue derives from preserving everything observed. See enough and write it down, I tell myself, and then some morning when the world seems drained of wonder, some day when I am only going through the motions of doing what I am supposed to do, which is write—on that bankrupt morning I will simply open my notebook and there it will all be, a forgotten account with accumulated interest, paid passage back to the world out there: dialogue overheard in hotels and elevators and at the hat-check counter in Pavillon (one middle-aged man shows his hat check to another and says, "That's my old football number"); impressions of Bettina Aptheker and Benjamin Sonnenberg and Teddy ("Mr. Acapulco") Stauffer; careful *aperçus* about tennis bums and failed fashion models and Greek shipping heiresses, one of whom taught me a significant lesson (a lesson I could have learned from F. Scott Fitzgerald, but perhaps we must 8

meet the very rich for ourselves) by asking, when I arrived to interview her in her orchid-filled sitting room on the second day of a paralyzing New York blizzard, whether it was snowing outside.

9   I imagine, in other words, that the notebook is about other people. But of course it is not. I have no real business with what one
stranger said to another at the hat-check counter in Pavillon; in fact I
suspect that the line "That's my old football number" touched not my
own imagination at all, but merely some memory of something once
read, probably "The Eighty-Yard Run." Nor is my concern with a
woman in a dirty crêpe-de-Chine wrapper in a Wilmington bar. My
stake is always, of course, in the unmentioned girl in the plaid silk
dress. *Remember what it was to be me*: that is always the point.

10   It is a difficult point to admit. We are brought up in the ethic that
others, any others, all others, are by definition more interesting than
ourselves; taught to be diffident, just this side of self-effacing. ("You're
the least important person in the room and don't forget it," Jessica
Mitford's governess would hiss in her ear on the advent of any social
occasion; I copied that into my notebook because it is only recently
that I have been able to enter a room without hearing some such
phrase in my inner ear.) Only the very young and the very old may recount their dreams at breakfast, dwell upon self, interrupt with memories of beach picnics and favorite Liberty lawn dresses and the rain-
bow trout in a creek near Colorado Springs. The rest of us are
expected, rightly, to affect absorption in other people's favorite
dresses, other people's trout.

11   And so we do. But our notebooks give us away, for however dutifully we record what we see around us, the common denominator of
all we see is always, transparently, shamelessly, the implacable "I."
We are not talking here about the kind of notebook that is patently for
public consumption, a structural conceit for binding together a series
of graceful *pensées*: we are talking about something private, about bits
of the mind's string too short to use, an indiscriminate and erratic assemblage with meaning only for its maker.

12   And sometimes even the maker has difficulty with the meaning.
There does not seem to be, for example, any point in my knowing for
the rest of my life that, during 1964, 720 tons of soot fell on every
square mile of New York City, yet there it is in my notebook, labeled
"FACT." Nor do I really need to remember that Ambrose Bierce liked
to spell Leland Stanford's* name "£eland \$tanford" or that "smart
women almost always wear black in Cuba," a fashion hint without
much potential for practical application. And does not the relevance of
these notes seem marginal at best?:

---

*Railroad magnate (1834–1893) who founded the university.—ED.

In the basement museum of the Inyo Country Courthouse in Independence, California, sign pinned to a mandarin coat: "This MANDARIN COAT was often worn by Mrs. Minnie S. Brooks when giving lectures on her TEAPOT COLLECTION."

Redhead getting out of car in front of Beverly Wilshire Hotel, chinchilla stole, Vuitton bags with tags reading:

MRS LOU FOX

HOTEL SAHARA

VEGAS

Well perhaps not entirely marginal. As a matter of fact, Mrs. Minnie S. Brooks and her MANDARIN COAT pull me back into my own childhood, for although I never knew Mrs. Brooks and did not visit Inyo County until I was thirty, I grew up in just such a world, in houses cluttered with Indian relics and bits of gold ore and ambergris and the souvenirs my Aunt Mercy Farnsworth brought back from the Orient. It is a long way from that world to Mrs. Lou Fox's world, where we all live now, and is it not just as well to remember that? Might not Mrs. Minnie S. Brooks help me to remember what I am? Might not Mrs. Lou Fox help me to remember what I am not? 13

But sometimes the point is harder to discern. What exactly did I have in mind when I noted down that it cost the father of someone I know $650 a month to light the place on the Hudson in which he lived before the Crash? What use was I planning to make of this line by Jimmy Hoffa: "I may have my faults, but being wrong ain't one of them"? And although I think it interesting to know where the girls who travel with the Syndicate have their hair done when they find themselves on the West coast, will I ever make suitable use of it? Might I not be better off just passing it on to John O'Hara? What is a recipe for sauerkraut doing in my notebook? What kind of magpie keeps this notebook? "*He was born the night the Titanic went down.*" That seems a nice enough line, and I even recall who said it, but is it not really a better line in life than it could ever be in fiction? 14

But of course that is exactly it: not that I should ever use the line, but that I should remember the woman who said it and the afternoon I heard it. We were on her terrace by the sea, and we were finishing the wine left from lunch, trying to get what sun there was, a California winter sun. The woman whose husband was born the night the *Titanic* went down wanted to rent her house, wanted to go back to her children in Paris. I remember wishing that I could afford the house, which cost $1,000 a month. "Someday you will," she said lazily. "Someday it all comes." There in the sun on her terrace it seemed easy to believe in someday, but later I had a low-grade afternoon hang- 15 over and ran over a black snake on the way to the supermarket and was flooded with inexplicable fear when I heard the checkout clerk explaining to the man ahead of me why she was finally divorcing her husband. "He left me no choice," she said over and over as she punched the register. "He has a little seven-month-old baby by her, he left me no choice." I would like to believe that my dread then was for the human condition, but of course it was for me, because I wanted a baby and did not then have one and because I wanted to own the house that cost $1,000 a month to rent and because I had a hangover.

16   It all comes back. Perhaps it is difficult to see the value in having one's self back in that kind of mood, but I do see it; I think we are well advised to keep on nodding terms with the people we used to be, whether we find them attractive company or not. Otherwise they turn up unannounced and surprise us, come hammering on the mind's door at 4 A.M. of a bad night and demand to know who deserted them, who betrayed them, who is going to make amends. We forget all too soon the things we thought we could never forget. We forget the loves and the betrayals alike, forget what we whispered and what we screamed, forget who we were. I have already lost touch with a couple of people I used to be; one of them, a seventeen-year-old, presents little threat, although it would be of some interest to me to know again what it feels like to sit on a river levee drinking vodka-and-orange-juice and listening to Les Paul and Mary Ford and their echoes sing "How High the Moon" on the car radio. (You see I still have the scenes, but I no longer perceive myself among those present, no longer could even improvise the dialogue.) The other one, a twenty-three-year-old, bothers me more. She was always a good deal of trouble, and I suspect she will reappear when I least want to see her, skirts too long, shy to the point of aggravation, always the injured party, full of recriminations and little hurts and stories I do not want to hear again, at once saddening me and angering me with her vulnerability and ignorance, an apparition all the more insistent for being so long banished.

17   It is a good idea, then, to keep in touch, and I suppose that keeping in touch is what notebooks are all about. And we are all on our own when it comes to keeping those lines open to ourselves: your notebook will never help me, nor mine you. *"So what's new in the whiskey business?"* What could that possibly mean to you? To me it means a blonde in a Pucci bathing suit sitting with a couple of fat men by the pool at the Beverly Hills Hotel. Another man approaches, and they all regard one another in silence for a while. "So what's new in the whiskey business?" one of the fat men finally says by way of welcome, and the blonde stands up, arches one foot and dips it in the pool, looking all the while at the cabaña where Baby Pignatari is talking on the telephone. That is all there is to that, except that several years later I saw the blonde coming out of Saks Fifth Avenue in New York

with her California complexion and a voluminous mink coat. In the harsh wind that day she looked old and irrevocably tired to me, and even the skins in the mink coat were not worked the way they were doing them that year, not the way she would have wanted them done, and there is the point of the story. For a while after that I did not like to look in the mirror, and my eyes would skim the newspapers and pick out only the deaths, the cancer victims, the premature coronaries, the suicides, and I stopped riding the Lexington Avenue IRT because I noticed for the first time that all the strangers I had seen for years—the man with the seeing-eye dog, the spinster who read the classified pages every day, the fat girl who always got off with me at Grand Central—looked older than they once had.

It all comes back. Even that recipe for sauerkraut: even that 18 brings it back. I was on Fire Island when I first made this sauerkraut, and it was raining, and we drank a lot of bourbon and ate the sauerkraut and went to bed at ten, and I listened to the rain and the Atlantic and felt safe. I made the sauerkraut again last night and it did not make me feel any safer, but that is, as they say, another story.

_____ CONSIDERATIONS _____

1. Read the selections from Henry David Thoreau's journal and comment on the differences you find between his idea of a journal and Didion's idea of a writer's notebook.

2. How far must you read in Didion's piece before you know her real reason for keeping a journal? Why does she delay that announcement so long? Might such a delay work well in one of your essays?

3. "You're the least important person in the room and don't forget it" is a line from Didion's journal. Does she believe that statement? If not, why does she include it in her essay?

4. Didion discusses the randomness of a notebook. How does she use this randomness, or lack of order or purpose, to bring order and purpose to her essay? Take paragraphs 14 and 15 and study the method she derives from her seeming madness.

5. In paragraph 16, Didion says she has already "lost touch with a couple of people I used to be." Is self-awareness a key to Nora Ephron's essay (page 159), or Louise Bogan's (page 81)? Have you ever had similar feelings about some of the people you used to be? What significant details in your memory come to mind?

6. Using a periodical index in your college library, see how quickly you can locate one of Didion's many journalistic essays.

Annie Dillard (b. 1945) was born in Pittsburgh, went to Hollins College, and lived for a while in Virginia in the Roanoke Valley—the area she describes so beautifully in her writing. She currently lives in Connecticut. In 1974 she published her first book of poems, Tickets for a Prayer Wheel, *and her first book of prose,* Pilgrim at Tinker Creek, *which won a Pulitzer Prize. In 1977 she published* Holy the Firm, *and in 1982* Living by Fiction. *Other books include* An American Childhood *(1987),* The Writing Life *(1989), and* The Living *(1992). The* Annie Dillard Reader *appeared in 1994.*

Teaching a Stone to Talk (1982) gathered Annie Dillard's miscellaneous essays from periodicals. Book reviewers often condescend to such collections; in her introduction to the work Annie Dillard wants to be certain that readers understand and tell us ". . . this is my real work." Indeed, the brief essay is her literary form, and she masters it as Chekhov mastered the short story.

22

ANNIE DILLARD
Sojourner

1   If survival is an art, then mangroves are artists of the beautiful: not only that they exist at all—smooth-barked, glossy-leaved, thickets of lapped mystery—but that they can and do exist as floating islands, as trees upright and loose, alive and homeless on the water.

2   I have seen mangroves, always on tropical ocean shores, in Florida and in the Galápagos. There is the red mangrove, the yellow, the button, and the black. They are all short, messy trees, waxy-leaved, laced all over with aerial roots, woody arching buttresses, and weird leathery berry pods. All this tangles from a black muck soil, a black muck matted like a mud-sopped rag, a muck without any other

plants, shaded, cold to the touch, tracked at the water's edge by herons and nosed by sharks.

It is these shoreline trees which, by a fairly common accident, 3 can become floating islands. A hurricane flood or a riptide can wrest a tree from the shore, or from the mouth of a tidal river, and hurl it into the ocean. It floats. It is a mangrove island, blown.

There are floating islands on the planet; it amazes me. Credulous 4 Pliny described some islands thought to be mangrove islands floating on a river. The people called these river islands *the dancers*, "because in any consort of musicians singing, they stir and move at the stroke of the feet, keeping time and measure."

Trees floating on rivers are less amazing than trees floating on 5 the poisonous sea. A tree cannot live in salt. Mangrove trees exude salt from their leaves; you can see it, even on shoreline black mangroves, as a thin white crust. Lick a leaf and your tongue curls and coils; your mouth's a heap of salt.

Nor can a tree live without soil. A hurricane-born mangrove is- 6 land may bring its own soil to the sea. But other mangrove trees make their own soil—and their own islands—from scratch. These are the ones which interest me. The seeds germinate in the fruit on the tree. The germinated embryo can drop anywhere—say, onto a dab of floating muck. The heavy root end sinks; a leafy plumule unfurls. The tiny seedling, afloat, is on its way. Soon aerial roots shooting out in all directions trap debris. The sapling's networks twine, the interstices narrow, and water calms in the lee. Bacteria thrive on organic broth; amphipods swarm. These creatures grow and die at the trees' wet feet. The soil thickens, accumulating rainwater, leaf rot, seashells, and guano; the island spreads.

More seeds and more muck yield more trees on the new island. A 7 society grows, interlocked in a tangle of dependencies. The island rocks less in the swells. Fish throng to the backwaters stilled in snarled roots. Soon, Asian mudskippers—little four-inch fish—clamber up the mangrove roots into the air and peer about from periscope eyes on stalks, like snails. Oysters clamp to submersed roots, as do starfish, dog whelk, and the creatures that live among tangled kelp. Shrimp seek shelter there, limpets a holdfast, pelagic birds a rest.

And the mangrove island wanders on, afloat and adrift. It walks 8 teetering and wanton before the wind. Its fate and direction are random. It may bob across an ocean and catch on another mainland's shores. It may starve or dry while it is still a sapling. It may topple in a storm, or pitchpole. By the rarest of chances, it may stave into another mangrove island in a crash of clacking roots, and mesh. What it is most likely to do is drift anywhere in the alien ocean, feeding on death and growing, netting a makeshift soil as it goes, shrimp in its toes and terns in its hair.

9   We could do worse.

10   I alternate between thinking of the planet as home—dear and familiar stone hearth and garden—and as a hard land of exile in which we are all sojourners. Today I favor the latter view. The word "sojourner" occurs often in the English Old Testament. It invokes a nomadic people's sense of vagrancy, a praying people's knowledge of estrangement, a thinking people's intuition of sharp loss: "For we are strangers before thee, and sojourners, as were all our fathers: our days on the earth are as a shadow, and there is none abiding."

11   We don't know where we belong, but in times of sorrow it doesn't seem to be here, here with these silly pansies and witless mountains, here with sponges and hard-eyed birds. In times of sorrow the innocence of the other creatures—from whom and with whom we evolved—seems a mockery. Their ways are not our ways. We seem set among them as among lifelike props for a tragedy—or a broad lampoon—on a thrust rock stage.

12   It doesn't seem to be here that we belong, here where space is curved, the earth is round, we're all going to die, and it seems as wise to stay in bed as budge. It is strange here, not quite warm enough, or too warm, too leafy, or inedible, or windy, or dead. It is not, frankly, the sort of home for people one would have thought of—although I lack the fancy to imagine another.

13   The planet itself is a sojourner in airless space, a wet ball flung across nowhere. The few objects in the universe scatter. The coherence of matter dwindles and crumbles toward stillness. I have read, and repeated, that our solar system as a whole is careering through space toward a point east of Hercules. Now I wonder: what could that possibly mean, east of Hercules? Isn't space curved? When we get "there," how will our course change, and why? Will we slide down the universe's inside arc like mud slung at a wall? Or what sort of welcoming shore is this east of Hercules? Surely we don't anchor there, and disembark, and sweep into dinner with our host. Does someone cry, "Last stop, last stop?" At any rate, east of Hercules, like east of Eden, isn't a place to call home. It is a course without direction; it is "out." And we are cast.

14   These are enervating thoughts, the thoughts of despair. They crowd back, unbidden, when human life as it unrolls goes ill, when we lose control of our lives or the illusion of control, and it seems that we are not moving toward any end but merely blown. Our life seems cursed to be a wiggle merely, and a wandering without end. Even nature is hostile and poisonous, as though it were impossible for our vulnerability to survive on these acrid stones.

15   Whether these thoughts are true or not I find less interesting than the possibilities for beauty they may hold. We are down here in time, where beauty grows. Even if things are as bad as they could pos-

sibly be, and as meaningless, then matters of truth are themselves indifferent; we may as well please our sensibilities and, with as much spirit as we can muster, go out with a buck and wing.

The planet is less like an enclosed spaceship—spaceship earth— 16 than it is like an exposed mangrove island beautiful and loose. We the people started small and have since accumulated a great and solacing muck of soil, of human culture. We are rooted in it; we are bearing it with us across nowhere. The word "nowhere" is our cue: the consort of musicians strikes up, and we in the chorus stir and move and start twirling our hats. A mangrove island turns drift to dance. It creates its own soil as it goes, rocking over the salt sea at random, rocking day and night and round the sun, rocking round the sun and out toward east of Hercules.

_____ CONSIDERATIONS _____

1. In many passages, Annie Dillard's prose verges on poetry, particularly in her high degree of compression in alluding to persons ("Pliny," paragraph 4), places ("Galápagos," paragraph 2, "east of Hercules," paragraph 13), and sources (see Psalm 39 for the quotation in paragraph 10) that may not be immediately recognizable to the hurried reader. You will enjoy her essay more and appreciate her skill if you take the time to determine the significance of these allusions.

2. One of the hallmarks of an accomplished writer like Dillard is the ability to integrate the various materials of an essay. As one example, study her closing paragraph to see how tightly she brings together elements she has introduced earlier.

3. Explain why a reader would be foolish to conclude that Dillard's essay is simply a study of the mangrove islands, of interest only to students of natural history. What elements of the essay might account for such a conclusion?

4. Dillard's diction (choice of words) mixes vocabularies. Find a few of the contrasts, such as the scientific ("plumule," "amphipods," "pelagic") versus the imaginative ("matted like a mud-sopped rag," or "shrimp in its toes and terns in its hair") versus the nautical ("pitchpole," "stave," "lee"), and discuss the delights and difficulties for a reader encountering such diversity.

5. Does Dillard offer any consolation for the sense of despairing rootlessness she expresses in paragraph 13? Explain in a short essay based on your own ideas about the destiny or purpose of humankind's presence on the planet.

Frederick Douglass (1817–1895) was born a slave in Maryland and escaped to Massachusetts in 1838. Later, he lectured against slavery and wrote of his experience. "Plantation Life" comes from A Narrative of the Life of Frederick Douglass, an American Slave, Written by Himself *(1845). During the Civil War he organized two regiments of black troops in Massachusetts: in the Reconstruction period he worked for the government.*

23

FREDERICK DOUGLASS
Plantation Life

1   My master's family consisted of two sons, Andrew and Richard; one daughter, Lucretia, and her husband, Captain Thomas Auld. They lived in one house, upon the home plantation of Colonel Edward Lloyd. My master was Colonel Lloyd's clerk and superintendent. He was what might be called the overseer of the overseers. I spent two years of childhood on this plantation in my old master's family. . . . As I received my first impressions of slavery on this plantation, I will give some description of it, and of slavery as it there existed. The plantation is about twelve miles north of Easton, in Talbot county, and is situated on the border of Miles River. The principal products raised upon it were tobacco, corn, and wheat. These were raised in great abundance; so that, with the products of this and the other farms belonging to him, he was able to keep in almost constant employment a large sloop, in carrying them to market at Baltimore. This sloop was named *Sally Lloyd*, in honor of one of the colonel's daughters. My master's son-in-law, Captain Auld, was master of the vessel; she was otherwise manned by the colonel's own slaves. Their names were Peter, Isaac, Rich, and Jake. These were esteemed very highly by the other slaves, and looked upon as the privileged ones of the plantation; for it was no small affair, in the eyes of the slaves, to be allowed to see Baltimore.

2   Colonel Lloyd kept from three to four hundred slaves on his home plantation, and owned a large number more on the neighboring farms belonging to him. The names of the farms nearest to the home

plantation were Wye Town and New Design. "Wye Town" was under the overseership of a man named Noah Willis. New Design was under the overseership of a Mr. Townsend. The overseers of these, and all the rest of the farms, numbering over twenty, received advice and direction from the managers of the home plantation. This was the great business place. It was the seat of government for the whole twenty farms. All disputes among the overseers were settled here. If a slave was convicted of any high misdemeanor, became unmanageable, or evinced a determination to run away, he was brought immediately here, severely whipped, put on board the sloop, carried to Baltimore, and sold to Austin Woolfolk, or some other slave-trader, as a warning to the slaves remaining.

Here, too, the slaves of all the other farms received their monthly   3
allowance of food, and their yearly clothing. The men and women slaves received, as their monthly allowance of food, eight pounds of pork, or its equivalent in fish, and one bushel of corn meal. Their yearly clothing consisted of two coarse linen shirts, one pair of linen trousers, like the shirts, one jacket, one pair of trousers for winter, made of coarse negro cloth, one pair of stockings, and one pair of shoes; the whole of which could not have cost more than seven dollars. The allowance of the slave children was given to their mothers, or the old women having the care of them. The children unable to work in the field had neither shoes, stockings, jackets, nor trousers, given to them; their clothing consisted of two coarse linen shirts per year. When these failed them, they went naked until the next allowance-day. Children from seven to ten years old, of both sexes, almost naked, might be seen at all seasons of the year.

There were no beds given the slaves, unless one coarse blanket   4
be considered such, and none but the men and women had these. This, however, is not considered a very great privation. They find less difficulty from the want of beds, than from the want of time to sleep; for when their day's work in the field is done, the most of them having their washing, mending, and cooking to do, and having few or none of the ordinary facilities for doing either of these, very many of their sleeping hours are consumed in preparing for the field the coming day; and when this is done, old and young, male and female, married and single, drop down side by side, on one common bed,—the cold, damp floor,—each covering himself or herself with their miserable blankets; and here they sleep till they are summoned to the field by the driver's horn. At the sound of this, all must rise, and be off to the field. There must be no halting; every one must be at his or her post; and woe betides them who hear not this morning summons to the field; for if they are not awakened by the sense of hearing, they are by the sense of feeling: no age nor sex finds any favor. Mr. Severe, the overseer, used to stand by the door of the quarter, armed with a large hickory stick

and heavy cowskin, ready to whip any one who was so unfortunate as not to hear, or, from any other cause, was prevented from being ready to start for the field at the sound of the horn.

5   Mr. Severe was rightly named: he was a cruel man. I have seen him whip a woman, causing the blood to run half an hour at the time; and this, too, in the midst of her crying children, pleading for their mother's release. He seemed to take pleasure in manifesting his fiendish barbarity. Added to his cruelty, he was a profane swearer. It was enough to chill the blood and stiffen the hair of an ordinary man to hear him talk. Scarce a sentence escaped him but that was commenced or concluded by some horrid oath. The field was the place to witness his cruelty and profanity. His presence made it both the field of blood and of blasphemy. From the rising till the going down of the sun, he was cursing, raving, cutting, and slashing among the slaves of the field, in the most frightful manner. His career was short. He died very soon after I went to Colonel Lloyd's; and he died as he lived, uttering, with his dying groans, bitter curses and horrid oaths. His death was regarded by the slaves as the result of a merciful providence.

6   Mr. Severe's place was filled by a Mr. Hopkins. He was a very different man. He was less cruel, less profane, and made less noise, than Mr. Severe. His course was characterized by no extraordinary demonstrations of cruelty. He whipped, but seemed to take no pleasure in it. He was called by the slaves a good overseer.

7   The home plantation of Colonel Lloyd wore the appearance of a country village. All the mechanical operations for all the farms were performed here. The shoemaking and mending, the blacksmithing, cartwrighting, coopering, weaving, and grain-grinding, were all performed by the slaves on the home plantation. The whole place wore a businesslike aspect very unlike the neighboring farms. The number of houses, too, conspired to give it advantage over the neighboring farms. It was called by the slaves the *Great House Farm*. Few privileges were esteemed higher, by the slaves of the out-farms, than that of being selected to do errands at the Great House Farm. It was associated in their minds with greatness. A representative could not be prouder of his election to a seat in the American Congress, than a slave on one of the out-farms would be of his election to do errands at the Great House Farm. They regarded it as evidence of great confidence reposed in them by their overseers; and it was on this account, as well as a constant desire to be out of the field from under the driver's lash, that they esteemed it a high privilege, one worth careful living for. He was called the smartest and most trusty fellow, who had this honor conferred upon him the most frequently. The competitors for this office sought as diligently to please their overseers, as the office-seekers in the political parties seek to please and deceive the people. The same

traits of character might be seen in Colonel Lloyd's slaves, as are seen in the slaves of the political parties.

The slaves selected to go to the Great House Farm, for the monthly allowance for themselves and their fellow-slaves, were peculiarly enthusiastic. While on their way, they would make the dense old woods, for miles around, reverberate with their wild songs, revealing at once the highest joy and the deepest sadness. They would compose and sing as they went along, consulting neither time nor tune. The thought that came up, came out—if not in the word, in the sound;—and as frequently in the one as in the other. They would sometimes sing the most pathetic sentiment in the most rapturous tone, and the most rapturous sentiment in the most pathetic tone. Into all of their songs they would manage to weave something of the Great House Farm. Especially would they do this, when leaving home. They would then sing most exultingly the following words:— 8

> I am going away to the Great House Farm!
> A, yea! O, Yea! O!

This they would sing, as a chorus, to words which to many would seem unmeaning jargon, but which, nevertheless, were full of meaning to themselves. I have sometimes thought that the mere hearing of those songs would do more to impress some minds with the horrible character of slavery, than the reading of whole volumes of philosophy on the subject could do.

I did not, when a slave, understand the deep meaning of those rude and apparently incoherent songs. I was myself within the circle; so that I neither saw nor heard as those without might see and hear. They told a tale of woe which was then altogether beyond my feeble comprehension; they were tones loud, long, and deep; they breathed the prayer and complaint of souls boiling over with the bitterest anguish. Every tone was a testimony against slavery, and a prayer to God for deliverance from chains. The hearing of those wild notes always depressed my spirit, and filled me with ineffable sadness. I have frequently found myself in tears while hearing them. The mere recurrence of those songs, even now, afflicts me; and while I am writing these lines, an expression of feeling has already found its way down my cheek. To those songs I trace my first glimmering conception of the dehumanizing character of slavery. I can never get rid of that conception. Those songs still follow me, to deepen my hatred of slavery, and quicken my sympathies for my brethren in bonds. If any one wishes to be impressed with the soul-killing effects of slavery, let him go to Colonel Lloyd's plantation, and, on allowance-day, place himself in the deep pine woods, and there let him, in silence, analyze the 9 sounds that shall pass through the chambers of his soul,—and if he is not thus impressed, it will only be because "there is no flesh in his obdurate heart."

10   I have often been utterly astonished, since I came to the north, to find persons who could speak of the singing, among slaves, as evidence of their contentment and happiness. It is impossible to conceive of a greater mistake. Slaves sing most when they are most unhappy. The songs of the slave represent the sorrows of his heart; and he is relieved by them, only as an aching heart is relieved by its tears. At least, such is my experience. I have often sung to drown my sorrow, but seldom to express my happiness. Crying for joy, and singing for joy, were alike uncommon to me while in the jaws of slavery. The singing of a man cast away upon a desolate island might be as appropriately considered as evidence of contentment and happiness, as the signing of a slave; the songs of the one and of the other are prompted by the same emotion.

_____ CONSIDERATIONS _____

1. Is there anything to suggest, at the end of paragraph 7, that Douglass had a talent for satire?

2. In paragraphs 2 and 7, Douglass sketches the operations of the home plantation and its relationship to the outlying farms owned by the same man. Does the arrangement sound feudal? How did the plantation system differ from feudalism?

3. "I was myself within the circle; so that I neither saw nor heard as those without might see and hear," writes Douglass in paragraph 9. Is a fish aware that its medium is water? Are you, as a student, always conscious of the knowledge you acquire?

4. What single phenomenon, according to Douglass, taught him the most moving and enduring lesson about the dehumanizing character of slavery? In what way did that lesson surprise those who had not had Douglass's experience?

5. Paragraph 5 offers a good example of Douglass's typical sentence structure: a linear series of independent clauses, with little or no subordination, all of which produces a blunt, stop-and-go effect. Without losing any of the information provided, rewrite the paragraph, reducing the number of sentences from twelve to six. Do this by converting some of the sentences to phrases, modifying clauses, or, in some cases, single-word modifiers.

6. Read Brent Staples's essay "Just Walk On By" (page 484) and write an essay on the changes in race relations through the 146 years between Douglass's and Staples's accounts.

24

GRETEL EHRLICH
About Men

When I'm in New York but feeling lonely for Wyoming I look for the Marlboro ads in the subway. What I'm aching to see is horseflesh, the glint of a spur, a line of distant mountains, brimming creeks, and a reminder of the ranchers and cowboys I've ridden with for the last eight years. But the men I see in those posters with their stern, humorless looks remind me of no one I know here. In our hellbent earnestness to romanticize the cowboy we've ironically disesteemed his true character. If he's "strong and silent" it's because there's probably no one to talk to. If he "rides away into the sunset" it's because he's been on horseback since four in the morning moving cattle and he's trying, fifteen hours later, to get home to his family. If he's "a rugged individualist" he's also part of a team: ranch work is teamwork and even the glorified open-range cowboys of the 1880s rode up and down the Chisholm Trail in the company of twenty or thirty other riders. Instead of the macho, trigger-happy man our culture has perversely

1

wanted him to be, the cowboy is more apt to be convivial, quirky, and softhearted. To be "tough" on a ranch has nothing to do with conquests and displays of power. More often than not, circumstances—like the colt he's riding or an unexpected blizzard—are overpowering him. It's not toughness but "toughing it out" that counts. In other words, this macho, cultural artifact the cowboy has become is simply a man who possesses resilience, patience, and an instinct for survival. "Cowboys are just like a pile of rocks—everything happens to them. They get climbed on, kicked, rained and snowed on, scuffed up by wind. Their job is 'just to take it,' " one old-timer told me.

2   A cowboy is someone who loves his work. Since the hours are long—ten to fifteen hours a day—and the pay is $30 he has to. What's required of him is an odd mixture of physical vigor and maternalism. His part of the beef-raising industry is to birth and nurture calves and take care of their mothers. For the most part his work is done on horseback and in a lifetime he sees and comes to know more animals than people. The iconic myth surrounding him is built on American notions of heroism: the index of a man's value as measured in physical courage. Such ideas have perverted manliness into a self-absorbed race for cheap thrills. In a rancher's world, courage has less to do with facing danger than with acting spontaneously—usually on behalf of an animal or another rider. If a cow is stuck in a boghole he throws a loop around her neck, takes his dally (a half hitch around the saddle horn), and pulls her out with horsepower. If a calf is born sick, he may take her home, warm her in front of the kitchen fire, and massage her legs until dawn. One friend, whose favorite horse was trying to swim a lake with hobbles on, dove under water and cut her legs loose with a knife, then swam her to shore, his arm around her neck lifeguard-style, and saved her from drowning. Because these incidents are usually linked to someone or something outside himself, the westerner's courage is selfless, a form of compassion.

3   The physical punishment that goes with cowboying is greatly underplayed. Once fear is dispensed with, the threshold of pain rises to meet the demands of the job. When Jane Fonda asked Robert Redford (in the film *Electric Horseman*) if he was sick as he struggled to his feet one morning, he replied, "No, just bent." For once the movies had it right. The cowboys I was sitting with laughed in agreement. Cowboys are rarely complainers; they show their stoicism by laughing at themselves.

4   If a rancher or cowboy has been thought of as a "man's man"—laconic, hard-drinking, inscrutable—there's almost no place in which the balancing act between male and female, manliness and femininity, can be more natural. If he's gruff, handsome, and physically fit on the outside, he's androgynous at the core. Ranchers are midwives,

hunters, nurturers, providers, and conservationists all at once. What we've interpreted as toughness—weathered skin, calloused hands, a squint in the eye and a growl in the voice—only masks the tenderness inside. "Now don't go telling me these lambs are cute," one rancher warned me the first day I walked into the football-field-sized lambing sheds. The next thing I knew he was holding a black lamb. "Ain't this little rat good-lookin'?"

So many of the men who came to the West were Southerners— 5 men looking for work and a new life after the Civil War—that chivalrousness and strict codes of honor were soon thought of as western traits. There were very few women in Wyoming during territorial days, so when they did arrive (some as mail-order brides from places like Philadelphia) there was a standoffishness between the sexes and a formality that persists now. Ranchers still tip their hats and say, "Howdy, ma'am" instead of shaking hands with me.

Even young cowboys are often evasive with women. It's not that 6 they're Jekyll and Hyde creatures—gentle with animals and rough on women—but rather, that they don't know how to bring their tenderness into the house and lack the vocabulary to express the complexity of what they feel. Dancing wildly all night becomes a metaphor for the explosive emotions pent up inside, and when these are, on occasion, released, they're so battery-charged and potent that one caress of the face or one "I love you" will peal for a long while.

The geographical vastness and the social isolation here make 7 emotional evolution seem impossible. Those contradictions of the heart between respectability, logic, and convention on the one hand, and impulse, passion, and intuition on the other, played out wordlessly against the paradisical beauty of the West, give cowboys a wide-eyed but drawn look. Their lips pucker up, not with kisses but with immutability. They may want to break out, staying up all night with a lover just to talk, but they don't know how and can't imagine what the consequences will be. Those rare occasions when they do bare themselves result in confusion. "I feel as if I'd sprained my heart," one friend told me a month after such a meeting.

My friend Ted Hoagland wrote, "No one is as fragile as a woman 8 but no one is as fragile as a man." For all the women here who use "fragileness" to avoid work or as a sexual ploy, there are men who try to hide theirs, all the while clinging to an adolescent dependency on women to cook their meals, wash their clothes, and keep the ranch house warm in winter. But there is true vulnerability in evidence here. Because these men work with animals, not machines or numbers, because they live outside in landscapes of torrential beauty, because they are confined to a place and a routine embellished with awesome variables, because calves die in the arms that pulled others into life, because they go to the mountains as if on a pilgrimage to find out what makes a herd of elk tick, their strength is also a softness, their toughness, a rare delicacy.

_____ CONSIDERATIONS _____

1. Although Ehrlich writes informally, her vocabulary may give some readers a little trouble. Consider unfamiliar words such as "disesteemed," "artifact," "iconic," "stoicism," "laconic," "androgynous." Just looking them up in the dictionary may not be enough. Examine the same words in their immediate context: "we've ironically *disesteemed* his true character"; "this macho, cultural *artifact* the cowboy has become"; "the *iconic* myth surrounding him is built on American notions of heroism"; "cowboys are rarely complainers; they show their *stoicism* by laughing at themselves"; "a man's man—*laconic*, hard-drinking, inscrutable"; "he's *androgynous* at the core. Ranchers are midwives, hunters, nurturers, providers, and conservationists all at once." A third step, if you want to make these new words your own, would be to use them in your own writing.

2. The real nature of the cowboy, writes Ehrlich, is hidden beneath a set of myths and stereotypes implanted deeply in our consciousness by Hollywood movies and cheap fiction. Is this more true of the cowboy than of people in other walks of life, say a policeman, a sailor, an artist, a shopkeeper, a student, a teacher? Build an essay on your responses to the question.

3. Ehrlich closes her essay with a set of contradictions. In what way do such contradictions make sense, and why would an author risk confusing the reader with them?

4. Ehrlich's "About Men," Maxine Kumin's "Building Fence," Carol Bly's "Getting Tired," and Joyce Carol Oates's "On Boxing" are all concerned with habits of life conventionally thought of as masculine. Are these subjects distorted by the fact that the writers are women? Do their approaches differ from the way male writers might have written about the same topics?

5. Read the little dialog that opens Daniel Boorstin's essay "The Pseudo-Event." Then comment on Ehrlich's turning to Marlboro advertisements in her homesickness for the life she had known in Montana. How does she make the reader aware that she herself is conscious of the irony?

Ralph Ellison (1914–1994), born in Oklahoma, won the National Book Award in 1953 for his novel The Invisible Man. *His essays are collected in* Shadow and Act *(1964). For forty years and more, Ellison lectured and wrote on literature and race. A year after his death, the University Press of Mississippi published* Conversations with Ralph Ellison.

25

RALPH ELLISON
On Becoming a Writer

In the beginning writing was far from a serious matter; it was a reflex of reading, an extension of a source of pleasure, escape, and instruction. In fact, I had become curious about writing by way of seeking to understand the aesthetic nature of literary power, the devices through which literature could command my mind and emotions. It was not, then, the *process* of writing which initially claimed my attention, but the finished creations, the artifacts, poems, plays, novels. The act of learning writing technique was, therefore, an amusing investigation of what seemed at best a secondary talent, an exploration, like dabbling in sculpture, of one's potentialities as a "Renaissance Man." This, surely, would seem a most unlikely and even comic concept to introduce here; and yet, it is precisely because I come from where I do (the Oklahoma of the years between World War I and the Great Depression) that I must introduce it, and with a straight face.

Anything and everything was to be found in the chaos of Oklahoma; thus the concept of the Renaissance Man has lurked long within the shadow of my past, and I shared it with at least a half dozen of my Negro friends. How we actually acquired it I have never learned, and since there is no true sociology of the dispersion of ideas within the American democracy, I doubt if I ever shall. Perhaps we breathed it in with the air of the Negro community of Oklahoma City, the capital of that state whose Negroes were often charged by exasperated white Texans with not knowing their "place." Perhaps we took it defiantly from one of them. Or perhaps I myself picked it up from some transplanted New Englander whose shoes I had shined of a Saturday afternoon. After all, the most meaningful tips do not always come in the form of money, nor are they intentionally extended. Most likely, however, my friends and I acquired the idea from some book or some idealistic Negro teacher, some dreamer seeking to function responsibly in an environment which at its more normal took on some of the mixed character of nightmare and of dream.

3   One thing is certain, ours was a chaotic community, still characterized by frontier attitudes and by that strange mixture of the naive and sophisticated, the benign and malignant, which makes the American past so puzzling and its present so confusing; that mixture which often affords the minds of the young who grow up in the far provinces such wide and unstructured latitude, and which encourages the individual's imagination—up to the moment "reality" closes in upon him—to range widely and, sometimes, even to soar.

4   We hear the effects of this in the Southwestern jazz of the 30's, that joint creation of artistically free and exuberantly creative adventurers, of artists who had stumbled upon the freedom lying within the restrictions of their musical tradition as within the limitations of their social background, and who in their own unconscious way have set an example for any Americans, Negro or white, who would find themselves in the arts. They accepted themselves and the complexity of life as they knew it, they loved their art and through it they celebrated American experience definitively in sound. Whatever others thought or felt, this was their own powerful statement, and only non-musical assaults upon their artistic integrity—mainly economically inspired changes of fashion—were able to compromise their vision.

5   Much of so-called Kansas City jazz was actually brought to perfection in Oklahoma by Oklahomans. It is an important circumstance for me as a writer to remember, because while these musicians and their fellows were busy creating out of tradition, imagination, and the sounds and emotions around them, a freer, more complex, and driving form of jazz, my friends and I were exploring an idea of human versatility and possibility which went against the barbs or over the palings of almost every fence which those who controlled social and political power had erected to restrict our roles in the life of the country. Looking back, one might say that the jazzmen, some of whom we idolized, were in their own way better examples for youth to follow than were most judges and ministers, legislators and governors (we were stuck with the notorious Alfalfa Bill Murray). For as we viewed these pillars of society from the confines of our segregated community we almost always saw crooks, clowns, or hypocrites. Even the best were revealed

by their attitudes toward us as lacking the respectable qualities to which they pretended and for which they were accepted outside by others, while despite the outlaw nature of their art, the jazzmen were less torn and damaged by the moral compromises and insincerities which have so sickened the life of our country.

Be that as it may, our youthful sense of life, like that of many Negro children (though no one bothers to note it—especially the specialists and "friends of the Negro" who view our Negro-American life as essentially non-human) was very much like that of Huckleberry Finn, who is universally so praised and enjoyed for the clarity and courage of his moral vision. Like Huck, we observed, we judged, we imitated and evaded as we could the dullness, corruption, and blindness of "civilization." We were undoubtedly comic because, as the saying goes, we weren't supposed to know what it was all about. But to ourselves we were "boys," members of a wild, free, outlaw tribe which transcended the category of race. Rather we were Americans born into the forty-sixth state, and thus, into the context of Negro-American post-Civil War history, "frontiersmen." And isn't one of the implicit functions of the American frontier to encourage the individual to a kind of dreamy wakefulness, a state in which he makes—in all ignorance of the accepted limitations of the possible—rash efforts, quixotic gestures, hopeful testings of the complexity of the known and the given? 6

Spurring us on in our controlled and benign madness was the voracious reading of which most of us were guilty and the vicarious identification and empathetic adventuring which it encouraged. This was due, in part, perhaps to the fact that some of us were fatherless— my own father had died when I was three—but most likely it was because boys are natural romantics. We were seeking examples, patterns to live by, out of a freedom which for all its being ignored by the sociologists and subtle thinkers, was implicit in the Negro situation. Father and mother substitutes also have a role to play in aiding the child to help create himself. Thus we fabricated our own heroes and ideals catch-as-catch-can, and with an outrageous and irreverent sense of freedom. Yes, and in complete disregard of ideas of respectability or the surreal incongruity of some of our projections. Gamblers and scholars, jazz musicians and scientists, Negro cowboys and soldiers from the Spanish-American and First World Wars, movie stars and stunt men, figures from the Italian Renaissance and literature, both classical and popular, were combined with the special virtues of some local bootlegger, the eloquence of some Negro preacher, the strength and grace of some local athlete, the ruthlessness of some businessman-physician, the elegance in dress and manners of some headwaiter or hotel doorman. 7

8   Looking back through the shadows upon this absurd activity, I realize now that we were projecting archetypes, recreating folk figures, legendary heroes, monsters even, most of which violated all ideas of social hierarchy and order and all accepted conceptions of the hero handed down by cultural, religious, and racist tradition. But we, remember, were under the intense spell of the early movies, the silents as well as the talkies; and in our community, life was not so tightly structured as it would have been in the traditional South—or even in deceptively *"free"* Harlem. And our imaginations processed reality and dream, natural man and traditional hero, literature and folklore, like maniacal editors turned loose in some frantic film-cutting room. Remember, too, that being boys, yet in the play-stage of our development, we were dream-serious in our efforts. But serious nevertheless, for *culturally* play is a preparation, and we felt that somehow the human ideal lay in the vague and constantly shifting figures—sometimes comic but always versatile, picaresque, and self-effacingly heroic—which evolved from our wildly improvisatory projections: figures neither white nor black, Christian nor Jewish, but representative of certain desirable essences, of skills and powers, physical, aesthetic, and moral.

9   The proper response to these figures was, we felt, to develop ourselves for the performance of many and diverse roles, and the fact that certain definite limitations had been imposed upon our freedom did not lessen our sense of obligation. Not only were we to prepare but we were to perform—not with mere competence but with an almost reckless verve; with, may we say (without evoking the quaint and questionable notion of *négritude*) Negro-American style? Behind each artist there stands a traditional sense of style, a sense of the felt tension indicative of expressive completeness, a mode of humanizing reality and of evoking a feeling of being at home in the world. It is something which the artist shares with the group, and part of our boyish activity expressed a yearning to make any and everything of quality *Negro-American*; to appropriate it, possess it, recreate it in our own group and individual images.

10   And we recognized and were proud of our group's own style wherever we discerned it, in jazzmen and prize-fighters, ballplayers, and tap dancers; in gesture, inflection, intonation, timbre, and phrasing. Indeed, in all those nuances of expression and attitude which reveal a culture. We did not fully understand the cost of that style, but we recognized within it an affirmation of life beyond all question of our difficulties as Negroes.

11   Contrary to the notion currently projected by certain specialists in the "Negro problem" which characterizes the Negro American as self-hating and defensive, we did not so regard ourselves. We felt, among ourselves at least, that we were supposed to be whoever we

would and could be and do anything and everything which other boys did, and do it better. Not defensively, because we were ordered to do so; nor because it was held in the society at large that we were naturally, as Negroes, limited—but because we demanded it of ourselves. Because to measure up to our own standards was the only way of affirming our notion of manhood.

Hence it was no more incongruous, as seen from our own particular perspective in this land of incongruities, for young Negro Oklahomans to project themselves as Renaissance men than for white Mississippians to see themselves as ancient Greeks or noblemen out of Sir Walter Scott. Surely our fantasies have caused far less damage to the nation's sense of reality, if for no other reason than that ours were expressive of a more democratic ideal. Remember, too, as William Faulkner made us so vividly aware, that the slaves often took the essence of the aristocratic ideal (as they took Christianity) with far more seriousness than their masters, and that we, thanks to the tight telescoping of American history, were but two generations from that previous condition. Renaissance men, indeed! 12

I managed, by keeping quiet about it, to cling to our boyish ideal during three years in Alabama, and I brought it with me to New York, where it not only gave silent support to my explorations of what was then an unknown territory, but served to mock and caution me when I became interested in the Communist ideal. And when it was suggested that I try my hand at writing it was still with me. 13

The act of writing requires a constant plunging back into the shadow of the past where time hovers ghostlike. When I began writing in earnest I was forced, thus, to relate myself consciously and imaginatively to my mixed background as American, as Negro-American, and as a Negro from what in its own belated way was a pioneer background. More important, and inseparable from this particular effort, was the necessity of determining my true relationship to that body of American literature to which I was most attracted and through which, aided by what I could learn from the literatures of Europe, I would find my own voice and to which I was challenged, by way of achieving myself, to make some small contribution, and to whose composite picture of reality I was obligated to offer some necessary modifications. 14

This was no matter of sudden insight but of slow and blundering discovery, of a struggle to stare down the deadly and hypnotic temptation to interpret the world and all its devices in terms of race. To avoid this was very important to me, and in light of my background far from simple. Indeed, it was quite complex, involving as it did, a ceaseless questioning of all those formulas which historians, politicians, sociologists, and an older generation of Negro leaders and writers—those of the so-called "Negro Renaissance"—had evolved to describe my 15 group's identity, its predicament, its fate, and its relation to the larger society and the culture which we share.

16   Here the question of reality and personal identity merge. Yes, and the question of the nature of the reality which underlies American fiction and thus the human truth which gives fiction viability. In this quest, for such it soon became, I learned that nothing could go unchallenged; especially that feverish industry dedicated to telling Negroes who and what they are, and which can usually be counted upon to deprive both humanity and culture of their complexity. I had undergone, not too many months before taking the path which led to writing, the humiliation of being taught in a class in sociology at a Negro college (from Park and Burgess, the leading textbook in the field) that Negroes represented the "lady of the races." This contention the Negro instructor passed blandly along to us without even bothering to wash his hands, much less his teeth. Well, I had no intention of being bound by any such humiliating definition of my relationship to American literature. Not even to those works which depicted Negroes negatively. Negro Americans have a highly developed ability to abstract desirable qualities from those around them, even from their enemies, and my sense of reality could reject bias while appreciating the truth revealed by achieved art. The pleasure which I derived from reading had long been a necessity, and in the *act* of reading, that marvelous collaboration between the writer's artful vision and the reader's sense of life, I had become acquainted with other possible selves; freer, more courageous and ingenuous and, during the course of the narrative at least, even wise.

17   At the time I was under the influence of Ernest Hemingway, and his description, in *Death in the Afternoon*, of his thinking when he first went to Spain became very important as translated in my own naïve fashion. He was trying to write, he tells us,

> and I found the greatest difficulty aside from knowing truly what you really felt, rather than what you were supposed to feel, and had been taught to feel, was to put down what really happened in action; what the actual things were which produced the emotion that you experienced. . . .

18   His statement of moral and aesthetic purpose which followed focused on my own search to relate myself to American life through literature. For I found the greatest difficulty for a Negro writer was the problem of revealing what he truly felt, rather than serving up what Negroes were supposed to feel, and were encouraged to feel. And linked to this was the difficulty, based upon our long habit of deception and evasion, of depicting what really happened within our areas of American life, and putting down with honesty and without bowing to ideological expediencies the attitudes and values which give Negro-

American life its sense of wholeness and which render it bearable and human and, when measured by our own terms, desirable.

I was forced to this awareness through my struggles with the 19 craft of fiction; yes, and by my attraction (soon rejected) to Marxist political theory, which was my response to the inferior status which society sought to impose upon me (I did not then, now, or ever *consider* myself inferior).

I did not know my true relationship to America—what citizen of 20 the U.S. really does?—but I did know and accept how I felt inside. And I also knew, thanks to the old Renaissance Man, what I expected of myself in the matter of personal discipline and creative quality. Since by the grace of the past and the examples of manhood picked willy-nilly from the continuing present of my background, I rejected all negative definitions imposed upon me by others, there was nothing to do but search for those relationships which were fundamental.

In this sense fiction became the agency of my efforts to answer 21 the questions, Who am I, what am I, how did I come to be? What shall I make of the life around me, what celebrate, what reject, how confront the snarl of good and evil which is inevitable? What does American society *mean* when regarded out of my *own* eyes, when informed by my *own* sense of the past and viewed by my *own* complex sense of the present? How, in other words, should I think of myself and my pluralistic sense of the world, how express my vision of the human predicament, without reducing it to a point which would render it sterile before that necessary and tragic—though enhancing—reduction which must occur before the fictive vision can come alive? It is quite possible that much potential fiction by Negro Americans fails precisely at this point: through the writers' refusal (often through provincialism or lack of courage or through opportunism) to achieve a vision of life and resourcefulness of craft commensurate with the complexity of their actual situation. Too often they fear to leave the uneasy sanctuary of race to take their chances in the world of art.

_____ CONSIDERATIONS _____

1. Ellison's opening statement that writing was "a reflex of reading" points to the experience of many other students and writers (see Richard Wright's "The Library Card") and implies an important relationship between the two activities. Are reading and writing two sides of the same coin? (See also the editors' "Preface" to this volume.)

2. Look in a good dictionary for a definition of "Renaissance man" and explain why this concept is central to an understanding of Ellison's essay.

3. How, in paragraph 7, does Ellison specify, and thus clarify, what he means by "ours was a chaotic community" in paragraph 3?

4. At several points in his essay, Ellison is critical of "specialists and 'friends of the Negro.'" What is his primary criticism of their efforts?

5. Does Ellison's remark "boys are natural romantics" in paragraph 7 help explain his first sentence in paragraph 8? Do you think that sentence is limited to the boys of one race or class? Use your own experience to write an essay on the subject.

6. Which of these authors would be most likely to agree with the first sentence of Ellison's paragraph 14—Joan Didion, Alice Walker, or George Orwell?

*Nora Ephron (b. 1941), daughter of two screenwriters,
grew up in Hollywood wanting to move to New York and
become a writer. She did. She began by working for*
Newsweek, *and soon was contributing articles to the* New
Yorker *and a monthly column to* Esquire. *Most of her
writing is about women, and manages to be at once funny
and serious, profound and irreverent—and on occasion
outrageous. In 1983 she published a novel entitled*
Heartburn *that, in 1986, was made into a film. Her essays
are collected in* Wallflower at the Orgy *(1970),* Crazy Salad
*(1975), from which we take this essay on growing up flat-
chested, and most recently in* Nora Ephron Collected
(1991).

26

NORA EPHRON

A Few Words About Breasts: Shaping Up Absurd

I have to begin with a few words about androgyny. In grammar   1
school, in the fifth and sixth grades, we were all tyrannized by a rigid
set of rules that supposedly determined whether we were boys or girls.
The episode in *Huckleberry Finn* where Huck is disguised as a girl and
gives himself away by the way he threads a needle and catches a ball—
that kind of thing. We learned that the way you sat, crossed your legs,
held a cigarette and looked at your nails, your wristwatch, the way
you did these things instinctively was absolute proof of your sex. Now
obviously most children did not take this literally, but I did. I thought
that just one slip, just one incorrect cross of my legs or flick of an
imaginary cigarette ash would turn me from whatever I was into the
other thing; that would be all it took, really. Even though I was out-
wardly a girl and had many of the trappings generally associated with
the field of girldom—a girl's name, for example, and dresses, my own

telephone, an autograph book—I spent the early years of my adolescence absolutely certain that I might at any point gum it up. I did not feel at all like a girl. I way boyish. I was athletic, ambitious, outspoken, competitive, noisy, rambunctious. I had scabs on my knees and my socks slid into my loafers and I could throw a football. I wanted desperately not to be that way, not to be a mixture of both things but instead just one, a girl, a definite indisputable girl. As soft and as pink as a nursery. And nothing would do that for me, I felt, but breasts.

2   I was about six months younger than everyone in my class, and so for about six months after it began, for six months after my friends had begun to develop—that was the word we used, develop—I was not particularly worried. I would sit in the bathtub and look down at my breasts and know that any day now, any second now, they would start growing like everyone else's. They didn't. "I want to buy a bra," I said to my mother one night. "What for?" she said. My mother was really hateful about bras, and by the time my third sister had gotten to the point where she was ready to want one, my mother had worked the whole business into a comedy routine. "Why not use a Band-Aid instead?" she would say. It was a source of great pride to my mother that she had never even had to wear a brassiere until she had her fourth child, and then only because her gynecologist made her. It was incomprehensible to me that anyone would ever be proud of something like that. It was the 1950s, for God's sake. Jane Russell. Cashmere sweaters. Couldn't my mother see that? *"I am too old to wear an undershirt."* Screaming. Weeping. Shouting. "Then don't wear an undershirt," said my mother. "But I want to buy a bra," "What for?"

3   I suppose that for most girls, breasts, brassieres, that entire thing, has more trauma, more to do with the coming of adolescence, of becoming a woman, than anything else. Certainly more than getting your period, although that too was traumatic, symbolic. But you could *see* breasts; they were there; they were visible. Whereas a girl could claim to have her period for months before she actually got it and nobody would ever know the difference. Which is exactly what I did. All you had to do was make a great fuss over having enough nickels for the Kotex machine and walk around clutching your stomach and moaning for three to five days a month about The Curse and you could convince anybody. There is a school of thought somewhere in the women's lib/women's mag/gynecology establishment that claims that menstrual cramps are purely psychological, and I lean toward it. Not that I didn't have them finally. Agonizing cramps, heating-pad cramps, go-down-to-the-school-nurse-and-lie-on-the-cot cramps. But unlike any pain I have ever suffered, I adored the pain of cramps, welcomed it, wallowed in it, bragged about it. "I can't go. I have cramps." "I can't do that. I have cramps." And most of all, gigglingly, blush-

ingly: "I can't swim. I have cramps." Nobody ever used the hard-core word. Menstruation. God, what an awful word. Never that. "I have cramps."

The morning I first got my period, I went into my mother's bed- 4
room to tell her. And my mother, my utterly-hateful-about-bras mother, burst into tears. It was really a lovely moment, and I remember it so clearly not just because it was one of the two times I ever saw my mother cry on my account (the other was when I was caught being a six-year-old kleptomaniac), but also because the incident did not mean to me what it meant to her. Her little girl, her firstborn, had finally become a woman. That was what she was crying about. My reaction to the event, however, was that I might well be a woman in some scientific, textbook sense (and could at least stop faking every month and stop wasting all those nickels). But in another sense—in a visible sense—I was as androgynous and as liable to tip over into boyhood as ever.

I started with a 28AA bra. I don't think they made them any 5
smaller in those days, although I gather that now you can buy bras for five year olds that don't have any cups whatsoever in them; trainer bras they are called. My first brassiere came from Robinson's Department Store in Beverly Hills. I went there alone, shaking, positive they would look me over and smile and tell me to come back next year. An actual fitter took me into the dressing room and stood over me while I took off my blouse and tried the first one on. The little puffs stood out on my chest. "Lean over," said the fitter (to this day I am not sure what fitters in bra departments do except to tell you to lean over). I leaned over, with the fleeting hope that my breasts would miraculously fall out of my body and into the puffs. Nothing.

"Don't worry about it," said my friend Libby some months later, 6
when things had not improved. "You'll get them after you're married."

"What are you talking about?" I said. 7

"When you get married," Libby explained, "your husband will 8
touch your breasts and rub them and kiss them and they'll grow."

That was the killer. Necking I could deal with. Intercourse I 9
could deal with. But it had never crossed my mind that a man was going to touch my breasts, that breasts had something to do with all that, petting, my God they never mentioned petting in my little sex manual about fertilization of the ovum. I became dizzy. For I knew instantly—as naïve as I had been only a moment before—that only part of what she was saying was true: the touching, rubbing, kissing part, not the growing part. And I knew that no one would ever want to marry me. I had no breasts. I would never have breasts.

10   My best friend in school was Diana Raskob. She lived a block from me in a house full of wonders. English muffins, for instance. The Raskobs were the first people in Beverly Hills to have English muffins for breakfast. They also had an apricot tree in the back, and a badminton court, and a subscription to *Seventeen* magazine, and hundreds of games like Sorry and Parcheesi and Treasure Hunt and Anagrams. Diana and I spent three or four afternoons a week in their den reading and playing and eating. Diana's mother's kitchen was full of the most colossal assortment of junk food I have ever been exposed to. My house was full of apples and peaches and milk and homemade chocolate-chip cookies—which were nice, and good for you, but-not-right-before-dinner-or-you'll-spoil-your-appetite. Diana's house had nothing in it that was good for you, and what's more, you could stuff it in right up until dinner and nobody cared. Bar-B-Q potato chips (they were the first in them, too), giant bottles of ginger ale, fresh popcorn with melted butter, hot fudge sauce on Baskin-Robbins jamoca ice cream, powdered-sugar doughnuts from Van de Kamps. Diana and I had been best friends since we were seven; we were about equally popular in school (which is to say, not particularly), we had about the same success with boys (extremely intermittent) and we looked much the same. Dark. Tall. Gangly.

11   It is September, just before school begins. I am eleven years old, about to enter the seventh grade, and Diana and I have not seen each other all summer. I have been to camp and she has been somewhere like Banff with her parents. We are meeting, as we often do, on the street midway between our two houses and we will walk back to Diana's and eat junk and talk about what has happened to each of us that summer. I am walking down Walden Drive in my jeans and my father's shirt hanging out and my old red loafers with the socks falling into them and coming toward me is ... I take a deep breath ... a young woman. Diana. Her hair is curled and she has a waist and hips and a bust and she is wearing a straight skirt, an article of clothing I have been repeatedly told that I will be unable to wear until I have the hips to hold it up. My jaw drops, and suddenly I am crying, crying hysterically, can't catch my breath sobbing. My best friend has betrayed me. She has gone ahead without me and done it. She has shaped up.

12   Here are some things I did to help:

13   Bought a Mark Eden Bust Developer.

14   Slept on my back for four years.

15   Splashed cold water on them every night because some French actress said in *Life* magazine that that was what *she* did for her perfect bustline.

16   Ultimately, I resigned myself to a bad toss and began to wear padded bras. I think about them now, think about all those years in high school I went around in them, my three padded bras, every single

one of them with different sized breasts. Each time I changed bras I changed sizes: one week nice perky but not too obtrusive breasts, the next medium-sized slightly pointed ones, the next week knockers, true knockers; all the time, whatever size I was, carrying around this rubberized appendage on my chest that occasionally crashed into a wall and was poked inward and had to be poked outward—I think about all that and wonder how anyone kept a straight face through it. My parents, who normally had no restraints about needling me—why did they say nothing as they watched my chest go up and down? My friends, who would periodically inspect my breasts for signs of growth and reassure me—why didn't they at least counsel consistency?

And the bathing suits. I die when I think about the bathing suits. 17 That was the era when you could lay an uninhabited bathing suit on the beach and someone would make a pass at it. I would put one on, an absurd swimsuit with its enormous bust built into it, the bones from the suit stabbing me in the rib cage and leaving little red welts on my body, and there I would be, my chest plunging straight downward absolutely vertically from my collarbone to the top of my suit and then suddenly, wham, out came all that padding and material and wiring absolutely horizontally.

Buster Klepper was the first boy who ever touched them. He was 18 my boyfriend my senior year of high school. There is a picture of him in my high-school yearbook that makes him look quite attractive in a Jewish, horn-rimmed glasses sort of way, but the picture does not show the pimples, which were air-brushed out, or the dumbness. Well, that isn't really fair. He wasn't dumb. He just wasn't terribly bright. His mother refused to accept it, refused to accept the relentlessly average report cards, refused to deal with her son's inevitable destiny in some junior college or other. "He was tested," she would say to me, apropos of nothing, "and it came out 145. That's near-genius." Had the word underachiever been coined, she probably would have lobbed that one at me, too. Anyway, Buster was really very sweet—which is, I know, damning with faint praise, but there it is. I was the editor of the front page of the high-school newspaper and he was editor of the back page; we had to work together, side by side, in the print shop, and that was how it started. On our first date, we went to see *April Love* starring Pat Boone. Then we started going together. Buster had a green coupe, a 1950 Ford with an engine he had handchromed until it shone, dazzled, reflected the image of anyone who looked into it, anyone usually being Buster polishing it or the gas-station attendants he constantly asked to check the oil in order for them to be overwhelmed by the sparkle on the valves. The car also had a boot stretched over the back seat for reasons I never understood; hanging from the rearview mirror, as was the custom, was a pair of angora dice. A previous girl friend named Solange who was famous throughout Beverly Hills High School for having no pigment in her right eyebrow had knitted them for him. Buster and I would ride around town, the two of us seated to the left of the steering wheel. I would shift gears. It was nice.

19   There was necking. Terrific necking. First in the car, overlooking Los Angeles from what is now the Trousdale Estates. Then on the bed of his parents' cabana at Ocean House. Incredibly wonderful, frustrating necking, I loved it, really, but no further than necking, please don't, please, because there I was absolutely terrified of the general implications of going-a-step-further with a near-dummy and also terrified of his finding out there was next to nothing there (which he knew, of course; he wasn't that dumb).

20   I broke up with him at one point. I think we were apart for about two weeks. At the end of that time I drove down to see a friend at a boarding school in Palos Verdes Estates and a disc jockey played *April Love* on the radio four times during the trip. I took it as a sign. I drove straight back to Griffith Park to a golf tournament Buster was playing in (he was the sixth-seeded teen-age golf player in Southern California) and presented myself back to him on the green of the 18th hole. It was all very dramatic. That night we went to a drive-in and I let him get his hand under my protuberances and onto my breasts. He really didn't seem to mind at all.

21   *"Do you want to marry my son?" the woman asked me.*

22   *"Yes," I said.*

23   *I was nineteen years old, a virgin, going with this woman's son, this big strange woman who was married to a Lutheran minister in New Hampshire and pretended she was Gentile and had this son, by her first husband, this total fool of a son who ran the hero-sandwich concession at Harvard Business School and whom for one moment one December in New Hampshire I said—as much out of politeness as anything else—that I wanted to marry.*

24   *"Fine," she said. "Now, here's what you do. Always make sure you're on top of him so you won't seem so small. My bust is very large, you see, so I always lie on my back to make it look smaller, but you'll have to be on top most of the time."*

25   *I nodded. "Thank you," I said.*

26   *"I have a book for you to read," she went on. "Take it with you when you leave. Keep it." She went to the bookshelf, found it, and gave it to me. It was a book on frigidity.*

27   *"Thank you," I said.*

28   This is a true story. Everything in this article is a true story, but I feel I have to point out that that story in particular is true. It happened on December 30, 1960. I think about it often. When it first happened, I naturally assumed that the woman's son, my boyfriend, was responsi-

ble. I invented a scenario where he had had a little heart-to-heart with his mother and had confessed that his only objection to me was that my breasts were small; his mother then took it upon herself to help out. Now I think I was wrong about the incident. The mother was acting on her own, I think: that was her way of being cruel and competitive under the guise of being helpful and maternal. You have small breasts, she was saying; therefore you will never make him as happy as I have. Or you have small breasts; therefore you will doubtless have sexual problems. Or you have small breasts; therefore you are less woman than I am. She was, as it happens, only the first of what seems to me to be a never-ending string of women who have made competitive remarks to me about breast size. "I would love to wear a dress like that," my friend Emily says to me, "but my bust is too big." Like that. Why do women say these things to me? Do I attract these remarks the way other women attract married men or alcoholics or homosexuals? This summer, for example. I am at a party in East Hampton and I am introduced to a woman from Washington. She is a minor celebrity, very pretty and Southern and blonde and outspoken and I am flattered because she has read something I have written. We are talking animatedly, we have been talking no more than five minutes, when a man comes up to join us. "Look at the two of us," the woman says to the man, indicating me and her. "The two of us together couldn't fill an A cup." Why does she say that? It isn't even true, dammit, so why? Is she even more addled than I am on this subject? Does she honestly believe there is something wrong with her size breasts, which, it seems to me, now that I look hard at them, are just right. Do I unconsciously bring out competitiveness in women? In that form? What did I do to deserve it?

As for men. 29

There were men who minded and let me know they minded. 30 There were men who did not mind. In any case, I always minded.

And even now, now that I have been countlessly reassured that 31 my figure is a good one, now that I am grown up enough to understand that most of my feelings have very little to do with the reality of my shape, I am nonetheless obsessed by breasts. I cannot help it. I grew up in the terrible Fifties—with rigid stereotypical sex roles, the insistence that men be men and dress like men and women be women and dress like women, the intolerance of androgyny—and I cannot shake it, cannot shake my feelings of inadequacy. Well, that time is gone, right? All those exaggerated examples of breast worship are gone, right? Those women were freaks, right? I know all that. And yet, here I am, stuck with the psychological remains of it all, stuck with my own peculiar version of breast worship. You probably think I am crazy to go on like this: here I have set out to write a confession that is meant to hit you with the shock of recognition and instead you are sitting there thinking I am thoroughly warped. Well, what can I tell you? If I had had them, I would have been a completely different person. I honestly believe that.

32   After I went into therapy, a process that made it possible for me to tell total strangers at cocktail parties that breasts were the hang-up of my life, I was often told that I was insane to have been bothered by my condition. I was also frequently told, by close friends, that I was extremely boring on the subject. And my girl friends, the ones with nice big breasts, would go on endlessly about how their lives had been far more miserable than mine. Their bra straps were snapped in class. They couldn't sleep on their stomachs. They were stared at whenever the word "mountain" cropped up in geography. And *Evangeline*, good God what they went through every time someone had to stand up and recite the Prologue to Longfellow's *Evangeline*: "... *stand like druids of eld* ... / *With beards that rest on their bosoms.*" It was much worse for them, they tell me. They had a terrible time of it, they assure me. I don't know how lucky I was, they say.

33   I have thought about their remarks, tried to put myself in their place, considered their point of view. I think they are full of shit.

_____ CONSIDERATIONS _____

1. Nora Ephron's account offends some readers and attracts others for the same reason—the frank and casual exploration of a subject that generations have believed unmentionable. This problem is worth investigating: Are there, in fact, subjects that should not be discussed in the popular press? Are there words a writer must not use? Why? And who should make the list of things not to be talked about?

2. Imagine an argument about Ephron's article between a feminist and an antifeminist. What ammunition could each find in the article? Write the dialogue as you hear it.

3. Ephron reports that from a very early age she worried that she might not be "a girl, a definite indisputable girl." Is this anxiety as uncommon as she thought it was? Is worry about one's sex an exclusively female problem?

4. Are our ideas about masculinity and femininity changing? How are such ideas determined? How important are they in shaping personality and in channeling thoughts? See Margaret Atwood's "Alien Territory," (page 37).

5. Ephron's article is a good example of the very informal essay. What does she do that makes it so informal? Consider both diction and sentence structure.

6. How can one smile at others' problems—or at one's own disappointments, for that matter? How can Ephron see humor now in what she thought of as tragic then? Provide an example from your own experience.

Louise Erdrich (b. 1954) grew up in North Dakota and travelled east to attend Dartmouth College. Her heritage is partly German-American and partly Turtle Mountain Chippewa. She lives in New Hampshire with her husband, the writer Michael Dorris, and their four children. Best known as a novelist, she has also published two collections of poetry and most recently her first collection of essays, The Blue Jay's Dance *(1995)—subtitled "A Birth Year"—from which we take this essay.*

27

LOUISE ERDRICH
Skunk Dreams

When I was fourteen, I slept alone on a North Dakota football   1
field under the cold stars on an early spring night. May is unpredictable in the Red River Valley, and I happened to hit a night when frost formed in the grass. A skunk trailed a plume of steam across the forty-yard line near moonrise. I tucked the top of my sleeping bag over my head and was just dozing off when the skunk walked onto me with simple authority.

Its ripe odor must have dissipated in the frozen earth of its win-   2
terlong hibernation, because it didn't smell all that bad, or perhaps it was just that I took shallow breaths in numb surprise. I felt him—her, whatever—pause on the side of my hip and turn around twice before evidently deciding I was a good place to sleep. At the back of my knees, on the quilting of my sleeping bag, it trod out a spot for itself and then, with a serene little groan, curled up and lay perfectly still. That made two of us. I was wildly awake, trying to forget the sharpness and number of skunk teeth, trying not to think of the high percentage of skunks with rabies, or the reason that on camping trips my father always kept a hatchet underneath his pillow.

Inside the bag, I felt as if I might smother. Carefully, making only   3
the slightest of rustles, I drew the bag away from my face and took a

deep breath of the night air, enriched with skunk, but clear and watery and cold. It wasn't so bad, and the skunk didn't stir at all, so I watched the moon—caught that night in an envelope of silk, a mist—pass over my sleeping field of teenage guts and glory. The grass in spring that has lain beneath the snow harbors a sere dust both old and fresh. I smelled that newness beneath the rank tone of my bag-mate—the stiff fragrance of damp earth and the thick pungency of newly manured fields a mile or two away—along with my sleeping bag's smell, slightly mildewed, forever smoky. The skunk settled even closer and began to breathe rapidly; its feet jerked a little like a dog's. I sank against the earth, and fell asleep too.

4   Of what easily tipped cans, what molten sludge, what dogs in yards on chains, what leftover macaroni casseroles, what cellar holes, crawl spaces, burrows taken from meek woodchucks, of what miracles of garbage did my skunk dream? Or did it, since we can't be sure, dream the plot of *Moby Dick*, how to properly age parmesan, or how to restore the brick-walled, tumbledown creamery that was its home? We don't know about the dreams of any other biota, and even much about our own. If dreams are an actual dimension, as some assert, then the usual rules of life by which we abide do not apply. In that place, skunks may certainly dream themselves into the vests of stockbrokers. Perhaps that night the skunk and I dreamed each other's thoughts or are still dreaming them. To paraphrase the problem of the Chinese sage, I may be a woman who has dreamed herself a skunk, or a skunk still dreaming that she is a woman.

5   In a book called *Death and Consciousness*, David H. Lund—who wants very much to believe in life after death—describes human dream-life as a possible model for a disembodied existence:

> Many of one's dreams are such that they involve the activities of an apparently embodied person whom one takes to be oneself as long as one dreams. . . . Whatever is the source of the imagery . . . apparently has the capacity to bring about images of a human body and to impart the feeling that the body is mine. It is, of course, just an image body, but it serves as a perfectly good body for the dream experience. I regard it as mine, I act on the dream environment by means of it, and it constitutes the center of the perceptual world of my dream.

6   Over the years I have acquired and reshuffled my beliefs and doubts about whether we live on after death—in any shape or form, that is, besides the molecular level at which I am to be absorbed by the taproots of cemetery elms or pines and the tangled mats of fearfully poisoned, too-green lawn grass. I want something of the self on whom I have worked so hard to survive the loss of the body (which, incidentally, the self has done a fairly decent job of looking after, excepting spells of too much cabernet and a few idiotic years of rolling my own

cigarettes out of Virginia Blond tobacco). I am put out with the marvelous discoveries of the intricate biochemical configuration of our brains, though I realize that the processes themselves are quite miraculous. I understand that I should be self-proud, content to gee-whiz at the fact that I am the world's only mechanism that can admire itself. I should be grateful that life is here today, though gone tomorrow, but I can't help it. I want more.

Skunks don't mind each other's vile perfume. Obviously, they find each other more than tolerable. And even I, who have been in the presence of a direct skunk hit, wouldn't classify their weapon as mere smell. It is more on the order of a reality-enhancing experience. It's not so pleasant as standing in a grove of old-growth red cedars, or on a lyrical moonshed plain, or watching trout rise to the shadow of your hand on the placid surface of an Alpine lake. When the skunk lets go, you're surrounded by skunk presence: inhabited, owned, involved with something you can only describe as powerfully *there*.

I woke at dawn, stunned into that sprayed state of being. The dog that had approached me was rolling in the grass, half-addled, sprayed too. The skunk was gone. I abandoned my sleeping bag and started home. Up Eighth Street, past the tiny blue and pink houses, past my grade school, past all the addresses where I had baby-sat, I walked in my own strange wind. The streets were wide and empty; I met no one—not a dog, not a squirrel, not even an early robin. Perhaps they had all scattered before me, blocks away. I had gone out to sleep on the football field because I was afflicted with a sadness I had to dramatize. Mood swings had begun, hormones, feverish and brutal. They were nothing to me now. My emotions had seemed vast, dark, and sickeningly private. But they were minor, mere wisps, compared to skunk.

I have found that my best dreams come to me in cheap motels. One such dream about an especially haunting place occurred in a rattling room in Valley City, North Dakota. There, in the home of the Winter Show, in the old Rudolph Hotel, I was to spend a weeklong residency as a poet-in-the-schools. I was supporting myself, at the time, by teaching poetry to children, convicts, rehabilitation patients, high-school hoods, and recovering alcoholics. What a marvelous job it was, and what opportunities I had to dream, since I paid my own lodging and lived low, sometimes taking rooms for less than ten dollars a night in motels that had already been closed by local health departments.

The images that assailed me in Valley City came about because the bedspread was so thin and worn—a mere brown tissuey curtain—that I had to sleep beneath my faux fur Salvation Army coat, wearing all of my clothing, even a scarf. Cold often brings on the most spectacular of my dreams, as if my brain has been incited to fevered activity.

On that particular frigid night, the cold somehow seemed to snap boundaries, shift my time continuum, and perhaps even allow me to visit my own life in a future moment. After waking once, transferring the contents of my entire suitcase onto my person, and shivering to sleep again, I dreamed of a vast, dark, fenced place. The fencing was chain-link in places, chicken wire, sagging X wire, barbed wire on top, jerry-built with tipped-out poles and uncertain corners nailed to log posts and growing trees. And yet it was quite impermeable and solid, as time-tested, broken-looking things so often are.

11   Behind it, trees ran for miles—large trees, grown trees, big pines the likes of which do not exist on the Great Plains. In my dream I walked up to the fence, looked within, and saw tawny, humpbacked elk move among the great trunks and slashing green arms. Suave, imponderable, magnificently dumb, they lurched and floated through the dim-complexioned air. One turned, however, before they all vanished, and from either side of that flimsy-looking barrier there passed between us a look, a communion, a long and measureless regard that left me, on waking, with a sensation of penetrating sorrow.

12   I didn't think about my dreams for many years, until after I moved to New Hampshire. I had become urbanized and sedentary since the days when I slept with skunks, and I had turned inward. For several years I spent my days leaning above a strange desk, a green door on stilts, which was so high that to sit at it I bought a barstool upholstered in brown leatherette. Besides, the entire Northeast seemed like the inside of a house to me, the sky small and oddly lit, as if by an electric bulb. The sun did not pop over the great trees for hours—and then went down so soon. I was suspicious of Eastern land: the undramatic loveliness, the small scale, the lack of sky to watch, the way the weather sneaked up without enough warning.

13   The woods themselves seemed bogus at first—every inch of the ground turned over more than once, and even in the second growth of old pines so much human evidence. Rock walls ran everywhere, grown through and tumbled, as if the dead still had claims they imposed. The unkillable and fiercely contorted trees of old orchards, those revenants, spooked me when I walked in the woods. The blasted limbs spread a white lace cold as fire in the spring, and the odor of the blossoms was furiously spectral, sweet. When I stood beneath the canopies that hummed and shook with bees, I heard voices, other voices, and I did not understand what they were saying, where they had come from, what drove them into this earth.

14   Then, as often happens to sparring adversaries in 1940s movies, I fell in love.

15   After a few years of living in the country, the impulse to simply *get outside* hit me, strengthened, and became again a habit of thought, a reason for storytelling, an uneasy impatience with walls and roads.

At first, when I had that urge, I had to get into a car and drive fifteen hundred miles before I was back in a place that I defined as *out*. The West, or the edge of it anyway, the great level patchwork of chemically treated fields and tortured grazing land, was the outside I had internalized. In the rich Red River Valley, where the valuable cropland is practically measured in inches, environmental areas are defined and proudly pointed out as stretches of roadway where the ditches are not mowed. Deer and pheasants survive in shelter belts—rows of Russian olive, plum, sometimes evergreen—planted at the edges of fields. The former tall-grass prairie has now become a collection of mechanized gardens tended by an array of air-conditioned farm implements and bearing an increasing amount of pesticide and herbicide in each black teaspoon of dirt. Nevertheless, no amount of reality changed the fact that I still *thought* of eastern North Dakota as wild.

In time, though, *out* became outside my door in New England. 16 By walking across the road and sitting in my little writing house—a place surrounded by trees, thick plumes of grass, jets of ferns, and banks of touch-me-not—or just by looking out a screen door or window, I started to notice what there was to see. In time, the smothering woods that had always seemed part of Northeastern civilization— more an inside than an outside, more like a friendly garden—revealed themselves as forceful and complex. The growth of plants, the lush celebratory springs made a grasslands person drunk. The world turned dazzling green, the hills rode like comfortable and flowing animals. Everywhere there was the sound of water moving.

And yet, even though I finally grew closer to these woods, on 17 some days I still wanted to tear them from before my eyes.

I wanted to *see*. Where I grew up, our house looked out on the 18 western horizon. I could see horizon when I played. I could see it when I walked to school. It was always there, a line beyond everything, a simple line of changing shades and colors that ringed the town, a vast place. That was it. Down at the end of every grid of streets: vastness. Out the windows of the high school: vastness. From the drive-in theater where I went parking in a purple Duster: vast distance. That is why, on lovely New England days when everything should have been all right—a fall day, for instance, when the earth had risen through the air in patches and the sky lowered, dim and warm— I fell sick with longing for the horizon. I wanted the clean line, the simple line, the clouds marching over it in feathered masses. I suffered from horizon sickness. But it sounds crazy for a grown woman to throw herself at the sky, and the thing is, I wanted to get well. And so to compensate for horizon sickness, for the great longing that seemed both romantically German and pragmatically Chippewa in origin, I found solace in trees.

Trees are a changing landscape of sound—and the sound I grew 19 attached to, possible only near large deciduous forests, was the great hushed roar of thousands and millions of leaves brushing and touching one another. Windy days were like sitting just out of sight of an ocean, the great magnetic ocean of wind. All around me, I watched the trees tossing, their heads bending. At times the movement seemed passionate, as though they were flung together in an eager embrace, caressing each other, branch to branch. If there is a vegetative soul, an animating power that all things share, there must be great rejoicing out there on windy days, ecstasy, for trees move so slowly on calm days. At least it seems that way to us. On days of high wind they move so freely it must give them a cellular pleasure close to terror.

20   Unused to walking in the woods, I did not realize that trees dropped branches—often large ones—or that there was any possible danger in going out on windy days, drawn by the natural drama. There was a white pine I loved, a tree of the size foresters call *overgrown*, a waste, a thing made of long-since harvestable material. The tree was so big that three people couldn't reach around it. Standing at the bottom, craning back, fingers clenched in grooves of bark, I held on as the crown of the tree roared and beat the air a hundred feet above. The movement was frantic, the soft-needled branches long and supple. I thought of a woman tossing, anchored in passion: calm one instant, full-throated the next, hair vast and dark, shedding the piercing, fresh oil of broken needles. I went to visit her often, and walked onward, farther, though it was not so far at all, and then one day I reached the fence.

21   Chain-link in places, chicken wire, sagging X wire, barbed wire on top, jerry-built with tipped-out poles and uncertain corners nailed to log posts and growing trees, still it seemed impermeable and solid. Behind it, there were trees for miles: large trees, grown trees, big pines. I walked up to the fence, looked within, and could see elk moving. Suave, imponderable, magnificently dumb, they lurched and floated through the dim air.

22   I was on the edge of a game park, a rich man's huge wilderness, probably the largest parcel of protected land in western New Hampshire, certainly the largest privately owned piece I knew about. At forty square miles—25,000 acres—it was bigger than my mother's home reservation. And it had the oddest fence around it that I'd ever seen, the longest and the tackiest. Though partially electrified, the side closest to our house was so piddling that an elk could easily have tossed it apart. Certainly a half-ton wild boar, the condensed and living version of a tank, could have strolled right through. But then animals, much like most humans, don't charge through fences unless they have sound reasons. As I soon found out, because I naturally grew fascinated with the place, there were many more animals trying to get into the park than out, and they couldn't have cared less about ending up in a hunter's stew pot.

These were not animals, the elk—since they were grained at 23
feeding stations, how could they be? They were not domesticated either, however, for beyond the no-hunt boundaries they fled and vanished. They were game. Since there is no sport in shooting feedlot
steers, these animals—still harboring wild traits and therefore more
challenging to kill—were maintained to provide blood pleasure for the
members of the Blue Mountain Forest Association.

As I walked away from the fence that day, I was of two minds 24
about the place—and I am still. Shooting animals inside fences, no
matter how big the area they have to hide in, seems abominable and
silly. And yet, I was glad for that wilderness. Though secretly managed and off limits to me, it was the source of flocks of evening gros-
beaks and pine siskins, of wild turkey, ravens, and grouse, of Eastern
coyote, oxygen-rich air, foxes, goldfinches, skunk, and bears that tun-
neled in and out.

I had dreamed of this place in Valley City, or it had dreamed me. 25
There was affinity here, beyond any explanation I could offer, so I
didn't try. I continued to visit the tracts of big trees, and on deep
nights—windy nights, especially when it stormed—I liked to fall
asleep imagining details. I saw the great crowns touching, heard the
raving sound of wind and thriving, knocking cries as the blackest of
ravens flung themselves across acres upon indifferent acres of tossing,
old-growth pine. I could fall asleep picturing how, below that dark air,
taproots thrust into a deeper blankness, drinking the powerful rain.

Or was it so only in my dreams? The park, known locally as 26
Corbin's Park, after its founder, Austin Corbin, is knit together of land
and farmsteads he bought in the late nineteenth century from 275 individuals. Among the first animals released there, before the place became a hunting club, were thirty buffalo, remnants of the vast Western herds. Their presence piqued the interest of Ernest Harold Bayne, a
conservation-minded local journalist, who attempted to break a pair of
buffalo calves to the yoke. He exhibited them at county fairs and even
knit mittens out of buffalo wool, hoping to convince the skeptical of
their usefulness. His work inspired sympathy, if not a trend for buffalo
yarn, and collective zeal for the salvation of the buffalo grew until by
1915 the American Bison Society, of which Bayne was secretary,
helped form government reserves that eventually more than doubled
the herds that remained.

The buffalo dream seems to have been the park's most noble 27
hour. Since that time it has been the haunt of wealthy hunting enthu-
siasts. The owner of Ruger Arms currently inhabits the stunning, but-
ter-yellow original Corbin mansion and would like to buy the whole
park for his exclusive use, or so local gossip has it.

For some months I walked the boundary admiring the tangled 28
landscape, at least all that I could see. After my first apprehension, I

ignored the fence. I walked along it as if it simply did not exist, as if I really were part of that place which lay just beyond my reach. The British psychotherapist Adam Phillips has examined obstacles from several different angles, attempting to define their emotional use. "It is impossible to imagine desire without obstacles," he writes, "and wherever we find something to be an obstacle we are at the same time desiring something. It is part of the fascination of the Oedipus story in particular, and perhaps narrative in general, that we and the heroes and heroines of our fictions never know whether obstacles create desire or desire creates obstacles." He goes on to characterize the Unconscious, our dream world, as a place without obstacles: "A good question to ask of a dream is: What are the obstacles that have been removed to make this extraordinary scene possible?"

29   My dream, however, was about obstacles still in place. The fence was the main component, the defining characteristic of the forbidden territory that I watched but could not enter or experience. The obstacles that we overcome define us. We are composed of hurdles we set up to pace our headlong needs, to control our desires, or against which to measure our growth. "Without obstacles," Phillips writes, "the notion of development is inconceivable. There would be nothing to master."

30   Walking along the boundary of the park no longer satisfied me. The preciousness and deceptive stability of that fence began to rankle. Longing filled me. I wanted to brush against the old pine bark and pass beyond the ridge, to see specifically what was there: what Blue Mountain, what empty views, what lavender hillside, what old cellar holes, what unlikely animals. I was filled with poacher's lust, except I wanted only to smell the air. The linked web restraining me began to grate, and I started to look for weak spots, holes, places where the rough wire sagged. From the moment I began to see the fence as permeable, it became something to overcome. I returned time after time—partly to see if I could spot anyone on the other side, partly because I knew I must trespass.

31   Then, one clear, midwinter morning, in the middle of a half-hearted thaw, I walked along the fence until I came to a place that looked shaky—and was. I went through. There were no trails that I could see, and I knew I needed to stay away from any perimeter roads or snowmobile paths, as well as from the feeding stations where the animals congregated. I wanted to see the animals, but only from a distance. Of course, as I walked on, leaving a trail easily backtracked, I encountered no animals at all. Still, the terrain was beautiful, the columns of pine tall and satisfyingly heavy, the patches of oak and elderly maple from an occasional farmstead knotted and patient. I was satisfied, and sometime in the early afternoon, I decided to turn back and head toward the fence again. Skirting a low, boggy area that teemed with wild turkey tracks, heading toward the edge of a deadfall

of trashed dead branches and brush, I stared too hard into the sun, and stumbled.

In a half crouch, I looked straight into the face of a boar, massive 32
as a boulder. Cornfed, razor-tusked, alert, sensitive ears pricked, it edged slightly backward into the convening shadows. Two ice picks of light gleamed from its shrouded, tiny eyes, impossible to read. Beyond the rock of its shoulder, I saw more: a sow and three cinnamon-brown farrows crossing a small field of glare snow, lit by dazzling sun. The young skittered along, lumps of muscled fat on tiny hooves. They reminded me of snowsuited toddlers on new skates. When they were out of sight the boar melted through the brush after them, leaving not a snapped twig or crushed leaf in his wake.

I almost didn't breathe in the silence, letting the fact of that pres 33
ence settle before I retraced my own tracks.

Since then, I've been to the game park via front gates, driven 34
down the avenues of tough old trees, and seen herds of wild pigs and elk meandering past the residence of the gamekeeper. A no-hunting zone exists around the house, where the animals are almost tame. But I've been told by privileged hunters that just beyond that invisible boundary they vanish, becoming suddenly and preternaturally elusive.

There is something in me that resists the notion of fair use of 35
this land if the only alternative is to have it cut up, sold off in lots, condominiumized. Yet the dumb fervor of the place depresses me— the wilderness locked up and managed but not for its sake; the animals imported and cultivated to give pleasure through their deaths. All animals, that is, except for skunks.

Not worth hunting, inedible except to old trappers like my uncle 36
Ben Gourneau, who boiled his skunk with onions in three changes of water, skunks pass in and out of Corbin's Park without hindrance, without concern. They live off the corn in the feeding cribs (or the mice it draws), off the garbage of my rural neighbors, off bugs and frogs and grubs. They nudge their way onto our back porch for catfood, and even when disturbed they do not, ever, hurry. It's easy to get near a skunk, even to capture one. When skunks become a nuisance, people either shoot them or catch them in crates, cardboard boxes, Havahart traps, plastic garbage barrels.

Natives of the upper Connecticut River valley have neatly solved 37
the problem of what to do with such catches. They hoist their trapped mustelid into the back of a pickup truck and cart the animal across the river to the neighboring state—New Hampshire to Vermont, Vermont to New Hampshire—before releasing it. The skunk population is estimated as about even on both sides.

We should take comfort from the skunk, an arrogant creature so 38
pleased with its own devices that it never runs from harm, just turns its back in total confidence. If I were an animal, I'd choose to be a skunk: live fearlessly, eat anything, gestate my young in just two

months, and fall into a state of dreaming torpor when the cold bit hard. Wherever I went, I'd leave my sloppy tracks. I wouldn't walk so much as putter, destinationless, in a serene belligerence—past hunters, past death overhead, past death all around.

———— CONSIDERATIONS ————————————————

1. In paragraph 6, Erdrich makes the interesting and startling statement, "I understand . . . the fact that I am the world's only mechanism that can admire itself." However, two questions arise as one ponders the sentence: (a) How does she know? and (b) Doesn't she contradict herself later in the essay?

2. Why does Erdrich use the French word "faux" instead of the English word "fake" to describe her fur, in paragraph 10?

3. What brought on what Erdrich describes in paragraph 18 as "horizon sickness"?

4. In her closing paragraphs Erdrich returns us to the skunk that in paragraph 1, "walked onto me with simple authority." Where have we been in the meantime?

5. There are moments of wonderment, even moments of terror in Erdrich's unusual essay. Can you find her sense of humor at work as well?

6. When do you realize that Erdrich's dream of the fence came true, and how does she account for that fact?

Louise Erdrich's two books of poems are Jacklight *(1984) and* Baptism of Desire *(1989), from which we take "Owls."*

28

LOUISE ERDRICH
Owls

The barred owls scream in the black pines,
searching for mates. Each night
the noise wakes me, a death
rattle, everything in sex that wounds.
There is nothing in the sound but raw need   5
of one feathered body for another.
Yet, even when they find one another,
there is no peace.

In Ojibwa, the owl is Kokoko, and not
even the smallest child loves the gentle sound   10
of the word. Because the hairball
of bones and vole teeth can be hidden
under snow, to kill the man who walks over it.
Because the owl looks behind itself to see you coming,
the vane of the feather does not disturb   15
air, and the barb is ominously soft.

Have you ever seen, at dusk,
an owl take flight from the throat of a dead tree?
Mist, troubled spirit.
You will notice only after   20
its great silver body has turned to bark.
The flight was soundless.

That is how we make love,
when there are people in the halls around us,
clashing dishes, filling their mouths   25

with air, with debris, pulling
switches and filters as the whole machinery
of life goes on, eliminating and eliminating
until there are just the two bodies
30   fiercely attached, the feathers
floating down and cleaving to their shapes.

Louise Erdrich's novels began with Love Medicine
*(1984), which won the National Book Award. She followed
it with* Beet Queen *(1986),* Tracks *(1988), and* Bingo Palace
*(1994). With her husband Michael Dorris, she collaborated
on a novel called* The Crown of Columbus *in 1992. She
published this short story in* Harper's *in 1990.*

29

LOUISE ERDRICH
The Leap

My mother is the surviving half of a blindfold trapeze act, not a
fact I think about much even now that she is sightless, the result of
encroaching and stubborn cataracts. She walks slowly through her
house here in New Hampshire, lightly touching her way along walls
and running her hands over knickknacks, books, the drift of a grown
child's belongings and castoffs. She has never upset an object or as
much as brushed a magazine onto the floor. She has never lost her balance or bumped into a closet door left carelessly open.

It has occurred to me that the catlike precision of her movements in old age might be the result of her early training, but she
shows so little of the drama or flair one might expect from a performer
that I tend to forget the Flying Avalons. She has kept no sequined cos-
tume, no photographs, no fliers or posters from that part of her youth.
I would, in fact, tend to think that all memory of double somersaults
and heart-stopping catches had left her arms and legs were it not for
the fact that sometimes, as I sit sewing in the room of the rebuilt
house in which I slept as a child, I hear the crackle, catch a whiff of
smoke from the stove downstairs, and suddenly the room goes dark,
the stitches burn beneath my fingers, and I am sewing with a needle of
hot silver, a thread of fire.

I owe her my existence three times. The first was when she saved
herself. In the town square a replica tent pole, cracked and splintered,
now stands cast in concrete. It commemorates the disaster that put

our town smack on the front page of the Boston and New York tabloids. It is from those old newspapers, now historical records, that I get my information. Not from my mother, Anna of the Flying Avalons, nor from any of her in-laws, nor certainly from the other half of her particular act, Harold Avalon, her first husband. In one news account it says, "The day was mildly overcast, but nothing in the air or temperature gave any hint of the sudden force with which the deadly gale would strike."

4   I have lived in the West, where you can see the weather coming for miles, and it is true that out here we are at something of a disadvantage. When extremes of temperature collide, a hot and cold front, winds generate instantaneously behind a hill and crash upon you without warning. That, I think, was the likely situation on that day in June. People probably commented on the pleasant air, grateful that no hot sun beat upon the striped tent that stretched over the entire center green. They bought their tickets and surrendered them in anticipation. They sat. They ate caramelized popcorn and roasted peanuts. There was time, before the storm, for three acts. The White Arabians of Ali-Khazar rose on their hind legs and waltzed. The Mysterious Bernie folded himself into a painted cracker tin, and the Lady of the Mists made herself appear and disappear in surprising places. As the clouds gathered outside, unnoticed, the ringmaster cracked his whip, shouted his introduction, and pointed to the ceiling of the tent, where the Flying Avalons were perched.

5   They loved to drop gracefully from nowhere, like two sparkling birds, and blow kisses as they threw off their plumed helmets and high-collared capes. They laughed and flirted openly as they beat their way up again on the trapeze bars. In the final vignette of their act, they actually would kiss in midair, pausing, almost hovering as they swooped past one another. On the ground, between bows, Harry Avalon would skip quickly to the front rows and point out the smear of my mother's lipstick, just off the edge of his mouth. They made a romantic pair all right, especially in the blindfold sequence.

6   That afternoon, as the anticipation increased, as Mr. and Mrs. Avalon tied sparkling strips of cloth onto each other's face and as they puckered their lips in mock kisses, lips destined "never again to meet," as one long breathless article put it, the wind rose, miles off, wrapped itself into a cone, and howled. There came a rumble of electrical energy, drowned out by the sudden roll of drums. One detail not mentioned by the press, perhaps unknown—Anna was pregnant at the time, seven months and hardly showing, her stomach muscles were that strong. It seems incredible that she would work high above the ground when any fall could be so dangerous, but the explanation—I know from watching her go blind—is that my mother lives comfortably in extreme elements. She is one with the constant dark now, just

as the air was her home, familiar to her, safe, before the storm that afternoon.

From opposite ends of the tent they waved, blind and smiling, to 7 the crowd below. The ringmaster removed his hat and called for silence, so that the two above could concentrate. They rubbed their hands in chalky powder, then Harry launched himself and swung, once, twice, in huge calibrated beats across space. He hung from his knees and on the third swing stretched wide his arms, held his hands out to receive his pregnant wife as she dove from her shining bar.

It was while the two were in midair, their hands about to meet, 8 that lightning struck the main pole and sizzled down the guy wires, filling the air with a blue radiance that Harry Avalon must certainly have seen through the cloth of his blindfold as the tent buckled and the edifice toppled him forward, the swing continuing and not returning in its sweep, and Harry going down, down into the crowd with his last thought, perhaps, just a prickle of surprise at his empty hands.

My mother once said that I'd be amazed at how many things a 9 person can do within the act of falling. Perhaps, at the time, she was teaching me to dive off a board at the town pool, for I associate the idea with midair somersaults. But I also think she meant that even in that awful doomed second one could think, for she certainly did. When her hands did not meet her husband's, my mother tore her blindfold away. As he swept past her on the wrong side, she could have grasped his ankle, the toe-end of his tights, and gone down clutching him. Instead, she changed direction. Her body twisted toward a heavy wire and she managed to hang on to the braided metal, still hot from the lightning strike. Her palms were burned so terribly that once healed they bore no lines, only the blank scar tissue of a quieter future. She was lowered, gently, to the sawdust ring just underneath the dome of the canvas roof, which did not entirely settle but was held up on one end and jabbed through, torn, and still on fire in places from the giant spark, though rain and men's jackets soon put that out.

Three people died, but except for her hands my mother was not 10 seriously harmed until an overeager rescuer broke her arm in extricating her and also, in the process, collapsed a portion of the tent bearing a huge buckle that knocked her unconscious. She was taken to the town hospital, and there she must have hemorrhaged, for they kept her, confined to her bed, a month and a half before her baby was born without life.

Harry Avalon had wanted to be buried in the circus cemetery 11 next to the original Avalon, his uncle, so she sent him back with his brothers. The child, however, is buried around the corner, beyond this house and just down the highway. Sometimes I used to walk there just to sit. She was a girl, but I rarely thought of her as a sister or even as a separate person really. I suppose you could call it the egocentrism of a child, of all young children, but I considered her a less finished version of myself.

12   When the snow falls, throwing shadows among the stones, I can easily pick hers out from the road, for it is bigger than the others and in the shape of a lamb at rest, its legs curled beneath. The carved lamb looms larger as the years pass, though it is probably only my eyes, the vision shifting, as what is close to me blurs and distances sharpen. In odd moments, I think it is the edge drawing near, the edge of every-thing, the unseen horizon we do not really speak of in the eastern woods. And it also seems to me, although this is probably an idle fan-tasy, that the statue is growing more sharply etched, as if, instead of weathering itself into a porous mass, it is hardening on the hillside with each snowfall, perfecting itself.

13   It was during her confinement in the hospital that my mother met my father. He was called in to look at the set of her arm, which was complicated. He stayed, sitting at her bedside, for he was some-thing of an armchair traveler and had spent his war quietly, at an air force training grounds, where he became a specialist in arms and legs broken during parachute training exercises. Anna Avalon had been to many of the places he longed to visit—Venice, Rome, Mexico, all through France and Spain. She had no family of her own and was taken in by the Avalons, trained to perform from a very young age. They toured Europe before the war, then based themselves in New York. She was illiterate.

14   It was in the hospital that she finally learned to read and write, as a way of overcoming the boredom and depression of those weeks, and it was my father who insisted on teaching her. In return for stories of her adventures, he graded her first exercises. He bought her her first book, and over her bold letters, which the pale guides of the penman-ship pads could not contain, they fell in love.

15   I wonder if my father calculated the exchange he offered: one form of flight for another. For after that, and for as long as I can re-member, my mother has never been without a book. Until now, that is, and it remains the greatest difficulty of her blindness. Since my fa-ther's recent death, there is no one to read to her, which is why I re-turned, in fact, from my failed life where the land is flat. I came home to read to my mother, to read out loud, to read long into the dark if I must, to read all night.

16   Once my father and mother married, they moved onto the old farm he had inherited but didn't care much for. Though he'd been thinking of moving to a larger city, he settled down and broadened his practice in this valley. It still seems odd to me, when they could have gone anywhere else, that they chose to stay in the town where the dis-aster had occurred, and which my father in the first place had found so

constricting. It was my mother who insisted upon it, after her child did not survive. And then, too, she loved the sagging farmhouse with its scrap of what was left of a vast acreage of woods and hidden hay fields that stretched to the game park.

I owe my existence, the second time then, to the two of them 17 and the hospital that brought them together. That is the debt we take for granted since none of us asks for life. It is only once we have it that we hang on so dearly.

I was seven the year the house caught fire, probably from stand- 18 ing ash. It can rekindle, and my father, forgetful around the house and perpetually exhausted from night hours on call, often emptied what he thought were ashes from cold stoves into wooden or cardboard containers. The fire could have started from a flaming box, or perhaps a buildup of creosote inside the chimney was the culprit. It started right around the stove, and the heart of the house was gutted. The baby-sitter, fallen asleep in my father's den on the first floor, woke to find the stairway to my upstairs room cut off by flames. She used the phone, then ran outside to stand beneath my window.

When my parents arrived, the town volunteers had drawn water 19 from the fire pond and were spraying the outside of the house, preparing to go inside after me, not knowing at the time that there was only one staircase and that it was lost. On the other side of the house, the superannuated extension ladder broke in half. Perhaps the clatter of it falling against the walls woke me, for I'd been asleep up to that point.

As soon as I awakened, in the small room that I now use for 20 sewing, I smelled the smoke. I followed things by the letter then, was good at memorizing instructions, and so I did exactly what was taught in the second-grade home fire drill. I got up, I touched the back of my door before opening it. Finding it hot, I left it closed and stuffed my rolled-up rug beneath the crack. I did not hide under my bed or crawl into my closet. I put on my flannel robe, and then I sat down to wait.

Outside, my mother stood below my dark window and saw 21 clearly that there was no rescue. Flames had pierced one side wall, and the glare of the fire lighted the massive limbs and trunk of the vigorous old elm that had probably been planted the year the house was built, a hundred years ago at least. No leaf touched the wall, and just one thin branch scraped the roof. From below, it looked as though even a squirrel would have had trouble jumping from the tree onto the house, for the breadth of that small branch was no bigger than my mother's wrist.

Standing there, beside Father, who was preparing to rush back 22 around to the front of the house, my mother asked him to unzip her dress. When he wouldn't be bothered, she made him understand. He couldn't make his hands work, so she finally tore it off and stood there in her pearls and stockings. She directed one of the men to lean the broken half of the extension ladder up against the trunk of the tree. In surprise, he complied. She ascended. She vanished. Then she could be seen among the leafless branches of late November as she made her way up and, along her stomach, inched the length of a bough that curved above the branch that brushed the roof.

23   Once there, swaying, she stood and balanced. There were plenty of people in the crowd and many who still remember, or think they do, my mother's leap through the ice-dark air toward that thinnest extension, and how she broke the branch falling so that it cracked in her hands, cracked louder than the flames as she vaulted with it toward the edge of the roof, and how it hurtled down end over end without her, and their eyes went up, again, to see where she had flown.

24   I didn't see her leap through air, only heard the sudden thump and looked out my window. She was hanging by the backs of her heels from the new gutter we had put in that year, and she was smiling. I was not surprised to see her, she was so matter-of-fact. She tapped on the window. I remember how she did it, too. It was the friendliest tap, a bit tentative, as if she was afraid she had arrived too early at a friend's house. Then she gestured at the latch, and when I opened the window she told me to raise it wider and prop it up with the stick so it wouldn't crush her fingers. She swung down, caught the ledge, and crawled through the opening. Once she was in my room, I realized she had on only underclothing, a bra of the heavy stitched cotton women used to wear and step-in, lace-trimmed drawers. I remember feeling light-headed, of course, terribly relieved, and then embarrassed for her to be seen by the crowd undressed.

25   I was still embarrassed as we flew out the window, toward earth, me in her lap, her toes pointed as we skimmed toward the painted target of the fire fighter's net.

26   I know that she's right. I knew it even then. As you fall there is time to think. Curled as I was, against her stomach, I was not startled by the cries of the crowd or the looming faces. The wind roared and beat its hot breath at our back, the flames whistled. I slowly wondered what would happen if we missed the circle or bounced out of it. Then I wrapped my hands around my mother's hands. I felt the brush of her lips and heard the beat of her heart in my ears, loud as thunder, long as the roll of drums.

_____ CONSIDERATIONS _____

1. "I owe her my existence three times" writes Erdrich's narrator, but unless you read with some care, one or two of those times may escape you. Identify the paragraphs that signal the three times her mother saved her.

2. Find a couple of ironic incidents in the story, and explain why irony is such a useful tool for a writer.

3. What is there in our introduction to the speaker's mother that suggests she might laugh at the people described in the first paragraph of Donald Hall's "Keeping Things" (page 237)?

4. "I wonder if my father calculated the exchange he offered: one form of flight for another." (paragraph 15). Explain.

5. In an otherwise realistically written story, "The Leap" contains one sentence that could only be called fantastic—or, possibly, surreal. Find that sentence and explain its significance.

6. How much time is covered by the story?

7. Sometimes writers cannot resist burying a story yet to be told in the one they're telling us at the moment. Does that occur in "The Leap"?

William Faulkner (1897–1962) was a great novelist, born in Mississippi, who supported himself much of his life by writing screenplays and short fiction for magazines. He received the Nobel Prize for Literature in 1950. Among his novels are The Sound and the Fury *(1929),* As I Lay Dying *(1930),* Light in August *(1932), and a comic series:* The Hamlet *(1940),* The Town *(1957), and* The Mansion *(1960).* "A Rose for Emily" *is an expert piece of magazine fiction: remarkably, it also makes an emblem for the disease and decease of a society.*

30

WILLIAM FAULKNER
A Rose for Emily

I

1   When Miss Emily Grierson died, our whole town went to her funeral: the men through a sort of respectful affection for a fallen monument, the women mostly out of curiosity to see the inside of her house, which no one save an old manservant—a combined gardener and cook—had seen in at least ten years.

2   It was a big, squarish frame house that had once been white, decorated with cupolas and spires and scrolled balconies in the heavily lightsome style of the seventies, set on what had once been our most select street. But garages and cotton gins had encroached and obliterated even the august names of that neighborhood; only Miss Emily's house was left, lifting its stubborn and coquettish decay above the cotton wagons and the gasoline pumps—an eyesore among eyesores. And now Miss Emily had gone to join the representatives of those august

names where they lay in the cedar-bemused cemetery among the ranked and anonymous graves of Union and Confederate soldiers who fell at the battle of Jefferson.

Alive, Miss Emily had been a tradition, a duty, and a care; a sort   3
of hereditary obligation upon the town, dating from that day in 1894 when Colonel Sartoris, the mayor—he who fathered the edict that no Negro woman should appear on the streets without an apron—remitted her taxes, the dispensation dating from the death of her father on into perpetuity. Not that Miss Emily would have accepted charity. Colonel Sartoris invented an involved tale to the effect that Miss Emily's father had loaned money to the town, which the town, as a matter of business, preferred this way of repaying. Only a man of Colonel Sartoris' generation and thought could have invented it, and only a woman could have believed it.

When the next generation, with its more modern ideas, became   4
mayors and aldermen, this arrangement created some little dissatisfaction. On the first of the year they mailed her a tax notice. February came, and there was no reply. They wrote her a formal letter, asking her to call at the sheriff's office at her convenience. A week later the mayor wrote her himself, offering to call or to send his car for her, and received in reply a note on paper of an archaic shape, in a thin, flowing calligraphy in faded ink, to the effect that she no longer went out at all. The tax notice was also enclosed, without comment.

They called a special meeting of the Board of Aldermen. A depu-   5
tation waited upon her, knocked at the door through which no visitor had passed since she ceased giving china-painting lessons eight or ten years earlier. They were admitted by the old Negro into a dim hall from which a staircase mounted into still more shadow. It smelled of dust and disuse—a close, dank smell. The Negro led them into the parlor. It was furnished in heavy, leather-covered furniture. When the Negro opened the blinds of one window, a faint dust rose sluggishly about their thighs, spinning with slow motes in the single sun-ray. On a tarnished gilt easel before the fireplace stood a crayon portrait of Miss Emily's father.

They rose when she entered—a small, fat woman in black, with a   6
thin gold chain descending to her waist and vanishing into her belt, leaning on an ebony cane with a tarnished gold head. Her skeleton was small and spare; perhaps that was why what would have been merely plumpness in another was obesity in her. She looked bloated, like a body long submerged in motionless water, and of that pallid hue. Her eyes, lost in the fatty ridges of her face, looked like two small pieces of coal pressed into a lump of dough as they moved from one face to another while the visitors stated their errand.

She did not ask them to sit. She just stood in the door and lis-   7
tened quietly until the spokesman came to a stumbling halt. Then

they could hear the invisible watch ticking at the end of the gold chain.

8   Her voice was dry and cold. "I have no taxes in Jefferson. Colonel Sartoris explained it to me. Perhaps one of you can gain access to the city records and satisfy yourselves."

9   "But we have. We are the city authorities, Miss Emily. Didn't you get a notice from the sheriff, signed by him?"

10   "I received a paper, yes," Miss Emily said. "Perhaps he considers himself the sheriff. . . . I have no taxes in Jefferson."

11   "But there is nothing on the books to show that, you see. We must go by the—"

12   "See Colonel Sartoris. I have no taxes in Jefferson."

13   "But, Miss Emily—"

14   "See Colonel Sartoris." (Colonel Sartoris had been dead almost ten years.) "I have no taxes in Jefferson. Tobe!" The Negro appeared. "Show these gentlemen out."

II

15   So she vanquished them, horse and foot, just as she had vanquished their fathers thirty years before about the smell. That was two years after her father's death and a short time after her sweetheart—the one we believed would marry her—had deserted her. After her father's death she went out very little; after her sweetheart went away, people hardly saw her at all. A few of the ladies had the temerity to call, but were not received, and the only sign of life about the place was the Negro man—a young man then—going in and out with a market basket.

16   "Just as if a man—any man—could keep a kitchen properly," the ladies said, so they were not surprised when the smell developed. It was another link between the gross, teeming world and the high and mighty Griersons.

17   A neighbor, a woman, complained to the mayor, Judge Stevens, eighty years old.

18   "But what will you have me do about it, madam?" he said.

19   "Why, send her word to stop it," the woman said. "Isn't there a law?"

20   "I'm sure that won't be necessary," Judge Stevens said. "It's probably just a snake or a rat that nigger of hers killed in the yard. I'll speak to him about it."

21   The next day he received two more complaints, one from a man who came in diffident deprecation. "We really must do something about it, Judge. I'd be the last one in the world to bother Miss Emily, but we've got to do something." That night the Board of Aldermen

met—three graybeards and one younger man, a member of the rising generation.

"It's simple enough," he said. "Send her word to have her place 22
cleaned up. Give her a certain time to do it in, and if she don't . . . "

"Dammit, sir," Judge Stevens said, "will you accuse a lady to her 23
face of smelling bad?"

So the next night, after midnight, four men crossed Miss Emily's 24
lawn and slunk about the house like burglars, sniffing along the base
of the brickwork and at the cellar openings while one of them performed a regular sowing motion with his hand out of a sack slung
from his shoulder. They broke open the cellar door and sprinkled lime
there, and in all the outbuildings. As they recrossed the lawn, a window that had been dark was lighted and Miss Emily sat in it, the light
behind her, and her upright torso motionless as that of an idol. They
crept quietly across the lawn and into the shadow of the locusts that
lined the street. After a week or two the smell went away.

That was when people had begun to feel sorry for her. People in 25
our town remembering how old lady Wyatt, her great-aunt, had gone
completely crazy at last, believed that the Griersons held themselves a
little too high for what they really were. None of the young men were
quite good enough for Miss Emily and such. We had long thought of
them as a tableau: Miss Emily a slender figure in white in the background, her father a spraddled silhouette in the foreground, his back to
her and clutching a horsewhip, the two of them framed by the back-
flung front door. So when she got to be thirty and was still single, we
were not pleased exactly, but vindicated; even with insanity in the
family she wouldn't have turned down all of her chances if they had
really materialized.

When her father died, it got about that the house was all that was 26
left to her; and in a way, people were glad. At last they could pity Miss
Emily. Being left alone, and a pauper, she had become humanized.
Now she too would know the old thrill and the old despair of a penny
more or less.

The day after his death all the ladies prepared to call at the house 27
and offer condolence and aid, as is our custom. Miss Emily met them
at the door, dressed as usual and with no trace of grief on her face. She
told them that her father was not dead. She did that for three days,
with the ministers calling on her, and the doctors trying to persuade
her to let them dispose of the body. Just as they were about to resort to
law and force, she broke down, and they buried her father quickly.

We did not say she was crazy then. We believed she had to do 28
that. We remembered all the young men her father had driven away,
and we knew that with nothing left, she would have to cling to that
which had robbed her, as people will.

III

29   She was sick for a long time. When we saw her again, her hair was cut short, making her look like a girl, with a vague resemblance to those angels in colored church windows—sort of tragic and serene.

30   The town had just let the contracts for paving the sidewalks, and in the summer after her father's death they began to work. The construction company came with niggers and mules and machinery, and a foreman named Homer Barron, a Yankee—a big, dark, ready man, with a big voice and eyes lighter than his face. The little boys would follow in groups to hear him cuss the niggers, and the niggers singing in time to the rise and fall of pricks. Pretty soon he knew everybody in town. Whenever you heard a lot of laughing anywhere about the square, Homer Barron would be in the center of the group. Presently we began to see him and Miss Emily on Sunday afternoons driving in the yellow-wheeled buggy and the matched team of bays from the livery stable.

31   At first we were glad that Miss Emily would have an interest, because the ladies all said, "Of course a Grierson would not think seriously of a Northerner, a day laborer." But there were still others, older people, who said that even grief could not cause a real lady to forget *noblesse oblige*—without calling it *noblesse oblige*. They just said, "Poor Emily. Her kinsfolk should come to her." She had some kin in Alabama; but years ago her father had fallen out with them over the estate of old lady Wyatt, the crazy woman, and there was no communication between the two families. They had not even been represented at the funeral.

32   And as soon as the old people said, "Poor Emily," the whispering began. "Do you suppose it's really so?" they said to one another. "Of course it is. What else could . . ." This behind their hands; rustling of craned silk and satin behind jalousies closed upon the sun of Sunday afternoon as the thin, swift clop-clop-clop of the matched team passed: "Poor Emily."

33   She carried her head high enough—even when we believed that she was fallen. It was as if she demanded more than ever the recognition of her dignity as the last Grierson; as if it had wanted that touch of earthliness to reaffirm her imperviousness. Like when she bought the rat poison, the arsenic. That was over a year after they had begun to say "Poor Emily," and while the two female cousins were visiting her.

34   "I want some poison," she said to the druggist. She was over thirty then, still a slight woman, though thinner than usual, with cold, haughty black eyes in a face the flesh of which was strained across the temples and about the eyesockets as you imagine a lighthouse-keeper's face ought to look. "I want some poison," she said.

"Yes, Miss Emily. What kind? For rats and such? I'd recom—" 35

"I want the best you have. I don't care what kind." 36

The druggist named several. "They'll kill anything up to an ele- 37
phant. But what you want is—"

"Arsenic," Miss Emily said. "Is that a good one?" 38

"Is . . . arsenic? Yes ma'am. But what you want—" 39

"I want arsenic." 40

The druggist looked down at her. She looked back at him, erect, 41
her face like a strained flag. "Why, of course," the druggist said. "If
that's what you want. But the law requires you to tell what you are going to use it for."

Miss Emily just stared at him, her head tilted back in order to 42
look him eye for eye, until he looked away and went and got the arsenic and wrapped it up. The Negro delivery boy brought her the package; the druggist didn't come back. When she opened the package at
home there was written on the box, under the skull and bones: "For
rats."

IV

So the next day we all said, "She will kill herself"; and we said it 43
would be the best thing. When she had first begun to be seen with
Homer Barron, we had said, "She will marry him." Then we said, "She
will persuade him yet," because Homer himself had remarked—he
liked men, and it was known that he drank with the younger men in
the Elk's Club—that he was not a marrying man. Later we said, "Poor
Emily," behind the jalousies as they passed on Sunday afternoon in
the glittering buggy, Miss Emily with her head high and Homer Barron
with his hat cocked and a cigar in his teeth, reins and whip in a yellow
glove.

Then some of the ladies began to say that it was a disgrace to the 44
town and a bad example to the young people. The men did not want to
interfere, but at last the ladies forced the Baptist minister—Miss
Emily's people were Episcopal—to call upon her. He would never di-
vulge what happened during that interview, but he refused to go back
again. The next Sunday they again drove about the streets and the following day the minister's wife wrote to Miss Emily's relations in
Alabama.

So she had blood-kin under her roof again and we sat back to 45
watch developments. At first nothing happened. Then we were sure
that they had to be married. We learned that Miss Emily had been to
the jeweler's and ordered a man's toilet set in silver, with the letters
H.B. on each piece. Two days later we learned that she had bought a
complete outfit of men's clothing, including a nightshirt, and we said

"They are married." We were really glad. We were glad because the two female cousins were even more Grierson than Miss Emily had ever been.

46   So we were surprised when Homer Barron—the streets had been finished some time since—was gone. We were a little disappointed that there was not a public blowing-off, but we believed that he had gone on to prepare for Miss Emily's coming, or to give a chance to get rid of the cousins. (By that time it was a cabal, and we were all Miss Emily's allies to help circumvent the cousins.) Sure enough, after another week they departed. And, as we had expected all along, within three days Homer Barron was back in town. A neighbor saw the Negro man admit him at the kitchen door at dusk one evening.

47   And that was the last we saw of Homer Barron. And of Miss Emily for some time. The Negro man went in and out with the market basket, but the front door remained closed. Now and then we would see her at a window for a moment, as the men did that night when they sprinkled the lime, but for almost six months she did not appear on the streets. Then we knew that this was to be expected too; as if that quality of her father which had thwarted her woman's life so many times had been too virulent and too furious to die.

48   When we next saw Miss Emily, she had grown fat and her hair was turning gray. During the next few years it grew grayer and grayer until it attained an even pepper-and-salt iron-gray, when it ceased turning. Up to the day of her death at seventy-four it was still that vigorous iron-gray, like the hair of an active man.

49   From that time on her front door remained closed, save for a period of six or seven years, when she was about forty, during which she gave lessons in china-painting. She fitted up a studio in one of the downstairs rooms, where the daughters and granddaughters of Colonel Sartoris' contemporaries were sent to her with the same regularity and in the same spirit that they were sent on Sundays with a twenty-five cent piece for the collection plate. Meanwhile her taxes had been remitted.

50   Then the newer generation became the backbone and the spirit of the town, and the painting pupils grew up and fell away and did not send their children to her with boxes of color and tedious brushes and pictures cut from the ladies' magazines. The front door closed upon the last one and remained closed for good. When the town got free postal delivery Miss Emily alone refused to let them fasten the metal numbers above her door and attach a mailbox to it. She would not listen to them.

51   Daily, monthly, yearly we watched the Negro grow grayer and more stooped, going in and out with the market basket. Each December we sent her a tax notice, which would be returned by the post office a week later, unclaimed. Now and then we would see her in one of

the downstairs windows—she had evidently shut up the top floor of the house—like the carven torso of an idol in a niche, looking or not looking at us, we could never tell which. Thus she passed from generation to generation—dear, inescapable, impervious, tranquil, and perverse.

And so she died. Fell ill in the house filled with dust and shadows, with only a doddering Negro man to wait on her. We did not even know she was sick; we had long since given up trying to get any information from the Negro. He talked to no one, probably not even to her, for his voice had grown harsh and rusty, as if from disuse. 52

She died in one of the downstairs rooms, in a heavy walnut bed with a curtain, her gray head propped on a pillow yellow and moldy with age and lack of sunlight. 53

V

The Negro met the first of the ladies at the front door and let them in, with their hushed, sibilant voices and their quick, curious glances, and then he disappeared. He walked right through the house and out the back and was not seen again. 54

The two female cousins came at once. They held the funeral on the second day, with the town coming to look at Miss Emily beneath a mass of bought flowers, with the crayon face of her father musing profoundly above the bier and the ladies sibilant and macabre; and the very old men—some in their brushed Confederate uniforms—on the porch and the lawn, talking of Miss Emily as if she had been a contemporary of theirs, believing that they had danced with her and courted her perhaps, confusing time with its mathematical progression, as the old do, to whom all the past is not a diminishing road, but, instead, a huge meadow which no winter ever quite touches, divided from them now by the narrow bottleneck of the most recent decade of years. 55

Already we knew that there was one room in the region above the stairs which no one had seen in forty years, and which would have to be forced. They waited until Miss Emily was decently in the ground before they opened it. 56

The violence of breaking down the door seemed to fill this room with pervading dust. A thin, acrid pall as of the tomb seemed to lie everywhere upon this room decked and furnished as for a bridal: upon the valance curtains of faded rose color, upon the rose-shaded lights, upon the dressing table, upon the delicate array of crystal and the man's toilet things backed with tarnished silver, silver so tarnished that the monogram was obscured. Among them lay a collar and tie, as if they had just been removed, which, lifted, left upon the surface a pale crescent in the dust. Upon a chair hung the suit, carefully folded; beneath it the two mute shoes and the discarded socks. 57

58   The man himself lay in the bed.

59   For a long while we just stood there, looking down at the profound and fleshless grin. The body had apparently once lain in the attitude of an embrace, but now the long sleep that outlasts love, that conquers even the grimace of love, had cuckolded him. What was left of him, rotted beneath what was left of the nightshirt, had become inextricable from the bed in which he lay; and upon him and upon the pillow beside him lay that even coating of the patient and biding dust.

60   Then we noticed that in the second pillow was the indentation of a head. One of us lifted something from it, and leaning forward, that faint and invisible dust dry and acrid in the nostrils, we saw a long strand of iron-gray hair.

____ CONSIDERATIONS ____

1. The art of narration, some say, is the successful management of a significant sequence of actions through time. But "through time" does not necessarily imply chronological order. Identify the major events of Faulkner's story according to when they actually happened, then arrange them in the order in which they are given by the author. Try the same technique with "A Worn Path" by Eudora Welty.

2. Faulkner uses the terms "Negro" and "nigger" to refer to nonwhite persons in the story. Does he intend distinction between the two words? If he were writing the story today, instead of in 1930, might he substitute the word "black"? Why? Can you think of parallel terms used to designate other minority peoples, say, Jews, Catholics, Italians, or Japanese? Of what significance is the variety of such terms?

3. In what ways, if any, is Emily Grierson presented as a sympathetic character? Why?

4. In part III, Faulkner puts considerable emphasis on the phrase *noblesse oblige*. Look up the meaning of that phrase, then comment on the author's use of it.

5. Who is the "we" in the story? Does "we" play any significant part?

6. Obviously death is a significant element in this story. Could Faulkner also have had in mind the death of a particular society or a way of life? Discuss Faulkner's use of symbolism, using examples from the story.

7. While the events of Faulkner's story span a considerable period of time, they fall roughly halfway between the accounts of Frederick Douglass (1845) and Shelby Steele (1988). Looking through the eyes of these three writers, what changes do you see in attitudes toward African Americans over the 143 years?

Richard Feynman (1918–1988) has been called the most brilliant theoretical physicist of his generation. He helped to develop the atomic bomb, and in 1965 shared the Nobel Prize for Physics. For most of his adult life he taught at the California Institute of Technology. Along with his many scientific books and papers, he wrote an autobiography— Surely You're Joking, Mr. Feynman *(1985)—which was a best-seller, followed by* What Do You Care What Other People Think? *(1988), from which we take this excerpt.* Genius, *a biography of Richard Feynman by James Glieck, appeared in 1992.*

31

RICHARD FEYNMAN
It's as Simple as One, Two, Three . . .

When I was a kid growing up in Far Rockaway, I had a friend 1
named Bernie Walker. We both had "labs" at home, and we would do
various "experiments." One time, we were discussing something—we
must have been eleven or twelve at the time—and I said, "But thinking is nothing but talking to yourself inside."

"Oh yeah?" Bernie said. "Do you know the crazy shape of the 2
crankshaft in a car?"

"Yeah, what of it?" 3

"Good. Now, tell me: how did you describe it when you were 4
talking to yourself?"

So I learned from Bernie thoughts can be visual as well as verbal. 5

Later on, in college, I became interested in dreams. I wondered 6
how things could look so real, just as if light were hitting the retina of

the eye, while the eyes are closed: are the nerve cells on the retina actually being stimulated in some other way—by the brain itself, perhaps—or does the brain have a "judgment department" that gets slopped up during dreaming? I never got satisfactory answers to such questions from psychology, even though I became very interested in how the brain works. Instead, there was all this business about interpreting dreams, and so on.

7　　When I was in graduate school at Princeton a kind of dumb psychology paper came out that stirred up a lot of discussion. The author had decided that the thing controlling the "time sense" in the brain is the chemical reaction involving iron. I thought to myself. "Now, how the hell could he figure that?"

8　　Well, the way he did it was, his wife had a chronic fever which went up and down a lot. Somehow he got the idea to test her sense of time. He had her count seconds to herself (without looking at a clock), and checked how long it took her to count up to 60. He had her counting—the poor woman—all during the day: when her fever went up, he found she counted quicker: when her fever went down, she counted slower. Therefore, he thought, the thing that governed the "time sense" in the brain must be running faster when she's got fever than when she hasn't got fever.

9　　Being a very "scientific" guy, the psychologist knew that the rate of a chemical reaction varies with the surrounding temperature by a certain formula that depends on the energy of the reaction. He measured the differences in speed of his wife's counting, and determined how much the temperature changed the speed. Then he tried to find a chemical reaction whose rates varied with temperature in the same amounts as his wife's counting did. He found that iron reactions fit the pattern best. So he deduced that his wife's sense of time was governed by a chemical reaction in her body involving iron.

10　　Well, it all seemed like a lot of baloney to me—there were so many things that could go wrong in his long chain of reasoning. But it *was* an interesting question: what *does* determine the "time sense"? When you're trying to count at an even rate, what does that rate depend on? And what could you do to yourself to change it?

11　　I decided to investigate. I started by counting seconds—without looking at a clock, of course—up to 60 in a slow, steady rhythm: 1, 2, 3, 4, 5. . . . When I got to 60, only 48 seconds had gone by, but that didn't bother me: the problem was not to count for exactly one minute, but to count at a standard rate. The next time I counted to 60, 49 seconds had passed. The next time, 48. Then 47, 48, 49, 48, 48. . . . So I found I could count at a pretty standard rate.

12　　Now, if I just sat there, without counting, and waited until I thought a minute had gone by, it was very irregular—complete variations. So I found it's very poor to estimate a minute by sheer guessing. But by counting, I could get very accurate.

Now that I knew I could count at a standard rate, the next ques-   13
tion was—what affects the rate?

Maybe it has something to do with the heart rate. So I began to   14
run up and down the stairs, up and down, to get my heart beating fast.
Then I'd run into my room, throw myself down on the bed, and count
up to 60.

I also tried running up and down the stairs and counting to my-   15
self *while* I was running up and down.

The other guys saw me running up and down the stairs, and   16
laughed. "What are you doing?"

I couldn't answer them—which made me realize I couldn't talk   17
while I was counting to myself—and kept right on running up and
down the stairs, looking like an idiot.

(The guys at the graduate college were used to me looking like an   18
idiot. On another occasion, for example, a guy came into my room—I
had forgotten to lock the door during the "experiment"—and found
me in a chair wearing my heavy sheepskin coat, leaning out of the
wide-open window in the dead of winter, holding a pot in one hand
and stirring with the other. "Don't bother me! Don't bother me!" I
said. I was stirring Jell-O and watching it closely: I had gotten curious
as to whether Jell-O would coagulate in the cold if you kept it moving
all the time.)

Anyway, after trying every combination of running up and down   19
the stairs and lying on the bed, surprise! The heart rate had no effect.
And since I got very hot running up and down the stairs, I figured temperature had nothing to do with it either (although I must have known
that your temperature doesn't really go up when you exercise). In fact,
I couldn't find anything that affected my rate of counting.

Running up and down stairs got pretty boring, so I started count-   20
ing while I did things I had to do anyway. For instance, when I put out
the laundry, I had to fill out a form saying how many shirts I had, how
many pants, and so on. I found I could write down "3" in front of
"pants" or "4" in front of "shirts," but I couldn't count my socks.
There were too many of them: I'm already using my "counting machine"—36, 37, 38—and here are all these socks in front of me—39,
40, 41. . . . How do I count the socks?

I found I could arrange them in geometrical patterns—like a   21
square, for example: a pair of socks in this corner, a pair in that one: a
pair over here, and a pair over there—eight socks.

I continued this game of counting by patterns, and found I could   22
count the lines in a newspaper article by grouping the lines into patterns of 3, 3, 3, and 1 to get 10; then 3 of those patterns, 3 of those patterns, 3 of those patterns, and 1 of those patterns made 100. I went
right down the newspaper like that. After I had finished counting up
to 60, I knew where I was in the patterns and could say, "I'm up to 60,
and there are 113 lines." I found that I could even *read* the articles

while I counted to 60, and it didn't affect the rate! In fact, I could do anything while counting to myself—except talk out loud, of course.

23   What about typing—copying words out of a book? I found that I could do that, too, but here my time was affected. I was excited: finally, I've found something that appears to affect my counting rate! I investigated it more.

24   I would go along, typing the simple words rather fast, counting to myself 19, 20, 21, typing along, counting 27, 28, 29, typing along, until—What the hell is that word?—Oh, yeah—and then continue counting 30, 31, 32, and so on. When I'd get to 60, I'd be late.

25   After some introspection and further observation, I realized what must have happened: I would interrupt my counting when I got to a difficult word that "needed more brains," so to speak. My counting rate wasn't slowing down, rather, the counting itself was being held up temporarily from time to time. Counting to 60 had become so automatic that I didn't even notice the interruptions at first.

26   The next morning, over breakfast, I reported the results of all these experiments to the other guys at the table. I told them all the things I could do while counting to myself, and said the only thing I absolutely could not do while counting to myself was talk.

27   One of the guys, a fella named John Tukey, said, "I don't believe you can read, and I don't see why you can't talk. I'll bet you I can talk while counting to myself, and I'll bet you you can't read."

28   So I gave a demonstration: they gave me a book and I read it for a while, counting to myself. When I reached 60 I said, "Now!"—48 seconds, my regular time. Then I told them what I had read.

29   Tukey was amazed. After we checked him a few times to see what his regular time was, he started talking: "Mary had a little lamb; I can say anything I want to, it doesn't make any difference; I don't know what's bothering you"—blah, blah, blah, and finally, "Okay!" He hit his time right on the nose! I couldn't believe it!

30   We talked about it a while, and we discovered something. It turned out that Tukey was counting in a different way: he was visualizing a tape with numbers on it going by. He would say, "Mary had a little lamb," and he would *watch* it! Well, now it was clear: he's "looking" at this tape going by, so he can't read, and I'm "talking" to myself when I'm counting, so I can't speak!

31   After that discovery, I tried to figure out a way of reading out loud while counting—something neither of us could do. I figured I'd have to use a part of my brain that wouldn't interfere with the seeing or speaking departments, so I decided to use my fingers, since that involved the sense of touch.

32   I soon succeeded in counting with my fingers and reading out loud. But I wanted the whole process to be mental, and not rely on any physical activity. So I tried to imagine the feeling of my fingers moving while I was reading out loud.

I never succeeded. I figured that was because I hadn't practiced   33
enough, but it might be impossible: I've never met anybody who can
do it.

By that experience Tukey and I discovered that what goes on in   34
different people's heads when they *think* they're doing the same
thing—something as simple as *counting*—is different for different people. And we discovered that you can externally and objectively test
how the brain works: you don't have to ask a person how he counts
and rely on his own observations of himself; instead, you observe
what he can and can't do while he counts. The test is absolute.
There's no way to beat it: no way to fake it.

It's natural to explain an idea in terms of what you already have   35
in your head. Concepts are piled on top of each other: this idea is
taught in terms of that idea, and that idea is taught in terms of another
idea, which comes from counting, which can be so different for different people!

I often think about that, especially when I'm teaching some eso-   36
teric technique such as integrating Bessel functions. When I see equa-
tions, I see the letters in colors—I don't know why. As I'm talking, I
see vague pictures of Bessel functions from Jahnke and Emde's book,
with light-tan *j*'s, slightly violet-bluish *n*'s, and dark brown *x*'s flying
around. And I wonder what the hell it must look like to the students.

____ CONSIDERATIONS _____

1. What surprises you most about Feynman's style?

2. Feynman uses his own experiments at different ages to encourage
others to respect their curiosity, no matter how odd it might seem to someone
else. Which of his experiments would make the best material for a cartoonist?
Why?

3. Feynman, Sven Birkerts, and Molly Ivins write in extremely informal
ways. List a few examples of what you mean by "informal" in each. Do their
essays sound alike? Why?

4. "It's natural," writes Feynman, "to explain an idea in terms of what
you already have in your head." How might his statement apply to your work
as a student?

5. Devise your own experiment along the lines of Feynman's in order to
test some idea you question. Notice how he begins, in paragraph 10, by calling
the idea "baloney," but then moves on to try different ways of actually testing
it. Report your findings.

Robert Finch (b. 1943) was born in New Jersey beside the Passaic River, which he has called "one of the ten dirtiest rivers in America." He settled on Cape Cod full time in 1972, where he has been director of publications for the Cape Cod Museum of Natural History. He has written Common Ground: A Naturalist's Cape Cod *(1981),* The Primal Place *(1983), and* Outlands *(1986). In 1990 he edited* The Norton Book of Nature Writing. *In 1993 the National Park Service issued Finch's official handbook,* Cape Cod: Its Natural and Cultural History. *In the same year he edited a Cape Cod reader called* A Place Apart. *The essays in* Common Ground, *from which we take "Very Like a Whale," first appeared as weekly columns syndicated in four Cape Cod newspapers.*

32

ROBERT FINCH
Very Like a Whale

1   One day last week at sunset I went back to Corporation Beach in Dennis to see what traces, if any, might be left of the great, dead finback whale that had washed up there several weeks before. The beach was not as hospitable as it had been that sunny Saturday morning after Thanksgiving when thousands of us streamed over the sand to gaze and look. A few cars were parked in the lot, but these kept their inhabitants. Bundled up against a sharp wind, I set off along the twelve-foot swath of trampled beach grass, a raw highway made in a few hours by ten thousand feet that day.

2   I came to the spot where the whale had beached and marveled that such a magnitude of flesh could have been there one day and gone the next. But the carcass had been hauled off and the tide had smoothed and licked clean whatever vestiges had remained. The cold,

salt wind had lifted from the sands the last trace of that pervasive stench of decay that clung to our clothes for days, and now blew clean and sharp into my nostrils.

The only sign that anything unusual had been there was that the   3
beach was a little too clean, not quite so pebbly and littered as the surrounding areas, as the grass above a new grave is always fresher and greener. What had so manifestly occupied this space a short while ago was now utterly gone. And yet the whale still lay heavily on my mind; a question lingered, like a persistent odor in the air. And its dark shape, though now sunken somewhere beneath the waves, still loomed before me, beckoning, asking something.

What was it? What had we seen? Even the several thousand of us   4
that managed to get down to the beach before it was closed off did not see much. Whales, dead or alive, are protected these days under the Federal Marine Mammals Act, and shortly after we arrived, local police kept anyone from actually touching the whale. I could hardly regret this, since in the past beached whales, still alive, have had cigarettes put out in their eyes and bits of flesh hacked off with pocket knives by souvenir seekers. And so, kept at a distance, we looked on while the specialists worked, white-coated, plastic-gloved autopsists from the New England Aquarium, hacking open the thick hide with carving knives and plumbing its depth for samples to be shipped to Canada for analysis and determination of causes of death. What was it they were pulling out? What fetid mystery would they pluck from that huge coffin of dead flesh? We would have to trust them for the answer.

But as the crowds continued to grow around the whale's body   5
like flies around carrion, the question seemed to me, and still seems, not so much why did the whale die, but why had we come to see it? What made this dark bulk such a human magnet, spilling us over onto private lawns and fields? I watched electricians and oil truck drivers pulling their vehicles off the road and clambering down to the beach. Women in high heels and pearls, on their way to Filene's, stumbled through the loose sand to gaze at a corpse. The normal human pattern was broken and a carnival atmosphere was created, appropriate enough in the literal sense of "a farewell to the flesh." But there was also a sense of pilgrimage in those trekking across the beach, an obligation to view such a thing. But for what? Are we really such novices to death? Or so reverent toward it?

I could understand my own semiprofessional interest in the   6
whale, but what had drawn these hordes? There are some obvious answers, of course: a break in the dull routine, "something different." An old human desire to associate ourselves with great and extraordinary events. We placed children and sweethearts in front of the corpse and clicked cameras. "Ruthie and the whale." "Having a whale of a time on Cape Cod."

7   Curiosity, the simplest answer, doesn't really answer anything. What, after all, did we learn by being there? We were more like children at a zoo, pointing and poking, or Indians on a pristine beach, gazing in innocent wonder at strange European ships come ashore. Yet, as the biologists looted it with vials and plastic bags and the press captured it on film, the spectators also tried to *make* something of the whale. Circling around it as though for some hold on its slippery bulk, we grappled it with metaphors, lashed similes around its immense girth. It lay upside down, overturned "like a trailer truck." Its black skin was cracked and peeling, red underneath, "like a used tire." The distended, corrugated lower jaw, "a giant accordion," was afloat with the gas of putrefaction and, when pushed, oscillated slowly "like an enormous waterbed." Like our primitive ancestors, we still tend to make images to try to comprehend the unknown.

8   But what were we looking at? Or more to the point, from what perspective were we looking at it? What did we see in it that might tell us why we had come? A male finback whale—*Balaenoptera physalus*—a baleen cetacean. The second largest creature ever to live on earth. An intelligent and complex mammal. A cause for conservationists. A remarkably adapted swimming and eating machine. Perfume, pet food, engineering oil. A magnificent scientific specimen. A tourist attraction. A media event, a "day to remember." A health menace, a "possible carrier of a communicable disease." A municipal headache and a navigational hazard. Material for an essay.

9   On the whale's own hide seemed to be written its life history, which we could remark but not read. The right fluke was almost entirely gone, lost in some distant accident or battle and now healed over with a white scar. The red eye, unexpectedly small and mammalian, gazed out at us with fiery blankness. Like the glacial scratches sometimes found on our boulders, there were strange marks or grooves in the skin around the anal area, perhaps caused by scraping the ocean bottom.

10   Yet we could not seem to scratch its surface. The whale—dead, immobile, in full view—nonetheless shifted kaleidoscopically before our eyes. The following morning it was gone, efficiently and sanitarily removed, like the week's garbage. What was it we saw? I have a theory, though probably (as they say in New England) it hardly does.

11   There is a tendency these days to defend whales and other endangered animals by pointing out their similarities to human beings. Cetaceans, we are told, are very intelligent. They possess a highly complex language and have developed sophisticated communications systems that transmit over long distances. They form family groups, develop social structures and personal relationships, and express loyalty and affection toward one another. Much of their behavior seems to be recreational: they sing, they play. And so on.

These are not sentimental claims. Whales apparently do these 12
things, at least as far as our sketchy information about their habits
warrants such interpretations. And for my money, any argument that
helps to preserve these magnificent creatures can't be all bad.

I take exception to this approach not because it is wrong, but be- 13
cause it is wrongheaded and misleading. It is exclusive, anthropocentric, and does not recognize nature in its own right. It implies that
whales and other creatures have value only insofar as they reflect man
himself and conform to his ideas of beauty and achievement. This attitude is not really far removed from that of the whalers themselves. To
consume whales solely for their nourishment of human values is only a
step from consuming them for meat and corset staves. It is not only pre-
sumptuous and patronizing, but it is misleading and does both whales
and men a grave disservice. Whales have an inalienable right to exist,
not because they resemble man *or* because they are useful to him, but
simply because they do exist, because they have a proven fitness to the
exactitudes of being on a global scale matched by few other species. If
they deserve our admiration and respect, it is because, as Henry Beston
put it, "They are other nations, caught with ourselves in the net of life
and time, fellow prisoners of the splendour and travail of life."

But that still doesn't explain the throngs who came pell-mell to 14
stare and conjecture at the dead whale that washed up at Corporation
Beach and dominated it for a day like some extravagant *memento
mori.* Surely we were not flattering ourselves, consciously or unconsciously, with any human comparisons to that rotting hulk. Nor was
there much, in its degenerate state, that it had to teach us. And yet we
came—why?

The answer may be so obvious that we have ceased to recognize 15
it. Man, I believe, has a crying need to confront otherness in the universe. Call it nature, wilderness, the "great outdoors," or what you
will—we crave to look out and behold something other than our own
human faces staring back at us, expectantly and increasingly frustrated. What the human spirit wants, as Robert Frost said, "Is not its
own love back in copy-speech,/ But counter-love, original response."

This sense of otherness is, I feel, as necessary a requirement to 16
our personalities as food and warmth are to our bodies. Just as an individual, cut off from human contact and stimulation, may atrophy and
die of loneliness and neglect, so mankind is today in a similar, though
more subtle, danger of cutting himself off from the natural world he
shares with all creatures. If our physical survival depends upon our devising a proper use of earth's materials and produce, our growth as a
species depends equally upon our establishing a vital and generative
relationship with what surrounds us.

We need plants, animals, weather, unfettered shores and unbro- 17
ken woodland, not merely for a stable and healthy environment, but

as an antidote to introversion, a preventive against human inbreeding. Here in particular, in the splendor of natural life, we have an extraordinary reservoir of the Cape's untapped possibilities and modes of being, ways of experiencing life, of knowing wind and wave. After all, how many neighborhoods have whales wash up in their backyards? To confine this world in zoos or in exclusive human terms does injustice not only to nature, but to ourselves as well.

18   Ever since his beginnings, when primitive man adopted totems and animal spirits to himself and assumed their shapes in ritual dance, *Homo sapiens* has been a superbly imitative animal. He has looked out across the fields and seen and learned. Somewhere along the line, though, he decided that nature was his enemy, not his ally, and needed to be confined and controlled. He abstracted nature and lost sight of it. Only now are we slowly realizing that nature can be confined only by narrowing our own concepts of it, which in turn narrows us. That is why we came to see the whale.

19   We substitute human myth for natural reality and wonder why we starve for nourishment. "Your Cape" becomes "your Mall," as the local radio jingle has it. Thoreau's "huge and real Cape Cod . . . a wild, rank place with no flattery in it," becomes the Chamber of Commerce's "Rural Seaside Charm"—until forty tons of dead flesh wash ashore and give the lie to such thin, flattering conceptions, flesh whose stench is still the stench of life that stirs us to reaction and response. That is why we came to see the whale. Its mute, immobile bulk represented that ultimate, unknowable otherness that we both seek and recoil from, and shouted at us louder than the policeman's bullhorn that the universe is fraught, not merely with response or indifference, but incarnate assertion.

20   Later that day the Dennis Board of Health declared the whale carcass to be a "health menace" and warned us off the beach. A health menace? More likely an intoxicating, if strong, medicine that might literally bring us to our senses.

21   But if those of us in the crowd failed to grasp the whale that day, others did not have much better luck. Even in death the whale escaped us: the tissue samples taken in the autopsy proved insufficient for analysis and the biologists concluded, "We will never know why the whale died." The carcass, being towed tail-first by a Coast Guard cutter for a final dumping beyond Provincetown, snapped a six-inch hawser. Eluding further attempts to reattach it, it finally sank from sight. Even our powers of disposal, it seemed, were questioned that day.

22   And so, while we are left on shore with the memory of a deflated and stinking carcass and of bullhorns that blared and scattered us like flies, somewhere out beyond the rolled waters and the shining winter sun, the whale sings its own death in matchless, sirenian strains.

_____ **CONSIDERATIONS** _____

1. A feature of Finch's style in "Very Like a Whale" is his skillful use of figurative language. In paragraph 3, for example, h_ compares the cleaned-up beach to "grass above a new grave," and his question to the whale that "still lay heavily on my mind." Other examples are the question that "lingered like a persistent odor," and the dark shape of the whale, long gone beneath the waves, that "still loomed" before him. Locate and underline a dozen more figures of speech in the essay. Decide whether they are merely decorative or significantly functional in the essay.

2. Does Finch's title sound familiar, but you just can't place it? Look up the phrase in _Familiar Quotations_ by John Bartlett. Does it take on a new meaning when used as the title of this essay? How much thought do you give to the titles of your own essays?

3. Where does Finch first set forth the thesis of his essay? What responsibility does a thesis expressed as a question place on the writer? Does Finch meet that responsibility?

4. With the exception of the first three lines, what is the conspicuous grammatical form used in paragraph 8? Try changing each of the items in the series to a more conventional form. Can you now justify Finch's style in this paragraph?

5. Why does Finch object to a common approach by people concerned about preserving "nature"? See paragraph 13. Would he, for instance, find George Orwell's response to the death of an elephant (see "Shooting an Elephant") "sentimental," "exclusive," or "anthropocentric"?

6. What is the significance of the next to last word of Finch's essay?

*M. F. K. Fisher (1908–1992) was author of more than a
dozen books of fiction, reminiscence, and essays about
cooking.* How to Cook a Wolf *(1942) was her best-known
title. Born in Michigan, she grew up in California—* Among
Friends *(1970) is her memoir of childhood in Whittier—
and lived most of her life in France and California. She
was the first writer about food to be elected to the
American Academy of Arts and Letters.*

33

M. F. K. FISHER
One Way to Give Thanks

1   There could not be a better place for Thanksgiving than the vineyards of northern California, where we were. There could not, in
truth, be more to give thanks for: two of the sisters and their families
living within calling distance over the bright leaves of the plucked
frost-nipped vines, in the valley rimmed with blue mountains, and another sister not more than a hundred miles away. All of us were
friendly to the point of open enjoyment, a good rare thing in a family
and especially to be savored at this turn-point of the year.

2   Norah would have us all at her house for the solemn, giddy festival. Anne would bring the wines. I would, I said, roast two birds of
proper age and size.

3   Norah would set out the long table, which with help from lend-
ings could stretch from the middle of the farmhouse kitchen through
the big folding doors into the living room, with my red-checked table-
cloths, her glasses, a general assemblage of plates and silver. Anne
would assemble, too, a colossal pile of greenery for the salad, and keep
it mixed, in batches as needed: all the children are part rabbit. I would
make Elsa's Orange Torte, for a light, delicately dry dessert with
coffee.

4   We would meet at midday, all the friends. . . .

I found that a mind of rebellion teased me, about the turkeys. It 5
was because of the peculiarly poignant setting in the wine valley with
all of us there: I did not want to do what any fool could do time and
again, as I had often done, with oysters and dry bread and sage. I
wanted to roast our dainty birds as they would never have been
roasted before, and still keep them simple and succulent enough for
the children, those perceptive creatures of unsullied palate, innocent
of nicotine and alcohol and God knows what other decadent titilla-
tors. I wanted to produce something that they would smile on, and
their parents, too.

Then, as I knew I would, I got out Sheila Hibben's *Kitchen Man-* 6
ual, which remains for me the simplest and most sensible essay ever
written in good English on the proper behavior when faced with a fish,
fowl, or cut-off-the-joint. (It is the only cookery book I own which I've
marked and added to, and from which clippings spew out.)

Stuck in at page forty-seven, where Mrs. Hibben gets off to a fine 7
start on the subject of roast chicken by taking a ladylike poke at Bril-
lat-Savarin, was a chipped yellowing sheet from an Iowan collection of
"The Ladies' Guild's Best," which had fairly brutal directions for the
Thanksgiving rites (dated 1879): ". . . place in hot oven, but not too hot
at first until flour dredgings blacken; look in often and you will be able
to tell if your fire is too brisk or too slow."

There was a column torn from a supermarket throwaway, which 8
gave some good tips on tempering deep-freeze birds to the local winds.
One of the best ones, from frozen turkeys or those caught on the hoof,
was to let the roasted beauty "set" for half an hour or so before carving it.

Then there was a colored card about trussing a bird, which I 9
think I cut from a dime-store set of skewers I once bought. I have since
located the same excellent directions in several good cookbooks, but it
is nice to know, in my own private filing system, just where they are
for *me*: pasted in the back of Mrs. Hibben's *Manual*. I always follow
them as if they were new to me, armed with needles, skewers, twine,
scissors. . . .

Then there was a Christmas card printed years ago by Ward 10
Ritchie, with a Landacre woodcut on it . . . "How to Cook a Turkey,"
by Morton Thompson. The method is as odd as the text, and all of
Thompson's pseudo-real quotations from sages like Gisantius Pracep-
tus and so on are not as true as his own dictum, "If you want a well-
cooked dinner the labor of preparing must be equal to the pleasure of
your enjoying."

This is my theory too, for ceremonial feasting at least, and this is 11
how I proved it, in a somewhat tedious but never-faltering pattern,
with all the children and several friends and now and then Norah and
Anne wandering about me in the kitchen, sniffing, yearning, exclaiming, doubting, commenting. . . .

12   The two birds weighed about twelve pounds each. I gave them by best attention and tweaked out even more than the usual number of feather ends, both before and after I had washed them well in cold running water and dried them gently. I swished out the insides with a cup of *vin rosé*, unnecessarily but all to the good, and salted them lightly, and laid them away in a cool, airy place until the next day, to be stuffed and roasted.

13   The stuffing, or dressing as you may call it, depending on how and by whom you were raised, is enough for these two trim little birds or one big one, and would as far as I know be as good in a goose, if you are of the stuffed-goose school. It might even be good with a domestic duck. It is robust and yet light and subtle, like some Chinese dishes, and its preparation is, as Mr. Thompson and many another cook would recommend, a finicky and odorous one.

Turkey Stuffing

8 *slices lean bacon*
3 *cups chopped mild onions*
3 *cups chopped celery stalks and*
   tops
1/2 *orange and* 1/2 *lemon, finely*
   chopped (skins and all)
1 *large green pepper, chopped*
Livers, hearts, and so on of the
   bird(s), coarsely chopped
1/2 *cup butter*
8 *cups cooked rice*

1 *cup slivered blanched almonds*
   or whole pine nuts
1 *cup chopped fresh parsley or 2*
   tablespoons dried
1 *teaspoon dried marjoram*
   (optional)
2 *pounds cooked cleaned, peeled*
   shrimp (or prawns)
1/2 *teaspoon cayenne pepper*
Butter and cream
Salt, pepper to taste

14   Sauté the bacon, drain on paper, and crumble. Sauté the onion in the bacon fat until golden. Pour off the excess fat into another skillet. Add the celery to the onions, and sauté gently. Add the orange and lemon and the green pepper, return the bacon to the mixture, and set aside.

15   Sauté the chopped livers and so on in the butter, and add to the mixture.

16   How much raw rice will make 8 cups of cooked rice depends on whether it is polished, brown, precooked, and so on, but no matter what kind you use, it is best browned slightly in the bacon fat left from the first step, and then cooked in the Italian style, with adequate chicken stock or water in a tightly covered pan, until done and fluffy. Then add the nuts and parsley and (if you wish) the marjoram to it, toss all together lightly, and combine in the same manner with the same mixture.

17   Cover the fresh or frozen shrimps (or prawns) deeply with cold water, add the cayenne pepper, bring to a quick boil, and let cool in

the water. Peel and clean, and cut into bite-size pieces. Sauté until golden in adequate butter, and add to the mixture.

Toss all together very lightly, and let stand for a few hours, or 18 overnight in a cool place.

Allowing plenty of time before the roasting should begin, pack 19 the stuffing lightly into the bird(s), adding some melted butter or cream if it seems too dry. Correct seasoning to taste, using salt and freshly ground pepper if wished. Truss with string and skewers, according to custom and common sense, and rub all the skin well with soft butter. Then weigh it, and put it in a 300-degree oven, counting between ten and twelve minutes for each pound.

It should be basted every ten or fifteen minutes, with its own 20 juices and a warm mixture of one part butter, one part good olive oil, and one part sherry or vermouth. (Very sweet vermouth adds to the fine glaze. . . .)

And that was the basic formula, a kind of distillation of what a 21 dozen cooks had hinted to me in their pages, and what I myself was hoping for. I went on from there, realizing my limitations and accepting my blessings. I found that in my electric oven I did not need to cover the birds with butter-soaked cloths as I would have done in a gas oven, especially if they had been older. I found that my somewhat inexpert trussing presented several little holes where I could squirt the juices from my glass baster. I found that every time I opened the oven several people wanted to look, so I added fifteen minutes to the cooking time.

I did the two birds separately, because of my small stove and be- 22 cause of the general enjoyment of the slow, demanding ritual. The children would drift in and out, from the vineyards or the redwood trees, to watch the ceremony and to breathe the smells, which grew by the minute into a kind of cloud of herb and orange peel and turkeyness. They leaned forward and then away, stunned and tempted, and the dance went on.

We took the birds up to Norah's in the back of the station wagon, 23 past the blazing vines, and there was the long table, three different patchy shapes under the stretch of red and white cloths and three different heights, but with chairs all around it for us the diners, so varied too in shapes and heights and even purposes. One thing we all did know: we wanted to sit down together and eat and drink.

We had sipped Wente Brothers Dry Semillon all morning, slowly 24 and peacefully. Gnats fell into it whenever we stepped outside the two little farmhouses we moved between: the vineyards and indeed the whole valley still gave off a winey, rotting perfume of discarded grapeskins and forgotten raisins.

Inside Norah's place the children prepared and then presented 25 some sort of pageant about Pilgrims and Indians sitting down together to a feast of corn pudding and baked pumpkins and firewater. Anne patted the ten thousand leaves of a series of "tossed green salads" and stirred a large bowl of dressing made firm but mild for the young palates. On the sideboard Norah put the Danish coffee mugs, the dark rum for them as wished it, and the handsome torte dusted with white sugar.

26   Down the table marched breadbaskets, and ripe grapes on their flat bright leaves, and the wine bottles, a noble motley for the various tastes, but all from the valley where we stayed so thankfully: Charles Krug and Louis Martini had made the whites, and Inglenook, Beaulieu, and Krug again the reds; and there were pitchers of milk for the children. . . .

27   The birds were noble and enough, thus bolstered. Their juices followed the course of the knife, as Mrs. Hibben had said they would, and the meat fell away like waves before a fine ship's bow. All down the table the people held up their plates as fast as the server could carve again, and their eyes shone, and they reached happily for bread, salad, wine, milk, the silver bowl of cranberry sauce in honor of the Pilgrims, and a stone jar of ancient jelly, which one of us three sisters had brought dutifully from our childhood home.

28   I sat near the carver. I was hot and weary and exalted. I looked down the long gay table, into the living room from the kitchen and past the hearth and out through the big window toward the mountains. The grapes were harvested. The vines were starting, brilliantly, a short beneficent sleep, and in here in the warm cluttered rich room were my sisters and those they loved and those I did too. It was a good moment in life.

29   Everything was fine, and so was the dressing. It was light, tantalizing, essentially Oriental. And before we ever tasted it, through the long exercise of our sense while it was prepared and while it fumed slowly in the dainty birds, we all as one (and that is an important fine thing to happen at least a couple of times in anybody's life), we all as one bowed our heads in thanksgiving. It was part of the pageant that none of us had rehearsed. . . .

_____ CONSIDERATIONS _____

1. Fisher's essay is an example of a type of exposition—the process or how-to-do-it piece. How does it differ from the conventional attempt of that type, say, "How to Clean a Carburetor," or "Four Steps Toward a Successful Neighborhood Street Dance"?

2. What, if anything, does Fisher gain by spending so much time (paragraphs 6–10) flipping through her favorite cookbook?

3. In paragraph 13, Fisher gives us a choice of words—"The stuffing, or dressing as you may call it. . . ." What does your family call it? What other words do you know that vary from family to family or region to region? Of what significance are these variations to writers?

4. Who is the "Mr. Thompson" mentioned in paragraph 13? And how do you know?

5. Considering the deep feelings of satisfaction that Fisher expresses in her essay, especially in the last three paragraphs, how does she avoid sentimentalizing the event?

Robert Frost (1874–1963) was born in California and became the great poet of New England. He published many books of poetry and won the Pulitzer Prize three times. A popular figure, Frost was admired as a gentle, affectionate, avuncular figure given to country sayings. The private Frost, however, was another man—guilty, jealous, bitter, sophisticated, occasionally triumphant, and always complicated. President Kennedy asked Robert Frost to read a poem at his inauguration in 1962. Because the sunlight dazzled his eyes, the old man could not read the poem that he had composed for the occasion, and instead recited "The Gift Outright" from memory. In the last line, thinking of the occasion, Frost changed "would" to "will." In 1995 the Library of America issued Robert Frost's work in one volume.

34

ROBERT FROST
The Gift Outright

The land was ours before we were the land's.
She was our land more than a hundred years
Before we were her people. She was ours
In Massachusetts, in Virginia,
5 But we were England's, still colonials,
Possessing what we still were unpossessed by,
Possessed by what we now no more possessed.
Something we were withholding made us weak
Until we found out that it was ourselves
10 We were withholding from our land of living,
And forthwith found salvation in surrender.
Such as we were we gave ourselves outright
(The deed of gift was many deeds of war)
To the land vaguely realizing westward,
15 But still unstoried, artless, unenhanced,
Such as she was, such as she would become.

From *The Poetry of Robert Frost* edited by Edward Connery Lathem. Copyright © 1942 by Robert Frost. Copyright © 1970 by Lesley Frost Ballantine. Copyright © 1969 by Henry Holt and Co., Inc. Reprinted by permission of Henry Holt & Co., Inc.

*Martin Gansberg (b. 1920) edited and reported for the
New York Times for forty years. This story, written in
1964, has been widely reprinted. Largely because of
Gansberg's account, the murder of Kitty Genovese has
become an infamous example of citizen apathy. When
Gansberg returned to the neighborhood fifteen years
afterward, revisiting the place of the murder with a
television crew, the people had not changed: still, no one
wanted to get involved.*

35

MARTIN GANSBERG

38 Who Saw Murder Didn't Call the Police

For more than half an hour 38 respectable, law-abiding citizens   1
in Queens watched a killer stalk and stab a woman in three separate
attacks in Kew Gardens.

Twice their chatter and the sudden glow of their bedroom lights   2
interrupted him and frightened him off. Each time he returned, sought
her out, and stabbed her again. Not one person telephoned the police
during the assault; one witness called after the woman was dead.

That was two weeks ago today.   3

Still shocked is Assistant Chief Inspector Frederick M. Lussen, in   4
charge of the borough's detectives and a veteran of 25 years of homicide investigations. He can give a matter-of-fact recitation on many
murders. But the Kew Gardens slaying baffles him—not because it is a
murder, but because the "good people" failed to call the police.

"As we have reconstructed the crime," he said, "the assailant   5
had three chances to kill this woman during a 35-minute period. He
returned twice to complete the job. If we had been called when he first
attacked, the woman might not be dead now."

6   This is what the police say happened beginning at 3:20 A.M. in the staid, middle-class, tree-lined Austin Street area:

7   Twenty-eight-year-old Catherine Genovese, who was called Kitty by almost everyone in the neighborhood, was returning home from her job as manager of a bar in Hollis. She parked her red Fiat in a lot adjacent to the Kew Gardens Long Island Rail Road Station, facing Mowbray Place. Like many residents of the neighborhood, she had parked there day after day since her arrival from Connecticut a year ago, although the railroad frowns on the practice.

8   She turned off the lights of her car, locked the door, and started to walk the 100 feet to the entrance of her apartment at 82–70 Austin Street, which is in a Tudor building, with stores in the first floor and apartments on the second.

9   The entrance to the apartment is in the rear of the building because the front is rented to retail stores. At night the quiet neighborhood is shrouded in the slumbering darkness that marks most residential areas.

10   Miss Genovese noticed a man at the far end of the lot, near a seven-story apartment house at 82–40 Austin Street. She halted. Then nervously, she headed up Austin Street towards Lefferts Boulevard, where there is a call box to the 102nd Police Precinct in nearby Richmond Hill.

11   She got as far as a street light in front of a bookstore before the man grabbed her. She screamed. Lights went on in the 10-story apartment house at 82–67 Austin Street, which faces the bookstore. Windows slid open and voices punctuated the early-morning stillness.

12   Miss Genovese screamed: "Oh, my God, he stabbed me! Please help me! Please help me!"

13   From one of the upper windows in the apartment house, a man called down: "Let that girl alone!"

14   The assailant looked up at him, shrugged and walked down Austin Street toward a white sedan parked a short distance away. Miss Genovese struggled to her feet.

15   Lights went out. The killer returned to Miss Genovese, now trying to make her way around the side of the building by her parking lot to get to her apartment. The assailant stabbed her again.

16   "I'm dying!" she shrieked. "I'm dying!"

17   Windows were opened again, and lights went on in many apartments. The assailant got into his car and drove away. Miss Genovese staggered to her feet. A city bus, O–10, the Lefferts Boulevard line to Kennedy International Airport, passed. It was 3:35 A.M.

18   The assailant returned. By then, Miss Genovese had crawled to the back of the building where the freshly painted doors to the apartment house held out hope for safety. The killer tried the first door; she wasn't there. At the second door, 82–62 Austin Street, he saw her

slumped on the floor at the foot of the stairs. He stabbed her a third time—fatally.

It was 3:50 by the time the police received their first call, from a   19
man who was a neighbor of Miss Genovese. In two minutes they were at the scene. The neighbor, a 70-year-old woman, and another woman were the only persons on the street. Nobody else came forward.

The man explained that he had called the police after much de-   20
liberation. He had phoned a friend in Nassau County for advice and then he had crossed the roof of the building to the apartment of the elderly woman to get her to make the call.

"I didn't want to get involved," he sheepishly told the police.   21

Six days later, the police arrested Winston Moseley, a 29-year-old   22
business-machine operator, and charged him with homicide. Moseley had no previous record. He is married, has two children and owns a home at 133–19 Sutter Avenue, South Ozone Park, Queens. On Wednesday, a court committed him to Kings County Hospital for psychiatric observation.

When questioned by the police, Moseley also said that he had   23
slain Mrs. Annie May Johnson, 24, of 146–12 133rd Avenue, Jamaica, on Feb. 29 and Barbara Kralik, 15, of 174–17 140th Avenue, Springfield Gardens, last July. In the Kralik case, the police are holding Alvin L. Mitchell, who is said to have confessed that slaying.

The police stressed how simple it would have been to have got-   24
ten in touch with them. "A phone call," said one of the detectives, "would have done it." The police may be reached by dialing "O" for operator or SPring 7–3100.

Today witnesses from the neighborhood, which is made up of   25
one-family homes in the $35,000 to $60,000 range with the exception of the two apartment houses near the railroad station, find it difficult to explain why they didn't call the police.

A housewife, knowingly if quite casually, said, "We thought it   26
was a lover's quarrel." A husband and wife both said, "Frankly, we were afraid." They seemed aware of the fact that events might have been different. A distraught woman, wiping her hands on her apron, said, "I didn't want my husband to get involved."

One couple, now willing to talk about that night, said they heard   27
the first screams. The husband looked thoughtfully at the bookstore where the killer first grabbed Miss Genovese.

"We went to the window to see what was happening," he said,   28
"but the light from our bedroom made it difficult to see the street." The wife, still apprehensive, added: "I put out the light and we were able to see better."

Asked why they hadn't called the police, she shrugged and   29
replied: "I don't know."

A man peeked out from a light opening in the doorway to his   30
apartment and rattled off an account of the killer's second attack. Why

hadn't he called the police at the time? "I was tired," he said without emotion. "I went back to bed."

31   It was 4:25 A.M. when the ambulance arrived to take the body of Miss Genovese. It drove off. "Then," a solemn police detective said, "the people came out."

_____ CONSIDERATIONS _____

1. Obviously—though not overtly—Gansberg's newspaper account con-demns the failure of ordinary citizens to feel socially responsible. Explain how the writer makes his purpose obvious without openly stating it. Compare his method with Orwell's use of implication in "A Hanging."

2. In paragraph 7, Gansberg tells us that Catherine Genovese was called Kitty and that she drove a red Fiat. Are these essential details? If not, why does this writer use them?

3. Newspapers use short paragraphs for visual relief. If you were making this story into a narrative essay, how might you change the paragraphing?

4. Is Gansberg's opening sentence a distortion of the facts? Read his ac-count carefully before you answer; then explain and support your answer with reference to other parts of the story.

5. Gansberg's newspaper report was published nearly thirty years ago. Are similar incidents more common now? Were they more common in the 1960s than in the 1940s or 1930s or 1920s? How about the 1970s, 1980s, and 1990s? In what way does media coverage alter our impressions? What sources could you use to find the facts?

*Stephen Jay Gould (b. 1941) is a paleontologist who teaches at Harvard and writes scientific essays for the general reader. He calls himself "an evolutionist," for Darwin and the theory of evolution live at the center of his mind. Five of his books collect periodical essays—*Ever Since Darwin *(1977),* The Panda's Thumb *(1980),* Hen's Teeth and Horse's Toes *(1983),* Bully for Brontosaurus *(1991), and* Eight Little Piggies *(1993). This criticism of textbooks comes from* Bully for Brontosaurus. *Gould's lively mind, eager to use scientific method for public thinking, seeks out diverse subjects and often discovers a political flavor in matters not usually perceived as political.*

36

STEPHEN JAY GOULD

The Case of the Creeping Fox Terrier Clone

When Asta the fox terrier exhumed the body of the Thin Man, his delightfully tipsy detective master, Nick Charles, exclaimed, "You're not a terrier; you're a police dog" (*The Thin Man*, MGM 1934 original with William Powell and Myrna Loy). May I now generalize for Asta's breed in the case of the telltale textbook.

The wisdom of our culture abounds with mottoes that instruct us to acknowledge the faults within ourselves before we criticize the failings of others. These words range from clichés about pots and kettles to various sayings of Jesus: "And why beholdest thou the mote that is in thy brother's eye, but perceivest not the beam that is in thine own eye?" (Luke 6:41); "He that is without sin among you, let him first cast a stone at her" (John 8:7). I shall follow this wisdom by exposing my own profession in trying to express what I find so desperately wrong about the basic tool of American teaching, the textbook.

3   In March 1987, I spent several hours in the exhibit hall of the National Science Teachers Association convention in Washington, D.C. There I made an informal, but reasonably complete, survey of evolution as treated (if at all) in major high-school science textbooks. I did find some evidence of adulteration, pussyfooting, and other forms of capitulation to creationist pressure. One book, *Life Science*, by L. K. Bierer, K. F. Liem, and E. P. Silberstein (Heath, 1987), in an accommodation that at least makes you laugh while you weep for lost integrity in education, qualifies every statement about the ages of fossils—usually in the most barbarous of English constructions, the passive infinitive. We discover that trilobites are "believed to have lived 500–600 million years ago," while frozen mammoths are "thought to have roamed the tundra 22,000 years ago." But of one poor bird, we learn with terrible finality, "There are no more dodoes living today." Their extinction occurred within the bounds of biblical literalism and need not be hedged.

4   But I was surprised and pleased to note that most books contained material at reasonable length about evolution, and with no explicit signs of tampering to appease creationists. Sins imposed by others were minimal. But I then found the beam in our own eye and became, if anything, more distressed than by any capitulation to the yahoos. The problem does not lie in what others are doing to us, but in what we are doing to ourselves. In book after book, the evolution section is virtually cloned. Almost all authors treat the same topics, usually in the same sequence, and often with illustrations changed only enough to avoid suits for plagiarism. Obviously, authors of textbooks are copying material on a massive scale and passing along to students an ill-considered and virtually Xeroxed version with a rationale lost in the mists of time.

5   Just two months after making this depressing observation, I read Diane B. Paul's fascinating article "The Nine Lives of Discredited Data" (*The Sciences*, May 1987). Paul analyzed the sections on heritability of IQ from twenty-eight textbooks on introductory genetics published between 1978 and 1984. She paid particular attention to their treatment of Sir Cyril Burt's data on identical twins raised separately. We now know that these "studies" represent one of the most striking cases of fraud in twentieth-century science—for Burt invented both data and coworkers. His sad story had been well publicized, and all authors of texts published since 1978 surely knew that Burt's data had been discredited and could not be used. Several texts even included discussions of the Burt scandal as a warning about caution and scrutiny in science.

But Paul then found that nearly half these books continued to   6
cite and use Burt's data, probably unconsciously. Of nineteen textbooks that devoted more than a paragraph to the subject of genetics
and IQ, eleven based their conclusions about high heritability on a review article published in *Science* in 1963. This review featured a figure that ten of these textbooks reproduced either directly or in slightly
altered and simplified form. This figure includes, as a prominent feature, the results of Sir Cyril Burt (not yet suspect in 1963). We must
conclude that the authors of these texts either had not read the 1963
article carefully or had not consulted it at all. Paul infers (correctly, I
am sure) that this carelessness arises because authors of textbooks
copy from other texts and often do not read original sources. How else
to explain the several books that discussed the Burt scandal explicitly
and then, unbeknownst to their authors, used the same discredited
data in a figure?

Paul argues that the increasing commercialization of textbooks   7
has engendered this virtual cloning of contents. Textbook publishing
is a big business, replete with market surveys, fancy art programs, and
subsidiary materials in the form of slide sets, teachers' guides, even
test-making and grading services. The actual text of the book can become secondary and standardized; and departure from a conventional
set of topics could derail an entire industry of supporting materials.
Teachers are also locked into a largely set curriculum based on this
flood of accoutrements. Paul concludes: "Today's textbooks are
thicker, slicker, more elaborate, and more expensive than they used to
be. They are also more alike. Indeed, many are virtual clones, both
stylistic and substantive, of a market leader."

The marketplace rules. Most publishing houses are now owned   8
by conglomerates—CBS, Raytheon, and Coca-Cola among them—
with managers who never raise their eyes from the financial bottom
line, know little or nothing about books, and view the publishing arm
of their diversified empire as but one more item for the ultimate balance. I received a dramatic reminder of this trend last week when I
looked at the back cover of my score for Mozart's *Coronation Mass*,
now under rehearsal in my chorus. It read: "Kalmus Score. Belwin
Mills Publishing Company, distributed by Columbia Pictures Publication, a unit of the Coca-Cola Company." I don't say that Bill Cosby or
Michael Jackson or whoever advertises the stuff doesn't like Mozart; I
merely suspect that Don Giovanni can't be high on the executive
agenda when the big boys must worry about such really important issues as whether or not to market Cherry Coke (a resounding "yes"
vote from this old New York soda fountain junkie).

Paul quotes a leading industry analyst from the 1984 *Book Pub-*   9
lishing Annual. Future textbooks, the analyst argues, will have "more

elaborate designs and greater use of color. . . . The ancillary packages will become more comprehensive. . . . New, more aggressive marketing plans will be needed just to maintain a company's position. The quality of marketing will make the difference." Do note the conspicuous absence of any mention whatsoever about the quality of the text itself.

10   Paul is obviously correct in arguing that this tendency to cloning has accelerated remarkably as concerns of the market overwhelm scholarly criteria in the composition of textbooks. But I believe that the basic tendency has always been present and has a human as well as a corporate face. Independent thought has always been more difficult than borrowing, and authors of textbooks have almost always taken the easier way out. Of course I have no objection to the similar recording of information by textbooks. No author can know all the byways of a profession, and all must therefore rely on written sources for areas not enlightened by personal expertise. I speak instead of the thoughtless, senseless, and often false copying of phrase, anecdote, style of argument, and sequence of topics that perpetuates itself by degraded repetition from text to text and thereby loses its anchor in nature.

11   I present an example that may seem tiny and peripheral in import. Nevertheless, and perhaps paradoxically, such cases provide our best evidence for thoughtless copying. When a truly important and well-known fact graces several texts in the same form, we cannot know whether it has been copied from previous sources or independently extracted from any expert's general knowledge. But when a quirky little senseless item attains the frequency of the proverbial bad penny, copying from text to text is the only reasonable interpretation. There is no other source. My method is no different from the standard technique of bibliographic scholars, who establish lineages of texts by tracing errors (particularly for documents spread by copyists before the invention of printing).

12   When textbooks choose to illustrate evolution with an example from the fossil record, they almost invariably trot out that greatest warhorse among case studies—the history of horses themselves. The standard story begins with an animal informally called *Eohippus* (the dawn horse), or more properly, *Hyracotherium*. Since evolutionary increase in size is a major component of the traditional tale, all texts report the diminutive stature of ancestral *Hyracotherium*. A few give actual estimates or measurements, but most rely upon a simile with some modern organism. For years, I have been much amused (and mildly bothered) that the great majority of texts report *Hyracotherium* as "like a fox-terrier" in size. I was jolted into action when I found myself writing the same line, and then stopped. "Wait a minute," said my inner voice, "beyond some vague memories of Asta last time I

watched a Thin Man movie, I haven't the slightest idea what a fox terrier is. I can't believe that the community of textbook authors includes only dog fanciers—so if I don't know, I'll bet most of them don't either." Clearly, the classic line has been copied from text to text. Where did it begin? What has been its history? Is the statement even correct?

My immediate spur to action came from a most welcome and unexpected source. I published a parenthetical remark about the fox terrier issue ending with a serious point: "I also wonder what the textbook tradition of endless and thoughtless copying has done to retard the spread of original ideas." 13

I have, over the years, maintained a correspondence about our favorite common subject with Roger Angell of the *New Yorker*, who is, among other things, the greatest baseball writer ever. I assumed that his letter of early April would be a scouting report for the beginning of a new season. But I found that Roger Angell is a man of even more dimensions than I had realized; he is also a fox terrier fancier. He had read my parenthetical comment and wrote, "I am filled with excitement and trepidation at the prospect of writing you a letter about science instead of baseball." 14

Angell went on to suggest a fascinating and plausible explanation for the origin of the fox terrier simile (no excuse, of course, for its later cloning). Fox terriers were bred "to dig out foxes from their burrows, when a fox had gone to earth during a traditional British hunt." Apparently, generations of fox-hunting gentlemen selected fox terriers not only for their functional role in the hunt but also under a breeder's artifice to make them look as much like horses as possible. Angell continues, "The dogs rode up on the saddle during the hunt, and it was a pretty conceit for the owner-horseman to appear to put down a little simulacrum of a horse when the pack of hounds and the pink-coated throng had arrived at an earth where the animal was to do his work." He also pointed out that fox terriers tend to develop varied patches of color on a basically white coat and that a "saddle" along the back is "considered desirable and handsome." Thus, Angell proposed his solution: "Wouldn't it seem possible that some early horse geologist, in casting about for the right size animal to fit his cliché-to-be, might have settled, quite unconsciously, on a breed of dog that fitted the specifications in looks as well as size?" 15

This interesting conjecture led me to devise the following, loosely controlled experiment. I asked David Backus, my research assistant, to record every simile for *Hyracotherium* that he could find in the secondary literature of texts and popular books during more than a century since O. C. Marsh first recognized this animal as a "dawn horse." We would then use these patterns in attempting to locate original sources for favored similes in the primary literature of vertebrate 16 paleontology. We consulted the books in my personal library as a sample, and compiled a total of eighty-six descriptions. The story turns out to be much more ascertainable and revealing than I had imagined.

17   The tradition of simile begins at the very beginning. Richard Owen, the great British anatomist and paleontologist, described the genus *Hyracotherium* in 1841. He did not recognize its relationship with horses (he considered this animal, as his chosen name implies, to be a possible relative of hyraxes, a small group of Afro-Asian mammals, the "coneys" of the Bible). In this original article, Owen likened his fossil to a hare in one passage and to something between a hog and a hyrax in another. Owen's simile plays no role in later history because other traditions of comparison had been long established before scientists realized that Owen's older discovery represented the same animal that Marsh later named *Eohippus*. (Hence, under the rules of taxonomy, Owen's inappropriate and uneuphonious name takes unfortunate precedence over Marsh's lovely *Eohippus*.)

18   The modern story begins with Marsh's description of the earliest horses in 1874. Marsh pressed "go" on the simile machine by writing, "This species was about as large as a fox." He also described the larger descendant *Miohippus* as sheeplike in size.

19   Throughout the nineteenth century all sources that we have found (eight references, including such major figures as Joseph Le Conte, Archibald Geikie, and even Marsh's bitter enemy E. D. Cope) copy Marsh's favored simile—they all describe *Eohippus* as fox-sized. We are confident that Marsh's original description is the source because most references also repeat his statement the *Miohippus* is the size of a sheep. How, then, did fox terriers replace their prey?

20   The first decade of our century ushered in a mighty Darwinian competition among three alternatives and led to the final triumph of fox terriers. By 1910, three similes were battling for survival. Marsh's original fox suffered greatly from competition, but managed to retain a share of the market at about 25 percent (five of twenty citations between 1900 and 1925 in our sample—a frequency that has been maintained ever since (see accompanying figure)). Competition came from two stiff sources, however—both from the American Museum of Natural History in New York.

21   First, in 1903, W. D. Matthew, vertebrate paleontologist at the Museum, published his famous pamphlet *The Evolution of the Horse* (it remained in print for fifty years, and was still being sold at the Museum shop when I was a child). Matthew wrote: "The earliest known ancestors of the horse were small animals not larger than the domestic cat." Several secondary sources picked up Matthew's simile during this quarter century (also five of twenty references between 1900 and 1925), but felines have since faded (only one of fifteen references since 1975), and I do not know why.

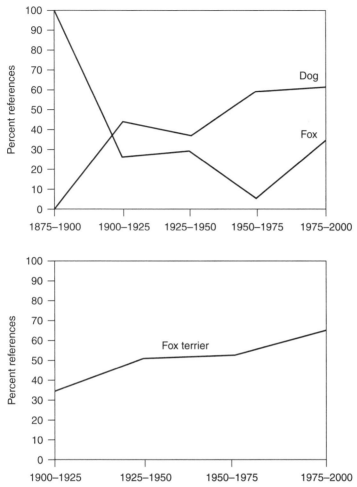

The rise to dominance of fox terriers as similes for the size of the earliest horses. Top graph: Increasing domination of dogs over foxes through time. Lower graph: Increase in percentage of fox terrier references among sources citing dogs as their simile. Graph by Iromie Weeramantry. Reprinted by permission of *Natural History* magazine.

Second, the three-way carnivorous competition of vulpine, feline, and canine began in earnest when man's best friend made his belated appearance in 1904 under the sponsorship of Matthew's boss, American Museum president and eminent vertebrate paleontologist Henry Fairfield Osborn. Remember that no nineteenth-century source (known to us) had advocated a canine simile, so Osborn's late entry suffered a temporal handicap. But Osborn was as commanding (and enigmatic) a figure as American natural history has ever produced—a powerful patrician in science and politics, imperious but kind, prolific and pompous, crusader for natural history and for other causes of opposite merit (Osborn wrote, for example, a glowing preface to the most influential tract of American scientific racism, *The Passing of the Great Race*, by his friend Madison Grant).

23   In the *Century Magazine* for November 1904, Osborn published a popular article, "The Evolution of the Horse in America." (Given Osborn's almost obsessively prolific spate of publications, we would not be surprised if we have missed an earlier citation.) His first statement about *Eohippus* introduces the comparison that would later win the competition:

> We may imagine the earliest herds of horses in the Lower Eocene (*Eohippus*, or "dawn horse" stage) as resembling a lot of small fox-terriers in size. . . . As in the terrier, the wrist (knee) was near the ground, the hand was still short, terminating in four hoofs, with a part of the fifth toe (thumb) dangling at the side.

24   Osborn provides no rationale for his choice of breeds. Perhaps he simply carried Marsh's old fox comparison unconsciously in his head and chose the dog most similar in name to the former standard. Perhaps Roger Angell's conjecture is correct. Osborn certainly came from a social set that knew about fox hunting. Moreover, as the quotation indicates, Osborn extended the similarity of *Eohippus* and fox terrier beyond mere size to other horselike attributes of this canine breed (although, in other sources, Osborn treated the whippet as even more horselike, and even mounted a whippet's skeleton for an explicit comparison with *Eohippus*). Roger Angell described his fox terrier to me: "The back is long and straight, the tail is held jauntily upward like a trotter's, the nose is elongated and equine, and the forelegs are strikingly thin and straight. In motion, the dog comes down on these forelegs in a rapid and distinctive, stiff, flashy style, and the dog appears to walk on his tiptoes—on hooves, that is."

25   In any case, we can trace the steady rise to domination of dog similes in general, and fox terriers in particular, ever since. Dogs reached nearly 50 percent of citations (nine of twenty) between 1900 and 1925, but have now risen to 60 percent (nine of fifteen) since 1975. Meanwhile, the percentage of fox terrier citations among dog similes had also climbed steadily, from one-third (three of nine) between 1900 and 1925 to one-half (eight of sixteen) between 1925 and 1975, to two-thirds (six of nine) since 1975. Osborn's simile has been victorious.

25   Copying is the only credible source for these shifts of popularity—first from experts; then from other secondary sources. Shifts in fashion cannot be recording independent insights based on observation of specimens. *Eohippus* could not, by itself, say "fox" to every nineteenth-century observer and "dog" to most twentieth-century writers. Nor can I believe that two-thirds of all dog-inclined modern

writers would independently say, "Aha, fox terrier" when contemplating the dawn horse. The breed is no longer so popular, and I suspect that most writers, like me, have only the vaguest impression about fox terriers when they copy the venerable simile.

In fact, we can trace the rise to dominance of fox terriers in our 27 references. The first post-Osborn citation that we can find (Ernest Ingersoll, *The Life of Animals*, Macmillan, 1906) credits Osborn explicitly as author of the comparison with fox terriers. Thereafter, no one cites the original, and I assume that the process of text copying text had begun.

Two processes combined to secure the domination of fox terriers. 28 First, experts began to line up behind Osborn's choice. The great vertebrate paleontologist W. B. Scott, for example, stood in loyal opposition in 1913, 1919, and 1929 when he cited both alternatives of fox and cat. But by 1937, he had switched: "*Hyracotherium* was a little animal about the size of a fox-terrier, but horse-like in all parts." Second, dogs became firmly ensconced in major textbooks. Both leading American geology textbooks of the early twentieth century (Chamberlin and Salisbury, 1909 edition, and Pirsson and Schuchert, 1924 edition) opt for canines, as does Hegner's zoology text (1912) and W. Maxwell Read's fine children's book (a mainstay of my youth) *The Earth for Sam* (1930 edition).

Fox terriers have only firmed up their position ever since. Experts 29 cite this simile, as in A. S. Romer's leading text, *Vertebrate Paleontology* (3rd edition, 1966): "'*Eohippus*' was a small form, some specimens no larger than a fox terrier." They have also entered the two leading high-school texts: (1) Otto and Towle (descendant of Moon, Mann, and Otto, the dominant text for most of the past fifty years): "This horse is called *Eohippus*. It had four toes and was about the size of a fox-terrier" (1977 edition); (2) the *Biological Sciences Curriculum Study, Blue Edition* (1968): "The fossil of a small four-toed animal about the size of a fox-terrier was found preserved in layers of rock." College texts also comply. W. T. Keeton, in his *Biological Science*, the Hertz of the profession, writes (1980 edition): "It was a small animal, only about the size of a fox-terrier." Baker and Allen's *The Study of Biology*, a strong Avis, agrees (1982 edition): "This small animal *Eohippus* was not much bigger than a fox-terrier."

You may care little for dawn horses or fox terriers and might feel 30 that I have made much of nothing in this essay. But I cite the case of the creeping fox terrier clone not for itself, but rather as a particularly clear example of a pervasive and serious disease—the debasement of our textbooks, the basic tool of written education, by endless, thoughtless copying.

My younger son started high school last month. For a biology 31 text, he is using the 4th edition of *Biology: Living Systems*, by R. F. Oram, with consultants P. J. Hummer and R. C. Smoot (Charles E.

Merrill, 1983, but listed on the title page, following our modern reality of conglomeration, as a Bell and Howell Company). I was sad and angered to find several disgraceful passages of capitulation to creationist pressure. Page one of the chapter on evolution proclaims in a blue sidebar: "The theory of evolution is the most widely accepted scientific explanation of the origin of life and changes in living things. You may wish to investigate other theories." Similar invitations are not issued for any other well-established theory. Students are not told that "most folks accept gravitation, but you might want to check out levitation" or that "most people view the earth as a sphere, but you might want to consider the possibility of a plane." When the text reaches human history, it doesn't even grant majority status to our evolutionary consensus: "Humans are indeed unique, but because they are also organisms, many scientists believe that humans have an evolutionary history."

32   Yet, as I argued at the outset, I find these compromises to outside pressure, disgraceful though they be, less serious than the internal disease of cloning from text to text. There is virtually only one chapter on evolution in all high-school biology texts, copied and degraded, then copied and degraded again. My son's book is no exception. This chapter begins with a discussion of Lamarck and the inheritance of acquired characters. It then moves to Darwin and natural selection and follows this basic contrast with a picture of a giraffe and a disquisition of Lamarckian and Darwinian explanations for long necks. A bit later, we reach industrial melanism in moths and dawn horses of you-know-what size.

33   What is the point of all this? I could understand this development if Lamarckism were a folk notion that must be dispelled before introducing Darwin, or if Lamarck were a household name. But I will lay 100 to 1 that few high-school students have ever heard of Lamarck. Why begin teaching evolution by explicating a false theory that is causing no confusion? False notions are often wonderful tools in pedagogy, but not when they are unknown, are provoking no trouble, and make the grasp of an accepted theory more difficult. I would not teach more sophisticated college students this way; I simply can't believe that this sequence works in high school. I can only conclude that someone once wrote the material this way for a reason lost in the mists of time, and that authors of textbooks have been dutifully copying "Lamarck . . . Darwin . . . giraffe necks" ever since.

34   (The giraffe necks, by the way, make even less sense. This venerable example rests upon no data at all for the superiority of Darwinian explanation. Lamarck offered no evidence for his interpretation and only introduced the case in a few lines of speculation. We have no proof that the long neck evolved by natural selection for eating leaves at the tops of acacia trees. We only prefer this explanation because it matches current orthodoxy. Giraffes do munch the topmost leaves,

and this habit obviously helps them to thrive, but who knows how or why their necks elongated? They may have lengthened for other reasons and then been fortuitously suited for acacia leaves.)

If textbook cloning represented the discovery of a true educational optimum, and its further honing and propagation, then I would not object. But all evidence—from my little story of fox terriers to the larger issue of a senseless but nearly universal sequence of Lamarck, Darwin, and giraffe necks—indicates that cloning bears an opposite and discouraging message. It is the easy way out, a substitute for thinking and striving to improve. Somehow I must believe—for it is essential to my notion of scholarship—that good teaching requires fresh thought and genuine excitement, and that rote copying can only indicate boredom and slipshod practice. A carelessly cloned work will not excite students, however pretty the pictures. As an antidote, we need only the most basic virtue of integrity—not only the usual, figurative meaning of honorable practice but the less familiar, literal definition of wholeness. We will not have great texts if authors cannot shape content but must serve a commercial master as one cog in an ultimately powerless consortium with other packagers.   35

To end with a simpler point amid all this tendentiousness and generality: Thoughtlessly cloned "eternal verities" are often false. The latest estimate I have seen for the body size of *Hyracotherium* (MacFadden, 1986), challenging previous reconstructions congenial with the standard simile of much smaller fox-terriers, cites a weight of some twenty-five kilograms, or fifty-five pounds.   36

Lassie come home!   37

───── CONSIDERATIONS ─────────────────────

1. In paragraph 3, Gould refers to "the most barbarous of English constructions, the passive infinitive." Why is he so exercised over that construction?

2. Look briefly at a writer who prefers long paragraphs—Henry Thoreau, for instance, in his "Civil Disobedience" (page 537) or Igor Stravinsky "The Dearest City" (page 510)—then at a writer on the other end of the scale, such as Sven Birkerts (page 71) or Martin Gansberg (page 213). Where would Gould fall on such a scale? Is there such a thing as a standard paragraph length?

3. Does Gould have a distinct thesis statement? If so, where does it first appear?

4. In paragraph 4, Gould uses the term "yahoos." What does it mean, and what is its source?

5. Are all of Gould's statements to be taken seriously?

6. Gould does not get down to the main example of his thesis until paragraph 11. What is the point of all the material in those preceding paragraphs?

Harvey Green (b. 1946) published The Uncertainty of
Everyday Life, *from which we take "The Radio Age," in
1992. He is professor of history at Northeastern University,
and his earlier books include* The Life of the Home: An
Intimate View of Women in Victorian America, *and* Fit for
America: Health, Fitness, Sport, and American Society
1830–1940. *He lives in New Ipswich, New Hampshire.*

37

HARVEY GREEN
The Radio Age 1915–1945

1   In the three decades preceding the end of World War II the
amount of time expended at ease and the variety of leisure activities
had expanded for millions. Innovations in the industries of play were
both enduring, such as radio and the talking cinema, and faddish and
ephemeral, such as mah-jongg. Americans of nearly all classes experienced in one way or another what has been rightly termed the "golden
age" of sport and dancing. Prohibition may have cramped the style of
some for a while, but speakeasies and other "clubs" eased that difficulty. A drink could be had with considerable speed in most cities if
the thirsty knew where to look and were stout of heart, since the quality of the hooch was often frightening. Ultimately there were enough
forms of entertainment that were cheap enough that many of them became true mass media and mass diversions, in spite of the Depression.

A Cultural Revolution

2   The most important leisure-time innovation of the era was the
radio. For Secretary of Commerce Herbert Hoover in 1921, it was "an
instrument of beauty and learning." But for others, such as Bruce
Bliven, editor of *The New Republic*, radio programming was "outrageous rubbish, both verbal and musical." Undaunted by Bliven's condemnation and perhaps encouraged by Hoover's hyperbole, the popu-

larity of radio grew rapidly. By 1924, 5 million homes nationwide had at least one set, and Americans had spent $350 million on radios and radio parts, or one-third of all the money spent on furniture. Within the first eight years of the industry's life it had become a $500 million industry with more than 500 local stations. For every 1,000 Americans in 1928, 50 radios were owned. A January 1, 1929, survey conducted for the National Broadcasting Company by Massachusetts Institute of Technology professor Daniel Starch found that one-third of all American homes owned a radio, and that 80 percent of all radio owners listened daily. In addition, he found that rural and urban listener programming preferences were virtually identical, which suggested to some optimists that radio programmers had discovered—or created—some of the unifying elements in American culture.

The severity of the Depression did not slow radio's phenomenal growth. By 1934, 60 percent of all American homes had radios, and radio listening had become Americans' favorite pastime, according to a survey conducted by the National Recreation Association, published as *The Leisure of 5,000 People*. Americans owned 43.2 percent of all the radios in the world. By 1939 the number of radios in American homes totaled 44 million, 86 percent of all households owned at least one set, and the average listener tuned in for four and one-half hours daily. There were, in addition, 6.5 million radios in automobiles. In 1940, the entire population spent 1 billion hours weekly listening to the radio, about seven times as much time as they passed at the movies.

Working-class Americans often saved money by building their own sets. After buying a germanium crystal for about $2 at a hardware or department store, the do-it-yourself radio builder only had to connect it to a wire wound in a coil, and attach the whole thing to a board. Then, after wiring a headset into the apparatus and twisting the coil until sound began to crackle, all that remained were adjustments until a comprehensible sound came through. Putting the headset in a hollow vessel created a loudspeaker of sorts.

Early Programming

Radio in the 1920s was for the most part a local affair, and it reflected the interests and talents of either urban neighborhoods or farming areas. Much of the early urban programming was nonprofit, operated by ethnic, religious, and labor groups. In 1925, 28 percent of the nation's 571 stations were owned by educational or religious groups. Many predominantly English-language stations broadcast "nationality hours" in the languages of the most powerful or most numerous ethnic groups of the cities they served. In the countryside commercial stations were at first more common, for the most part because businesses were about the only source of capital available to those who wanted to begin operating a station.

6   Commercial radio soon infiltrated all areas of the country, because broadcasting in areas in which people were highly concentrated could be very profitable. The commercial alleged to have been the first of the genre was aired on August 28, 1922. It was for real estate, and was broadcast over station WEAF in New York City. By the mid-1920s radio station managers discovered that manufacturers would pay for air time providing they could have some fraction of a fifteen-minute time slot to pitch their wares. Some advertisers at first declined to use the medium, fearing that the radio ad was too much of an intrusion into the intimacy of the parlor or bedroom. But by 1927, when the National Broadcasting Company established the first national network, the advertising business had shed its reservations. The radio was an immediate personal experience—as the cinema was not—and was for many advertisers a dream come true. One slick trick was to buy enough time to name the show after a product. The *Eveready Hour* debuted in 1926 on fourteen stations, and in the 1927–1928 season thirty-nine companies sponsored shows on NBC, while four did so on the newer Columbia Broadcasting System. The next year sixty-five sponsors bought time from the networks for a total of more than $25 million.

7   By the 1930s, tuning in the radio (which was at times a testing task requiring an attentive listener) brought Americans advertisements that were louder, more frequent, and more boisterous in their claims for products than the subdued descriptive ads of the late 1920s had been. Radio ads took up an increasing percentage of corporations' advertising budgets, and led to a corresponding drop in monies spent on advertising in other media. Between 1928 and 1934, radio ads grew 316 percent nationally, newspaper ads declined by 30 percent, and magazine ads dropped 45 percent; 246 daily newspapers ceased publication, in part a result of the Depression and in part because of their losses in advertising revenue.

8   Early commercially made radio sets were often crude, industrial-looking objects, conglomerations of dials, diodes, wires, resistors, capacitors, and speakers. At first, and until about 1927, the technology of the thing was miraculous, and the look of it was properly scientific and laboratorylike. But by the late twenties diodes were not enough of a statement: The miracle of sound was taken for granted, and a newer sign of the future and of technology was marketed. The workings, like those of the appliances of the era, were encased in new materials, such as Bakelite, or in basic box furniture forms designed to indicate "future" or "modern." Veneering the cases with different colored woods using the linear and streamlined decorative designs of the era's graphic arts gave a sense of movement to radios, and many floor consoles were designed to look like a piece of parlor furniture that was more tech-

moderne than a sofa. The latter merely provided a comfortable place to sit or recline; the radio cabinet contained the wizardry of science and technology. Machine-age designs did not appeal to every radio owner, however. "Colonial" and other "historical" forms were also broadly popular, in spite of the incongruity of encasing a thoroughly modern communication system in furniture that represented the preindustrial world. Perhaps these forms of eras long gone were an unconscious comfort to those who wanted the benefits of the new technology and the illusion of "simpler" times before machines and industry had taken over American culture.

Music was the most common form of programming broadcast in the early 1920s. Sporting events and plays were distant second and third most common broadcast genres, and news reports occurred every hour on the hour. In cities classical music dominated early radio programming, consistent with the conviction that the medium had its greatest potential as an agent of uplift and that classical European music was the best form of "higher" culture. The first live symphony concert was broadcast in 1926, as Serge Koussevitzky led the Boston Symphony Orchestra in a concert heard by an estimated 1 million listeners. Music appreciation shows and weekly concerts were aired through the 1930s, and the Metropolitan Opera began broadcasts in 1931. In 1938 an estimated 12 million people heard the Met broadcasts regularly during the opera season. WQXR, New York, began a classical-only program in 1937, and the New York Yankees baseball team sponsored a program of classical music interspersed with major league scores. 9

Popular music gradually surpassed, but did not completely supplant, classical music on urban radio stations. In 1938 the Federal Communications Commission conducted a survey of the content of 62,000 radio hours, and found that one-third of the air time was devoted to commercials. Of the remaining 40,000 hours, one-half were devoted to music, and popular music dominated that segment; 9 percent of the time was for drama, 9 percent for variety programming, 8.5 percent for new and sports, 5.2 percent for religion, 2.2 percent for special events, and 13.7 percent for "miscellaneous," mostly talking, shows. Country music stations operated in nearly all the nation's rural areas, sometimes bringing the music of Nashville's Grand Old Opry (which began broadcasting the show under that name in 1927, after a few years as station WSM's "Barn Dance"), but usually carrying the performances of itinerant singers and bands that played at the station for a week or two and then moved on. West Virginia miner Aaron Barkham remembered when "the first radio come to Mingo County . . . in 1934. That was a boon. It was a little job, got more squeals and squeaks than anything else. Everybody came from miles around to look at it. We didn't have any electricity. So we hooked up two car batteries. We got 'Grand Old Opry' on it." 10

11   The radio brought a new style of singing, termed "crooning," to Americans, in addition to comic songs, ditties, and country music. The most famous of the crooners—Bing Crosby and Rudy Vallee were two of the best known—developed a slow and smooth delivery that featured sliding into notes as opposed to the clipped style of more formal singers. In 1935 another unique American form of music and song joined the airwaves when the "singing cowboy," Gene Autry, began his evening show and enormously lucrative career as movie star, singer, and entrepreneur. Radio play of recorded music did not actually cut into record or sheet music sales, but record sales became the measure of how often and for how long tunes were aired.

Amos 'n' Andy; The "Soaps"

12   Perhaps as significant because of their national popularity, if not their percentage of the air time, were two other types of programs—comedy and daytime drama. The great age of radio comedy began (on a national scale) in the summer of 1929. Just a couple of months before the crash, two Chicago radio actors went national with a show that had been a local success for a few years. Freeman Gosden and Charles J. Correll "blacked up" their voices as Sam 'n' Henry, two "indigent colored boys" known as "the Gumps" in Chicago.

13   After changing stations in Chicago, and their names to Amos 'n' Andy, they linked up with NBC and shuffled into American homes with the help of Pepsodent toothpaste. The most popular radio show of the 1930s, it eventually dominated the listening lives of middle-class and working Americans, including some African-Americans, in spite of the show's demeaning racial stereotypes. First aired at eleven P.M. eastern time, the network switched to seven because parents complained that their children refused to go to sleep until the show was over. When people in the mountain and Pacific time zones complained that they were still at work when the show aired, the network broadcast it again at eleven-thirty P.M. eastern time. Restaurants broadcast the show, and movie houses scheduled showings around the fifteen-minute adventures of the two urban hustlers, sometimes actually stopping a film to bring in the broadcast. Telephone calls dropped off precipitously at seven and eleven-thirty, and only the president had air rights over them.

14   *Amos 'n' Andy* succeeded brilliantly among the white middle-class audience that loved them because they epitomized coping with the Depression in a manner that posed no threat to the established order. The black protagonists—one a middle-class aspirant who never quite got it right in spite of his schemes (Amos), and the other a lazy, clownish, but ultimately shrewd manipulator (Andy)—were obsessed with money and money-getting. The show's hokey moralism reinforced the idea that hard work and industriousness (and implicitly not

labor organization or strikes) were the keys to success. Their struggles were those of the population as a whole, but they were depicted as if the scuffling of everyday life were appropriate for them, and not for the white folks. Three-quarters of a million blacks didn't think so: They signed a petition protesting the depiction of African-Americans on the show. Nothing much happened. *Amos 'n' Andy* became a television show after World War II, still steeped in stereotypes, but at least with black actors.

Other comedy shows brought vaudeville performers such as Eddie Cantor and George Burns and his allegedly dingbat wife, Gracie Allen, to the radio, and made-for-radio shows such as *Fibber McGee and Molly* made fun of everything about American married life, often with barely disguised slights of ethnic groups.   15

Daytime drama programs, originally sponsored by soap companies, seized a significant market share during the afternoons. Figuring that the bulk of the listeners at home during the day were women, and that they were the major purchasers of soap products, the companies put their money behind an array of extremely successful serial dramas that soon after their introduction were termed "soap operas." Three such shows were on the air in 1931. There were ten in 1934, nineteen in 1935, thirty-one in 1936 and 1937, and sixty-one in 1939.   16

Most offered plots revolving around personal struggle—with finance, with lovers and husbands, or between classes. Most had strong women as central characters, reflecting the gender, the problems, and the desires of their listeners. The shows' formulaic plots oversimplified the problems of personal interaction, and in keeping with the experience and identity of their working- and middle-class audiences, the characters were plain simple folk. Like "Old Ma Perkins," they embodied the mythic American culture that had been overwhelmed by the greedy and unprincipled economic onslaught that had caused the Depression.   17

Ma Perkins was a widow who had "spent all her life taking care of her home, washing and cooking and raising her family." When her husband died she took over the lumberyard that he had run. She was a fountain of down-home wisdom in Rushville Center, reaffirming the "basic" social values of accommodation, cooperation, and comfort with one's social and economic position. In these dramas men were largely irrelevant, or absent, with the exception of older, nonthreatening figures. What order there was in the turmoil of Rushville Center or in the class-conscious lives of Stella Dallas, Helen Trent, or Our Gal Sunday (other famous "soap" heroines) was the result of wise, struggling, and strong women. Maybe the promise of the machine and the modern was a hollow one after all, a slick urban sophisticated hoax on the basically sound values of town, farm, and village. The villains were the easily identifiable (and overdrawn) stereotypes of city life: rich men, hollow socialites, painted women, shysters, crooks, hoods,   18 and hustlers. Amos 'n' Andy were urban but safe: They were clownish, almost rural chicken-stealers in the city, nonthreatening because they were black, unsuccessful, and segregated. In the "soaps" the greedy high-rollers were white, successful, and everywhere.

19   Evening radio serial dramas often starred motion-picture cowboy heroes such as Gene Autry or radio creations such as the Lone Ranger. The masked man was a typical Depression-era hero: a renegade Texas Ranger who rode with an outcast and sage Indian who had rescued him and nursed him back to health. The Lone Ranger, like Dashiell Hammett's Sam Spade and other detectives in the popular mystery novels of the era, was an outlaw, and a symbol of a society with little faith in its established institutions. The regular lawmen in this and other western series were usually good men at best buffaloed by crime, and at worst simply inept and occasionally crooked. The Ranger was a vigilante, and potentially a dangerous example of the man who took the law into his own hands, a Machiavellian do-gooder who rejected the limitations of law and law enforcement, even though his goals were justice. By the middle of 1939 the Ranger had ridden more than 1,000 times, on hundreds of stations, as often as three times in a week. For the Lone Ranger, Gene Autry, and other western heroes, as well as for Ma Perkins and the rest of the "soap" heroes, the key was to return, if not to "those thrilling days of yesteryear," as the Ranger and Tonto did, then to the values of those years, as Ma, Stella, and Helen did.

News and Sports

20   News and sports shows were often spectacularly popular, gathering as much as one-half the audience if the event was truly monumental. These were often one-shot affairs, such as the second Joe Louis–Max Schmeling heavyweight fight, which got a "Crosley" rating of 57.6 percent of the radios turned on and measured by the Crosley company. Politics entered the radio era in 1928, when an estimated 40 million listeners heard Al Smith and Herbert Hoover speak on election eve. The largest single line item (20 percent of the total) in the Republican party's campaign budget in 1928 was for radio ads. The Republicans bought 30 more hours of radio time in 1932 than they had in 1928, when they purchased 42.5 hours, to the Democrats' 51.5 hours (the same amount as in 1928). It backfired on Hoover, who came across as stodgy and distant in the face of a great human crisis. Roosevelt used radio to convey a personal and caring presence. Later, his "Fireside Chats" were also big scorers, garnering 30 to 40 percent of the listening audience. The World Series, the Kentucky Derby, and the Rose Bowl were similar big winners. Workers in the plant and on the farm regularly listened to baseball games all through the spring and summer if they could bring them in on the radio.

Listeners perhaps were comforted by the repetition of the hourly 21
news that punctuated the day. News stories did not break with regularity or very often, but the news bulletin and its dramatic urgency (especially as World War II began to take shape in 1938 and 1939) kept
many radios on, even if the listeners were only half attentive. In 1934
there were 4,670 interruptions of normal programming for news bulletins, nearly one-half of them relating to the "crime of the century,"
the kidnapping and death of the Lindbergh baby.

The war in Europe provided radio news with its greatest opportu- 22
nity to establish the medium as the most reliable medium for the delivery of information. The crisis of the late 1930s also provided CBS
with the opportunity to make up ground on NBC, the first and largest
network. Pictures did not lie, but they were not instantaneous and
they were not personal. Live reporting brought the crisis home and did
it with immediacy and drama. A legendary group of reporters—among
them H. V. Kaltenborn, Edward R. Murrow, and Robert Trout—
brought interviews with political leaders, battlefield reports from
Spain in 1936, and later from eastern Europe as Hitler began to overrun the region. Daily broadcasts from Berlin, Prague, Rome, London,
and Munich began in 1938, and bulletins from two minutes to two
hours in length during the Czechoslovakian crisis of September 1938
established news as more popular than entertainment and CBS as the
top news network. Murrow's famous "This is London" opening
brought the reality of the Blitz to Americans in a way that comple-
mented and perhaps outdid the power of the photograph. In early
1938, the Columbia University Office of Radio Research reported that
its surveys found that less than one-half of the public preferred radio
to print journalism; after the Munich crisis, two-thirds preferred radio
news to newspapers and magazines.

CONSIDERATIONS

1. In the 1930s, questionnaires directed at householders asked if there
was a radio in the home. Ten years later, they simply asked how many radios—as today, the question is not, do you have a television set, but, how
many? Think about this rapid multiplication of the mass media in American
life and build an essay around your conclusions.

2. Why did advertisers at first decline to use the medium of radio? Can
you imagine that happening today?

3. In his account of the famous *Amos 'n' Andy* show, which attained an
enormous following, does Green express his opinions of the show or does he
simply report the history and nature of its success?

4. Conduct a survey of your own among older men and women of your
acquaintance as a way of testing Green's statements about the loyalty of listeners, especially women, to such long-running shows as *Ma Perkins, Stella*

Dallas, Helen Trent, or *Our Gal Sunday.* Sum up your findings in an essay that might be classed as social commentary.

5. Writers often find it difficult to use statistics without boring their readers. Examine three or four paragraphs in which Green employs statistics. How does he keep the figures from dominating his essay?

6. One of Charles Dickens' criticisms of American life in 1842 was the sameness he found in the people and their towns. How does Green express something similar in his essay?

Donald Hall (b. 1928), co-editor of A Writer's Reader, *was born in Connecticut and has spent the last twenty years writing on an ancestral farm in New Hampshire. Best known as a poet, he is author of* The One Day, *a book length poem, which won the National Books Critics Circle Award and The Los Angeles Times Book Award in 1989. He has also published a book of short stories, books for children (including* Ox Cart Man, *which was awarded the Caldecott Medal in 1980), and many essays. We take "Keeping Things" from his collection,* Here at Eagle Pond.

38

DONALD HALL
Keeping Things

On the second floor of our house there is a long, unfinished room   1
that my family has always called the back chamber. It is the place the
broken chair ascends to when it is too weak for sitting on; the broken
lamp finds its shelf there, the toolbox its roost after the carpenter's
death. You do not throw things away: You cannot tell when they
might come in handy. My great-grandfather was born in 1826 and died
in 1914; some of his clothes remain in the back chamber, waiting to
come in handy.

His name was Benjamin Keneston, and he had two sons and   2
three daughters, the youngest my grandmother Kate, who died at
ninety-seven in 1975. Most of Ben's children were long-lived; when
they survived their spouses they would come home, bringing a house-
ful of furniture with them. They never called this place anything but
home, or used the word for any other place, though they might have
lived and worked elsewhere for fifty years. Both Luther and Nannie returned to live in cottages near the farm, and Kate kept bedrooms at the
house in their names—Luther's room, Nannie's room—for when they
were sick. Their extra furniture went to the back chamber, or above

the back chamber in a loft, or in the dark hole that extends under eaves in the old part of the house without windows or electric lights.

3   When we potter in the back chamber today, we find a dozen knocked-down double beds, one painted with gold designs and the slogan *Sleep Balmy Sleep* on dark veneer. We find something like thirty chairs: captain's chairs, rockers with a rocker missing, Morris chairs, green painted kitchen chairs, pressed-wood upright dining room chairs, uncomfortable stuffed parlor chairs; most of them lack a strut or a leg but live within distance of repair. We find a sewing machine that my grandmother sewed on for sixty years and a 1903 perambulator she wheeled my mother in. Two sisters came after my mother, and the back chamber is well furnished with dolls' furniture: tiny chests of drawers, small rockers and small captain's chairs, prams, cradles, and a miniature iron cookstove, like the big Glenwood range in the kitchen below, with an oven door that swings open, firebox, stove lids, and a tiny iron skillet that fits a stovetop opening. We find fat old wooden skis and sleds with bentwood runners. One ancient stove, with castiron floral reliefs, we cleaned up and use in Jane's study, which used to be Nannie's room. We find toolboxes, postcard collections, oil lamps, electric lamps, pretty cardboard boxes, books by Joe Lincoln and Zane Grey, cribs, carpetbags, loveseats, and a last for making shoes. We find three spinning wheels, two of them broken and a third intact, dispatched upstairs when Ward's replaced homespun; as the family remembers, Benjamin's wife Lucy Buck Keneston was a wonderful spinner. We find a dozen quilts too frail for cleaning, showing bright squares of the cut-up dresses of seamstresses born to the early Republic. We find six or seven chests full of dead people's clothing, Ben Keneston's among them. In a dark row stand four baby highchairs; one made from stout brown wood is more than seventy years old, first used by my mother's younger sister Nan, next by me, later by my children; two wicker highchairs are older, and a frail wooden one older still. I don't know which of them my grandmother sat in.

4   In the back chamber we keep the used and broken past. Of course it is also a dispensary. When my daughter moved from her University of New Hampshire dormitory to an apartment in Dover, she outfitted her flat from unbroken furniture out of the back chamber. With glue and dowels, the apartments of children and grandchildren could be filled for fifty years. In, and out again: the past hovering in the dusty present like motes, a future implicit in shadowy ranks of used things, usable again. We do not call these objects antiques; they were never removed from use as testimony to affluence. Twice a year, as I show somebody through the house, somebody decides that I am in need of counseling: "You've got a fortune here." I keep my temper. None of it would fetch a great price, but even if it would, I would as soon sell my

ancestors' bones for soup as I would sell their top hats, chairs, tool chests, and pretty boxes. Someday when we are dead let them go to auction, if they are not repaired and dispersed.

Continually we discover new saved things, and my wonder is not   5
for the things themselves but for the saving of them. Could Kate really have thought, when she put away a 1917 agricultural bulletin, that it might come in handy someday? The back chamber bespeaks attachment to the outlived world. On a long, narrow cardboard box an old hand has written, "Wool was from B. C. Keneston's sheep carded and ready for spinning at Otterville"—where there was a carding mill—"in 1848." When we open it, we find protected by mothballs a few pounds of one-hundred-and-forty-year-old sheep's wool, preserved for preservation's sake, so that we may touch our fingers to the wool our ancestor's fingers sheared. (Was 1848 his first crop from his first sheep? He was twenty-two that year.) This back chamber is like the parlor walls covered with family portraits, like the graveyard with its Vermont slate and New Hampshire granite; it keeps the dead.

When we moved into the old house after my grandmother's   6
death, it needed work. (She was seventy-four when my grandfather died. He had kept the house up, and after his death she could not afford to hire help. My mother paid to keep the house painted and the roof dry.) Now as we painted and shingled, dug out the cesspool, planted daffodils, put in a leachfield, fertilized hayfields, jacked up the woodshed for a new sill, replaced clapboards, and mulched old roses, our neighbors let us know that they were pleased. In this countryside, everyone over fifty had watched white wooden houses lose paint and tilt inward as their roofs sagged, and finally whole square-built houses collapse into their own cellarholes. Everyone here takes interest in preserving things, in landscape and buildingscape, even if everyone knows that in a hundred years fire will consume all these houses.

One outbuilding was too far gone for us to bring it back. Built at   7
the turn of this century just north of the house, the saphouse had been the site of prodigious syrup making. In 1913 my grandfather, with the help of his father-in-law and Freeman Morrison, made five hundred gallons to sell for a dollar each, and put the windfall into land. Because it takes about forty gallons of sap to make a gallon of syrup—the pale sap is watery; it is hard to taste the sweetness—he hauled twenty thousand gallons of maple sap that year, in the two or three weeks of sugaring. First he tapped the huge old trees of the sugarbush on Ragged Mountain, setting one or more buckets at each tree to collect the dripping liquid; then he visited each tree each day, emptying the buckets into twenty-gallon pails he carried on a yoke across his shoulders; then he walked through the snowy woods to the ox sledge, where he

poured the sap into milk cans; when the cans were full he eased his oxen to a funnel uphill from the saphouse and piped his crop down to the saphouse's holding tank.

8   When I was little and visited the farm in March, if I hit upon sugaring time, I walked the sugarbush with him. The crop is best when days are warm and nights freezing. To keep the sap boiling, somebody has to tend the fire twenty-four hours a day; Freeman, who was a night owl, stayed up all night and much of the day to feed the fire. He pushed whole trees, foot by foot, over the snow through the saphouse's open doors into the firebox. Freeman and my grandfather had built the saphouse under the supervision of my grandfather's father-in-law, informally called Uncle Ben. (Formally he was Benjamin Cilley Keneston, to distinguish him from his father, who was plain Benjamin. When I was a child I liked knowing that I was part Cilley.) BCK died in 1914, sixty-six years after he sheared the sheep's wool in the back chamber. Although I never knew him, I have been aware of his presence since I was a child, and living in his house I feel him every day, not only in the photograph on the living room wall or the top hat under the stairs. If we find a tar-brand for sheep it is *K*. He was diminutive and powerful, and it must have been hard for my grandfather Wesley Wells to marry his daughter, move into his house, and take direction from him. Yet I never caught a shade of resentment in the stories my grandfather told me.

9   We hated to pull the saphouse down. My grandfather used it last to make a few gallons in March 1950. That autumn he had a heart attack, sold the cows, and never used the saphouse again. He died in March 1953. When we moved into his house in 1975 we found an unopened quart from his last crop of syrup on a shelf in the rootcellar. Maybe if I had been truest to family practices I would have carried it up to the back chamber unopened but labeled for future generations to wonder at. However, we opened it, we ate it on pancakes, and when we had almost finished it, we poured the last drops into a store-bought gallon—figuring that for a few decades at least, if we continued emptying old gallons into new ones, we could imagine molecular survival for my grandfather's final quart.

10   The saphouse leaned over, a third out of the vertical. The shed-like door gapped loose. I no longer entered it, because sometime the roof would collapse and I would not let it collapse on me. Rot feathered the timbers up from the ground, the tarpaper roof was swaybacked, and the lead pipe sagged as it rose up-mountain from the rotten galvanized holding tank. Twenty years before, my grandmother Kate had sold the evaporator—big tin tray over the firebox—to somebody building a new saphouse; somebody else had bought the buckets. Every now and then, a pickup braked in front of the house and a

stranger offered to tear the saphouse down for us, in return for the old wood that he could salvage. There's a market for old wood: beams for what is called restoration, planks to be cut up for picture frames. I refused these offers, wanting to keep the old wood, and probably because I inherited or acquired the desire to keep things. Also I remembered the sheepbarn. Two men tore it down for my grandmother when it started to lean over; they promised, as all the pickup people promised, to clean it up real good. But when these fellows had removed the solid wood they left a mess of rotten board and shingle that weeds grew to cover, a treacherous vegetal-archaeological heap you could break a leg in, where woodchucks bred for generations until we hired a dozer and a truck to haul the mess to the dump.

We tied a cable around the saphouse walls, hitched the cable to a 11 four-wheel-drive pickup, and pulled it down. The frail boards stretched apart like a clasped bunch of straw when you unclench your fist. Sun touched bright unweathered boards that had seen no light since Wesley and Freeman lifted them from the sawmill's pile and hammered them in place. Store nails pulled from the corner four-by-fours. At the door we found long, irregular hammered iron pins, which Freeman had pounded out at his forge in the shop that stood not twenty yards away—the shop also gone now, all traces gone except the grindstone's base that leaned beside it.

We tossed rotten boards in the pickup's bed, stacked the good 12 wood and hauled it for storage to the cowbarn with its kept-up roof. At day's end we drove the junk to the town dump. In a wheelbarrow we collected old bottles, one intact sap bucket, a float, an enamel funnel, and an elegantly shaped handmade shovel. Two huge tapered iron hinges bore a hammer's prints. We tucked the ironwork in a corner of the woodshed (where firewood covers it half the year) among ax heads, scythe blades, and the frail graceful trident of a pitchfork. Freeman forged some of this iron with his engineering-generalist's skill—who turned baseball bats on a lathe, tanned leather and made shoes, built ladders and hayricks and playhouses and wooden spoons and stone walls, repaired cutlery and milk pails, moved rocks and pulled stumps—but some of the work is finer than Freeman's; I fancy the hand of John Wells, Wesley's father, who fought at Vicksburg and returned to be blacksmith and farrier on a hill west of Danbury.

Soon grass and saplings would cover the debris we left behind, 13 bricks and small pieces of wood, chowder of rusted metal, spread now in a drift of old leaves that blew into the saphouse autumns past, gray-brown and fragile. High in the center stood the one monument that remained like the saphouse's tombstone, the long brick hive of fire, firebox into which Freeman had pushed whole trees. Seventy-five-year-old mortar spilled at the edge of bricks pink as a baby's mouth. I remember hearing that BCK liked to butter bricks; he must have done this work. Maybe in a hundred years a hiker walking down Ragged Mountain will find this brickwork among new maples.

14   When we were done, birches cast late-day shadows across the little field between the house and the place where the saphouse used to be. Then we noticed an odd-shaped white stone where there had been a corner four-by-four. It was flat and looked carved. We lifted it up and saw that beneath it there was another piece just like it, and when we turned the top one over, we understood two things at once: The two pieces fitted where they had broken in the middle, and it was a tombstone. Cleaning it off, I read the name and dates of my great-greatgrandfather, BCK's father, BENJAMIN KENISTON 1789–1863. Because I knew his grave in the old Andover graveyard, because I remembered the sturdy, legible stone above it, I understood that this was his *first* gravestone, that it had broken, that his son BCK had replaced it—and brought it home and put it to use.

15   The first month we moved here, going through an old desk, we found a yellowed piece of stationery headed by an indistinct photograph of Mount Kearsarge and the words *B. C. Keneston Eagle Pond Farm.* (It was BCK who changed the spelling of the family name, to distance himself from some Keniston cousins.) The pond is west of the farm, thirty acres of water—a lake anywhere else. No one alive remembered that name for the place. Although it had not stuck, I decided to make use of it, not for piety of reference but to ease the minds of urban and suburban correspondents who find it hard to believe that a town's name can be address enough. So BCK solved a problem: All that first year, the dead helped out.

16   Mostly they demanded attention. I could not decide whether Freeman or BCK demanded more. (My grandparents, whom I knew so well and loved so much, demanded little; I thought of them without being reminded.) BCK, whom I had never known, had picked this place out; it was he who deserved credit for staking the claim to Kearsarge and to Eagle Pond. It was he who bought the pew at the South Danbury church he helped to found, where his daughter Kate played the organ Sundays from the age of fourteen to ninety-two. (Is seventy-eight years at the same organ a neo-Calvinist record?) It was fitting, then, that my one glimpse of his ghost, looking suspiciously like my favorite photograph of him, occurred in church one Sunday. He vanished as soon as I saw him. If every Sunday I caught sight of my grandmother's black sequined hat, bobbing next to the green glass lampshade above the organ, that vision seemed natural enough.

17   Freeman insisted on his presence in a manner perfectly material. He had stenciled his name all over the house. Cousin Freeman moved in as a boy when his family was burned out; he preferred Uncle Ben

and Aunt Lucy to his parents and loved Kate like a little sister. His father took him away and put him to work when he was sixteen, but for the rest of his life he kept returning to this place that he loved. I remember him old and sick, wrapped in a blanket, tucked into the rocker by the kitchen range, attended by Kate grown old. He stenciled his name on the underside of stairs leading to the back chamber, which we could see as we walked down to the rootcellar. He stenciled his name on the bottom of a drawer in the pantry, on the underside of the windowsill in his room, and on shingles we found wedged under a box in the toolshed. When we turned something over or lifted something up, we half expected to see Freeman's name, as if his face with its playful eyes leapt up like a jack-in-the-box. He stenciled his name, as it were, on everybody who knew him.

My ghost stories are mostly unconscious memory. When we had   18 lived here only a few weeks a stranger knocked on the front door; his trailer had broken down and he needed a large monkey wrench. I started to say that I had no big wrench, but before I could speak something took hold of me. Asking the man to wait I gave myself over to whatever possessed me and let it direct me out of the kitchen, into the toolshed toward the woodshed door; my right hand rose unbidden toward a flat shelf over that door where the big wrench resided, and had resided forever, covered now with thirty years of dust and spider webs. Something similar happened when I bought a sickle at Thornley's store to chop down weeds in the backyard. I cut Lexington plant until my back stopped me, then walked with my silvery crescent into the toolshed where I would find something to hang it on; I did not know why I headed for a particular place, but when I raised my hand toward the naily ceiling, I saw three frail rusted sickles hanging there already.

Not everything that happened was memory. Once my wife heard   19 her name called repeatedly in the barn when no one was there to say it. Once after someone helping us cleaned a shed loft, and threw away old shoes and clothing we would not have thrown away, Jane felt in the loft some violence, anger, or even evil, as if something terrible had happened there; maybe it was only resentment over things lost. And there was something else soon after we moved in, although we did not hear about it for two years. It happened to a visitor—skeptical, secular, unsuperstitious, hesitant to speak of it, unable to understand what she saw. It was just a *seeing*. As she stood in our living room, she saw someone in the doorway of the kitchen, someone who was not there: a short man, bearded, wearing overalls and a hat. Both BCK and Freeman were short, bearded, wore overalls and a hat.

These experiences virtually stopped after that first year, but   20 there was an exception. When we had lived here six years, we finally afforded a new bathroom. The old one was Sears 1937: cold, shabby, showerless. We tore it off the side of the house and put a new bathroom (with shower and laundry) into our old bedroom, extending a new bedroom onto the north lawn. For warmth in winter we extended the rootcellar under the new room, which obliged us to raise the north side of the house on jacks and bulldoze underneath it. We dug out rotten sills and replaced them; ripping a wall from the old bedroom we exposed 1803 carpentry; the wallpaper of the family Troy was nine layers deep; in one wall we found cardboard insulation from a box of breakfast cereal, Washington's Crisps, and a picture of the general with bright red lips.

21   It was the first major alteration of the house's shape since BCK expanded it in 1865, when it became the extended farmhouse familiar in New Hampshire—outbuildings not separated but linked one to one, moving in slow file backward to the hill. To haul firewood in winter we pass through a kitchen door into the toolshed, which is another repository almost like the back chamber: saws, levels, crowbars, old nails, screws, bolts, shovels, rakes, hoes, sickles, awls, drills and their bits, hammers, hammerheads, traps, stovepipe, lanterns, wrenches, screwdrivers; and the practice organ Kate learned to play on, moved from the parlor to the toolshed in 1927 when my mother and father displayed wedding presents in the parlor—and at the southeast corner of the toolshed we go through another door into the woodshed. This door is made from planks nailed to crossplanks, and it latches by a smooth oblong of wood—touched ten million times like Saint Peter's toe to a soft and shiny texture—which turns on a bolt and sticks at a thumb of wood below. Because we must carry wood many times a day, much of the year, we have unfixed the latch to open this door thousands of times, walked into the woodshed, loaded up with logs, and walked back out again, latching the door behind us. But while we were tearing things up, something new happened, not once or twice but seven times: While we were fetching logs, this woodshed door swung closed behind us, and the wooden latch turned by itself and locked us inside the woodshed.

22   It never happened once in the years before; in the years since we stopped sawing and hammering, it has not happened again. This locking up was not malicious, because it is easy enough to get out of the woodshed by a door that leads outside. Not malicious, just an annoying prank.

23   The steadiest presence remains in the possessions, rooms, and artifacts of the dead. Living in their house, we take over their practices and habits, which makes us feel close to them and to the years that they knew. I always wanted to live in this house with the old people, and now I do, even though they are dead. I don't live in their past; they

inhabit my present, where I live as I never lived before. I used to survive, like many people, half in a daydream of future reward that is a confession of present malaise: the vacation trip, the miraculous encounter. When I moved here, at first I feared the fulfillment of desire, as if I would be punished for possessing what I wanted so much; there was a brief time when I drove ten miles under the speed limit and buckled up to move the car in the driveway; but contentment was relentless and would not let me go until I studied the rapture of the present tense. It turns out that the fulfillment of desire is to stop desiring, to live in the full moon and the snow, in the direction the wind comes from, in the animal scent of the alive second.

The dead were welcoming. I worried about usurping their place 24 until two dreams helped me. In one I discovered that my grandfather—who was working the farm, now, in my dream—had disappeared and I thought him dead, only to see him striding up the dirt road from Andover (a road paved before I was born), leading a file of zoo animals: ostrich, bear, elephant, lion, tiger. He had traded the cows and sheep for these exotic creatures, proving (as I take the dream) that I was permitted to raise poems on this farm instead of stock. The other dream was more to the point of disappearances; a large voice pronounced, "The blow of the ax resides in the acorn."

If there is no connected past, we lack the implication of persis- 25 tence after our own death. The preserved or continuous past implies the possibility that oneself may continue, in place or object or even in spirit, a ring of time that revolves, revisits, and contains. As a child I heard about a bone ring. When John Wells fought at Vicksburg he stood next to a young man named George Henry Butler, who came from a farm on New Canada Road; people from the same neighborhoods fought together in that war. As they were shelled, Wells took cover behind a great tree, which allowed him to stand upright; Butler squatted in a hole beside him. When the cannonade continued Wells offered to switch places with Butler, to let him stretch for a bit, and when they had changed places, a cannonball crashed through the tree and took off the young man's head. My great-grandfather emptied Butler's pockets, and when he mustered out and walked home to Danbury turned over the dead soldier's possessions to his family.

John Wells's son Wesley married George Henry Butler's cousin 26 Kate Keneston, and one object from those pockets came down to her. A few years ago it disappeared. No one could find it in the house, and we thought it was gone forever. We lamented the lost connection with a young man killed in the Civil War. Then we discovered it in a box of buttons in the back chamber: a finger ring carved out of bone, eight-sided, scratched with little decorations, small and yellowed—a bone ring I take as emblem of this place.

___ CONSIDERATIONS _____

1. How does Hall avoid the vague meanderings so characteristic of such reminiscing?

2. How does his account amount to more than a sentimental memoir of the past?

3. What trait of Hall's great grandfather is illustrated by the anecdote about an odd-shaped white stone found in the remnants of the leveled sap-house?

4. Examine some older houses in your town, paying particular attention to parts that were additions to the original structure and keeping in mind the changes Hall describes in paragraph 21. Report your findings by reconstructing—a little imagination will help—the routines and ways of life, changes in the family, and the economic ups and downs reflected in those changes of the house.

5. "... a bone ring I take as emblem of this place." Hall's concluding sentence. What does he mean by "emblem," and why does he think the bone ring a suitable one for his place?

6. Two other authors in your text, Patricia Hampl and E. B. White, also make important use of the past in their essays. Read one (or both) of them and then explain, with examples, how Hall's essay differs from the others.

*Patricia Hampl (b. 1946) was born in St. Paul,
Minnesota, where she lives now. She received an MFA at
the Iowa Writers Workshop, and was a founding member
of The Loft, a twin cities institution promoting literature
and the arts. She has published stories, poems, and essays
in the* New Yorker, Paris Review, *and* American Poetry
Review. *In 1981 she received a Houghton Mifflin Literary
Fellowship for her memoir,* A Romantic Education.

39

PATRICIA HAMPL
Holding Old Negatives Up to the Light

I was five and was sitting on the floor of the vestibule hallway of   1
my grandmother's house where the one bookcase had been pushed.
The bookcase wasn't in the house itself—ours wasn't a reading family.
I was holding in my lap a book of sepia photographs bound in a soft
brown cover, stamped in flaking gold with the title *Zlatá Praha*,
Golden Prague, views of the nineteenth century.

The album felt good, soft. First, the Hradčany Castle and its gar-   2
dens, then a close-up of the astronomical clock, a view of the baroque
jumble of Malá Strana. Then a whole series of photographs of the Vl-
tava River, each showing a different bridge, photograph after pale photograph like a wild rose that opens petal by petal, exposing itself ef-
fortlessly, as if there were no such thing as regret. All the buildings in
the pictures were hazy, making it seem that the air, not the stone,
held the contour of the baroque villas intact.

I didn't know how to read yet, and the Czech captions under the   3
pictures were no more incomprehensible to me than English would
have been. I liked the soft, fleshlike pliancy of the book. I knew the
pictures were of Europe, and that Europe was far away, unreachable.

From *A Romantic Education* by Patricia Hampl, published by Houghton Mifflin.
Copyright © 1981 by Patricia Hampl. Reprinted by permission of The Rhoda Weyr
Agency, New York.

Still, it had something to do with me, with my family. I sat in the cold vestibule, turning the pages of the Prague album. I was flying; I was somewhere else. I was not in St. Paul, Minnesota, and I was happy.

4 My grandmother appeared at the doorway. Her hands were on her stout hips, and she wanted me to come out of the unheated hallway. She wanted me to eat coffee cake in the kitchen with everybody else, and I had been hard to find. She said, "Come eat," as if this were the family motto.

5 As she turned to go, she noticed the album. In a second she was down on the floor with me, taking the album carefully in her hands, turning the soft, felt pages. "Oh," she said, "Praha." She looked a long time at one picture, I don't remember which one, and then she took a white handkerchief out of her pinafore apron pocket, and dabbed at the tears under her glasses. She took off the wire-rim glasses and made a full swipe.

6 Her glasses had made deep hollows on either side of her nose, two small caves. They looked as if, with a poke, the skin would give way like a ripe peach, and an entrance would be exposed into her head, into the skull, a passageway to the core of her brain. I didn't want her head to have such wounds. Yet I liked them, these unexpected dips in a familiar landscape.

7 "So beautiful," she was crying melodramatically over the album. "So beautiful." I had never seen an adult cry before. I was relieved, in some odd way, that there was crying in adulthood, that crying would not be taken away.

8 My grandmother hunched down next to me in the hallway; she held the album, reciting the gold-stamped captions as she turned the pages and dabbed at her eyes. She was having a good cry. I wanted to put my small finger into the two little caves of puckered skin, the eyeless sockets on either side of her large, drooping nose. Strange wounds, I wanted to touch them. I wanted to touch her, my father's mother. She was so *foreign*.

9 Looking repeatedly into the past, you do not necessarily become fascinated with your own life, but rather with the phenomenon of memory. The act of remembering becomes less autobiographical; it begins to feel tentative, aloof. It becomes blessedly impersonal.

10 The self-absorption that seems to be the impetus and embarrassment of autobiography turns into (or perhaps always was) a hunger for the world. Actually, it begins as hunger for *a* world, one gone or lost, effaced by time or a more sudden brutality. But in the act of remembering, the personal environment expands, resonates beyond itself, beyond its "subject," into the endless and tragic recollection that is history.

11 We look at old family photographs in which we stand next to black, boxy Fords and are wearing period costumes, and we do not

gaze fascinated because there we are young again, or there we are standing, as we never will again in life, next to our mother. We stare and drift because there we are . . . historical. It is the dress, the black car that dazzle us now and draw us beyond our mother's bright arms which once caught us. We reach into the attractive impersonality of something more significant than ourselves.

We embrace the deathliness and yet we are not dead. We are im- 12 personal and yet ourselves. The astonishing power and authority of memory derive from this paradox. Here, in memory, we live *and* die. We do "live again" in memory, but differently: in history as well as in biography. And when these two come together, forming a narrative, they approach fiction. The imprecision of memory causes us to create, to extend remembrance into narrative. It sometimes seems, therefore, that what we remember is not—could not be—true. And yet it is *accurate*. The imagination, triggered by memory, is satisfied that this is so.

We trust memory against all the evidence: it is selective, subjec- 13 tive, cannily defensive, unreliable as fact. But a single red detail remembered—a hat worn in 1952, the nail polish applied one summer day by an aunt to her toes, separated by balls of cotton, as we watched—has more real blood than the creatures around us on a bus as, for some reason, we think of that day, that hat, those bright feet. That world. This power of memory probably comes from its kinship with the imagination. In memory each of us is an artist: each of us creates. The Kingdom of God, the nuns used to tell us in school, is within you. We may not have made a religion of memory, but it is our passion, and along with (sometimes in opposition to) science, our authority. It is a kingdom of its own.

Psychology, which is somehow *our* science, the claustrophobic 14 discipline of the century, has made us acknowledge the value of remembering—even at the peril of shame. But it is especially difficult to reach back into the merely insignificant, into a family life where, it seemed, nothing happened, where there wasn't the ghost of a pretension. That is a steelier resistance because to break through what is unimportant and as anonymous as dirt a greater sense of worthlessness must be overcome. At least shame is interesting; at least it is hidden, the sign of anything valuable. But for a past to be overlooked, discarded because it was not only useless but simply without interest—that is a harsher heritage. In fact, is it a heritage?

It seems as if I spent most of my twenties holding a lukewarm 15 cup of coffee, hunched over a table, talking. Innumerable cups of coffee, countless tables: the booths of the Gopher Grill at the University of Minnesota where, probably around 1965, I first heard myself use the word *relationship*; a little later, the orange formica table of a federal prison where "the man I live with" (there still is no other term) was serving a sentence for draft resistance; and the second-hand tables of a dozen apartments, the wooden farmhouse table of a short-lived commune—table after table, friend after friend, rehashing our hardly ended (or not ended) childhoods. I may have the tables wrong; maybe the formica one was in the farmhouse, the oak one in the prison, maybe the chairs in the prison were orange and the table gray. But they are fixtures, nailed down, not to be moved: memories.

16   This generation has written its memoirs early; we squeezed every childhood lemon for all it was worth: my mother this, my father that. Our self-absorption was appalling. But I won't go back—not yet—on that decade. It was also the time when my generation, as "a generation," was most political, most involved. The people I sat with, picking at our individual pasts, wearing nightgowns till noon as we analyzed within a millimeter our dreams and their meanings (that is, how they proved this or that about our parents), finally put on our clothes, went outside and, in various ways that are too easily forgotten, tried to end a war which we were the first, as a group, to recognize was disastrous. In fact, our protest against the war is what made us a generation, even to ourselves.

17   Perhaps no American generation—certainly not our parents who were young during the Depression—had a childhood as long as ours. The war kept us young. We stayed in school, endlessly, it seemed, and our protest kept us in the child's position: we alternately "rebelled" against and pestered the grownups for what we wanted—an end to the war. Those who fought the war had no such long, self-reflective youths. Childhood belonged to us, who stayed at home. And we became the "sixties generation."

18   Our certainty that the war was strong became entangled with our analysis of our families and our psyches not only because we were given to self-reflection and had a lot of time on our hands. We combed through our dreams and our childhoods with Jung's *Man and His Symbols* at the ready, and were looking for something, I now think, that was neither personal nor familial and perhaps not even psychological. We had lost the national connection and were heartsick in a cultural way. I don't think we knew that; I didn't, anyway. But at home I didn't talk psychology, I talked politics, arguing with a kind of angry misery whose depths confused me and made my family frightened for me, and probably of me. But there was no real argument—I did all the talking; my family, gathered for Sunday dinner, looked glumly at the gravy on their plates as if at liquid Rorschach blots that might suggest why I, the adored child, had come to this strange pass. They weren't "for the way," but the belligerent way I was against it dismayed them and caused them to fall silent, waiting for me to stop. I had opinions, I spoke of my "position" on things.

19   One night my uncle, trying to meet me halfway, said, "Well, when I was in Italy during the War . . . "

"How do you defend that analogy?" I snapped at him, perhaps 20
partly because for them "the War" was still the Second World War.
My family couldn't seem, for a long time, to *focus* on Vietnam. But
my uncle retreated in the face of the big guns of my new English-ma-
jor lingo.

On Thanksgiving one year I left the table to find *I. F. Stone's* 21
Weekly and read parts of it to the assembled family in a ringing, tri-
umphantly angry voice. "But," my father said when I finished, as if I.
F. Stone had been compiling evidence about me and not the Johnson
administration, "you used to be so *happy*—the happiest person I ever
met."

"What does that have to do with anything?" I said.   22

Yet he was right. My unhappiness (but I didn't think of myself as 23
unhappy) was a confusion of personal and public matters, and it was
made more intense by the fact that I had been happy ("the happiest
person!") and now I couldn't remember what that happiness had
been—just childhood? But many childhoods are miserable. And I
couldn't remember exactly how the happiness stopped. I carry from
that time the feeling that private memory is not just private and not
just memory. Yet the resistances not against memory but against the
significance of memory remain strong.

I come from people who have always been polite enough to feel 24
that nothing has ever happened to them. They have worked, raised
families, played cards, gone on fishing trips together, risen to grief and
admirable bitterness and, then, taken patiently the early death that
robbed them of a brother, a son. They have not dwelt on things. To
dwell, that appropriate word, as if the past were a residence, faintly
morbid and barbaric: the dwellings of prehistoric men. Or, the language of the Bible: "The Word was made flesh, and dwelt amongst us."

I have dwelt, though. To make a metaphor is to make a fuss, and 25
I am a poet, though it seems that is something one cannot claim for
oneself; anyway, I write poetry. I am enough of them, my kind family,
to be repelled by the significance of things, to find poetry, with its tendency to make connections and to break the barriers between past and
present, slightly embarrassing.

It would be impossible to look into the past, even a happy one 26
(especially a happy one), were it not for the impersonality that dwells
in the most intimate fragments, the integuments that bind even obscure lives to history and, eventually, history to fiction, to myth.

I will hold up negative after family negative to the light. I will 27
dwell. Dwell in the house of the dead and in the living house of my
relatives. I'm after junk. I want to make something out of what my
family says is nothing. I suppose that is what I was up to when my
grandmother called me out of the vestibule, away from the bookcase
and the views of Prague, to eat my dinner with everybody else.

_____ **CONSIDERATIONS** _____

1. Two authors, working at different times and places for different reasons, come together on the same idea! After reading Hampl, especially paragraphs 9–12, read Joan Didion's "On Keeping a Notebook," page 131, especially paragraphs 6–8. In what important way might the two writers be saying the same thing?

2. Why, according to Hampl, is psychology "our" science?

3. Hampl writes in paragraph 25, "To make a metaphor is to make a fuss. . . ." What does she mean?

4. As a poet, Hampl makes expert use of images, both literal and figurative. Underline a few examples and discuss their value versus more abstract language, such as that of paragraph 14.

5. What do you think of Hampl as a representative of the "sixties generation," especially its opposition to the Vietnam war?

Jean Hegland (b. 1956) did graduate work and taught composition at Eastern Washington University. Now she lives with her family in northern California, writing fiction and essays, and teaches creative writing at Santa Rosa Junior College. "The Fourth Month"—part of Life Within: Celebration of a Pregnancy *(1991)—appeared in* Spiritual Mothering *in 1989. In 1996, she published her first novel,* In the Forest.

40

JEAN HEGLAND
The Fourth Month

Woman is the artist of the imagination and the child in the womb is the canvas whereon she painteth her pictures.

Paracelsus (1493–1541)

For several days I thought they were just the soft rumblings of my own guts, these dim twistings low in my belly. But then one morning as we lay in bed, the twister's father put his hand on my stomach and felt a nudge at the same time I felt a poke. After months of gyrating unobserved, this creature had finally made itself indisputably known, its delicate flutters like a message from a distant planet or a deserted island—there is life here, too! It tapped against its father's palm once more, and then was still, indifferent to our sudden joy, to the hot blaze of tears in its parents' eyes.

It feels like a kiss, this quickening, like another's tongue slipping and curling inside my mouth. The Eskimos said that the aurora borealis was the playing of unborn children. I have seen only the dim, southern version of those northern lights, but still, this sensation is like that, ghostly, lovely, a dance performed in the darkness of another world.

Now as I go about my days, I am aware of the baby brewing inside me, and it surprises me that the pattern of my life is not completely transformed by this quickening. At night, when I lie next to

Douglas, I feel the tumbling of the child we have set in motion, and I think I am a priestess privy to the mysteries of the gods. But at other times this tickling in my guts comes as no surprise. Like the passing of gas, or the beating of a heart, it is a familiar feeling, comfortable, homey, and often it seems usual, normal, to have this movement inside me.

4   I feel newly fond of this old body, now that it is more than just the vehicle of my own continuance. I have forgiven its many curves and softnesses, and I am proud of the neat little bulge of my belly, pleased with my swollen breasts and their thick brown nipples. No longer mine, more than myself, I have become a catalyst, a resource, a riddle. I am a boat which contains an ocean, a basket filling with a single egg. I am a cradle, a crucible, a garden.

5   "Quicken" means to come to life, and it does seem as though this baby had just begun, now that I can feel its presence. And now that I can distinguish between us, I feel more connection to it than I did before. With these first quiet nudges comes the nascence of love.

6   In Egypt, they say that the heart sees the baby before the eye. But even a heart must be able to see before it can love. Our organs cannot love themselves, and even a heart can only love what is outside of and other than itself, because such a great part of loving is that longing to bridge that distance. Now that it is tangibly separate from me, I find myself asking the lover's question of this finger-length child tucked beneath my heart: dear Riddle, what is it like for you? They say that already your face, with its newly finished lips, is like no one else's face. Already, the lines that tell your fortune are etched into your pea-sized palms. Already, the whorls have risen on the pads of your fingertips and in the flesh of your feet. What is it like to have that face, those feet and hands?

7   I wish I could be a twin in your womb, to know what it is you know. I wish I could hear the sounds and silences that your ears have just begun to hear, could feel the currents of amniotic fluid on your raw skin, and the elastic give of the walls that contain you. I wish I could learn exactly what this time is like for you. But as I ask those questions to which I know I will never find answers, I learn something else. I learn that imagination is the essence of love.

_____ **CONSIDERATIONS** _____

1. In what way does the author of "The Fourth Month" prepare us for the surprising conclusion: "I learn that imagination is the essence of love"?

2. Although "The Fourth Month" is a subjective expression of what the pregnant woman experiences, the writer's research is skillfully put to work in this short essay. Find examples of that research.

3. How does her awareness of her developing baby affect the mother's image of herself?

4. Each of the chapters of Hegland's book, *The Life Within*, from which "The Fourth Month" was taken, begins with a quotation from a different source. What do you think of an author's use of such material? Can you imagine using one of Ambrose Bierce's "Devil's Definitions" at the head of an essay you might write?

5. How might Diane Ackerman have made use of Hegland's essay in "The Importance of Touch" (page 10)?

Lillian Hellman (1905–1984) was a playwright, born in New Orleans, who grew up in New Orleans and New York City. After graduating from New York University, she went to work in publishing. The Children's House *(1934), her first great success on Broadway, was followed by her most famous play,* The Little Foxes *(1939), and* Watch on the Rhine *(1941). She also wrote the book for Leonard Bernstein's musical* Candide.

Hellman's later works were autobiographical, and include Pentimento *(1973),* Scoundrel Time *(1977), and* An Unfinished Woman, *which won the National Book Award in 1970. These narratives were collected into one volume with new commentary by the author:* Three *(1979). In 1980 she published* Maybe: A Story.

The anecdote below, which is from An Unfinished Woman, *tells of a climactic episode in the transition from childhood to adolescence, and shows the rebelliousness, strong feeling, and independence that become themes of the autobiography.*

41

LILLIAN HELLMAN
Runaway

1   It was that night that I disappeared, and that night that Fizzy said I was disgusting mean, and Mr. Stillman said I would forever pain my mother and father, and my father turned on both of them and said he would handle his family affairs himself without comments from strangers. But he said it too late. He had come home very angry with me: the jeweler, after my father's complaints about his unreliability, had found the lock of hair in the back of the watch. What started out to be a mild reproof on my father's part soon turned angry when I wouldn't explain about the hair. (My father was often angry when I

From *An Unfinished Woman: A Memoir* by Lillian Hellman. Copyright © 1969 by Lillian Hellman. Reprinted by permission of Little, Brown and Co.

was most like him.) He was so angry that he forgot that he was attacking me in front of the Stillmans, my old rival Fizzy, and the delighted Mrs. Dreyfus, a new, rich boarder who only that afternoon had complained about my bad manners. My mother left the room when my father grew angry with me. Hannah, passing through, put up her hand as if to stop my father and then, frightened of the look he gave her, went out to the porch. I sat on the couch, astonished at the pain in my head. I tried to get up from the couch, but one ankle turned and I sat down again, knowing for the first time the rampage that could be caused in me by anger. The room began to have other forms, the people were no longer men and women, my head was not my own. I told myself that my head had gone somewhere and I have little memory of anything after my Aunt Jenny came into the room and said to my father, "Don't you remember?" I have never known what she meant, but I knew that soon after I was moving up the staircase, that I slipped and fell a few steps, that when I woke up hours later in my bed, I found a piece of angel cake—an old love, an old custom—left by my mother on my pillow. The headache was worse and I vomited out of the window. Then I dressed, took my red purse, and walked a long way down St. Charles Avenue. A St. Charles Avenue mansion had on its back lawn a famous doll's-house, an elaborate copy of the mansion itself, built years before for the small daughter of the house. As I passed this showpiece, I saw a policeman and moved swiftly back to the doll palace and crawled inside. If I had known about the fantasies of the frightened, that ridiculous small house would not have been so terrible for me. I was surrounded by ornate, carved reproductions of the mansion furniture, scaled for children, bisque figurines in miniature, a working toilet seat of gold leaf in suitable size, small draperies of damask with a sign that said "From the damask of Marie Antoinette," a miniature samovar with small bronze cups, and a tiny Madame Récamier couch on which I spent the night, my legs on the floor. I must have slept, because I woke from a nightmare and knocked over a bisque figurine. The noise frightened me, and since it was now almost light, in one of those lovely mist mornings of late spring when every flower in New Orleans seems to melt and mix with the air, I crawled out. Most of that day I spent walking, although I had a long session in the ladies' room of the railroad station. I had four dollars and two bits, but that wasn't much when you meant it to last forever and when you knew it would not be easy for a fourteen-year-old girl to find work in a city where too many people knew her. Three times I stood in line at the railroad ticket windows to ask where I could go for four dollars, but each time the question seemed too dangerous and I knew no other way of asking.

Toward evening, I moved to the French Quarter, feeling sad and envious as people went home to dinner. I bought a few Tootsie Rolls and a half loaf of bread and went to the St. Louis Cathedral in Jackson

Square. (It was that night that I composed the prayer that was to become, in the next five years, an obsession, mumbled over and over through the days and nights: "God forgive me, Papa forgive me, Mama forgive me, Sophronia, Jenny, Hannah, and all others, through this time and that time, in life and in death." When I was nineteen, my father, who had made several attempts through the years to find out what my lip movements meant as I repeated the prayer, said, "How much would you take to stop that? Name it and you've got it." I suppose I was sick of the nonsense by that time because I said, "A leather coat and a feather fan," and the next day he bought them for me.) After my loaf of bread, I went looking for a bottle of soda pop and discovered, for the first time, the whorehouse section around Bourbon Street. The women were ranged in the doorways of the cribs, making the first early evening offers to sailors, who were the only men in the streets. I wanted to stick around and see how things like that worked, but the second or third time I circled the block, one of the girls called out to me. I couldn't understand the words, but the voice was angry enough to make me run toward the French Market.

3   The Market was empty except for two old men. One of them called to me as I went past, and I turned to see that he had opened his pants and was shaking what my circle called "his thing." I flew across the street into the coffee stand, forgetting that the owner had known me since I was a small child when my Aunt Jenny would rest from her marketing tour with a cup of fine, strong coffee.

4   He said, in the patois, "*Que faites, ma 'fant? Je suis fermé.*"

5   I said, "*Rein. My tante attend*"—Could I have a doughnut?

6   He brought me two doughnuts, saying one was *lagniappe*, but I took my doughnuts outside when he said, "*Mais où est vo' tante à c'heure?*"

7   I fell asleep with my doughnuts behind a shrub in Jackson Square. The night was damp and hot and through the sleep were many voices and, much later, there was music from somewhere near the river. When all sounds had ended, I woke, turned my head, and knew I was being watched. Two rats were sitting a few feet from me. I urinated on my dress, crawled backwards to stand up, screamed as I ran up the steps of St. Louis Cathedral and pounded on the doors. I don't know when I stopped screaming or how I got to the railroad station, but I stood against the wall trying to tear off my dress and only knew I was doing it when two women stopped to stare at me. I began to have cramps in my stomach of a kind I had never known before. I went to the ladies' room and sat bent in a chair, whimpering with pain. After a while the cramps stopped, but I had an intimation, when I looked into the mirror, of something happening to me: my face was blotched, and there seemed to be circles and twirls I had never seen before, the

straight blonde hair was damp with sweat, and a paste of green from the shrub had made lines on my jaw. I had gotten older.

Sometime during that early morning I half washed my dress, 8 threw away my pants, put cold water on my hair. Later in the morning a cleaning woman appeared, and after a while began to ask questions that frightened me. When she put down her mop and went out of the room, I ran out of the station. I walked, I guess, for many hours, but when I saw a man on Canal Street who worked in Hannah's office, I realized that the sections of New Orleans that were known to me were dangerous for me.

Years before, when I was a small child, Sophronia and I would go 9 to pick up, or try on, pretty embroidered dresses that were made for me by a colored dressmaker called Bibettera. A block up from Bibettera's there had been a large ruin of a house with a sign, ROOMS— CLEAN—CHEAP, and cheerful people seemed always to be moving in and out of the house. The door of the house was painted a bright pink. I liked that and would discuss with Sophronia why we didn't live in a house with a pink door.

Bibettera was long since dead, so I knew I was safe in this Negro 10 neighborhood. I went up and down the block several times, praying that things would work and I could take my cramps to bed. I knocked on the pink door. It was answered immediately by a small young man.

I said, "Hello." He said nothing. 11

I said, "I would like to rent a room, please." 12

He closed the door but I waited, thinking he had gone to get the 13 lady of the house. After a long time, a middle-aged woman put her head out of a second-floor window and said, "What you at?"

I said, "I would like to rent a room, please. My mama is a widow 14 and has gone to work across the river. She gave me money and said to come here until she called for me."

"Who your mama?" 15

"Er. My mama." 16

"What you at? Speak out." 17

"I told you. I have money . . ." But as I tried to open my purse, 18 the voice grew angry.

"This is a nigger house. Get you off. *Vite.*" 19

I said, in a whisper, "I know. I'm part nigger." 20

The small young man opened the front door. He was laughing. 21 "You part mischief. Get the hell out of here."

I said, "Please"—and then, "I'm related to Sophronia Mason. She 22 told me to come. Ask her."

Sophronia and her family were respected figures in New Orleans 23 Negro circles, and because I had some vague memory of her stately bow to somebody as she passed this house, I believed they knew her. If they told her about me I would be in trouble, but phones were not usual then in poor neighborhoods, and I had no other place to go.

24   The woman opened the door. Slowly I went into the hall.

25   I said, "I won't stay long. I have four dollars and Sophronia will give more if . . . "

26   The woman pointed up the stairs. She opened the door of a small room. "Washbasin place down the hall. Toilet place behind the kitchen. Two-fifty and no fuss, no bother."

27   I said, "Yes, ma'am, yes ma'am," but as she started to close the door, the young man appeared.

28   "Where your bag?"

29   "Bag?"

30   "Nobody put up here without no bag."

31   "Oh. You mean the bag with my clothes? It's at the station. I'll go and get it later . . ." I stopped because I knew I was about to say I'm sick, I'm in pain, I'm frightened.

32   He said, "I say you lie. I say you trouble. I say you get out."

33   I said, "And I say you shut up."

34   Years later, I was to understand why the command worked, and to be sorry that it did, but that day I was very happy when he turned and closed the door. I was asleep within minutes.

35   Toward evening, I went down the stairs, saw nobody, walked a few blocks and bought myself an oyster loaf. But the first bite made me feel sick, so I took my loaf back to the house. This time, as I climbed the steps, there were three women in the parlor, and they stopped talking when they saw me. I went back to sleep immediately, dizzy and nauseated.

36   I woke to a high, hot sun and my father standing at the foot of the bed staring at the oyster loaf.

37   He said, "Get up now and get dressed."

38   I was crying as I said, "Thank you, Papa, but I can't."

39   From the hall, Sophronia said, "Get along up now. *Vite.* The morning is late."

40   My father left the room. I dressed and came into the hall carrying my oyster loaf. Sophronia was standing at the head of the stairs. She pointed out, meaning my father was on the street.

41   I said, "He humiliated me. He did. I won't . . . "

42   She said, "Get you going or I will never see you whenever again."

43   I ran past her to the street. I stood with my father until Sophronia joined us, and then we walked slowly, without speaking, to the street-car line. Sophronia bowed to us, but she refused my father's hand when he attempted to help her into the car. I ran to the car meaning to ask her to take me with her, but the car moved and she raised her hand as if to stop me. My father and I walked again for a long time.

He pointed to a trash can sitting in front of a house. "Please put 44 that oyster loaf in the can."

At Vanalli's restaurant, he took my arm. "Hungry?" 45

I said, "No, thank you, Papa." 46

But we went through the door. It was, in those days, a New Or- 47 leans custom to have an early black coffee, go to the office, and after a few hours have a large breakfast at a restaurant. Vanalli's was crowded, the headwaiter was so sorry, but after my father took him aside, a very small table was put up for us—too small for my large father, who was accommodating himself to it in a manner most unlike him.

He said, "Jack, my rumpled daughter would like cold crayfish, a 48 nice piece of pompano, separate bowl of Béarnaise sauce, don't ask me why, French fried potatoes . . . "

I said, "Thank you, Papa, but I am not hungry. I don't want to be 49 here."

My father waved the waiter away and we sat in silence until the 50 crayfish came. My hand reached out instinctively and then drew back.

My father said, "Your mother and I have had an awful time." 51

I said, "I'm sorry about that. But I don't want to go home, Papa." 52

He said, angrily, "Yes, you do. But you want me to apologize 53 first. I do apologize but you should not have made me say it."

After a while I mumbled, "God forgive me, Papa forgive me, 54 Mama forgive me, Sophronia, Jenny, Hannah . . . "

"Eat your crayfish." 55

I ate everything he had ordered and then a small steak. I suppose 56 I had been mumbling throughout my breakfast.

My father said, "You're talking to yourself. I can't hear you. 57 What are you saying?"

"God forgive me, Papa forgive me, Mama forgive me, Sophronia, 58 Jenny . . . "

My father said, "Where do we start your training as the first Jew- 59 ish nun on Prytania Street?"

When I finished laughing, I liked him again. I said, "Papa, I'll tell 60 you a secret. I've had very bad cramps and I am beginning to bleed. I'm changing life."

He stared at me for a while. Then he said, "Well, it's not the way 61 it's usually described, but it's accurate, I guess. Let's go home now to your mother."

We were never, as long as my mother and father lived, to men- 62 tion that time again. But it was of great importance to them and I've thought about it all my life. From that day on I knew my power over my parents. That was not to be too important: I was ashamed of it and did not abuse it too much. But I found out something more useful and more dangerous: if you are willing to take the punishment, you are halfway through the battle. That the issue may be trivial, the battle ugly, is another point.

____ CONSIDERATIONS _____

1. Hellman's recollection of running away at fourteen is complicated by her refusal to tell it in strict chronology. Instead, she interrupts the narrative with flashbacks and episodes of later years. How can one justify such interruptions?

2. On page 260, as she is trying to talk her way into the rooming house in the black district, Hellman tells a young man to shut up and then adds, "Years later, I was to understand why the command worked, and to be sorry that it did." What did she later understand?

3. What was the "power over my parents" that Hellman learned from her runaway experience? Have you ever wielded such power?

4. Accounts of childhood escapades often suffer as the author idealizes or glamorizes them. Does Hellman successfully resist the temptation? What is your evidence?

5. The bases the fourteen-year-old runaway touched in her flight were actually part of a familiar world: a doll's house, a cathedral, a market, a railroad station. How does Hellman give her flight more than a touch of horror?

6. In what specific ways did her first menstrual period heighten and distort some of the things that happened—or seemed to happen—to the fourteen-year-old runaway? Discuss the ways in which physiological and psychological conditions seem to feed on each other.

Edward Hoagland (b. 1932) was born in New York City and lives there much of the year, alternating between Manhattan and the countryside of northern Vermont. He has written novels but is best known for his essays, many like "The Urge for and End" published in Harper's. *His recent books are* The Final Fate of the Alligators *and* Balancing Acts *(both 1992).*

42

EDWARD HOAGLAND
The Urge for an End

A friend of mine, a peaceable soul who has been riding the New York subways for thirty years, finds himself stepping back from the tracks once in a while and closing his eyes as the train rolls in. This, he says, is not only to suppress an urge to throw himself in front of it but because every couple of weeks an impulse rises in him to push a stranger onto the tracks, any stranger, thus ending his own life too. He blames this partly on apartment living—"pigeonholes without being able to fly."   1

It is profoundly startling not to trust oneself after decades of doing so. I don't dare keep ammunition in my country house for a small rifle I bought secondhand two decades ago. The gun sat in a cupboard in the back room with the original box of .22 bullets under the muzzle all that time, seldom fired except at a few apples hanging in a tree every fall to remind me of my army training near the end of the Korean War, when I'd been considered quite a marksman. When I bought the gun I didn't trust either my professional competence as a writer or my competence as a father as much as I came to do, but certainly believed I could keep myself alive. I bought it for protection, and the idea that someday I might be afraid of shooting myself with the gun would have seemed inconceivable—laughable.   2

One's fifties can be giddy years, as anybody fifty knows. Chest pains, back pains, cancer scares, menopausal or prostate complications are not the least of it, and the fidelities of a lifetime, both personal and professional, may be called into question. Was it a mistake   3

Reprinted by permission of the author.

to have stuck so long with one's marriage, and to have stayed with a lackluster well-paying job? (Or *not* to have stayed and stuck?) People not only lose faith in their talents and their dreams or values; some simply tire of them. Grow tired, too, of the smell of fried-chicken grease, once such a delight, and the cold glutinosity of ice cream, the boredom of beer, the stop-go of travel, the hiccups of laughter, and of two rush hours a day, then the languor of weekends, of athletes as well as accountants, and even the frantic birdsong of spring—red-eyed vireos that have been clocked singing 22,000 times in a day. Life is a matter of cultivating the five senses (the sixth too), and an equilibrium with nature and what I think of as its subdivision, human nature, trusting no one completely but almost everyone at least a little; but this is easier said than done.

4   More than 30,000 Americans took their own lives last year, men mostly, with the highest rate being among those older than sixty-five. When I asked a friend of mine why three times as many men kill themselves as members of her own sex, she replied with sudden anger, "I'm not going to go into the self-indulgence of men." Suicide is an exasperating act as often as it is pitiable. "Committing" suicide is in bad odor in our culture even among those who don't believe that to cash in your chips ahead of time and hand back to God his gifts to you is a blasphemous sin. We the living, in any case, are likely to feel accused by this person who "voted with his feet." It appears to cast a subversive judgment upon the social polity as a whole that what was supposed to work in life—religion, family, friendship, commerce, and industry—did not; and furthermore, it "frightens the horses in the street," as Virginia Woolf once defined wrongful behavior (before she killed herself).

5   Many suicides inflict outrageous trauma, burning permanent injuries into the minds of their children, though they may have joked beforehand only of "taking a dive." And sometimes the gesture has a peevish or cowardly aspect, or seems to have been senselessly short-sighted as far as an outside observer can tell. There are desperate suicides and crafty suicides, people who do it to cause others trouble and people who do it to save others trouble, deranged exhibitionists who yell from a building ledge and closedmouthed, secretive souls who swim out into the ocean's anonymity. Suicide may in fact be an attempt to escape death, shortcut the dreadful deteriorating processes, abort one's natural trajectory, elude "the ruffian on the stairs," in A. E. Housman's phrase for a cruelly painful and anarchic death—make it neat and not messy. The deed can be grandiose or self-abnegating, vindictive or drably mousy, rationally plotted or plainly insane. People sidle toward death, intent upon outwitting their own bodies' defenses, or they may dramatize the chance to make one last, unambiguous, irrevocable decision, like a captain scuttling his ship—death before dishonor—leaping toward oblivion through a curtain of pain, like a frog

going down the throat of a snake. One man I knew hosted a quietly affectionate evening with several unknowing friends on the night before he swallowed too many pills. Another waved an apologetic good-bye to a bystander on a bridge; rarely considerate, he turned apologetic in the last moment of life. Never physically inclined, he made a great vault toward the ice on the Mississippi.

In the army, we wore dog tags with a notch at one end by which   6
these numbered pieces of metal could be jammed between our teeth, if we lay dead and nameless on a battlefield, for later sorting. As "servicemen" our job would be to kill people who were pointed out to us as enemies, or make "the supreme sacrifice" for a higher good than enjoying the rest of our lives. Life was very much a possession, in other words—not only God's, but the soldier's own to dispose of. Working in an army hospital, I frequently did handle dead bodies, but this never made me feel I would refuse to kill another man whose uniform was pointed out to me as being inimical, or value my life more tremulously and vigilantly. The notion of dying for my country didn't appeal to me as much as dying free-lance for my ideas (in the unlikely event I *could* do that), but I was ready. People were taught during the 1940s and '50s that one should be ready to die for one's beliefs. Heroes were revered because they had deliberately chosen to give up their lives. Life would not be worth living under the tyranny of an invader, and Nathan Hale apparently hadn't paused to consider whether God might have other uses for him besides being hanged. Nor did the pilot Colin Kelly hesitate before crashing his plane into a Japanese battleship, becoming America's first well-publicized hero in World War II.

I've sometimes wondered why people who know that they are   7
terminally ill, or who are headed for suicide, so very seldom have paused to take a bad guy along with them. It is lawless to consider an act of assassination, yet hardly more lawless, really, than suicide is regarded in some quarters. Government bureaucracies, including our own, in their majesty and as the executors of laws, regularly weigh the pros and cons of murdering foreign antagonists. Of course the answer is that most individuals are fortunately more timid as well as humbler in their judgment than government officialdom; but beyond that, when dying or suicidal, people no longer care enough to devote their final energies to doing good works of any kind—Hitler himself in their gun sights they would have passed up. Some suicides become so crushed and despairing that they can't recognize the consequences of anything they do; and it's not primarily vindictiveness that wreaks such havoc upon their survivors but their derangement from ordinary life.

Courting the idea is different from the real impulse. "When he   8
begged for help, we took him and locked him up," another friend of

mine says, speaking of her husband. "Not till then. Wishing to be out of the situation you are in—feeling helpless and unable to cope—is not the same as wishing to be dead. If I actually wished to be dead, even my children's welfare would have no meaning."

9   You might think the ready option of divorce available lately would have cut suicide rates, offering an escape to battered wives, lovelorn husbands, and other people in despair. But it doesn't work that way. When the number of choices people have is increased, an entire range of possibilities opens up. The suicide rate among teenagers has nearly quadrupled since 1950, although the standard of comfort that their families enjoy has gone up. Black Americans, less affluent than white Americans, have a suicide rate about half that of whites.

10   Still, if a fiftyish fellow with fine teeth and a foolproof pension plan, a cottage at the beach and the Fourth of July weekend coming up, kills himself, it seems truculent. We would look at him bafflingly if he told us he no longer likes the Sturm und Drang of banging fireworks.

11   *Then stay at your hideaway!* we'd argue with him.

12   "Big mouths eat little mouths. Nature isn't 'timeless.' Whole lives are squeezed into three months or three days."

13   *What about your marriage?*

14   "She's become more mannish than me. I loved women. I don't believe in marriage between men."

15   *Remarry, then!*

16   "I've gone impotent, and besides, when I see somebody young and pretty I guess I feel like dandling her on my knee."

17   *Marriage is friendship. You can find someone your own age.*

18   "I'm tired of it."

19   *But how about your company?—it's positioned itself on the cutting edge of the silicon frontier. That's interesting.*

20   "I know what wins. It's less and less appetizing."

21   *You're not scared of death anymore?*

22   "It interests me less than it did."

23   *What are you so sick of? The rest of us keep going.*

24   "I'm tired of weathermen and sportscasters on the screen. Of being patient and also of impatience. I'm tired of the President, whoever the President happens to be, and sleeping badly, with forty-eight half hours in the day—of breaking two eggs every morning and putting sugar on something. I'm tired of the drone of my voice, but also of us jabbering like parrots at each other—of all our stumpy ways of doing everything."

25   *You're bored with yourself?*

26   "I'm maybe the least interesting person I know."

27   *But to* kill *yourself?*

28   "You know, it's a tradition, too," he remarks quietly, not making so bold as to suggest that the tradition is an honorable one, though his

tone of voice might be imagined to imply this. "I guess I've always been a latent maverick."

Except in circumstances which are themselves a matter of life and death, I'm reluctant to agree with the idea that suicide is not the result of mental illness. No matter how reasonably the person appears to have examined his options, it goes against the grain of nature for him to destroy himself. And any illness that threatens his life changes a person. Suicidal thinking, if serious, can be a kind of death scare, comparable to suffering a heart attack or undergoing a cancer operation. One survives such a phase both warier and chastened. When—two years ago—I emerged from a bad dip into suicidal speculation, I felt utterly exhausted and yet quite fearless of ordinary dangers, vastly afraid of myself but much less scared of extraneous eventualities. The fact of death may not be tragic; many people die with a bit of a smile that captures their mouths at the last instant, and some who are revived after a deadly accident are reluctant to be brought to life, resisting resuscitation, and carrying back confusing, beamish, or ecstatic memories. But the same impetuosity that made him throw himself out of a window might have enabled that person to love life all the more if he'd been calibrated somewhat differently at the time of the emergency. Death's edge is so abrupt and near that many who expect a short, momentary dive may be astounded to find that it is bottomless and change their minds and start to scream when they are only halfway down.

Although my fright at my mind's anarchy superseded my fear of death in the conventional guise of heart seizures, airplane crashes, and so on, nightmares are more primitive, and in my dreams I continued to be scared of a death not sought after—dying from driving too fast and losing control of the car, breaking through thin ice while skating and drowning in the cold, or falling off a cliff. When I am tense and sleeping raggedly, my worst nightmare isn't drawn from anxious prepschool memories or the bad spells of my marriages or any of adulthood's vicissitudes. Nothing else from the past half-century has the staying power in my mind of the elevated train rides that my father and I used to take down Third Avenue to the Battery in New York City on Sunday afternoons when I was three or four or five, so I could see the fish at the aquarium. We were probably pretty good companions in those years, but the wooden platforms forty feet up shook terribly as trains from both directions pulled in and out. To me they seemed worse than rickety—ready to topple. And the roar was fearful, and the railings left large gaps for a child to fall through, after the steep climb up the slatsided, windy, shaking stairway from street level. It's a rare dream, but several times a year I still find myself on such a perch, without his company or anybody else's, on a boyish or a grownup's mission, when the elevated platform begins to rattle desperately, seesaw, heel over, and finally come apart, disintegrate, while I cling to struts and trusses.

31   My father, as he lay dying at home of bowel cancer, used to enjoy watching Tarzan reruns on the children's hour of television. Like a strong green vine, they swung him far away from his deathbed to a world of skinnydipping, friendly animals, and scenic beauty linked to the lost realities of his adolescence in Kansas City. Earlier, when he was still able to walk without much pain, he'd paced the house for several hours at night, contemplating suicide, I expect, along with other anguishing thoughts, regrets, remembrances, and yearnings. I don't know how much of that decision was for his wife and children, how much was because he didn't want to be a "quitter," as he sometimes put it, and how much was due to his believing that life belongs to God (which I'm not even sure he did). He was not a churchgoer after his thirties. He had belonged to J. P. Morgan's church, St. George's, on Stuyvesant Square—Morgan was a hero of his—but when things went a little wrong for him at the Wall Street law firm he worked for, and he changed jobs and moved out to the suburbs, he became a skeptic on religious matters, and gradually, in the absence of faith of that previous kind, he adhered to a determined allegiance to the social order. Dwight D. Eisenhower instead of J. P. Morgan became the sort of hero he admired, and suicide would have seemed an act of insurrection against the laws and conventions of the society, internationalist-Republican, that he believed in.

32   I was never particularly afraid that I might plan a suicide, swallowing a bunch of pills and keeping them down—only of what I think of as Anna Karenina's kind of death. This most plausible self-killing in all of literature is frightening because it was unwilled, regretted at midpoint, and came as a complete surprise to Anna herself. After rushing impulsively, in great misery, to the Moscow railway station to catch a train, she ended up underneath another one, dismayed, astonished, and trying to climb out from under the wheels even as they crushed her. Many people who briefly verge on suicide undergo a mental somersault for a terrifying interval during which they're upside down, their perspective topsy-turvy, skidding, churning; and this is why I got rid of the bullets for my .22.

33   Nobody expects to trust his body overmuch after the age of fifty. Incipient cataracts or arthritis, outlandish snores, tooth-grinding, ankles that threaten to turn are part of the game. But not to trust one's *mind?* That's a surprise. The single attribute that older people were sure to have (we thought as boys) was a stodgy dependability, a steady temperance and caution. Adults might be vain, unimaginative, pompous, and callous, but they did have their affairs tightly in hand. It was not till my thirties that I began to know friends who were in their fifties on equal terms, and I remember being amused, piqued, and bewildered to learn that some of them still felt as marginal or rebellious or in a quandary about what to do with themselves for the next dozen

years as my contemporaries were likely to. Even that close to retirement, some of them harbored a deep-seated contempt for the organizations they had been working for, ready to walk away from almost everybody they had known and the efforts of whole decades with very little sentiment. Nor did twenty years of marriage necessarily mean more than two or three—they might be just as ready to walk away from that also, and didn't really register it as twenty years at all. Rather, life could be about to begin all over again. "Bummish" was how one man described himself, with a raffish smile—"Lucky to have a roof over my head"—though he'd just put a child through Yale. He was quitting his job and claimed with exasperation that his wife still cried for her mother in her sleep, as if they'd never been married.

The great English traveler Richard Burton quoted an Arab 34
proverb that speaks for many middle-aged men of the old-fashioned variety: "Conceal thy Tenets, thy Treasure and thy Travelling." These are serious matters, in other words. People didn't conceal their tenets in order to betray them, but to fight for them more opportunely. And except for kings and princelings, concealing whatever treasure one had went without saying. As for travel, a man's travels were also a matter of gravity. Travel was knowledge, ambiguity, dalliances or misalliances, divided loyalty, forbidden thinking; and besides, someday he might need to make a run for it and go to ground someplace where he had made some secret friends. Friends of mine whose husbands or whose wives have died have been quite startled afterward to discover caches of money or traveler's checks concealed around the house, or a bundle of cash in a safe-deposit box.

Burton, like any other desert adage-spinner (and most individuals 35
over fifty), would have agreed to an addition so obvious that it wasn't included to begin with: "Conceal thy Illnesses." I can remember how urgently my father worried that word would get out, after a preliminary operation for his cancer. He didn't want to be written off, counted out of the running at the corporation he worked for and in other enclaves of competition. Men often compete with one another until the day they die; comradeship consists of rubbing shoulders jocularly with a competitor. As breadwinners, they must be considered fit and sound by friend as well as foe, and so there's lots of truth to the most common answer I heard when asking why three times as many men as women kill themselves: "They keep their troubles to themselves"; "They don't know how to ask for help."

I'm not entirely like that, and I discovered that when I confided 36
something of my perturbation to a woman friend, she was likely to keep telephoning me or mailing cheery postcards, whereas a man would usually listen with concern, communicate his sympathy, and maybe intimate that he had pondered the same drastic course of action himself a few years back and would end up respecting my decision either way. Open-mindedness seems an important attribute to a

good many men who pride themselves on being objective, hearing all sides of an issue, on knowing that truth and honesty do not always coincide with social dicta, and who may even cherish a subterranean outlaw streak that, like being ready to violently defend one's family, reputation, and country, is by tradition male.

37   Men, having been so much freer than women in society, used to feel they had less of a stake in the maintenance of certain churchly conventions and enjoyed speaking irreverently about various social truisms, including even the principle that people ought to die on schedule, not cutting in ahead of their assigned place in line. Contemporary women, after their triumphant irreverence during the 1960s and 1970s, cannot be generalized about so easily. They turn as skeptical and saturnine as any man. In fact, women attempt suicide more frequently, but favor pills or other methods, whereas two-thirds of the men who kill themselves use a gun: in 1985, 85 percent of suicides by means of firearms were committed by men. An overdose of medication hasn't the same finality. It may be reversible if the person is discovered quickly, or be subject to benign miscalculation to start with. Even if it works, perhaps it can be fudged by a kindly doctor in the recordkeeping. Like an enigmatic drowning or a single-car accident that baffles the suspicions of the insurance company, a suicide by drugs can be a way to avoid making a loud statement, and merely illustrate the final modesty of a person who didn't wish to ask for too much of the world's attention.

38   Unconsummated attempts at suicide can strike the rest of us as self-pitying, self-aggrandizing, or as plaintive plea-bargaining—"childish," we say, though actually the helplessness that echoes through a child's suicide is ghastly beyond any stunt of self-mutilation an adult may indulge in. It would be hard to define chaos better than as a world where children decide that they don't want to live.

39   Love is the solution to all dilemmas, we sometimes hear; and in those moments when the spirit bathes itself in beneficence and manages to transcend the static of personalities rubbing fur off of each other, indeed it is. Without love nothing matters, Paul told the Corinthians, a mystery which, if true, has no ready Darwinian explanation. Love without a significant sexual component and for people who are unrelated to us serves little practical purpose. It doesn't help us feed our families, win struggles, thrive, and prosper. It distracts us from the ordinary business of sizing people up and making a living, and is not even conducive to intellectual observation, because instead of seeing them, we see right through them to the bewildered child and dreaming adolescent who inhabited their bodies earlier, the now tired idealist who fell in and out of love, got hired and quit, bought cars and wore them out, like black-eyed susans, blueberry muffins, and roosters crowing—liked roosters crowing better than skyscrapers but now

likes skyscrapers better than roosters crowing. As swift as thought, we select the details that we need to see in order to be able to love them.

Yet at other times we'll dispense with these same poignancies 40 and choose only their grunginess to look at, their pinched mouths and shifty eyes, their thirst for gin at noon and indifference to their kids, their greed for the best tidbit on the buffet table, and their penchant for poking their penises up the excretory end of other human beings. I tend to gaze quite closely at the faces of priests I meet on the street to see if a lifetime of love has marked them noticeably. Real serenity or asceticism I no longer expect, and I take for granted the beefy calm that often goes with Catholic celibacy, but I am watching for the marks of love and often see mere resignation or tenacity.

Many men are romantics, likely to plunge, go for broke, take ac- 41 tion in a spirit of exigency rather than waiting for the problem to re- solve itself. Then, still as romantics, they may drift into despairing passivity, stare at the TV all day long, and binge with a bottle. Women too may turn frenetic for a while and then throw up their hands; but though they may not seem as grandiosely fanciful and romantic at the outset, they are more frequently believers—at least they seem to me to believe in God or in humanity, the future, and so on. We have above us the inviting eternity of "the heavens," if we choose to look at it, ly- ing on our backs in the summer grass under starlight, some of which had left its source before mankind became man. But because we live in our heads more than in nature nowadays, even the summer sky is a mine field for people whose memories are mined. With the sky no longer humbling, and sunshine only a sort of convenience, and no god- head located anywhere outside of our own heads, every problem may seem insolubly interlocked. When the telephone has become impossi- ble to answer at home, sometimes it finally becomes impossible to stride down the gangplank of a cruise ship in Mombasa too, although no telephones will ring for you there.

But if escapist travel is ruled out in certain emergencies, surely 42 you can *pray*? Pray, yes; but to whom? That requires a bit of prepara- tion. Rarely do people obtain much relief from praying if they haven't stood in line awhile to get a visa. It's an appealing idea that you can just *go*, and in a previous era perhaps you could have. But it's not so simple now. What do you believe in? Whom are you praying to? What are you praying for? There's no crèche on the courthouse lawn; you're not supposed to adhere exactly even to what your parent believed. Like psychotherapy, praying takes time, even if you know which di- rection to face when you kneel.

Love is powerfully helpful when the roof falls in—loving other 43 people with a high and hopeful heart and as a kind of prayer. That feat too, however, requires new and sudden insights or long practice. The beatitude of loving strangers as well as friends—loving them on sight with a leap of empathy and intuition—is a form of inspiration, edging, of course, in some cases toward madness, as other states of beatitude can do. But there's no question that a genuine love for the living will stymie suicidal depressions not chemical in origin. Love is an elixir, changing the life of the lover. And many of us have experienced this— a temporary lightening of our leery, prickly disapproval of much of the rest of the world, when at a wedding or a funeral of shared emotion, or when we have fallen in love.

44   Yet the zest for life of those unusual men and women who make a great zealous success of living is due more often in good part to the crafty pertinacity with which they manage to overlook the misery of others. You can watch them watch life beat the stuffing out of the faces of their friends and acquaintances, yet they themselves seem to outwit the dense delays of social custom, the tedious tick-tock of bureaucratic obfuscation, accepting loss and age and change and disappointment without suffering punctures in their stomach lining. Breathlessness or strange dull pains from their nether organs don't nonplus them. They fret and doubt in moderation, and love a lobster roast, squeeze lemon juice on living clams on the half shell to prove that the clams are alive, laugh as a robin tussles a worm out of the ground or a kitten flees a dog. Like the problem drinkers, pork eaters, and chain smokers who nevertheless finish out their allotted years, succumbing to a stroke at a nice round biblical age when the best vitamin-eating vegetarian has long since died, their faces become veritable walnuts of fine character, with the same smile lines as the rarer individual whose grin has been affectionate all of his life.

45   We spend our lives getting to know ourselves, yet wonders never cease. During my adolescent years my states of mind, though undulant, seemed seamless; even when I was unhappy, no cracks or fissures made me wonder if I was a danger to myself. My confidence was such that I treaded the slippery lips of waterfalls, fought forest fires, drove ancient cars cross-country night and day, and scratched the necks of menagerie leopards in the course of various adventures which enhanced the joy of being alive. The chemistry of the mind, because unfathomable, is more frightening. In the city, I live on the waterfront and occasionally will notice an agitated-looking figure picking his way along the pilings and stringpieces of the timbered piers nearby, staring at the sliding whorls on the surface of the Hudson as if teetering over an abyss. Our building, across the street, seems imposing from the water and over the years has acted as a magnet for a number of suicides— people who have dreaded the clammy chill, the onerous smothering essential to their first plan. One woman climbed out after jumping in and took the elevator to our roof (my neighbors remember how wringing wet she was), and leapt off, banging window ledges on the way down, and hit with the whap of a sack of potatoes, as others have.

But what is more remarkable than that a tiny minority of souls   46
reach a point where they entrust their bodies to the force of gravity is
that so few of the rest of us splurge an hour of a summer day gazing at
the trees and sky. How many summers do we *have*?

People with sunny natures do seem to live longer than people   47
who are nervous wrecks; yet mankind didn't evolve out of the animal
kingdom by being unduly sunny-minded. Life was fearful and phantas-
magoric, supernatural and preternatural, as well as encompassing the
kind of clockwork regularity of our well-governed day. It had numerous superstitious elements, such as we are likely to catch a whiff of
only when we're peering at a dead body. And it was not just our opti-
mism but our pessimistic premonitions, our dark moments as a
species, our irrational, frightful speculations, our strange mutations
upon the simple theme of love, and our sleepless, obsessive inventive-
ness—our dread as well as our faith—that made us human beings.
Staking one's life on the more general good came to include risking
suicide also. Brilliant, fecund people sometimes kill themselves.

Joy to the world! . . . Let heaven and nature sing, and heaven and   48
nature sing. The famous Christmas carol invokes not only glee but
unity: heaven with nature, not always a Christian combination. It's a
rapturous hymn, and no one should refuse to surrender to such a pitch
of revelation when it comes. But the flip side of rapture can be a riptide of panic, or hysterical gloom. Our faces are not molded as if joy
were a preponderant experience. (Nor is a caribou's or a thrush's.) Our
faces in repose look stoic or battered, and people of the sunniest temperament sometimes die utterly unstrung, doubting everything they
have ever believed in.

Let heaven and nature sing! But *is* there such harmony? Are God   49
and Mother Nature really the same? And will we risk burning our
wings if we mount high enough to try to see? I've noticed that woods
soil in Italy smells the same as woods soil in New England when you
pick up a handful of it and enjoy its aromas—but is God there the
same? It can be precarious to wonder. I don't rule out suicide as being
unthinkable for people who have tried to live full lives, and don't regard it as negating the work and faith and even ecstasy they may have
known before. In killing himself a person acknowledges his failures
during a time span when perhaps heaven and earth had caught him
like a pair of scissors—but not his life span. Man is different from animals in that he speculates, a high-risk activity.

_____ CONSIDERATIONS _____

1. In paragraph 3, Hoagland includes the one reason for suicide with which it is probably most difficult to argue. Identify that reason.

2. What do you see as the unifying idea of paragraph 5, in which no main idea is overtly stated?

3. Why, according to Hoagland, do so few people—terminally ill or headed for suicide—seize the opportunity to rid the world of a public enemy?

4. "The Urge for an End" is an informal, personal essay in that Hoagland writes in the first person, relies heavily on his personal experience, and adopts a casual, slangy, almost playful tone. With an eye (and an ear) open to Hoagland's tone, study the essay and collect examples of language that create and maintain the writer's attitude.

5. Our expectations of each other figure frequently in Hoagland's essay. In paragraph 33, what was he surprised to learn about his expectations of older people?

6. In paragraphs 34 and 35, Hoagland refers to the tendency among older people to conceal their illnesses. Use your own experience with older people and/or your reading to build an essay confirming or refuting Hoagland's idea.

7. In the last third of his essay, Hoagland presents what he calls the world's best definition of chaos. What has that to do with suicide? (Hint: In paragraph 9, he reports that "The suicide rate among teenagers has nearly quadrupled since 1950. . . .")

8. In paragraph 41, the author writes ". . . we live in our heads more than in nature nowadays," and in paragraph 46, he wonders that "so few of the rest of us splurge an hour of a summer day gazing at the trees and sky." Read Robert Finch's essay "Very Like a Whale," especially paragraphs 15, 16, 17, and 18, and/or the entry from Henry David Thoreau's journal of November 30, 1858. Draw from those readings and your own life to develop into an essay Hoagland's implications that nature might have a preventive or curative effect on would-be suicides.

Andrew Holleran (b. 1943) has written essays for New York *magazine and* Christopher Street, *as well as two novels:* Dancer from the Dance *(1978) and* Nights in Aruba *(1984).* Ground Zero *(1988) collects his essays, including "Bedside Manners."*

43

ANDREW HOLLERAN

Bedside Manners

"There is no difference between men so profound," wrote Scott 1
Fitzgerald, "as that between the sick and the well."

There are many thoughts that fill someone's head as he walks 2
across town on a warm July afternoon to visit a friend confined to a
hospital room—and that is one of them. Another occurs to you as you
wait for the light to change and watch the handsome young basketball
players playing on the public court behind a chicken wire fence:
Health is everywhere. The world has a surreal quality to it when you
are on your way to the hospital to visit someone you care for who is
seriously ill: Everyone in it, walking down the sidewalk, driving by in
cars, rushing about on a basketball court with sweat-stained chests,
exhausted faces, and wide eyes, seems to you extremely peculiar.
They are peculiar because they are free: walking under their own
power, nicely dressed, sometimes beautiful. Beauty does not lose its
allure under the spell of grief. The hospital visitor still notices the
smooth chests of the athletes in their cotton shorts as they leap to recover the basketball after it bounces off the rim. But everything seems
strangely quiet—speechless—as if you were watching a movie on television with the sound turned off, as if everyone else in the world but
you is totally unaware of something: that the act of walking across
York Avenue under one's own power is essentially miraculous.

Every time he enters a hospital, the visitor enters with two si- 3
multaneous thoughts: He hates hospitals, and only people working in
them lead serious lives. Everything else is selfish. Entering a hospital

he always thinks, *I should work for a year as a nurse, an aide, a volunteer helping people, coming to terms with disease and death.* This feeling will pass the moment he leaves the hospital. In reality the visitor hopes his fear and depression are not evident on his face as he walks down the gleaming, silent hall from the elevator to his friend's room. He is trying hard to stay calm.

4   The door of the room the receptionist downstairs has told the visitor his friend is in is closed—and on it are taped four signs that are not on any of the other doors and are headlined, WARNING. The visitor stops as much to read them as to allow his heartbeat to subside before going in. He knows—from the accounts of friends who have already visited—he must don a robe, gloves, mask, and even a plastic cap. He is not sure if the door is closed because his friend is asleep inside or because the door to this room is always kept closed. So he pushes it open a crack and peers in. His friend is turned on his side, a white mound of bed linen, apparently sleeping.

5   The visitor is immensely relieved. He goes down the hall and asks a nurse if he may leave the *Life* magazine he brought for his friend and writes a note to him saying he was here. Then he leaves the hospital and walks west through the summer twilight as if swimming through an enchanted lagoon. The next day—once more crossing town—he is in that surreal mood, under a blue sky decorated with a few photogenic, puffy white clouds, certain that no one else knows . . . knows he or she is absurdly, preposterously, incalculably fortunate to be walking on the street. He feels once again that either the sound has been turned off or some other element (his ego, perhaps with all its anger, ambition, jealousy) has been removed from the world. The basketball players are different youths today but just as much worth pausing to look at. He enters the hospital one block east more calmly this time and requests to see his friend—who is allowed only two visitors at a time, and visits lasting no more than ten minutes. He goes upstairs, peeks around the door, and sees his friend utterly awake. The visitor's heart races as he steps back and puts on the gloves, mask, cap, and robe he has been told his friends all look so comical in. He smiles because he hopes the photograph that made him bring the copy of *Life* to the hospital—Russian women leaning against a wall in Leningrad in bikinis and winter coats, taking the sun on a February day—has amused his friend as much as it tickled him.

6   "Richard?" the visitor says as he opens the door and peeks in. His friend blinks at him. Two plastic tubes are fixed in his nostrils bringing him oxygen. His face is emaciated and gaunt, his hair longer, softer in appearance, wisps rising above his head. But the one feature the visitor cannot get over are his friend's eyes. His eyes are black, huge, and furious. Perhaps because his face is gaunt or perhaps because they really are larger than usual, they seem the only thing alive in his face; as if his whole being were distilled and concentrated, poured, drained,

into his eyes. They are shining, alarmed, and—there is no other word—furious. He looks altogether like an angry baby—or an angry old man—or an angry bald eagle.

And just as the hospital visitor is absorbing the shock of these   7
livid eyes, the sick man says in a furious whisper, "Why did you bring that dreadful magazine? I hate *Life* magazine! With that stupid picture! I wasn't amused! I wasn't amused at all! You should never have brought that dreck into this room!"

The visitor is momentarily speechless: It is the first time in their   8
friendship of ten years that anything abusive or insulting has ever been said; it is as astonishing as the gaunt face in which two huge black eyes burn and shine. But he sits down and recovers his breath and apologizes. The visitor thinks, *He's angry because I haven't visited him till now. He's angry that he's here at all, that he's sick.* And they begin to talk. They talk of the hospital food (which he hates too), of the impending visit of his mother (whose arrival he dreads), of the drug he is taking (which is experimental), and of the other visitors he has had. The patient asks the visitor to pick up a towel at the base of the bed and give it to him. The visitor complies. The patient places it across his forehead—and the visitor, who, like most people, is unsure what to say in this situation, stifles the question he wants to ask, *Why do you have a towel on your forehead?* The patient finally says, "Don't you think I look like Mother Theresa?" And the visitor realizes his friend has made a joke—as he did years ago in their house on Fire Island: doing drag with bedspreads, pillow cases, towels, whatever was at hand. The visitor does not smile—he is so unprepared for a joke in these circumstances—but he realizes, with relief, he is forgiven. He realizes what people who visit the sick often learn: It is the patient who puts the visitor at ease. In a few moments his ten minutes are up. He rises and says, "I don't want to tire you." He goes to the door and once beyond it he turns and looks back. His friend says to him, "I'm proud of you for coming."

"Oh—!" the visitor says and shakes his head. "Proud of *me* for   9
coming!" he tells a friend later that evening, after he has stripped off his gown and mask and gone home, through the unreal city of people in perfect health. "Proud of me! Can you imagine! To say that to me, to make *me* feel good! When he's the one in bed!" The truth is he is proud of himself the next time he visits his friend, for he is one of those people who looks away when a nurse takes a blood test and finds respirators frightening. He is like almost everyone—everyone except these extraordinary people who work in hospitals, he thinks, as he walks into the building. The second visit is easier, partly because it is the second, and partly because the patient is better—the drug has worked.

But he cannot forget the sight of those dark, angry eyes and the   10
plastic tubes and emaciated visage—and as he goes home that evening,

he knows there is a place whose existence he was not aware of before: the foyer of death. It is a place many of us will see at least once in our lives. Because modern medicine fights for patients who a century ago would have died without its intervention, it has created an odd place between life and death. One no longer steps into Charon's boat to be ferried across the River Styx—ill people are now detained, with one foot in the boat and the other still on shore. It is a place where mercy looks exactly like cruelty to the average visitor. It is a place that one leaves, if one is only a visitor, with the conviction that ordinary life is utterly miraculous, so that, going home from the hospital on the subway, one is filled with things one cannot express to the crowd that walks up out of the station or throngs the street of the block where he lives. But if the people caught in the revolving door between health and death could speak, would they not say—as Patrick Cowley reportedly did as he watched the men dancing to his music while he was fatally ill, "Look at those stupid queens. Don't they *know*?" Guard your health. It is all you have. It is the thin line that stands between you and hell. It is your miraculous possession. Do nothing to threaten it. Treat each other with kindness. Comfort your suffering friends. Help one another. Revere life. Do not throw it away for the momentous pleasures of lust, or even the obliteration of loneliness.

11   Many homosexuals wonder how they will die: where, with whom. Auden went back to Oxford, Santayana to the Blue Nuns in Rome. We are not all so lucky. Some men afflicted with AIDS returned to die in their family's home. Others have died with friends. Some have died bitterly and repudiated the homosexual friends who came to see them; others have counted on these people. Volunteers from the Gay Men's Health Crisis have cooked, cleaned, shopped, visited, taken care of people they did not even know until they decided to help. One thing is sure—we are learning how to help one another. We are discovering the strength and goodness of people we knew only in discotheques or as faces on Fire Island. We are following a great moral precept by visiting the sick. We are once again learning the awful truth Robert Penn Warren wrote years ago: "Only through the suffering of the innocent is the brotherhood of man confirmed." The most profound difference between men may well be that between the sick and the well, but compassionate people try to reach across the chasm and bridge it. The hospital visitor who conquers his own fear of something facing us all takes the first step on a journey that others less fearful than he have already traveled much further on: They are combining eros and agape as they rally round their stricken friends. As for the courage and dignity and sense of humor of those who are sick, these are beyond praise, and one hesitates where words are so flimsy. As for a disease whose latency period is measured in years, not months, there is no telling which side of the line dividing the sick and the well each of us will be on before this affliction is conquered. We may disdain the

hysteria of policemen and firemen who call for masks, and people who ask if it is safe to ride the subway, and television crews who will not interview AIDS patients. For they are not at risk—those who are, are fearlessly helping their own. This is the greatest story of the plague.

_____ CONSIDERATIONS _____

1. In his long closing paragraph, Holleran uses the words "eros" and "agape" in the same clause. Both Greek words could be translated "love." What difference is the author after? Or is he careless and guilty of redundancy?

2. Locate in that same closing paragraph the theme Holleran borrows from the Scott Fitzgerald quotation that opens the essay. Note that the sentence following that restatement begins with a "but," as though to imply that what follows the "but" is more important than what precedes it. How does that "but" alter Holleran's thesis?

3. In paragraph 2, Holleran uses on four occasions a device of punctuation few writers employ. Review what you know of that device, study Holleran's use of it to determine what function(s) it performs in this passage, then try using it yourself in one of your own essays.

4. Holleran does not mention the word "AIDS" until his closing paragraph. How soon do you suspect that this is the disease his friend suffers from? What clues does Holleran give you?

5. In explaining what he means by "the foyer of death" (paragraph 10), Holleran reminds his readers of Charon, a figure in Greek mythology. What is the most immediately available source that you could expect to tell you enough about that figure to understand the author's use of it in "Bedside Manners"? What are some alternative sources?

6. How does Holleran avoid thrusting himself unduly into the reader's attention in discussing a situation as obviously intimate and personal as Holleran's concern for his friend hospitalized with AIDS?

7. Would Holleran's essay be as moving if the friend were dying of cancer rather than AIDS? What elements of important interest to contemporary Americans would be missing? What elements would remain the same?

James D. Houston (b. 1933) was born in San Francisco and attended San Jose State University as well as Stanford University. He has received a grant from the National Endowment for the Arts, a Wallace Stegner Fellowship, and a Joseph Henry Jackson Award for Fiction. In 1973 he wrote Farewell to Manzanar *with his wife Jeanne Wakatsuki Houston, about her family's experience during the internment of Japanese-Americans. A television show based on the book received a Humanitas Prize in 1976. Some of his novels are* Gig *(1969),* Continental Drift *(1978), and* Love Life *(1985). The* Men in My Life *(1987) is a memoir, recently reprinted in paperback. In 1982,* Californians: Searching for the Golden State, *won an* American Book Award *from* The Before Columbus Foundation. *We take this essay from* Californians.

__44__

JAMES D. HOUSTON

Sand, Tattoo, and the
Golden Gate

1 One Sunday when I was eight, the entire city of San Francisco was reduced to the size of a billboard. This was the Sunday we received the news that Japanese aircraft had bombed Pearl Harbor and crippled America's Pacific Fleet. The billboard stood at the corner of 25th Avenue and Irving Street, half a block from the house my father had made his first payment on three years earlier. In what is now the classic scene of how Americans received the news that launched us into World War II, we all sat around the radio staring at the floor or at the speaker. When the somber announcement ended, my father switched off the radio. The mood in the room was so heavy I went out-

---

From *Californians: Searching for the Golden State,* originally published by Alfred Knopf Inc. Copyright © 1982 by James D. Houston. Reprinted by permission of the author.

side, wandered up to the corner and huddled down behind the billboard I had come to rely on in times of stress and uncertainty.

It was a sandlot billboard with two surfaces to plaster ads across. 2 They made a right angle just inside the concrete, one side facing 25th, the other facing Irving. I never knew what the ads said. My world was behind the signs, where all the struts, cross-pieces, and footings met and overlapped. Back there, when I was eight, you felt secure. The western wall broke the wind that usually poured down Irving from the ocean, twenty-five blocks away. If you fell from one of the cross-beams, or jumped, as we often did, like pirates abandoning ship or pilots leaving a flaming cockpit, the sand was there to break your fall. This whole district was built on sand, miles and miles of what had once been dunes were covered with houses. In those days there were still more miles waiting to be covered, dunes dotted with spiny beach grass of the same variety growing in this vacant corner lot. Wherever a parcel of houses ended and the dunes began, a little skirmish was going on. Half a sidewalk would be disappearing under wind-blown sand, sometimes half an avenue would be disappearing. People who lived in the final row of houses could look out across a mile or so of dunes and wonder how long before the next row would go in, so that *their* lawns and cars would no longer have to bear the brunt.

As a kid, I always wanted the sand to win. I loved the sand, hot or 3 cold, dry or wet, day or night. In that district, the Sunset District of San Francisco, which was the world of my boyhood, sand was the alternative to civilization and its discontents, and so it is no wonder that on the day World War II broke out I wandered up to the corner sandlot to think.

None of my buddies were there, and I was glad. I wanted solitude. 4 I was not in the mood that day for abandoning ship or leaping from the cockpit. Real planes could be appearing in the sky at any moment. This is what my parents were talking about. This is what I expected. Hawaii was twenty-four hundred miles west, with nothing between here and there but open water. My father had been to Hawaii. He had been stationed at Pearl Harbor for a couple of years during the 1920s, with a submarine crew.

"If they have a mind to keep on bombing," he said, "they'll have 5 to fly clear over here 'fore they've got anything else to hit."

"You think they'll do it?" my mother asked. 6

"No tellin," he said. "They might be able to git here. But I don't 7 know how they'd ever git back. And if you cain't git back, there ain't much use in gittin' here."

A tall strip of lattice separated the two sides of the billboard, 8 right at the corner, splintery boards painted green and nailed diagonally so you could squat back there, hidden from cars, and peer through the diamonds down Irving Street. I sat for a long time peering at the cloud bank above the distant ocean, expecting to see planes emerge, fighters, bombers. At times it seemed that the clouds *were* bombers, ingeniously disguised as broken clouds and moving toward the city like an inexorable fog.

9   Never before had the sky taken on such a threatening look. As the clouds drew nearer, my childish fears ebbed and flowed, and the air grew damp and cold. By the time they had covered the sun, my fearful solitude lost its savor. The day's news had emptied the streets. There was nothing else to do but go home. I came over the back fence, by way of another vacant lot, and from the yard I heard strange noises. I heard voices up on our roof.

10   It wasn't easy to get onto the roof. Counting the street-level garage, our house was actually three stories high. To reach the roof you had to carry a ladder up the back stairs to the second landing, and from there hoist yourself over the gutter. I saw the ladder leaning up there, climbed the stairs, climbed the ladder, got my chin to the gutter level, and found my mother and grandmother standing on the roof gazing west. This had never happened before. No one went up onto the roof but my father, from time to time, when a skylight needed putty. Seeing the women on the roof added to the strangeness of this day. Their panicky conversation confirmed the half-shaped worry I was carrying around. They too were looking for Japanese bombers and trying to decide what to do.

11   My grandmother was doing most of the deciding. Her idea was that we should head back to west Texas where it was safe. They had all come out from Texas the year before I was born, from a little Panhandle town right at the edge of the Dust Bowl. Shading her eyes, like a pioneer woman trying to see through mirages on a desert horizon, she kept saying things like, "Look! Look out there! Isn't that something flying to'rd the city? Look! Can you see it now?" Not only could she see and hear bombers over the Cliff House, she was certain San Francisco Bay was filling with enemy subs and that hidden infantry divisions would soon be marching out of Chinatown.

12   By the next afternoon a plan had taken shape. Three of us would leave first, me, my five-year-old sister, and Grandma. That way, at least the children would be saved. We would travel by train to Texas, where she still owned a farmhouse and a quarter-section of land. Grandma called the Southern Pacific terminal and reserved seats on the overnight train to Los Angeles, where we would meet up tomorrow with the southwest special heading east toward Phoenix and El Paso. She drew all her savings out of the Bank of America, which amounted to $300 or $400, money she had earned as a seamstress, doing alterations and hemstitching in her apartment here on the second floor. My mother packed our bags, cleaned us up and dressed us, so that by the time my father came home from work we were too baffled to cry, protest, or even speak.

The plan was perfect in all details but one: my father had not been   13
consulted. The plan had taken shape after he had driven off to work
that morning. When his old Plymouth pulled up to the curb, we were
standing on the stairs waiting for him to drive us downtown to the terminal—me in my woolen suit, my sister in a pinafore Grandma had
sewn and over the pinafore a red coat with simulated fur collar. My
mother twisted at her sweater sleeve, caught between having to watch
her children ride out of her life for who knew how many months or
years, and her dread of the first air raid. Grandma stood over us, dressed
in her city clothes, her long cloth coat, her round black pillbox hat garnished with cherries; but underneath these clothes she was the ranch-
country matriarch, determined to protect her herd.

Dad climbed out of the car, still wearing his overalls. He was a   14
painting contractor, worked jobs in all parts of the city—homes, apartment houses, office buildings. He smelled like paint. His bill cap was
spotted with it, his shirt and his shoes. His hands were covered with a
chalky film made of thinner and enamel residue. He had rolled up the
sleeves of his blue shirt, so you could see a line across his wrists.

My mother broke into tears. "Dudley, please hurry. Load up as   15
fast as you can!"

Grandma, looking mournful, waited until he had reached the   16
stairs. "It's got to be, Dudley, it's just got to be."

He looked the situation over and finally said, "What has got to   17
be?"

While they explained, he listened in stoic silence. He was not a   18
talker. He took great pride in all forms of handiwork, but never put
much stock in words. When they finished explaining, he stood there
for a long time saying nothing. He squinted down at my sister and me
and blinked and worked his jaws and fingered one of the brass buttons
on his overalls, testing the callused tip of his forefinger.

The air was so charged, it was painful. I was looking around for   19
anything else to concentrate on, and that was when I noticed his tattoo. It was a purple anchor. A rope curled around the anchor's stem, a
purple eagle perched upon the crosspiece. At age eight my eyes were
just about even with his forearm. What a relief to see his tattoo inches
away. I gave it my full attention. I had looked at it many times, but on
this day it occurred to me that the tattoo had not always been a feature of my father's arm. Someone had put it there. For the first time I
wondered why, and when? His forearm was thick and brown, the hairs
fine around the squinting eagle and the navy anchor. I thought I saw
the eagle move. Was it breathing? Or was Dad barely squeezing his
fist?

My mother had reached her limit. She cried, "Well, Dudley! My   20
goodness! You going to stand here all day?"

He waited a while longer. I saw a trapped look come into his   21
eyes, the voiceless alarm of a trapped animal. Then he blinked and the

look went away. His jaws clenched one final time and his mouth opened. "Maybe I will," he said. "Maybe I'll stand here all day."

22   Grandma was a twenty-year widow who had raised her two children—my mother and my uncle—all by herself on that semi-fertile, semi-prairie quarter-section. It had put iron in her eyes. She fixed this iron glare on my father. "I *do* believe we ought to be gittin' along, Dudley."

23   The eagle stopped breathing. The anchor came to rest. He said, "I believe we ought to hold off a few days."

24   My mother was appalled: "HOLD OFF!"

25   Grandma was willing to bargain. "Now Dudley," she began, "if it's the money you're thinkin' about, you needn't . . . "

26   He passed between them, up the stairs, into the house.

27   For three weeks the bags stayed packed, while we waited on his approval of the plan. During those weeks the city braced itself for invasion by land or sea or air. The west sides of all the street lamps were painted chocolate brown. We draped our windows, taped up every place where light might leak, and sat through practice blackouts, staying off the streets, listening for bombers. They never came. The landing barges never landed. Grandma put her money back into the Bank of America. The sand continued to creep toward the last row of houses where the dunes began. My father never again mentioned the escape plan, nor did he ever acknowledge or even hint that such a plan had existed.

28   Twenty-five years later, I was again looking closely at his tattoo. We were at the University of California Medical Center on Parnassus Avenue, and a nurse was probing around on his arm with a transfusion needle.

29   "Your veins are very thin," she said.

30   He looked insulted, misjudged, but said nothing. She tried his left arm. "This one will do," she said. "The veins are stronger." And she slanted the needle through his white flesh.

31   He glanced at her with eyes full of suspicion, eyes that knew his right arm should be stronger, since that was the one he used most. With lips pursed she adjusted a valve on the thin, clear tube rising from his arm, watched the tube turn red. A scarlet bubble rose in the jar above his bed.

32   "This will take about four hours."

33   The trapped look came into his eyes. He wanted to ask her why so long. I knew he wouldn't ask. It was not his style. He rarely asked— for advice, for assistance, for answers. She noted something on her clipboard and padded out into the corridor, while I sat staring at the purple tattoo shielding his tender vein, watching that old eagle's slitted and arrogant eye.

After a while he said to me, "Why does it take so long?"   34

"Probably makes it easier for your system to adjust, assimilate   35
the new blood."

A faint smile, while his body shifted restlessly under the sheet,   36
impatient with the forced waiting. His jaws squeezed, the bunched
muscles bulged, his lips began to part. He was framing another sentence, but he wouldn't speak it yet. His eyes roamed the room and
gradually came to rest on the red bottle. It was always that way with
him, the long slow pondering. I was never sure whether that reserve
came from indecision or from caring too much, brooding too long over
what was right and best.

"You'd think," he said at last, "that they could get somethin'   37
like this done in less than four hours."

His eyes followed the infrequent climb of bubbles through the   38
blood drawn from my arm earlier that day. My eyes were fixed again
on his tattoo, wondering if this new blood had yet flowed under it. I
searched for a richer hue in the eagle's wing, along the rope curling
down behind the anchor's stem. He was grizzled by that time, coming
through his third bout with intestinal cancer, a chronic ailment I connected to his lifetime habit of holding too much inside. His skin was
pale and his blood thin, but the tattoo had not changed, the ink had
not faded much at all. The eagle had not moved, the rope had not
frayed, nor had the anchor rusted since I first took careful note of it in
December 1941, or for that matter since his young right arm was decorated by the Filipino master on Hotel Street in downtown Honolulu
one night back in 1926.

He saw me staring at his arm. I looked away, out the window, to-   39
ward the vista to the north. The medical center stands high up the
side of a steep wooded hill under the eucalyptus groves of Sutro Forest.
From his room you could gaze out across several blocks of vintage
flats and rooming houses pressed wall to wall in the San Francisco
manner and cascading down the slope below. The houses end at
Golden Gate Park. Beyond the park, beyond the Richmond District,
beyond the city, rose the orange spires of the bridge, peeking over the
forested hills around the Presidio.

That view was easier to watch, and it started me thinking about   40
his life and mine. The spires had not been there when he first sailed
into San Francisco Bay, on his way home from Hawaii, on his way
home to Texas, when his tattoo was new. In those days there was a
legendary waterway known around the world as the Golden Gate, but
as yet no bridge had come rising out of the water to span it. He didn't
stay long in Texas. A few years later he was back, with his bride.
Something glittered for him here. I'm still not sure what it was, maybe
all those things the bridge has come to symbolize, maybe something
else entirely. I can only guess. We never talked about it. I do know

this: the bridge and I are of the same generation. As it happens, construction began in the year I was born. I was three when police motorcycles escorted the first cars across. I grew up taking it for granted.

41   As I sat next to the bed of my father, I remembered the times I played along beaches in full view of the bridge, explored the Fort Point ruins in the shadow of its towers, bicycled out to stop in the middle, between spires, to watch the ruffling, endless Pacific, framed by the city on one side, the moss-ridged Coast Range on the other. On a sunny day the hills of white buildings still quiver with a brightness you only see in cities next to water. I wonder where I would have cycled had Grandma's plan carried through, and what other skylines might have beguiled me? And I wonder still at my father's particular form of delay. Was it uncertainty, or caution, or wisdom, or stubbornness, or fear that kept us in San Francisco till the war was past and the smoke had cleared?

42   Whatever anchored us, I know now that it shapes you to grow up in a city whose gate is golden. You leave, you return through its golden gate. Such a glitter can blind you to certain things. It can color all your expectations. Sooner or later you learn that from those railings people regularly plunge to their death, sometimes traveling thousands of miles to make the famous leap. But by the time you know that, the spires have already imprinted their gleaming image, and it takes more than suicides or heavy traffic to erase the eldorados flickering there.

_____ CONSIDERATIONS _____

1. As many another child had done in moments of anxiety, the eight-year-old Houston sought security in a special place after he heard the frightening news of the Pearl Harbor attack. He describes that hide-out in paragraph 2. Write an essay about your own childhood secret place that you relied on in times of stress and uncertainty. Use your descriptive skills, as Houston has done, but develop your essay around an attempt to explain the phenomenon.

2. What role does sand play in this essay of reminiscence?

3. How does Houston make use of his father's tattoo?

4. What is notable in Houston's depiction of his father's reaction to Grandma's evacuation plan?

5. Several other writers in your text discuss or touch significantly on the idea of sense of place, most explicitly Wallace Stegner, (page 503). What passage in Houston's essay is most clearly a statement of that idea?

Langston Hughes (1902–1967) was a poet, novelist, playwright, and essayist who wrote with wit and energy; he was a leader in the emergence of black American literature in the twentieth century. More than twenty of his books remain in print, including Selected Poems *(1959) and his autobiography,* I Wonder as I Wander *(1956). He argues as well as he sings the blues—and he knows how to tell a story.*

45

LANGSTON HUGHES
Salvation

I was saved from sin when I was going on thirteen. But not really 1
saved. It happened like this. There was a big revival at my Auntie
Reed's church. Every night for weeks there had been much preaching,
singing, praying, and shouting, and some very hardened sinners had
been brought to Christ, and the membership of the church had grown
by leaps and bounds. Then just before the revival ended, they held a
special meeting for children, "to bring the young lambs to the fold."
My aunt spoke of it for days ahead. That night I was escorted to the
front row and placed on the mourners' bench with all the other young
sinners, who had not yet been brought to Jesus.

My aunt told me that when you were saved you saw a light, and 2
something happened to you inside! And Jesus came into your life! And
God was with you from then on! She said you could see and hear and
feel Jesus in your soul. I believed her. I had heard a great many old people say the same thing and it seemed to me they ought to know. So I
sat there calmly in the hot, crowded church, waiting for Jesus to come
to me.

The preacher preached a wonderful rhythmical sermon, all 3
moans and shouts and lonely cries and dire pictures of hell, and then
he sang a song about the ninety and nine safe in the fold, but one little

lamb was left out in the cold. Then he said: "Won't you come? Won't you come to Jesus? Young lambs, won't you come?" And he held out his arms to all us young sinners there on the mourners' bench. All the little girls cried. And some of them jumped up and went to Jesus right away. But most of us just sat there.

4   A great many old people came and knelt around us and prayed, old women with jet-black faces and braided hair, old men with work-gnarled hands. And the church sang a song about the lower lights are burning, some poor sinners to be saved. And the whole building rocked with prayer and song.

5   Still I kept waiting to *see* Jesus.

6   Finally all the young people had gone to the altar and were saved, but one boy and me. He was a rounder's son named Westley. Westley and I were surrounded by sisters and deacons praying. It was very hot in the church, and getting late now. Finally Westley said to me in a whisper: "God damn! I'm tired o' sitting here. Let's get up and be saved." So he got up and was saved.

7   Then I was left all alone on the mourners' bench. My aunt came and knelt at my knees and cried, while prayers and songs swirled all around me in the little church. The whole congregation prayed for me alone, in a mighty wail of moans and voices. And I kept waiting serenely for Jesus, waiting, waiting—but he didn't come. I wanted to see him, but nothing happened to me. Nothing! I wanted something to happen to me, but nothing happened.

8   I heard the songs and the minister saying: "Why don't you come? My dear child, why don't you come to Jesus? Jesus is waiting for you. He wants you. Why don't you come? Sister Reed, what is this child's name?"

9   "Langston," my aunt sobbed.

10   "Langston, why don't you come? Why don't you come and be saved? Oh, Lamb of God! Why don't you come?"

11   Now it was really getting late. I began to be ashamed of myself, holding everything up so long. I began to wonder what God thought about Westley, who certainly hadn't seen Jesus either, but who was now sitting proudly on the platform, swinging his knickerbockered legs and grinning down at me, surrounded by deacons and old women on their knees praying. God had not struck Westley dead for taking his name in vain or for lying in the temple. So I decided that maybe to save further trouble, I'd better lie, too, and say that Jesus had come, and get up and be saved.

12   So I got up.

13   Suddenly the whole room broke into a sea of shouting, as they saw me rise. Waves of rejoicing swept the place. Women leaped in the air. My aunt threw her arms around me. The minister took me by the hand and led me to the platform.

When things quieted down, in a hushed silence, punctuated by a 14
few ecstatic "Amens," all the new young lambs were blessed in the
name of God. Then joyous singing filled the room.

That night, for the last time in my life but one—for I was a big 15
boy twelve years old—I cried. I cried, in my bed alone, and couldn't
stop. I buried my head under the quilts, but my aunt heard me. She
woke up and told my uncle I was crying because the Holy Ghost had
come into my life, and because I had seen Jesus. But I was really crying
because I couldn't bear to tell her that I had lied, that I had deceived
everybody in the church, and I hadn't seen Jesus, and that now I didn't
believe there was a Jesus any more, since he didn't come to help me.

____ CONSIDERATIONS _____

1. Hughes tells this critical episode of his childhood in a simple,
straightforward, unelaborated fashion, almost as though he were still a child
telling the story as it happened. Why is it necessary to say "*almost* as though
he were still a child"? How would you go about recounting a critical moment
in your childhood? Where does simple childhood memory stop and adult judgment take over?

2. Hughes's disillusionment is an example of what people call "an initi-
ation story." Compare it with the autobiographical essay by Lillian Hellman,
or the girlhood memories of Louise Bogan, or James D. Houston's re-tracing of
a boyhood awakening. Discuss the *degrees* of awareness noticeable among
these varied characters.

3. Why is it so important to the congregation of Auntie Reed's church
that everyone, children included, acknowledge their salvation?

4. Why does Westley finally proclaim that he is saved?

5. In his final paragraph, Hughes writes, "That night, for the last time in
my life but one . . . I cried." He does not tell us, in this account, what that
other time was. Read a little more about his life, or simply use your imagination, and write a brief account of the other time.

Molly Ivins (b. 1948) grew up in Texas, where she lives and writes her political journalism. She put in some years with the New York Times *before moving back home. She does a monthly column for the* Progressive *and writes frequently for the* Nation. *Many outrageous essays compose* Molly Ivins Can't Say That, Can She? *(1991) and its successor,* Nothin' But Good Times Ahead *(1993).*

46

MOLLY IVINS

As Thousands Cheer

1   Some days you open the paper and it's kind of like finding Fidel Castro in the refrigerator, smoking a cigar. Hard to know what to think. For instance, when the lead story is that fourteen Dallas Cowboy Cheerleaders have resigned because they believe the team's new owner is trying to make them into sex objects. Says I to myself, "No doo-doo?" (That's the George Bush influence.)

2   While the rest of the world has been following China's crushing of the pro-democracy movement, here in Texas we have been absorbed in the complex issues presented by the rebellion of the Dallas Cowboy Cheerleaders. The uprising, you might call it.

3   Here's the deal: The Dallas Cowboys, America's Team, got bought a few months back by a rich guy from Arkansas named Jerry Jones. Seemed like pretty much the end of the world at the time—the Dallas Cowboys owned by some Arkie. Alas, how far we have fallen.

4   Then the new owner fired Tom Landry, the only coach the Cowboys have ever had. And then he fired Tex Schramm, the only manager the team has ever had. And now he's messing with the franchise.

5   The girls (we all call them girls) want to retain their clean-cut, wholesome image. You may not have been aware until now that they had a clean-cut, wholesome image, but that's only because you have not studied the matter deeply. As the *Fort Worth Star-Telegram* noted in its caption under a particularly fine picture of two Cheerleaders jig-

gling up a storm, "Dallas Cowboy Cheerleaders Frequently Visit Nursing Homes."

But the barbarian from Arkansas wanted the girls to wear reveal- 6 ing costumes—halter tops and spandex bicycle pants, as opposed to the Puritanical outfits they wear now. He further said the girls could socialize with football players. Yes, I'm telling you! And he was going to scrap the rule that says the Cheerleaders can't perform where alcoholic beverages are served. There was even a rumor that he wanted the girls to make a beer commercial.

Debbie Bond, director of the Cheerleaders for ten years, resigned, 7 saying, "I couldn't ask these girls to do something which was against my beliefs. And I would not want my daughter wearing the uniform under the present regime. It's image, reputation, standards, morals, character, principles. They all go hand in hand."

Alona Wood, a four-year veteran of the squad, said, "We wanted 8 to be different from the other cheerleading squads. That's why we were so popular. That's why nobody could touch us. Sure it's purity— high moral standards."

Tina Miller, a three-year veteran, said, "When you tell somebody 9 you don't associate with the Cowboy players, they love that—they put you on a pedestal."

Toni Atwater, a rookie, said, "I feel like we are a sacred, sacred 10 organization. You can imagine—or, actually, you probably can't—the public outpouring of support and sympathy for the Cheerleaders."

In Dallas, we like girls who will stand up against tanks for tradi- 11 tional virtues like that. Jones backed down and tried to claim it was all just a misunderstanding, but he also kept referring to "our girls" who he claims are "the pick of the litter." He should probably shut up. No one is fooled. He has named a new director of cheerleading, and he's still going to change the uniforms.

One of the more brain-spraining aspects of Texan culture is Bap- 12 tist sex. As we all know, Baptists (who stand here metaphorically for the entire Southern fundamentalist world view) are agin sin, which they define as drinkin', dancin', and carryin' on. Carryin' on is the worst.

That Baptists see nothing wrong with the Dallas Cowboy Cheer- 13 leaders, who are indisputably open-air coochie girls, is one of those anomalies we all live with here. Because football requires the suspension of rational thought, just as theater requires the suspension of disbelief, we see nothing odd in such phenomena as the Kilgore Rangerettes, the Apache Belles, and other noted practitioners of the close-order drill and baton-twirling arts.

Objectively, there's no denying that what those girls do is dress 14 up in costumes that would do credit to a striptease artiste and then prance about in front of thousands of people, shaking their bums and jiggling their tits. This display is considered not just decent but proper, as Jim Schutze put it, "as long as the presentation is locked inside a bulletproof sugar-coating of overdone, over-made-up, over-hairsprayed, ultra-exaggerated nicey-nicey wholesomeness."

15   Well, is that any more irrational than most other American attitudes toward sex? It is not a subject that has ever motivated people to do a lot of real clear thinking.

_____ CONSIDERATIONS _____

1. One of the features of Molly Ivins's brassy, irreverent style is her use of slang, especially as she mixes it into sentences with more respectable diction. Study an example or two of this mixing and comment on its effects.

2. Is Ivins satirical, witty, ironic, humorous, sarcastic, cynical? None of these? All of these?

3. Much of the appeal of Molly Ivins's writing is that it sounds like talk. Study "As Thousands Cheer" to see what gives it that conversational quality.

4. How would you answer the question Ivins puts to the reader in paragraph 15?

Thomas Jefferson (1743–1826) was the third president of the United States, and perhaps more truly the Father of his Country than George Washington was; or maybe we would only like to think so, for such paternity flatters the offspring. Jefferson was a politician, philosopher, architect, inventor, and writer. With an energy equal to his curiosity, he acted to improve the world: he wrote the Declaration of Independence; he wrote a life of Jesus; and he founded the University of Virginia, whose original buildings he designed. An arch-Republican, fearful of Alexander Hamilton's monarchical reverence for authority, Jefferson withheld support from the Constitution until he saw the Bill of Rights added to it.

We take this text from Garry Wills's Inventing America *(1978); by juxtaposition, Wills demonstrates the revision of a classic.*

47

THOMAS JEFFERSON
The Declarations of Jefferson and of the Congress

I will state the form of the declaration as originally reported. The parts struck out by Congress shall be distinguished by a black line drawn under them; & those inserted by them shall be placed in the margin or in a concurrent column:

1   A Declaration by the representatives of the United States of America, in [General] Congress assembled.

2   When in the course of human events it becomes necessary for one people to dissolve the political bands which have connected them with another, and to assume the powers of the earth the separate & equal station to which the laws of nature and of nature's god en-

title them, a decent respect to the opinions of mankind requires that they should declare the causes which impel them to the separation.

3   We hold these truths to be self evident: that all men are created equal; that they are endowed by their creator with ^ [inherent and] inalienable rights; that   certain
among these are life, liberty & the pursuit of happiness: that to secure these rights, governments are instituted among men, deriving their just powers from the consent of the governed; that whenever any form of government becomes destructive of these ends, it is the right of the people to alter or to abolish it, & to institute new government, laying it's foundation on such principles, & organising it's powers in such form, as to them shall seem most likely to effect their safety & happiness. Prudence indeed will dictate that governments long established should not be changed for light & transient causes; and accordingly all experience hath shewn that mankind are more disposed to suffer while evils are sufferable than to right themselves by abolishing the forms to which they are accustomed. But when a long train of abuses & usurpations [begun at a distinguished period and] pursuing invariably the same object, evinces a design to reduce them under absolute despotism it is their right, it is their duty to throw off such government, & to provide new guards for their future security. Such has been the patient sufferance of these colonies; & such is now the necessity which constrains them to ^ [expunge] their former systems of   alter
government. The history of the present king of Great Britain is a history of ^ [unremitting] injuries & usurpa-   repeated
tions, [among which appears no solitary fact to contradict the uniform tenor of the rest but all have] ^ in di-   all having
rect object the establishment of an absolute tyranny over these states. To prove this let facts be submitted to a candid world [for the truth of which we pledge a faith yet unsullied by falsehood].

4   He has refused his assent to laws the most wholesome & necessary for the public good.

5   He has forbidden his governors to pass laws of immediate & pressing importance, unless suspended in their operation till his assent should be obtained; & when so suspended, he has utterly neglected to attend to them.

6   He has refused to pass other laws for the accommodation of large districts of people, unless those people would relinquish the right of representation in the legislature, a right inestimable to them, & formidable to tyrants only.

7   He has called together legislative bodies at places unusual, uncomfortable, and distant from the depository of their public records, for the sole purpose of fatiguing them into compliance with his measures.

8   He has dissolved representative houses repeatedly [& continually] for opposing with manly firmness his invasions on the rights of the people.

9   He has refused for a long time after such dissolutions to cause others to be elected, whereby the legislative powers, incapable of annihilation, have returned to the people at large for their exercise, the state remaining in the mean time exposed to all the dangers of invasion from without & convulsions within.

10   He has endeavored to prevent the population of these states; for that purpose obstructing the laws for naturalization of foreigners, refusing to pass others to encourage their migrations hither, & raising the conditions of new appropriations of lands.

11   He has ∧ [suffered] the administration of justice   obstructed
     [totally to cease in some of these states] ∧ refusing his   by
     assent to laws for establishing judiciary powers.

12   He has made [our] judges dependant on his will alone, for the tenure of their offices, & the amount & paiment of their salaries.

13   He has erected a multitude of new offices [by a self assumed power] and sent hither swarms of new officers to harrass our people and eat out their substance.

14   He has kept among us in times of peace standing armies [and ships of war] without the consent of our legislatures.

15   He has affected to render the military independent of, & superior to the civil power.

16   He has combined with others to subject us to jurisdiction foreign to our constitutions & unacknowledged by our laws, giving his assent to their acts of pretended legislation for quartering large bodies of armed troops among us; for protecting them by a mock-trial from punishment for any murders which they should commit on the inhabitants of these states; for cutting off our trade with all parts of the world; for imposing

taxes on us without our consent; for depriving us ∧ of ~~in many cases~~ the benefits of trial by jury; for transporting us beyond seas to be tried to pretended offences; for abolishing the free system of English laws in a neighboring province, establishing therein an arbitrary government, and enlarging it's boundaries, so as to render it at once an example and fit instrument for introducing the same absolute rule into these ∧ [states]; for taking away our ~~colonies~~ charters, abolishing our most valuable laws, and altering fundamentally the forms of our governments; for suspending our own legislatures, & declaring themselves invested with power to legislate for us in all cases whatsoever.

17   He has abdicated government here ∧ [withdrawing ~~by declaring us~~ his governors, and declaring us out of his allegiance & ~~out of his~~ protection.] ~~protection & waging war against us~~

18   He has plundered our seas, ravaged our coasts, burnt our towns, & destroyed the lives of our people.

19   He is at this time transporting large armies of foreign mercenaries to compleat the works of death, desolation & tyranny already begun with circumstances of cruelty and perfidy ∧ unworthy the head of a civilized ~~scarcely~~ nation. ~~paralleled in the most bar-~~

20   He has constrained our fellow citizens taken cap- ~~barous ages, &~~ tive on the high seas to bear arms against their country, ~~totally~~ to become the executioners of their friends & brethren, or to fall themselves by their hands.

21   He has ∧ endeavored to bring on the inhabitants of ~~excited domes-~~ our frontiers the merciless Indian savages, whose ~~tic insurrec-~~ known rule of warfare is an undistinguished destruc- ~~tions amongst~~ tion of all ages, sexes, & conditions [of existence.] ~~us, & has~~

22   [He has incited treasonable insurrections of our fellow-citizens, with the allurements of forfeiture & confiscation of our property.

23   He has waged cruel war against human nature itself, violating it's most sacred rights of life and liberty in the persons of a distant people who never offended him, captivating & carrying them into slavery in another hemisphere or to incur miserable death in their transportation thither. This piratical warfare, the opprobrium of *infidel* powers, is the warfare of the *Christian* king of Great Britain. Determined to keep open a market where *Men* should be bought & sold, he has prostituted his negative for suppressing every legisla-

tive attempt to prohibit or to restrain this execrable commerce. And that this assemblage of horrors might want no fact of distinguished die, he is now exciting those very people to rise in arms among us, and to purchase that liberty of which he has deprived them, by murdering the people on whom he also obtruded them: thus paying off former crimes committed against the *Liberties* of one people, with crimes which he urges them to commit against the *lives* of another.]

24 In every stage of these oppressions we have petitioned for redress in the most humble terms: our repeated petitions have been answered only by repeated injuries. A prince whose character is thus marked by every act which may define a tyrant is unfit to be the ruler of a ∧ people [who mean to be free. Future ages   free will scarcely believe that the hardiness of one man adventured, within the short compass of twelve years only, to lay a foundation so broad & so undisguised for tyranny over a people fostered & fixed in principles of freedom.]

25 Nor have we been wanting in attentions to our British brethren. We have warned them from time to time of attempts by their legislature to extend ∧ [a] ju-   an unwarrantable risdiction over ∧ [these our states.] We have reminded   us them of the circumstances of our emigration & settlement here, [no one of which could warrant so strange a pretension: that these were effected at the expence of our own blood & treasure, unassisted by the wealth or the strength of Great Britain: that in constituting indeed our several forms of government, we had adopted one common king, thereby laying a foundation for perpetual league & amity with them: but that submission to their parliament was no part of our constitution, nor ever in idea, if history may be credited: and,] we ∧   have appealed to their native justice and magnanimity ∧ [as   and we have well as to] the ties of our common kindred to disavow   conjured them by these usurpations which ∧ [were likely to] interrupt our   would inevitably connection and correspondence. They too have been deaf to the voice of justice & of consanguinity, [and when occasions have been given them, by the regular course of their laws, of removing from their councils the disturbers of our harmony, they have, by their free election, reestablished them in power. At this very time too they are permitting their chief magistrate to send over not only souldiers of our common blood, but

Scotch & foreign mercenaries to invade & destroy us. These facts have given the last stab to agonizing affection, and manly spirit bids us to renounce for ever these unfeeling brethren. We must endeavor to forget our former love for them, and to hold them as we hold the rest of mankind enemies in war, in peace friends. We might have been a free and a great people together; but a communication of grandeur & of freedom it seems is below their dignity. Be it so, since they will have it. The road to happiness & to glory is open to us too. We will tread it apart from them, and] ∧ acquiesce in the necessity which denounces our [eternal] separation ∧!

we must therefore

and hold them as we hold the rest of mankind enemies in war in peace friends.

26   We therefore the representatives of the United States of America in General Congress assembled do in the name, & by the authority of the good people of these [states reject & renounce all allegiance & subjection to the kings of Great Britain & all others who may hereafter claim by, through or under them: we utterly dissolve all political connection which may heretofore have subsisted between us & the people of parliament of Great Britain: & finally we do assert & declare these colonies to be free & independent states,] & that as free & independant states, they have full power to levy war, conclude peace, contract alliances, establish commerce, & to do all other acts & things which independant states may of right do. And for the support of this declaration we mutually pledge to each

We therefore the representatives of the United States of America in General Congress assembled, appealing to the supreme judge of the world for the rectitude of our intentions, do in the name, & by the authority of the good people of these colonies, solemnly publish & declare that these United colonies are & of right ought to be free & independant states; that they are absolved from all allegiance to the British crown, and that all political connection between them & the state of Great Britain is, & ought to be, totally dissolved; & that as free & independant states they have full power to levy war, conclude peace, contract alliances, establish commerce & to do all other acts & things which independant states may of right do.

And for the support

other our lives, our for-
tunes & our sacred hon-
our.

of this declaration, with a
firm reliance on the pro-
tection of divine provi-
dence we mutually pledge
to each other our lives,
our fortunes & our sacred
honour.

_____ CONSIDERATIONS _____

1. What part of the original Declaration deleted by Congress most surprises you? Why?

2. Make a careful study of the first eight or ten changes imposed by
Congress on Jefferson's original Declaration. Why do you think each was
made?

3. Garry Wills says in his book *Inventing America* that the Declaration
is easy to misunderstand because it "is written in the lost language of the Enlightenment." What was the Enlightenment? How does the language of that
period differ from that of today? Perhaps the Declaration should be rewritten
in modern English?

4. If you conclude that the Declaration should be rewritten, try your
hand at it. Try, for instance, rewriting the famous third paragraph: "We hold
these truths. . . ." Can you be sure you're not writing a parody? For an example
of parody, see paragraphs 9, 10, and 11 in George Orwell's "Politics and the
English Language" (page 422).

5. How is the Declaration organized? Does it break down into distinct
parts? If so, what is the function of those parts?

Doris Kearns (b. 1943), a former professor of government at Harvard, interned in the State Department in 1963 and in the House of Representatives in 1965. Later she wrote an essay for the New Republic *called "How to Remove LBJ in 1968." Attending a White House party shortly thereafter, she was surprised when President Johnson asked her to dance. She became a special consultant to Johnson from 1969 to 1977, and in 1976 published* Lyndon Johnson and the American Dream. *Her* The Fitzgeralds and the Kennedys: An American Saga *followed in 1987, and in 1994* No Ordinary Time, *subtitled, "Franklin And Eleanor Roosevelt: The Home Front in World War II."*

48

DORIS KEARNS
Angles of Vision

1   The search after "the whole man" is the biographer's dream. We rummage through letters, memos, pictures, memories, diaries, and conversations in an attempt to develop our subject's character from youth to manhood to death. Yet, in the end, if we are honest with ourselves, the best we can offer is a partial rendering, a subjective portrait of the subject from a particular angle of vision shaped as much by our own biography—our attitudes, perceptions, and feelings toward the subject—as by the raw materials themselves.

2   Over the long years of research and writing, a biographer perceives his or her subject through inevitably shifting angles of vision. One cannot live with and worry about a subject for years without alternating feelings of anger, admiration, aggression, and affection.

3   I decided to write a study of Lyndon Johnson after having known him for a period of three years, the first on the White House staff, followed by two more, intermittently visiting his ranch. Initially, my feelings toward Johnson were a troubled mix of admiration and bitter-

"Angles of Vision" by Doris Kearns. From *Telling Lives: The Biographer's Art* edited by Marc Pachter, 1979, pp. 91–103. Reprinted by permission of the *New Republic.*

ness, affection and even fear. On the one hand his sheer power—and he still remains the most compelling individual I have ever met—utterly fascinated me. One could sense his extraordinary power the moment he entered a room. There was a strange texture to the mere act of standing next to him; it seemed as if he were violating the physical space of those around him by closing in—clasping and even hugging so tightly—that people felt they had no private space left.

The other side to that fascination was fright. For the very compulsion involved in the exercise of large power, the bending of other people's wills to his, was a frightening thing to observe. His associates often worried themselves sick about entering his office, worried that he would deride their work. I heard real fear in their voices and saw it on their faces. Lyndon Johnson made you feel larger at first, because he paid so much attention to you, almost as though he were courting. And he did that with everybody, man or woman alike, until he had won them. And then, almost as if these were all passing high school romances, people's feeling suddenly became of little interest to him. You felt diminished rather than enlarged, as a result of being with him.   4

So despite the pull of fascination, there was always a counterbalancing need to get away, to leave, not to be owned. I kept leaving and then returning. The fascination alone would not have brought me back; it was simply too wearing. But at the time that I knew him, the last five years of his life, that peculiar power of personality was coupled with a visible and growing vulnerability. And in that stage of his life, particularly after he retired to the ranch, he shared with me a side of himself that he had not shared with many before, his longings, his private thoughts, his memories, his dreams. As I began to write, I had to learn how to distance myself, in order to describe both his ruthless power while tempering my own angry reaction to it and his vulnerability without allowing my sympathy for it to overly soften my portrait.   5

My original angle of vision toward Johnson was also shaped, as a biographer's always is, by the training one brings to the task. I came to my material as a political scientist. My organizing questions revolved around leadership and government: the stuff of political science. What was it about this man that made him so phenomenally suited for the Senate of the 1950s and as president so mismatched to the turbulent sixties? For me, the question was one of process, not an evaluation of outcomes, but rather an attempt to understand how they had happened.   6

Johnson preferred to manipulate men, not ideas. He recognized, for example, that Wayne Morse wanted to seem influential in foreign affairs. So he described in great detail a proposed delegation to India, telling Morse that five other senators were begging him to appoint   7 them, making Morse feel that if only he was on that delegation, he would be a "figure" in foreign affairs. In fact, not one single senator had requested the appointment since no one had yet heard of the delegation, but when Johnson did appoint Morse one week later, Morse was eternally grateful.

8   Having understood some of the sources of Johnson's leadership, I was led to a larger question on historical context: What made Johnson's one-to-one-bargaining, his superb behind-the-scenes leadership, so suitable for the world of the fifties, so faltering in the 1960s—the world of television, civil wars in Asia, and a civil rights movement at home? The confounding of Johnson's leadership in the sixties mirrored the larger confusion of the American dream. Thus the title of my book.

9   In retrospect, however, though the plot I perceived from that original angle of vision worked to some extent, to a much larger extent the real story, the human truth, was something different, something I never fully understood as I was writing the biography, and only came to see afterwards. The real story was that of the gradual destruction of a giant of a man, forced to witness the smashing of his hopes for greatness and to live his last years removed from all real power, the only source of energy he had ever known. Having been so obsessive about the pursuit of power for so many years, he had no other purpose. So in retirement he had to invent an imitation power. He was so used to staff meetings each morning with men from Capitol Hill, or with cabinet officials and White House aides, that he had to replicate those sessions back on the ranch, meeting with four or five field hands. He would call conferences to decide which fields should be plowed at what time, which cows should be given what medicine, and which tractors would be fixed when. He would force his field hands to write out assignments, so that he could check up on them in the afternoon. And at night, so accustomed was he to reading reports from vast staffs across the country that he demanded detailed reports on how many eggs had been laid at the ranch that day, how many postcards had been sold at the L. B. J. Birth House, or how many people had entered the L. B. J. Library.

10   Yet when all the reports were put aside, as he fell asleep and when he awakened, increasingly this lonely man would ask of his years near and at the pinnacle of power: Was it really worth it? The American people he had tried all his life to do something for, he worried, no longer appreciated him. Indeed the young for whom he had cared so much seemed to hate him. Should he have given the time instead to his wife and children; at least he could have depended on them. All of this cut him to the quick; it also cut to the very nature of the presidency, and perhaps to the pursuit of success in any field. The real question, the one I wished I had asked from the start—was

whether the effort required to reach the top so distorts most personalities that they lose those human qualities that are necessary to a proportionate exercise of power.

A biographer's original angle of vision also encompasses an image of the place and the time span within which the subject's life story is played out. One would hope that the fascination most biographers feel toward the person extends equally to the place and the time. For me this was not so. For the place meant largely Texas and the times meant the first decades of the twentieth century. I was not fascinated by the first and felt I lacked perspective on the second. 11

Texas is a place, almost a country, in fact, that I had always seen largely in stereotype. And despite all the reading I did, all the trips I took, all the interviews I conducted, I never felt that I really came to terms with Texas. Perhaps the Irish easterner was too much inside me, both in reality and in the hidden myth of what I hoped to be, to ever allow me to comprehend Texas in other than an academic sense. 12

Texas did come to life, however, in the early chapters of the book, due not to me, but to Johnson's vivid recall. His memories of childhood had a physical texture. Unlike most people any easterner knows, he was living his last years in the very place he had been born—his ranch was literally one mile from his birthplace. He could walk every afternoon—and many afternoons he did—to and from these places, up the same path he had wandered as a child. Taken together these memories created a visual picture of what it was like to grow up in Texas in the first part of the century. The book lost much of this vividness when it followed Johnson away from home to college. 13

I believe the book became visually alive again only when Johnson came to Washington, for that city has been a deeply engaging place for me. I have found myself reacting to Washington as I did to Lyndon Johnson, with alternating awe, admiration, fascination, fear, and disdain. During my time on the White House staff, I was both drawn to and repelled by the same obsession that I was to witness in Johnson. For months I put my private life aside, saying to myself that "history" matters more and I could be helping to make it. So what if I missed a picnic or canceled a movie date—I could speak to the president of the United States. He would call me three or four times a week, ask me to wait around for a conversation with him that would usually take place between ten and eleven at night. All the other claims seemed irrelevant compared to that. 14

By the time I began to write the book my feelings toward Washington were as mixed as my feelings toward Johnson. I realized that if I had stayed there, given the attraction I felt for that world of power, I might have endlessly submerged my private life into a public one. Even if I had married and raised children, that never would have been 15 central. So I felt that I had to escape that kind of obsession in myself. And that choice in that stage of my life, as Erik Erikson would say, inevitably affected the way I analyzed choices that Johnson made differently.

16   The dissonance between Johnson as subject and me as biographer influenced the choice of subject matter in my next book, which follows three generations of the Kennedy family. On the one hand, I did not want to turn immediately to another close study of one powerful person. I know now how fragile such an enterprise is. Despite all the memories, dreams, and conversations Lyndon Johnson shared with me—perhaps the richest material that a biographer could have—I knew I had drawn an incomplete picture. To attempt another such book about an historical figure I had never seen would have been impossible for me. So I broadened the angle of vision, choosing three generations of one family rather than one person. And yet as the vision broadened, I decided that at least the place had to be brought closer to my own geographical and intellectual home. I chose the Irish, the East, the Kennedy family.

17   I feel comfortable writing about the Progressive Era at the turn of the century, which will be a large part of my story. Had I been a politician, I probably would rather have been a ward boss in Boston in 1900 than one of today's media compounds of polls, hypes, and sixty-second spots. Growing up with my father, Michael Alousius Kearns, has left me naturally comfortable with both the Irish and the Catholic parts of the story. I think I have some sense of what Catholicism might have meant to the Kennedys because I know what it has meant to me.

18   Yet if the tale of two cultures involved in this story leans toward the Irish and against the Yankees, I suspect the Kennedys expressed the same longings that I did to be fully accepted, which meant then— and to an extent that we may not like to recognize, still means now— to become a Yankee. In fact, the Kennedys were the first family to fulfill this longing as they became the first Irish Brahmins.

19   Another reason for choosing the Kennedy family as my subject is that I am at a stage in my own life when family is the dominant concern. The question I bring to the Kennedy story, well aware that the biographer's real challenge is to ask the right question, not simply the one satisfactory to oneself, is how it was that Ambassador Kennedy, a man as strong and as controversial as Lyndon Johnson, could shape a family unit in which each of his children led lives certainly influenced by him, but not narrowed by his influence?

20   A biographer's own persona necessarily affects the biographies he writes. The best chance one has is to put the line and the style of his own life interests, fascinations, and myths in consonance with his subject's. To pull against that grain, not so much against the grain of active dislike as against the grain of nodding disinterest, would make

for an uninteresting book. In other words, it is impossible to write a book about a bore without becoming boring.

The angle of vision that I have been describing thus far is the one that focuses on the subject himself. I would like to turn now to those other shifting angles of vision through which a biographer perceives and evaluates his or her materials. 21

Here, as elsewhere, politicians present special problems to the biographer. Though they leave behind hundreds of reams of words, we can never be exactly sure which ones are theirs and exactly what they mean. It is a politician's occupational hazard that effect comes to matter more than literal truth. So accustomed are they to speaking before audiences that most often what counts most is how the audiences react. Politicians tend to regard words as verbal and temporary, rather than written and permanent. Articulation, not analysis, is the coin of their kingdom. 22

This lesson was painfully driven home to me, when after listening to Johnson's proud description of his great-great-grandfather's heroic death at the Battle of San Jacinto, in Texas, I discovered that the grandfather had never even been at the battle. He was a real estate trader and had died at home in bed. But Johnson wanted an heroic relative so badly that he simply created the tale, and after retelling it dozens of times, the grandfather really came to exist in Johnson's mind. 23

So the powers of direct observation, as vivid as they might be, both in the White House and at the L. B. J. ranch, had to be balanced by a recognition of what Johnson was trying to convey and why. That meant checking everything, not just for its truth per se, but for the particular form in which it was expressed at a given time and how that rendition might reveal more about the continuing development of his character. 24

A second source of materials—interviews with associates—present a different kind of problem. The Johnson biography and Kennedy book provide contrasting examples of the problem. The tendency of President Johnson's associates is to be critical, while the tendency of President Kennedy's associates is to be admiring. This is not merely a reflection on the respective personalities of the two men. The central figures in the Johnson circle seem to be trying to break free of the intimacy and the fusion they experienced with Johnson, trying to live a life of some detachment, proving that they deserve their liberty by criticizing their former master. One first saw this passage to freedom in George Reedy's book *The Twilight of the Presidency;* one saw it later in Hubert Humphrey's memoirs. On the other hand, few of the Kennedy associates were ever as intimate with him as the Johnson associates were with Johnson. Kennedy tended to separate his social and 25 his political friends far more sharply than Johnson did. The Kennedy men, in my judgment, are often seeking through the written word to tie bonds that they never had to the president. The admiring works become a rite of passage to a Camelot that never really existed for them.

26   What of *memoirs?* I had the opportunity of watching the creation of Lyndon Johnson's memoirs on what was virtually a literary assembly line. I learned how unauthentic memoirs can be, unless one understands the stage of life in which they are written, why they are being written at that time, and what audience they aim to please.

27   At first, Johnson expressed the hope that his book would live on in history. This quickly yielded to the immediate necessity of proving that his critics had wronged him, especially about Vietnam. Like other presidents who wrote their memoirs, he wanted to help history along toward vindicating him. But unlike them, and like his own years in the White House, he wanted it all, all at once.

28   Still, the memoirs might have been a vital book if they had been written in Johnson's own tongue. For his language was colorful, metaphorical, fascinating, and equal to that of many novelists. But his book was stilted, formal, bureaucratic, and tedious. He felt he had to write like a statesman; he had to speak like a "Harvard" as he would put it; he had to drain the color from his life in order to give it the appropriate dignity. I worked on two chapters of the memoirs, one on economics and one on civil rights. Initially, I simply honed his own accounts as I had heard them from him. When he read them, he turned red in the face. "Are you serious?" he asked incredulously. "Do you think you're going to have me saying these awful words in front of all those people of the United States? What will they think?" I had recounted, for example, his wonderful description of Wilbur Mills as a cautious politician, who would never let anything come out of his Ways and Means Committee unless he was certain that it would pass the House. Johnson had said, "He is always so concerned about saving his face, that someday that man will fall on his ass."

29   Little did he know how prescient he would have seemed had he just left the prediction in his memoirs. But when he read that passage that he himself had said and that I had dutifully recorded, he got angry: "Don't you dare put such things in there; who am I to speak of Wilbur Mills that way? I may need him some day to get something passed in the Congress." Even in retirement, Johnson continued to be painstakingly presidential, hoping to prove that he had indeed belonged in the White House.

30   But before the end, as time took its toll on Johnson physically, as two heart attacks ravished him in the last years of his life, he became less guarded, almost as though, despite all his defenses, he had to tell his tale to someone in bits and pieces before it was too late. Otherwise, who would there ever be to tell the world about him?

The first heart attack was followed by a momentary euphoria. 31
His presidential memoirs were done; there was little pressure to begin
a book on the earlier years. Instead he could reminisce about them. He
even seemed now to want to stay alive; he quit smoking, he drank
less, he exercised regularly. For the first time since he had left the
White House, he appeared, if only briefly, to be relatively contented.
Not so coincidentally, his mind focused on a happier time in his career, his years as majority leader in the Senate. The control that he felt
during those years now seemed in the retelling to become a metaphor
to the control he was finally feeling at the ranch. There was a slower
pace to his conversation now. His words went far deeper than a plastic
presentation of public deeds; his candor became more than occasional.
He was willing to reveal himself as both the lion and the fox.

His second heart attack turned the psychic tide. I believe that he 32
knew in the last year and a half of his life that he was dying. And during that period he was obsessive about never being alone. It was during
this time, as I described it in the book, that he would awaken me at
five in the morning because he could not sleep and had to talk. His
sense that he was dying unlocked his earliest memories. Over and
over he recreated the scenes in which he had talked with his mother
about her past. As he described her to me, she was not the same model
mother he had praised two years before. The biographer finds that the
past is not simply the past, but a prism through which the subject filters his own changing self-image. Before, Johnson had pictured his
mother as loving, sensitive, and spiritual. Now, she was the demanding, ambitious, frustrated woman who loved him when he succeeded
for her and scorned him when he failed. He decided not to go to college after high school, because in high school he had felt so pressured
by her. She literally refused to talk to him for six months, to the point
where he finally ran away to California to try to make it on his own.
He could not; he came back in one year and acceded to all her demands, telling her that if she got him into college he would finally go.
And she did get him in, though it meant staying in his room for three
nights while he took the entrance exams. After that, he continued to
send his essays and book reports to her, which she corrected at once
and returned. The two together made a successful pair. Yet there was
always the sense as Johnson described her to me, that she would love
him only if he continued to succeed.

He would reveal such things in fits and starts. The next morning 33
he would sound guilty for blaming her; he would try to take his tale
back, saying: "Now, I didn't mean anything bad about my mother,
she was the most wonderful, beautiful woman, and she always loved
me no matter what." Soon he would offer another episode of her
darker side, but this slow exorcism seemed as painful as it now was
irrepressible.

34   Sadness welled up even more in those last years when he spoke of "the other beautiful woman" he had hoped to create—the Great Society. He had wanted her, he said, to be big and beneficent, fat and beautiful: In other words, when the federal government, through the laws he put on the books, became as fat or fatter even than the New Deal government, then he, Lyndon Johnson, would be even more loved than Franklin D. Roosevelt. Johnson lived to watch Nixon, month by month, cut his appropriations for the Great Society, and he felt, he said, that she was going to get so skinny and so ugly and so bony, that someday the American people were going to put her in a closet, refusing to look at her anymore. And alone in that closet she would die, and if she died, he said, then he too would die.

35   Johnson's curious metaphor became a part of his own life and death. Two days before he died he listened to President Nixon's second inaugural and the following day to Nixon's plan for dismantling the Great Society. Then, that afternoon, this man who was so afraid of being alone that he would ask friends to sit outside his door while he napped, had a heart attack in his bed when no one else was in the house. He called the secret service but by the time they reached his room, he was dead. The fear he had felt all his life—of dying alone— had been realized.

36   Surfeited with such rich, dramatic material, I wish I could have waited to write the book for ten or twenty years, so that I could really understand and convey its human value. But I was a young professor at Harvard, I had to publish. I also think, if I had it to do over again, that I would have written the book backwards rather than forwards, starting with his last years on the ranch, then going back to the Senate and House years, and finally to the sources of his character in childhood: In other words, following the tale in the order he presented it to me. It might have meant a loss of analytical details, since I couldn't have built up the patterns of traits shown in his childhood and early adulthood and later in his leadership. And it might have made the narrative telling more personal and difficult. But it would have allowed me to accompany Johnson on his search for his own past, to go with him, backwards in time, as he tried, in the last years of his life, to understand who and what he was. And that journey, however difficult to describe, would have been, I believe now, a richer tale.

_____ CONSIDERATIONS _____

1. In her final paragraph, as she muses over the possibility of writing the Johnson biography backwards, Kearns writes, "It would have allowed me to accompany Johnson on his search for his own past, to go with him, backwards in time, as he tried, in the last years of his life, to understand who and what he was." Read Patricia Hampl's short essay, page 247, and see whether she is do-

ing what LBJ tried to do. Build your conclusions into an essay about the difficulty of trying to go backward in time.

2. Study Johnson's use of metaphor, as Kearns reports it in paragraphs 34 and 35. Then experiment by rewriting paragraph 34 to remove the figurative language. What do you think of the change?

3. Biographers often use contrasting qualities of their subjects as a way of organizing their work. Write out in tabular form some of the contrasts that Kearns employs.

4. One way to appreciate biographical writing is to make some comparisons. After reading Kearns on LBJ, read William McFeely on another president, U.S. Grant, page 330. Then write a comparison-contrast essay about your findings—either about the two presidents or about the two biographers.

5. How did LBJ occupy his time when he retired to his Texas ranch? What significance did Kearns attach to his behavior?

6. "It is a politician's occupational hazard," writes Kearns in paragraph 22, "that effect comes to matter more than literal truth." Looking back at the 1996 presidential race, can you find examples to substantiate Kearns's statement? How do campaign strategies and techniques affect the truth? Are some truths more truthful than others?

Jane Kenyon (1947–1995) grew up in Ann Arbor, Michigan, where she won a Hopwood Award at the University of Michigan. After 1975 she lived on a farm in New Hampshire, writing essays and poems, and in 1992 received a Guggenheim Fellowship. In her lifetime she published four books of poems, starting with From Room to Room *in 1978 and concluding with* Constance *in 1993. She died of leukemia in 1995, and in 1996 her publisher issued* Otherwise: New and Selected Poems.

This poem grew out of Kenyon's 1991 visit to the battlefield in Pennsylvania, just as the Gulf War was ending.

49

JANE KENYON

Gettysburg: July 1, 1863

The young man, hardly more
than a boy, who fired the shot
had looked at him with an air
not of anger but of concentration,
5   as if he were surveying a road,
or feeding a length of wood into a saw:
it had to be done just so.

The bullet passed through
his upper chest, below the collarbone.
10   The pain was not what he might
have feared. Strangely exhilarated
he staggered out of the pasture
and into a grove of trees.

He pressed and pressed

15   the wound, trying to staunch
the blood, but he could only press
what he could reach, and he could
not reach his back, where the bullet
had exited.

20   He lay on the earth
smelling the leaves and mosses,
musty and damp and cool
after the blaze of open afternoon.
How good the earth smelled,

25   as it had when he was a boy
hiding from his father who was
intent on strapping him for doing
his chores late one time too many.

A cowbird razzed from a rail fence.

30   It isn't mockery, he thought,
no malice in it . . . just a noise.
Stray bullets nicked the oaks
overhead. Leaves and splinters fell.

Someone near him groaned.

35   But it was his own voice he heard.
His fingers and feet tingled,
the roof of his mouth,
and the bridge of his nose . . .

He became dry, dry, and thought

40   of Christ, who said, *I thirst.*
His man-smell—the smell of his hair
and skin, his sweat, the salt smell
of his cock and the little ferny hairs
that two women had known—

45   left him, and a sharp, almost sweet
smell began to rise from his open mouth
in the warm shade of the oaks.
A streak of sun climbed the rough
trunk of a tree, but he did not

50   see it with his open eye.

Yusef Komunyakaa (b. 1947) comes from Bogalusa, Louisiana, and teaches creative writing and Afro-American studies at Indiana University. In 1969 and 1970 he served with the Army in Vietnam. In 1992, his Magic City *won the Pulitzer Prize for Poetry, and in 1993 he published* Neon Vernacular: New and Selected Poems.

50

YUSEF KOMUNYAKAA
Facing It

My black face fades,
hiding inside the black granite.
I said I wouldn't,
dammit: No tears.
5　I'm stone, I'm flesh.
My clouded reflection eyes me
like a bird of prey, the profile of night
slanted against morning. I turn
this way—the stone lets me go.
10　I turn that way—I'm inside
the Vietnam Veterans Memorial
again, depending on the light
to make a difference.
I go down the 58,022 names,
15　half-expecting to find
my own in letters like smoke.
I touch the name Andrew Johnson;
I see the booby trap's white flash.
Names shimmer on a woman's blouse
20　but when she walks away
the names stay on the wall.
Brushstrokes flash, a red bird's
wings cutting across my stare.

Reprinted by permission of the author from *Dien Cai Dau* 1988, Wesleyan University Press.

The sky. A plane in the sky.
25   A white vet's image floats
closer to me, then his pale eyes
look through mine. I'm a window.
He's lost his right arm
inside the stone. In the black mirror
30   a woman's trying to erase names:
No, she's brushing a boy's hair.

Maxine Kumin (b. 1925) came north from Philadelphia to attend Radcliffe College and has remained in New England since 1976 in her beloved New Hampshire countryside, where she farms and raises horses. She is a poet, with a Pulitzer Prize won in 1973 for her collection Up Country. *Her other books include* Our Ground Time Here Will Be Brief *(1982) and most recently* Looking for Luck *(1992). In 1989 she became Poet Laureate of New Hampshire. She has also published novels, a collection of short stories, many children's books, and three essay collections, most recently* Women, Animals, and Vegetables *(1994). We take this essay from* In Deep: Country Essays *(1987).*

51

MAXINE KUMIN
Building Fence

1   Making fences presupposes not only pastures but a storehouse of diligence. When you start from a tangle of sumac and blackberry, every reclaimed square yard seems more precious than an acre of riverbottom land. For a dozen years we've been pushing back the forest, clearing, seeding, and sustaining what now adds up to fourteen up-and-down acres of the once two hundred-odd that nurtured a dairy herd between the two world wars.

2   Building the fence itself is an imperfect science. Despite actual measurements, you have to yield to the contours of the land. Post holes are soul destroyers. Technology hasn't done much for the fence line on a hill farm. Even if you hire a neighbor's tractor with auger attachment, at least half the holes will have to be hand crafted as you ease them this side or that of expectation. Stones annoy, rocks impede, boulders break your heart as you tunnel down at a slant, hunting in vain for the earth bottom. If obdurate ledge or obstinate pudding

stone does not require acts of faith and leaps of imagination, here and there you can count on a slope too steep for machinery to navigate. The gasoline-powered two-man auger is more adaptable, but even that ingenious tool will not maneuver between stump and bedrock with the same agility as the old manual clamshell tool.

Setting the posts exacts more faith from the dogged fence-pilgrim. Somehow there is never enough dirt in the pile you took out, even after you've placed a ring of stones in the bottom of the hole to brace the post. Even with a ring of stones stomped in nearly at the top for further support, your supply of loose dirt has vanished. You end up digging part of a second hold to make enough friable earth to hold the first pole solid. Clearly, you do not come out even.

You've set 225 posts, roughly ten feet apart. From an appropriate distance, if you squint, it's merely a toothpick stockade, inconclusive and raw-looking. You long to get on with it, to establish the feeling of fence, the ethos of enclosure.

The best part of building the fence is tacking up the string that denotes where the line of top boards means to be. You go around importantly to do this light work, trailing your ball of twine, wearing your apron of nails. You measure with your fold-up rule fifty-two inches from the ground—but where exactly *is* the ground? This mound, this declivity, this solitary flat patch? You tap in a nail, pull the string taut from the previous post, catch it with a few easy twists around, and so on. String stands in for wood, a notion, a suggestion of what's to come. Foreshadowing, you could call it.

Because this is New England, the fence travels uphill and down; only little bits of it are on the level. Although string lightheartedly imitates the contours of the land, boards have to be held in place, the angle of cut defined by pencil. Invariably, both ends of the boards want cutting. The eye wants readjustments despite the ruler. Sometimes bottom boards catch on hummocks, outcroppings, or earth bulges which must be shoveled out or the board rearranged. But let's say you've tacked up your whole top line for the day, you've stepped back, eye-balled and readjusted it. Oh, the hammering home! The joy and vigor of sending nails through hemlock into the treated four-by-four uprights. Such satisfying whacks, such permanence, such vengeance against the mass bustications of horses and heifers through the puny electric wire of yore. Visions of acres and acres of fences, field after field tamed, groomed, boarded in; that is the meaning of gluttony.

Finishing the fence—painting, staining, or applying preservative—requires the same constancy as the slow crafting of it. You put in your two hours a day, rejoice when rain interrupts the schedule and your Calvinist soul is permitted to tackle some other chore. Cleaning tack, for example, provides a pleasurable monotony compared to the servitude of the four-inch roller and the can of Noxious Mixture. In our case, it's composed of one-third diesel oil, one-third used crankcase oil, and one-third creosote. You are properly garbed to apply this Grade C syrup, wearing cast-off overalls, a battered felt hat, decayed boots, and thick neoprene gloves. You stand almost an arm's length away from the fence in order to get enough leverage so the mixture will penetrate wood grain—here tough, there smooth, here cracked and warty, there slick as a duck's feather. You invent methods for relieving the dreary sameness of the job. On one course you begin left to right, top to bottom, back to front. On the next you reverse the order. Sometimes you do all the undersides first, or all the backs. Sometimes you spring ahead, lavishly staining all the front-facing boards just to admire the dark wood lines dancing against the hummocky terrain of these young—yea, virginal—fields. The process gets you in the shoulder blades, later in the knees. You spatter freckles of the stuff on your protected body. Your protective eyeglasses are now freckled with iridescent dots. The stench of the mix premeates your hair, your gloved hands, becomes a way of life. You can no longer gain a new day without putting in your two hours staining board fences. More compelling than tobacco or alcohol, that addictive odor of char, of disinfectant, of grease pits. The horses follow you along the fence lines, curious, but even the fresh-faced filly keeps a respectful distance from you and your repellent mixture.

8   A year later you sit atop the remnants of a six-foot-wide stone wall unearthed along the perimeter of number two field and look across to the remarkable pear tree that stands alone in the third and newest field. Behind you, the first field; behind it, the barn. Between fields, hedgerow and hickory trees, red pine and hemlock. An intermittent brook further defines the boundary between number one and number two. A tributary meanders at the foot of number three. Beyond, a life-time of second-growth woodland awaits. In your mind's eye, an infinity of fenced fields recedes but never vanishes. And all the livestock of a lifetime safely graze.

____ CONSIDERATIONS _____

1. Make a little list of products you have seen advertised as "hand crafted." Then look at Kumin's use of the term to describe a hole in the ground. Is there something odd about that usage?

2. Can you remember jobs in which you had to invent "methods for relieving the dreary sameness" of a job, as Kumin puts it in paragraph 7? See also "Getting Tired," especially paragraph 13, for Carol Bly's method of keeping herself awake while driving a tractor back and forth across a field in Min-

nesota. Write an essay about the tricks and diversions we invent to get ourselves through a tedious job.

3. Do you find the word "bustications," as used in paragraph 6, in your dictionary? What does that suggest to you, first, about that particular word, and, second, about any newly invented word?

4. What phrase in paragraph 4 do the last two sentences of paragraph 8 elucidate?

5. What do you think of "Building Fence" as a "process" essay? Compare it with M. F. K. Fisher's "One Way to Give Thanks," page 206.

Phillip Lopate (b. 1943) writes poems and nonfiction: this essay comes from **Against Joie de Vivre** *(1989). He has received fellowships from the Guggenheim Foundation and the National Endowment for the Arts, and his work has appeared in* **Best American Essays.** *He teaches at the University of Houston and Columbia University. In 1994 he edited* The Art of the Personal Essay.

52

PHILLIP LOPATE
On Shaving a Beard

1   I have just made a change that feels as dramatic, for the moment, as switching from Democrat to Republican. I have shaved off my beard. Actually I clipped it away with scissors first, the I went in for the kill with a safety razor. The first snip is the most tentative: you can still allow yourself the fantasy that you are only shaping and trimming, perhaps a raffish Vandyke will emerge. Then comes the moment when you make a serious gash in the carpet. You rub the neighboring whiskers over the patch to see if it can still be covered, but the die is cast, and with a certain glee the energy turns demolitionary.

2   As I cut away the clumps of darkness, a moon rises out of my face. It lights up the old canyon line of the jawbone. I am getting my face back. I lather up again and again and shave away the bristles until the skin is smooth as a newborn's—the red irritation spots where the skin has reacted to the unaccustomed blade seem a sort of diaper rash. When I am done, I look in the glass and my face itself is like a mirror, so polished and empty are the cheeks. I feel a little sorry for the tender boy-man reflected before me, his helpless features open to assault. The unguarded vacancy of that face! Now I will have to come to terms again with the weak chin, the domineering nose, the thin, sarcastic-pleading lips.

3   I look down at the reddish-gray curls in the sink. The men in my family have always been proud that our beards grew in red, though the

tops of our heads were black. It seems an absurd triviality for Nature to waste a gene on, but it is one of the most tangible ways that my father has felt united to his sons and we to him. A momentary regret passes through me.

Never mind: I have taken an action. I grew the beard originally 4 because I had been restless and dissatisfied with myself; I shaved it for the same reason. How few cut-rate stratagems there are to better our mood; you can take a trip, go shopping, change your hair, see every movie in town—and the list is exhausted. Now I will have to be contented for a while. It is summer, the wrong time to start growing a beard again.

Because of the hot weather, I also have a ready-made excuse for 5 anyone who might ask why I gave up my beard. I know that the real reasons are more murky—they go to the heart of my insecurities as a man and my envy of others of my sex. When I meet a man I admire and he is wearing a beard, I immediately think about emulating him. The tribe of bearded men have a patriarchal firmness, a rabbinical kindly wisdom in their faces. They strike me as good providers. They resemble trees (their beards are nests) or tree cutters. In any case, mentally I place them in the forest, with flannel shirt and axe.

So I join this fraternity, and start to collect the equivalent of ap- 6 proving winks from other beardies, fellow conspirators in the League of Hirsutes. It feels good to be taken for an ancestor or pioneer. Then the novelty begins to wear off, the beard starts to itch, and I realize that inside I am no more rooted or masculinely capable than before. I start to envy clean-shaven men—their frank, open, attractively "vulnerable" faces. Some women will trust you more if you are clean-shaven; they profess to see beards as Mephistophelian masks, hiding the emotions. Early in the relationship, this may be a good reason to keep a beard. At a later point shaving it off becomes tantamount to a giddy declaration of love.

Other women, on the other hand, will tell you that a kiss with- 7 out facial hair is like a roast beef sandwich without mustard. *They* consider beards a mark of virility, trustworthiness, and bohemian sensitivity. Obviously, the image systems break down in the face of individual tastes. Nevertheless, it is still possible to say that beards connote freedom, telling the boss off, an attitude of "gone fishing"; men often grow them on vacations, or after being booted from the White House staff, like Ehrlichman. (Even Admiral Poindexter grew a mustache.) Clean-shavenness, on the other hand, implies a subscription to the rules of society.

A major division in the bearded kingdom exists between those 8 who revel in no longer having to bother with maintenance, letting Nature have its luxuriant bushy way, and those who continue to keep a razor nearby, prudently pruning or shaving the cheeks every few days.

A well-clipped beard on a kindly man looks as proper as a well-kept lawn on Sunday. On the other hand, there are beards with a glint of cruelty—beards trimmed to Caligulaesque exactitude. I had thought to be one of the pruners, but went too far, lacking the razor-sharp finesse.

9   Having shaved the beard off, I take my first cautious steps into society. I am dreading those who will ask why I did it, then settle back for a long soul-bearing explanation. What will I reply to those who are quick to say, "I liked you better the other way"? My impulse is to step on their toes, but we must not punish honesty. Once, when I was teaching in P.S. 90, I shaved off my beard, and the children, who were familiar with me as a hairy man, were so outraged that all through the first day of the new regime, they ran alongside and punched me. Children are good at expressing a sense of betrayal at change.

10   Those who are bearded for the long haul either tend to view the new me with something like a Mennonite's disapproval at backsliding, or are relieved that one who had appeared a member of the brotherhood was exposed in the nick of time as turncoat. A few friends, who pride themselves on their observational powers, make helpful comments like: You look fatter. You look thinner. You look younger. You look older. The majority say nothing. At first I think they are being polite, not meaning to broach a subject that might make me self-conscious. Then, out of frustration at their not having noticed, I finally call my naked face to their attention. They say: "I *thought* there was something different about you but I couldn't put my finger on it. Besides, you keep going back and forth, Lopate, who can keep up?"

_____ CONSIDERATIONS _____

1. In his first sentence, Lopate had to make a choice between "from Democrat to Republican," and "from Republican to Democrat." Did he make the right choice? Explain.

2. Why is Lopate unable to state decisively how a man's beard affects the opposite sex?

3. Lopate's smoothly written essay seems effortless, but a careful reader will find many unusually apt word choices, evidence that the writer did not toss off the piece casually. Note some of those choices and explain why they are real contributions to the essay.

4. In what sense, if any, does Lopate's essay explore deeper territory than the whiskers on his face?

5. There are a few capitalized words and phrases in the essay that you may not recognize: Vandyke, League of Hirsutes, Mephisophelian, Caligulaesque, P.S. 90, and so on. What do you lose if you do not bother to look them up?

Thomas Lynch (b. 1948) was born in Detroit and now lives in the town of Milford, Michigan, where he has been a funeral director since 1974. His first book of poems, Skating with Heather Grace, *was published by Knopf in 1988.* "Burying" *appeared in the* Quarterly.

53

THOMAS LYNCH

Burying

Every year I bury one hundred and fifty of my townspeople. Another dozen or two I take to the crematory to be burned. I sell caskets, burial vaults, and urns for the ashes. I have a sideline in headstones and monuments. I do flowers on commission. 1

Apart from the tangibles, I sell the use of my building eleven thousand square feet, furnished and fixtured with an abundance of pastel and chair rail and crown moldings. The whole lash-up is mortgaged and remortgaged well into the next century. My rolling stock includes a hearse, a limo, two Fleetwoods, and a mini-van with darkened windows our price list calls a service vehicle and everyone in town calls the Dead Wagon. 2

I used to use the "unit pricing method"—the old package deal. It meant you had only one number to look at. It was a large number. Now everything is itemized. It's the law. So now there is a long list of items and numbers and italicized disclaimers, something like a menu or the Sears, Roebuck wish book, and sometimes the federally mandated options begin to look like cruise control or rear-window defrost. I wear black most of the time, to keep folks in mind of the fact we're not talking Buicks here. At the bottom of the list is still a large number. 3

In a good year the gross is close to half a million, 5 percent of which we hope to call profit. I am the only undertaker in this town. I have a corner on the market. 4

---

[1]From the *Quarterly*. Reprinted by permission of the author.

5   The market, such as it is, is figured on what is called the "crude death rate"—the number of deaths every year out of every thousand of persons.

6   Here is how it works.

7   Imagine a large room into which you coax one thousand people. You slam the doors in January, leaving them plenty of food and drink, color TVs, magazines, condoms. Your sample should have an age distribution heavy on Baby Boomers and their children—1.2 children per boomer. For every four normal people, there is one Old-Timer, who, if he or she wasn't in this big room, would probably be in Florida or Arizona or a nursing home. You get the idea. The group will include fifteen lawyers, one faith healer, three dozen real-estate agents, a video technician, several licensed counselors, and an Amway distributor. The rest will be between jobs, middle managers, ne'er-do-wells, or retired.

8   Now the magic part—come late December, when you throw open the doors, only 991.3, give or take, will shuffle out upright. Two hundred and sixty will now be selling Amway. The other 8.7 have become the crude death rate.

9   Here's another stat.

10   Of the 8.7 corpses, two-thirds will have been Old-Timers, 5 percent will be children, and the rest (2.75) will be Boomers—realtors and attorneys—one of whom was, no doubt, elected to public office during the year. What's more, three will have died of cerebral vascular or coronary difficulties, two of cancer, one each of vehicular mayhem, diabetes, and domestic violence. The spare change will be by act of God or suicide—most likely the faith healer.

11   The figure most often and most conspicuously missing from the insurance charts and demographics is the one I call THE BIG ONE, which refers to the number of people out of every one hundred born who will die. Over the long haul, THE BIG ONE hovers right around . . . well—dead nuts on 100. If this were on the charts, they would call it "Death expectancy" and no one would buy futures of any kind. But it is a useful number and has its lessons. Maybe you will want to figure out what to do with your life. Maybe it will make you feel a certain kinship to the rest of us. Maybe it will make you hysterical. Whatever the implications of a one hundred death expectancy, calculate how big a town this is and why mine produces for me steady, if sometimes unpredictable, labor.

12   They die around the clock here, without apparent preference for a day of the week, month of the year; there is no clear favorite in the way of season. Nor does the alignment of the stars, fullness of moon, or liturgical calendar have very much to do with it. The whereabouts are neither here nor there. They go off upright or horizontally, in Chevrolets and nursing homes, in bathtubs, on the interstates, in ERs,

ORs, BMWs. And while it may be so that we assign more equipment or more importance to deaths that create themselves in places marked by initials—ICU being somehow better than Greenbrier Convalescent Home—it is also true that the dead don't care. In this way, the dead I bury and burn are like the dead before them, for whom time and space have become mortally unimportant. This loss of interest is, in fact, one of the first sure signs that something serious is about to happen. The next thing is they quit breathing. At this point, to be sure, a "gunshot wound to the chest" or "shock and trauma" will get more ink than a CVA or ASHD, but no condition of death is any less permanent than any other. All will do. The dead don't care.

13   Nor does *who* much matter, either. To say "I'm okay, you're okay, and by the way, he's dead!" is, for the living, a kind of comfort.

14   It is why we drag rivers and comb plane wrecks.

15   It is why MIA is more painful than DOA.

16   It is why we have open caskets and classified obits.

17   Knowing is better than not knowing, and knowing it is you is terrifically better than knowing it is me. Once I'm the dead guy, whether you're okay or he's okay won't much interest me. You can both go bag your asses, because the dead don't care.

18   Of course, the living, bound by their adverbs and their actuarials, still do. Now there's the difference and why I'm in business. The living are careful and oftentimes caring. The dead are careless, or maybe it's care-less. Either way, they don't care. These are unremarkable and verifiable truths.

19   My former mother-in-law, herself an unremarkable and verifiable truth, was always fond of holding forth with Cagneyesque bravada—to wit, "When I'm dead, just put me in a box and throw me in a hole." But whenever I would remind her that we did substantially that with *everyone*, the woman would grow sullen and a little cranky.

20   Later, over meat loaf and green beans, she would invariably give out with "When I'm dead, just cremate me and scatter the ashes."

21   My former mother-in-law was trying to make carelessness sound like fearlessness. The kids would stop eating and look at each other. The kids' mother would whine, "Oh, Mom, don't talk like that." I'd take out my lighter and begin to play with it.

22   In the same way, the priest that married me to this woman's daughter—a man who loved gold and gold ciboria and vestments made of Irish linen; a man who drove a great black sedan with a wine-red interior and who always had his eye on the cardinal's job—this same fellow, leaving the cemetery one day, felt called upon to instruct me thus: "No bronze coffin for me. No Sir! No orchids or roses or limousines. The plain pine box is the one I want, a quiet Low Mass, and the pauper's grave. No pomp and circumstances."

23   He wanted, he explained, to be an example of simplicity, of prudence, of piety and austerity—all priestly and, apparently, Christian virtues. When I told him that he needn't wait, that he could begin his ministry of good example yet today, that he could quit the country club and do his hacking at the public links and trade his brougham for a used Chevette, that free of his Florsheims and cashmeres and prime ribs, free of his bingo nights and building funds, he could become, for Christ's sake, the very incarnation of Francis himself, or Anthony of Padua; when I said, in fact, that I would be willing to assist him in this, that I would gladly distribute his CDs and credit cards among the needy of the parish, and that I would, when the sad duty called, bury him for nothing in the manner he would have by then become accustomed to; when I told the priest who had married me these things, he said nothing at all, but turned his wild eye on me in the manner in which the cleric must have looked on Sweeney years ago, before he cursed him, irreversibly, into a bird.*

24   What I was trying to tell the fellow was, of course, that being a dead saint is no more worthwhile than being a dead philodendron or a dead angelfish. Living is the rub, and always has been. Living saints still feel the flames and stigmata, the ache of chastity and the pangs of conscience. Once dead, they let their relics do the legwork, because, as I was trying to tell this priest, the dead don't care.

25   Only the living care.

26   And I am sorry to be repeating myself, but this is the central fact of my business—that there is nothing, once you are dead, that can be done *to you* or *for you* or *with you* or *about you* that will do you any good or any harm; that any damage or decency we do accrues to the living, to whom your death happens if it really happens to anyone. The living have to live with it; you don't. Theirs is the grief or gladness your death brings. And there is the truth, abundantly self-evident, that seems, now that I think of it, the one most elusive to my old in-laws, to the parish priest, and to perfect strangers who are forever accosting me in barbershops and in cocktail bars and at parent-teacher conferences, hell-bent or duty-bound on telling me what it is they want done with them when they are dead.

27   Give it a rest is the thing I say.

28   Once you are dead, put your feet up, call it a day, and let the old man or the missus or the thankless kids decide whether you are to be buried or burned or blown out of a cannon or left to dry out in a ditch. It's not your day to watch it, because the dead don't care.

---

*Lynch alludes to a medieval Irish poem in which Sweeney attacks a priest, who puts a curse on Sweeney and changes him into a bird. The poem was recently translated from the Celtic by the Irish poet Seamus Heaney who called it, "Sweeney Astray."

Another reason people are always rehearsing their obsequies 29
with me has to do with the fear of death, which is something anyone
in his right mind has. It is healthy. It keeps us from playing in the traffic. I say pass it on to the kids.

There is a belief—widespread among the women I have dated, lo- 30
cal Rotarians, and friends of my children—that I, being the undertaker
here, have some irregular fascination with, special interest in, inside
information about, even attachment to, *the dead*. They assume, these
people, some perhaps with good reason, that I want their bodies.

It is an interesting concept. 31

But here's the truth. 32

Being dead is one—the worst, the last—but only one in a series of 33
calamities that afflicts our own and several other species. The list may
include, but is not limited to, gingivitis, bowel obstruction, contested
divorce, tax audit, spiritual vexation, money trouble, political mischief,
and on and on and on. There is no shortage of *misery*. And I am no more
attracted to the dead than the dentist is to your bad gums, the doctor to
your rotten innards, or the accountant to your sloppy expense records. I
have no more stomach for misery than the banker or the lawyer, the
pastor or the politico—because misery is careless and is everywhere.
Misery is the bad check, the exwife, the mob in the street, and the IRS—
who, like the dead, feel nothing, and, like the dead, *don't care*.

Which is not to say that the dead do not matter. 34

They do. 35

Last Monday morning, Milo Hornsby died. Mrs. Hornsby called 36
at 2:00 A.M. to say that Milo had "expired" and would I take care of it,
as if his condition were like any other that could be renewed or somehow improved upon. At 2:00 A.M., yanked from sleep, I am thinking,
put a quarter in Milo and call me in the morning. But Milo is dead. In
a moment, in a twinkling, Milo has slipped irretrievably out of our
reach, beyond Mrs. Hornsby and the children, beyond the women at
the laundromat he owned, beyond his comrades at the Legion Hall,
the Grand Master of the Masonic Lodge, his pastor at First Baptist, beyond the mailman, zoning board, town council, and Chamber of Commerce; beyond us all, and any treachery or any kindness we had in
mind for him.

Milo is dead. 37

X's on his eyes, lights out, curtains. 38

Helpless, harmless. 39

Milo's dead. 40

Which is why I do not haul to my senses, coffee and a quick 41
shave, Homburg and great coat, warm up the Dead Wagon, and make
for the freeway in the early o'clock for Milo's sake but for his missus's
sake, for she who has become, in the same moment and same twinkling, like water to ice, the widow Hornsby. I go for her—because she
still can cry and care and pray and pay my bill.

42   .   The hospital that Milo died in is state of the art. There are signs on every door declaring a part or process or bodily function. I like to think that, taken together, the words would add up to something like the Human Condition, but they never do. What's left of Milo, the remains, are in the basement, between SHIPPING & RECEIVING and LAUNDRY ROOM. Milo would like that if he were still liking anything. Milo's room is called PATHOLOGY.

43   The medical-technical parlance of death emphasizes disorder. We are forever dying of failures, of anomalies, of insufficiencies, of dysfunctions, arrests, accidents. These are either chronic or acute. The language of death certificates—Milo's says "Cardiopulmonary Failure"—is like the language of weakness. Likewise, Mrs. Hornsby, in her grief, will be said to be breaking down or falling apart or going to pieces, as if there were something structurally awry with her. It is as if death and grief were not part of the Order of Things, as if Milo's failure and his widow's weeping were, or ought to be, sources of embarrassment. "Doing well" for Mrs. Hornsby would mean that she is bearing up, braving the storm, or being strong for the children. We have willing pharmacists to help her with this. Of course, for Milo, doing well would mean he was back upstairs, holding his own, keeping the meters and monitors bleeping.

44   But Milo is downstairs, between SHIPPING & RECEIVING and LAUNDRY ROOM, in a stainless-steel drawer, wrapped in white plastic top to toe, and—because of his small head, wide shoulders, ponderous belly, and skinny legs, and the trailing white binding cord from his ankles and toe tags—he looks, for all the world, like a larger than life-size sperm.

45   I sign for him and get him out of there. At some level, I am still thinking Milo gives a shit, which by now we all know he doesn't—because the dead don't care.

46   Back at my place of business, upstairs in the embalming room, behind a door marked PRIVATE, Milo Hornsby is floating on a porcelain table under fluorescent lights. Unwrapped, outstretched, Milo is beginning to look a little more like himself—eyes wide open, mouth agape, returning to our gravity. I shave him, close his eyes, his mouth. We call this "setting the features." These are the features—eyes and mouth—that, in death, will never look the way they would look in life, when they are always opening, closing, focusing, signaling, telling us something. In death, what they tell us is they will not be doing anything anymore. The last detail to be managed is Milo's hands—one folded over the other, over the umbilicus, in an attitude of ease, of repose, of retirement.

47   They will not be doing anything anymore, either.

48   I wash his hands before positioning them.

When my wife moved out some years ago, I kept the children and   49
the dirty laundry. It was big news in a small town. There was the gossip and the goodwill that places like this are famous for. And while
there was plenty of talk, no one knew exactly what to say to me. They
felt hopeless, I suppose. So they brought casseroles and beef stews,
took the kids out to the movies or canoeing, brought their younger sisters around to visit me. What Milo did was sent his laundry van by
twice a week for two months, until I had found a housekeeper. Milo
would pick up five loads in the morning and return them by
lunchtime, fresh and folded. I never asked him to do this. I hardly
knew him. I had never been in his home or in his laundromat. His
wife had never known my wife. His children were too old to play with
my children.

After my housekeeper was installed, I went to thank Milo and to   50
pay my bill. The invoices detailed the number of loads, the washers
and the dryers, detergent, bleaches, fabric softeners. I think the total
came to sixty dollars. When I asked Milo what the charges were for
pickup and delivery, for stacking and folding, for saving my life and
the lives of my children, for keeping us in clean clothes and towels
and bed linens, "Never mind that," Milo said, "one hand washes the
other."

I place Milo's right hand over his left hand, then try the other   51
way. Then back again. Then I decide that it does not matter, that one
hand washes the other either way.

The embalming takes me about two hours.   52

It is daylight by the time I am done.   53

Every Monday morning Paddy Fulton comes to my office. He was   54
damaged in some profound way in Korea. The details of his damage
are unknown to the locals. Paddy Fulton has no limp or anything
missing—so everyone thinks it was something he saw in Korea that
left him a little simple, occasionally perplexed, the type to draw rein
abruptly in his daylong walks, to consider the meaning of litter, pausing over bottle caps and gum wrappers. Paddy Fulton has a nervous
smile and a deadfish handshake. He wears a baseball cap and thick
eyeglasses. Every Sunday night Paddy goes to the I.G.A. and buys up
the tabloids at the checkout stands with headlines that usually involve Siamese twins or movie stars or UFOs. Paddy is a speed reader
and a math whiz—but because of his damage, he has never held a job
and never applied for one. Every Monday morning, Paddy brings me
clippings of stories under headlines like: 601 LB. MAN FALLS THRU COFFIN—A GRAVE SITUATION or EMBALMER FOR THE STARS SAYS ELVIS IS FOREVER. The Monday morning Milo died, Paddy's clipping had to do with
an urn full of ashes that made grunting and groaning noises, that whistled sometimes, and that was expected to begin talking. Certain scientists in England could make no sense of it. They had run several tests.

The ashes' widow, however—left with nine children and no estate—is convinced that her dearly beloved and greatly reduced husband is trying to give her winning numbers for the lottery. "Jacky would never leave us without good prospects," she says. "He loved his family more than anything." There is a picture of the two of them—the widow and the urn, the living and the dead, flesh and bronze, the Victrola and the Victrola's dog. She has her ear cocked, waiting.

We are always waiting. Waiting for some good word or for the 55 winning numbers. Waiting for a sign or wonder, some signal from our dear dead that the dead still care. We are gladdened when they do outstanding things, when they arise from their graves or appear to us in dreams or fall from their caskets. It pleases us no end, as if there were no end; as if the dead still cared, had agendas, were yet alive.

But the sad and well-known fact of the matter is that most of us 56 will stay in our caskets and be dead a long time, and that our urns and graves will never make a sound. Our reason and requiems, our headstones and High Masses, will neither get us in nor keep us out of heaven. The meaning of our lives, and the memories of them, will belong only to the living, just as our funerals do.

We heat graves here for winter burials, as a kind of foreplay be- 57 fore digging in, to loosen the frost's hold on the ground before the sexton and his backhoe do the opening. We buried Milo in the ground last Wednesday. It was, by then, the only thing to do. The mercy is that what we buried there, in an oak casket, just under the frost line, had ceased to be Milo. It was something else. Milo had become the idea of himself, a permanent fixture of the third person and past tense, his widow's loss of appetite and trouble sleeping, the absence in places where we look for him, our habits of him breaking, our phantom limb, our one hand washing the other.

____ **CONSIDERATIONS** _____

1. Why is Thomas Lynch less than reverential toward the dead? Is he disrespectful toward them?

2. Are the following words synonymous: *ironic, satiric, sardonic, cynical, humorous, witty, sarcastic*? After comparing their definitions in a good dictionary, which one would you select as the most descriptive of Lynch's tone (attitude) in his essay? Be prepared to back up your choice by referring to illustrative words, phrases, or passages in "Burying." If you think none of these words is appropriate, make a case for any other word you think would be better.

3. In paragraph 43, Lynch tells us of something he discovers by looking at the "parlance of death." What is his criticism of that jargon?

4. In paragraph 46, find an example of Lynch making fun of his own parlance. What other evidence do you find that Lynch enjoys playing with language?

5. Some readers feel that Lynch is coldly commercial about his work. What passages might give them that impression? What evidence do you find that Lynch is not without feelings about the dead and their survivors?

6. What do you make of Lynch's method of explaining the "crude death rate"?

7. Look at some of Lynch's one-sentence paragraphs. How do you suppose he might defend them as paragraphs?

8. What did Milo's remark "One hand washes the other" mean to Lynch?

William S. McFeeley (b. 1930) is a historian born in New York and educated at Amherst College and Yale University. His Grant: A Biography *(1981) won him the Pulitzer Prize as well as the Francis Parkman Prize. He has taught at Yale University, Mt. Holyoke College, and the University of Georgia. Here, he introduces a reprint of the autobiography of Ulysses S. Grant, the best book ever written by a president of the United States.*

54

WILLIAM S. MCFEELY

U. S. Grant, Writer

1   Every good story has a story. *The Personal Memoirs of U. S. Grant,* the general's own account of his wars—of his life, is a case in point. No one expected him to tell it, but he told it so well it won't be forgotten. Recently in England there appeared a lament that Grant is no longer remembered primarily for his patriotic valor as a soldier: "It is, perhaps, a sign of our times that we should be asked to admire the greatest nineteenth-century American general for his authorship of a now unread book." Without bothering to read the sign, it can be said, unequivocally, that this assessment of his writing is wrong; the book is read. Its readers, enemies of cant, include Gore Vidal, who, in one of his brilliantly iconoclastic essays, wrote, "it simply is not possible to read Grant's memoirs without realizing that the author is a man of first-rate intelligence." The book is one of the most unflinching studies of war in our literature.

2   If the book has a flourishing present-day reputation, it has a vivid history as well. And, in one sense, it is a very brief history. Ulysses S. Grant began writing in the late summer of 1884 just as he learned that he had cancer. He finished less than a year later when he completed his splendidly-cadenced two volumes. His last work on the proofs was done on July 14; on July 23, 1885, he died. Grant's accomplishment has daunted writers every since, but the *Personal Memoirs* is far more

than a *tour de force*. It is the record not only of the martial accomplishments of a great general, but also of the workings of that man's mind. The book's history runs back deeply into Grant's life.

That life has always seemed mysterious. How could a failed peacetime soldier, failed farmer, failed woodcutter, failed bill collector—a thirty-eight year old clerk in a harness store in the spring of 1861—become, by 1862, the object of sober speculation about the presidency of the United States? How was it that this unexceptional small man was, by 1864, the general commanding all the armies on one side of a vast and fierce civil war? And then, having become his republic's Alexander and Caesar, how did he earn so poor a reputation as its president? Henry Adams had one explanation; there was an elemental force in Grant that had little to do with conventional tests of success and nothing at all to do with intellect. Adams's assessment that "one had only to look at the evolution from Washington to Grant to disprove Darwin" has scathing force of its own, but it does not take into account Grant's book. One wonders if Adams read it.

The energy Adams felt in Grant worked with awesome effectiveness in the Civil War. Taking a terrible toll, he had pressed through and won it. When it was over he had nowhere to go except back into obscurity—which, once fame had come, was the equivalent of failure—or forward into the White House. He chose the latter course and, near the close of the second term, he reported to the Congress more frankly than any president before or since about his disappointing performance in office. That remarkable message might have become a model and the *Personal Memoirs* a revelation of peacetime self-doubt and confusion, but no such thing happened. Instead, when he did get to the task of writing about himself, he chose to tell of the steady, alert, controlled days of warring.

No book at all seems to have been in his mind as he left the White House, which had been the most secure (and permanent) place that Julia and Ulysses Grant had lived. They left reluctantly. "Waifs" was their word for themselves as they wandered the world in an extraordinary two-and-a-half year trip around the world. The modest republican couple was celebrated as exemplifying everything American, and the two travelers cheerfully enjoyed almost endless rounds of public dinners and sight-seeing. Grant took it all in, but he kept no journal—no record of either the events of which he was the center or, more disappointingly, of his reactions to them. A *New York Herald* reporter who was along, J. Russell Young, produced *Around the World with General Grant*, which holds an honorable place in the nineteenth century's long list of fascinating travel accounts, but it is Young's book, not Grant's.

In Japan, Grant worried about what he would do with himself when at a healthy fifty-six he went back to a country in which he was

3

4

5

6

the most famous citizen and in which he had no home. Apparently writing did not occur to him and, once again, the White House seemed the only refuge. Grant sought a third term, but his new reputation as a world leader did not offset his earlier presidential record. He, if not Julia, proved less skillful than the other politicians maneuvering at the Republican national convention of 1880, and Grant did not get the nomination. The Grants then moved to New York City, where he followed the trail of many other Civil War generals into business as a railroad president—the road was to be built in Mexico—and, even less promisingly, as a stock broker. Grant & Ward had been founded by his second son, Ulysses, and a quicksilver entrepreneur, Fernando Ward. The entrance of the general into the firm brought some customers, but no business acumen. Grant & Ward failed in 1884 and Ward left the country amid well-founded reports of illegal transactions. The best that can be said about the Grants, father and son, is that they had been monumentally inattentive.

7   Now in his sixties, as he had been in his thirties, Grant was broke. As he had once had to go to his father to explain, contritely, that he had failed and needed a job, so now he had to go to William H. Vanderbilt for a loan. He got it and held off his creditors, but all of his private resources were gone. He needed to make some money.

8   Writing about past battles had become a flourishing cottage industry for Civil War veterans. Magazines competed for the articles, fanning controversy between rival generals, but much of this literature proved to be one general's defense of his every move, while attacking the moves of every other general. (The enemy, of course, consisted almost entirely of officers in one's own army. Only rarely was the Confederacy or, conversely, the Union the primary foe.) Much of this writing is worth little, either as narrative or military history, although some books, like *Lew Wallace: An Autobiography of 1906*, and *Memoirs of General William T. Sherman*, published in 1875, are distinguished works. The Century Company, whose editors were compiling material for its famous anthology *Battles and Leaders of the Civil War*, had approached Grant for articles on Shiloh and Vicksburg. Now, with the general's pecuniary needs common knowledge and with the Sherman work as a challenge, Century approached Grant about a book.

9   The negotiations took place late in the summer of 1884 and Grant was well along toward a contract with Century when, enter Mark Twain. People have written of the friendship of Samuel Clemens and Ulysses S. Grant as a curiosity when, in fact, it was totally logical. Both were midwestern ducks out of water; they had scooted about as far as they could get from the great Mississippi River each had made more famous. Each took a sardonic view of the concept of America as the promised land; each was expecting to be cheated by the next charlatan to come along. Clemens spent only two weeks in

the war, on the side of the Confederacy, while Grant had fought a bit longer for the Union; yet, when Clemens mocked the great general at a vast testimonial dinner in 1880, he got away with it. As a phalanx of deferential generals sat staring at their commander wondering how he would respond to being likened to a baby trying to swallow his toe, Grant laughed. The two men became staunch friends. And when Clemens heard that Century had made Grant a very modest offer for his book, he was incensed. He had just created his own publishing company (as his only defense against a particular breed of charlatans) for *Huckleberry Finn*, and he proposed to Grant that *he* publish his memoirs at a handsome royalty rate. (In time, Grant's widow received close to a half-million dollars.)

In Clemen's telling of the story, he casts himself in the role of 10
the man who almost instantaneously rescued Grant from the rascals; in fact the negotiations went on for several months and Grant, for once, proved shrewd. He knew the publisher also stood to make a good deal of money, and delayed just enough to keep Clemens hungry and cause him to come across with the excellent royalty arrangement.

There have been suggestions that Grant did not write the *Per-* 11
sonal Memoirs and reports that Clemens did. Both are false. Clemens encouraged Grant, but he did not write the book. Neither did Adam Badeau, a former aide of Grant's and the author of *Military History of General Ulysses S. Grant, from April, 1861, to April, 1865.* Badeau moved into Grant's house on 66th Street in New York, at the general's invitation, to assist in the writing of the book. Badeau assumed Grant could not do the job, and perhaps at the start Grant believed that too. But soon Grant knew that he, and he alone, could write the book. Badeau departed (and began a nasty suit in which he claimed, unsuccessfully, that his work was used unethically by Grant and his son; the charge was dismissed in court after Grant's death). Grant's oldest son, Frederick Dent Grant, helped his father as a research assistant, but the writing was done by Ulysses Grant, in pencil on lined pads of writing paper. A splendid opportunity is available to the scholar who undertakes a textual analysis of the manuscript and a comparison of it to the first edition, on which all subsequent editions, including the present one, are based. Until we have such a study, which would probably tell us much about how Grant worked as a writer, the best means we have to explain how he came, seemingly so suddenly, to a mastery of prose is to look back at the way he wrote during the war.

On his first night in Chattanooga—after an overnight trip made 12
worse by an injured leg, on horseback over a scarred mountain trail in miserable weather—Grant listened to the conflicting stories of generals, each seeking to excuse himself for his part in maneuvers that had left the Union forces almost trapped in the southeastern Tennessee town. When he had heard them all out, Grant moved to a table and, in pencil, wrote orders that moved almost every unit of the western

armies. These orders, like hundreds he wrote in the four years of the war, were models of terse, clear prose. He almost never lost control of syntax; only rarely did he have to enter, with a caret, a word omitted in the quick, steady movement of his pencil. Grant demonstrated a remarkable grasp both of the totality of actions he was contemplating and the certainty that whatever was expected for the morning would be subject to change by night. Already, he had the mind of a historian, to which he would give full play when he wrote military history of the first order in the *Personal Memoirs*.

13   Of the present 588 pages in his book, eight are devoted to a provocative discussion of his ancestry and his boyhood experiences, eight more to his "weary" years at West Point (which he did not enjoy, except when he was reading novels, drawing, or riding a horse). Another 20 tell of his marriage to Julia Dent and the dispiriting peacetime years between the wars; there is virtually nothing on the presidency, and, finally, there is a strange seven page "Conclusion" which exposes Grant in an oddly disjointed and disquietingly prophetic mood. It is not impossible that these final pages also show how huge doses of morphine had began to take their toll on the dying writer.

14   The rest of the book is all war. Grant gives us the best account we have of the Mexican War, complete with telling observations on the politics of slavery and, more particularly, of expansionist aggression. His watchful eye does not fail him as he scans the social and natural landscape of Texas and Mexico. The Mexican War chapters are masterful, but the Civil War is his true subject. There is a splendid demonstration of the entanglement of politics and war and an even more impressive grasp of the wholeness of the conflict. There is no false humility; he allows himself to stay at the center of his story (which he does not permit to do him discredit) but he maintains a quiet grasp of the total experience. The individual anguish of dying men is lost, but the contours of the ceaselessly changing events of the war are strongly drawn. As Edmund Wilson noted in *Patriotic Gore*, it is a "literary construct," the "purified fervor and force" of which might "still invigorate the reader," and Grant's force informed the work of other bold writers including Gertrude Stein and Sherwood Anderson. His biographers, Hamlin Garland among them, seeking to explain Grant and his America, have been acutely aware how much the *Personal Memoirs* do not tell us; nonetheless, we have always known it was he who told his story best.

_____ **CONSIDERATIONS** _____

1. Why in paragraph 4 does McFeely make a point of what Grant chose *not* to do in his book?

2. In the rest of his essay, McFeely is precise and definite, but he closes paragraph 6 with a peculiarly vague remark. Can you think why?

3. "He almost never lost control of syntax," writes McFeely about Grant's written orders to his various army units. What is "syntax," and what is amusing about one student writing of another's essay, "Well, for one thing, it's just full of syntax"?

4. Why do historians describe Mark Twain, who ridiculed Grant when he was President, as a great friend of the general?

5. Why does McFeely say that a comparison of Grant's manuscript and the published version of his *Memoirs* may be valuable?

6. The introduction of a book might be thought of as a kind of book review. How successful is McFeely in fulfilling such review requirements as (a) providing factual information about what the book consists of; (b) making judgments about strong points and weaknesses; (c) explaining why the book is (or is not) important; (d) giving readers some idea of the author's style; and (e) putting the book into the context of comparable works?

· John McPhee (b. 1931) was born in Princeton, New
Jersey, where he graduated from college, and where he still
lives. His writing, largely for the New Yorker, *has taken*
him far afield, to Florida for a book about oranges, to
Maine for a book about birchbark canoes, and all over the
country for encounters with the American wilderness. In
1977 he published a report on Alaska called Coming into
the Country. *Some of his recent titles are* Assembling
California *(1993) and* The Ransom of Russian Art *(1994).*

55

JOHN MCPHEE
The Search for Marvin Gardens

1   Go. I roll the dice—a six and a two. Through the air I move my
token, the flatiron, to Vermont Avenue, where dog packs range.

●

2   The dogs are moving (some are limping) through ruins, rubble,
fire damage, open garbage. Doorways are gone. Lath is visible in the
crumbling walls of the buildings. The street sparkles with shattered
glass. I have never seen, anywhere, so many broken windows. A sign—
"Slow, Children at Play"—has been bent backward by an automobile.
At the lighthouse, the dogs turn up Pacific and disappear. George
Meade, Army engineer, built the lighthouse—brick upon brick, six
hundred thousand bricks, to reach up high enough to throw a beam
twenty miles over the sea. Meade, seven years later, saved the Union
at Gettysburg.

●

3   I buy Vermont Avenue for $100. My opponent is a tall, shadowy
figure, across from me, but I know him well, and I know his game like

a favorite tune. If he can, he will always go for the quick kill. And when it is foolish to go for the quick kill he will be foolish. On the whole, though, he is a master assessor of percentages. It is a mistake to underestimate him. His eleven carries his top hat to St. Charles Place, which he buys for $140.

●

The sidewalks of St. Charles Place have been cracked to shards 4
by through-growing weeds. There are no buildings. Mansions, hotels once stood here. A few street lamps now drop cones of light on broken glass and vacant space behind a chain-link fence that some great machine has in places bent to the ground. Five plane trees—in full summer leaf, flecking the light—are all that live on St. Charles Place.

●

Block upon block, gradually, we are cancelling each other out— 5
in the blues, the lavenders, the oranges, the greens. My opponent follows a plan of his own devising. I use the Hornblower & Weeks opening and the Zuricher defense. The first game draws tight, will soon finish. In 1971, a group of people in Racine, Wisconsin, played for seven hundred and sixty-eight hours. A game begun a month later in Danville, California, lasted eight hundred and twenty hours. These are official records, and they stun us. We have been playing for eight minutes. It amazes us that Monopoly is thought of as a long game. It is possible to play to a complete, absolute, and final conclusion in less than fifteen minutes, all within the rules as written. My opponent and I have done so thousands of times. No wonder we are sitting across from each other now in this best-of-seven series for the international singles championship of the world.

●

On Illinois Avenue, three men lean out from second-story win- 6
dows. A girl is coming down the street. She wears dungarees and a bright-red shirt, has ample breasts and a Hadendoan Afro, a black halo, two feet in diameter. Ice rattles in the glasses in the hands of the men.
"Hey, sister!"   7
"Come on up!"   8
She looks up, looks from one to another to the other, looks them 9
flat in the eye.
"What for?" she says, and she walks on.   10

●

I buy Illinois for $240. It solidifies my chances, for I already own 11
Kentucky and Indiana. My opponent pales. If he had landed first on Illinois, the game would have been over then and there, for he has

houses built on Boardwalk and Park Place, we share the railroads equally, and we have cancelled each other everywhere else. We never trade.

•

12   In 1852, R. B. Osborne, an immigrant Englishman, civil engineer, surveyed the route of a railroad line that would run from Camden to Absecon Island, New Jersey, traversing the state from the Delaware River to the barrier beaches of the sea. He then sketched in the plan of a "bathing village" that would surround the eastern terminus of the line. His pen flew glibly, framing and naming spacious avenues parallel to the shore—Mediterranean, Baltic, Oriental, Ventnor—and narrower transsecting avenues: North Carolina, Pennsylvania, Vermont, Connecticut, States, Virginia, Tennessee, New York, Kentucky, Indiana, Illinois. The place as a whole had no name, so when he had completed the plan Osborne wrote in large letters over the ocean, "Atlantic City." No one ever challenged the name, or the names of Osborne's streets. Monopoly was invented in the early nineteen-thirties by Charles B. Darrow, but Darrow was only transliterating what Osborne had created. The railroads, crucial to any player, were the making of Atlantic City. After the rails were down, houses and hotels burgeoned from Mediterranean and Baltic to New York and Kentucky. Properties—building lots—sold for as little as six dollars apiece and as much as a thousand dollars. The original investors in the railroads and the real estate called themselves the Camden & Atlantic Land Company. Reverently, I repeat their names: Dwight Bell, William Coffin, John DaCosta, Daniel Deal, William Fleming, Andrew Hay, Joseph Porter, Jonathan Pitney, Samuel Richards—founders, fathers, forerunners, archetypical masters of the quick kill.

•

13   My opponent and I are now in a deep situation of classical Monopoly. The torsion is almost perfect—Boardwalk and Park Place versus the brilliant reds. His cash position is weak, though, and if I escape him now he may fade. I land on Luxury Tax, contiguous to but in sanctuary from his power. I have four houses on Indiana. He lands there. He concedes.

•

14   Indiana Avenue was the address of the Brighton Hotel, gone now. The Brighton was exclusive—a word that no longer has retail value in the city. If you arrived by automobile and tried to register at the Brighton, you were sent away. Brighton-class people came in private railroad cars. Brighton-class people had other private railroad cars for their horses—dawn rides on the firm sand at water's edge, skirts fly-

ing. Colonel Anthony J. Drexel Biddle—the sort of name that would constrict throats in Philadelphia—lived, much of the year, in the Brighton.

●

Colonel Sanders' fried chicken is on Kentucky Avenue. So is   15
Clifton's Club Harlem, with the Sepia Revue and the Sepia Follies, featuring the Honey Bees, the Fashions, and the Lords.

●

My opponent and I, many years ago, played 2,428 games of Mo-   16
nopoly in a single season. He was then a recent graduate of the Harvard Law School, and he was working for a downtown firm, looking up law. Two people we knew—one from Chase Manhattan, the other from Morgan, Stanley—tried to get into the game, but after a few rounds we found that they were not in the conversation and we sent them home. Monopoly should always be *mano a mano* anyway. My opponent won 1,199 games, and so did I. Thirty were ties. He was called into the Army, and we stopped just there. Now, in Game 2 of the series, I go immediately to jail, and again to jail while my opponent seines property. He is dumbfoundingly lucky. He wins in twelve minutes.

●

Visiting hours are daily, eleven to two; Sunday, eleven to one;   17
evenings, six to nine. "NO MINORS, NO FOOD, Immediate Family Only Allowed in Jail." All this above a blue steel door in a blue cement wall in the windowless interior of the basement of the city hall. The desk sergeant sits opposite the door to the jail. In a cigar box in front of him are pills in every color, a banquet of fruit salad an inch and a half deep—leapers, co-pilots, footballs, truck drivers, peanuts, blue angels, yellow jackets, redbirds, rainbows. Near the desk are two soldiers, waiting to go through the blue door. They are about eighteen years old. One of them is trying hard to light a cigarette. His wrists are in steel cuffs. A military policeman waits, too. He is a year or so older than the soldiers, taller, studious in appearance, gentle, fat. On a bench against a wall sits a good-looking girl in slacks. The blue door rattles, swings heavily open. A turnkey stands in the doorway. "Don't you guys kill yourselves back there now," says the sergeant to the soldiers.

"One kid, he overdosed himself about ten and a half hours ago,"   18
says the M.P.

The M.P., the soldiers, the turnkey, and the girl on the bench are   19
white. The sergeant is black. "If you take off the handcuffs, take off the belts," says the sergeant to the M.P. "I don't want them hanging

themselves back there." The door shuts and its tumblers move. When it opens again, five minutes later, a young white man in sandals and dungarees and a blue polo shirt emerges. His hair is in a ponytail. He has no beard. He grins at the good-looking girl. She rises, joins him. The sergeant hands him a manila envelope. From it he removes his belt and a small notebook. He borrows a pencil, makes an entry in the notebook. He is out of jail, free. What did he do? He offended Atlantic City in some way. He spent a night in the jail. In the nineteen-thirties, men visiting Atlantic City went to jail, directly to jail, did not pass Go, for appearing in topless bathing suits on the beach. A city statute requiring all men to wear full-length bathing suits was not seriously challenged until 1937, and the first year in which a man could legally go bare-chested on the beach was 1940.

●

20   Game 3. After seventeen minutes, I am ready to begin construction on overpriced and sluggish Pacific, North Carolina, and Pennsylvania. Nothing else being open, opponent concedes.

●

21   The physical profile of streets perpendicular to the shore is something like a playground slide. It begins in the high skyline of Boardwalk hotels, plummets into warrens of "side-avenue" motels, crosses Pacific, slopes through church missions, convalescent homes, burlesque houses, rooming houses, and liquor stores, crosses Atlantic, and runs level through the bombed out ghetto as far—Baltic, Mediterranean—as the eye can see. North Carolina Avenue, for example, is flanked at its beach end by the Chalfonte and the Haddon Hall (908 rooms, air-conditioned), where, according to one biographer, John Philip Sousa (1854–1932) first played when he was twenty-two, insisting, even then, that everyone call him by his entire name. Behind these big hotels, motels—Barbizon, Catalina—crouch. Between Pacific and Atlantic is an occasional house from 1910—wooden porch, wooden mullions, old yellow paint—and two churches, a package store, a strip show, a dealer in fruits and vegetables. Then, beyond Atlantic Avenue, North Carolina moves on into the vast ghetto, the bulk of the city, and it looks like Metz in 1919, Cologne in 1944. Nothing has actually exploded. It is not bomb damage. It is deep and complex decay. Roofs are off. Bricks are scattered in the street. People sit on porches, six deep, at nine on a Monday morning. When they go off to wait in unemployment lines, they wait sometimes two hours. Between Mediterranean and Baltic runs a chain-link fence, enclosing rubble. A patrol car sits idling by the curb. In the back seat is a German shepherd. A sign on the fence says, "Beware of Bad Dogs."

Mediterranean and Baltic are the principal avenues of the ghetto. 22
Dogs are everywhere. A pack of seven passes me. Block after block,
there are three-story brick row houses. Whole segments of them are
abandoned, a thousand broken windows. Some parts are intact, occupied. A mattress lies in the street, soaking in a pool of water. Wet
stuffing is coming out of the mattress. A postman is having a rye and a
beer in the Plantation Bar at nine-fifteen in the morning. I ask him
idly if he knows where Marvin Gardens is. He does not. "HOOKED AND
NEED HELP? CONTACT N.A.R.C.O." "REVIVAL NOW GOING ON, CONDUCTED
BY REVEREND H. HENDERSON OF TEXAS." These are signboards on
Mediterranean and Baltic. The second one is upside down and leans
against a boarded-up window of the Faith Temple Church of God in
Christ. There is an old peeling poster on a warehouse wall showing a
figure in an electric chair. "The Black Panther Manifesto" is the title
of the poster, and its message is, or was, that "the fascists have already
decided in advance to murder Chairman Bobby Seale in the electric
chair." I pass an old woman who carries a bucket. She wears blue
sneakers, worn through. Her feet spill out. She wears red socks, rolled
at the knees. A white handkerchief, spread over her head, is knotted at
the corners. Does she know where Marvin Gardens is? "I sure don't
know," she says, setting down the bucket. "I sure don't know. I've
heard of it somewhere, but I just can't say where." I walk on, through
a block of shattered glass. The glass crunches underfoot like coarse
sand. I remember when I first came here—a long train ride from Tren-
ton, long ago, games of poker in the train—to play basketball against
Atlantic City. We were half black, they were all black. We scored forty
points, they scored eighty, or something like it. What I remember
most is that they had glass backboards—glittering, pendent, expensive
glass backboards, a rarity then in high schools, even in colleges, the
only ones we played on all year.

I turn on Pennsylvania, and start back toward the sea. The win- 23
dows of the Hotel Astoria, on Pennsylvania near Baltic, are boarded
up. A sheet of unpainted plywood is the door, and in it is a triangular
peephole that now frames an eye. The plywood door opens. A man answers my question. Rooms there are six, seven, and ten dollars a week.
I thank him for the information and move on, emerging from the
ghetto at the Catholic Daughters of America Women's Guest House,
between Atlantic and Pacific. Between Pacific and the Boardwalk are
the blinking vacancy signs of the Aristocrat and Colton Manor motels.
Pennsylvania terminates at the Sheraton-Seaside—thirty-two dollars a
day, ocean corner. I take a walk on the Boardwalk and into the Holiday Inn (twenty-three stories). A guest is registering. "You reserved for
Wednesday, and this is Monday," the clerk tells him. "But that's all
right. We have *plenty* of rooms." The clerk is very young, female, and

has soft brown hair that hangs below her waist. Her superior kicks her.

24   He is a middle-aged man with red spiderwebs in his face. He is jacketed and tied. He takes her aside. "Don't say 'plenty,' " he says. "Say 'You are fortunate, sir. We have rooms available.' "

25   The face of the young woman turns sour. "We have all the rooms you need," she says to the customer, and, to her superior, "How's that?"

●

26   Game 4. My opponent's luck has become abrasive. He has Boardwalk and Park Place, and has sealed the board.

●

27   Darrow was a plumber. He was, specifically, a radiator repairman who lived in Germantown, Pennsylvania. His first Monopoly board was a sheet of linoleum. On it he placed houses and hotels that he had carved from blocks of wood. The game he thus invented was brilliantly conceived, for it was an uncannily exact reflection of the business milieu at large. In its depth, range, and subtlety, in its luck-skill ratio, in its sense of infrastructure and socioeconomic parameters, in its philosophical characteristics, it reached to the profundity of the financial community. It was as scientific as the stock market. It suggested the manner and means through which an underdeveloped world had been developed. It was chess at Wall Street level. "Advance token to the nearest Railroad and pay owner twice the rental to which he is otherwise entitled. If Railroad is unowned, you may buy it from the Bank. Get out of Jail, free. Advance token to nearest Utility. If unowned, you may buy it from Bank. If owned, throw dice and pay owner a total ten times the amount thrown. You are assessed for street repairs: $40 per house, $115 per hotel. Pay poor tax of $15. Go to Jail. Go directly to Jail. Do not pass Go. Do not collect $200.

●

28   The turnkey opens the blue door. The turnkey is known to the inmates as Sidney K. Above his desk are ten closed-circuit TV screens—assorted viewpoints of the jail. There are three cellblocks—men, women, juvenile boys. Six days is the average stay. Showers are twice a week. The steel doors and the equipment that operates them were made in San Antonio. The prisoners sleep on bunks of butcher block. There are no mattresses. There are three prisoners to a cell. In winter, it is cold in here. Prisoners burn newspapers to keep warm. Cell corners are black with smudge. The jail is three years old. The men's block echoes with chatter. The man in the cell nearest Sidney K. is pacing. His shirt is covered with broad stains of blood. The block

for juvenile boys is, by contrast, utterly silent—empty corridor, empty cells. There is only one prisoner. He is small and black and appears to be thirteen. He says he is sixteen and that he has been alone in here for three days.

"Why are you here? What did you do?" 29

"I hit a jitney driver." 30

●

The series stands at three all. We have split the fifth and sixth 31 games. We are scrambling for property. Around the board we fairly fly. We move so fast because we do our own banking and search our own deeds. My opponent grows tense.

●

Ventnor Avenue, a street of delicatessens and doctors' offices, is 32 leafy with plane trees and hydrangeas, the city flower. Water Works is on the mainland. The water comes over in submarine pipes. Electric Company gets power from across the state, on the Delaware River, in Deepwater. States Avenue, now a wasteland like St. Charles, once had gardens running down the middle of the street, a horse-drawn trolley, private homes. States Avenue was as exclusive as the Brighton. Only an apartment house, a small motel, and the All Wars Memorial Building—monadnocks spaced widely apart—stand along States Avenue now. Pawnshops, convalescent homes, and the Paradise Soul Saving Station are on Virginia Avenue. The soul-saving station is pink, orange, and yellow. In the windows flanking the door of the Virginia Money Loan Office are Nikons, Polaroids, Yashicas, Sony TVs, Underwood typewriters, Singer sewing machines, and pictures of Christ. On the far side of town, beside a single track and locked up most of the time, is the new railroad station, a small hut made of glazed firebrick, all that is left of the lines that built the city. An authentic phrenologist works on New York Avenue close to Frank's Extra Dry Bar and a church where the sermon today is "Death in the Pot." The church is of pink brick, has blue and amber windows and two red doors. St. James Place, narrow and twisting, is lined with boarding houses that have wooden porches on each of three stories, suggesting a New Orleans made of salt-bleached pine. In a vacant lot on Tennessee is a white Ford station wagon stripped to the chassis. The windows are smashed. A plastic Clorox bottle sits on the driver's seat. The wind has pressed newspaper against the chain-link fence around the lot. Atlantic Avenue, the city's principal thoroughfare, could be seventeen American Main Streets placed end to end—discount vitamins and Vienna Corset shops, movie theatres, shoe stores, and funeral homes. The Boardwalk is made of yellow pine and Douglas fir, soaked in pentachlorophenol. Downbeach, it reaches far beyond the city. Signs everywhere—on windows, lampposts, trash baskets—proclaim "Bien-venue Canadiens!" The salt air is full of Canadian French. In the Clar-idge Hotel, on Park Place, I ask a clerk if she knows where Marvin Gardens is. She asks, "Is it a floral shop?" I ask a cabdriver, parked outside. He says, "Never heard of it." Park Place is one block long. Pa-cific to Boardwalk. On the roof of the Claridge is the Solarium, the highest point in town—panoramic view of the ocean, the bay, the salt-water ghetto. I look down at the rooftops of the side-avenue motels and into swimming pools. There are hundreds of people around the rooftop pools, sunbathing, reading—many more people than are on the beach. Walls, windows, and a block of sky are all that is visible from these pools—no sand, no sea. The pools are craters, and with the peo-ple around them they are countersunk into the motels.

●

33   The seventh, and final, game is ten minutes old and I have hotels on Oriental, Vermont, and Connecticut. I have Tennessee and St. James. I have North Carolina and Pacific. I have Boardwalk, Atlantic, Ventnor, Illinois, Indiana. My fingers are forming a "V." I have mort-gaged most of these properties in order to pay for others, and I have mortgaged the others to pay for the hotels. I have seven dollars. I will pay off the mortgages and build my reserves with income from the three hotels. My cash position may be low, but I feel like a rocket in an underground silo. Meanwhile, if I could just go to jail for a time I could pause there, wait there, until my opponent, in his inescapable rounds, pays the rates of my hotels. Jail, at times, is the strategic place to be. I roll boxcars from the Reading and move the flatiron to Com-munity Chest. "Go to Jail. Go directly to Jail."

●

34   The prisoners, of course, have no pens and no pencils. They take paper napkins, roll them tight as crayons, char the ends with matches, and write on the walls. The things they write are not entirely id-iomatic; for example, "In God We Trust." All is in carbon. Time is re-quired in the writing. "Only humanity could know of such pain." "God So Loved the World." "There is no greater pain than life itself." In the women's block now, there are six blacks, giggling, and a white asleep in red shoes. She is drunk. The others are pushers, prostitutes, an auto thief, a burglar caught with pistol in purse. A sixteen-year-old accused of murder was in here last week. These words are written on the wall of a now empty cell: "Laying here I see two bunks about six inches thick, not counting the one I'm laying on, which is hard as brick. No cushion for my back. No pillow for my head. Just a couple scratchy blankets which is best to use it's said. I wake up in the morn-ing so shivery and cold, waiting and waiting till I am told the food is

coming. It's on its way. It's not worth waiting for, but I eat it anyway. I know one thing when they set me free I'm gonna be good if it kills me."

●

How many years must a game be played to produce an Anthony 35 J. Drexel Biddle and chestnut geldings on the beach? About half a century was the original answer, from the first railroad to Biddle at his peak. Biddle, at his peak, hit an Atlantic City streetcar conductor with his fist, laid him out with one punch. This increased Biddle's legend. He did not go to jail. While John Philip Sousa led his band along the Boardwalk playing "The Stars and Stripes Forever" and Jack Dempsey ran up and down in training for his fight with Gene Tunney, the city crossed the high curve of its parabola. Al Capone held conventions here—upstairs with his sleeves rolled, apportioning among his lieutenant governors the states of the Eastern seaboard. The natural history of an American resort proceeds from Indians to French Canadians via Biddles and Capones. French Canadians, whatever they may be at home, are Visigoths here. Bienvenue Visigoths!

●

My opponent plods along incredibly well. He has got his fourth 36 railroad, and patiently, unbelievably, he has picked up my potential winners until he has blocked me everywhere but Marvin Gardens. He has avoided, in the fifty-dollar zoning, my increasingly petty hotels. His cash flow swells. His railroads are costing me two hundred dollars a minute. He is building hotels on States, Virginia, and St. Charles. He has temporarily reversed the current. With the yellow monopolies and my blue monopolies, I could probably defeat his lavenders and his railroads. I have Atlantic and Ventnor. I need Marvin Gardens. My only hope is Marvin Gardens.

●

There is a plaque at Boardwalk and Park Place, and on it in relief 37 is the leonine profile of a man who looks like an officer in a metropolitan bank—"Charles B. Darrow, 1889–1967, inventor of the game of Monopoly." "Darrow," I address him, aloud. "Where is Marvin Gardens?" There is, of course, no answer. Bronze, impassive, Darrow looks south down the Boardwalk. "Mr. Darrow, please, where is Marvin Gardens?" Nothing. Not a sign. He just looks south down the Boardwalk.

●

My opponent accepts the trophy with his natural ease and I 38 make, from notes, remarks that are even less graceful than his.

●

39   Marvin Gardens is the one color-block Monopoly property that is not in Atlantic City. It is a suburb within a suburb, secluded. It is a planned compound of seventy-two handsome houses set on curvilinear private streets under yews and cedars, poplars and willows. The compound was built around 1920, in Margate, New Jersey, and consists of solid buildings of stucco, brick, and wood, with slate roofs, tile roofs, multimullioned porches, Giraldic towers, and Spanish grilles. Marvin Gardens, the ultimate outwash of Monopoly, is a citadel and sanctuary of the middle class. "We're heavily patrolled by police here. We don't take no chances. Me? I'm living here nine years. I paid seventeen thousand dollars and I've been offered thirty. Number one, I don't want to move. Number two, I don't need the money. I have four bedrooms, two and a half baths, front den, back den. No basement. The Atlantic is down there. Six feet down and you float. A lot of people have a hard time finding this place. People that lived in Atlantic City all their life don't know how to find it. They don't know where the hell they're going. They just know it's south, down the Boardwalk."

_____ CONSIDERATIONS _____

1. What is the most obvious stylistic feature of McPhee's essay?

2. On first reading, you might complain that McPhee provides no transitional aids as he jumps from the world of the game to the world of Atlantic City. A second reading should make you aware of McPhee's skillful transitional devices. Point out some of them and adapt them in your writing.

3. In what sense might one call McPhee's final paragraph a postscript?

4. Why could not McPhee find Marvin Gardens in his walks around Atlantic City?

5. What evidence do you find that McPhee's research was not confined to walking about the streets of Atlantic City?

6. How does McPhee provide continuity through his essay?

7. How much information about your own city or town could you find by walking a few of its streets? Try it. Take copious notes on your observations and impressions. Then devise a thesis that would help you organize your material into an interesting essay.

8. Monopoly was an enormous success, making its inventor a millionaire. What caused the game's appeal? Consider the time in history when it appeared.

Nancy Mairs (b. 1943) began life in California, went east to attend college in Massachusetts, and has worked as a technical writer and editor as well as a teacher at the high school and college levels. She has published a book of poems, In All the Rooms of the Yellow House *(1984), and a collection of essays,* Plain Text: Deciphering a Woman's Life *(1986), as well as* Remembering the Bone House: An Erotics of Place and Space *(1989).* Ordinary Time *appeared in 1993, and in 1994* Voice Lessons: On Becoming a (Woman) Writer.

56

NANCY MAIRS
The Unmaking of a Scientist

My daughter is dissecting a chicken. Her first. Her father, whose job this usually is, has been derelict in his duties, and my hands are now too weak to dissect much more than a zucchini. If she wants dinner (and she does), she will make this pale, flabby carcass into eight pieces I can fit into the skillet. I act as coach. To encourage her, I tell her that her great-great-grandfather was a butcher. This is true, not something I have made up to con her into doing a nasty job. 1

Now that she's gotten going, she is having a wonderful time. She has made the chicken crow and flap and dance all over the cutting board, and now it lies quiet under her short, strong fingers as she slices the length of its breastbone. She pries back the ribs and peers into the cavity. "Oh, look at its mesenteries!" she cries. I tell her I thought mesentery was something you got from drinking the water in Mexico. She pokes at some filmy white webs. Mesenteries, she informs me, are the membranes that hold the chicken's organs in place. My organs too. She flips the chicken over and begins to cut along its spine. As her fingers search out joints and the knife severs wing from breast, leg from thigh, she gives me a lesson in the comparative anatomy of this 2

From *Plain Text: Deciphering a Woman's Life.* Reprinted by permission of the University of Arizona Press.

chicken and the frog she and her friend Emily have recently dissected at school.

3   I am charmed by her enthusiasm and self-assurance. Since she was quite small, she has talked of becoming a veterinarian, and now that she is approaching adulthood, her purpose is growing firmer. During this, her junior year in a special high school, she is taking a college-level introductory course in biology. I took much the same course when I was a freshman in college. But if I entered that course with Anne's self-confidence, and I may very well have done so, I certainly had none of it by the time I wrote the last word of my final examination in my blue book and turned it in the following spring. As the result of Miss White and the quadrat report, I am daunted to the point of dysfunction by the notion of thinking or writing "scientifically."

4   That woman—damn that woman!—turned me into a scientific cripple, and did so in the name of science at a prestigious women's college that promised to school me in the liberal arts that I might "have life and have it abundantly." And really, I have had it abundantly, so I suppose I oughtn't to complain if it's been a little short in *Paramecia* and *Amanita phalloides* and *Drosophila melanogaster*, whose eyes I have never seen.

5   Still, Miss White should not have been allowed to teach freshman biology because she had a fatal idiosyncracy (fatal, that is, to the courage of students, not to herself, though I believe she is dead now of some unrelated cause): She could not bear a well-written report. One could be either a writer or a scientist but not both, she told me one November afternoon, the grey light from a tall window sinking into the grain of the dark woodwork in her cramped office in the old Science Building, her fingers flicking the sheets of my latest lab write-up. She was washing her hands of me, I could tell by the weariness of her tone. She didn't even try to make me a scientist. For that matter, she didn't even point to a spot where I'd gone wrong and show me what she wanted instead. She simply wrinkled her nose at the odor of my writing, handed me the sheets, and sent me away. We never had another conference. At the end of the semester, I wrote my quadrat report, and Miss White failed it. She allowed me to rewrite it. I wrote it again, and she failed it again. Neither of us went for a third try.

6   All the same, I liked my quadrat, which was a twenty-by-twenty plot in the College Woods behind the Library. Mine was drab compared to some others: Pam Weprin's, I remember, had a brook running through it, in which she discovered goldfish. It turned out that her magical discovery had a drab explanation: In a heavy rain the water from Peacock Pond backed up and spilled its resident carp into the brook. Even so, her quadrat briefly held an excitement mine never did. Mine was, in fact, as familiar as a living room, since I had spent large portions of my youth tramping another such woods sixty miles north.

The lichen grew on the north side of the trees. In the rain the humus turned black and rank. Afterwards, a fallen log across one corner would sprout ears of tough, pale fungus.

Each freshman biology student received a quadrat. There were 7 enough of us that we had to double up, but I never met my quadrat-mate or even knew her name. It occurs to me that I ought to have found out, ought to have asked her what she got on her quadrat report, but I was new to failure and knew no ways to profit from it. I simply did as I was told—visited my quadrat to observe its progress through the seasons and wrote up my observations—and then discovered that I had somehow seen and spoken wrong. I wish now that I had kept the report. I wonder exactly what I said in it. Probably something about ears of fungus. Good God.

With a D+ for the first semester I continued, perversely, to like 8 biology, but I also feared it more and more. Not the discipline itself. I pinned and opened a long earthworm, marveling at the delicately tinted organs. I dissected a beef heart, carefully, so as not to spoil it for stuffing and roasting at the biology department's annual beef-heart feast. For weeks I explored the interior of my rat, which I had opened neatly, like the shutters over a window. He was a homely thing, stiff, his fur yellow and matted from formaldehyde, and because he was male, not very interesting. Several students got pregnant females, and I envied them the intricate organs, the chains of bluish-pink fetuses. At the end of each lab, I would reluctantly close the shutters, swaddle my rat in his plastic bag, and slip him back into the crock.

No, biology itself had more fascination and delight than fear. But 9 with each report I grew more terrified of my own insidious poetic nature, which Miss White sniffed out in the simplest statement about planaria or left ventricles. Years later, when I became a technical editor and made my living translating the garbled outbursts of scientists, I learned that I had done nothing much wrong. My understanding was limited, to be sure, but Miss White would have forgiven me ignorance, even stupidity I think, if I had sufficiently muddled the language. As it was, I finished biology with a C−, and lucky I was to get it, since the next year the college raised the passing grade from C− to C. I have always thought, indeed, that the biology departments awarded me a passing grade simply so that they wouldn't have to deal with me another year.

And they didn't. Nor did anyone else. I never took another sci- 10 ence course, although I surprised myself long afterward by becoming, perforce and precipitously, a competent amateur herpetologist. My husband arrived home one afternoon with a shoebox containing a young bull snake, or gopher snake as this desert variety is called, which he had bought for a quarter from some of his students at a school for emotionally disturbed boys so that they wouldn't try to find out how long a snake keeps wriggling without its head. This was Ferdinand, who was followed by two more bull snakes, Squeeze and Beowulf, and by a checkered garter snake named Winslow J. Tweed, a black racer named Jesse Owens, a Yuma king snake named Hrothgar, and numerous nameless and short-lived blind snakes, tiny and translucent, brought to us by our cats Freya, Burton Rustle, and Vanessa Bell. I grew so knowledgeable that when my baby boa constrictor, Crictor, contracted a respiratory ailment, I found that I was more capable of caring for him than were any of the veterinarians in the city. In fact, I learned, veterinarians do not do snakes; I could find only one to give Crictor the shot of a broad-spectrum antibiotic he needed.

11   So I do do snakes. I have read scientific treatises on them. I know that the Latin name for the timber rattlesnake is *Crotalus horridus horridus.* I know that Australia has more varieties of venomous snakes than any other continent, among them the lethal sea snakes and the willfully aggressive tiger snake. I know how long one is likely to live after being bitten by a mamba (not long). I read the treatises; but I don't, of course, write them. Although as a technical editor I grew proficient at unraveling snarls in the writing of scientists. I have never, since Miss White, attempted scientific experimentation or utterance.

12   Aside from my venture into herpetology, I remain a scientific booby. I mind my stupidity. I feel diminished by it. And I know now that it is unnecessary, the consequence of whatever quirk of fate brought me into Miss White's laboratory instead of Miss Chidsey's or Dr. McCoy's. Miss White, who once represented the whole of scientific endeavor to me, was merely a woman with a hobbyhorse. I see through her. Twenty years later, I am now cynical enough to write a quadrat report badly enough to pass her scrutiny, whereas when I had just turned seventeen I didn't even know that cynicism was an option—knowledge that comes, I suppose, from having life abundantly. I've learned, too, that Miss White's bias, though unusually strong, was not peculiar to herself but arose from a cultural rift between the humanities and the sciences resulting in the assumption that scientists will naturally write badly, that they are, in fact, rhetorical boobies. Today I teach technical writing. My students come to me terrified of the word-world from which they feel debarred, and I teach them to breach the boundaries in a few places, to step with bravado at least a little way inside. Linguistic courage is the gift I can give them.

13   In return, they give me gifts that I delight in—explanations of vortex centrifuges, evaluations of copper-smelting processes, plans for extracting gums from paloverde beans. These help me compensate for my deficiencies, as do the works of the popularizers of science. Carl Sagan. Loren Eiseley. Lewis Thomas and his reverential reflections subtitled *Notes of a Biology Watcher.* Stephen Jay Gould. James Burke

and Jacob Bronowski. Pierre Teilhard de Chardin. John McPhee, who has made me love rocks. Isaac Asimov. Elaine Morgan. I watch television too. *Nova. Odyssey. The Undersea World of Jacques Cousteau. The Body in Question.* But always I am aware that I am having translated for me the concepts of worlds I will never now explore for myself. I stand with my toes on the boundaries, peering, listening.

Anne has done a valiant job with the chicken. She's had a little 14
trouble keeping its pajamas on, and one of the thighs has a peculiar trapezoidal shape, but she's reduced it to a workable condition. I brown it in butter and olive oil. I press in several cloves of garlic and then splash in some white wine. As I work, I think of the worlds Anne is going to explore. Some of them are listed in the college catalogues she's begun to collect: "Genetics, Energetics, and Evolution"; "Histology of Animals"; "Vertebrate Endocrinology"; "Electron Microscopy"; "Organic Synthesis"; "Animal Morphogenesis."

Anne can write. No one has yet told her that she can be a scien- 15
tist or a writer but not both, and I trust that no one ever will. The complicated world can ill afford such lies to its children. As she plunges from my view into the thickets of calculus, embryology, and chemical thermodynamics, I will wait here for her to send me back messages. I love messages.

____ CONSIDERATIONS _____

1. What, precisely, is a quadrat? (*Hint:* It is not a member of the family *Muridae* or of the genus *Rattus*, one specimen of which Mairs dissected as a girl in biology class. It does, however, figure importantly in Mairs's disillusionment with science education.)

2. Mairs does some interesting things with tenses in her essay. Study the changes carefully. How might you try them in your own writing?

3. "The complicated world can ill afford such lies to its children," Mairs writes in her closing paragraph. What lies does she mean? Why is she particularly well qualified to point them out?

4. Another aspect to the preceding question opens up if one thinks about the "cultural rift" Mairs writes about in paragraph 12 "between the humanities and the sciences." What does she know about that?

5. Are any of the science writers so admired by Mairs in paragraph 13 immediately available to you?

6. What is the meaning of "mesentery," and how do the writer and her daughter have a bit of fun with the word?

Peter Marin (b. 1936) teaches at the University of California at Santa Barbara in the departments of sociology and of English—a double profession that probably makes him unique among American academics. He has taught at colleges all over the country, has directed a free school, has worked for the government, and has written in many genres: poems, a novel, and many essays of social criticism. He likes especially to investigate people and ideas that appear excluded from the center of American society. For several years he has spent much of his time in shelters and on the streets of American cities. He is currently writing a book about the homeless. In 1994 he collected Freedom and Its Discontents, *subtitled "Reflections on Four Decades of American Moral Experience."*

57

PETER MARIN
Helping and Hating the Homeless

1   When I was a child, I had a recurring vision of how I would end as an old man: alone, in a sparsely furnished second-story room I could picture quite precisely, in a walk-up on Fourth Avenue in New York, where the secondhand bookstores then were. It was not a picture which frightened me. I liked it. The idea of anonymity and solitude and marginality must have seemed to me, back then, for reasons I do not care to remember, both inviting and inevitable. Later, out of college, I took to the road, hitchhiking and traveling on freights, doing odd jobs here and there, crisscrossing the country. I liked that too: the anonymity and the absence of constraint and the rough community I sometimes found. I felt at home on the road, perhaps because I felt at home nowhere else, and periodically, for years, I would return to that world, always with a sense of relief and release.

Reprinted by permission of the author.

I have been thinking a lot about that these days, now that tran-   2
sience and homelessness have made their way into the national consciousness, and especially since the town I live in, Santa Barbara, has
become well known because of the recent successful campaign to do
away with the meanest aspects of its "sleeping ordinances"—a set of
foolish laws making it illegal for the homeless to sleep at night in public places. During that campaign I got to know many of the homeless
men and women in Santa Barbara, who tend to gather, night and day,
in a small park at the lower end of town, not far from the tracks and
the harbor, under the rooflike, overarching branches of a gigantic fig
tree, said to be the oldest on the continent. There one enters much the
same world I thought, as a child, I would die in, and the one in which I
traveled as a young man: a "marginal" world inhabited by all those
unable to find a place in "our" world. Sometimes, standing on the
tracks close to the park, you can sense in the wind, or in the smell of
tar and ties, the presence and age of that material world: the way it
stretches backward and inevitably forward in time, parallel to our own
world, always present, always close, and yet separated from us—at
least in the mind—by a gulf few of us are interested in crossing.

Late last summer, at a city council meeting here in Santa Bar-   3
bara, I saw, close up, the consequences of that strange combination of
proximity and distance. The council was meeting to vote on the repeal
of the sleeping ordinances, though not out of any sudden sense of compassion or justice. Council members had been pressured into it by the
threat of massive demonstrations—"The Selma of the Eighties" was
the slogan one heard among the homeless. But this threat that frightened the council enraged the town's citizens. Hundreds of them
turned out for the meeting. One by one they filed to the microphone
to curse the council and castigate the homeless. Drinking, doping, loitering, panhandling, defecating, urinating, molesting, stealing—the
litany went on and on, was repeated over and over, accompanied by
fantasies of disaster: the barbarian hordes at the gates, civilization
ended.

What astonished me about the meeting was not what was said;   4
one could have predicted that. It was the power and depth of the emotion revealed: the mindlessness of the fear, the vengefulness of the
fury. Also, almost none of what was said had anything to do with the
homeless people I know—not the ones I once traveled with, not the
ones in town. They, the actual homeless men and women, might not
have existed at all.

If I write about Santa Barbara, it is not because I think the atti-   5
tudes at work here are unique. They are not. You find them everywhere in America. In the last few months I have visited several cities
around the country, and in each of them I have found the same thing:
more and more people in the streets, more and more suffering. (There

are at least 350,000 homeless people in the country, perhaps as many as 3 million.) And, in talking to the good citizens of these cities, I found, almost always, the same thing: confusion and ignorance, or simple indifference, but anger too, and fear.

6   What follows here is an attempt to explain at least some of that anger and fear, to clear up some of the confusion, to chip away at the indifference. It is not meant to be definitive; how could it be? The point is to try to illuminate some of the darker corners of homelessness, those we ordinarily ignore, and those in which the keys to much that is now going on may be hidden.

7   The trouble begins with the word "homeless." It has become such an abstraction, and is applied to so many different kinds of people, with so many different histories and problems, that it is almost meaningless.

8   Homelessness, in itself, is nothing more than a condition visited upon men and women (and, increasingly, children) as the final stage of a variety of problems about which the word "homelessness" tells us almost nothing. Or, to put it another way, it is a catch basin into which pour all of the people disenfranchised or marginalized or scared off by processes beyond their control, those which lie close to the heart of American life. Here are the groups packed into the single category of "the homeless":

- Veterans, mainly from the war in Vietnam. In many American cities, vets make up close to 50 percent of all homeless males.
- The mentally ill. In some parts of the country, roughly a quarter of the homeless would, a couple of decades ago, have been institutionalized.
- The physically disabled or chronically ill, who do not receive any benefits or whose benefits do not enable them to afford permanent shelter.
- The elderly on fixed incomes whose funds are no longer sufficient for their needs.
- Men, women, and whole families pauperized by the loss of a job.
- Single parents, usually women, without the resources or skills to establish new lives.
- Runaway children, many of whom have been abused.
- Alcoholics and those in trouble with drugs (whose troubles often begin with one of the other conditions listed here).
- Immigrants, both legal and illegal, who often are not counted among the homeless because they constitute a "problem" in their own right.
- Traditional tramps, hobos, and transients, who have taken to the road or the streets for a variety of reasons and who prefer to be there.

You can quickly learn two things about the homeless from this   9
list. First, you can learn that many of the homeless, before they were
homeless, were people more or less like ourselves: members of the
working or middle class. And you can learn that the world of the
homeless has its roots in various policies, events, and ways of life for
which some of us are responsible and from which some of us actually
prosper.

We decide, as a people, to go to war, we ask our children to kill   10
and to die, and the result, years later, is grown men homeless on the
street.

We change, with the best intentions, the laws pertaining to the   11
mentally ill, and then, without intention, neglect to provide them
with services; and the result, in our streets, drives some of us crazy
with rage.

We cut taxes and prune budgets, we modernize industry and shift   12
the balance of trade, and the result of all these actions and errors can
be read, sleeping form by sleeping form, on our city streets.

The liberals cannot blame the conservatives. The conservatives   13
cannot blame the liberals. Homelessness is the *sum total* of our
dreams, policies, intentions, errors, omissions, cruelties, kindnesses,
all of it recorded, in flesh, in the life of the streets.

You can also learn from this list one of the most important   14
things there is to know about the homeless—that they can be roughly
divided into two groups: those who have had homelessness forced
upon them and want nothing more than to escape it; and those who
have at least in part *chosen* it for themselves, and now accept, or in
some cases, embrace it.

I understand how dangerous it is to introduce the idea of choice   15
into a discussion of homelessness. It can all too easily be used to justify indifference or brutality toward the homeless, or to argue that
they are only getting what they "deserve." And yet it seems to me
that it is only by taking choice into account, in all of the intracacies of
its various forms and expressions, that one can really understand certain kinds of homelessness.

The fact is, many of the homeless are not only hapless victims   16
but voluntary exiles, "domestic refugees," people who have turned
not against life itself but against *us*, our life, American life. Look for a
moment at the vets. The price of returning to America was to forget
what they had seen or learned in Vietnam, to "put it behind them."
But some could not do that, and the stress of trying showed up as alcoholism, broken marriages, drug addiction, crime. And it showed up
too as life on the street, which was for some vets a desperate choice
made in the name of life—the best they could manage. It was a way of
avoiding what might have occurred had they stayed where they were:
suicide, or violence done to others.

17   We must learn to accept that there may indeed be people, and not only vets, who have seen so much of our world, or seen it so clearly, that to live in it becomes impossible. Here, for example, is the story of Alice, a homeless middle-aged woman in Los Angeles, where there are, perhaps, 50,000 homeless people. It was set down a few months ago by one of my students at the University of California, Santa Barbara, where I taught for a semester. I had encouraged them to go find the homeless and listen to their stories. And so, one day, when this student saw Alice foraging in a dumpster outside a McDonald's, he stopped and talked to her:

> She told me she had led a pretty normal life as she grew up and eventually went to college. From there she went on to Chicago to teach school. She was single and lived in a small apartment.
>
> One night, after she got off the train after school, a man began to follow her to her apartment building. When she got to her door she saw a knife and the man hovering behind her. She had no choice but to let him in. The man raped her.
>
> After that, things got steadily worse. She had a nervous breakdown. She went to a mental institution for three months, and when she went back to her apartment she found her belongings gone. The landlord had sold them to cover the rent she hadn't paid.
>
> She had no place to go and no job because the school had terminated her employment. She slipped into depression. She lived with friends until she could muster enough money for a ticket to Los Angeles. She said she no longer wanted to burden her friends, and that if she had to live outside, at least Los Angeles was warmer than Chicago.
>
> It is as if she began back then to take on the mentality of a street person. She resolved herself to homelessness. She's been out West since 1980, without a home or job. She seems happy, with her best friend being her cat. But the scars of memories still haunt her, and she is running from them, or should I say *him*.

18   This is, in essence, the same story one hears over and over again on the street. You begin with an ordinary life; then an event occurs—traumatic, catastrophic; smaller events follow, each one deepening the original wound; finally, homelessness becomes inevitable, or begins to *seem* inevitable to the person involved—the only way out of an intolerable situation. You are struck continually, hearing these stories, by something seemingly unique in American life, the absolute isolation involved. In what other culture would there be such an absence or failure of support from familial, social, or institutional sources? Even more disturbing is the fact that it is often our supposed sources of support—family, friends, government organizations—that have caused the problem in the first place.

19   Everything that happened to Alice—the rape, the loss of job and apartment, the breakdown—was part and parcel of a world gone radi-

cally wrong, a world, for Alice, no longer to be counted on, no longer worth living in. Her homelessness can be seen as flight, as failure of will or nerve, even, perhaps, as *disease*. But it can also be seen as a mute, furious refusal, a self-imposed exile far less appealing to the rest of us than ordinary life, but *better*, in Alice's terms.

We like to think, in America, that everything is redeemable, that 20 everything broken can be magically made whole again, and that what has been "dirtied" can be cleansed. Recently I saw on television that one of the soaps had introduced the character of a homeless old woman. A woman in her thirties discovers that her long-lost mother has appeared in town, on the streets. After much searching the mother is located and identified and embraced; and then she is scrubbed and dressed in style, restored in a matter of days to her former upper-class habits and role.

A triumph—but one more likely to occur on television than in 21 real life. Yes, many of these on the streets could be transformed, rehabilitated. But there are others whose lives have been irrevocably changed, damaged beyond repair, and who no longer want help, who no longer recognize the need for help, and whose experience in our world has made them want only to be left alone. How, for instance, would one restore Alice's life, or reshape it in a way that would satisfy *our* notion of what a life should be? What would it take to return her to the fold? How to erase the four years of homelessness, which have become as familiar to her, and as much a home, as her "normal" life once was? Whatever we think of the way in which she has resolved her difficulties, it constitutes a sad peace made with the world. Intruding ourselves upon it in the name of redemption is by no means as simple a task—or as justifiable a task—as one might think.

It is important to understand too that however disorderly and 22 dirty and unmanageable the world of homeless men and women like Alice appears to us, it is not without its significance, and its rules and rituals. The homeless in our cities mark out for themselves particular neighborhoods, blocks, buildings, doorways. They impose on themselves often obsessively strict routines. They reduce their world to a small area, and thereby protect themselves from a world that otherwise be too much to bear.

Pavlov, the Russian psychologist, once theorized that the two 23 most fundamental reflexes in all animals, including humans, are those involving freedom and orientation. Grab any animal, he said, and it will immediately struggle to accomplish two things: to break free and to orient itself. And this is what one sees in so many of the homeless. Having been stripped of all other forms of connection, and of most kinds of social identity, they are left only with this: the raw stuff of nature, something encoded in the cells—the desire to be free, the need for familiar space. Perhaps this is why so many of them struggle so vehemently against us when we offer them aid. They are clinging to their freedom and their space, and they do not believe that this is what we, with our programs and our shelters, mean to allow them.

24   Years ago, when I first came to California, bumming my way west, the marginal world, and the lives of those in it, were very different from what they are now. In those days I spent much of my time in hobo jungles or on the skid rows of various cities, and just as it was easier back then to "get by" in the easygoing beach towns on the California coast, or in the bohemian and artistic worlds in San Francisco or Los Angeles or New York, it was also far easier than it is now to survive in the marginal world.

25   It is important to remember this—important to recognize the immensity of the changes that have occurred in the marginal world in the past twenty years. Whole sections of many cities—the Bowery in New York, the Tenderloin in San Francisco—were once ceded to the transient. In every skidrow area in America you could find what you needed to survive: hash houses, saloons offering free lunches, pawnshops, surplus-clothing stores, and, most important of all, cheap hotels and flophouses and two-bit employment agencies specializing in the kinds of labor (seasonal, shape-up) transients have always done.

26   It was by no means a wonderful world. But it *was* a world. Its rituals were spelled out in ways most of the participants understood. In hobo jungles up and down the tracks, whatever there was to eat went into a common pot and was divided equally. Late at night, in empties crisscrossing the country, men would speak with a certain anonymous openness, as if the shared condition of transience created among them a kind of civility.

27   What most people in that world wanted was simply to be left alone. Some of them had been on the road for years, itinerant workers. Others were recuperating from wounds they could never quite explain. There were young men and a few women with nothing better to do, and older men who had no families or had lost their jobs or wives, or for whom the rigor and pressure of life had proved too demanding. The marginal world offered them a respite from the other world, a world grown too much for them.

28   But things have changed. There began to pour into the marginal world—slowly in the sixties, a bit faster in the seventies, and then faster still in the eighties—more and more people who neither belonged nor knew how to survive there. The sixties brought the counterculture and drugs; the streets filled with young dropouts. Changes in the law loosed upon the streets mentally ill men and women. Inflation took its toll, then recession. Working-class and even middle-class men and women—entire families—began to fall into a world they did not understand.

29   At the same time the transient world was being inundated by new inhabitants, its landscape, its economy, was shrinking radically.

Jobs became harder to find. Modernization had something to do with it; machines took the place of men and women. And the influx of workers from Mexico and points farther south created a class of semi-permanent workers who took the place of casual transient labor. More important, perhaps, was the fact that the forgotten parts of many cities began to attract attention. Downtown areas were redeveloped, reclaimed. The skid-row sections of smaller cities were turned into "old townes." The old hotels that once catered to transients were upgraded or torn down or became warehouses for welfare families—an arrangement far more profitable to the owners. The price of housing increased; evictions increased. The mentally ill, who once could afford to house themselves in cheap rooms, the alcoholics, who once would drink themselves to sleep at night in their cheap hotels, were out on the street—exposed to the weather and to danger, and also in plain and public view: "problems" to be dealt with.

Nor was it only cheap shelter that disappeared. It was also those 30 "open" spaces that had once been available to those without other shelter. As property rose in value, the nooks and crannies in which the homeless had been able to hide became more visible. Doorways, alleys, abandoned buildings, vacant lots—these "holes" in the cityscape, these gaps in public consciousness, became *real estate*. The homeless, who had been there all the time, were overtaken by economic progress, and they became intruders.

You cannot help thinking, as you watch this process, of what 31 happened in parts of Europe in the eighteenth and nineteenth centuries: the effects of the enclosure laws, which eliminated the "commons" in the countryside and drove the rural poor, now homeless, into the cities. The centuries-old tradition of common access and usage was swept away by the beginnings of industrialism; land became *privatized*, a commodity. At the same time something occurred in the cultural psyche. The world itself, space itself, was subtly altered. It was no longer merely to be lived in; it was now to be owned. What was enclosed was not only the land. It was also *the flesh itself*; it was cut off from, denied access to, the physical world.

And one thinks too, when thinking of the homeless, of the 32 American past, the settlement of the "new" world which occurred at precisely the same time that the commons disappeared. The dream of freedom and equality that brought men and women here had something to do with *space,* as if the wilderness itself conferred upon those arriving here a new beginning: the Eden that had been lost. Once God had sent Christ to redeem men; now he provided a new world. Men discovered, or believed, that this world, and perhaps time itself, had no edge, no limit. Space was a sign of God's magnanimity. It was a kind of grace.

Somehow, it is all this that is folded into the sad shapes of the 33 homeless. In their mute presence one can sense, however faintly, the dreams of a world gone aglimmering, and the presence of our failed hopes. A kind of claim is made, silently, an ethic is proferred, or, if you will, a whole cosmology, one older than our own ideas of privilege and property. It is as if flesh itself were seeking, this one last time, the home in the world it has been denied.

34   Daily the city eddies around the homeless. The crowds flowing past leave a few feet, a gap. We do not touch the homeless world. Perhaps we cannot touch it. It remains separate even as the city surrounds it.

35   The homeless, simply because they are homeless, are strangers, alien—and therefore a threat. Their presence, in itself, comes to constitute a kind of violence; it deprives us of our sense of safety. Let me use myself as an example. I know, and respect, many of those now homeless on the streets of Santa Barbara. Twenty years ago, some of them would have been my companions and friends. And yet, these days, if I walk through the park near my home and see strangers bedding down for the night, my first reaction, if not fear, is a sense of annoyance and intrusion, of worry and alarm. I think of my teenage daughter, who often walks through the park, and then of my house, a hundred yards away, and I am tempted—only tempted, but tempted, still—to call the "proper" authorities to have the strangers moved on. Out of sight, out of mind.

36   Notice: I do not bring them food. I do not offer them shelter or a shower in the morning. I do not even stop to talk. Instead, I think: my daughter, my house, my privacy. What moves me is not the threat of *danger*—nothing as animal as that. Instead there pops up inside of me, neatly in a row, a set of anxieties, ones you might arrange in a dollhouse living room and label: Family of bourgeois fears. The point is this: our response to the homeless is fed by a complex set of cultural attitudes, habits of thought, and fantasies and fears so familiar to us, so common, that they have become a *second* nature and might as well be instinctive, for all the control we have over them. And it is by no means easy to untangle this snarl of responses. What does seem clear is that the homeless embody all that bourgeois culture has for centuries tried to eradicate and destroy.

37   If you look to the history of Europe you find that homelessness first appears (or is first acknowledged) at the very same moment that bourgeois culture begins to appear. The same processes produced them both: the breakup of feudalism, the rise of commerce and cities, the combined triumphs of capitalism, industrialism, and individualism. The historian Fernand Braudel, in *The Wheels of Commerce*, describes, for instance, the armies of impoverished men and women who began to haunt Europe as far back as the eleventh century. And the makeup of these masses? Essentially the same then as it is now: the unfortunates, the throwaways, the misfits, the deviants.

> In the eighteenth century, all sorts and conditions were to be found in this human dross . . . widows, orphans, cripples . . . journeymen who had broken their contracts, out-of-work labourers, homeless priests with no living, old men, fire victims . . . war victims, deserters, discharged soldiers, would-be vendors of useless articles, vagrant preachers with or without licenses, "pregnant servant-girls and unmarried mothers driven from home," children sent out "to find bread or to maraud."

Then, as now, distinctions were made between the "homeless"   38
and the supposedly "deserving" poor, those who knew their place and willingly sustained, with their labors, the emergent bourgeois world.

> The good paupers were accepted, lined up and registered on the official list; they had a right to public charity and were sometimes allowed to solicit it outside churches in the prosperous districts, when the congregation came out, or in market places. . . .
>
> When it comes to beggars and vagrants, it is a very different story, and different pictures meet the eye: crowds, mobs, processions, sometimes mass emigrations, "along the country highways or the streets of the Towns and Villages," by beggars "whom hunger and nakedness has driven from home." . . . The towns dreaded these alarming visitors and drove them out as soon as they appeared on the horizon.

And just as the distinctions made about these masses were the   39
same then as they are now, so too was the way society saw them. They seemed to bourgeois eyes (as they still do) the one segment of society that remained resistant to progress, unassimilable and incorrigible, inimical to all order.

It is in the nineteenth century, in the Victorian era, that you can   40
find the beginnings of our modern strategies for dealing with the homeless: the notion that they should be controlled and perhaps eliminated through "help." With the Victorians we begin to see the entangling of self-protection with social obligation, the strategy of masking self-interest and the urge to control as *moral duty.* Michel Foucault has spelled this out in his books on madness and punishment: the zeal with which the overseers of early bourgeois culture tried to purge, improve, and purify all of urban civilization—whether through schools and prisons, or, quite literally, with public baths and massive new water and sewage systems. Order, ordure—this is, in essence, the tension at the heart of bourgeois culture, and it was the singular genius of the Victorians to make it the main component of their medical, aesthetic, *and* moral systems. It was not a sense of justice or even empathy which called for charity or new attitudes toward the poor; it was *hygiene.* The very same attitudes appear in nineteenth-century America. Charles Loring Brace, in an essay on homeless and vagrant children written in 1876, described the treatment of delinquents in this way:

"Many of their vices drop from them like the old and verminous clothing they left behind. . . . The entire change of circumstances seems to cleanse them of bad habits." Here you have it all: *vices, verminous clothing, cleansing them of bad habits*—the triple association of poverty with vice with dirt, an equation in which each term comes to stand for all of them.

41   These attitudes are with us still; that is the point. In our own century the person who has written most revealingly about such things is George Orwell, who tried to analyze his own middle-class attitudes toward the poor. In 1933, in *Down and Out in Paris and London*, he wrote about tramps:

> In childhood we are taught that tramps are blackguards . . . a repulsive, rather dangerous creature, who would rather die than work or wash, and wants nothing but to beg, drink or rob henhouses. The tramp monster is no truer to life than the sinister Chinaman of the magazines, but he is very hard to get rid of. The very word "tramp" evokes his image.

42   All of this is still true in America, though now it is not the word "tramp" but the word "homeless" that evokes the images we fear. It is the homeless who smell. Here, for instance, is part of a paper a student of mine wrote about her first visit to a Rescue Mission on skid row.

> The sermon began. The room was stuffy and smelly. The mixture of body odors and cooking was nauseating. I remember thinking: how can these people share this facility? They must be repulsed by each other. They had strange habits and dispositions. They were a group of dirty, dishonored, weird people to me.
>   When it was over I ran to my car, went home, and took a shower. I felt extremely dirty. Through the day I would get flashes of that disgusting smell.

43   To put it as bluntly as I can, for many of us the homeless are *shit*. And our policies toward them, our spontaneous sense of disgust and horror, our wish to be rid of them—all of this has hidden in it, close to its heart, our feelings about excrement. Even Marx, that most bourgeois of revolutionaries, described the deviant *lumpen* in *The Eighteenth Brumaire of Louis Bonaparte* as "scum, offal, refuse of all classes." These days, in puritanical Marxist nations, they are called "parasites"—a word, perhaps not incidentally, one also associates with human waste.

44   What I am getting at here is the *nature* of the desire to help the homeless—what is hidden behind it and why it so often does harm. Every government program, almost every private project, is geared as much to the needs of those giving help as it is to the needs of the homeless. Go to any government agency, or, for that matter, to most private charities, and you will find yourself enmeshed, at once, in a

bureaucracy so tangled and oppressive, or confronted with so much moral arrogance and contempt, that you will be driven back out into the streets for relief.

Santa Barbara, where I live, is as good an example as any. There 45 are three main shelters in the city—all of them private. Between them they provide fewer than a hundred beds a night for the homeless. Two of the three shelters are religious in nature: the Rescue Mission and the Salvation Army. In the mission, as in most places in the country, there are elaborate and stringent rules. Beds go first to those who have not been there for two months, and you can stay for only two nights in any two-month period. No shelter is given to those who are not sober. Even if you go to the mission only for a meal, you are required to listen to sermons and participate in prayer, and you are regularly proselytized—sometimes overtly, sometimes subtly. There are obligatory, regimented showers. You go to bed precisely at ten: lights out, no reading, no talking. After the lights go out you will find fifteen men in a room with double-decker bunks. As the night progresses the room grows stuffier and hotter. Men toss, turn, cough, and moan. In the morning you are awakened precisely at five forty-five. Then breakfast. At seven-thirty you are back on the street.

The town's newest shelter was opened almost a year ago by a 46 consortium of local churches. Families and those who are employed have first call on the beds—a policy which excludes the congenitally homeless. Alcohol is not simply forbidden *in* the shelter; those with a history of alcoholism must sign a "contract" pledging to remain sober and chemical-free. Finally, in a paroxysm of therapeutic bullying, the shelter has added a new wrinkle: if you stay more than two days you are required to fill out and then discuss with a social worker a complex form listing what you perceive as your personal failings, goals, and strategies—all of this for men and women who simply want a place to lie down out of the rain!

It is these attitudes, in various forms and permutations, that you 47 find repeated endlessly in America. We are moved either to "redeem" the homeless or to punish them. Perhaps there is nothing consciously hostile about it. Perhaps it is simply that as the machinery of bureaucracy cranks itself up to deal with these problems, attitudes assert themselves automatically. But whatever the case, the fact remains that almost every one of our strategies for helping the homeless is simply an attempt to rearrange the world *cosmetically*, in terms of how it looks and smells to *us*. Compassion is little more than the passion for control.

The central question emerging from all this is, What does a soci- 48 ety owe to its members in trouble, and *how* is that debt to be paid? It is a question which must be answered in two parts: first, in relation to the men and women who have been marginalized against their will, and then, in a slightly different way, in relation to those who have chosen (or accept or even prize) their marginality.

49   As for those who have been marginalized against their wills, I think the general answer is obvious: A society owes its members whatever it takes for them to regain their places in the social order. And when it comes to specific remedies, one need only read backward the various processes which have created homelessness and then figure out where help is likely to do the most good. But the real point here is not the specific remedies required—affordable housing, say— but the basis upon which they must be offered, the necessary underlying ethical notion we seem in this nation unable to grasp: that those who are the inevitable casualties of modern industrial capitalism and the free-market system are entitled, *by right*, and by the simple virtue of their participation in that system, to whatever help they need. They are entitled to have to find and hold their places in the society whose social contract they have, in effect, signed and observed.

50   Look at that for just a moment: the notion of a contract. The majority of homeless Americans have kept, insofar as they could, to the terms of that contract. In any shelter these days you can find men and women who have worked ten, twenty, forty years, and whose lives have nonetheless come to nothing. These are people who cannot afford a place in the world they helped create. And in return? Is it life on the street they have earned? Or the cruel charity we so grudgingly grant them?

51   But those marginalized against their will are only half the problem. There remains, still, the question of whether we owe anything to those who are voluntarily marginal. What about them: the street people, the rebels, and the recalcitrants, those who have torn up their social contracts or returned them unsigned?

52   I was in Las Vegas last fall, and I went out to the Rescue Mission at the lower end of town, on the edge of the black ghetto, where I first stayed years ago on my way west. It was twilight, still hot; in the vacant lot next door to the mission 200 men were lining up for supper. A warm wind blew along the street lined with small houses and salvage yards, and in the distance I could see the desert's edge and the smudge of low hills in the fading light. There were elderly alcoholics in line, and derelicts, but mainly the men were the same sort I had seen here years ago: youngish, out of work restless and talkative, the drifters and wanderers for whom the word "wanderlust" was invented.

53   At supper—long communal tables, thin gruel, stale sweet rolls, ice water—a huge black man in his twenties, fierce and muscular, sat across from me. "I'm from the Coast, man," he said. "Never been away from home before. Ain't sure I like it. Sure don't like *this* place. But I lost my job back home a couple of weeks ago and figured, why

wait around for another. I thought I'd come out here, see me something of the world."

After supper, a squat Portuguese man in his mid-thirties, hunkered down against the mission wall, offered me a smoke and told me: "Been sleeping in my car, up the street, for a week. Had my own business back in Omaha. But I got bored, man. Sold everything, got a little dough, came out here. Thought I'd work construction. Let me tell you, this is one tough town."   54

In a world better than ours, I suppose, men (or women) like this might not exist. Conservatives seem to have no trouble imagining a society so well disciplined and moral that deviance of this kind would disappear. And leftists envision a world so just, so generous, that deviance would vanish along with inequity. But I suspect that there will always be something at work in some men and women to make them restless with the systems others devise for them, and to move them outward toward the edges of the world, where life is always riskier, less organized, and easier going.   55

Do we owe anything to these men and women, who reject our company and what we offer and yet nonetheless seem to demand *something* from us?   56

We owe them, I think, at least a place to exist, a way to exist. That may not be a *moral* obligation, in the sense that our obligation to the involuntarily marginal is clearly a moral one, but it is an obligation nevertheless, one you might call an existential obligation.   57

Of course, it may be that I think we owe these men something because I have liked men like them, and because I want their world to be there always, as a place to hide or rest. But there is more to it than that. I think we as a society need men like these. A society needs its margins as much as it needs art and literature. It needs holes and gaps, *breathing spaces*, let us say, into which men and women can escape and live, when necessary, in ways otherwise denied them. Margins guarantee to society a flexibility, an elasticity, and allow it to accommodate itself to the natures and needs of its members. When margins vanish, society becomes too rigid, too oppressive by far, and therefore inimical to life.   58

It is for such reasons that, in cultures like our own, marginal men and women take on a special significance. They are all we have left to remind us of the narrowness of the received truths we take for granted. "Beyond the pale," they somehow redefine the pale, or remind us, at least, that *something* is still out there, beyond the pale. They preserve, perhaps unconsciously, a dream that would otherwise cease to exist, the dream of having a place in the world, and of being *left alone*.   59

Quixotic? Infantile? Perhaps. But remember Pavlov and his reflexes coded in the flesh: animal, and therefore as if given by God.   60

What we are talking about here is *freedom*, and with it, perhaps, an echo of the dream men brought, long ago, to wilderness America. I use the word "freedom" gingerly, in relation to lives like these: skewed, crippled, emptied of everything we associate with a full, or realized, freedom. But perhaps this is the condition into which freedom has fallen among us. Art has been "appreciated" out of existence; literature has become an extension of the university, replete with tenure and pensions; and as for politics, the ideologies which ring us round seem too silly or shrill by far to speak for life. What is left, then, is this mute and intransigent independence, this "waste" of life which refuses even interpretation, and which cannot be assimilated to any ideology, and which therefore can be put to no one's use. In its crippled innocence and the perfection of its superfluity it amounts, almost, to a rebellion against history, and that is no small thing.

61   Let me put it as simply as I can: what we see on the streets of our cities are two dramas, both of which cut to the troubled heart of the culture and demand from us a response we may not be able to make. There is the drama of those struggling to survive by regaining their place in the social order. And there is the drama of those struggling to survive outside of it.

62   The resolution of both struggles depends on a third drama occurring at the heart of the culture: the tension and contention between the magnanimity we owe to life and the darker tendings of the human psyche: our fear of strangeness, our hatred of deviance, our love of order and control. How we mediate by default or design between those contrary forces will determine not only the destinies of the homeless but also something crucial about the nation, and perhaps—let me say it—about our own souls.

_____ CONSIDERATIONS _____

1. What advantage does Marin gain by starting his essay with his own youthful experience on the road?

2. What causes a word like "homeless" to lose much of its meaning?

3. Paragraphs 10, 11, and 12 form a sequence of short, one-sentence units of very similar construction: "We decide . . . ," "We change . . . ," "We cut . . . " What, if anything, does the writer gain that is worth the risk of sounding monotonous?

4. In more than one place in his essay, Marin divides the homeless into the involuntary and the voluntary. Why, then, in paragraph 15, does he say that it is "dangerous to introduce the idea of choice into a discussion of homelessness"?

5. Why, according to Marin, do some of the homeless react violently to any offer of aid?

6. Marin's paragraph 29, in which he talks about what has happened to old neighborhoods, brings to mind a word that Marin does not use—"gentrification." Why might it have been an idea to work into that paragraph?

7. In paragraph 43, Marin puts it as "bluntly" as he can. Do you find his bluntness offensive or justifiable in this context?

8. How might Marin have made use of Hellman's essay "Runaway," page 256? or John McPhee's "The Search for Marvin Gardens," page 336?

Edwin Muir (1887–1959) was born on an isolated rural island of the Orkneys off Scotland. In his early teens he moved with his family to the poor and crowded city of Glasgow—and his life and work derive in part from the contrast of places. He edited, he wrote criticism and book reviews, but his best work is his poetry, although it was not until 1952 that his Collected Poems *won him the recognition he deserved. "The Horses" was written in 1952, when the world had spent seven years thinking about what happened in Hiroshima and Nagasaki.*

58

EDWIN MUIR
The Horses (1952)

Barely a twelvemonth after
The seven days war that put the world to sleep,
Late in the evening the strange horses came.
By then we had made our covenant with silence,
5   But in the first few days it was so still
We listened to our breathing and were afraid.
On the second day
The radios failed; we turned the knobs; no answer.
On the third day a warship passed us, heading north,
10   Dead bodies piled on the deck. On the sixth day
A plane plunged over us into the sea. Thereafter
Nothing. The radios dumb;
And still they stand in corners of our kitchens,
And stand, perhaps, turned on, in a million rooms
15   All over the world. But now if they should speak,
If on a sudden they should speak again,
If on the stroke of noon a voice should speak,
We would not listen, we would not let it bring
That old bad world that swallowed its children quick

"The Horses," pages 246–247, 52 lines. From *Collected Poems* by Edwin Muir. Copyright © 1960 by Willa Muir. Reprinted by permission of Oxford University Press, Inc. and Faber and Faber Limited.

At one great gulp. We would not have it again.   20
Sometimes we think of the nations lying asleep,
Curled blindly in impenetrable sorrow,
And then the thought confounds us with its strangeness.
The tractors lie about our fields; at evening
They look like dank sea-monsters couched and waiting.   25
We leave them where they are and let them rust:
'They'll moulder away and be like other loam.'
We make our oxen drag our rusty ploughs,
Long laid aside. We have gone back
Far past our fathers' land.   30
                              And then, that evening
Late in the summer the strange horses came.
We heard a distant tapping on the road,
A deepening drumming; it stopped, went on again
And at the corner changed to hollow thunder.   35
We saw the heads
Like a wild wave charging and were afraid.
We had sold our horses in our fathers' time
To buy new tractors. Now they were strange to us
As fabulous steeds set on an ancient shield   40
Or illustrations in a book of knights.
We did not dare go near them. Yet they waited,
Stubborn and shy, as if they had been sent
By an old command to find our whereabouts
And that long-lost archaic companionship.   45
In the first moment we had never a thought
That they were creatures to be owned and used.
Among them were some half-a-dozen colts
Dropped in some wilderness of the broken world,
Yet new as if they had come from their own Eden.   50
Since then they have pulled our ploughs and borne our loads
But that free servitude still can pierce our hearts.
Our life is changed; their coming our beginning.

Joyce Carol Oates (b. 1938) grew up in New York State and attended Syracuse University. She has published many novels, collections of short stories, essay collections, and books of poetry. A Guggenheim Fellow and winner of the National Book Award, she currently teaches at Princeton University. Recent fiction includes Foxfire *(1993),* Haunted *(1994), and* Zombie *(1995). Her book* On Boxing, *from which the following is excerpted, appeared in 1987.*

59

JOYCE CAROL OATES
On Boxing

1   No sport is more physical, more direct, than boxing. No sport appears more powerfully homoerotic: the confrontation in the ring—the disrobing—the sweaty, heated combat that is part dance, courtship, coupling—the frequent urgent pursuit by one boxer of the other in the fight's natural and violent movement toward the "knockout." Surely boxing derives much of its appeal from this mimicry of a species of erotic love in which one man overcomes the other in an exhibition of superior strength.

2   Most fights, however fought, lead to an embrace between the boxers after the final bell—a gesture of mutual respect and apparent affection that appears to the onlooker to be more than perfunctory. Rocky Graziano, often derided for being a slugger rather than a "classic" boxer, sometimes kissed his opponents out of gratitude for the fight. Does the boxing match, one almost wonders, lead irresistibly to this moment: the public embrace of two men who otherwise, in public or in private, could not approach each other with such passion. Are men privileged to embrace with love only after having fought? A woman is struck by the tenderness men will express for boxers who have been hurt, even if it is only by way of commentary on photographs: the startling picture of Ray (Boom Boom) Mancini after his

second losing fight with Livingston Bramble, for instance, when Mancini's face was hideously battered (photographs in *Sports Illustrated* and elsewhere were gory, near-pornographic); the much-reprinted photograph of the defeated Thomas Hearns being carried to his corner in the arms of an enormous black man in formal attire—the "Hit Man" from Detroit now helpless, only semiconscious, looking precisely like a black Christ taken from the cross. These are powerful, haunting, unsettling images, cruelly beautiful, very much bound up with the primitive appeal of the sport.

Yet to suggest that men might love one another directly without   3
the violent ritual of combat is to misread man's greatest passion—for war, not peace. Love, if there is to be love, comes second.

Boxing is, after all, about lying. It is about cultivating a double   4
personality. As José Torres, the ex-light-heavyweight champion who is now the New York State Boxing Commissioner, says, "We fighters understand lies. What's a feint? What's a left hook off the jab? What's an opening? What's thinking one thing and doing another . . . ?"

There is nothing fundamentally playful about boxing, nothing   5
that seems to belong to daylight, to pleasure. At its moments of greatest intensity it seems to contain so complete and so powerful an image of life—life's beauty, vulnerability, despair, incalculable and often reckless courage—that boxing *is* life, and hardly a mere game. During a superior boxing match we are deeply moved by the body's communion with itself by way of another's flesh. The body's dialogue with its shadow-self—or Death. Baseball, football, basketball—these quintessentially American pastimes are recognizably sports because they involve play: They are games. One *plays* football; one doesn't *play* boxing.

Observing team sports, teams of adult men, one sees how men   6
are children in the most felicitous sense of the word. But boxing in its elemental ferocity cannot be assimilated into childhood—though very young men box, even professionally, and numerous world champions began boxing when they were hardly more than children. Spectators at public games derive much of their pleasure from reliving the communal emotions of childhood, but spectators at boxing matches relive the murderous infancy of the race. Hence the notorious cruelty of boxing crowds and the excitement when a man begins to bleed. ("When I see blood," says Marvin Hagler, "I become a bull." He means his own.)

The boxing ring comes to seem an altar of sorts, one of those leg-   7
endary magical spaces where the laws of a nation are suspended: Inside the ropes, during an officially regulated three-minute round, a man may be killed at his opponent's hands but he cannot be legally murdered. Boxing inhabits a sacred space predating civilization; or, to use D. H. Lawrence's phrase, before God was love. If it suggests a savage ceremony or a rite of atonement, it also suggests the futility of

such rites. For what atonement is the fight waged, if it must shortly be waged again . . .?

8   All this is to speak of the paradox of boxing—its obsessive appeal for many who find in it not only a spectacle involving sensational feats of physical skill but an emotional experience impossible to convey in words; an art form, as I have suggested, with no natural analogue in the arts. And of course this accounts, too, for the extreme revulsion it arouses in many people. ("Brutal," "disgusting," "barbaric," "inhuman," "a terrible, terrible sport"—typical comments on the subject.)

9   In December 1984, the American Medical Association passed a resolution calling for the abolition of boxing on the principle that it is the only sport in which the *objective* is to cause injury. This is not surprising. Humanitarians have always wanted to reform boxing—or abolish it altogether. The 1896 heavyweight title match between Ruby Robert Fitzsimmons and Peter Maher was outlawed in many parts of the United States, so canny promoters staged it across the Mexican border four hundred miles from El Paso. (Some three hundred people made the arduous journey to see what must have been one of the most disappointing bouts in boxing history—Fitzsimmons knocked out his opponent in a mere ninety-five seconds.)

10   During the prime of Jack Dempsey's career in the 1920s, boxing was illegal in many states, like alcohol, and like alcohol, seems to have aroused a hysterical public enthusiasm. Photographs of jammed outdoor arenas taken in the 1920s with boxing rings like postage-sized altars at their centers, the boxers themselves scarcely visible, testify to the extraordinary emotional appeal boxing had at that time, even as reform movements were lobbying against it. When Jack Johnson won the heavyweight title in 1908 (he had to pursue the white champion Tommy Burns all the way to Australia to confront him), the special "danger" of boxing was also that it might expose and humiliate white men in the ring. After Johnson's victory over the "White Hope" contender Jim Jeffries, there were race riots and lynchings throughout the United States; even films of some of Johnson's fights were outlawed in many states. And because boxing has become a sport in which black and Hispanic men have lately excelled, it is particularly vulnerable to attack by white middle-class reformers, who seem uninterested in lobbying against equally dangerous but "establishment" sports like football, auto racing, and thoroughbred horse racing.

11   There is something peculiarly American in the fact that, while boxing is our most controversial sport, it is also the sport that pays its top athletes the most money. In spite of the controversy, boxing has never been healthier financially. The three highest paid athletes in the world in both 1983 and 1984 were boxers; a boxer with a long career like heavyweight champion Larry Holmes—forty-eight fights in thir-

teen years as a professional—can expect to earn somewhere beyond $50 million. (Holmes said that after retirement what he would miss about boxing is his million-dollar checks.) Dempsey, who said that a man fights for one thing only—money—made somewhere beyond $3,500,000 in the ring in his long and varied career. Now $1.5 million is a fairly common figure for a single fight. Thomas Hearns made at least $7 million in his fight with Hagler while Hagler made at least $7.5 million. For the first of his highly publicized matches with Roberto Duran in 1980—which he lost on a decision—the popular black welterweight champion Sugar Ray Leonard received a staggering $10 million to Duran's $1.3 million. And none of these figures takes into account various subsidiary earnings (from television commercials, for instance) which in Leonard's case are probably as high as his income was from boxing.

Money has drawn any number of retired boxers back into the ring, very often with tragic results. The most notorious example is perhaps Joe Louis, who, owing huge sums in back taxes, continued boxing well beyond the point at which he could perform capably. After a career of seventeen years he was stopped by Rocky Marciano—who was said to have felt as upset by his victory as Louis by the defeat. (Louis then went on to a degrading second career as a professional wrestler. This, too, ended abruptly when 300-pound Rocky Lee stepped on the forty-two-year-old Louis's chest and damaged his heart.) Ezzard Charles, Jersey Joe Walcott, Joe Frazier, Muhammad Ali—each continued fighting when he was no longer in condition to defend himself against young heavyweight boxers on the way up. Of all heavyweight champions, only Rocky Marciano, to whom fame and money were not of paramount significance, was prudent enough to retire before he was defeated. In any case, the prodigious sums of money a few boxers earn do not account for the sums the public is willing to pay them.   12

Though boxing has long been popular in many countries and under many forms of government, its popularity in the United States since the days of John L. Sullivan has a good deal to do with what is felt as the spirit of the individual—his "physical" spirit—in conflict with the constrictions of the state. The rise of boxing in the 1920s in particular might well be seen as a consequence of the diminution of the individual vis-à-vis society; the gradual attrition of personal freedom, will, and strength—whether "masculine" or otherwise. In the Eastern bloc of nations, totalitarianism is a function of the state; in the Western bloc it has come to seem a function of technology, or history—"fate." The individual exists in his physical supremacy, but does the individual matter?   13

In the magical space of the boxing ring so disquieting a question has no claim. There, as in no other public arena, the individual as a   14 unique physical being asserts himself; there, for a dramatic if fleeting period of time, the great world with its moral and political complexities, its terrifying impersonality, simply ceases to exist. Men fighting one another with only their fists and their cunning are all contemporaries, all brothers, belonging to no historical time. "He can run, but he can't hide"—so said Joe Louis before his famous fight with young Billy Conn in 1941. In the brightly lighted ring, man is *in extremis*, performing an atavistic rite or agon for the mysterious solace of those who can participate only vicariously in such drama: the drama of life in the flesh. Boxing has become America's tragic theater.

_____ CONSIDERATIONS _____

1. In her opening paragraph, Oates uses the term "homoerotic." How does this differ from "homosexual"? Or does it?

2. What, according to Oates, is "man's greatest passion"? How does she try to support this assertion?

3. In paragraphs 11 and 12, Oates cites remarks by great fighters like Larry Holmes and Jack Dempsey, who claim that the most important thing about boxing is the money. How do their statements affect the writer's assertion (in paragraph 5) that boxing is hardly a game, it is life itself?

4. A research question: What happened to the resolution passed in 1984 by the American Medical Association calling for the abolition of boxing? Does Oates's essay provide any answers? How would you go about finding an answer in your college library?

5. In what ways does it make sense for Oates to describe gory photographs of battered boxers as "near-pornographic"? See Margaret Atwood's essay, "Pornography," page 31, for help in answering this question.

6. Oates compares boxing to love (paragraph 2), sacrifice (paragraph 6), religious rites (paragraph 7), and the theater (paragraph 14). Are such notions merely fanciful or do they point up significant aspects of the sport?

Flannery O'Connor (1925–1964) was born in Savannah and moved with her family to her mother's birthplace, Milledgeville, Georgia, at the age of twelve. When she was fifteen her father died of the inherited degenerative disease lupus. She received her B.A. at Milledgeville's Georgia State College for Women (now Georgia College) and then studied fiction writing at the University of Iowa. From 1947 until 1951 she spent time in New York, Connecticut, and Georgia. When she discovered that she was ill, she returned to live with her mother on the Milledgeville farm called Andalusia, surrounded by pet peacocks and peahens, writing her remarkable fiction and staying in touch with friends by letter. She died of lupus when she was thirty-eight. The Library of America published her Collected Works *in one volume in 1988.*

In 1979 a selection of Flannery O'Connor's letters, edited by Sally Fitzgerald, appeared as The Habit of Being. *The letters are affectionate, often funny, rich with literary and religious thought.*

The following excerpts begin with two letters about "A Good Man Is Hard to Find." The first is a passage from a letter addressed to the novelist John Hawkes, a leading writer of O'Connor's generation, author of The Lime Twig, The Blood Oranges, *and* The Passion Artist *among other novels. In the passage found here, O'Connor speaks of the theology of her story. The second letter, "To a Professor of English," is prefaced by Sally Fitzgerald's explanatory note. The letter that follows is another to John Hawkes. In it O'Connor's Catholicism is clear and certain; Hawkes is of another mind. The last letter is addressed to Alfred Corn, who is now a well-known poet. In 1962 he was an undergraduate at Emory University in Atlanta, Georgia; when he heard Flannery O'Connor speak to an English class, he wrote her about a subject that troubled him.*

60

FLANNERY O'CONNOR
From Flannery O'Connor's Letters

To John Hawkes

14 April 60

1   Thanks for your letter of some time back. I have been busy keeping my blood pressure down while reading various reviews of my book. Some of the favorable ones are as bad as the unfavorable; most reviewers seem to have read the book in fifteen minutes and written the review in ten. . . . I hope that when yours comes out you'll fare better.

2   It's interesting to me that your students naturally work their way to the idea that the Grandmother in "A Good Man" is not pure evil and may be a medium for Grace. If they were Southern students I would say this was because they all had grandmothers like her at home. These old ladies exactly reflect the banalities of the society and the effect of the comical rather than the seriously evil. But Andrew [Lytle] insists that she is a witch, even down to the cat. These children, yr. students, know their grandmothers aren't witches.

3   Perhaps it is a difference in theology, or rather the difference that ingrained theology makes in the sensibility. Grace, to the Catholic way of thinking, can and does use as its medium the imperfect, purely human, and even hypocritical. Cutting yourself off from Grace is a very decided matter, requiring a real choice, act of will, and affecting the very ground of the soul. The Misfit is touched by the Grace that comes through the old lady when she recognizes him as her child, as she has been touched by the Grace that comes through him in his particular suffering. His shooting her is a recoil, a horror at her humanness, but after he has done it and cleansed his glasses, the Grace has worked in him and he pronounces his judgment: she would have been

a good woman if *he* had been there every moment of her life. True enough. In the Protestant view, I think Grace and nature don't have much to do with each other. The old lady, because of her hypocrisy and humanness and banality couldn't be a medium for Grace. In the sense that I see things the other way, I'm a Catholic writer.

To a Professor of English

A professor of English had sent Flannery the following letter: "I am writing as spokesman for three members of our department and some ninety university students in three classes who for a week now have been discussing your story 'A Good Man Is Hard to Find.' We have debated at length several possible interpretations, none of which fully satisfies us. In general we believe that the appearance of the Misfit is not 'real' in the same sense that the incidents of the first half of the story are real. Bailey, we believe, imagines the appearance of the Misfit, whose activities have been called to his attention on the night before the trip and again during the stopover at the roadside restaurant. Bailey, we further believe, identifies himself with the Misfit and so plays two roles in the imaginary last half of the story. But we cannot, after great effort, determine the point at which reality fades into illusion or reverie. Does the accident literally occur, or is it a part of Bailey's dream? Please believe me when I say we are not seeking an easy way out of our difficulty. We admire your story and have examined it with great care, but we are convinced that we are missing something important which you intended for us to grasp. We will all be very grateful if you comment on the interpretation which I have outlined above and if you will give us further comments about your intention in writing 'A Good Man Is Hard to Find.' "

She replied:

28 March 61

The interpretation of your ninety students and three teachers is 1 fantastic and about as far from my intentions as it could get to be. If it were a legitimate interpretation, the story would be little more than a trick and its interest would be simply for abnormal psychology. I am not interested in abnormal psychology.

There is a change of tension from the first part of the story to the 2 second where the Misfit enters, but this is no lessening of reality. This story is, of course, not meant to be realistic in the sense that it portrays the everyday doings of people in Georgia. It is stylized and its conventions are comic even though its meaning is serious.

3   Bailey's only importance is as the Grandmother's boy and the driver of the car. It is the Grandmother who first recognizes the Misfit and who is most concerned with him throughout. The story is a duel of sorts between the Grandmother and her superficial beliefs and the Misfit's more profoundly felt involvement with Christ's action which set the world off balance for him.

4   The meaning of a story should go on expanding for the reader the more he thinks about it, but meaning cannot be captured in an interpretation. If teachers are in the habit of approaching a story as if it were a research problem for which any answer is believable so long as it is not obvious, then I think students will never learn to enjoy fiction. Too much interpretation is certainly worse than too little, and where feeling for a story is absent, theory will not supply it.

5   My tone is not meant to be obnoxious. I am in a state of shock.

To John Hawkes

28 November 61

1   I have been fixing to write you ever since last summer when we saw the goat man.* We went up to north Georgia to buy a bull and when we were somewhere above Conyers we saw up ahead a pile of rubble some eight feet high on the side of the road. When we got about fifty feet from it, we could begin to make out that some of the rubble was distributed around something like a cart and that some of it was alive. Then we began to make out the goats. We stopped in front of it and looked back. About half the goats were asleep, venerable and exhausted, in a kind of heap. I didn't see Chess. Then my mother located an arm around the neck of one of the goats. We also saw a knee. The old man was lying on the road, asleep amongst them, but we never located his face.

2   That is wonderful about the new baby. I can't equal that but I do have some new additions to my ménage. For the last few years I have been hunting a pair of swans that I could afford. Swans cost $250 a pair and that was beyond me. My friend in Florida, the one I wrote you about once, took upon herself to comb Florida for cheap swans. What she sets out to do, she does. . . . So now I am the owner of a one-eyed swan and her consort. They are Polish, or immutable swans and very tractable and I radiate satisfaction every time I look at them.

---

*The founder of the Free Thinking Christian Mission, a wandering witness who traveled with a cart and a clutch of goats.

I had brief notes from Andrew [Lytle][†] a couple of times lately. In
fact he has a story of mine but I haven't heard from him whether he's
going to use it or not. He said he had asked you to write an article
about my fiction and that if he used my story I might want to send it
to you. If he does take it and you write an article and want to see the
story ["The Lame Shall Enter First"], I'll send it. It's about one of Tarwater's terrible cousins, a lad named Rufus Johnson, and it will add
fuel to your theory though not legitimately I think.

You haven't convinced me that I write with the Devil's will or
belong in the romantic tradition and I'm prepared to argue some more
with you on this if I can remember where we left off at. I think the reason we can't agree on this is because there is a difference in our two
devils. My Devil has a name, a history and a definite plan. His name is
Lucifer, he's a fallen angel, his sin is pride, and his aim is the destruction of the Divine plan. Now I judge that your Devil is co-equal to
God, not his creature; that pride is his virtue, not his sin; and that his
aim is not to destroy the Divine plan because there isn't any Divine
plan to destroy. My Devil is objective and yours is subjective. You say
one becomes "evil" when one leaves the herd. I say that depends entirely on what the herd is doing.

The herd has been known to be right, in which case the one who
leaves it is doing evil. When the herd is wrong, the one who leaves it is
not doing evil but the right thing. If I remember rightly, you put that
word, evil, in quotation marks which means the standards you judge it
by there are relative; in fact you would be looking at it there with the
eyes of the herd.

I think I would admit to writing what Hawthorne called "romances," but I don't think that has anything to do with the romantic
mentality. Hawthorne interests me considerably. I feel more of a kinship with him than with any other American, though some of what he
wrote I can't make myself read through to the end.

I didn't write the note to *Wise Blood*. I just let it go as is. I
thought here I am wasting my time saying what I've written when I've
already written it and I could be writing something else. I couldn't
hope to convince anybody anyway. A friend of mine wrote me that he
had read a review in one of the university magazines of *The Violent
Bear etc.* that said that since the seeds that had opened one at a time
in Tarwater's blood were put there in the first place by the great uncle
that the book was about homosexual incest. When you have a generation of students who are being taught to think like that, there's nothing to do but wait for another generation to come along and hope it
won't be worse. . . .

———————

[†]Novelist and editor of the *Sewanee Review*.

8   I've introduced *The Lime Twig* to several people and they're all enthusiastic. Somebody has gone off with my copy now. I hope you are at another one.

To Alfred Corn

30 May 62

1   I think that this experience you are having of losing your faith, or as you think, of having lost it, is an experience that in the long run belongs to faith; or at least it can belong to faith if faith is still valuable to you, and it must be or you would not have written me about this.

2   I don't know how the kind of faith required of a Christian living in the 20th century can be at all if it is not grounded on this experience that you are having right now of unbelief. This may be the case always and not just in the 20th century. Peter said, "Lord, I believe. Help my unbelief." It is the most natural and most human and most agonizing prayer in the gospels, and I think it is the foundation prayer of faith.

3   As a freshman in college you are bombarded with new ideas, or rather pieces of ideas, new frames of reference, an activation of the intellectual life which is only beginning, but which is already running ahead of your lived experience. After a year of this, you think you cannot believe. You are just beginning to realize how difficult it is to have faith and the measure of a commitment to it, but you are too young to decide you don't have faith just because you feel you can't believe. About the only way we know whether we believe or not is by what we do, and I think from your letter that you will not take the path of least resistance in this matter and simply decide that you have lost your faith and that there is nothing you can do about it.

4   One result of the stimulation of your intellectual life that takes place in college is usually a shrinking of the imaginative life. This sounds like a paradox, but I have often found it to be true. Students get so bound up with difficulties such as reconciling the clashing of so many different faiths such as Buddhism, Mohammedanism, etc., that they cease to look for God in other ways. Bridges once wrote Gerard Manley Hopkins and asked him to tell him how he, Bridges, could believe. He must have expected from Hopkins a long philosophical answer. Hopkins wrote back, "Give alms." He was trying to say to Bridges that God is to be experienced in Charity (in the sense of love for the divine image in human beings). Don't get so entangled with intellectual difficulties that you fail to look for God in this way.

5   The intellectual difficulties have to be met, however, and you will be meeting them for the rest of your life. When you get a reasonable hold on one, another will come to take its place. At one time, the

clash of the different world religions was a difficulty for me. Where you have absolute solutions, however, you have no need of faith. Faith is what you have in the absence of knowledge. The reason this clash doesn't bother me any longer is because I have got, over the years, a sense of the immense sweep of creation, of the evolutionary process in everything, of how incomprehensible God must necessarily be to be the God of heaven and earth. You can't fit the Almighty into your intellectual categories. I might suggest that you look into some of the works of Pierre Teilhard de Chardin (*The Phenomenon of Man* et al.). He was a paleontologist—helped to discover Peking man—and also a man of God. I don't suggest you go to him for answers but for different questions, for that stretching of the imagination that you need to make you a skeptic in the face of much that you are learning, much of which is new and shocking but which when boiled down becomes less so and takes its place in the general scheme of things. What kept me a skeptic in college was precisely my Christian faith. It always said: wait, don't bite on this, get a wider picture, continue to read.

If you want your faith, you have to work for it. It is a gift, but for very few it is a gift given without any demand for equal time devoted to its cultivation. For every book you read that is anti-Christian, make it your business to read one that presents the other side of the picture; if one isn't satisfactory read others. Don't think that you have to abandon reason to be a Christian. A book that might help you is *The Unity of Philosophical Experience* by Etienne Gilson. Another is Newman's *The Grammar of Assent*. To find out about faith, you have to go to the people who have it and you have to go to the most intelligent ones if you are going to stand up intellectually to agnostics and the general run of pagans that you are going to find in the majority of people around you. Much of the criticism of belief that you find today comes from people who are judging it from the standpoint of another and narrower discipline. The Biblical criticism of the 19th century, for instance, was the product of historical disciplines. It has been entirely revamped in the 20th century by applying broader criteria to it, and those people who lost their faith in the 19th century because of it, could better have hung on in blind trust. 6

Even in the life of a Christian, faith rises and falls like the tides of an invisible sea. It's there, even where he can't see it or feel it, if he wants it to be there. You realize, I think, that it is more valuable, more mysterious, altogether more immense than anything you can learn or decide upon in college. Learn what you can, but cultivate Christian scepticism. It will keep you free—not free to do anything you please, but free to be formed by something larger than your own intellect or the intellects of those around you. 7

I don't know if this is the kind of answer that can help you, but any time you care to write me, I can try to do better. 8

———— CONSIDERATIONS ——————————————————

Letter to John Hawkes, April 14, 1960

1. What does O'Connor mean when she says that some of the favorable reviews of her book "are as bad as the unfavorable"? How do you go about judging the quality of a book review? As a writer, how do you judge your instructors' comments on your own papers?

2. In paragraph 2, O'Connor suggests that the grandmother in her story is like a lot of grandmothers in the South, but in her letter to the professor of English she says her story is not realistic in the "everyday" sense. Can you reconcile this apparent contradiction?

3. What does O'Connor mean by the term "grace" in paragraph 3? Pursue the word in a good dictionary where you will find at least a dozen different definitions of the word. Keep in mind that she is using the word according to her own view of Catholic theology.

4. O'Connor says at the end of paragraph 3 that she is a Catholic writer. Does she mean that Protestant readers are not welcome or that Protestants could not understand her work? Is it possible to disagree with—or even disapprove of—a writer's ideas and still appreciate that writer's work? Explain.

5. While she does not always agree with John Hawkes's interpretations of her stories, O'Connor's letters to him (see also that of 11/28/61) express a good deal more respect for his ideas than can be found in her letter to a professor of English. Read a little of the work of John Hawkes to see if you can discover qualities he shares with O'Connor.

Letter to a Professor of English, March 28, 1961

1. O'Connor says her story is realistic, not in an "everyday" but "stylized" sense. Compare a paragraph or two of her story with a passage in Eudora Welty's "A Worn Path" to see if you can determine what O'Connor means by "stylized." You might also get some help on that word by consulting a history of art.

2. Find passages in "A Good Man Is Hard to Find" that will illustrate what O'Connor means by the grandmother's "superficial beliefs" and The Misfit's "more profoundly felt involvement." Does such a close examination of the story push you closer to or further away from O'Connor's belief that the heart of the story is a "duel of sorts" between the grandmother and The Misfit?

3. In paragraph 4, O'Connor makes an interesting distinction between "meaning" and "interpretation" as she deplores the "habit of approaching a story as if it were a research problem for which any answer is believable so long as it is not obvious." Discuss some experience of your own in which insistence on a particular interpretation (yours or anyone else's) interfered with the expanded meaning O'Connor mentions.

4. O'Connor says in her last paragraph that her tone in the letter "is not meant to be obnoxious." If you were the professor to whom she had written, what particular lines or words in the letter might you think gave it an obnox-

ious tone? Can you find any other writers in this book whose tone is obnoxious? Explain.

5. In what sense, if any, do you think a short story (or poem or novel or play or essay for that matter) can be taught? What assistance do you expect or want from your own instructor and/or text in reading a story like O'Connor's?

Letter to John Hawkes, November 28, 1961

1. O'Connor's remarkable versatility in the use of the English language is demonstrated in her letters as well as in her stories. This letter to John Hawkes, for example, shows her ability to shift from one voice to another at will. Find examples.

2. At the end of paragraph 4, O'Connor tells Hawkes, "You say one becomes 'evil' when one leaves the herd. I say that depends entirely on what the herd is doing." Write an essay on relative versus absolute morality.

3. O'Connor, speaking of her interest in Hawthorne, makes a distinction between writing "romances" and having a "romantic mentality." What did Hawthorne mean by "romances," and why does O'Connor "feel more of a kinship with him than with any other American"?

4. O'Connor's letters are filled with brief reports on local events and people, like the one on the goat man in the letter to John Hawkes. Eudora Welty, in discussing one of her own short stories—see her essay "The Point of the Story"—says that her story began when she observed an old woman in Mississippi. How might O'Connor's observations of her surroundings have contributed to "A Good Man Is Hard to Find"?

Letter to Alfred Corn, May 30, 1962

1. "You can't fit the Almighty into your intellectual categories," says O'Connor. Does she advise her correspondent to ignore the intellectual challenges of college? Study her discussion of the clash between intellectual inquiry and faith, especially in paragraphs 5 and 6, and write an essay on her conclusions.

2. How, according to O'Connor, can we know whether we believe or not?

3. Look over Consideration 1 regarding O'Connor's 1961 letter to John Hawkes and think about voice. How would you describe the voice in this letter to Alfred Corn? Does O'Connor play with changes of voice in this letter? Why?

4. Read Langston Hughes's essay "Salvation"; how might O'Connor have consoled the disillusioned boy?

Flannery O'Connor's first novel, Wise Blood, *appeared in 1952: her second and last,* The Violent Bear It Away, *in 1960. Most critics prefer her stories to her novels. All of her fiction—stories and novels together—is gathered together in one volume of The Library of America. During her lifetime she published one collection of stories, bearing the title of the story that follows. This was the story she usually read aloud when asked to read.*

61

FLANNERY O'CONNOR
A Good Man Is Hard to Find

1   The grandmother didn't want to go to Florida. She wanted to visit some of her connections in east Tennessee and she was seizing every chance to change Bailey's mind. Bailey was the son she lived with, her only boy. He was sitting on the edge of his chair at the table, bent over the orange sports section of the *Journal.* "Now look here, Bailey," she said, "see here, read this," and she stood with one hand on her thin hip and the other rattling the newspaper at his bald head. "Here this fellow that calls himself The Misfit is aloose from the Federal Pen and headed toward Florida and you read here what it says he did to these people. Just you read it. I wouldn't take my children in any direction with the criminal like that aloose in it. I couldn't answer to my conscience if I did."

2   Bailey didn't look up from his reading so she wheeled around then and faced the children's mother, a young woman in slacks, whose face was as broad and innocent as a cabbage and was tied around with a green headkerchief that had two points on the top like rabbit's ears. She was sitting on the sofa, feeding the baby his apricots out of a jar. "The children have been to Florida before," the old lady said. "You all ought to take them somewhere else for a change so they

would see different parts of the world and be broad. They never have been to east Tennessee."

The children's mother didn't seem to hear her, but the eight-   3
year-old boy, John Wesley, a stocky child with glasses, said, "If you don't want to go to Florida, why dontcha stay at home?" He and the little girl, June Star, were reading the funny papers on the floor.

"She wouldn't stay at home to be queen for a day," June Star said   4
without raising her yellow head.

"Yes, and what would you do if this fellow, The Misfit, caught   5
you?" the grandmother asked.

"I'd smack his face," John Wesley said.   6

"She wouldn't stay at home for a million bucks," June Star said.   7
"Afraid she'd miss something. She has to go everywhere we go."

"All right, Miss," the grandmother said. "Just remember that the   8
next time you want me to curl your hair."

June Star said her hair was naturally curly.   9

The next morning the grandmother was the first one in the car,   10
ready to go. She had her big black valise that looked like the head of a hippopotamus in one corner, and underneath it she was hiding a basket with Pitty Sing, the cat, in it. She didn't intend for the cat to be left alone in the house for three days because he would miss her too much and she was afraid he might brush against one of the gas burners and accidentally asphyxiate himself. Her son, Bailey, didn't like to arrive at a motel with a cat.

She sat in the middle of the back seat with John Wesley and June   11
Star on either side of her. Bailey and the children's mother and the baby sat in the front and they left Atlanta at eight forty-five with the mileage on the car at 55890. The grandmother wrote this down because she thought it would be interesting to say how many miles they had been when they got back. It took them twenty minutes to reach the outskirts of the city.

The old lady settled herself comfortably, removing her white cot-   12
ton gloves and putting them up with her purse on the shelf in front of the back window. The children's mother still had on slacks and still had her head tied up in a green kerchief, but the grandmother had on a navy blue straw sailor hat with a bunch of white violets on the brim and a navy blue dress with a small white dot in the print. Her collar and cuffs were white organdy trimmed with lace and at her neckline she had pinned a purple spray of cloth violets containing a sachet. In case of an accident, anyone seeing her dead on the highway would know at once that she was a lady.

She said she thought it was going to be a good day for driving,   13
neither too hot nor too cold, and she cautioned Bailey that the speed limit was fifty-five miles an hour and that the patrolmen hid themselves behind billboards and small clumps of trees and sped out after

you before you had a chance to slow down. She pointed out interesting details of the scenery: Stone Mountain; the blue granite that in some places came up to both sides of the highway; the brilliant red clay banks slightly streaked with purple; and the various crops that made rows of green lace-work on the ground. The trees were full of silver-white sunlights and the meanest of them sparkled. The children were reading comic magazines and their mother had gone back to sleep.

14   "Let's go through Georgia fast so we don't have to look at it much," John Wesley said.

15   "If I were a little boy," said the grandmother, "I wouldn't talk about my native state that way. Tennessee has the mountains and Georgia has the hills."

16   "Tennessee is just a hillbilly dumping ground," John Wesley said, "and Georgia is a lousy state too."

17   "You said it," June Star said.

18   "In my time," said the grandmother, folding her thin veined fingers, "children were more respectful of their native states and their parents and everything else. People did right then. Oh look at the cute little pickaninny!" she said and pointed to a Negro child standing in the door of a shack. "Wouldn't that make a picture now?" she asked and they all turned and looked at the little Negro out of the back window. He waved.

19   "He didn't have any britches on," June Star said.

20   "He probably didn't have any," the grandmother explained. "Little niggers in the country don't have things like we do. If I could paint, I'd paint that picture," she said.

21   The children exchanged comic books.

22   The grandmother offered to hold the baby and the children's mother passed him over the front seat to her. She set him on her knee and bounced him and told him about the things they were passing. She rolled her eyes and screwed up her mouth and stuck her leathery thin face into his smooth bland one. Occasionally he gave her a faraway smile. They passed a large cotton field with five or six graves fenced in the middle of it, like a small island. "Look at the graveyard!" the grandmother said, pointing it out. "That was the old family burying ground. That belonged to the plantation."

23   "Where's the plantation?" John Wesley asked.

24   "Gone With the Wind," said the grandmother. "Ha. Ha."

25   When the children finished all the comic books they had brought, they opened the lunch and ate it. The grandmother ate a peanut butter sandwich and an olive and would not let the children throw the box and the paper napkins out the window. When there was nothing else to do they played a game by choosing a cloud and making the other two guess what shape it suggested. John Wesley took one the shape of a cow and June Star guessed a cow and John Wesley said, no,

an automobile, and June Star said he didn't play fair, and they began to slap each other over the grandmother.

The grandmother said she would tell them a story if they would 26 keep quiet. When she told a story, she rolled her eyes and waved her head and was very dramatic. She said once when she was a maiden lady she had been courted by a Mr. Edgar Atkins Teagarden from Jasper, Georgia. She said he was a very good-looking man and a gentleman and that he brought her a watermelon every Saturday afternoon with his initials cut in it, E.A.T. Well, one Saturday, she said, Mr. Teagarden brought the watermelon and there was nobody at home and he left it on the front porch and returned in his buggy to Jasper, but she never got the watermelon, she said, because a nigger boy ate it when he saw the initials, E.A.T.! This story tickled John Wesley's funny bone and he giggled and giggled but June Star didn't think it was any good. She said she wouldn't marry a man that just brought her a watermelon on Saturday. The grandmother said she would have done well to marry Mr. Teagarden because he was a gentleman and had bought Coca-Cola stock when it first came out and that he had died only a few years ago, a very wealthy man.

They stopped at The Tower for barbecued sandwiches. The 27 Tower was a part-stucco and part-wood filling station and dance hall set in a clearing outside of Timothy. A fat man named Red Sammy Butts ran it and there were signs stuck here and there on the building and for miles up and down the highway saying, TRY RED SAMMY'S FAMOUS BARBECUE. NONE LIKE FAMOUS RED SAMMY'S! RED SAM! THE FAT BOY WITH THE HAPPY LAUGH. A VETERAN! RED SAMMY'S YOUR MAN!

Red Sammy was lying on the bare ground outside The Tower 28 with his head under a truck while a gray monkey about a foot high, chained to a small chinaberry tree, chattered nearby. The monkey sprang back into the tree and got on the highest limb as soon as he saw the children jump out of the car and run toward him.

Inside, The Tower was a long dark room with a counter at one 29 end and tables at the other and dancing space in the middle. They all sat down at a broad table next to the nickelodeon and Red Sam's wife, a tall burnt-brown woman with hair and eyes lighter than her skin, came and took their order. The children's mother put a dime in the machine and played "The Tennessee Waltz," and the grandmother said that tune always made her want to dance. She asked Bailey if he would like to dance but he only glared at her. He didn't have a naturally sunny disposition like she did and trips made him nervous. The grandmother's brown eyes were very bright. She swayed her head from side to side and pretended she was dancing in her chair. June Star said play something she could tap to so the children's mother put in another dime and played a fast number and June Star stepped out onto the dance floor and did her tap routine.

30   "Ain't she cute?" Red Sam's wife said, leaning over the counter. "Would you like to come be my little girl?"

31   "No, I certainly wouldn't," June Star said. "I wouldn't live in a broken-down place like this for a million bucks!" and she ran back to the table.

32   "Ain't she cute?" the woman repeated, stretching her mouth politely.

33   "Aren't you ashamed?" hissed the grandmother.

34   Red Sam came in and told his wife to quit lounging on the counter and hurry up with these people's order. His khaki trousers reached just to his hip bones and his stomach hung over them like a sack of meal swaying under his shirt. He came over and sat down at a table nearby and let out a combination sigh and yodel. "You can't win," he said. "You can't win," and he wiped his sweating red face off with a gray handkerchief. "These days you don't know who to trust," he said. "Ain't that the truth?"

35   "People are certainly not nice like they used to be," said the grandmother.

36   "Two fellers come in here last week," Red Sammy said, "driving a Chrysler. It was an old beat-up car but it was a good one and these boys looked all right to me. Said they worked at the mill and you know I let them fellers charge the gas they bought? Now why did I do that?"

37   "Because you're a good man!" the grandmother said at once.

38   "Yes'm, I suppose so," Red Sam said as if he were struck with this answer.

39   His wife brought the orders, carrying the five plates all at once without a tray, two in each hand and one balanced on her arm. "It isn't a soul in this green world of God's that you can trust," she said. "And I don't count nobody out of that, not nobody," she repeated, looking at Red Sammy.

40   "Did you read about that criminal, The Misfit, that's escaped?" asked the grandmother.

41   "I wouldn't be a bit surprised if he didn't attack this place right here," said the woman. "If he hears about it being here, I wouldn't be none surprised to see him. If he hears it's two cent in the cash register, I wouldn't be a tall surprised if he . . ."

42   "That'll do," Red Sam said. "Go bring these people their Co'-Colas," and the woman went off to get the rest of the order.

43   "A good man is hard to find," Red Sammy said. "Everything is getting terrible. I remember the day you could go off and leave your screen door unlatched. Not no more."

44   He and the grandmother discussed better times. The old lady said that in her opinion Europe was entirely to blame for the way things were now. She said the way Europe acted you would think we were made of money and Red Sam said it was no use talking about it, she

was exactly right. The children ran outside into the white sunlight and looked at the monkey in the lacy chinaberry tree. He was busy catching fleas on himself and biting each one carefully between his teeth as if it were a delicacy.

They drove off again into the hot afternoon. The grandmother 45 took cat naps and woke up every few minutes with her own snoring. Outside of Toombsboro she woke up and recalled an old plantation that she had visited in this neighborhood once when she was a young lady. She said the house had six white columns across the front and that there was an avenue of oaks leading up to it and two little wooden trellis arbors on either side in front where you sat down with your suitor after a stroll in the garden. She recalled exactly which road to turn off to get to it. She knew that Bailey would not be willing to lose any time looking at an old house, but the more she talked about it, the more she wanted to see it once again and find out if the little twin arbors were still standing. "There was a secret panel in this house," she said craftily, not telling the truth but wishing that she were, "and the story went that all the family silver was hidden in it when Sherman came through but it was never found. . . ."

"Hey!" John Wesley said. "Let's go see it! We'll find it! We'll 46 poke at the wood work and find it! Who lives there? Where do you turn off at? Hey Pop, can't we turn off there?"

"We never have seen a house with a secret panel!" June Star 47 shrieked. "Let's go to the house with the secret panel! Hey, Pop, can't we go see the house with the secret panel!"

"It's not far from here, I know," the grandmother said. "It 48 wouldn't take over twenty minutes."

Bailey was looking straight ahead. His jaw was as rigid as a horse- 49 shoe. "No," he said.

The children began to yell and scream that they wanted to see 50 the house with the secret panel. John Wesley kicked the back of the front seat and June Star hung over her mother's shoulder and whined desperately into her ear that they never had any fun even on their vacation, that they could never do what THEY wanted to do. The baby began to scream and John Wesley kicked the back of the seat so hard that his father could feel the blows in his kidney.

"All right!" he shouted and drew the car to a stop at the side of 51 the road. "Will you all shut up? Will you all just shut up for one second? If you don't shut up, we won't go anywhere."

"It would be very educational for them," the grandmother mur- 52 mured.

"All right," Bailey said, "but get this. This is the only time we're 53 going to stop for anything like this. This is the one and only time."

"The dirt road that you have to turn down is about a mile back," 54 the grandmother directed. "I marked it when we passed."

"A dirt road," Bailey groaned.   55

56   After they had turned around and were headed toward the dirt road, the grandmother recalled other points about the house, the beautiful glass over the front doorway and the candle lamp in the hall. John Wesley said that the secret panel was probably in the fireplace.

57   "You can't go inside the house," Bailey said. "You don't know who lives there."

58   "While you all talk to the people in front, I'll run around behind and get in a window," John Wesley suggested.

59   "We'll all stay in the car," his mother said.

60   They turned onto the dirt road and the car raced roughly along in a swirl of pink dust. The grandmother recalled the times when there were no paved roads and thirty miles was a day's journey. The dirt road was hilly and there were sudden washes in it and sharp curves on dangerous embankments. All at once they would be on a hill, looking down over the blue tops of trees for miles around, then the next minute, they would be in a red depression with the dust-coated trees looking down on them.

61   "This place had better turn up in a minute," Bailey said, "or I'm going to turn around."

62   The road looked as if no one had traveled on it in months.

63   "It's not much further," the grandmother said and just as she said it, a horrible thought came to her. The thought was so embarrassing that she turned red in the face and her eyes dilated and her feet jumped up, upsetting her valise in the corner. The instant the valise moved, the newspaper top she had over the basket under it rose with a snarl and Pitty Sing, the cat, sprang onto Bailey's shoulder.

64   The children were thrown to the floor and their mother, clutching the baby, was thrown out the door onto the ground; the old lady was thrown into the front seat. The car turned over once and landed right-side-up in a gulch on the side of the road. Bailey remained in the driver's seat with the cat—gray-striped with a broad white face and an orange nose—clinging to his neck like a caterpillar.

65   As soon as the children saw they could move their arms and legs, they scrambled out of the car shouting, "We've had an ACCIDENT!" The grandmother was curled up under the dashboard, hoping she was injured so that Bailey's wrath would not come down on her all at once. The horrible thought she had had before the accident was that the house she had remembered so vividly was not in Georgia but in Tennessee.

66   Bailey removed the cat from his neck with both hands and flung it out the window against the side of a pine tree. Then he got out of the car and started looking for the children's mother. She was sitting against the side of the red gutted ditch, holding the screaming baby, but she only had a cut down her face and a broken shoulder. "We've had an ACCIDENT!" the children screamed in a frenzy of delight.

"But nobody's killed," June Star said with disappointment as the 67
grandmother limped out of the car, her hat still pinned to her head but
the broken front brim standing up at a jaunty angle and the violet
spray hanging off the side. They all sat down in the ditch, except the
children, to recover from the shock. They were all shaking.

"Maybe a car will come along," said the children's mother 68
hoarsely.

"I believe I have injured an organ," said the grandmother, press- 69
ing her side, but no one answered her. Bailey's teeth were clattering.
He had on a yellow sport shirt with bright parrots designed in it and
his face was as yellow as the shirt. The grandmother decided that she
would not mention that the house was in Tennessee.

The road was about ten feet above and they could see only the 70
tops of the trees on the other side of it. Behind the ditch they were sitting in there were more woods, tall and dark and deep. In a few minutes they saw a car some distance away on top of a hill, coming slowly
as if the occupants were watching them. The grandmother stood up
and waved both arms dramatically to attract their attention. The car
continued to come on slowly, disappeared around a bend and appeared
again, moving even slower, on top of the hill they had gone over. It
was a big black battered hearselike automobile. There were three men
in it.

It came to a stop just over them and for some minutes, the driver 71
looked down with a steady expressionless gaze to where they were sitting, and didn't speak. Then he turned his head and muttered something to the other two and they got out. One was a fat boy in black
trousers and a red sweat shirt with a silver stallion embossed on the
front of it. He moved around on the right side of them and stood staring, his mouth partly open in a kind of loose grin. The other had on
khaki pants and a blue striped coat and a gray hat pulled down very
low, hiding most of his face. He came around slowly on the left side.
Neither spoke.

The driver got out of the car and stood by the side of it, looking 72
down at them. He was an older man than the other two. His hair was
just beginning to gray and he wore silver-rimmed spectacles that gave
him a scholarly look. He had a long creased face and didn't have on
any shirt or undershirt. He had on blue jeans that were too tight for
him and he was holding a black hat and a gun. The two boys also had
guns.

"We've had an ACCIDENT!" the children screamed. 73

The grandmother had the peculiar feeling that the bespectacled 74
man was someone she knew. His face was as familiar to her as if she
had known him all her life but she could not recall who he was. He
moved away from the car and began to come down the embankment,
placing his feet carefully so that he wouldn't slip. He had on tan and

white shoes and no socks, and his ankles were red and thin. "Good afternoon," he said, "I see you all had you a little spill."

75   "We turned over twice!" said the grandmother.

76   "Oncet," he corrected. "We see it happen. Try their car and see will it run, Hiram," he said quietly to the boy with the gray hat.

77   "What you got that gun for?" John Wesley asked. "Whatcha gonna do with that gun?"

78   "Lady," the man said to the children's mother, "would you mind calling them children to sit down by you? Children make me nervous. I want all you all to sit down right together there where you're at."

79   "What are you telling us what to do for?" June Star asked.

80   Behind them the line of woods gaped like a dark open mouth. "Come here," said their mother.

81   "Look here now," Bailey began suddenly, "we're in a predicament! We're in . . ."

82   The grandmother shrieked. She scrambled to her feet and stood staring.

83   "You're The Misfit!" she said. "I recognized you at once!"

84   "Yes'm," the man said, smiling slightly as if he were pleased in spite of himself to be known. "But it would have been better for all of you, lady, if you hadn't of reckernized me."

85   Bailey turned his head sharply and said something to his mother that shocked the children. The old lady began to cry and The Misfit reddened.

86   "Lady," he said, "don't you get upset. Sometimes a man says things he don't mean. I don't reckon he meant to talk to you that-away."

87   "You wouldn't shoot a lady, would you?" the grandmother said and removed a clean handkerchief from her cuff and began to slap at her eyes with it.

88   The Misfit pointed the toe of his shoe into the ground and made a little hole and then covered it up again. "I would hate to have to," he said.

89   "Listen," the grandmother almost screamed, "I know you're a good man. You don't look a bit like you have common blood. I know you must come from nice people!"

90   "Yes mam," he said, "finest people in the world." When he smiled he showed a row of strong white teeth. "God never made a finer woman than my mother and my daddy's heart was pure gold," he said. The boy with the red sweat shirt had come around behind them and was standing with his gun at his hip. The Misfit squatted down on the ground. "Watch them children, Bobby Lee," he said. "You know they make me nervous." He looked at the six of them huddled together in front of him and he seemed to be embarrassed as if he couldn't think of anything to say. "Ain't a cloud in the sky," he re-

marked, looking up at it. "Don't see no sun but don't see no cloud neither."

"Yes, it's a beautiful day," said the grandmother. "Listen," she 91 said, "you shouldn't call yourself The Misfit because I know you're a good man at heart. I can just look at you and tell."

"Hush!" Bailey yelled. "Hush! Everybody shut up and let me 92 handle this!" He was squatting in the position of a runner about to spring forward but he didn't move.

"I pre-chate that, lady," The Misfit said and drew a little circle in 93 the ground with the butt of his gun.

"It'll take a half a hour to fix this here car," Hiram called, look- 94 ing over the raised hood of it.

"Well, first you and Bobby Lee get him and that little boy to step 95 over yonder with you," The Misfit said, pointing to Bailey and John Wesley. "The boys want to ask you something," he said to Bailey. "Would you mind stepping back in them woods there with them?"

"Listen," Bailey began, "we're in a terrible predicament! Nobody 96 realizes what this is," and his voice cracked. His eyes were as blue and intense as the parrots in his shirt and he remained perfectly still.

The grandmother reached up to adjust her hat brim as if she were 97 going to the woods with him but it came off in her hand. She stood staring at it and after a second she let it fall on the ground. Hiram pulled Bailey up by the arm as if he were assisting an old man. John Wesley caught hold of his father's hand and Bobby Lee followed. They went off toward the woods and just as they reached the dark edge. Bailey turned and supporting himself against a gray naked pine trunk, he shouted, "I'll be back in a minute, Mamma, wait on me!"

"Come back this instant!" his mother shrilled but they all disap- 98 peared into the woods.

"Bailey Boy!" the grandmother called in tragic voice but she 99 found she was looking at The Misfit squatting on the ground in front of her. "I just know you're a good man," she said desperately. "You're not a bit common!"

"Nome, I ain't a good man," The Misfit said after a second as if 100 he had considered her statement carefully, "but I ain't the worst in the world neither. My daddy said I was a different breed of dog from my brothers and sisters. 'You know,' Daddy said, 'it's some that can live their whole life out without asking about it and it's others has to know why it is, and this boy is one of the latters. He's going to be into everything!' " He put on his black hat and looked up suddenly and then away deep into the woods as if he were embarrassed again. "I'm sorry, I don't have on a shirt before you ladies," he said, hunching his shoulders slightly. "We buried our clothes that we had on when we escaped and we're just making do until we can get better. We borrowed these from some folks we met," he explained.

101   "That's perfectly all right," the grandmother said. "Maybe Bailey has an extra shirt in his suitcase."

102   "I'll look and see terrectly," The Misfit said.

103   "Where are they taking him?" the children's mother screamed.

104   "Daddy was a card himself," The Misfit said. "You couldn't put anything over on him. He never got in trouble with the Authorities though. Just had the knack of handling them."

105   "You could be honest too if you'd only try," said the grandmother. "Think how wonderful it would be to settle down and live a comfortable life and not have to think about somebody chasing you all the time."

106   The Misfit kept scratching in the ground with the butt of his gun as if he were thinking about it. "Yes'm, somebody is always after you," he murmured.

107   The grandmother noticed how thin his shoulder blades were just behind his hat because she was standing up looking down on him. "Do you ever pray?" she asked.

108   He shook his head. All she saw was the black hat wiggle between his shoulder blades. "Nome," he said.

109   There was a pistol shot from the woods, followed closely by another. Then silence. The old lady's head jerked around. She could hear the wind move through the tree tops like a long satisfied insuck of breath. "Bailey Boy!" she called.

110   "I was a gospel singer for a while," The Misfit said. "I been most everything. Been in the arm service, both land and sea, at home and abroad, been twict married, been an undertaker, been with the railroads, plowed Mother Earth, been in a tornado, seen a man burnt alive oncet," and he looked up at the children's mother and the little girl who were sitting close together, their faces white and their eyes glassy; "I even seen a woman flogged," he said.

111   "Pray, pray," the grandmother began, "pray, pray . . . "

112   "I never was a bad boy that I remember of," The Misfit said in an almost dreamy voice, "but somewheres along the line I done something wrong and got sent to the penitentiary. I was buried alive," and he looked up and held her attention to him by a steady stare.

113   "That's when you should have started to pray," she said. "What did you do to get sent to the penitentiary that first time?"

114   "Turn to the right, it was a wall," The Misfit said, looking up again at the cloudless sky. "Turn to the left, it was a wall. Look up it was a ceiling, look down it was a floor. I forgot what I done, lady. I set there and set there, trying to remember what it was I done and I ain't recalled it to this day. Oncet in a while, I would think it was coming to me, but it never come."

115   "Maybe they put you in by mistake," the old lady said vaguely.

116   "Nome," he said. "It wasn't no mistake. They had the papers on me."

"You must have stolen something," she said.   117

The Misfit sneered slightly. "Nobody had nothing I wanted," he   118
said. "It was a head-doctor at the penitentiary said what I had done
was kill my daddy but I known that for a lie. My daddy died in nineteen ought nineteen of the epidemic flu and I never had a thing to do
with it. He was buried in the Mount Hopewell Baptist churchyard and
you can go there and see for yourself."

"If you would pray," the old lady said, "Jesus would help you."   119

"That's right," The Misfit said.   120

"Well then, why don't you pray?" she asked trembling with de-   121
light suddenly.

"I don't want no hep," he said, "I'm doing all right by myself."   122

Bobby Lee and Hiram came ambling back from the woods. Bobby   123
Lee was dragging a yellow shirt with bright blue parrots in it.

"Throw me that shirt, Bobby Lee," The Misfit said. The shirt   124
came flying at him and landed on his shoulder and he put it on. The
grandmother couldn't name what the shirt reminded her of. "No,
lady," The Misfit said while he was buttoning it up, "I found out the
crime don't matter. You can do one thing or you can do another, kill a
man or take a tire off his car, because sooner or later you're going to
forget what it was you done and just be punished for it."

The children's mother had begun to make heaving noises as if   125
she couldn't get her breath. "Lady," he asked, "would you and that little girl like to step off yonder with Bobby Lee and Hiram and join your
husband?"

"Yes, thank you," the mother said faintly. Her left arm dangled   126
helplessly and she was holding the baby, who had gone to sleep, in the
other. "Hep that lady up, Hiram," The Misfit said as she struggled to
climb out of the ditch, "and Bobby Lee, you hold onto that little girl's
hand."

"I don't want to hold hands with him," June Star said. "He re-   127
minds me of a pig."

The fat boy blushed and laughed and caught her by the arm and   128
pulled her off into the woods after Hiram and her mother.

Alone with The Misfit, the grandmother found that she had lost   129
her voice. There was not a cloud in the sky nor any sun. There was
nothing around her but woods. She wanted to tell him that he must
pray. She opened and closed her mouth several times before anything
came out. Finally she found herself saying, "Jesus. Jesus," meaning, Jesus will help you, but the way she was saying it, it sounded as if she
might be cursing.

"Yes'm," The Misfit said as if he agreed. "Jesus thrown every-   130
thing off balance. It was the same case with Him as with me except
He hadn't committed any crime and they could prove I had committed one because they had the papers on me. Of course," he said, "they
never shown me any papers. That's why I sign myself now, I said long

ago, you get you a signature and sign everything you do and keep a copy of it. Then you'll know what you done and you can hold up the crime to the punishment and see do they match and in the end you'll have something to prove you ain't been treated right. I call myself The Misfit," he said, "because I can't make what all I done wrong fit with all I gone through in punishment."

131   There was a piercing scream from the woods, followed closely by a pistol report. "Does it seem right to you, lady, that one is punished a heap and another ain't punished at all?"

132   "Jesus!" the old lady cried. "You've got blood! I know you wouldn't shoot a lady! I know you come from nice people! Pray! Jesus, you ought not to shoot a lady. I'll give you all the money I've got!"

133   "Lady," The Misfit said, looking beyond her far into the woods, "there was never a body that give the undertaker a tip."

134   There were two more pistol reports and the grandmother raised her head like a parched old turkey hen crying for water and called, "Bailey Boy, Bailey Boy!" as if her heart would break.

135   "Jesus was the only One that ever raised the dead," The Misfit continued, "and He shouldn't have done it. He thrown everything off balance. If He did what He said, then it's nothing for you to do but throw away everything and follow Him, and if He didn't then it's nothing for you to do but enjoy the few minutes you got left the best way you can—by killing somebody or burning down his house or doing some other meanness to him. No pleasure but meanness," he said and his voice had become almost a snarl.

136   "Maybe He didn't raise the dead," the old lady mumbled, not knowing what she was saying and feeling so dizzy that she sank down in the ditch with her legs twisted under her.

137   "I wasn't there so I can't say He didn't," The Misfit said. "I wisht I had of been there," he said, hitting the ground with his fist. "It ain't right I wasn't there because if I had of been there I would of known. Listen lady," he said in a high voice, "if I had of been there I would of known and I wouldn't be like I am now." His voice seemed about to crack and the grandmother's head cleared for an instant. She saw the man's face twisted close to her own as if he were going to cry and she murmured, "Why, you're one of my babies. You're one of my own children!" She reached out and touched him on the shoulder. The Misfit sprang back as if a snake had bitten him and shot her three times through the chest. Then he put his gun down on the ground and took off his glasses and began to clean them.

138   Hiram and Bobby Lee returned from the woods and stood over the ditch, looking down at the grandmother who half sat and half lay in a puddle of blood with her legs crossed under her like a child's and her face smiling up at the cloudless sky.

139   Without his glasses, The Misfit's eyes were red-rimmed and pale and defenseless-looking. "Take her off and throw her where you

thrown the others," he said, picking up the cat that was rubbing itself against his leg.

"She was a talker, wasn't she?" Bobby Lee said, sliding down the 140 ditch with a yodel.

"She would of been a good woman," The Misfit said, "if it had 141 been somebody there to shoot her every minute of her life."

"Some fun!" Bobby Lee said.   142

"Shut up, Bobby Lee," The Misfit said. "It's no real pleasure in 143 life."

____ CONSIDERATIONS _____

1. To keep the children quiet, the grandmother tells the ridiculous story of Mr. Edgar Atkins Teagarden, who cut his initials E.A.T. in a watermelon. How do you account for O'Connor's including such an anecdote in a story about a psychopathic murderer?

2. One respected scholar and critic describes O'Connor's story as a "satire on the half-and-half Christian faced with nihilism and death." In what sense would the grandmother qualify as a "half-and-half Christian"? Is there anything in O'Connor's letters to John Hawkes and Alfred Corn that might help you understand what O'Connor thought a real Christian was?

3. Does this story contain characteristics of satire as seen in Molly Ivins's "As Thousands Cheer," Stephen Jay Gould's "The Case of the Creeping Fox Terrier Clone," Swift's "A Modest Proposal," or Twain's "Was the World Made for Man"? If so, does that make all these pieces somewhat alike?

4. O'Connor borrows a line from her own story to serve as a title. Find the line, study the context and comment on it as a title.

5. When The Misfit tells the grandmother, "it would have been better for all of you, lady, if you hadn't of reckernized me," what purpose does his warning serve in furthering the story?

6. Study three elderly women: the grandmother in this story, Faulkner's Emily in "A Rose for Emily," page 186, and Welty's Phoenix Jackson in "A Worn Path," page 597. Do you think it accurate to say that all three are used to convey the point of their respective authors' stories? Explain.

Flannery O'Connor also wrote essays, collected after her death in a volume called Mystery and Manners: Occasional Prose *(1969). This essay, which originally appeared in the* Georgia Bulletin *in 1963, addressed local and immediate problems. In the American 1990s its insights remain urgent, as our culture, in O'Connor's word, becomes increasingly "fractured."*

62

FLANNERY O'CONNOR

The Total Effect and the Eighth Grade

1   In two recent instances in Georgia, parents have objected to their eighth- and ninth-grade children's reading assignments in modern fiction. This seems to happen with some regularity in cases throughout the country. The unwitting parent picks up his child's book, glances through it, comes upon passages of erotic detail or profanity, and takes off at once to complain to the school board. Sometimes, as in one of the Georgia cases, the teacher is dismissed and hackles rise in liberal circles everywhere.

2   The two cases in Georgia, which involved Steinbeck's *East of Eden* and John Hersey's *A Bell for Adano*, provoked considerable newspaper comment. One columnist, in commending the enterprise of the teachers, announced that students do not like to read the fusty works of the nineteenth century, that their attention can best be held by novels dealing with the realities of our own time, and that the Bible, too, is full of racy stories.

3   Mr. Hersey himself addressed a letter to the State School Superintendent in behalf of the teacher who had been dismissed. He pointed out that his book is not scandalous, that it attempts to convey an

---

earnest message about the nature of democracy, and that it falls well within the limits of the principle of "total effect," that principle followed in legal cases by which a book is judged not for isolated parts but by the final effect of the whole book upon the general reader.

I do not want to comment on the merits of these particular cases. 4 What concerns me is what novels ought to be assigned in the eighth and ninth grades as a matter of course, for if these cases indicate anything, they indicate the haphazard way in which fiction is approached in our high schools. Presumably there is a state reading list which contains "safe" books for teachers to assign; after that it is up to the teacher.

English teachers come in Good, Bad, and Indifferent, but too fre- 5 quently in high schools anyone who can speak English is allowed to teach it. Since several novels can't easily be gathered into one textbook, the fiction that students are assigned depends upon their teacher's knowledge, ability, and taste: variable factors at best. More often than not, the teacher assigns what he thinks will hold the attention and interest of the students. Modern fiction will certainly hold it.

Ours is the first age in history which has asked the child what he 6 would tolerate learning, but that is a part of the problem with which I am not equipped to deal. The devil of Educationism that possesses us is the kind that can be "cast out only by prayer and fasting." No one has yet come along strong enough to do it. In other ages the attention of children was held by Homer and Virgil, among others, but, by the reverse evolutionary process, that is no longer possible; our children are too stupid now to enter the past imaginatively. No one asks the student if algebra pleases him or if he finds it satisfactory that some French verbs are irregular, but if he prefers Hersey to Hawthorne, his taste must prevail.

I would like to put forward the proposition, repugnant to most 7 English teachers, that fiction, if it is going to be taught in the high schools, should be taught as a subject and as a subject with a history. The total effect of a novel depends not only on its innate impact, but upon the experience, literary and otherwise, with which it is approached. No child needs to be assigned Hersey or Steinbeck until he is familiar with a certain amount of the best work of Cooper, Hawthorne, Melville, the early James, and Crane, and he does not need to be assigned these until he has been introduced to some of the better English novelists of the eighteenth and nineteenth centuries.

The fact that these works do not present him with the realities of 8 his own time is all to the good. He is surrounded by the realities of his own time, and he has no perspective whatever from which to view them. Like the college student who wrote in her paper on Lincoln that he went to the movies and got shot, many students go to college unaware that the world was not made yesterday; their studies began with the present and dipped backward occasionally when it seemed necessary or unavoidable.

9   There is much to be enjoyed in the great British novels of the nineteenth century, much that a good teacher can open up in them for the young student. There is no reason why these novels should be either too simple or too difficult for the eighth grade. For the simple, they offer simple pleasures; for the more precocious, they can be made to yield subtler ones if the teacher is up to it. Let the student discover, after reading the nineteenth-century British novel, that the nineteenth-century American novel is quite different as to its literary characteristics, and he will thereby learn something not only about these individual works but about the sea-change which a new historical situation can effect in a literary form. Let him come to modern fiction with this experience behind him, and he will be better able to see and to deal with the more complicated demands of the best twentieth-century fiction.

10   Modern fiction often looks simpler than the fiction that preceded it, but in reality is more complex. A natural evolution has taken place. The author has for the most part absented himself from direct participation in the work and has left the reader to make his own way amid experiences dramatically rendered and symbolically ordered. The modern novelist merges the reader in experience; he tends to raise the passions he touches upon. If he is a good novelist, he raises them to effect by their order and clarity a new experience—the total effect—which is not in itself sensuous or simply of the moment. Unless the child has had some literary experience before, he is not going to be able to resolve the immediate passions the book arouses into any true, total picture.

11   It is here the moral problem will arise. It is one thing for a child to read about adultery in the Bible or in *Anna Karenina*, and quite another for him to read about it in most modern fiction. This is not only because in both the former instances adultery is considered a sin, and in the latter, at most, an inconvenience, but because modern writing involves the reader in the action with a new degree of intensity, and literary mores now permit him to be involved in any action a human being can perform.

12   In our fractured culture, we cannot agree on morals; we cannot even agree that moral matters should come before literary ones when there is a conflict between them. All this is another reason why the high schools would do well to return to their proper business of preparing foundations. Whether in the senior year students should be assigned modern novelists should depend both on their parents' consent and on what they have already read and understood.

13   The high-school English teacher will be fulfilling his responsibility if he furnishes the student a guided opportunity, through the best writing of the past, to come, in time, to an understanding of the best

writing of the present. He will teach literature, not social studies or little lessons in democracy or the customs of many lands.

And if the student finds that this is not to his taste? Well, that is   14 regrettable. Most regrettable. His taste should not be consulted; it is being formed.

____ CONSIDERATIONS _____

1. How far must you read in O'Connor's essay before you know her chief concern? Does it occupy her attention in her first three paragraphs? If not, how can you defend the organization of this essay?

2. O'Connor argues in paragraph 8 that "it is all to the good" that the so-called classics do not present the child "with the realities of his own time." How does her reference to the college student writing about Lincoln apply to her argument? How would she offset a reader's insistence that children's reading be relevant to their own time?

3. To what extent does O'Connor's paragraph 10 help explain the principle of "total effect" mentioned in paragraph 3? Do you consider that principle a reasonable means of sorting out acceptable from unacceptable reading matter?

4. How would Margaret Atwood (see "Pornography") respond to O'Connor's solution to the moral problem mentioned in paragraph 12?

5. Write a response to O'Connor's answer to her question at the beginning of paragraph 14. Take into account the rest of her essay as well as your own feelings.

6. What nineteenth-century British and American novels do you remember well enough to compare with modern novels? If your answer is "none," are you in any position to argue with O'Connor?

Frank O'Connor (1903–1966), the pseudonym of Michael Francis O'Donovan, was a great Irish story-writer born in Cork. He wrote novels, criticism (most notably The Lonely Voice: A Study of the Short Story, *in 1962), and biography, but his short stories are his most celebrated work. We take "Christmas" from his volume of autobiography called* An Only Child *(1961).*

63

FRANK O'CONNOR
Christmas

1   Christmas was always the worst time of the year for me, though it began well, weeks before Christmas itself, with the Christmas numbers. Normally I read only boys' weeklies, but at this time of year all papers, juvenile and adult, seemed equally desirable, as though the general magic of the season transcended the particular magic of any one paper. School stories, detective stories, and adventure stories all emerged into one great Christmas story.

2   Christmas numbers were, of course, double numbers; their pale-green and red covers suddenly bloomed into glossy colours, with borders of red-berried holly. Even their titles dripped with snow. As for the pictures within, they showed roads under snow, and old houses under snow, with diamond-paned windows that were brilliant in the darkness. I never knew what magic there was in snow for me because in Ireland we rarely saw it for more than two or three days in the year, and that was usually in the late spring. In real life it meant little to me except that Father—who was always trying to make a manly boy of me as he believed himself to have been at my age—made me wash my face and hands in it to avert chilblains. I think its magic in the Christmas numbers depended on the contrast between it and the Christmas candles, the holly branches with the red berries, the log fires, and the gleaming windows. It was the contrast between light and dark, life

From *An Only Child* by Frank O'Connor. Reprinted by arrangement with the Joan Daves Agency c/o Writer's House as agents for the proprietor.

and death; the cold and darkness that reigned when life came into the world. Going about her work, Mother would suddenly break into song:

Natum videte
Regem angelorum . . .*

and I would join in. It was the season of imagination. My trouble was that I already had more than my share of imagination.

Then there were no more Christmas numbers, but I managed to   3
preserve the spirit of them, sitting at my table with pencil and paper, trying to draw Christmas scenes of my own—dark skies and walls, bright snow and windows. When I was older and could trace figures, these turned into the figures of the manger scene, cut out and mounted on cardboard to make a proper crib.

Christmas Eve was the culmination of this season, the day when   4
the promise of the Christmas numbers should be fulfilled. The shops already had their green and red streamers, and in the morning Mother decorated the house with holly and ivy. Much as I longed for it, we never had red-berried holly, which cost more. The Christmas candle, two feet high and a couple of inches thick, was set in a jam crock, wrapped in coloured paper, and twined about with holly. Everything was ready for the feast. For a lot of the day I leaned against the front door or wandered slowly down the road to the corner, trying to appear careless and indifferent so that no one should know I was really waiting for the postman. Most of the Christmas mail we got came on Christmas Eve, and though I don't think I ever got a present through the post, that did not in the least diminish my expectations of one. Whatever experience might have taught me, the Christmas numbers taught differently.

Father had a half-day on Christmas Eve, and came home at noon   5
with his week's pay in his pocket—that is, when he got home at all. Mother and I knew well how easily he was led astray by out-of-works who waited at the street corners for men in regular jobs, knowing that on Christmas Eve no one could refuse them a pint. But I never gave that aspect of it much thought. It wasn't for anything so commonplace as Father's weekly pay that I was waiting. I even ignored the fact that when he did come in, there was usually an argument and sometimes a quarrel. At ordinary times when he did not give Mother enough to pay the bills, she took it with resignation, and if there was a

---

*From the 17th-century Latin hymn, "Adeste Fideles" ("O Come, All Ye Faithful"). ("Behold the birth of the King of angels.") St. Stephen's Day is observed in Catholic communities. O'Connor explains the custom in paragraphs 12 and 13.

row it was he who provoked it by asking: 'Well, isn't that enough for you?' But at Christmas she would fight and fight desperately. One Christmas Eve he came home and handed her the housekeeping money with a complacent air, and she looked at the coins in her hand and went white. 'Lord God, what am I to do with that?' I heard her whisper despairingly, and I listened in terror because she never invoked the name of God. Father suddenly blew up into the fury he had been cooking up all the way home—a poor, hardworking man deprived of his little bit of pleasure at Christmas time because of an extravagant wife and child. 'Well, what do you want it for?' he snarled. 'What do I want it for?' she asked distractedly, and went through her shopping list, which, God knows, must have been modest enough. And then he said something that I did not understand, and I heard her whispering in reply and there was a frenzy in her voice that I would not have believed possible; 'Do you think I'll leave him without it on the one day of the year?'

6   Years later I suddenly remembered the phrase because of its beauty, and realized that it was I who was to be left without a toy, and on this one day of the year that seemed to her intolerable. And yet I did not allow it to disturb me; I had other expectations, and I was very happy when the pair of us went shopping together, down Blarney Lane, past the shop in the big old house islanded in Goulnaspurra, where they sold the coloured cardboard cribs I coveted, with shepherds and snow, manger and star, and across the bridge to Myles's Toy Shop on the North Main Street. There in the rainy dusk, jostled by prams and drunken women in shawls, and thrust on one side by barefooted children from the lanes, I stood in wonder, thinking which treasure Santa Claus would bring me from the ends of the earth to show his appreciation of the way I had behaved in the past twelve months. As he was a most superior man, and I a most superior child, I saw no limit to the possibilities of the period, and no reason why Mother should not join in my speculations.

7   It was usually dark when we tramped home together, up Wyse's Hill, from which we saw the whole city lit up beneath us and the trams reflected in the water under Patrick's Bridge; or later—when we lived in Barrackton, up Summerhill, Mother carrying the few scraps of meat and the plum pudding from Thompson's and me something from the Penny Bazaar. We had been out a long time, and I was full of expectations of what the postman might have brought in the meantime. Even when he hadn't brought anything, I didn't allow myself to be upset, for I knew that the poor postmen were dreadfully overworked at this time of year. And even if he didn't come later, there was always the final Christmas-morning delivery. I was an optimistic child, and the holly over the mirror in the kitchen and the red paper in the lighted window of the huxter shop across the street assured me that the Christmas numbers were right and anything might happen.

There were lesser pleasures to look forward to, like the lighting   8
of the Christmas candle and the cutting of the Christmas cake. As the
youngest of the household I had the job of lighting the candle and saying solemnly: 'The light of Heaven to our souls on the last day,' and
Mother's principal worry was that before the time came Father might
slip out to the pub and spoil the ritual, for it was supposed to be carried out by the oldest and the youngest, and Father, by convention,
was the oldest, though, in fact, as I later discovered, he was younger
than Mother.

In those days the cake and candle were supposed to be presented   9
by the small shopkeeper from whom we bought the tea, sugar, paraffin
oil, and so on. We could not afford to shop in the big stores where
everything was cheaper, because they did not give credit to poor people, and most of the time we lived on credit. But each year our 'presents' seemed to grow smaller, and Mother would comment impatiently on the meanness of Miss O' or Miss Mac in giving us a tiny
candle or a stale cake. (When the 1914 War began they stopped giving
us the cake.) Mother could never believe that people could be so mean,
but, where we were concerned, they seemed to be capable of anything.
The lighted candle still left me with two expectations. However late it
grew I never ceased to expect the postman's knock, and even when
that failed, there was the certainty that Christmas Morning would set
everything right.

But when I woke on Christmas Morning, I felt the season of   10
imagination slipping away from me and the world or reality breaking
in. If all Santa Claus could bring me from the North Pole was something I could have bought in Myles's Toy Shop for a couple of pence,
he seemed to me to be wasting his time. Then the postman came, on
his final round before a holiday that already had begun to seem eternal, and either he brought nothing for us, or else he brought the dregs
of the Christmas mail, like a Christmas card from somebody who had
just got Mother's card and remembered her existence at the last moment. Often, even this would be in an unsealed envelope and it would
upset her for hours. It was strange in a woman to whom a penny was
money that an unsealed envelope seemed to her the worst of ill-breed-
ing, equivalent to the small candle or the stale cake—not a simple
measure of economy, but plain, unadulterated bad taste.

Comparing Christmas gifts with other kids didn't take long or   11
give much satisfaction, and even then the day was overshadowed by
the harsh rule that I was not supposed to call at other children's
houses or they at mine. This, Mother said, was the family season,
which was all very well for those who had families but death to an
only child. It was the end of the season of imagination, and there was
no reason to think it would ever come again. Nothing had happened as
it happened in the Christmas numbers. There was no snow; no relative had returned from the States with presents for everyone; there

was nothing but Christmas Mass and the choir thundering out *Natum videte regem angelorum* as though they believed it, when any fool could see that things were just going on in the same old way. Mother would sigh and say: 'I never believe it's really Christmas until I hear the *Adeste,'* but if that was all that Christmas meant to her she was welcome to it. Most Christmas days I could have screamed with misery. I argued with Mother that other kids were just as depressed as I was, and dying to see me, but I never remember that she allowed me to stray far from the front door.

12   But, bad as Christmas Day was, St. Stephen's Day was terrible. It needed no imagination, only as much as was required to believe that you really had a dead wren on the holly bush you carried from door to door, singing:

> I up with me stick and I gave him a fall,
> And I brought him here to visit ye all.

13   Father was very contemptuous, watching this, and took it as another sign of the disappearance of youthful manliness, for in his young days not only did they wash their faces in snow, but on Christmas Day they raised the countryside with big sticks, killing wrens—or droleens, as we called them. Everyone knew that it was the droleen's chirping that had alerted the Roman soldiers in the Garden of Gethsemane and pointed out to them where Christ was concealed, and in Father's young days they had carried it around with great pomp, all the mummers disguised. It seemed to him positively indecent to ask for money on the strength of a dead wren that you didn't have. It wasn't the absence of the wren that worried Mother, even if he was an informer, for she adored birds and supported a whole regiment of them through the winter, but the fear that I would be a nuisance to other women as poor as herself who didn't have a penny to give the wren boys.

14   In the afternoon she and I went to see the cribs in the chapels. (There were none in the parish churches.) She was never strong enough to visit the seven cribs you had to visit to get the special blessing, but we always went to the chapel of the Good Shepherd Convent in Sunday's Well where she had gone to school. She was very loyal to those she called 'the old nuns,' the nuns who had been kind to her when she was a child.

15   One Christmas Santa Claus brought me a toy engine. As it was the only present I had received, I took it with me to the convent, and played with it on the floor while Mother and 'the old nuns' discussed old times and how much nicer girls used to be then. But it was a young man who brought us in to see the crib. When I saw the Holy Child in the manger I was very distressed, because little as I had, he had nothing at all. For me it was fresh proof of the incompetence of

Santa Claus—an elderly man who hadn't even remembered to give the Infant Jesus a toy and who should have been retired long ago. I asked the young nun politely if the Holy Child didn't like toys, and she replied composedly enough: 'Oh, he does, but his mother is too poor to afford them.' That settled it. My mother was poor too, but at Christmas she at least managed to buy me something, even if it was only a box of crayons. I distinctly remember getting into the crib and putting the engine between his outstretched arms. I probably showed him how to wind it as well, because a small baby like that would not be clever enough to know. I remember too the tearful feeling of reckless generosity with which I left him there in the nightly darkness of the chapel, clutching my toy engine to his chest.

Because somehow I knew even then exactly how that child felt—   16 the utter despondency of realizing that he had been forgotten and that nobody had brought him anything; the longing for the dreary, dreadful holidays to pass till his father got to hell out of the house, and the postman returned again with the promise of better things.

____ **CONSIDERATIONS** _____

1. The pleasures of anticipation, we are told, rarely match the reality that follows. Does O'Connor's account of his boyhood Christmas support this commonplace? Referring to "Christmas," write an argumentative essay on the subject.

2. O'Connor's preoccupation with the "magic" of snow, in paragraph 2, prompts a question: Why did snow and holly berries and the red and green covers of the Christmas magazines strike the adult writer as he tells of his boyhood?

3. O'Connor describes himself on Christmas Eve, loitering about, "trying to appear careless and indifferent," as he waited for the postman to bring the Christmas mail. What current slang word would perfectly fit the boy's behavior, and why didn't O'Connor use it?

4. What happened to the toy engine O'Connor remembers receiving one Christmas, and what had it to do with the boy's feeling that Santa Claus was an incompetent old man "who should have been retired long ago"?

5. If the O'Connors were so poor, how did they manage a Christmas cake and a Christmas candle?

Tillie Olsen (b. 1913) has spent most of her life as a resident of San Francisco. When she was the young mother of four children, she lacked time and energy to write; her first book did not appear until 1962—her celebrated short story collection, Tell Me A Riddle, *from which we take "I Stand Here Ironing." Later, she brought out* Yonnondio *in 1974 and in 1978 published* Silences, *a meditation or investigation into writers—particularly women—who have written little.*

64

TILLIE OLSEN

I Stand Here Ironing

1   I stand here ironing, and what you asked me moves tormented back and forth with the iron.

2   "I wish you would manage the time to come in and talk with me about your daughter. I'm sure you can help me understand her. She's a youngster who needs help and whom I'm deeply interested in helping."

3   "Who needs help." Even if I came, what good would it do? You think because I am her mother I have a key, or that in some way you could use me as a key? She has lived for nineteen years. There is all that life that has happened outside of me, beyond me.

4   And when is there time to remember, to sift, to weigh, to estimate, to total? I will start and there will be an interruption and I will have to gather it all together again. Or I will become engulfed with all I did or did not do, with what should have been and what cannot be helped.

5   She was a beautiful baby. The first and only one of our five that was beautiful at birth. You do not guess how new and uneasy her tenancy in her now-loveliness. You did not know her all those years she

was thought homely, or see her poring over her baby pictures, making me tell her over and over how beautiful she had been—and would be, I would tell her—and was now, to the seeing eye. But the seeing eyes were few or nonexistent. Including mine.

I nursed her. They feel that's important nowadays. I nursed all 6 the children, but with her, with all the fierce rigidity of first mother-hood, I did like the books then said. Though her cries battered me to trembling and my breasts ached with swollenness, I waited till the clock decreed.

Why do I put that first? I do not even know if it matters, or if it 7 explains anything.

She was a beautiful baby. She blew shining bubbles of sound. She 8 loved motion, loved light, loved color and music and textures. She would lie on the floor in her blue overalls patting the surface so hard in ecstasy her hands and feet would blur. She was a miracle to me, but when she was eight months old I had to leave her daytimes with the woman downstairs to whom she was no miracle at all, for I worked or looked for work and for Emily's father, who "could no longer endure" (he wrote in his good-bye note) "sharing want with us."

I was nineteen. It was the pre-relief, pre-WPA world of the de- 9 pression. I would start running as soon as I got off the streetcar, run-ning up the stairs, the place smelling sour, and awake or asleep to star-tle awake, when she saw me she would break into a clogged weeping that could not be comforted, a weeping I can hear yet.

After a while I found a job hashing at night so I could be with her 10 days, and it was better. But it came to where I had to bring her to his family and leave her.

It took a long time to raise the money for her fare back. Then she 11 got chicken pox and I had to wait longer. When she finally came, I hardly knew her, walking quick and nervous like her father, looking like her father, thin, and dressed in a shoddy red that yellowed her skin and glared at the pockmarks. All the baby loveliness gone.

She was two. Old enough for nursery school they said, and I did 12 not know then what I know now—the fatigue of the long day, and the lacerations of group life in nurseries that are only parking places for children.

Except that it would have made no difference if I had known. It 13 was the only place there was. It was the only way we could be to-gether, the only way I could hold a job.

And even without knowing, I knew. I knew the teacher that was 14 evil because all these years it has curled into my memory, the little boy hunched in the corner, her rasp, "why aren't you outside, because Alvin hits you? that's no reason, go out, scaredy." I knew Emily hated it even if she did not clutch and implore "don't go Mommy" like the other children, mornings.

15   She always had a reason why we should stay home. Momma, you look sick, Momma. I feel sick. Momma, the teachers aren't there today, they're sick. Momma, we can't go, there was a fire there last night. Momma, it's a holiday today, no school, they told me.

16   But never a direct protest, never rebellion. I think of our others in their three-, four-year-oldness—the explosions, the tempers, the denunciations, the demands—and I feel suddenly ill. I put the iron down. What in me demanded that goodness in her? And what was the cost, the cost to her of such goodness?

17   The old man living in the back once said in his gentle way: "You should smile at Emily more when you look at her." What *was* in my face when I looked at her? I loved her. There were all the acts of love.

18   It was only with the others I remembered what he said, and it was the face of joy, and not of care or tightness or worry I turned to them—too late for Emily. She does not smile easily, let alone almost always as her brothers and sisters do. Her face is closed and sombre, but when she wants, how fluid. You must have seen it in her pantomimes, you spoke of her rare gift for comedy on the stage that rouses a laughter out of the audience so dear they applaud and applaud and do not want to let her go.

19   Where does it come from, that comedy? There was none of it in her when she came back to me that second time, after I had had to send her away again. She had a new daddy now to learn to love, and I think perhaps it was a better time.

20   Except when we left her alone nights, telling ourselves she was old enough.

21   "Can't you go some other time, Mommy, like tomorrow?" she would ask. "Will it be just a little while you'll be gone? Do you promise?"

22   The time we came back, the front door open, the clock on the floor in the hall. She rigid awake. "It wasn't just a little while. I didn't cry. Three times I called you, just three times, and then I ran downstairs to open the door so you could come faster. The clock talked loud. I threw it away, it scared me what it talked."

23   She said the clock talked loud again that night I went to the hospital to have Susan. She was delirious with the fever that comes before red measles, but she was fully conscious all the week I was gone and the week after we were home when she could not come near the new baby or me.

24   She did not get well. She stayed skeleton thin, not wanting to eat, and night after night she had nightmares. She would call for me, and I would rouse from exhaustion to sleepily call back: "You're all right, darling, go to sleep, it's just a dream," and if she still called, in a sterner voice, "now go to sleep, Emily, there's nothing to hurt you."

Twice, only twice, when I had to get up for Susan anyhow, I went in to sit with her.

Now when it is too late (as if she would let me hold and comfort 25 her like I do the others) I get up and go to her at once at her moan or restless stirring. "Are you awake, Emily? Can I get you something?" And the answer is always the same: "No, I'm all right, go back to sleep, Mother."

They persuaded me at the clinic to send her away to a convales- 26 cent home in the country where "she can have the kind of food and care you can't manage for her, and you'll be free to concentrate on the new baby." They still send children to that place. I see pictures on the society page of sleek young women planning affairs to raise money for it, or dancing at the affairs, or decorating Easter eggs or filling Christmas stockings for the children.

They never have a picture of the children so I do not know if the 27 girls still wear those gigantic red bows and the ravaged looks on the every other Sunday when parents can come to visit "unless otherwise notified"—as we were notified the first six weeks.

Oh it is a handsome place, green lawns and tall trees and fluted 28 flower beds. High up on the balconies of each cottage the children stand, the girls in their red bows and white dresses, the boys in white suits and giant red ties. The parents stand below shrieking up to be heard and the children shriek down to be heard, and between them the invisible wall "Not To Be Contaminated by Parental Germs or Physical Affection."

There was a tiny girl who always stood hand in hand with Emily. 29 Her parents never came. One visit she was gone. "They moved her to Rose College," Emily shouted in explanation. "They don't like you to love anybody here."

She wrote once a week, the labored writing of a seven-year-old. "I 30 am fine. How is the baby. If I write my leter nicly I will have a star. Love." There never was a star. We wrote every other day, letters she could never hold or keep but only hear read—once. "We simply do not have room for children to keep any personal possessions," they patiently explained when we pieced one Sunday's shrieking together to plead how much it would mean to Emily, who loved so to keep things, to be allowed to keep her letters and cards.

Each visit she looked frailer. "She isn't eating," they told us.   31

(They had runny eggs for breakfast or mush with lumps, Emily 32 said later, I'd hold it in my mouth and not swallow. Nothing ever tasted good, just when they had chicken.)

It took us eight months to get her released home, and only the 33 fact that she gained back so little of her seven lost pounds convinced the social worker.

34   I used to try to hold and love her after she came back, but her body would stay stiff, and after a while she'd push away. She ate little. Food sickened her, and I think much of life too. Oh she had physical lightness and brightness, twinkling by on skates, bouncing like a ball up and down up and down over the jump rope, skimming over the hill; but these were momentary.

35   She fretted about her appearance, thin and dark and foreign-looking at a time when every little girl was supposed to look or thought she should look a chubby blonde replica of Shirley Temple. The doorbell sometimes rang for her, but no one seemed to come and play in the house or be a best friend. Maybe because we moved so much.

36   There was a boy she loved painfully through two school semesters. Months later she told me how she had taken pennies from my purse to buy him candy. "Licorice was his favorite and I brought him some every day, but he still liked Jennifer better'n me. Why, Mommy?" The kind of question for which there is no answer.

37   School was a worry to her. She was not glib or quick in a world where glibness and quickness were easily confused with ability to learn. To her overworked and exasperated teachers she was an overconscientious "slow learner" who kept trying to catch up and was absent entirely too often.

38   I let her be absent, though sometimes the illness was imaginary. How different from my now-strictness about attendance with the others. I wasn't working. We had a new baby, I was home anyhow. Sometimes, after Susan grew old enough, I would keep her home from school, too, to have them all together.

39   Mostly Emily had asthma, and her breathing, harsh and labored, would fill the house with a curiously tranquil sound. I would bring the two old dresser mirrors and her boxes of collections to her bed. She would select beads and single earrings, bottle tops and shells, dried flowers and pebbles, old postcards and scraps, all sorts of oddments; then she and Susan would play Kingdom, setting up landscapes and furniture, peopling them with action.

40   Those were the only times of peaceful companionship between her and Susan. I have edged away from it, that poisonous feeling between them, that terrible balancing of hurts and needs I had to do between the two, and did so badly, those earlier years.

41   Oh there are conflicts between the others too, each one human, needing, demanding, hurting, taking—but only between Emily and Susan, no, Emily toward Susan that corroding resentment. It seems so obvious on the surface, yet it is not obvious. Susan, the second child, Susan, golden- and curly-haired and chubby, quick and articulate and assured, everything in appearance and manner Emily was not; Susan, not able to resist Emily's precious things, losing or sometimes clum-

sily breaking them; Susan telling jokes and riddles to company for applause while Emily sat silent (to say to me later: that was *my* riddle, Mother, I told it to Susan); Susan, who for all the five years' difference in age was just a year behind Emily in developing physically.

I am glad for that slow physical development that widened the 42 difference between her and her contemporaries, though she suffered over it. She was too vulnerable for that terrible world of youthful competition, of preening and parading, of constant measuring of yourself against every other, of envy. "If I had that copper hair," "If I had that skin. . . ." She tormented herself enough about not looking like the others, there was enough of the unsureness, the having to be conscious of words before you speak, the constant caring—what are they thinking of me? without having it all magnified by the merciless physical drives.

Ronnie is calling. He is wet and I change him. It is rare there is 43 such a cry now. That time of motherhood is almost behind me when the ear is not one's own but must always be racked and listening for the child cry, the child call. We sit for a while and I hold him, looking out over the city spread in charcoal with its soft aisles of light. "*Shoogily,*" he breathes and curls closer. I carry him back to bed, asleep. *Shoogily.* A funny word, a family word, inherited from Emily, invented by her to say: *comfort.*

In this and other ways she leaves her seal, I say aloud. And startle 44 at my saying it. What do I mean? What did I start to gather together, to try and make coherent? I was at the terrible, growing years. War years. I do not remember them well. I was working, there were four smaller ones now, there was not time for her. She had to help be a mother, and housekeeper, and shopper. She had to set her seal. Mornings of crisis and near hysteria trying to get lunches packed, hair combed, coats and shoes found, everyone to school or Child Care on time, the baby ready for transportation. And always the paper scribbled on by a smaller one, the book looked at by Susan then mislaid, the homework not done. Running out to that huge school where she was one, she was lost, she was a drop; suffering over the unpreparedness, stammering and unsure in her classes.

There was so little time left at night after the kids were bedded 45 down. She would struggle over books, always eating (it was in those years she developed her enormous appetite that is legendary in our family) and I would be ironing, or preparing food for the next day, or writing V-mail to Bill, or tending the baby. Sometimes, to make me laugh, or out of her despair, she would imitate happenings or types at school.

I think I said once: "Why don't you do something like this in the 46 school amateur show?" One morning she phoned me at work, hardly understandable through the weeping: "Mother, I did it. I won, I won; they gave me first prize; they clapped and clapped and wouldn't let me go."

47   Now suddenly she was Somebody, and as imprisoned in her difference as she had been in anonymity.

48   She began to be asked to perform at other high schools, even in colleges, then at city and statewide affairs. The first one we went to, I only recognized her that first moment when thin, shy, she almost drowned herself into the curtains. Then: Was this Emily? The control, the command, the convulsing and deadly clowning, the spell, then the roaring, stamping audience, unwilling to let this rare and precious laughter out of their lives.

49   Afterwards: You ought to do something about her with a gift like that—but without money or knowing how, what does one do? We have left it all to her, and the gift has as often eddied inside, clogged and clotted, as been used and growing.

50   She is coming. She runs up the stairs two at a time with her light graceful step, and I know she is happy tonight. Whatever it was that occasioned your call did not happen today.

51   "Aren't you ever going to finish the ironing, Mother? Whistler painted his mother in a rocker. I'd have to paint mine standing over an ironing board." This is one of her communicative nights and she tells me everything and nothing as she fixes herself a plate of food out of the icebox.

52   She is so lovely. Why did you want me to come in at all? Why were you concerned? She will find her way.

53   She starts up the stairs to bed. "Don't get me up with the rest in the morning." "But I thought you were having midterms." "Oh, those," she comes back in, kisses me, and says quite lightly, "in a couple of years when we'll all be atom-dead they won't matter a bit."

54   She has said it before. She *believes* it. But because I have been dredging the past, and all that compounds a human being is so heavy and meaningful in me, I cannot endure it tonight.

55   I will never total it all. I will never come in to say: She was a child seldom smiled at. Her father left me before she was a year old. I had to work her first six years when there was work, or I sent her home and to his relatives. There were years she had care she hated. She was dark and thin and foreign-looking in a world where the prestige went to blondeness and curly hair and dimples, she was slow where glibness was prized. She was a child of anxious, not proud, love. We were poor and could not afford for her the soil of easy growth. I was a young mother, I was a distracted mother. There were the other children pushing up, demanding. Her younger sister seemed all that she was not. There were years she did not want me to touch her. She kept too much in herself, her life was such she had to keep too much

in herself. My wisdom came too late. She has much to her and probably nothing will come of it. She is a child of her age, of depression, of war, of fear.

Let her be. So all that is in her will not bloom—but in how many 56 does it? There is still enough left to live by. Only help her to know—help make it so there is cause for her to know—that she is more than this dress on the ironing board, helpless before the iron.

___ **CONSIDERATIONS** _____

1. Who is the "I" in the story? Actually, there are two of them. Identify them both.

2. In the concluding paragraphs of the story, what is so shocking to the mother that she says, "I cannot endure it tonight"?

3. What is there about the story that makes the title memorable?

4. Some readers find themselves arguing about which character the story is about—Emily or the nameless mother. Can you settle that dispute?

5. The mother worries that she and Emily had not had enough closeness and demonstrations of mutual affection—as in paragraph 34. Read Diane Ackerman's "Speaking of Touch," especially paragraph 11, (page 10), and discuss the relevance of her report to Tillie Olson's story.

6. What two experiences when Emily was little seemed to heighten the mother's worry about a growing distance between her and her daughter?

George Orwell (1903–1950) was the pen name of Eric Blair, who was born in India of English parents, attended Eton on a scholarship, and returned to the East as a member of the Imperial Police. He quit his position after five years because he wanted to write, and because he came to feel that imperialism was "very largely a racket." For eight years he wrote with small success and lived in considerable poverty. His first book, Down and Out in Paris and London *(1933), described those years. Further memoirs and novels followed, including* Burmese Days *(1935) and* Keep the Aspidistra Flying *(1938). His last books were the political fable* Animal Farm *(1945) and his great anti-utopia* 1984, *which appeared in 1949, shortly before his death. He died of tuberculosis, his health first afflicted when he was a police officer in Burma, undermined by years of poverty, and further worsened by a wound he received during the civil war in Spain.*

*Best known for his fiction, Orwell was essentially an essayist; even his novels are essays. He made his living most of his adult life by writing reviews and articles for English weeklies. His collected essays, reviews, and letters form an impressive four volumes. Politics is at the center of his work—a personal politics. After his disaffection from imperialism, he became a leftist and fought on the Loyalist side against Franco in Spain. (*Homage to Catalonia *comes out of this time.) But his experience of Communist duplicity there, and his early understanding of the paranoid totalitarianism of Stalin, turned him anti-Communist. He could swear allegiance to no party. His anti-Communism made him in no way conservative; he considered himself a socialist until his death, but other socialists would have nothing to do with him. He found politics shabby and politicians dishonest. With an empirical, English turn of mind, he looked skeptically at all saviors and panaceas.*

65

GEORGE ORWELL
A Hanging

It was in Burma, a sodden morning of the rains. A sickly light, 1
like yellow tinfoil, was slanting over the high walls into the jail yard.
We were waiting outside the condemned cells, a row of sheds fronted
with double bars, like small animal cages. Each cell measured about
ten feet by ten and was quite bare within except for a plank bed and a
pot for drinking water. In some of them brown, silent men were squatting at the inner bars, with their blankets draped around them. These
were the condemned men, due to be hanged within the next week or
two.

One prisoner had been brought out of his cell. He was a Hindu, a 2
puny wisp of a man, with a shaven head and vague liquid eyes. He had
a thick, sprouting moustache, absurdly too big for his body, rather like
the moustache of a comic man on the films. Six tall Indian warders
were guarding him and getting him ready for the gallows. Two of them
stood by with rifles and fixed bayonets, while the others handcuffed
him, passed a chain through his handcuffs and fixed it to their belts,
and lashed his arms tight to his sides. They crowded very close about
him, with their hands always on him in a careful, caressing grip, as
though all the while feeling him to make sure he was there. It was like
men handling a fish which is still alive and may jump back into the
water. But he stood quite unresisting, yielding his arms limply to the
ropes, as though he hardly noticed what was happening.

Eight o'clock struck and a bugle call, desolately thin in the wet 3
air, floated from the distant barracks. The superintendent of the jail,
who was standing apart from the rest of us, moodily prodding the
gravel with his stick, raised his head at the sound. He was an army
doctor, with a grey toothbrush moustache and a gruff voice. "For
God's sake hurry up, Francis," he said irritably. "The man ought to
have been dead by this time. Aren't you ready yet?"

Francis, the head jailer, a fat Dravidian in a white drill suit and 4
gold spectacles, waved his black hand. "Yes sir, yes sir," he bubbled.

"All iss satisfactorily prepared. The hangman iss waiting. We shall proceed."

5   "Well, quick march, then. The prisoners can't get their breakfast till this job's over."

6   We set out for the gallows. Two warders marched on either side of the prisoner, with their rifles at the slope; two others marched close against him, gripping him by arm and shoulder, as though at once pushing and supporting him. The rest of us, magistrates and the like, followed behind. Suddenly, when we had gone ten yards, the procession stopped short without any order or warning. A dreadful thing had happened—a dog, come goodness knows whence, had appeared in the yard. It came bounding among us with a loud volley of barks and leapt round us wagging its whole body, wild with glee at finding so many human beings together. It was a large woolly dog, half Airedale, half pariah. For a moment it pranced around us, and then, before anyone could stop it, it had made a dash for the prisoner, and jumping up tried to lick his face. Everybody stood aghast, too taken aback even to grab the dog.

7   "Who let that bloody brute in here?" said the superintendent angrily. "Catch it, someone!"

8   A warder detached from the escort, charged clumsily after the dog, but it danced and gambolled just out of his reach, taking everything as part of the game. A young Eurasian jailer picked up a handful of gravel and tried to stone the dog away, but it dodged the stones and came after us again. Its yaps echoed from the jail walls. The prisoner, in the grasp of the two warders, looked on incuriously, as though this was another formality of the hanging. It was several minutes before someone managed to catch the dog. Then we put my handkerchief through its collar and moved off once more, with the dog still straining and whimpering.

9   It was about forty yards to the gallows. I watched the bare brown back of the prisoner marching in front of me. He walked clumsily with his bound arms, but quite steadily, with that bobbing gait of the Indian who never straightens his knees. At each step his muscles slid neatly into place, the lock of hair on his scalp danced up and down, his feet printed themselves on the wet gravel. And once, in spite of the men who gripped him by each shoulder, he stepped lightly aside to avoid a puddle on the path.

10   It is curious; but till that moment I had never realized what it means to destroy a healthy, conscious man. When I saw the prisoner step aside to avoid the puddle I saw the mystery, the unspeakable wrongness, of cutting a life short when it is in full tide. This man was not dying, he was alive just as we are alive. All the organs of his body were working—bowels digesting food, skin renewing itself, nails growing, tissues forming—all toiling away in solemn foolery. His nails

would still be growing when he stood on the drop, when he was falling through the air with a tenth-of-a-second to live. His eyes saw the yellow gravel and the grey walls, and his brain still remembered, foresaw, reasoned—even about puddles. He and we were a party of men walking together, seeing, hearing, feeling, understanding the same world; and in two minutes, with a sudden snap, one of us would be gone— one mind less, one world less.

The gallows stood in a small yard, separate from the main 11 grounds of the prison, and overgrown with tall prickly weeds. It was a brick erection like three sides of a shed, with planking on top, and above that two beams and a crossbar with the rope dangling. The hangman, a greyhaired convict in the white uniform of the prison, was waiting beside his machine. He greeted us with a servile crouch as we entered. At a word from Francis the two wards, gripping the prisoner more closely than ever, half led, half pushed him to the gallows and helped him clumsily up the ladder. Then the hangman climbed up and fixed the rope round the prisoner's neck.

We stood waiting, five yards away. The warders had formed in a 12 rough circle round the gallows. And then, when the noose was fixed, the prisoner began crying out to his god. It was a high, reiterated cry of "Ram! Ram! Ram! Ram!" not urgent and fearful like a prayer or cry for help, but steady, rhythmical, almost like the tolling of a bell. The dog answered the sound with a whine. The hangman, still standing on the gallows, produced a small cotton bag like a flour bag and drew it down over the prisoner's face. But the sound, muffled by the cloth, still persisted, over and over again: "Ram! Ram! Ram! Ram! Ram!"

The hangman climbed down and stood ready, holding the lever. 13 Minutes seemed to pass. The steady, muffled crying from the prisoner went on and on, "Ram! Ram! Ram!" never faltering for an instant. The superintendent, his head on his chest, was slowly poking the ground with his stick; perhaps he was counting the cries, allowing the prisoner a fixed number—fifty, perhaps, or a hundred. Everyone had changed colour. The Indians had gone grey like bad coffee, and one or two of the bayonets were wavering. We looked at the lashed, hooded man on the drop, and listened to his cries—each cry another second of life; the same thought was in all our minds; oh, kill him quickly, get it over, stop that abominable noise!

Suddenly the superintendent made up his mind. Throwing up his 14 head he made a swift motion with his stick. "Chalo!" he shouted almost fiercely.

There was a clanking noise, and then dead silence. The prisoner 15 had vanished, and the rope was twisting on itself. I let go of the dog, and it galloped immediately to the back of the gallows; but when it got there it stopped short, barked, and then retreated into a corner of the yard, where it stood among the weeds, looking timorously out at us. We went round the gallows to inspect the prisoner's body. He was dangling with his toes pointed straight downwards, very slowly revolving, as dead as a stone.

16   The superintendent reached out with his stick and poked the bare brown body; it oscillated slightly. "*He's* all right," said the superintendent. He backed out from under the gallows, and blew out a deep breath. The moody look had gone out of his face quite suddenly. He glanced at his wrist-watch. "Eight minutes past eight. Well, that's all for this morning, thank God."

17   The warders unfixed bayonets and marched away. The dog, sobered and conscious of having misbehaved itself, slipped after them. We walked out of the gallows yard, past the condemned cells with their waiting prisoners, into the big central yard of the prison. The convicts, under the command of warders armed with lathis, were already receiving their breakfast. They squatted in long rows, each man holding a tin pannikin, while two warders with buckets marched round ladling out rice; it seemed quite a homely, jolly scene, after the hanging. An enormous relief had come upon us now that the job was done. One felt an impulse to sing, to break into a run, to snigger. All at once everyone began chatting gaily.

18   The Eurasian boy walking beside me nodded towards the way we had come, with a knowing smile: "Do you know, sir, our friend (he meant the dead man) when he heard his appeal had been dismissed, he pissed on the floor of his cell. From fright. Kindly take one of my cigarettes, sir. Do you not admire my new silver case, sir? From the boxwallah, two rupees eight annas. Classy European style."

19   Several people laughed—at what, nobody seemed certain.

20   Francis was walking by the superintendent, talking garrulously: "Well, sir, all has passed off with the utmost satisfactoriness. It was all finished—flick! Like that. It iss not always so—oah, no! I have known cases where the doctor wass obliged to go beneath the gallows and pull the prisoner's legs to ensure decease. Most disagreeable!"

21   "Wriggling about, eh? That's bad," said the superintendent.

22   "Ach, sir, it iss worse when they become refractory! One man, I recall, clung to the bars of hiss cage when we went to take him out. You will scarcely credit, sir, that it took six wards to dislodge him, three pulling at each leg. We reasoned with him, 'My dear fellow,' we said, 'think of all the pain and trouble you are causing to us!' But no, he would not listen! Ach, he wass very troublesome!"

23   I found that I was laughing quite loudly. Everyone was laughing. Even the superintendent grinned in a tolerant way. "You'd better all come out and have a drink," he said quite genially. "I've got a bottle of whisky in the car. We could do with it."

24   We went through the big double gates of the prison into the road. "Pulling at his legs!" exclaimed a Burmese magistrate suddenly, and burst into a loud chuckling. We all began laughing again. At that mo-

ment Francis' anecdote seemed extraordinarily funny. We all had a
drink together, native and European alike, quite amicably. The dead
man was a hundred yards away.

___ CONSIDERATIONS ___

1. Many readers have described Orwell's "A Hanging" as a powerful
condemnation of capital punishment. Study Orwell's technique in drawing
from his readers the desired inference.

2. Point out examples of Orwell's skillful use of detail to establish the
place and mood of "A Hanging." Adapt his technique to your purpose in your
next essay.

3. What minor incident caused Orwell suddenly to see "the unspeakable wrongness . . . of cutting a life short"? Why?

4. What effect, in paragraph 6, does the boisterous dog have on the players of this scene? On you, the reader? Explain in terms of the whole essay.

5. "One mind, one world less" is the way Orwell sums up the demise of
the Hindu prisoner. Obviously, Orwell's statement is highly compressed, jam-
ming into its short length many ideas, hopes, and fears. Write a short essay,
opening up his aphorism so that your readers get some idea of what can be
packed into five short words. For additional examples of compressed expression, see Ambrose Bierce's "Devil's Dictionary," and any of the poems in this
book.

6. The warden and others present were increasingly disconcerted by the
prisoner's continued cry, "Ram! Ram! Ram! Ram!" But note Orwell's description of that cry in paragraphs 12 and 13. Does that description give you a clue
as to the nature of the man's cry? Why doesn't Orwell explain it?

In this famous essay, Orwell attacks the rhetoric of politics. He largely attacks the left—because his audience was an English intellectual class that was largely leftist.

66

GEORGE ORWELL

Politics and the English Language

1   Most people who bother with the matter at all would admit that the English language is in a bad way, but it is generally assumed that we cannot by conscious action do anything about it. Our civilization is decadent and our language—so the argument runs—must inevitably share in the general collapse. It follows that any struggle against the abuse of language is a sentimental archaism, like preferring candles to electric light or hansom cabs to aeroplanes. Underneath this lies the half-conscious belief that language is a natural growth and not an instrument which we shape for our own purposes.

2   Now, it is clear that the decline of a language must ultimately have political and economic causes: it is not due simply to the bad influence of this or that individual writer. But an effect can become a cause, reinforcing the original cause and producing the same effect in an intensified form, and so indefinitely. A man may take to drink because he feels himself to be a failure, and then fail all the more completely because he drinks. It is rather the same thing that is happening to the English language. It becomes ugly and inaccurate because our thoughts are foolish, but the slovenliness of our language makes it easier for us to have foolish thoughts. The point is that the process is reversible. Modern English, especially written English, is full of bad habits which spread by imitation and which can be avoided if one is willing to take the necessary trouble. If one gets rid of these habits one can think more clearly, and to think clearly is a necessary first step to-

wards political regeneration: so that the fight against bad English is not frivolous and is not the exclusive concern of professional writers. I will come back to this presently, and I hope that by that time the meaning of what I have said here will have become clearer. Meanwhile, here are five specimens of the English language as it is now habitually written.

These five passages have not been picked out because they are especially bad—I could have quoted far worse if I had chosen—but because they illustrate various of the mental vices from which we now suffer. They are a little below the average, but are fairly representative samples. I number them so that I can refer back to them when necessary: 3

> (1) I am not, indeed, sure whether it is not true to say that the Milton who once seemed not unlike a seventeenth-century Shelley had not become, out of an experience ever more bitter in each year, more alien [*sic*] to the founder of that Jesuit sect which nothing could induce him to tolerate.
>
> Professor Harold Laski
[Essay in Freedom of Expression]

> (2) Above all, we cannot play ducks and drakes with a native battery of idioms which prescribes such egregious collocations of vocables as the Basic *put up with* for *tolerate* or *put at a loss* for *bewilder*.
>
> Professor Lancelot Hogben [Interglossa]

> (3) On the one side we have the free personality: by definition it is not neurotic, for it has neither conflict nor dream. Its desires, such as they are, are transparent, for they are just what institutional approval keeps in the forefront of consciousness; another institutional pattern would alter their number and intensity, there is little in them that is natural, irreducible, or culturally dangerous. But *on the other side*, the social bond itself is nothing but the mutual reflection of these self-secure integrities. Recall the definition of love. Is not this the very picture of a small academic? Where is there a place in this hall of mirrors for either personality or fraternity?
>
> Essay on psychology in Politics [New York]

> (4) All the "best people" from the gentlemen's clubs, and all the frantic fascist captains, united in common hatred of Socialism and bestial horror of the rising tide of the mass revolutionary movement, have turned to acts of provocation, to foul incendiarism, to medieval legends of poisoned wells, to legalize their own destruction of proletarian organizations, and rouse the agitated petty-bourgeoisie to chauvinistic fervor on behalf of the fight against the revolutionary way out of the crisis.
>
> Communist pamphlet

(5) If a new spirit is to be infused into this old country, there is one thorny and contentious reform which must be tackled, and that is the humanization and galvanization of the B.C.C. Timidity here will bespeak canker and atrophy of the soul. The heart of Britain may be sound and of strong beat, for instance, but the British lion's roar at present is like that of Bottom in Shakepeares's *Midsummer Night's Dream*—as gentle as any sucking dove. A virile new Britain cannot continue indefinitely to be traduced in the eyes, or rather ears, of the world by the effete languors of Langham Place brazenly masquerading as "standard English." When the Voice of Britain is heard at nine o'clock, better far and infinitely less ludicrous to hear aitches honestly dropped than the present priggish, inflated, inhibited, schoolma'amish arch braying of blameless bashful mewing maidens!

Letter in *Tribune*

4   Each of these passages has faults of its own, but, quite apart from avoidable ugliness, two qualities are common to all of them. The first is staleness of imagery; the other is lack of precision. The writer either has a meaning and cannot express it, or he inadvertently says something else, or he is almost indifferent as to whether his words mean anything or not. This mixture of vagueness and sheer incompetence is the most marked characteristic of modern English prose, and especially of any kind of political writing. As soon as certain topics are raised, the concrete melts into the abstract and no one seems able to think of turns of speech that are not hackneyed: prose consists less and less of *words* chosen for the sake of their meaning, and more and more of *phrases* tacked together like the sections of a prefabricated hen-house. I list below, with notes and examples, various of the tricks by means of which the work of prose-construction is habitually dodged:

Dying Metaphors

5   A newly invented metaphor assists thought by evoking a visual image, while on the other hand a metaphor which is technically "dead" (e.g. *iron resolution*) has in effect reverted to being an ordinary word and can generally be used without loss of vividness. But in between these two classes there is a huge dump of worn-out metaphors which have lost all evocative power and are merely used because they save people the trouble of inventing phrases for themselves. Examples are: *Ring the changes on, take up the cudgels for, toe the line, ride roughshod over, stand shoulder to shoulder with, play into the hands of, no axe to grind, grist to the mill, fishing in troubled waters, on the order of the day, Achilles' heel, swan song, hotbed.* Many of these are used without knowledge of their meaning (what is a "rift," for instance?), and incompatible metaphors are frequently mixed, a sure

sign that the writer is not interested in what he is saying. Some metaphors now current have been twisted out of their original meaning without those who use them even being aware of the fact. For example, *toe the line* is sometimes written *tow the line*. Another example is *the hammer and the anvil*, now always used with the implication that the anvil gets the worst of it. In real life it is always the anvil that breaks the hammer, never the other way about: a writer who stopped to think what he was saying would be aware of this, and would avoid perverting the original phrase.

Operators or Verbal False Limbs

These save the trouble of picking out appropriate verbs and   6
nouns, and at the same time pad each sentence with extra syllables which give it an appearance of symmetry. Characteristic phrases are *render inoperative, militate against, make contact with, be subjected to, give rise to, give grounds for, have the effect of, play a leading part (role) in, make itself felt, take effect, exhibit a tendency to, serve the purpose of,* etc., etc. The keynote is the elimination of simple verbs. Instead of being a single word, such as *break, stop, spoil, men, kill* a verb becomes a *phrase*, made up of a noun or adjective tacked on to some general-purpose verb such as *prove, serve, form, play, render*. In addition, the passive voice is wherever possible used in preference to the active, and noun constructions are used instead of gerunds (*by examination of* instead of *by examining*). The range of verbs is further cut down by means of the *-ize* and *de-* formations, and the banal statements are given an appearance of profundity by means of the *not un-* formation. Simple conjunctions and prepositions are replaced by such phrases as *with respect to, having regard to, the fact that, by dint of, in view of, in the interests of, on the hypothesis that;* and the ends of sentences are saved from anticlimax by such resounding commonplaces as *greatly to be desired, cannot be left out of account, a development to be expected in the near future, deserving of serious consideration, brought to a satisfactory conclusion* and so on and so forth.

Pretentious Diction

Words like *phenomenon, element, individual* (as noun), *objec-*   7
tive, categorical, effective, virtual, basic, primary, promote, constitute, exhibit, exploit, utilize, eliminate, liquidate, are used to dress up simple statements and give an air of scientific impartiality to biased judgments. Adjectives like *epoch-making, epic, historic, unforgettable, triumphant, age-old, inevitable, inexorable, veritable,* are used to dignify the sordid processes of international politics, while writing that aims at glorifying war usually takes on an archaic color, its characteristic words being: *realm, throne, chariot, mailed first, trident,*

sword, shield, buckler, banner, jackboot, clarion. Foreign words and expressions such as *cul de sac, ancien régime, deux ex machina, mutatis mutandis, status quo, gleichschaltung, weltanschauung,* are used to give an air of culture and elegance. Except for the useful abbrecations *i.e., e.g.,* and *etc.,* there is no real need for any of the hundreds of foreign phrases now current in English. Bad writers, and especially scientific, political and sociological writers, are nearly always haunted by the notion that Latin or Greek words are grander than Saxon ones, and unnecessary words like *expedite, ameliorate, predict, extraneous, deracinated, clandestine, subaqueous* and hundreds of others constantly gain ground from their Anglo-Saxon opposite numbers.* The jargon peculiar to Marxist writing (*hyena, hangman, cannibal, petty bourgeois, these gentry, lacquey, flunkey, mad dog, White Guard,* etc.) consists largely of words and phrases translated from Russian, German or French; but the normal way of coining a new word is to use a Latin or Greek root with the appropriate affix and, where necessary, the *-ize* formation. It is often easier to make up words of this kind (*derogionalize, impermissible, extramarital, nonfragmentary* and so forth) than to think up the English words that will cover one's meaning. The result, in general, is an increase in slovenliness and vagueness.

Meaningless Words

8   In certain kinds of writing, particularly in an art criticism and literary criticism, it is normal to come across long passages which are almost completely lacking in meaning.** Words like *romantic, plastic, values, human, dead, sentimental, natural, vitality,* as used in art criticism, are strictly meaningless, in the sense that they not only do not point to any discoverable object, but are hardly ever expected to do so by the reader. When one critic writes, "The outstanding features of Mr. X's work is its living quality," while another writes, "The immediately striking thing about Mr. X's work is its peculiar deadness," the reader accepts this as a simple difference of opinion. If words like *black* and *white* were involved, instead of the jargon words *dead* and

---

*An interesting illustration of this is the way in which the English flower names which were in use till very recently are being ousted by Greek ones, *snapdragons* becoming *antirrhinum, forget-me-not* becoming *myosotis,* etc. It is hard to see any practical reason for this change of fashion: it is probably due to an instinctive turning-away from the more homely word and a vague feeling that the Greek is scientific.

**Example: "Comfort's catholicity of perception and image, strangely Whitmanesque in range, almost the exact opposite in aesthetic compulsion, continues to evoke that trembling atmosphere accumulative hinting at a cruel, an inexorably serene timelessness. . . .Wrey Gardiner scores by aiming at simple bull's-eyes with precision. Only they are not so simple, and through his contented sadness runs more than the surface bitter-sweet of resignation." (*Poetry Quarterly.*)

living, he would see at once that language was being used in an improper way. Many political words are similarly abused. The word *Fascism* has now no meaning in so far as it signifies "something not desirable." The words *democracy, socialism, freedom, patriotic, realistic, justice*, have each of them several different meanings which cannot be reconciled with one another. In the case of a word like *democracy*, not only is there no agreed definition, but the attempt to make one is resisted from all sides. It is almost universally felt that when we call a country democratic we are praising it: consequently the defenders of every kind of régime claim that it is a democracy, and fear that they might have to stop using the word if it were tied down to any one meaning. Words of this kind are often used in a consciously dishonest way. That is, the person who uses them has his own private definition, but allows his hearer to think he means something quite different. Statements like *Marshal Pétain was a true patriot, The Soviet Press is the freest in the world, The Catholic Church is opposed to persecution*, are almost always made with intent to deceive. Other words used in variable meanings, in most cases more or less dishonestly, are: *class, totalitarian, science, progressive, reactionary, bourgeois, equality*.

Now that I have made this catalogue of swindles and perversions, let me give another example of the kind of writing that they lead to. This time it must of its nature be an imaginary one. I am going to translate a passage of good English into modern English of the worst sort. Here is a well-known verse from *Ecclesiastes*: 9

> *I returned and saw under the sun, that the race is not to the swift, nor the battle to the strong, neither yet bread to the wise, nor yet riches to men of understanding, nor yet favour to men of skill, but time and chance happeneth to them all.*

Here it is in modern English: 10

> Objective consideration of contemporary phenomena compels the conclusion that success or failure in competitive activities exhibits no tendency to be commensurate with innate capacity, but that a considerable element of the unpredictable must invariably be taken into account.

This is a parody, but not a very gross one. Exhibit (3), above, for instance, contains several patches of the same kind of English. It will be seen that I have not made a full translation. The beginning and ending of the sentence follow the original meaning fairly closely, but in the middle the concrete illustrations—race, battle, bread—dissolve into the vague phrase "success or failure in competitive activities." This had to be so, because no modern writer of the kind I am discussing—no one capable of using phrases like "objective consideration 11 of contemporary phenomena"—would ever tabulate his thoughts in that precise and detailed way. The whole tendency of modern prose is away from concreteness. Now analyse these two sentences a little more closely. The first contains forty-nine words but only sixty syllables, and all its words are those of everyday life. The second contains thirty-eight words of ninety syllables: eighteen of its words are from Latin roots, and one from Greek. The first sentence contains six vivid images, and only one phrase ("time and chance") that could be called vague. The second contains not a single fresh, arresting phrase, and in spite of its ninety syllables it gives only a shortened version of the meaning contained in the first. Yet without a doubt it is the second kind of sentence that is gaining ground in modern English. I do not want to exaggerate. This kind of writing is not yet universal, and out-crops of simplicity will occur here and there in the worst-written page. Still, if you or I were told to write a few lines on the uncertainty of human fortunes, we should probably come much nearer to my imaginary sentence than to the one from *Ecclesiastes*.

12   As I have tried to show, modern writing at its worst does not consist in picking out words for the sake of their meaning and inventing, images in order to make the meaning clearer. It consists in gumming together long strips of words which have already been set in order by someone else, and making the results presentable by sheer humbug. The attraction of this way of writing is that it is easy. It is easier—even quicker, once you have the habit—to say *In my opinion it is not an unjustifiable assumption that* than to say *I think*. If you use ready-made phrases, you not only don't have to hunt about for words; you also don't have to bother with the rhythms of your sentences, since these phrases are generally so arranged as to be more or less euphonious. When you are composing in a hurry—when you are dictating to a stenographer, for instance, or making a public speech—it is natural to fall into a pretentious, Latinized style. Tags like *a consideration which we should do well to bear in mind* or *a conclusion to which all of us would readily assent* will save many a sentence from coming down with a bump. By using stale metaphors, similes and idioms, you save much mental effort, at the cost of leaving your meaning vague, not only for your reader but for yourself. This is the significance of mixed metaphors. The sole aim of a metaphor is to call up visual image. When these images clash—as in *The Fascist octopus has sung its swan song, the jackboot is thrown into the melting pot*—it can be taken as certain that the writer is not seeing a mental image of the objects he is naming; in other words he is not really thinking. Look again at the examples I gave at the beginning of this essay. Professor Laski (1) uses five negatives in fifty-three words. One of these is superfluous, making nonsense of the whole passage, and in addition there is a slip *alien* for *akin*, making further nonsense, and several avoidable pieces of clumsiness which increase the general vagueness.

Professor Hogben (2) plays ducks and drakes with a battery which is able to write prescriptions, and, while disapproving of the everyday phrase *put up with*, is unwilling to look *egregious* up in the dictionary and see what it means; (3), if one takes an uncharitable attitude towards it, is simply meaningless: probably one could work out its intended meaning by reading the whole of the article in which it occurs. In (4), the writer knows more or less what he wants to say, but an accumulation of stale phrases chokes him, like tea leaves blocking a sink. In (5), words and meaning have almost parted company. People who write in this manner usually have a general emotional meaning—they dislike one thing and want to express solidarity with another—but they are not interested in the detail of what they are saying. A scrupulous writer, in every sentence that he writes, will ask himself at least four questions, thus: What am I trying to say? What words will express it? What image or idiom will make it clearer? Is this image fresh enough to have an effect? And he will probably ask himself two more: Could I put it more shortly? Have I said anything that is avoidably ugly? But you are not obliged to go to all this trouble. You can shirk it by simply throwing your mind open and letting the ready-made phrases come crowding in. They will construct your sentences for you—even think your thoughts for you, to a certain extent—and at need they will perform the important service of partially concealing your meaning even from yourself. It is at this point that the special connection between politics and the debasement of language becomes clear.

    In our time it is broadly true that political writing is bad writing. 13 Where it is not true, it will generally be found that the writer is some kind of rebel, expressing his private opinions and not a "party line." Orthodoxy, of whatever color, seems to demand a lifeless, imitative style. The political dialects to be found in pamphlets, leading articles, manifestos, White Papers and the speeches of undersecretaries do, of course, vary from party to party, but they are all alike in that one almost never finds in them a fresh, vivid, home-made turn of speech. When one watches some tired hack on the platform mechanically repeating the familiar phrases—*bestial atrocities, iron heel, blood-stained tyranny, free people of the world, stand shoulder to shoulder*—one often has a curious feeling that one is not watching a live human being but some kind of dummy: a feeling which suddenly becomes stronger at moments when the light catches the speaker's spectacles and turns them into blank discs which seem to have no eyes behind them. And this is not altogether fanciful. A speaker who uses that kind of phraseology has gone some distance towards turning himself into a machine. The appropriate noises are coming out of his larynx, but his brain is not involved as it would be if he were choosing his words for himself. If the speech he is making is one that he is accustomed to make over and over again, he may be almost unconscious of what he is saying, as one is when one utters the responses in church. And this reduced state of consciousness, if not indispensable, is at any rate favorable to political conformity.

14 In our time, political speech and writing are largely the defence of the indefensible. Things like the continuance of British rule in India, the Russian purges and deportations, the dropping of the atom bombs on Japan, can indeed be defended, but only by arguments which are too brutal for most people to face, and which do not square with the professed aims of political parties. Thus political language has to consist largely of euphemism, question-begging and sheer cloudy vagueness. Defenceless villages are bombarded from the air, the inhabitants driven out into the countryside, the cattle machine-gunned, the huts set on fire with incendiary bullets: this is called *pacification*. Millions of peasants are robbed of their farms and sent trudging along the roads with no more than they can carry: this is called *transfer of population* or *rectification of frontiers*. People are imprisoned for years without trial, or shot in the back of the neck or sent to die of scurvy in Arctic lumber camps: this is called *elimination of unreliable elements*. Such phraseology is needed if one wants to name things without calling up mental pictures of them. Consider for instance some comfortable English professor defending Russian totalitarianism. He cannot say outright: "I believe in killing off your opponents when you can get good results by doing so." Probably, therefore, he will say something like this:

15 "While freely conceding that the Soviet régime exhibits certain features which the humanitarian may be inclined to deplore, we must, I think, agree that a certain curtailment of the right to political opposition is an unavoidable concomitant of transitional periods, and that the rigors which the Russian people have been called upon to undergo have been amply justified in the sphere of concrete achievement."

16 The inflated style is itself a kind of euphemism. A mass of Latin words falls upon the facts like soft snow, blurring the outlines and covering up all the details. The great enemy of clear language is insincerity. When there is a gap between one's real and one's declared aims, one turns as it were instinctively to long words and exhausted idioms, like a cuttlefish squirting out ink. In our age there is no such thing as "keeping out of politics." All issues are political issues, and politics itself is a mass of lies, evasions, folly, hatred and schizophrenia. When the general atmosphere is bad, language must suffer. I should expect to find—this is a guess which I have not sufficient knowledge to verify—that the German, Russian and Italian languages have all deteriorated in the last ten or fifteen years, as a result of dictatorship.

17 But if thought corrupts language, language can also corrupt thought. A bad usage can spread by tradition and imitation, even among people who should and do know better. The debased language

that I have been discussing is in some ways very convenient. Phrases like *a not unjustifiable assumption, leaves much to be desired, would serve no good purpose, a consideration which we should do well to bear in mind*, are a continuous temptation, a packet of aspirins at one's elbow. Look back through this essay, and for certain you will find that I have again and again committed the very faults I am protesting against. By this morning's post I have received a pamphlet dealing with conditions in Germany. The author tells me that he "felt impelled" to write it. I open it at random, and here is almost the first sentence that I see: "[The Allies] have an opportunity not only of achieving a radical transformation of Germany's social and political structure in such a way as to avoid a nationalistic reaction in Germany itself, but at the same time of laying the foundations of a co-operative and unified Europe." You see, he "feels impelled" to write—feels, presumably, that he has something new to say—and yet his words, like cavalry horses answering the bugle, group themselves automatically into the familiar dreary pattern. This invasion of one's mind by ready-made phrases (*lay the foundations, achieve a radical transformation*) can only be prevented if one is constantly on guard against them, and every such phrase anaesthetizes a portion of one's brain.

I said earlier that the decadence of our language is probably curable. Those who deny this would argue, if they produced an argument at all, that language merely reflects existing social conditions, and that we cannot influence its development by any direct tinkering with words and constructions. So far as the general tone or spirit of a language goes, this may be true, but it is not true in detail. Silly words and expressions have often disappeared, not through any evolutionary process but owing to the conscious action of a minority. Two recent examples were *explore every avenue* and *leave no stone unturned*, which were killed by the jeers of a few journalists. There is a long list of flyblown metaphors which could similarly be got rid of if enough people would interest themselves in the job; and it should also be possible to laugh the *not un-* formation out of existence,* to reduce the amount of Latin and Greek in the average sentence, to drive out foreign phrases and strayed scientific words, and, in general, to make pretentiousness of unfashionable. But all these are minor points. The defence of the English language implies more than this, and perhaps it is best to start by saying what it does *not* imply. 18

To begin with it has nothing to do with archaism, with the salvaging of obsolete words and turns of speech, or with the setting up of 19

---

*One can cure oneself of the *not un-* formation by memorizing this sentence: *A not unblack dog was chasing a not unsmall rabbit across a not ungreen field.*

a "standard English" which must never be departed from. On the contrary, it is especially concerned with the scrapping of every word or idiom which has outworn its usefulness. It has nothing to do with correct grammar and syntax, which are of no importance so long as one makes one's meaning clear, or with the avoidance of Americanisms, or with having what is called a "good prose style." On the other hand it is not concerned with fake simplicity and the attempt to make written English colloquial. Nor does it even imply in every case preferring the Saxon word to the Latin one, though it does imply using the fewest and shortest words that will cover one's meaning. What is above all needed is to let the meaning choose the word, and not the other way about. In prose, the worst thing one can do with words is to surrender to them. When you think of a concrete object, you think wordlessly, and then, if you want to describe the thing you have been visualizing you probably hunt about till you find the exact words that seem to fit it. When you think of something abstract you are more inclined to use words from the start, and unless you make a conscious effort to prevent it, the existing dialect will come rushing in and do the job for you, at the expense of blurring or even changing your meaning. Probably it is better to put off using words as long as possible and get one's meaning as clear as one can through pictures or sensations. Afterwards one can choose—not simply *accept*—the phrases that will best cover the meaning, and then switch round and decide what impression one's words are likely to make on another person. This last effort of the mind cuts out all stale or mixed images, all prefabricated phrases, needless repetitions, and humbug and vagueness generally. But one can often be in doubt about the effect of a word or a phrase, and one needs rules that one can rely on when instinct fails. I think the following rules will cover most cases:

(i) Never use a metaphor, simile or other figure of speech which you are used to seeing in print.

(ii) Never use a long word where a short one will do.

(iii) If it is possible to cut a word out, always cut it out.

(iv) Never use the passive where you can use the active.

(v) Never use a foreign phrase, a scientific word or a jargon word if you can think of an everyday English equivalent.

(vi) Break any of these rules sooner than say anything outright barbarous.

These rules sound elementary, and so they are, but they demand a deep change of attitude in anyone who has grown used to writing in the style now fashionable. One could keep all of them and still write bad English, but one could not write the kind of stuff that I quoted in those five specimens at the beginning of this article.

I have not here been considering the literary use of language, but merely language as an instrument for expressing and not for conceal-ing or preventing thought. Stuart Chase and others have come near to claiming that all abstract words are meaningless, and have used this as a pretext for advocating a kind of political quietism. Since you don't know what Fascism is, how can you struggle against Fascism? One need not swallow such absurdities as this, but one ought to recognize that the present political chaos is connected with the decay of lan-guage, and that one can probably bring about some improvement by starting at the verbal end. If you simplify your English, you are freed from the worst follies of orthodoxy. You cannot speak any of the nec-essary dialects, and when you make a stupid remark its stupidity will be obvious, even to yourself. Political language—and with variations this is true of all political parties, from Conservatives to Anarchists— is designed to make lies sound truthful and murder respectable, and to give an appearance of solidity to pure wind. One cannot change this all in a moment, but one can at least change one's own habits, and from time to time one can even, if one jeers loudly enough, send some worn-out and useless phrase—some *jackboot, Achilles' heel, hotbed, melting pot, acid test, veritable inferno* or other lump of verbal refuse—into the dustbin where it belongs.

20

_____ **CONSIDERATIONS** _____

1. "Style is the man himself." How well, and in what ways, does Or-well's essay illustrate Buffon's aphorism? Select another author in the text, someone with a distinct style, and test it against Buffon's statement.

2. Assuming that Orwell's statement in paragraph 2, "the fight against bad English is not frivolous and is not the exclusive concern of professional writers," is the conclusion of a syllogism, reconstruct the major and minor premises of that syllogism by studying the steps Orwell takes to reach his conclusion.

3. Orwell documents his argument by quoting five passages by writers who wrote in the forties. From comparable sources, assemble a gallery of cur-rent specimens to help confirm or refute his contention that "the English lan-guage is in a bad way."

4. Orwell concludes with six rules. From the rest of his essay, how do you think he would define "anything outright barbarous" (in rule vi)?

5. Has Orwell broken some of his own rules? Point out and explain any examples you find. Look over his "Shooting an Elephant" and "A Hanging" as well as "Politics and the English Language."

6. In paragraph 16, Orwell asserts that "The inflated style is itself a kind of euphemism." Look up the meaning of "euphemism" and compile examples

from your local newspaper. Do you agree with Orwell that they are "swindles and perversions"? Note how Ambrose Bierce counts on our understanding of euphemisms in his Devil's Dictionary.

*Some of George Orwell's best essays, like "A Hanging"
and this one, derive from his experience as a colonial
police officer, upholder of law and order for the British
empire. Many political thinkers develop an ideology from
thought and theory; Orwell's politics grew empirically
from the life he lived. He provides us models for learning
by living—and for learning by writing out of one's life.*

67

GEORGE ORWELL
Shooting an Elephant

In Moulmein, in Lower Burma, I was hated by large numbers of 1
people—the only time in my life that I have been important enough
for this to happen to me. I was a sub-divisional police officer of the
town, and in an aimless, petty kind of way anti-European feeling was
very bitter. No one had the guts to raise a riot, but if a European
woman went through the bazaars alone somebody would probably spit
betel juice over her dress. As a police officer I was an obvious target
and was baited whenever it seemed safe to do so. When a nimble Burman tripped me on the football field and the referee (another Burman)
looked the other way, the crowd yelled with hideous laughter. This
happened more than once. In the end the sneering yellow faces of
young men that met me everywhere, the insults hooted after me when
I was at a safe distance, got badly on my nerves. The young Buddhist
priests were the worst of all. There were several thousands of them in
the town and none of them seemed to have anything to do except
stand on street corners and jeer at Europeans.

All this was perplexing and upsetting. For at that time I had al- 2
ready made up my mind that imperialism was an evil thing and the
sooner I chucked up my job and got out of it the better. Theoreti-
cally—and secretly, of course—I was all for the Burmese and all
against their oppressors, the British. As for the job I was doing, I hated

it more bitterly than I can perhaps make clear. In a job like that you see the dirty work of Empire at close quarters. The wretched prisoners huddling in the stinking cages of the lock-ups, the grey, cowed faces of the long-term convicts, the scarred buttocks of the men who had been flogged with bamboos—all these oppressed me with an intolerable sense of guilt. But I could get nothing into perspective. I was young and ill-educated and I had had to think out my problems in the utter silence that is imposed on every Englishman in the East. I did not even know that the British Empire is dying, still less did I know that it is a great deal better than the younger empires that are going to supplant it. All I knew was that I was stuck between my hatred of the empire I served and my rage against the evil-spirited little beasts who tried to make my job impossible. With one part of my mind I thought of the British Raj as an unbreakable tyranny, as something clamped down, in *saecula saeculorum*, upon the will of prostrate peoples; with another part I thought that the greatest joy in the world would be to drive a bayonet into a Buddhist priest's guts. Feelings like these are the normal by-products of imperialism; ask any Anglo-Indian official, if you can catch him off duty.

3   One day something happened which in a roundabout way was enlightening. It was a tiny incident in itself, but it gave me a better glimpse than I had had before of the real nature of imperialism—the real motives for which despotic governments act. Early one morning the sub-inspector at a police station the other end of town rang me up on the phone and said that an elephant was ravaging the bazaar. Would I please come and do something about it? I did not know what I could do, but I wanted to see what was happening and I got on to a pony and started out. I took my rifle, an old .44 Winchester and much too small to kill an elephant, but I thought the noise might be useful *in terrorem*. Various Burmans stopped me on the way and told me about the elephant's doings. It was not, of course, a wild elephant, but a tame one which had gone "must." It had been chained up, as tame elephants always are when their attack of "must" is due, but on the previous night it had broken its chain and escaped. Its mahout, the only person who could manage it when it was in that state, had set out in pursuit, but had taken the wrong direction and was now twelve hours' journey away, and in the morning the elephant had suddenly reappeared in the town. The Burmese population had no weapons and were quite helpless against it. It had already destroyed somebody's bamboo hut, killed a cow and raided some fruit-stalls and devoured the stock; also it had met the municipal rubbish van and, when the driver jumped out and took to his heels, had turned the van over and inflicted violences upon it.

4   The Burmese sub-inspector and some Indian constables were waiting for me in the quarter where the elephant had been seen. It was a very poor quarter, a labyrinth of squalid bamboo huts, thatched with

palmleaf, winding all over a steep hillside. I remember that it was a cloudy, stuffy morning at the beginning of the rains. We began questioning the people as to where the elephant had gone and, as usual, failed to get any definite information. That is invariably the case in the East; a story always sounds clear enough at a distance, but the nearer you get to the scene of events the vaguer it becomes. Some of the people said that the elephant had gone in one direction, some said that he had gone in another, some professed not even to have heard of any elephant. I had almost made up my mind that the whole story was a pack of lies, when we heard yells a little distance away. There was a loud, scandalized cry of "Go away, child! Go away this instant!" and an old woman with a switch in her hand came round the corner of hut, violently shooing away a crowd of naked children. Some more women followed, clicking their tongues and exclaiming; evidently there was something that the children ought not to have seen. I rounded the hut and saw a man's dead body sprawling in the mud. He was an Indian, a black Dravidian coolie, almost naked, and he could not have been dead many minutes. The people said that the elephant had come suddenly upon him round the corner of the hut, caught him with its trunk, put its foot on his back and ground him into the earth. This was the rainy season and the ground was soft, and his face had scored a trench a foot deep and a couple of yards long. He was lying on his belly with arms crucified and head sharply twisted to one side. His face was coated with mud, the eyes wide open, the teeth bared and grinning with an expression of unendurable agony. (Never tell me, by the way, that the dead look peaceful. Most of the corpses I have seen looked devilish.) The friction of the great beast's foot had stripped the skin from his back as neatly as one skins a rabbit. As soon as I saw the dead man I sent an orderly to a friend's house nearby to borrow an elephant rifle. I had already sent back the pony, not wanting it to go mad with fright and throw me if it smelt the elephant.

The orderly came back in a few minutes with a rifle and five cartridges, and meanwhile some Burmans had arrived and told us that the elephant was in the paddy fields below, only a few hundred yards away. As I started forward practically the whole population of the quarter flocked out of the houses and followed me. They had seen the rifle and were all shouting excitedly that I was going to shoot the elephant. They had not shown much interest in the elephant when he was merely ravaging their homes, but it was different now that he was going to be shot. It was a bit of fun to them, as it would be to an English crowd; besides they wanted the meat. It made me vaguely uneasy. I had no intention of shooting the elephant—I had merely sent for the rifle to defend myself if necessary—and it is always unnerving to have a crowd following you. I marched down the hill, looking and feeling a fool, with the rifle over my shoulder and an ever-growing army of people jostling at my heels. At the bottom, when you got away from the

5

huts, there was a metalled road and beyond that a miry waste of paddy fields a thousand yards across, not yet ploughed but soggy from the first rains and dotted with coarse grass. The elephant was standing eight yards from the road, his left side towards us. He took not the slightest notice of the crowd's approach. He was tearing up bunches of grass, beating them against his knees to clean them and stuffing them into his mouth.

6   I had halted on the road. As soon as I saw the elephant I knew with perfect certainty that I ought not to shoot him. It is a serious matter to shoot a working elephant—it is comparable to destroying a huge and costly piece of machinery—and obviously one ought not to do it if it can possibly be avoided. And at that distance, peacefully eating, the elephant looked no more dangerous than a cow. I thought then and I think now that his attack of "must" was already passing off; in which case he would merely wander harmlessly about until the mahout came back and caught him. Moreover, I did not in the least want to shoot him. I decided that I would watch him for a little while to make sure that he did not turn savage again, and then go home.

7   But at that moment, I glanced round at the crowd that had followed me. It was an immense crowd, two thousand at the least and growing every minute. It blocked the road for a long distance on either side. I looked at the sea of yellow faces above the garish clothes—faces all happy and excited over this bit of fun, all certain that the elephant was going to be shot. They were watching me as they would watch a conjuror about to perform a trick. They did not like me, but with the magical rifle in my hands I was momentarily worth watching. And suddenly I realized that I should have to shoot the elephant after all. The people expected it of me and I had got to do it; I could feel their two thousand wills pressing me forward, irresistibly. And it was at this moment, as I stood there with the rifle in my hands, that I first grasped the hollowness, the futility of the white man's dominion in the East. Here was I, the white man with his gun, standing in front of the unarmed native crowd—seemingly the leading actor of the piece; but in reality I was only an absurd puppet pushed to and fro by the will of those yellow faces behind. I perceived in this moment that when the white man turns tyrant it is his own freedom that he destroys. He becomes a sort of hollow, posing dummy, the conventionalized figure of a sahib. For it is the condition of his rule that he shall spend his life in trying to impress the "natives," and so in every crisis he has got to do what the "natives" expect of him. He wears a mask, and his face grows to fit it. I had got to shoot the elephant. I had committed myself to doing it when I sent for the rifle. A sahib has got to act like a sahib; he has got to appear resolute, to know his own mind and do definite things. To come all that way, rifle in hand, with two thousand people marching at my heels, and then to trail feebly away, having done nothing—no, that was impossible. The crowd would laugh at me. And my

whole life, every white man's life in the East, was one long struggle not to be laughed at.

But I did not want to shoot the elephant. I watched him beating his bunch of grass against his knees, with that preoccupied grand-motherly air that elephants have. It seemed to me that it would be murder to shoot him. At that age I was not squeamish about killing animals, but I had never shot an elephant and never wanted to. (Some-how it always seems worse to kill a *large* animal.) Besides, there was the beast's owner to be considered. Alive, the elephant was worth at least a hundred pounds; dead, he would only be worth the value of his tusks, five pounds, possibly. But I had got to act quickly. I turned to some experienced-looking Burmans who had been there when we ar-rived, and asked them how the elephant had been behaving. They all said the same things: he took no notice of you if you left him alone, but he might charge if you went too close to him. 8

It was perfectly clear to me what I ought to do. I ought to walk up to within, say, twenty-five yards of the elephant and test his behavior. If he charged, I could shoot; if he took no notice of me, it would be safe to leave him until the mahout came back. But also I knew that I was going to do no such thing. I was a poor shot with a rifle and the ground was soft mud into which one would sink at every step. If the elephant charged and I missed him, I should have about as much chance as a toad under a steam-roller. But even then I was not thinking particu-larly of my own skin, only of the watchful yellow faces behind. For at that moment, with the crowd watching me, I was not afraid in the or-dinary sense, as I would have been if I had been alone. A white man mustn't be frightened in front of "natives"; and so, in general, he isn't frightened. The sole thought in my mind was that if anything went wrong those two thousand Burmans would see me pursued, caught, trampled on and reduced to a grinning corpse like that Indian up the hill. And if that happened it was quite probable that some of them would laugh. That would never do. There was only one alternative. I shoved the cartridges into the magazine and lay down on the road to get a better aim. 9

The crowd grew very still, and a deep, low, happy sigh, as of peo-ple who see the theatre curtain go up at last, breathed from innumer-able throats. They were going to have their bit of fun after all. The rifle was a beautiful German thing with cross-hair sights. I did not then know that in shooting an elephant one would shoot to cut an imagi-nary bar running from ear-hole to ear-hole. I ought, therefore, as the elephant was sideways on, to have aimed straight at his ear-hole; actu-ally I aimed several inches in front of this, thinking the brain would be further forward. 10

When I pulled the trigger I did not hear the bang or feel the kick—one never does when a shot goes home—but I heard the devilish roar of glee that went up from the crowd. In that instant, in too short a 11 time, one would have thought, even for the bullet to get there, a mysterious, terrible change had come over the elephant. He neither stirred nor fell, but every line of his body had altered. He looked suddenly stricken, shrunken, immensely old, as though the frightful impact of the bullet had paralysed him without knocking him down. At last, after what seemed a long time—it might have been five seconds, I dare say—he sagged flabbily to his knees. His mouth slobbered. An enormous senility seemed to have settled upon him. One could have imagined him thousands of years old. I fired again into the same spot. At the second shot he did not collapse but climbed with desperate slowness to his feet and stood weakly upright, with legs sagging and head drooping. I fired a third time. That was the shot that did for him. You could see the agony of it jolt his whole body and knock the last remnant of strength from his legs. But in falling he seemed for a moment to rise, for as his hind legs collapsed beneath him he seemed to tower upward like a huge rock toppling, his trunk reaching skywards like a tree. He trumpeted, for the first and only time. And then down he came, his belly towards me, with a crash that seemed to shake the ground even where I lay.

12   I got up. The Burmans were already racing past me across the mud. It was obvious that the elephant would never rise again, but he was not dead. He was breathing very rhythmically with long rattling gasps, his great mound of a side painfully rising and falling. His mouth was wide open. I could see far down into caverns of pale pink throat. I waited a long time for him to die, but his breathing did not weaken. Finally I fired my two remaining shots into the spot where I thought his heart must be. The thick blood welled out of him like red velvet, but still he did not die. His body did not even jerk when the shots hit him, the tortured breathing continued without pause. He was dying, very slowly and in great agony, but in some world remote from me where not even a bullet could damage him further. I felt I had got to put an end to that dreadful noise. It seemed dreadful to see the great beast lying there, powerless to move and yet powerless to die, and not even to be able to finish him. I sent back for my small rifle and poured shot after shot into his head and down his throat. They seemed to make no impression. The tortured gasps continued as steadily as the ticking of a clock.

13   In the end I could not stand it any longer and went away. I heard later that it took him half an hour to die. Burmans were bringing dahs and baskets even before I left, and I was told they had stripped his body almost to the bones by the afternoon.

14   Afterwards, of course, there were endless discussions about the shooting of the elephant. The owner was furious, but he was only an Indian and could do nothing. Besides, legally I had done the right thing, for a mad elephant has to be killed, like a mad dog, if its owner fails to control it. Among the Europeans opinion was divided. The

older men said I was right, the younger men said it was a damn shame to shoot an elephant for killing a coolie, because the elephant was worth more than any damn Coringhee coolie. And afterwards I was very glad that the coolie had been killed; it put me legally in the right and it gave me sufficient pretext for shooting the elephant. I often wondered whether any of the others grasped that I had done it solely to avoid looking a fool.

____ CONSIDERATIONS _____

1. Some of Orwell's remarks about the Burmese make him sound like a racist; collect a half-dozen of them on a separate sheet of paper, then look for lines or phrases that counter the first samples. Discuss your findings, bearing in mind the purpose of Orwell's essay.

2. "In a job like that you see the dirty work of Empire at close quarters." If you ponder Orwell's capitalizing "Empire" (paragraph 2) and then substitute other abstract terms for "Empire"—say, Government, Poverty, War, Hatred—you may discover one of the most important principles of effective writing, a principle beautifully demonstrated by Orwell's whole account.

3. In paragraph 4, Orwell says, "the nearer you get to the scene of events the vaguer it becomes." Have you had an experience that would help you understand his remark? Would it hold true for the soldier caught in battle, a couple suffering a divorce, a football player caught in a pile-up on the line of scrimmage?

4. Some years after his experience in Burma, Orwell became a well-known opponent of fascism. How might shooting the elephant have taught him to detest totalitarianism?

5. "Somehow it always seems worse to kill a *large* animal," Orwell writes in paragraph 8. Why? Are some lives more valuable than others? See also "Very Like a Whale," by Robert Finch, page 200.

6. After two substantial paragraphs of agonizing detail, Orwell's elephant is still dying. Why does the writer inflict this punishment on the reader?

Noel Perrin (b. 1927) is Professor of Environmental Studies at Dartmouth College, where he was formerly Professor of English. He has written essays in scholarship, as well as articles about living in the country collected in a series of books beginning with First Person Rural *(1977). His most recent work is* Solo: Life with an Electric Car *(1992).* A Noel Perrin Sampler *appeared in 1991.*

68

NOEL PERRIN

A Book That Could Cure Suicide

1   The year is 1903. A thirteen-year-old boy in a little English town has started keeping a journal. At first it's practically all science. "Am writing an essay on the life-history of insects, and have abandoned the idea of writing on 'How Cats Spend Their Time,' " he notes. Later that year he takes a sort of vow to learn all about beetles.

2   The boy's name is Bruce Cummings, and he comes from a background as drab as his name. His father works for an obscure provincial newspaper, making just enough money to count as middle class. Nobody in that family goes to college. Everybody in it starts work young.

3   Bruce picked the wrong family to be born in. What *he* wants is first education—lots and lots of it, at the best schools—and then fame. He'd like to be a great biologist, preferably the greatest of his generation.

4   He knows he has the temperament. By the time he's fifteen, he is reading Darwin, dissecting leeches, teaching himself chemistry. At sixteen, when he catches measles, he can look at his own body with a calm scientific eye and note, "I have somewhere near 10,000 spots on me." He can look at his mind (he loves to do this—he is self-intoxicated) and suspect himself of genius. And all the time he is pouring thoughts into his journal. What he doesn't know yet is that he is an extraordinarily good writer.

But the English class system does not easily let go of people. 5
Eighty years ago, it hardly let go at all.

At barely seventeen, Bruce Cummings left school forever, and re- 6
luctantly signed what he called his Death Warrant—a five-year bond
of apprenticeship on his father's paper. Six days a week for five years
he must labor at what doesn't interest him. Being stubborn, he continued studying biology, physics, chemistry and German in the evenings,
and dissecting owls and frogs on Sundays. But he was trapped, and he
knew it.

There was one escape route. The British government supported a 7
tiny handful of scientific institutions. Staff jobs in them were filled by
competitive examination. Win the exam, and you got the job. Unfortunately for the self-educated, such exams were not open to just anybody. You had to be invited to take them. Ordinarily, smart young
graduates of Oxford, Cambridge, and London got invited, having been
nominated by their professors. No others need apply. But if a Devonshire apprentice could get nominated, he did have a right to sit the
exam.

The year he was twenty-one, Cummings managed to get a nomi- 8
nation. Three places were open in the British Museum of Natural History. He did pretty well for someone with no academic training—he
came in fourth.

The next year he did even better. There was another competi- 9
tion. Two jobs open. A roomful of eager university graduates, plus
Bruce Cummings, were there to take the exam.

He placed first by a wide margin. And so at twenty-two he 10
vaulted up in the social structure, moved to London, and became a scientist. "I'm in, in, in!" he writes in his journal. Soon his keen provincial eye is noting all the wonders of London. He begins to publish in
magazines like *The Journal of Botany* and *Science Progress*. He discovers Beethoven, and goes in ecstasy to hear Sir Henry Wood conduct the
Fifth. It's hard for someone in the radio-TV-VCR age even to imagine
the wonder of that evening. He drops his drab provincial name, and
flames out as W. N. P. Barbellion. (The whole name is charged with
significance. Besides its pleasing foreignness, Barbellion combines
"barbarian" and "rebellion." As for three initials, they were and still
are a class indicator in England—they indicate gentry. The three
names Barbellion hid behind those chaste initials . . . well, you'll see
later.)

This is a delightful success story, made still more delightful by 11
the fact that Barbellion was such a lively man. Many scientists are
brilliant, single-focused, and boring. Barbellion was brilliant, multi-
focused, and fascinating. From age sixteen on, his journal gradually expanded to include all the things that interested him.

12   For example, there were girls. Barbellion adored girls, both in the reverent Victorian fashion, and in every other fashion you can think of. He even adored them scientifically. Once in Devonshire he spent an evening with a girl named Mary, and achieved a modest degree of intimacy. Afterwards he wrote in his journal, "I hope to goodness she doesn't think I want to marry her. In the Park in the dark, kissing her. I was testing and experimenting with a new experience."

13   In London, he sits behind an Irish girl (and her date) in a theater. "She was dark, with shining blue eyes, and a delightful little nose of the utmost import to every male who should gaze upon her." They manage to exchange smiles—twice—and all night he can think of nothing else. Two days later a newspaper is indignantly refusing to run his ad trying to get in touch with her; they suspect he's recruiting prostitutes.

14   When he later gets engaged to Eleanor Benger, a young artist he truly reveres, he can be surprised to find that in the middle of what he calls a "devotional" embrace, a part of his mind is thinking, "Hot stuff, this witch." Few Englishmen allowed such thoughts to surface them, much less rushed home to record them in a diary.

15   If Barbellion had lived to be a Fellow of the Royal Society, an old professor with a knighthood, as he dreamed of doing, his journal would still be among the twenty or so best in English. Right up there with Thoreau, Pepys, and George Templeton Strong. But Barbellion didn't live. His knowledge that he wouldn't is what gives the journal its greatest poignancy. I have saved one aspect of his story until now. It is this aspect that led Barbellion to call his book *The Journal of a Disappointed Man*.

16   Back when he was twenty, still in Barnstaple, he got handed a second death warrant—and this was no metaphor for a disagreeable job, but a warrant in earnest. He had a terrible heart attack, and the doctor who saw him discovered that he'd been born with an incurable disease. He could expect to die at any time. Worse yet, if by chance he did live a while, he could expect to see his health gradually deteriorate. (He got his first slight partial paralysis at twenty-three, the same year that the sight of one eye was affected.)

17   From then until he actually did die, just after his thirtieth birthday, Barbellion reckoned his future in months, or at most single years. "I badly want to live say another twelve months," he wrote at age twenty-four, at a time when he was first deeply in love and first beginning to publish widely. It was not to be counted on.

18   Another man might have gone into depression, especially as the paralysis grew on him. Certainly Barbellion had his dark hours. And it is in that sense that this is the journal of a disappointed man.

19   But being who he was, he mostly responded by trying to cram fifty years of life into the little time he had. To an astonishing degree he succeeded. He did marry Eleanor (she knowing exactly what she

was getting into) and even had a child. He saw and embraced the whole life of his time. If he and Eleanor are staying on a farm, sitting together in a flowery glade exchanging kisses, he can still use his good eye to notice one of the farm hens wandering by in search of bugs and think from its point of view. "How nice to be a chicken in a field of Buttercups and see them as big as Sunflowers!" Or himself wandering through London, he can soar up and look at his fellow men and women from the heights—look in love, scorn, pity, and finally admiration, overcome with the drama of practically all lives, tender with the desire that all should be recorded, as in some great never-ending film of the cosmos. "If there be no living God to watch us, it's a pity for His sake as much as for our own."

This journal is one of the great affirmations in our literature. If I   20
had a friend who found life tedious, who was maybe even suicidal, and I had the power to make him or her read one book, it would be the soul-stirring diary of Wilhelm Nero Pilate Barbellion, alias plain Bruce Cummings.

____ **CONSIDERATIONS** _____

1. In what tense did Perrin write his essay? Discuss what you find.
2. Perrin's essay is a kind of book review, as is William McFeely's introduction to the *Memoirs of U.S. Grant,* page 330. What are some significant differences between the two pieces?
3. Perrin says in paragraph 10 that the young man's newly adopted name "is charged with significance." He then teases the reader by not revealing the whole name until the last line in the essay. What was Perrin counting on by *not* discussing what the initials W. N. P. stood for?
4. Use the quotation at the end of Perrin's paragraph 19 as the thesis for an essay.
5. Perrin describes Bruce Cummings' book as "one of the great affirmations in literature," the one book he would recommend to a friend in the depths of depression. Could you be as whole heartedly positive about a book you know? Describe and explain.

Ishmael Reed (b. 1938) was born in Tennessee. He has published eight novels, five books of poetry, and two essay collections. He has received awards from the National Institute of Arts and Letters, the American Civil Liberties Union, the National Endowment for the Arts, and the Guggenheim Foundation. New and Selected Poems *appeared in 1989. His most recent fiction is* Airing Dirty Laundry *(1994). "America: The Multinational Society" started its life in* San Francisco Focus.

69

ISHMAEL REED

America: The Multinational Society

> At the annual Lower East Side Jewish Festival yesterday, a Chinese woman ate a pizza slice in front of Ty Thuan Duc's Vietnamese grocery store. Beside her a Spanish-speaking family patronized a cart with two signs: "Italian Ices" and "Kosher by Rabbi Alper." And after the pastrami ran out, everybody ate knishes.
>
> (*New York Times*, 23 June 1983)

1   On the day before Memorial Day, 1983, a poet called me to describe a city he had just visited. He said that one section included mosques, built by the Islamic people who dwelled there. Attending his reading, he said, were large numbers of Hispanic people, forty thousand of whom lived in the same city. He was not talking about a fabled city located in some mysterious region of the world. The city he'd visited was Detroit.

2   A few months before, as I was leaving Houston, Texas, I heard it announced on the radio that Texas's largest minority was Mexican-American, and though a foundation recently issued a report critical of bilingual education, the taped voice used to guide the passengers on the air trams connecting terminals in Dallas Airport is in both Spanish and English. If the trend continues, a day will come when it will be

difficult to travel through some sections of the country without hearing commands in both English and Spanish; after all, for some western states, Spanish was the first written language and the Spanish style lives on in the western way of life.

Shortly after my Texas trip, I saw in an auditorium located on   3 the campus of the University of Wisconsin at Milwaukee as a Yale professor—whose original work on the influence of African cultures upon those of the Americas has led to his ostracism from some monocultural intellectual circles—walked up and down the aisle, like an old-time southern evangelist, dancing and drumming the top of the lectern, illustrating his points before some serious Afro-American intellectuals and artists who cheered and applauded his performance and his mastery of information. The professor was "white." After his lecture, he joined a group of Milwaukeeans in a conversation. All of the participants spoke Yoruban, though only the professor had ever traveled to Africa.

One of the artists told me that his paintings, which included   4 African and Afro-American mythological symbols and imagery, were hanging in the local McDonald's restaurant. The next day I went to McDonald's and snapped pictures of smiling youngsters eating hamburgers below paintings that could grace the walls of any of the country's leading museums. The manager of the local McDonald's said, "I don't know what you boys are doing, but I like it," as he commissioned the local painters to exhibit in his restaurant.

Such blurring of cultural styles occurs in everyday life in the   5 United States to a greater extent than anyone can imagine and is probably more prevalent than the sensational conflict between people of different backgrounds that is played up and often encouraged by the media. The result is what the Yale professor, Robert Thompson, referred to as a cultural bouillabaisse, yet members of the nation's present educational and cultural Elect still cling to the notion that the United States belongs to some vaguely defined entity they refer to as "Western civilization," by which they mean, presumably, a civilization created by the people of Europe, as if Europe can be viewed in monolithic terms. Is Beethoven's Ninth Symphony, which includes Turkish marches, a part of Western civilization, or the late nineteenth- and twentieth-century French paintings, whose creators were influenced by Japanese art? And what of the cubists, through whom the influence of African art changed modern painting, or the surrealists, who were so impressed with the art of the Pacific Northwest Indians that, in their map of North America, Alaska dwarfs the lower forty-eight in size?

Are the Russians, who are often criticized for their adoption of   6 "Western" ways by Tsarist dissidents in exile, members of Western civilization? And what of the millions of Europeans who have black

African and Asian ancestry, black Africans having occupied several countries for hundreds of years? Are these "Europeans" members of Western civilization, or the Hungarians, who originated across the Urals in a place called Greater Hungary, or the Irish, who came from the Iberian Peninsula?

7   Even the notion that North America is part of Western civilization because our "system of government" is derived from Europe is being challenged by Native American historians who say that the founding fathers, Benjamin Franklin especially, were actually influenced by the system of government that had been adopted by the Iroquois hundreds of years prior to the arrival of large numbers of Europeans.

8   Western civilization, then, becomes another confusing category like Third World, or Judeo-Christian culture, as man attempts to impose his small-screen view of political and cultural reality upon a complex world. Our most publicized novelist recently said that Western civilization was the greatest achievement of mankind, an attitude that flourishes on the street level as scribbles in public restrooms: "White Power," "Niggers and Spics Suck," or "Hitler was a prophet," the latter being the most telling, for wasn't Adolph Hitler the archetypal monoculturalist who, in his pigheaded arrogance, believed that one way and one blood was so pure that it had to be protected from alien strains at all costs? Where did such an attitude, which has caused so much misery and depression in our national life, which has tainted even our noblest achievements, begin? An attitude that caused the incarceration of Japanese-American citizens during World War II, the persecution of Chicanos and Chinese-Americans, the near-extermination of the Indians, and the murder and lynchings of thousands of Afro-Americans.

9   Virtuous, hardworking, pious, even though they occasionally would wander off after some fancy clothes, or rendezvous in the woods with the town prostitute, the Puritans are idealized in our schoolbooks as "a hardy band" of no-nonsense patriarchs whose discipline razed the forest and brought order to the New World (a term that annoys Native American historians). Industrious, responsible, it was their "Yankee ingenuity" and practicality that created the work ethic. They were simple folk who produced a number of good poets, and they set the tone for the American writing style, of lean and spare lines, long before Hemingway. They worshiped in churches whose colors blended in with the New England snow, churches with simple structures and ornate lecterns.

10   The Puritans were a daring lot, but they had a mean streak. They hated the theater and banned Christmas. They punished people in a cruel and inhuman manner. They killed children who disobeyed their parents. When they came in contact with those whom they considered

heathens or aliens, they behaved in such a bizarre and irrational manner that this chapter in the American history comes down to us as a late-movie horror film. They exterminated the Indians, who taught them how to survive in a world unknown to them, and their encounter with the calypso culture of Barbados resulted in what the tourist guide in Salem's Witches' House refers to as the Witchcraft Hysteria.

The Puritan legacy of hard work and meticulous accounting led 11 to the establishment of a great industrial society; it is no wonder that the American industrial revolution began in Lowell, Massachusetts, but there was the other side, the strange and paranoid attitudes toward those different from the Elect.

The cultural attitudes of that early Elect continue to be voiced in 12 everyday life in the United States: the president of a distinguished university, writing a letter to the *Times*, belittling the study of African civilizations; the television network that promoted its show on the Vatican art with the boast that this art represented "the finest achievements of the human spirit." A modern up-tempo state of complex rhythms that depends upon contacts with an international community can no longer behave as if it dwelled in a "Zion Wilderness" surrounded by beasts and pagans.

When I heard a schoolteacher warn the other night about the in- 13 vasion of the American educational system by foreign curriculums, I wanted to yell at the television set, "Lady, they're already here." It has already begun because the world is here. The world has been arriving at these shores for at least ten thousand years from Europe, Africa, and Asia. In the late nineteenth and early twentieth centuries, large numbers of Europeans arrived, adding their cultures to those of the European, African, and Asian settlers who were already here, and recently millions have been entering the country from South America and the Caribbean, making Yale Professor Bob Thompson's bouillabaisse richer and thicker.

One of our most visionary politicians said that he envisioned a 14 time when the United States could become the brain of the world, by which he meant the repository of all of the latest advanced information systems. I thought of that remark when an enterprising poet friend of mine called to say that he had just sold a poem to a computer magazine and that the editors were delighted to get it because they didn't carry fiction or poetry. Is that the kind of world we desire? A humdrum homogeneous world of all brains and no heart, no fiction, no poetry; a world of robots with human attendants bereft of imagination, of culture? Or does North America deserve a more exciting destiny? To become a place where the cultures of the world crisscross. This is possible because the United States is unique in the world: The world is here.

_____ **CONSIDERATIONS** _____

1. Reed's concluding sentence, "The world is here," runs, in one variation or another, through his essay as a sort of refrain. What, precisely, does he mean?

2. What word does Reed use in describing Adolph Hitler that might be seen as the antonym of Reed's term, "multinational"?

3. "America: the Multinational Society," in some ways, illustrates the difficulty of presenting broad, sweeping ideas in such a short essay. What is that difficulty and how does Reed attempt to avoid it?

4. Is it fair, as some have done, to stigmatize Reed as a rabble-rousing demagogue seeking to subvert the American way of life? Explain.

5. What is "bouillabaisse," and why is it such a useful metaphor in Reed's argument?

Bertrand Russell (1872–1970) was a philosopher and a leading intellectual figure of his times. As a modern philosopher, he was unusual because he wrote about matters of the moment—politics, education—as well as matters of lasting intellectual and mathematical interest. In 1950 he received the Nobel Prize for literature.

70

BERTRAND RUSSELL

Individual Liberty and Public Control

Society cannot exist without law and order, and cannot advance except through the initiative of vigorous innovators. Yet law and order are always hostile to innovations, and innovators are almost always to some extent anarchists. Those whose minds are dominated by fear of a relapse toward barbarism will emphasize the importance of law and order, while those who are inspired by the hope of an advance toward civilization will usually be more conscious of the need of individual initiative. Both temperaments are necessary, and wisdom lies in allowing each to operate freely where it is beneficent. But those who are on the side of law and order, since they are reinforced by custom and the instinct for upholding the *status quo*, have no need of a reasoned defense. It is the innovators who have difficulty in being allowed to exist and work. Each generation believes that this difficulty is a thing of the past, but each generation is tolerant only of *past* innovations. Those of its own day are met with the same persecution as if the principle of toleration had never been heard of. 1

On any matter of general interest, there is usually in any given community, at any given time, a received opinion, which is accepted as a matter of course by all who give no special thought to the matter. Any questioning of the received opinion arouses hostility, for a number of reasons. 2

3   The most important of these is the instinct of conventionality, which exists in all gregarious animals, and often leads them to put to death any markedly peculiar member of the herd. The next most important is the feeling of insecurity aroused by doubt as to the beliefs by which we are in the habit of regulating our lives. Whoever has tried to explain the philosophy of Berkeley to a plain man will have seen in its unadulterated form the anger aroused by this feeling. What the plain man derives from Berkeley's philosophy at a first hearing is an uncomfortable suspicion that nothing is solid, so that it is rash to sit on a chair or to expect the floor to sustain us. Because this suspicion is uncomfortable it is irritating, except to those who regard the whole argument as merely nonsense. And in a more or less analogous way any questioning of what has been taken for granted destroys the feeling of standing on solid ground, and produces a condition of bewildered fear.

4   A third reason which makes men dislike novel opinions is, that vested interests are bound up with old beliefs. The long fight of the Church against science, from Giordano Bruno to Darwin, is attributable to this motive, among others. The horror of socialism which existed in the remote past was entirely attributable to this cause. But it would be a mistake to assume, as is done by those who seek economic motives everywhere, that vested interests are the principal source of anger against novelties in thought. If this were the case, intellectual progress would be much more rapid than it is. The instinct of conventionality, horror of uncertainty, and vested interests, all militate against the acceptance of a new idea. And it is even harder to think of a new idea than to get it accepted: most people might spend a lifetime in reflection without ever making a genuinely original discovery.

5   In view of all these obstacles, it is not likely that any society at any time will suffer from a plethora of heretical opinions. Least of all is this likely in a modern civilized society, where the conditions of life are in constant rapid change, and demand, for successful adaptation, an equally rapid change in intellectual outlook. There should, therefore, be an attempt to encourage rather than discourage the expression of new beliefs and the dissemination of knowledge tending to support them. But the very opposite is in fact the case. From childhood upwards, everything is done to make the minds of men and women conventional and sterile. And if, by misadventure, some spark of imagination remains, its unfortunate possessor is considered unsound and dangerous, worthy only of contempt in time and peace and of prison or a traitor's death in time of war. Yet such men are known to have been in the past the chief benefactors of mankind, and are the very men who receive most honor as soon as they are safely dead.

6   The whole realm of thought and opinion is utterly unsuited to public control: it ought to be as free, and as spontaneous, as is possible to those who know what others have believed. The state is justified in insisting that children shall be educated, but it is not justified in forc-

ing their education to proceed on a uniform plan and to be directed to the production of a dead level of glib uniformity. Education, and the life of the mind generally, is a matter in which individual initiative is the chief thing needed; the function of the state should begin and end with insistence on *some* kind of education, and, if possible, a kind which promotes mental individualism, not a kind which happens to conform to the prejudices of government officials.

II

Questions of practical morals raise more difficult problems than   7
questions of mere opinion. The Thugs of India honestly believe it their duty to commit murders, but the government does not acquiesce. Conscientious objectors honestly hold the opposite opinion, and again the government does not acquiesce. The punishment of conscientious objectors seems clearly a violation of individual liberty within its legitimate sphere.

It is generally assumed without question that the state has a   8
right to punish certain kinds of sexual irregularity. No one doubts that the Mormons sincerely believed polygamy to be a desirable practice, yet the United States required them to abandon its legal recognition, and probably any other Christian country would have done likewise. Nevertheless, I do not think this prohibition was wise. Polygamy is legally permitted in many parts of the world, but is not much practiced except by chiefs and potentates. I think that in all such cases the law should intervene only when there is some injury inflicted without the consent of the injured person.

It is obvious that men and women would not tolerate having   9
their wives or husbands selected by the state, whatever eugenists might have to say in favor of such a plan. In this, it seems clear that ordinary public opinion is in the right, not because people choose wisely, but because any choice of their own is better than a forced marriage. What applies to marriage ought also to apply to the choice of a trade or profession: although some men have no marked preferences, most men greatly prefer some occupations to others, and are far more likely to be useful citizens if they follow their preferences than if they are thwarted by a public authority.

III

We may now arrive at certain general principles in regard to indi-   10
vidual liberty and public control.

The greater part of human impulses may be divided into two   11
classes, those which are possessive and those which are constructive or creative. Property is the direct expression of possessiveness; science

and art are among the most direct expressions of creativeness. Possessiveness is either defensive or aggressive: it seeks either to retain something against a robber, or to acquire something from a present holder. In either case, an attitude of hostility to others is of its essence.

12   The whole realm of the possessive impulses, and of the use of force to which they give rise, stands in need of control by a public neutral authority, in the interests of liberty no less than of justice. Within a nation, this public authority will naturally be the state; in relations between nations, if the present anarchy is to cease, it will have to be some international parliament. But the motive underlying the public control of men's possessive impulses should always be the increase of liberty, both by the prevention of private tyranny, and by the liberation of creative impulses. If public control is not to do more harm than good, it must be so exercised as to leave the utmost freedom of private initiative in all ways that do not involve the private use of force. In this respect, all governments have always failed egregiously, and there is no evidence that they are improving.

13   The creative impulses, unlike those that are possessive, are directed to ends in which one man's gain is not another man's loss. The man who makes a scientific discovery or writes a poem is enriching others at the same time as himself. Any increase in knowledge or good-will is a gain to all who are affected by it, not only to the actual possessor. Force cannot create such things, though it can destroy them; no principle of distributive justice applies to them, since the gain of each is the gain of all. For these reasons, the creative part of a man's activity ought to be as free as possible from all public control, in order that it may remain spontaneous and full of vigor. The only function of the state in regard to this part of the individual life should be to do everything possible toward providing outlets and opportunities.

14   Huge organizations, both political and economic, are one of the distinguishing characteristics of the modern world. These organizations have immense power, and often use their power to discourage originality in thought and action. They ought, on the contrary, to give the freest scope that is possible without producing anarchy or violent conflict.

15   The problem which faces the modern world is the combination of individual initiative with the increase in the scope and size of organizations. Unless it is solved, individuals will grow less and less full of life and vigor, more and more passively submissive to conditions imposed upon them. A society composed of such individuals cannot be progressive, or add much to the world's stock of mental and spiritual possessions.

16   Only personal liberty and the encouragement of initiative can secure these things. Those who resist authority when it encroaches

upon the legitimate sphere of the individual are performing a service to society, however little society may value it. In regard to the past, this is universally acknowledged; but it is no less true in regard to the present and the future.

____ **CONSIDERATIONS** _____

1. Russell writes at a high level of abstraction, suitable, most would agree, to the discussion of ideas themselves. He can thus quickly traverse large areas of thought, each of which, to be presented thoroughly, would require a book-length exposition. Especially when it seeks to convince the reader, there is an inevitable weakness in this kind of writing: the absence of concrete matter, that is, examples, illustrations, specifics. Explain why the absence of such material is, in fact, a weakness.

2. What does Russell mean by the phrase, "received opinion" in paragraph 2?

3. How does Russell account for the hostility aroused by any questioning of "received opinion"?

4. Does Russell place any limits on individual liberty?

5. "The creative impulses, unlike those that are possessive, are directed to ends in which one man's gain is not another man's loss," writes Russell in paragraph 12. He then argues that, contrary to the need for state control of the possessive impulses, "the only function of the state in regard to the creative part of the individual life should be to do everything possible toward providing outlets and opportunities." Can you provide examples of this function in the United States and of the state's violation of that function?

Edith Rylander (b. 1935) lives in Minnesota with her husband and three children in a house that she and her family built. Twice, she has been a Bush Arts Fellow for poetry. Rural Routes: Essays on Living in Rural Minnesota *appeared in 1993. She writes for the* Morrison County Record, *the* Long Prairie Leader, *and the* St. Cloud Daily Times. *We reprint two of her newspaper columns.*

_71_

EDITH RYLANDER
Picking Rock *and* Lambing

Picking Rock

1   John and Eric have picked some rock this spring, and one day Eric hired himself out to a neighbor for a day of rock picking. So far, they haven't needed my services. I don't know whether to feel good or bad about this. I've got lots of other things to do, and, no doubt about it, rock picking is hard work. On the other hand, there have been times when I've enjoyed picking rock.

2   I especially remember a day in early June a couple of years ago when we picked rock in the soybean field. The soybeans were big enough to be visible, small enough for the truck to straddle the rows without damage. It was a good day for the job—warm but with a breeze. The four of us, John and I and Shireen and Eric, moved out across the field to pick up the stones, every size from baseball up to basketball. We used pitchforks to help loosen the ones partly sunk in the ground; a few stones that were tombstone size we left for another day. We moved the truck forward a little when we had cleared a section of field. When we were done, we carried our near-truckload of

rocks over to the house and dumped most of them into the foundation footings for what is now our greenhouse.

I suppose rock picking must be as old as agriculture, at least in any rocky soil. Most of Minnesota was glacier country once, and glaciers leave not only lakes but rocks behind them. Frost brings rocks to the surface. No matter how many are picked each year, there always seems to be more next year. And when there's nothing else to do on the farm and the fields are open, one can always pick rock.   3

Picked rock is traditionally loaded onto a stone boat. I blinked several times the first time I heard the words "stone boat." Of course a stone boat isn't a boat made of stone, but a wheelless drag pulled by a tractor or, in the old days, by horses. But lots of people pick into pickups. Or they use a tractor pulling a hayrack or an old car hood equipped with chains and inverted.   4

Though there are mechanical rock pickers on the market, most rock picking is still not fully mechanized. As a result, it is somewhat communal and social: family units do it or half a dozen kids. Like hay baling, it produces a certain mild exhibitionism among the young, especially in warm weather. Boys strip to the waist "to keep cool." Girls wear shorts and halter-tops "to get a tan." Once I saw a young lady picking rock in a bright red bikini—sensible shoes on the feet, sensible chore gloves on the hands, not much between but bare young girl.   5

I've never heard any work songs for picking rock like the songs for and about picking and chopping cotton and hoeing corn. But John's maternal grandfather, a Swedish immigrant like all four of his grandparents, used to recite Norse sagas to his children while they picked rock.   6

The stone fences in Robert Frost's poem "Mending Wall" were undoubtedly an end product of rock picking. Maybe because a lot of Minnesota was broken to the plow after the introduction of barbed wire, we have no tradition of stone fences. But older barns sometimes have fieldstone foundations, and the hunting lodges wealthy men built for themselves up her in the twenties have fieldstone fireplaces.   7

Most fields in central Minnesota have piles of rocks in the corner, but these piles are nothing compared to the rock piles further north. Up in the pine country of Northern Minnesota, after the lumber companies cut off the white and Norway pines, land-hungry settlers bought cheap or homesteaded. Where the soil was stony, people have left permanent monuments, like crumbling fortifications—those great mounds and dikes of rock that they had cleared from their fields stone by stone. Some homesteaders are still there, managing in a country of short summers and forty-below winters. More have fought a losing battle trying to wring corn and rye and rutabagas and cream checks out of thin soil and have lost out to jack pines that retake land cleared by fire or the axe. The log cabins and barns and the saunas of   8 the Finns have crumbled away or have been buried in the brush, and almost nothing shows that anyone ever lived there but the nomadic Chippewa. A friend once showed me his grandparents' home farm, now in the Chippewa National Forest; nothing was left of the home-site but a well casing.

9   It's not possible to be too melancholy about those vanished farms. When the same land will grow straggly, yellow-leaved, waist-high corn or luxuriant hundred-and-fifty-foot trees, there is not much question about which crop better suits it. Most of that land is better growing what it now grows: pine and poplar and grouse and blueber-ries and white-tailed deer.

Lambing

1   Just before lambing, the ewes spend a lot of time lying around breathing heavily. They look like great bags of beige-grey wool, im-probably equipped with slim dark legs and melancholy, patient faces. Now and then the wool ripples or jerks as the unborn lambs kick in-side.

2   We have reached the time of year when it isn't sufficient to check the livestock morning and evening. It's 3:00 A.M., and I'm going out to check the ewes. Under winter stars I pick my way across the yard in thick, waffle-soled boots, crossing the icy patch by the end of the garage with caution, breaking through surface frost and sliding in greasy mud as I cross the driveway between the cattle shed and the pole barn.

3   I switch on the flashlight and count the sheep outside the corral. Ten, that's right. None in labor, so far as I can see. That leaves the two in the barn, the two we penned up because they'd been bred first.

4   As I open the door I can hear a hoarse, panting sound. I switch on the light. It's Granny, a big grey-nosed ewe in the second pen.

5   For a moment as she swings around, I am seeing something mon-strous. Granny is half squatting. In the cold night her nostrils jet stream. She's breathing harshly, making a pounding sound like a steam engine. Her muzzle is covered with froth and her teeth show. Below her pushing haunches, lurching as she strains to be delivered, is a slimy, dark lump.

6   I take one step closer, and the lump is a head—the head of a lamb still in its birth membrane, which puffs faintly in and out over the nostrils. I can see both ears. And a foot. One foot.

7   Lambs normally exit the intra-uterine world in the attitude of a diver, front feet under chin. I climb into the pen with Granny and pull the wool aside so I can see better. She flinches away, but I'm sure now.

There's only one foot out, which means the other front leg is hung up inside.

I've read through the section on deliveries in the book, the one   8
with the line drawings, one leg back, both legs back, hind legs presenting, back presenting, twins tangled together. I also have vivid memories of the ewe two years back that we found in this situation. I had read all the instructions in the book—how you reach in, how you move things around. But when I tried it that time the lamb wound up dead. It was nearly dead when we got there, and it was an enormous lamb. But it was my first try, and it failed.

I stand back. Granny is pushing with all her strength. I've never   9
seen an animal work like that. The head, breath faintly stirring the membrane, is still just where it was. Go in the house and wake up my husband? He could get her down and on her back, "cast" her, as they call it in the sheep book. It might make a delivery easier. But he's more tired than I am, he wakes up more easily and more often.

Granny heaves again. When she does that, my abdominal mus-   10
cles and lower back muscles tighten sympathetically. If this goes on much longer we may lose both ewe and lamb.

I step toward her, pretending a confidence I don't feel. She stands   11
when I touch her. I take a deep breath and slide my hand in.

The hot, slick inside of this different body clasps my hand with   12
alien muscles. What I feel doesn't seem to have much to do with those line drawings in the book, or with words. But this is neck, and what's this, shoulder? Pushing against the pelvic girdle? If I can just change the angle a little.

There's a little shifting, Granny's muscles are pushing down. I   13
yank my hand away, and now there are two legs out. Then a heave, and a lamb out to the hips. Then one more heave and the whole dark, glistening bag full of lamb is squirming on the straw.

I think about breaking the birth sack, stripping the membrane,   14
but Granny is licking the lamb off, tearing and eating away membrane. The lamb bleats. She answers, less a bleat than a reassuring mutter, cleaning forward along the body. The membrane comes away from the face.

Before all the membrane is off, the little black ewe lamb is up on   15
its knees, bleating like anything. Three-fourths of the way through the cleaning job, Granny delivers another lamb. I stand at the fence and watch, though there's nothing left for me to do, as Granny cleans and nuzzles and the lambs bleat and stagger around and look for milk. Two healthy little ewes.

I find I'm dozing against the fence. I stump back to the house,   16
wash my hands well, throw off my clothes, fall into bed. It's 4:20, and we have eleven ewes to go.

___ **CONSIDERATIONS** _____

Picking Rock

1. In what sense could Northern Minnesota farmers refer to their "rock crop"?

2. Why doesn't Rylander grieve over the abandoned farms in northern Minnesota?

3. Aside from the advantage of regaining a cleared field, is there anything else about picking rock to look forward to?

4. Compare and contrast Rylander's account with that of Maxine Kumin, "Building Fence," page 314.

Lambing

1. Although Rylander is dealing with the fundamental process of birth and the imminent possibility of death, and she finds herself identifying with the straining ewe, her writing style does not become dramatic. It remains terse, matter of fact, with a minimum of adjectives and adverbs. Why is such a style appropriate in this piece?

2. "Picking Rock" and "Lambing" have almost exactly the same number of words, yet the former has only nine paragraphs to the latter's sixteen. How do you account for that difference?

3. Are you attracted to the life of a farmer or repelled by Rylander's accounts of the work and the anxieties of life on a farm? Explain. See also Carol Bly's "Getting Tired," page 76, and Maxine Kumin's "Building Fence," page 314.

Don Sharp (b. 1938) was taught in Alaska, Hawaii, and Australia, and once owned and operated a garage in Pennsylvania called Discriminating Services. He now lives in Massachusetts, where he writes for magazines and works on old cars. This essay won the Ken Purdy Award for Excellence in Automobile Journalism in 1981.

72

DON SHARP
Under the Hood

The owner of this 1966 Plymouth Valiant has made the rounds of car dealers. They will gladly sell him a new car—the latest model of government regulation and industrial enterprise—for $8,000, but they don't want his clattering, emphysemic old vehicle in trade. It isn't worth enough to justify the paperwork, a classified ad, and space on the used-car lot. "Sell it for junk," they tell him. "Scrap iron is high now, and they'll give you $25 for it." 1

The owner is hurt. He likes his car. It has served him well for 90,000-odd miles. It has a functional shape and he can get in and out of it easily. He can roll down his window in a light rain and not get his shoulder wet. The rear windows roll down, and he doesn't need an air conditioner. He can see out of it fore, aft, and abeam. He can hazard it on urban parking lots without fear of drastic, insurance-deductible casualty loss. His teenage children reject it as passé, so it is always available to him. It has no buzzers, and the only flashing lights are those he controls himself when signaling a turn. The owner, clearly one of a vanishing tribe, brings the car to a kindred spirit and asks me to rebuild it. 2

We do not discuss the cost. I do not advertise my services and my sign is discreet. My shop is known by word of mouth, and those who spread the word emphasize my house rule: "A blank check and a free hand." That is, I do to your car what I think it needs and you pay for it; you trust me not to take advantage, I guarantee you good brakes, 3 sound steering, and prompt starting, and you pay without quarrel. This kind of arrangement saves a lot of time spent in making estimates and a lot of time haggling over the bill. It also imposes a tremendous burden of responsibility on me and on those who spread the word, and it puts a burden of trust on those who deliver their cars into my custody.

4   A relationship of that sort is about as profound as any that two people can enjoy, even if it lasts no longer than the time required to re-line a set of brakes. I think of hometown farmers who made sharecropping deals for the season on a handshake; then I go into a large garage and see the white-coated service writer noting the customer's every specification, calling attention to the fine print at the bottom of the work order, and requiring a contractual signature before even a brake-light bulb is replaced. I perceive in their transaction that ignorance of cause and effect breeds suspicion, and I wonder who is the smaller, the customer or the service writer, and how they came to be so small of spirit.

5   Under the hood of this ailing Valiant, I note a glistening line of seeping oil where the oil pan meets the engine block. For thousands of miles, a piece of cork—a strip of bark from a Spanish tree—has stood firm between the pan and block against churning oil heated to nearly 200 degrees, oil that sought vainly to escape its duty and was forced back to work by a stalwart gasket. But now, after years of perseverance, the gasket has lost its resilience and the craven oil escapes. Ecclesiastes allows a time for all things, and the time for this gasket has passed.

6   Higher up, between the block casting that forms the foundation of the engine and the cylinder-head casting that admits fresh air and exhausts oxidized air and fuel, is the head gasket, a piece of sheet metal as thin as a matchbook cover that has confined the multiple fires built within the engine to their proper domains. Now, a whitish-gray deposit betrays an eroded area from which blue flame spits every time the cylinder fires. The gasket is "blown."

7   Let us stop and think of large numbers. In the four-cycle engines that power all modern cars, a spark jumps a spark-plug gap and sets off a fire in a cylinder every time the crankshaft goes around twice. The crankshaft turns the transmission shaft, which turns the driveshaft, which turns the differential gears, which turn the rear axles, which turn the wheels (what could Aquinas have done with something like that, had he addressed himself to the source of the spark or the final destination of the wheels?). In 100,000 miles—a common life for modern engines—the engine will make some 260 million turns, and in half of those turns, 130 million of them, a gasoline-fueled fire with a maximum temperature of 2,000 degrees (quickly falling to about 1,200 degrees) is built in each cylinder. The heat generated by the fire raises

the pressure in the cylinder to about 700 pounds per square inch, if only for a brief instant before the piston moves and the pressure falls. A head gasket has to contend with heat and pressure like this all the time the engine is running, and, barring mishap, it will put up with it indefinitely.

This Plymouth has suffered mishap. I know it as soon as I raise   8 the hood and see the telltale line of rust running across the underside of the hood: the mark of overheating. A water pump bearing or seal gave way, water leaked out, and was flung off the fan blades with enough force to embed particles of rust in the undercoating. Without cooling water, the engine grew too hot, and that's why the head gasket blew. In an engine, no cause exists without an effect. Unlike a court of law, wherein criminals are frequently absolved of wrongdoing, no engine component is without duty and responsibility, and failure cannot be mitigated by dubious explanations such as parental neglect or a crummy neighborhood.

Just as Sherlock Holmes would not be satisfied with one clue if   9 he could find others, I study the oil filter. The block and oil pan are caked with seepings and drippings, but below the filter the caking is visibly less thick and somewhat soft. So: once upon a time, a careless service-station attendant must have ruined the gasket while installing a new oil filter. Oil en route to the bearings escaped and washed away the grime that had accumulated. Odds are that the oil level fell too low and the crankshaft bearings were starved for oil.

Bearings are flat strips of metal, formed into half-circles about as   10 thick as a matchbook and about an inch wide. The bearing surface itself—the surface that *bears* the crankshaft and that *bears* the load imposed by the fire-induced pressure above the piston—is half as thick. Bearing metal is a drab, gray alloy, the principal component of which is *babbitt*, a low-friction metal porous enough to absorb oil but so soft that it must be allowed to withstand high pressures. (I like to think that Sinclair Lewis had metallurgy in mind when he named his protagonist George Babbitt.) When the fire goes off above the piston and the pressure is transmitted to the crankshaft via the connecting rod, the babbitt-alloyed bearing pushes downward with a force of about 3,500 pounds per square inch. And it must not give way, must not be peened into foil and driven from its place in fragments.

Regard the fleshy end joint of your thumb and invite a 100-pound   11 woman (or a pre-teen child, if no such woman be near to hand) to stand on it. Multiply the sensation by thirty-five and you get an idea of what the bearing is up against. Of course, the bearing enjoys a favorable handicap in the comparison because it works in a metal-to-metal environment heated to 180 degrees or so. The bearing is equal to its task so long as it is protected from direct metal-to-metal contact by a layer of lubricating oil, oil that must be forced into the space between the bearing and the crankshaft against that 3,500 pounds of force. True, the oil gets a lot of help from hydrodynamic action as the spinning crankshaft drags oil along with it, but lubrication depends primarily on a pump that forces oil through the engine at around 40 pounds of pressure.

12   If the oil level falls too low, the oil pump sucks in air. The oil gets as frothy as whipped cream and doesn't flow. In time, oil pressure will fall so low that the "idiot" light on the dashboard will flash, but long before then the bearing may have run "dry" and suffered considerable amounts of its metal to be peened away by those 3,500-pound hammer blows. "Considerable" may mean only 0.005 inches, or about the thickness of one sheet of 75-percent-cotton, 25-pound-per-ream dissertation bond—not much metal, but enough to allow oil to escape from the bearing even after the defective filter gasket is replaced and the oil supply replenished. From the time of oil starvation onward, the beaten bearing is a little disaster waiting to spoil a vacation or a commute to an important meeting.

13   Curious, that an unseen 0.005 inches of drab, gray metal worthy only to inspire the name of a poltroonish bourgeois should enjoy more consequence for human life than almost any equal thickness of a randomly chosen doctoral dissertation. Life is full of ironies.

14   The car I confront does not have an "idiot" light. It has an old-fashioned oil-pressure gauge. As the driver made his rounds from condominium to committee room, he could—if he cared or was ever so alert—monitor the health of his engine bearings by noting the oil pressure. Virtually all cars had these gauges in the old days, but they began to disappear in the mid-'50s, and nowadays hardly any cars have them. In eliminating oil-pressure gauges, the car makers pleaded that, in their dismal experience, people didn't pay much attention to gauges. Accordingly, Detroit switched to the warning light, which was cheaper to manufacture anyway (and having saved a few bucks on the mechanicals, the manufacturer could afford to etch a design in the opera windows; this is called "progress"). Curious, in the midst of all this, that Chrysler Corporation, the maker of Plymouths and the victim of so much bad management over the past fifteen years, should have been the one car manufacturer to constantly assert, via a standard-equipment oil-pressure gauge, a faith in the awareness, judgment, and responsibility of drivers. That Chrysler did so may have something to do with its current problems.

15   The other car makers were probably right. Time was when most men knew how to replace their own distributor points, repair a flat tire, and install a battery. Women weren't assumed to know as much, but they were expected to know how to put a gear lever in neutral, set a choke and throttle, and crank a car by hand if the battery was dead. Now, odds are that 75 percent of men and a higher percentage of

women don't even know how to work the jacks that come with their cars. To be sure, a bumper jack is an abominable contraption—the triumph of production economies over good sense—but it will do what it is supposed to do, and the fact that most drivers cannot make one work says much about the way motorists have changed over the past forty years.

About all that people will watch on the downslide of this century 16 is the fuel gauge, for they don't like to be balked in their purpose. A lack of fuel will stop a car dead in its tracks and categorically prevent the driver from arriving at the meeting to consider tenure for a male associate professor with a black grandfather and a Chinese mother. Lack of fuel will stall a car in mid-intersection and leave dignity and image prey to the honks and curses of riffraff driving taxicabs and beer trucks, so people watch the fuel gauge as closely as they watch a pubescent daughter or a bearish stock.

But for the most part, once the key goes into the ignition, people 17 assign responsibility for the car's smooth running to someone else—to anybody but themselves. If the engine doesn't start, that's not because the driver has abused it, but because the manufacturer was remiss or the mechanic incompetent. (Both suspicions are reasonable, but they do not justify the driver's spineless passivity.) The driver considers himself merely a client of the vehicle. He proudly disclaims, at club and luncheon, any understanding of the dysfunctions of the machine. He must so disclaim, for to admit knowledge or to seek it actively would require an admission of responsibility and fault. To be wrong about inflation or the political aspirations of the Albanians doesn't cost anybody anything, but to claim to know why the car won't start and then to be proved wrong is both embarrassing and costly.

Few people would remove $500 from someone's pocket without 18 a qualm and put it in their own. Yet, the job-lot run of mechanics do it all the time. Mechanics and drivers are alike: they gave up worrying long ago about the intricacies and demands of cause and effect. The mechanics do not attend closely to the behavior of the vehicle. Rather, they consult a book with flow-charts that says, "Try this, and if it doesn't work, try that." Or they hook the engine up to another machine and read gauges or cathode-ray-tube squiggles, but without realizing that gauges and squiggles are not reality but only tools used to aid perception of reality. A microscope is also a wonderful tool, but you still have to comprehend what you're looking for; else, like James Thurber, you get back the reflection of your own eye.

Mechanics, like academics and bureaucrats, have retreated too 19 far from the realities of their tasks. An engine runs badly. They consult the book. The book says to replace part A. They replace A. The engine still runs badly, but the mechanic can deny the fact as handily as a socialist can deny that minimum-wage laws eventually lead to unemployment. Just as the driver doesn't care to know why his oil pressure drops from 40 to 30 to 20 pounds and then to zero, so the mechanic cares little for the casuistic distinctions that suggest that part A is in good order but that some subtle conjunction of wholesome part B with defective part C may be causing the trouble. (I don't know about atheists in foxholes, but I doubt that many Jesuits are found among incompetent mechanics.)

20   And why should the mechanic care? He gets paid in any event. From the mechanic's point of view, he should get paid, for he sees a federal judge hire academic consultants to advise about busing, and after the whites have fled before the imperious column of yellow buses and left the schools blacker than ever, the judge hires the consultants again to find out why the whites moved out. The consultant gets paid in public money, whatever effects his action have, even when he causes things he said would never happen.

21   Consider the garden-variety Herr Doktor who has spent a pleasant series of warm fall weekends driving to a retreat in the Catskills; his car has started with alacrity and run well despite a stuck choke. Then, when the first blue norther of the season sends temperatures toward zero, the faithful machine must be haggled into action and proceeds haltingly down the road, gasping and backfiring. "Needs a new carburetor," the mechanic says, and, to be sure, once a new carburetor is installed, the car runs well again. Our Herr Doktor is happy. His car did not run well; it got a new carburetor and ran well again; ergo, the carburetor was at fault. Q.E.D.

22   Curious that in personal matters the classic *post hoc* fallacy should be so readily accepted when it would be mocked in academic debate. Our Herr Doktor should know, or at least suspect, that the carburetor that functioned so well for the past several months could hardly have changed its nature overnight, and we might expect of him a more diligent inquiry into its problems. But "I'm no mechanic," he chuckles to his colleagues, and they nod agreeably. Such skinned-knuckle expertise would be unfitting in a man whose self-esteem is equivalent to his uselessness with a wrench. Lilies of the postindustrial field must concern themselves with weighty matters beyond the ken of greasy laborers who drink beer at the end of a workday.

23   Another example will illustrate the point. A battery cable has an end that is designed to connect to a terminal on the battery. Both cable-end and battery-terminal surfaces look smooth, but aren't. Those smooth surfaces are pitted and peaked, and only the peaks touch each other. The pits collect water from the air, and the chemistry of electricity-carrying metals causes lead oxides to form in the pits. The oxides progressively insulate the cable end and battery terminal from each other until the day that turning the key produces only a single, resounding *clunk* and no more. The road service mechanics installs a

new $75 battery and collects $25 for his trouble. Removing the cables from the old battery cleans their ends somewhat, so things work for a few days, and then the car again fails to start. The mechanic installs a $110 alternator, applies a $5 charge to the battery, and collects another $25; several days later he gives the battery another $5 charge, installs a $75 starter, and collects $25 more. In these instances, to charge the battery—to send current backwards from cable end to battery terminal—disturbs the oxides and temporarily improves their conductivity. Wriggling the charger clamps on the cable ends probably helps too. On the driver's last $25 visit, the mechanic sells another $5 battery charge and a pair of $25 battery cables. Total bill $400, and all the car needed was to have its cable ends and battery terminals cleaned. The mechanic wasn't necessarily a thief. Perhaps, like academic education consultants, he just wasn't very smart—and his ilk abound; they are as plentiful as the drivers who will pay generously for the privilege of an aristocratic disdain of elementary cause and effect in a vehicular electrical system.

24   After a tolerably long practice as a mechanic, I firmly believe that at least two-thirds of the batteries, starters, alternators, ignition coils, carburetors, and water pumps that are sold are not needed. Batteries, alternators, and starters are sold because battery-cable ends are dirty. A maladjusted or stuck automatic choke is cured by a new carburetor. Water pumps and alternators are sold to correct problems from loose fan belts. In the course of the replacement, the fan belt gets properly tightened, so the original problem disappears in the misguided cure, with mechanic and owner never the wiser.

25   I understand the venality (and laziness and ignorance) of mechanics, and understand the shop owner's need to pay a salary to someone to keep up with the IRS and OSHA forms. The shop marks up parts by 50 to 100 percent. When the car with the faulty choke comes in the door, the mechanic must make a choice: he can spend fifteen minutes fixing it and charge a half-hour's labor, or he can spend a half-hour replacing the carburetor (and charge for one hour) with one he buys for $80 and sells for $135. If the shop is a profit-making enterprise, the mechanic can hardly be blamed for selling the unneeded new carburetor, especially if the customer will stand still to be fleeced. Whether the mechanic acts from ignorance or larceny (the odds are about equal), the result is still a waste, one that arises from the driver's refusal to study the cause and effect of events that occur under the hood of his car.

26   The willingness of a people to accept responsibility for the machines they depend on is a fair barometer of their sense of individual worth and of the moral strength of a culture. According to popular reports, the Russian working folk are a sorrowfully vodka-besotted lot;

likewise, reports are that Russian drivers abuse their vehicles atrociously. In our unhappy country, as gauges for battery-charging (ammeters), cooling-water temperature, and oil pressure disappeared from the dashboards, they were replaced by a big-brotherly series of cacophonous buzzers and flashing lights, buzzers and lights mandated by regulatory edict for the sole purpose of reminding the driver that the government considers him a hopeless fool. Concurrent with these developments has come social agitation and law known as "consumer protection," which is, in fact, an extension of that philosophy that people are morons for whom the government must provide outpatient care. People pay handsome taxes to be taught that they are not responsible and do not need to be. This is a long way from what the Puritans paid their tithes for, and, Salem witch trials aside, the Puritans got a better product for their money.

27   What is astounding and dismaying is how quickly people came to believe in their own incompetence. In 1951, Eric Hoffer noted in *The True Believer* that a leader so disposed could make free people into slaves easier than he could turn slaves into free people (cf. Moses). Hoffer must be pained by the accuracy of his perception.

28   I do not claim that Everyman can be his own expert mechanic, for I know that precious few can. I do claim that disdain for the beautiful series of cause-and-effect relationships ("beautiful" in the way that provoked Archimedes to proclaim "Eureka!") that move machines, and particularly the automobile, measures not only a man's wit but also a society's morals.

____ CONSIDERATIONS _____

1. At the end of paragraph 4, Sharp poses a question. What sentence toward the end of his essay answers this question? Is that sentence the thesis of his essay? What do you think of his choice of a moral barometer?

2. What would James Thurber think of Sharp's use of "which" in paragraph 7? (See Thurber's short essay "Which.")

3. In paragraphs 10, 11, and 12, Sharp offers an exposition of a process. Study his success in explaining technical matters without lapsing into terminology too specialized for the general reader.

4. Sharp calls a particular device on the dashboard an "idiot light." Why? Connect this epithet with other ideas in his essay.

5. Sharp refers (in paragraph 9) to Sherlock Holmes's renowned skill in deduction, and (in paragraph 22) to a common logical fallacy called *post hoc ergo propter hoc*. Consult a good dictionary for the meaning of this Latin phrase.

6. Note Sharp's distinctive word choice throughout the essay. How do his words affect the tone?

Charles Simic (b. 1938) left Yugoslavia when he was fifteen to become a leading American poet. He has written two collections of essays and many volumes of poetry, of which A Wedding in Hell *(1994) is the most recent. In 1984 he was named a MacArthur Fellow, and he won the Pulitzer Prize for Poetry in 1990. He teaches at the University of New Hampshire. He wrote this essay for an issue of the literary magazine* Antaeus *devoted to the subject of food. Books of his essays are* Wonderful Words, Silent Truth *(1990) and* The Unemployed Fortune-Teller *(1994).*

73

CHARLES SIMIC
On Food and Happiness

Sadness and good food are incompatible. The old sages knew that   1
wine lets the tongue loose, but one can grow melancholy with even
the best bottle, especially as one grows older. The appearance of food,
however, brings instant happiness. A *paella*, a *choucroute garnie*, a
pot of *tripes à la mode de Caen*, and so many other dishes of peasant
origin guarantee merriment. The best talk is around that table. Poetry
and wisdom are its company. The true Muses are cooks. Cats and dogs
don't stray far from the busy kitchen. Heaven is a pot of chili simmer-
ing on the stove. If I were to write about the happiest days of my life,
many of them would have to do with food and wine and a table full of
friends.

> Homer never wrote on any empty stomach.
> —Rabelais

One could compose an autobiography mentioning every memo-   2
rable meal in one's life and it would probably make better reading
than what one ordinarily gets. Honestly, what would you rather have?
The description of a first kiss, or of stuffed cabbage done to perfection?

Reprinted by permission of the author.

469

3   I have to admit, I remember better what I ate than what I thought. My memory is especially vivid about those far-off days from 1944 to 1949 in Yugoslavia when we were mostly starving. The black market flourished. Women exchanged their wedding rings and silk underwear for hams. Occasionally someone invited us to an illicit feast on a day everyone else was hungry.

4   I'll begin with the day I realized that there was more to food than just stuffing yourself. I was nine years old. I ate Dobrosav Cvetkovic's *burek*, and I can still see it and taste it when I close my eyes.

5   *Burek* is a kind of pie made with fillo dough and stuffed with either ground meat, cheese, or spinach. It is eaten everywhere in the Near East and Balkans. Like pizza today, it's usually good no matter where you get it, but it can also be a work of art. My father said that when Dobrosav retired from his bakery in Skopje, the mayor and his cronies, after realizing that he was gone, sent a police warrant after him. The cops brought him back in handcuffs! "Dobrosav," they said visiting him in jail, "how can you do a thing like that to us? At least make us one last *burek*, and then you can go wherever your heart desires."

6   I ate that famous *burek* forty-four years ago on a cold winter morning with snow falling. Dobrosav made it illegally in his kitchen and sold it to select customers who used to knock on his door and enter looking like foreign agents making a pickup. The day I was his guest—for the sake of my poor exiled father who was so good to Dobrosav—the *burek* came with meat. I ate every greasy crumb that fell out of my mouth on the table while old Dobrosav studied me the way a cat studies a bird in a cage. He wanted my opinion. I understood this was no fluke. Dobrosav knew something other *burek* makers did not. I believe I told him so. This was my first passionate outburst to a cook.

7   Then there was my aunt, Ivanka Bajalović. Every time I wiped my plate clean she shook her head sadly. "One day," she'd say to me, "I'll make so much food you won't be able to finish it." With my appetite in those days that seemed impossible, but she did it! She found a huge pot ordinarily used to make soap and filled it with beans to "feed an army," as the neighbors said.

8   All Serbians, of whatever gender or age, have their own opinion as to how this dish ought to be made. Some folk like it thicker, others soupier. Between the two extremes there are many nuances. Almost everybody adds bacon, pork ribs, sausage, paprika, and hot peppers. It's a class thing. The upper classes make it lean, the lower fatty. My aunt, who was educated in London and speaks English with a British accent to this day, made it like a ditchdigger's wife. The beans were spicy hot.

My uncle was one of those wonders of nature everybody envies, a 9
skinny guy who could eat all day long and never gain any weight. I'm
sad to admit that I've no idea how much we actually ate that day.
Anywhere between three and five platefuls is a good guess. These
were European soup plates, nice and roomy, that could take loads of
beans. It was summer afternoon. We were eating on a big terrace
watched by nosy neighbors who kept score. At some point, I remember, I just slid off my chair onto the floor.

I'm dying, it occurred to me. My uncle was still wielding the 10
spoon with his face deep in the plate. There was a kind of hush. In the
beginning, everybody talked and kidded around, but now my aunt was
exhausted and had gone in to lie down. There were still plenty of
beans, but I was through. I couldn't move. Finally, even my uncle staggered off to bed, and I was left alone, sitting under the table, the heat
intolerable, the sun setting, my mind blurry, thinking this is how a pig
must feel.

On May 9, 1950, I asked all my relatives to give me money in- 11
stead of presents for my birthday. When they did, I spent the entire
day going with a friend from one pastry shop to another. We ate huge
quantities of cream puffs, custard rolls, *dobos torta*, rum balls,
pishingers, strudels with poppy seed, and other Viennese and Hungarian pastries. At dusk we had no money left. We were dragging ourselves in the general vicinity of the Belgrade railroad station when a
man, out of breath and carrying a large suitcase, overtook us. He wondered if we could carry it for him to the station and we said we could.
The suitcase was very heavy and it made a noise like it was full of sil-
verware or burglar's tools, but we managed somehow to get it to his
train. There, he surprised us by paying us handsomely for our good
deed. Without a moment's thought we returned to our favorite pastry
shop, which was closing at that hour and where the help eyed us with
alarm as we ordered more ice cream and cake.

In 1951, I lived an entire summer in a village on the Adriatic 12
coast. Actually, the house my mother, brother, and I roomed at was a
considerable distance from the village on a stretch of sandy beach. Our
landlady, a war widow, was a fabulous cook. In her home I ate squid
for the first time and began my lifelong long affair with olives. All her
fish was grilled with a little olive oil, garlic, and parsley. I still prefer it
that way.

My favorite dish was a plate of tiny surf fish called *girice*, which 13
were fried in corn flour. We'd eat them with our fingers, head and all.
Since it's no good to swim after lunch, all the guests would take a long
siesta. I remember our deliciously cool room, the clean sheets, the

soothing sound of the sea, the aftertaste and smell of the fish, and the long naps full of erotic dreams.

14   There were two females who obsessed me in that place. One was a theater actress from Zagreb in the room next to ours who used to sunbathe with her bikini top removed when our beach was deserted and I was hiding in the bushes. The other was our landlady's sixteen-year-old daughter. I sort of tagged along after her. She must have been bored out of her wits to allow a thirteen-year-old boy to keep her company. We used to swim out to a rock in the bay where there were wild grapes. We'd lie sunbathing and popping the little blue grapes in our mouths. And in the evening, once or twice, there was even a kiss, and then an exquisite risotto with mussels.

> He that with his soup will drink,
> When he's dead won't sleep a wink.
> —Old French Song

15   In Paris I went to what can only be described as a school for losers. These were youngsters who were not destined for further glories of French education, but were en route to being petty bureaucrats and tradespeople. We ate lunch in school, and the food was mostly tolerable. We even drank red wine. The vegetable soup served on Tuesdays, however, was out of this world. One of the fat ladies I saw milling in the kitchen must have been a southerner, because the soup had a touch of Provence. For some reason, the other kids didn't care for it. Since the school rule was that you had to *manger* everything in your plate, and since I loved the soup so much, my neighbors at the table would let me have theirs. I'd end up by eating three of four servings of that thick concoction with tomatoes, green and yellow beans, potatoes, carrots, white beans, noodles, and herbs. After that kind of eating, I usually fell asleep in class after lunch only to be rudely awakened by one of my teachers and ordered to a blackboard already covered with numbers. I'd stand there bewildered and feeling sleepy while time changed into eternity, and nobody budged or said anything, and my only solace was the lingering taste in my mouth of that divine soup.

16   Some years back I found myself in Genoa at an elegant reception in Palazzo Doria talking with the Communist mayor. "I love American food," he blurted out to me after I mentioned enjoying the local cuisine. I asked him what he had in mind. "I love potato chips," he told me. I had to agree, potato chips were pretty good.

17   When we came to the United States in 1954, it now seems like that's all my brother and I ate. We sat in front of the TV eating potato chips out of huge bags. Our parents approved. We were learning Eng-

lish and being American. It's a wonder we have any teeth left today. We visited the neighborhood supermarket twice a day to sightsee the junk food. There were so many things to taste, and we were interested in them all. There was deviled ham, marshmallows, Spam, Hawaiian Punch, Fig Newtons, V-8 Juice, Mounds, Planter's Peanuts, and so much else, all good. Everything was good in America except for Wonder Bread, which we found disgusting.

It took me a few years to come to my sense. One day I met Salvatore. He told me I ate like a dumb shit, and took me home to his mother. Sal and his three brothers were all well-employed, unmarried, living at home, and giving their paychecks to Mom. The father was dead, so there were just these four boys to feed. She did not stop cooking. Every meal was like a peasant wedding feast. Of course, her sons didn't appreciate it as far as she was concerned. "Are you crazy, Mom?" they'd shout in a chorus each time she brought in another steaming dish. The old lady didn't flinch. The day I came she was happy to have someone else at the table who was more appreciative, and I did not spare the compliments.   18

She cooked southern Italian dishes. Lots of olive oil and garlic. I recollect with a sense of heightened consciousness her linguine with anchovies. We drank red Sicilian wine with it. She'd put several open bottles on the table before the start of the meal. I never saw anything like it. She'd lie to us and say there was nothing more to eat so we'd have at least two helpings, and then she'd bring some sausage and peppers, and some kind of roast after that.   19

After the meal we'd remain at the table, drinking and listening to old records of Beniamino Gigli and Feruccio Tagliavini. The old lady would still be around, urging on us a little more cheese, a little more cake. And then, just when we thought she had given up and gone to bed, she'd surprise us by bringing out a dish of fresh figs.   20

My late father, who never in his life refused another helping at the table, had a peculiarity common among gastronomes. The more he ate the more he talked about food. My mother was always amazed. We'd be done with a huge turkey roasted over sauerkraut and my father would begin reminiscing about a little breakfast-like sausage he had in some village on the Rumanian border in 1929, or a fish soup a blind woman made for him in Marseilles in 1945. Well, she wasn't completely blind, and besides she was pretty to look at—in any case, after three or four stories like that we'd be hungry again. My father had a theory that if you were still hungry, say for a hot dog, after a meal at Lutece, that meant that you were extraordinarily healthy. If a casual visitor to your house was not eating and drinking three minutes after his arrival, you had no manners. For people who had no interest in food, he absolutely had no comprehension. He'd ask them   21 questions like an anthropologist, and go away seriously puzzled and worried. He told me toward the end of his life that the greatest mistake he ever made was accepting his doctor's advice to eat and drink less after he passed seventy-five. He felt terrible until he went back to his old ways.

22   One day we are walking up Second Avenue and talking. We get into an elaborate philosophical argument, as we often did. I feel like I've understood everything! I'm inspired! I'm quoting Kant, Descartes, Wittgenstein, when I notice he's no longer with me. I look around and locate him a block back staring into a shop window. I'm kind of pissed, especially since I have to walk to where he's standing, for he doesn't move or answer to my shouts. Finally, I tap him on the shoulder and he looks at me, dazed. "Can you believe that?" he says and points to a window full of Hungarian smoked sausages, salamis, and pork rinds.

23   My friend, Mike De Porte, whose grandfather was a famous St. Petersburg lawyer and who in his arguments combines a Dostoevskian probity and his grandfather's jurisprudence, claims that such obsession with food is the best proof that we have of the existence of the soul. Ergo, long after the body is satisfied, the soul is not. "Does that mean," I asked him, "that the soul is never satisfied?" He has not given me his answer yet. My own notion is that it is a supreme sign of happiness. When our souls are happy, they talk about food.

____ CONSIDERATIONS _____

1. "I have to admit," writes Simic in paragraph 3, "I remember better what I ate than what I thought." Discuss in an essay how remembered tastes, smells, textures, colors, or shapes sometimes become powerful influences on our feelings, understandings, or behavior.

2. Does Simic's essay provide sufficient support for his thesis statement?

3. Why does Simic italicize words like *paella, choucroute, garnie, tripes à la mode de Caen, burek, dobos torta,* and so on? How do you show italics in a typed manuscript?

4. In what ways are eating customs keys—or, at least, introductions—to different cultures?

5. How do you think Simic would respond to the old question, "Do we eat to live or live to eat?"

Gary Soto (b. 1952) was born in Fresno and teaches at the University of California in Berkeley. He has published many books of poems—including The Elements of San Joaquin *(1977) and* Black Hair *(1985)—and more recently has written essays and reminiscence out of the Chicano experience, as well as fiction for children. This memoir comes from* A Summer Life *(1990).*

74

GARY SOTO

The Grandfather

Grandfather believed a well-rooted tree was the color of money. His money he kept hidden behind portraits of sons and daughters or taped behind the calendar of an Aztec warrior. He tucked it into the sofa, his shoes and slippers, and into the tight-lipped pockets of his suits. He kept it in his soft brown wallet that was machine tooled with "MEXICO" and a campesino and donkey climbing a hill. He had climbed, too, out of Mexico, settled in Fresno and worked thirty years at Sun Maid Raisin, first as a packer and later, when he was old, as a watchman with a large clock on his belt. 1

After work, he sat in the backyard under the arbor, watching the water gurgle in the rose bushes that ran along the fence. A lemon tree hovered over the clothesline. Two orange trees stood near the alley. His favorite tree, the avocado, which had started in a jam jar from a seed and three toothpicks lanced in its sides, rarely bore fruit. He said it was the wind's fault, and the mayor's, who allowed office buildings so high that the haze of pollen from the countryside could never find its way into the city. He sulked about this. He said that in Mexico buildings only grew so tall. You could see the moon at night, and the stars were clear points all the way to the horizon. And wind reached all the way from the sea, which was blue and clean, unlike the oily water sloshing against a San Francisco pier. 2

3   During its early years, I could leap over that tree, kick my bicycling legs over the top branch and scream my fool head off because I thought for sure I was flying. I ate fruit to keep my strength up, fuzzy peaches and branch-scuffed plums cooled in the refrigerator. From the kitchen chair he brought out in the evening, Grandpa would scold, "Hijo, what's the matta with you? You gonna break it."

4   By the third year, the tree was as tall as I, its branches casting a meager shadow on the ground. I sat beneath the shade, scratching words in the hard dirt with a stick. I had learned "Nile" in summer school and a dirty word from my brother who wore granny sunglasses. The red ants tumbled into my letters, and I buried them, knowing that they would dig themselves back into fresh air.

5   A tree was money. If a lemon cost seven cents at Hanoian's Market, then Grandfather saved fistfuls of change and more because in winter the branches of his lemon tree hung heavy yellow fruit. And winter brought oranges, juicy and large as softballs. Apricots he got by the bagfuls from a son, who himself was wise for planting young. Peaches he got from a neighbor, who worked the night shift at Sun Maid Raisin. The chile plants, which also saved him from giving up his hot, sweaty quarters, were propped up with sticks to support an abundance of red fruit.

6   But his favorite tree was the avocado because it offered hope and the promise of more years. After work, Grandpa sat in the back yard, shirtless, tired of flagging trucks loaded with crates of raisins, and sipped glasses of ice water. His yard was neat: five trees, seven rose bushes, whose fruit were the red and white flowers he floated in bowls, and a statue of St. Francis that stood in a circle of crushed rocks, arms spread out to welcome hungry sparrows.

7   After ten years, the first avocado hung on a branch, but the meat was flecked with black, an omen, Grandfather thought, a warning to keep an eye on the living. Five years later, another avocado hung on a branch, larger than the first and edible when crushed with a fork into a heated tortilla. Grandfather sprinkled it with salt and laced it with a river of chile.

8   "It's good," he said, and let me taste.

9   I took a big bite, waved a hand over my tongue, and ran for the garden hose gurgling in the rose bushes. I drank long and deep, and later ate the smile from an ice cold watermelon.

10   Birds nested in the tree, quarreling jays with liquid eyes and cool, pulsating throats. Wasps wove a horn-shaped hive one year, but we smoked them away with swords of rolled up newspapers lit with matches. By then, the tree was tall enough for me to climb to look into the neighbor's yard. But by then I was too old for that kind of thing and went about with my brother, hair slicked back and our shades dark as oil.

After twenty years, the tree began to bear. Although Grandfather 11
complained about how much he lost because pollen never reached the
poor part of town, because at the market he had to haggle over the
price of avocados, he loved that tree. It grew, as did his family, and
when he died, all his sons standing on each other's shoulders, oldest to
youngest, could not reach the highest branches. The wind could move
the branches, but the trunk, thicker than any waist, hugged the
ground.

_____ **CONSIDERATIONS** _____

1. In what sense could one say that Soto's essay is a tribute to his grandfather?

2. Select for study a few examples of Soto's use of figurative language.
Then create some of your own in a short essay on a member of your family.

3. What evidence do you find that Soto has _not_ romanticized his childhood?

4. What was there about the tree's first avocado that made the grandfather think neither old men nor growing boys were angels?

5. Why are there so many references to money in Soto's essay?

75

WILLIAM STAFFORD
A Way of Writing

1   A writer is not so much someone who has something to say as he is someone who has found a process that will bring about new things he would not have thought of if he had not started to say them. That is, he does not draw on a reservoir; instead, he engages in an activity that brings to him a whole succession of unforeseen stories, poems, essays, plays, laws, philosophies, religions, or—but wait!

2   Back in school, from the first when I began to try to write things, I felt this richness. One thing would lead to another; the world would give and give. Now, after twenty years or so of trying, I live by that certain richness, an idea hard to pin, difficult to say, and perhaps offensive to some. For there are strange implications in it.

3   One implication is the importance of just plain receptivity. When I write, I like to have an interval before me when I am not likely to be interrupted. For me, this means usually the early morning, be-

From *Field: Contemporary Poetry and Poetics*, #2 Spring 1970. Reprinted by permission of *Field*. Oberlin College, Oberlin, Ohio.

fore others are awake. I get pen and paper, take a glance out the window (often it is dark out there), and wait. It is like fishing. But I do not wait very long, for there is always a nibble—and this is where receptivity comes in. To get started I will accept anything that occurs to me. Something always occurs, of course, to any of us. We can't keep from thinking. Maybe I have to settle for an immediate impression: it's cold, or hot, or dark, or bright, or in between! Or—well, the possibilities are endless. If I put down something, that thing will help the next thing come, and I'm off. If I let the process go on, things will occur to me that were not at all in my mind when I started. These things, odd or trivial as they may be, are somehow connected. And if I let them string out, surprising things will happen.

If I let them string out. . . . Along with initial receptivity, then,   4 there is another readiness: I must be willing to fail. If I am to keep on writing, I cannot bother to insist on high standards. I must get into action and not let anything stop me, or even slow me much. By "standards" I do not mean "correctness"—spelling, punctuation, and so on. These details become mechanical for anyone who writes for awhile. I am thinking about what many people would consider "important" standards, such matters as social significance, positive values, consistency, etc. I resolutely disregard these. Something better, greater, is happening! I am following a process that leads so wildly and originally into new territory that no judgment can at the moment be made about values, significance, and so on. I am making something new, something that has not been judged before. Later others—and maybe I myself—will make judgments. Now, I am headlong to discover. Any distraction may harm the creating.

So, receptive, careless of failure, I spin out things on the page.   5 And a wonderful freedom comes. If something occurs to me, it is all right to accept it. It has one justification: it occurs to me. No one else can guide me. I must follow my own weak, wandering, diffident impulses.

A strange bonus happens. At times, without my insisting on it,   6 my writings become coherent; the successive elements that occur to me are clearly related. They lead by themselves to new connections. Sometimes the language, even the syllables that happen along, may start a trend. Sometimes the materials alert me to something waiting in my mind, ready for sustained attention. At such times, I allow myself to be eloquent, or intentional, or for great swoops (treacherous! not to be trusted!) reasonable. But I do not insist on any of that; for I know that back of my activity there will be the coherence of my self, and that indulgence of my impulses will bring recurrent patterns and meanings again.

This attitude toward the process of writing creatively suggests a   7 problem for me, in terms of what others say. They talk about "skills" in writing. Without denying that I do have experience, wide reading, automatic orthodoxies and maneuvers of various kinds, I still must insist that I am often baffled about what "skill" has to do with the precious little area of confusion when I do not know what I am going to say and then I find out what I am going to say. That precious interval I am unable to bridge by skill. What can I witness about it? It remains mysterious, just as all of us must feel puzzled about how we are so inventive as to be able to talk along through complexities with our friends, not needing to plan what we are going to say, but never stalled for long in our confident forward progress. Skill? If so, it is the skill we all have, something we must have learned before the age of three or four.

8   A writer is one who has become accustomed to trusting that grace, or luck, or—skill.

9   Yet another attitude I find necessary: most of what I write, like most of what I say in casual conversation, will not amount to much. Even I will realize, and even at the time, that it is not negotiable. It will be like practice. In conversation I allow myself random remarks—in fact, as I recall, that is the way I learned to talk—, so in writing I launch many expendable efforts. A result of this free way of writing is that I am not writing for others, mostly; they will not see the product at all unless the activity eventuates in something that later appears to be worthy. My guide is the self, and its adventuring in the language brings about communications.

10   This process-rather-than-substance view of writing invites a final, dual reflection:

1. Writers may not be special—sensitive or talented in any usual sense. They are simply engaged in sustained use of a language skill we all have. Their "creations" come about through confident reliance on stray impulses that will, with trust, find occasional patterns that are satisfying.
2. But writing itself is one of the great, free human activities. There is scope for individuality, and elation, and discovery, in writing. For the person who follows with trust and forgiveness what occurs to him, the world remains always ready and deep, an inexhaustible environment, with the combined vividness of an actuality and flexibility of a dream. Working back and forth between experience and thought, writers have more than space and time can offer. They have the whole unexplored realm of human vision.

15 December 1969

A sample daily-writing sheet and the poem as revised.

```
                    Shadows
                       I
Out in places like Wyoming some of the shadows

are cut out and pasted on fossils.

There are mountains that erode when
clouds drag across them.  You can hear  the tick

         of the light breaking edges off white stones.

           a
At         fountain on Main Street I saw

our shadow.  It did not drink but

waited on cement and water while I drank.

There were two people and but one shadow.

I looked up so hard outward that a bird

flying past made a shadow on the sky. ✗


There is a place in the air where our house

used to be.


Once I crawled through grassblades to hear

the sounds of their shadows. One of the shadows

moved, and it was the earth where a mole

was passing.  I could hear little

paws in the dirt, and fur brush along

the tunnel, and even, somehow, the mole shadow.

                where
In churches        hearts pump sermons

from wells full of shadows.

      In my prayers I let yesterday begin

      and then go behind this hour now,
```

Shadows

Out in places like Wyoming some of the shadows
are cut out and pasted on fossils.
There are mountains that erode when
clouds drag across them. You hear the tick
of sunlight breaking edges off white stones.

5

At a fountain on Main Street I saw
our shadow. It did not drink but
waited on cement and water while I drank.
There were two people and but one shadow.
I looked up so hard outward that a bird   10
flying past made a shadow on the sky.
There is a place in the air where
our old house used to be.

Once I crawled through grassblades to hear
the sounds of their shadows. One shadow   15
moved, and it was the earth where a mole
was passing. I could hear little
paws in the dirt, and fur brush along
the tunnel, and even, somehow, the mole shadow.

In my prayers I let yesterday begin   20
and then go behind this hour now,
in churches where hearts pump sermons
from wells full of shadows.

____ CONSIDERATIONS _____

1. Stafford is clearly and openly talking about himself—how *he* writes, what writing means to *him*—and yet most readers agree that he successfully avoids the egotism or self-consciousness that sours many first-person essays. Compare his style with three or four other first-person pieces in this book to see how he does it.

2. In his first paragraph, Stafford tells of an idea that might be called writing as discovery. Thinking back through your own writing, can you recall this experience—when, after struggling to write an essay or letter that you *had* to write, you discovered something you *wanted* to write? What did you do about it? More important, what might you do next time it happens?

3. What, according to Stafford, is more important to a writer than "social significance, or positive values, or consistency"?

4. Stafford is talking about writing a poem. How do his discoveries and conclusions bear on *your* problems in writing an essay? Be specific.

5. Do the opening and closing paragraphs differ in style? If so, what is the difference, and why does Stafford allow it?

6. Study the three versions of Stafford's poem "Shadows." Do you find anything that belies the easygoing impression his essay gives of Stafford at work? Explain.

7. Compare Stafford's advice with the suggestions of other authors in the text who talk about writing: Sven Birkerts, Joan Didion, Ralph Ellison, or Alice Walker. What advice is most relevant to your current writing tasks?

Brent Staples (b. 1951) is Assistant Metropolitan Editor at the New York Times. He grew up in Chester, Pennsylvania, and received his Ph.D. in psychology at the University of Chicago. He taught briefly, then worked for several magazines and newspapers, including the Chicago Sun-Times, *before moving to New York. "Just Walk On By" appeared in* Ms. *magazine in 1986. He published* Parallel Time: Growing up in Black and White *in 1994.*

76

BRENT STAPLES

Just Walk On By

1   My first victim was a woman—white, well-dressed, probably in her early twenties. I came upon her late one evening on a deserted street in Hyde Park, a relatively affluent neighborhood in an otherwise mean, impoverished section of Chicago. As I swung onto the avenue behind her, there seemed to be a discreet, uninflammatory distance between us. Not so. She cast back a worried glance. To her, the youngish black man—a broad six feet two inches with a beard and billowing hair, both hands shoved into the pockets of a bulky military jacket—seemed menacingly close. After a few more quick glimpses, she picked up her pace and was soon running in earnest. Within seconds she disappeared into a cross street.

2   That was more than a decade ago. I was 22 years old, a graduate student newly arrived at the University of Chicago. It was in the echo of that terrified woman's footfalls that I first began to know the unwieldy inheritance I'd come into—the ability to alter public space in ugly ways. It was clear that she thought herself the quarry of a mugger, a rapist, or worse. Suffering a bout of insomnia, however, I was stalking sleep, not defenseless wayfarers. As a softy who is scarcely able to take a knife to a raw chicken—let alone hold it to a person's throat—I was surprised, embarrassed, and dismayed all at once. Her flight made me feel like an accomplice in tyranny. It also made it clear that I was indistinguishable from the muggers who occasionally

_____
Reprinted by permission of the author.

seeped into the area from the surrounding ghetto. That first encounter, and those that followed, signified that a vast, unnerving gulf lay between nighttime pedestrians—particularly women—and me. And I soon gathered that being perceived as dangerous is a hazard in itself. I only needed to turn a corner into a dicey situation, or crowd some frightened, armed person in a foyer somewhere, or make an errant move after being pulled over by a policeman. Where fear and weapons meet—and they often do in urban America—there is always the possibility of death.

In that first year, my first away from my hometown, I was to become thoroughly familiar with the language of fear. At dark, shadowy intersections in Chicago, I could cross in front of a car stopped at a traffic light and elicit the *thunk, thunk, thunk, thunk* of the driver—black, white, male, or female—hammering down the door locks. On less traveled streets after dark, I grew accustomed to but never comfortable with people who crossed to the other side of the street rather than pass me. Then there were the standard unpleasantries with police, doormen, bouncers, cab drivers, and others whose business it is to screen out troublesome individuals *before* there is any nastiness.   3

I moved to New York nearly two years ago and I have remained an avid night walker. In central Manhattan, the near-constant crowd cover minimizes tense one-on-one street encounters. Elsewhere—visiting friends in SoHo, where sidewalks are narrow and tightly spaced buildings shut out the sky—things can get very taut indeed.   4

Black men have a firm place in New York mugging literature. Norman Podhoretz in his famed (or infamous) 1963 essay, "My Negro Problem—And Ours," recalls growing up in terror of black males; they "were tougher than we were, more ruthless," he writes—and as an adult on the Upper West Side of Manhattan, he continues, he cannot constrain his nervousness when he meets black men on certain streets. Similarly, a decade later, the essayist and novelist Edward Hoagland extols a New York where once "Negro bitterness bore down mainly on other Negroes." Where some see mere panhandlers, Hoagland sees "a mugger who is clearly screwing up his nerve to do more than just *ask* for money." But Hoagland has "the New Yorker's quick-hunch posture for broken-field maneuvering," and the bad guy swerves away.   5

I often witness that "hunch posture," from women after dark on the warrenlike streets of Brooklyn where I live. They seem to set their faces on neutral and, with their purse straps strung across their chests bandolier style, they forge ahead as though bracing themselves against being tackled. I understand, of course, that the danger they perceive is not a hallucination. Women are particularly vulnerable to street violence, and young black males are drastically overrepresented among the perpetrators of that violence. Yet these truths are no solace against   6 the kind of alienation that comes of being ever the suspect, against being set apart, a fearsome entity with whom pedestrians avoid making eye contact.

7   It is not altogether clear to me how I reached the ripe old age of 22 without being conscious of the lethality nighttime pedestrians attributed to me. Perhaps it was because in Chester, Pennsylvania, the small, angry industrial town where I came of age in the 1960s, I was scarcely noticeable against a backdrop of gang warfare, street knifings, and murders. I grew up one of the good boys, had perhaps a half-dozen fist fights. In retrospect, my shyness of combat has clear sources.

8   Many things go into the making of a young thug. One of those things is the consummation of the male romance with the power to intimidate. An infant discovers that random flailings send the baby bottle flying out of the crib and crashing to the floor. Delighted, the joyful babe repeats those motions again and again, seeking to duplicate the feat. Just so, I recall the points at which some of my boyhood friends were finally seduced by the perception of themselves as tough guys. When a mark cowered and surrendered his money without resistance, myth and reality merged—and paid off. It is, after all, only manly to embrace the power to frighten and intimidate. We, as men, are not supposed to give an inch of our lane on the highway; we are to seize the fighter's edge in work and in play and even in love; we are to be valiant in the face of hostile forces.

9   Unfortunately, poor and powerless young men seem to take all this nonsense literally. As a boy, I saw countless tough guys locked away; I have since buried several, too. They were babies, really—a teenage cousin, a brother of 22, a childhood friend in his mid-twenties—all gone down in episodes of bravado played out in the streets. I came to doubt the virtues of intimidation early on. I chose, perhaps even unconsciously, to remain a shadow—timid, but a survivor.

10   The fearsomeness mistakenly attributed to me in public places often has a perilous flavor. The most frightening of these confusions occurred in the late 1970s and early 1980s when I worked as a journalist in Chicago. One day, rushing into the office of a magazine I was writing for with a deadline story in hand, I was mistaken for a burglar. The office manager called security and, with an *ad hoc* posse, pursued me through the labyrinthine halls, nearly to my editor's door. I had no way of proving who I was. I could only move briskly toward the company of someone who knew me.

11   Another time I was on assignment for a local paper and killing time before an interview. I entered a jewelry store on the city's affluent Near North Side. The proprietor excused herself and returned with an enormous red Doberman pinscher straining at the end of a leash. She stood, the dog extended toward me, silent to my questions, her

eyes bulging nearly out of her head. I took a cursory look around, nodded, and bade her good night. Relatively speaking, however, I never fared as badly as another black male journalist. He went to nearby Waukegan, Illinois, a couple of summers ago to work on a story about a murderer who was born there. Mistaking the reporter for the killer, police hauled him from his car at gunpoint and but for his press credentials would probably have tried to book him. Such episodes are not uncommon. Black men trade tales like this all the time.

In "My Negro Problem—And Ours," Podhoretz writes that the 12 hatred he feels for blacks makes itself known to him through a variety of avenues—one being his discomfort with that "special brand of paranoid touchiness" to which he says blacks are prone. No doubt he is speaking here of black men. In time, I learned to smother the rage I felt at so often being taken for a criminal. Not to do so would surely have led to madness—via that special "paranoid touchiness" that so annoyed Podhoretz at the time he wrote the essay.

I began to take precautions to make myself less threatening. I 13 move about with care, particularly late in the evening. I give a wide berth to nervous people on subway platforms during the wee hours, particularly when I have exchanged business clothes for jeans. If I happen to be entering a building behind some people who appear skittish, I may walk by, letting them clear the lobby before I return, so as not to seem to be following them. I have been calm and extremely congenial on those rare occasions when I've been pulled over by the police.

And on late-evening constitutionals along streets less traveled 14 by, I employ what has proved to be an excellent tension-reducing measure. I whistle melodies from Beethoven and Vivaldi and the more popular classical composers. Even steely New Yorkers hunching toward nighttime destinations seem to relax, and occasionally they even join in the tune. Virtually everybody seems to sense that a mugger wouldn't be warbling bright, sunny selections from Vivaldi's *Four Seasons*. It is my equivalent of the cowbell that hikers wear when they know they are in bear country.

____ CONSIDERATIONS _____

1. "Her flight made me feel like an accomplice in tyranny," writes Staples, in paragraph 2, of the young white woman who was frightened by his mere appearance. What "tyranny" is Staples talking about?

2. Why does Staples say that "being perceived as dangerous is a hazard in itself"?

3. What do hikers wearing cowbells in bear country have to do with Staples's techniques for easing tension on his evening walks?

4. Is there any connection between the fear Staples encounters when he meets lone white men or women on the street at night and the fear of the homeless that many middle-class people feel? See Peter Marin's essay "Helping and Hating the Homeless."

5. Why was the word "hunching" a good choice in the second sentence of paragraph 14?

Shelby Steele (b. 1946) teaches English at San Jose State University in California. He has published essays in Commentary, *the* New York Times Magazine, *and the* American Scholar, *as well as* Harper's, *which printed "I'm Black, You're White, Who's Innocent?" in 1988. His "On Being Black and Middle Class" appeared in* The Best American Essays of 1989. *His* The Content of Our Character: A New Vision of Race in America *won the National Book Critics Circle Award in 1991.*

_77_

SHELBY STEELE

I'm Black, You're White, Who's Innocent?

It is a warm, windless California evening, and the dying light   1
that covers the redbrick patio is tinted pale orange by the day's smog. Eight of us, not close friends, sit in lawn chairs sipping chardonnay. A black engineer and I (we had never met before) integrate the group. A psychologist is also among us, and her presence encourages a surprising openness. But not until well after the lovely twilight dinner had been served, when the sky has turned to deep black and the drinks have long since changed to scotch, does the subject of race spring awkwardly upon us. Out of nowhere the engineer announces, with a coloring of accusation in his voice, that it bothers him to send his daughter to a school where she is one of only three black children. "I didn't realize my ambition to get ahead would pull me into a world where my daughter would lose touch with her blackness," he says.

Over the course of the evening we have talked about money, infi-   2
delity, past and present addictions, child abuse, even politics. Intimacies have been revealed, fears named. But this subject, race, sinks us into one of those shaming silences where eye contact terrorizes. Our host looks for something in the bottom of his glass. Two women stare into the black sky as if to locate the Big Dipper and point it out to us.

Reprinted by permission of the author.

Finally, the psychologist seems to gather herself for a challenge, but it is too late. "Oh, I'm sure she'll be just fine," says our hostess, rising from her chair. When she excuses herself to get the coffee, the two sky gazers offer to help.

3   With three of us now gone, I am surprised to see the engineer still silently holding his ground. There is a willfulness in his eyes, an inner pride. He knows he has said something awkward, but he is determined not to give a damn. His unwavering eyes intimidate me. At last the host's head snaps erect. He has an idea. "The hell with coffee," he says. "How about some of the smoothest brandy you ever tasted?" An idea made exciting by the escape it offers. Gratefully we follow him back into the house, quickly drink his brandy, and say our good-byes.

4   An autopsy of this party might read: death induced by an abrupt and lethal injection of the American race issue. An accurate if superficial assessment. Since it has been my fate to live a rather integrated life, I have often witnessed sudden deaths like this. The threat of them, if not the reality, is a part of the texture of integration. In the late 1960s, when I was just out of college, I took a delinquent's delight in playing the engineer's role, and actually developed a small reputation for playing it well. Those were the days of flagellatory white guilt; it was such great fun to pinion some professor or housewife or, best of all, a large group of remorseful whites, with the knowledge of both their racism and their denial of it. The adolescent impulse to sneer at convention, to startle the middle-aged with doubt, could be indulged under the guise of racial indignation. And how could I lose? My victims—earnest liberals for the most part—could no more crawl out from under my accusations than Joseph K. in Kafka's *Trial* could escape the amorphous charges brought against him. At this odd moment in history the world was aligned to facilitate my immaturity.

5   About a year of this was enough: the guilt that follows most cheap thrills caught up to me, and I put myself in check. But the impulse to do it faded more slowly. It was one of those petty talents that is tied to vanity, and when there were ebbs in my self-esteem the impulse to use it would come alive again. In integrated situations I can still feel the faint itch. But then there are many youthful impulses that still itch, and now, just inside the door of mid-life, this one is least precious to me.

6   In the literature classes I teach, I often see how the presence of whites all but seduces some black students into provocation. When we come to a novel by a black writer, say Toni Morrison, the white students can easily discuss the human motivations of the black characters. But, inevitably, a black student, as if by reflex, will begin to set in relief the various racial problems that are the background of these characters' lives. The student's tone will carry a reprimand: the class is afraid to confront the reality of racism. Classes cannot be allowed to

die like dinner parties, however. My latest strategy is to thank that student for his or her moral vigilance, and then appoint the young man or woman as the class's official racism monitor. But even if I get a laugh—I usually do, but sometimes the student is particularly indignant, and it gets uncomfortable—the strategy never quite works. Our racial division is suddenly drawn in neon. Overcaution spreads like spilled paint. And, in fact, the black student who started it all does become a kind of monitor. The very presence of this student imposes a new accountability on the class.

I think those who provoke this sort of awkwardness are operating out of a black identity that obliges them to badger white people about race almost on principle. Content hardly matters. (For example, it made no sense for the engineer to expect white people to sympathize with his anguish over sending his daughter to school with *white* children.) Race indeed remains a source of white shame; the goal of these provocations is to put whites, no matter how indirectly, in touch with this collective guilt. In other words, these provocations I speak of are *power* moves, little shows of power that try to freeze the "enemy" in self-consciousness. They gratify and inflate the provocateur. They are the underdog's bite. And whites, far more secure in their power, respond with a self-contained and tolerant silence that is, itself, a show of power. What greater power than that of non-response, the power to let a small enemy sizzle in his own juices, to even feel a little sad at his frustration just as one is also complimented by it. Black anger always, in a way, flatters white power. In America, to know that one is not black is to feel an extra grace, a little boost of impunity.

I think the real trouble between the races in America is that the races are not just races but competing power groups—a fact that is easily minimized perhaps because it is so obvious. What is not so obvious is that this is true quite apart from the issue of class. Even the well-situated middle-class (or wealthy) black is never completely immune to that peculiar contest of power that his skin color subjects him to. Race is a separate reality in American society, an entity that carries its own potential for power, a mark of fate that class can soften considerably but not eradicate.

The distinction of race has always been used in American life to sanction each race's pursuit of power in relation to the other. The allure of race as a human delineation is the very shallowness of the delineation it makes. Onto this shallowness—mere skin and hair—men can project a false depth, a system of dismal attributions, a series of malevolent or ignoble stereotypes that skin and hair lack the substance to contradict. These dark projections then rationalize the pursuit of power. Your difference from me makes you bad, and your badness justifies, even demands, my pursuit of power over you—the oldest formula for aggression known to man. Whenever much importance is given to race, power is the primary motive.

10 But the human animal almost never pursues power without first convincing himself that he is *entitled* to it. And this feeling of entitlement has its own precondition: to be entitled one must first believe in one's innocence, at least in the area where one wishes to be entitled. By innocence I mean a feeling of essential goodness in relation to others and, therefore, superiority to others. Our innocence always inflates us and deflates those we seek power over. Once inflated we are entitled; we are in fact licensed to go after the power our innocence tells us we deserve. In this sense, *innocence is power*. Of course, innocence need not be genuine or real in any objective sense, as the Nazis demonstrated not long ago. Its only test is whether or not we can convince ourselves of it.

11 I think the racial struggle in America has always been primarily a struggle for innocence. White racism from the beginning has been a claim of white innocence and, therefore, of white entitlement to subjugate blacks. And in the '60s, as went innocence so went power. Blacks used the innocence that grew out of their long subjugation to seize more power, while whites lost some of their innocence and so lost a degree of power over blacks. Both races instinctively understand that to lose innocence is to lose power (in relation to each other). Now to be innocent someone else must be guilty, a natural law that leads the races to forge their innocence on each other's backs. The inferiority of the black always makes the white man superior; the evil might of whites makes blacks good. This pattern means that both races have a hidden investment in racism and racial disharmony, despite their good intentions to the contrary. Power defines their relations, and power requires innocence, which, in turn, requires racism and racial division.

12 I believe it was this hidden investment that the engineer was protecting when he made his remark—the white "evil" he saw in a white school "depriving" his daughter of her black heritage confirmed his innocence. Only the logic of power explained this—he bent reality to show that he was once again a victim of the white world and, as a victim, innocent. His determined eyes insisted on this. And the whites, in their silence, no doubt protected their innocence by seeing him as an ungracious troublemaker—his bad behavior underscoring their goodness. I can only guess how he was talked about after the party. But it isn't hard to imagine that his blunder gave everyone a lift. What none of us saw was the underlying game of power and innocence we were trapped in, or how much we needed a racial impasse to play that game.

13 When I was a boy of about twelve, a white friend of mine told me one day that his uncle, who would be arriving the next day for a visit, was a racist. Excited by the prospect of seeing such a man, I spent the

following afternoon hanging around the alley behind my friend's house, watching from a distance as this uncle worked on the engine of his Buick. Yes, here was evil and I was compelled to look upon it. And I saw evil in the tight angle of his elbow as he pumped his wrench to tighten nuts, I saw it in the blade-sharp crease of his chinos, in the pack of Lucky Strikes that threatened to slip from his shirt pocket as he bent, and in the way his concentration seemed to shut out the human world. He worked neatly and efficiently, wiping his hands constantly, and I decided that evil worked like this.

I felt a compulsion to have this man look upon me so that I could 14 see evil—so that I could see the face of it. But when he noticed me standing beside his toolbox, he said only, "If you're looking for Bobby, I think he went up to the school to play baseball." He smiled nicely and went back to work. I was stunned for a moment, but then I realized that evil could be sly as well, could smile when it wanted to trick you.

Need, especially hidden need, puts a strong pressure on percep- 15 tion, and my need to have this man embody white evil was stronger than any contravening evidence. As a black person you always hear about racists but never meet any. And I needed to incarnate this odious category of humanity, those people who hated Martin Luther King Jr. and thought blacks should "go slow" or not at all. So, in my mental dictionary, behind the term "white racist," I inserted this man's likeness. I would think of him and say to myself, "There is no reason for him to hate black people. Only evil explains unmotivated hatred." And this thought soothed me; I felt innocent. If I hated white people, which I did not, at least I had a reason. His evil commanded me to assert in the world the goodness he made me confident of in myself.

In looking at this man I was *seeing for innocence*—a form of see- 16 ing that has more to do with one's hidden need for innocence (and power) than with the person or group one is looking at. It is quite possible, for example, that the man I saw that day was not a racist. He did absolutely nothing in my presence to indicate that he was. I invested an entire afternoon in seeing not the man but in seeing my innocence through the man. *Seeing for innocence* is, in this way, the essence of racism—the use of others as a means to our own goodness and superiority.

The loss of innocence has always to do with guilt, Kierkegaard 17 tells us, and it has never been easy for whites to avoid guilt where blacks are concerned. For whites, *seeing for innocence* means seeing themselves and blacks in ways that minimize white guilt. Often this amounts to a kind of white revisionism, as when President Reagan declares himself "colorblind" in matters of race. The President, like many of us, may aspire to racial color blindness, but few would grant that he has yet reached this sublimely guiltless state. The statement

clearly revises reality, moves it forward into some heretofore unknown America where all racial determinism will have vanished. I do
not think that Ronald Reagan is a racist, as that term is commonly
used, but neither do I think that he is capable of seeing color without
making attributions, some of which may be negative—nor am I, or
anyone else I've ever met.

18   So why make such a statement? I think Reagan's claim of color
blindness with regard to race is really a claim of racial innocence and
guiltlessness—the preconditions for entitlement and power. This was
the claim that grounded Reagan's campaign against special entitlement programs—affirmative action, racial quotas, and so on—that
black power had won in the '60s. Color blindness was a strategic assumption of innocence that licensed Reagan's use of government
power against black power.

19   I do not object to Reagan's goals in this so much as the presumption of innocence by which he rationalized them. I, too, am strained to
defend racial quotas and any affirmative action that supersedes merit.
And I believe there is much that Reagan has to offer blacks. His emphasis on traditional American values—individual initiative, self-suf-
ficiency, strong families—offers what I think is the most enduring solution to the demoralization and poverty that continue to widen the
gap between blacks and whites in America. Even his de-emphasis of
race is reasonable in a society where race only divides. But Reagan's
posture of innocence undermines any beneficial interaction he might
have with blacks. For blacks instinctively sense that a claim of racial
innocence always precedes a power move against them. Reagan's pretense of innocence makes him an adversary, and makes his quite reasonable message seem vindictive. You cannot be innocent of a man's
problem and expect him to listen.

20   I'm convinced that the secret of Reagan's "teflon" coating, his
personal popularity apart from his policies and actions, has been his
ability to offer mainstream America a vision of itself as innocent and
entitled (unlike Jimmy Carter, who seemed to offer only guilt and
obligation). Probably his most far-reaching accomplishment has been
to reverse somewhat the pattern by which innocence came to be distributed in the '60s, when outsiders were innocent and insiders were
guilty. Corporations, the middle class, entrepreneurs, the military—
all villains in the '60s—either took on a new innocence in Reagan's vision or were designated as protectors of innocence. But again, for one
man to be innocent another man must be bad or guilty. Innocence imposes, *demands*, division and conflict, a right/wrong view of the
world. And this, I feel, has led to the underside of Reagan's achievement. His posture of innocence draws him into a partisanship that undermines the universality of his values. He can't sell these values to

blacks and others because he has made blacks into the bad guys and outsiders who justify his power. It is humiliating for a black person to like Reagan because Reagan's power is so clearly derived from a distribution of innocence that leaves a black with less of it, and the white man with more.

Black Americans have always had to find a way to handle white 21 society's presumption of racial innocence whenever they have sought to enter the American mainstream. Louis Armstrong's exaggerated smile honored the presumed innocence of white society—I will not bring you your racial guilt if you will let me play my music. Ralph Ellison calls this "masking"; I call it bargaining. But whatever it's called, it points to the power of white society to enforce its innocence. I believe this power is greatly diminished today. Society has reformed and transformed—Miles Davis never smiles. Nevertheless, this power has not faded altogether; blacks must still contend with it.

Historically, blacks have handled white society's presumption of 22 innocence in two ways: they have bargained with it, granting white society its innocence in exchange for entry into the mainstream; or they have challenged it, holding that innocence hostage until their demand for entry (or other concessions) was met. A bargainer says, *I already believe you are innocent (good, fair-minded) and have faith that you will prove it.* A challenger says, *If you are innocent, then prove it.* Bargainers *give* in hope of receiving; challengers *withhold* until they receive. Of course, there is risk in both approaches, but in each case the black is negotiating his own self-interest against the presumed racial innocence of the larger society.

Clearly the most visible black bargainer on the American scene 23 today is Bill Cosby. His television show is a perfect formula for black bargaining in the '80s. The remarkable Huxtable family—with its doctor/lawyer parent combination, its drug-free, college-bound children, and its wise yet youthful grandparents—is a blackface version of the American dream. Cosby is a subscriber to the American identity, and his subscription confirms his belief in its fair-mindedness. His vast audience knows this, knows that Cosby will never assault their innocence with racial guilt. Racial controversy is all but banished from the show. The Huxtable family never discusses affirmative action.

The bargain Cosby offers his white viewers—I will confirm your 24 racial innocence if you accept me—is a good deal for all concerned. Not only does it allow whites to enjoy Cosby's humor with no loss of innocence, but it actually enhances their innocence by implying that race is not the serious problem for blacks that it once was. If anything, the success of this handsome, affluent black family points to the fairmindedness of whites who, out of their essential goodness,

changed society so that black families like the Huxtables could succeed. Whites can watch *The Cosby Show* and feel complimented on a
job well done.

25   The power that black bargainers wield is the power of absolution.
On Thursday nights, Cosby, like a priest, absolves his white viewers,
forgives and forgets the sins of the past. (Interestingly, Cosby was one
of the first blacks last winter to publicly absolve Jimmy the Greek for
his well-publicized faux pas about black athletes.) And for this he is
rewarded with an almost sacrosanct status. Cosby benefits from what
might be called a gratitude factor. His continued number-one rating
may have something to do with the (white) public's gratitude at being
offered a commodity so rare in our time; he tells his white viewers
each week that they are okay, and that this black man is not going to
challenge them.

26   When a black bargains, he may invoke the gratitude factor and
find himself cherished beyond the measure of his achievement; when
he challenges, he may draw the dark projections of whites and become
a source of irritation to them. If he moves back and forth between
these two options, as I think many blacks do today, he will likely baffle whites. It is difficult for whites to either accept or reject such
blacks. It seems to me that Jesse Jackson is such a figure—many
whites see Jackson as a challenger by instinct and a bargainer by political ambition. They are uneasy with him, more than a little suspicious. His powerful speech at the 1984 Democratic convention was a
masterpiece of bargaining. In it he offered a Kinglike vision of what
America could be, a vision that presupposed Americans had the fair-
mindedness to achieve full equality—an offer in hope of a return. A
few days after this speech, looking for rest and privacy at a lodge in Big
Sur, he and his wife were greeted with standing ovations three times a
day when they entered the dining room for meals. So much about
Jackson is deeply American—his underdog striving, his irrepressible
faith in himself, the daring of his ambition, and even his stubbornness. These qualities point to his underlying faith that Americans can
respond to him despite his race, and this faith is a compliment to
Americans, an offer of innocence.

27   But Jackson does not always stick to the terms of his bargain—he
is not like Cosby on TV. When he hugs Arafat, smokes cigars with
Castro, refuses to repudiate Farrakhan, threatens a boycott of major
league baseball, or, more recently, talks of "corporate barracudas,"
"pension-fund socialism," and "economic violence," he looks like a
challenger in bargainer's clothing, and his positions on the issues look
like familiar protests dressed in white-paper formality. At these times
he appears to be revoking the innocence so much else about him
seems to offer. The old activist seems to come out of hiding once

again to take white innocence hostage until whites prove they deserve to have it. In his candidacy there is a suggestion of protest, a fierce insistence on his *right* to run, that sends whites a message that he may secretly see them as a good bit less than innocent. His dilemma is to appear the bargainer while his campaign itself seems to be a challenge.

There are, of course, other problems that hamper Jackson's bid 28 for the Democratic presidential nomination. He has held no elective office, he is thought too flamboyant and opportunistic by many, there are rather loud whispers of "character" problems. As an individual he may not be the best test of a black man's chances for winning so high an office. Still, I believe it is the aura of challenge surrounding him that hurts him most. Whether it is right or wrong, fair or unfair, I think no black candidate will have a serious chance at his party's nomination, much less the presidency, until he can convince white Americans that he can be trusted to preserve *their* sense of racial innocence. Such a candidate will have to use his power of absolution; he will have to flatly forgive and forget. He will have to bargain with white innocence out of a genuine belief that it really exists. There can be no faking it. He will have to offer a vision that is passionately raceless, a vision that strongly condemns any form of racial politics. This will require the most courageous kind of leadership, leadership that asks all the people to meet a new standard.

Now the other side of American's racial impasse: How do blacks 29 lay claim to their racial innocence?

The most obvious and unarguable source of black innocence is 30 the victimization that blacks endured for centuries at the hands of a race that insisted on black inferiority as a means to its own innocence and power. Like all victims, what blacks lost in power they gained in innocence—innocence that, in turn, entitled them to pursue power. This was the innocence that fueled the civil rights movement of the '60s, and that gave blacks their first real power in American life—victimization metamorphosed into power via innocence. But this formula carries a drawback that I believe is virtually as devastating to blacks today as victimization once was. It is a formula that binds the victim to his victimization by linking his power to his status as a victim. And this, I'm convinced, is the tragedy of black power in America today. It is primarily a victim's power, grounded too deeply in the entitlement derived from past injustice and in the innocence that Western/Christian tradition has always associated with poverty.

Whatever gains this power brings in the short run through political action, it undermines in the long run. Social victims may be collectively entitled, but they are all too often individually demoralized. Since the social victim has been oppressed by society, he comes to feel that his individual life will be improved more by changes *in* society than by his own initiative. Without realizing it, he makes society rather than himself the agent of change. The power he finds in his victimization may lead him to collective action against society, but it also encourages passivity within the sphere of his personal life.

32   This past summer I saw a television documentary that examined life in Detroit's inner city on the twentieth anniversary of the riots there in which forty-three people were killed. A comparison of the inner city then and now showed a decline in the quality of life. Residents feel less safe than they did twenty years ago, drug trafficking is far worse, crimes by blacks against blacks are more frequent, housing remains substandard, and the teenage pregnancy rate has skyrocketed. Twenty years of decline and demoralization, even as opportunities for blacks to better themselves have increased. This paradox is not peculiar to Detroit. By many measures, the majority of blacks—those not yet in the middle class—are further behind whites today than before the victories of the civil rights movement. But there is a reluctance among blacks to examine this paradox, I think, because it suggests that racial victimization is not our real problem. If conditions have worsened for most of us as racism has receded, then much of the problem must be of our own making. But to fully admit this would cause us to lose the innocence we derive from our victimization. And we would jeopardize the entitlement we've always had to challenge society. We are in the odd and self-defeating position where taking responsibility for bettering ourselves feels like a surrender to white power.

33   So we have a hidden investment in victimization and poverty. These distressing conditions have been the source of our only real power, and there is an unconscious sort of gravitation toward them, a complaining celebration of them. One sees evidence of this in the near happiness with which certain black leaders recount the horror of Howard Beach and other recent (and I think over-celebrated) instances of racial tension. As one is saddened by these tragic events, one is also repelled at the way some black leaders—agitated to near hysteria by the scent of victim-power inherent in them—leap forward to exploit them as evidence of black innocence and white guilt. It is as though they sense the decline of black victimization as a loss of standing and dive into the middle of these incidents as if they were reservoirs of pure black innocence swollen with potential power.

34   *Seeing for innocence* pressures blacks to focus on racism and to neglect the individual initiative that would deliver them from poverty—the only thing that finally delivers anyone from poverty. With our eyes on innocence we see racism everywhere and miss opportunity even as we stumble over it. About 70 percent of black students at my university drop out before graduating—a flight from opportunity that racism cannot explain. It is an injustice that whites can *see for innocence* with more impunity than blacks can. The price

whites pay is a certain blindness to themselves. Moreover, for white *seeing for innocence* continues to engender the bad faith of a long-disgruntled minority. But the price blacks pay is an ever-escalating poverty that threatens to make the worst off of them a permanent underclass. Not fair, but real.

Challenging works best for the collective, while bargaining is more the individual's suit. From this point on, the race's advancement will come from the efforts of its individuals. True, some challenging will be necessary for a long time to come. But bargaining is now—today—a way for the black individual to *join* the larger society, to make a place for himself or herself. 35

"Innocence is ignorance," Kierkegaard says, and if this is so, the claim of innocence amounts to an insistence on ignorance, a refusal to know. In their assertions of innocence both races carve out very functional areas of ignorance for themselves—territories of blindness that license a misguided pursuit of power. Whites gain superiority by *not* knowing blacks; blacks gain entitlement by *not* seeing their own responsibility for bettering themselves. The power each race seeks in relation to the other is grounded in a double-edged ignorance, ignorance of the self as well as the other. 36

The original sin that brought us to an impasse at the dinner party I mentioned at the outset occurred centuries ago, when it was first decided to exploit racial difference as a means to power. It was the determinism that flowed karmically from this sin that dropped over us like a net that night. What bothered me most was our helplessness. Even the engineer did not know how to go forward. His challenge hadn't worked, and he'd lost the option to bargain. The marriage of race and power depersonalized us, changed us from eight people to six whites and two blacks. The easiest thing was to let silence blanket our situation, our impasse. 37

I think the civil rights movement in its early and middle years offered the best way out of America's racial impasse: in this society, race must not be a source of advantage or disadvantage for anyone. This is fundamentally a *moral* position, one that seeks to breach the corrupt union of race and power with principles of fairness and human equality: if all men are created equal, then racial difference cannot sanction power. The civil rights movement was conceived for no other reason than to redress that corrupt union, and its guiding insight was that only a moral power based on enduring principles of justice, equality, and freedom could offset the lower impulse in man to exploit race as a means to power. Three hundred years of suffering had driven the point home, and in Montgomery, Little Rock, and Selma, racial power was the enemy and moral power the weapon. 38

39   An important difference between genuine and presumed innocence, I believe, is that the former must be earned through sacrifice,
while the latter is unearned and only veils the quest for privilege. And
there was much sacrifice in the early civil rights movement. The
Gandhian principle of non-violent resistance that gave the movement
a spiritual center as well as a method of protest demanded sacrifice, a
passive offering of the self in the name of justice. A price was paid in
terror and lost life, and from this sacrifice came a hard-earned innocence and a credible moral power.

40   Non-violent passive resistance is a bargainer's strategy. It as-
sumes the power that is the object of the protest has the genuine innocence to morally respond, and puts the protesters at the mercy of that
innocence. I think this movement won so many concessions precisely
because of its belief in the capacity of whites to be moral. It did not so
much demand that whites change as offer them relentlessly the opportunity to live by their own morality—to attain a true innocence based
on the sacrifice of their racial privilege, rather than a false innocence
based on presumed racial superiority. Blacks always bargain with or
challenge the larger society; but I believe that in the early civil rights
years, these forms of negotiation achieved a degree of integrity and
genuineness never seen before or since.

41   In the mid-'60s all this changed. Suddenly a sharp *racial* consciousness emerged to compete with the moral consciousness that
had defined the movement to that point. Whites were no longer welcome in the movement, and a vocal "black power" minority gained
dramatic visibility. Increasingly, the movement began to seek racial as
well as moral power, and thus it fell into a fundamental contradiction
that plagues it to this day. Moral power precludes racial power by denouncing race as a means to power. Now suddenly the movement itself was using race as a means to power, and thereby affirming the
very union of race and power it was born to redress. In the end, black
power can claim no higher moral standing than white power.

42   It makes no sense to say this shouldn't have happened. The sacrifices that moral power demands are difficult to sustain, and it was inevitable that blacks would tire of these sacrifices and seek a more
earthly power. Nevertheless, a loss of genuine innocence and moral
power followed. The movement, splintered by a burst of racial mili-
tancy in the late '60s, lost its hold on the American conscience and descended more and more to the level of secular, interest-group politics.
Bargaining and challenging once again became racial rather than
moral negotiations.

43   You hear it asked, why are there no Martin Luther Kings around
today? I think one reason is that there are no black leaders willing to
resist the seductions of racial power, or to make the sacrifices moral
power requires. King understood that racial power subverts moral
power, and he pushed the principles of fairness and equality rather

than black power because he believed those principles would bring blacks their most complete liberation. He sacrificed race for morality, and his innocence was made genuine by that sacrifice. What made King the most powerful and extraordinary black leader of this century was not his race but his morality.

Black power is a challenge. It grants white no innocence; it de- 44 nies their moral capacity and then demands that they be moral. No power can long insist on itself without evoking an opposing power. Doesn't an insistence on black power call up white power? (And could this have something to do with what many are now calling a resurgence of white racism?) I believe that what divided the races at the dinner party I attended, and what divides them in the nation, can only be bridged by an adherence to those moral principles that disallow race as a source of power, privilege, status, or entitlement of any kind. In our age, principles like fairness and equality are ill-defined and all but drowned in relativity. But this is the fault of people, not principles. We keep them muddled because they are the greatest threat to our presumed innocence and our selective ignorance. Moral principles, even when somewhat ambiguous, have the power to assign responsibility and therefore to provide us with knowledge. At the dinner party we were afraid of so severe an accountability.

What both black and white Americans fear are the sacrifices and 45 risks that true racial harmony demands. This fear is the measure of our racial chasm. And though fear always seeks a thousand justifications, none is ever good enough, and the problems we run from only remain to haunt us. It would be right to suggest courage as an antidote to fear, but the glory of the word might only intimidate us into more fear. I prefer the word effort—relentless effort, moral effort. What I like most about this word are its connotations of everydayness, earnestness, and practical sacrifice. No matter how badly it might have gone for us that warm summer night, we should have talked. We should have made the effort.

_____ CONSIDERATIONS _____

1. "It was one of those petty talents that is tied to vanity, and when there were ebbs in my self-esteem the impulse to use it would come alive again," writes Steele in paragraph 5. What petty talent is he talking about, and what other similar "talents" can you think of?

2. In paragraph 17, Steele writes, "I do not think that Ronald Reagan is a racist, as that term is commonly used, but neither do I think that he is capable of seeing color without making attributions, some of which may be negative—nor am I, or anyone else I've ever met." Read Brent Staples's short report of his experiences in "Just Walk On By" and decide whether or not he would agree with Steele.

3. In his lengthy discussion of the racial struggle for innocence, beginning with the first sentence of paragraph 11, how does Steele make use of two well-known but different black figures?

4. How does Steele's essay become more than a superficial glance at the racial problems of the United States?

5. How does Steele explain his belief that black power is "the enemy," but moral power is "the weapon" in the blacks' fight for equality?

6. To what extent does Steele employ comparison and contrast in organizing his materials?

7. How could Steele justify devoting his first three paragraphs to a dinner party?

Wallace Stegner (1909–1993) was a novelist of the western United States and an essayist devoted to the natural world. He won the Pulitzer Prize for Angle of Repose *(1971) and the National Book Award for* The Spectator Bird *(1976). In 1990 he published his* Collected Stories *and in 1992* Where the Blackbird Sings to the Lemonade Springs. *He taught for many years at Stanford University.*

78

WALLACE STEGNER
The Sense of Place

If you don't know where you are, says Wendell Berry, you don't 1 know *who* you are. Berry is a writer, one of our best, who after some circling has settled on the bank of the Kentucky River, where he grew up and where his family has lived for many generations. He conducts his literary explorations inward, toward the core of what supports him physically and spiritually. He belongs to an honorable tradition, one that even in America includes some great names: Thoreau, Burroughs, Frost, Faulkner, Steinbeck—lovers of known earth, known weathers, and known neighbors both human and nonhuman. He calls himself a "placed" person.

But if every American is several people, and one of them is or 2 would like to be a placed person, another is the opposite, the displaced person, cousin not to Thoreau but to Daniel Boone, dreamer not of Walden Ponds but of far horizons, traveler not in Concord but in wild unsettled places, explorer not inward but outward. Adventurous, restless, seeking, asocial or antisocial, the displaced American persists by the million long after the frontier has vanished. He exists to some extent in all of us, the inevitable by-product of our history: the New World transient. He is commoner in the newer parts of America—the West, Alaska—than in the older parts, but he occurs everywhere, always in motion.

3   To the placed person he seems hasty, shallow, and restless. He
has a current like the Platte, a mile wide and an inch deep. As a
species, he is nonterritorial, he lacks a stamping ground. Acquainted
with many places, he is rooted in none. Culturally he is a discarder or
transplanter, not a builder or conserver. He even seems to like and
value his rootlessness, though to the placed person he shows the
symptoms of nutritional deficiency, as if he suffered from some obscure scurvy or pellagra of the soul.

4   Migratoriness has its dangers, unless it is the traditional, seasonal, social migratoriness of shepherd tribes, or of the academic
tribes who every June leave Cambridge or New Haven for summer
places in Vermont, and every September return to their winter range.
Complete independence, absolute freedom of movement, are exhila-
rating for a time but may not wear well. That romantic atavist we
sometimes dream of being, who lives alone in a western or arctic
wilderness, playing Natty Bumppo and listening to the loons and living on moose meat and moving on if people come within a hundred
miles, is a very American figure but he is not a full human being. He is
a wild man of the woods, a Sasquatch.

5   He has many relatives who are organized as families—migrant
families that would once have followed the frontier but that now follow construction booms from Rock Springs to Prudhoe Bay, or pursue
the hope of better times from Michigan to Texas, or retire from the
midwestern farm to St. Petersburg or Sunshine City, or still hunt the
hippie heaven from Sedona to Telluride to Sand Point. These migrants
drag their exposed roots and have trouble putting them down in new
places. Some don't *want* to put them down, but at retirement climb
into their RVs and move with the seasons from national park to national park, creating a roadside society out of perpetual motion. The
American home is often a mobile home.

6   I know about this. I was born on wheels, among just such a family. I know about the excitement of newness and possibility, but I also
know the dissatisfaction and hunger that result from placelessness.
Some towns that we lived in were never real to me. They were only
the raw material of places, as I was the raw material of a person. Neither place nor I had a chance of being anything unless we could live together for a while. I spent my youth envying people who had lived all
their lives in the houses they were born in, and had attics full of proof
that they *had* lived.

7   The deep ecologists warn us not to be anthropocentric, but I
know no way to look at the world, settled or wild, except through my
own human eyes. I know that it wasn't created especially for my use,
and I share the guilt for what members of my species, especially the
migratory ones, have done to it. But I am the only instrument that I
have access to by which I can enjoy the world and try to understand it.
So I must believe that, at least to human perception, a place is not a

place until people have been born in it, have grown up in it, lived in it, known it, died in it—have both experienced and shaped it, as individuals, families, neighborhoods, and communities, over more than one generation. Some are born in their place, some find it, some realize after long searching that the place they left is the one they have been searching for. But whatever their relation to it, it is made a place only by slow accrual, like a coral reef.

Once, as George Stewart reminded us in *Names on the Land*, the 8 continent stretched away westward without names. It had no places in it until people had named them, and worn the names smooth with use. The fact that Daniel Boone killed a bear at a certain spot in Kentucky did not make it a place. It began to be one, though, when he remembered the spot as Bear Run, and other people picked up the name and called their settlement by it, and when the settlement became a landmark or destination for travelers, and when children had worn paths through its woods to schoolhouse or swimming hole. The very fact that people remembered Boone's bear-killing, and told about it, added something of placeness.

No place is a place until things that have happened in it are re- 9 membered in history, ballads, yarns, legends, or monuments. Fictions serve as well as facts. Rip Van Winkle, though a fiction, enriches the Catskills. Real-life Mississippi spreads across unmarked boundaries into Yoknapatawpha County. Every one of the six hundred rocks from which the Indian maiden jumped to escape her pursuers grows by the legend, and people's lives get lived around and into it. It attracts family picnics and lovers' trysts. There are names carved in the trees there. Just as surely as do the quiet meadows and stone walls of Gettysburg, or the grassy hillside above the Little Big Horn where the Seventh Cavalry died, even a "phony" place like the Indian maiden's rock grows by human association.

In America the process of cumulative association has gone a good 10 way by now in stable, settled, and especially rural areas—New England, the Midwest, the South—but hardly any way at all in the raw, migrant West. For one thing, the West has been raided more often than settled, and raiders move on when they have got what they came for. Many western towns never lasted a single human lifetime. Many others have changed so fast that memory cannot cling to them; they are unrecognizable to anyone who knew them twenty years ago. And as they change, they may fall into the hands of planners and corporations, so that they tend to become more and more alike. Change too often means stereotype. Try Gillette, Wyoming, not too long ago a sleepy cowtown on the verge of becoming a real place, now a coal boomtown that will never be a place.

Changing everywhere, America changes fastest west of the 100th 11 meridian. Mining booms, oil booms, irrigation booms, tourist booms, culture booms as at Aspen and Sun Valley, crowd out older populations and bring in new ones. Communities lose their memory along with their character. For some, the memory can over time be reinstated. For many, the memory too will be a transient, for irrigation agribusiness from California and Arizona to Idaho has by now created a whole permanent underclass of the migrant and dispossessed, totally placeless people who will never have a chance to settle down anywhere, who will know a place briefly during the potato or cantaloupe or grape harvest, and then move on.

12   As with life, so with literature. Except in northern California, the West has never had a real literary outpouring, a flowering of the sort that marked New England, the Midwest, and the South. As I have noted elsewhere, a lot of what *has* been written is a literature of motion, not of place. There is a whole tradition of it, from Mark Twain's *Roughing It* to Kerouac's *On the Road.* Occasionally we get loving place-oriented books such as Ivan Doig's *This House of Sky* and Norman Maclean's *A River Runs Through It,* but even while we applaud them we note that they are memorials to places that *used* to be, not celebrations of ongoing places. They are nostalgic before history has taken its second step, as much a looking-back as *Huckleberry Finn* was for Mark Twain.

13   And that is a curious phenomenon, that nostalgia that has marked American writing ever since Irving and Cooper. From our very beginnings, and in the midst of our perpetual motion, we have been homesick for the old folks at home and the old oaken bucket. We have been forever bidding farewell to the last of the Mohicans, or the last of the old-time cattlemen, or the last of the pioneers with the bark on, or the vanishing wilderness. Just at random, read Willa Cather's *A Lost Lady* or Conrad Richter's *The Sea of Grass* or Larry McMurtry's *Horseman, Pass By,* or even William Dean Howells's *The Rise of Silas Lapham*, with its portrait of a businessman possessed of an antique and doomed integrity. We have made a tradition out of mourning the passing of things we never had time really to know, just as we have made a culture out of the open road, out of movement without place.

14   Freedom, especially free land, has been largely responsible. Nothing in our history has bound us to a plot of ground as feudalism once bound Europeans. In older, smaller, more homogeneous and traditional countries, life was always more centripetal, held in tight upon its center. In Ireland, for example, Yeats tells us, "there is no river or mountain that is not associated in the memory with some event or legend. . . . I would have our writers and craftsmen of many kinds master this history and these legends, and fix upon their memory the appearance of mountains and rivers and make it all visible again in their arts, so that Irishmen, even though they had gone thousands of miles away, would still be in their own country."

15   America is both too large and too new for that sort of universal recognition. It was just the lack of such recognitions and acceptances,

the lack of a complex American society rooted in richly remembered places, that led Washington Irving to transplant European legends to the Catskills, and Hawthorne to labor at creating what he called a usable past. The same lacks drove Henry James, later, to exploit his countrymen not as dwellers in their own country but more often as pilgrims and tourists abroad, hunting what their own country did not provide. When native themes, characters, and places did emerge, they were likely to be local-colorish, exploiting the local picturesque and probably mourning its passing, or expressions of our national restlessness, part of the literature of the road.

Indifferent to, or contemptuous of, or afraid to commit ourselves 16 to, our physical and social surroundings, always hopeful of something better, hooked on change, a lot of us have never stayed in one place long enough to learn it, or have learned it only to leave it. In our displaced condition we are not unlike the mythless man that Carl Jung wrote about, who lives "like one uprooted, having no true link either with the past, or with the ancestral life which continues within him, or yet with contemporary human society. He . . . lives a life of his own, sunk in a subjective mania of his own devising, which he believes to be the newly discovered truth."

Back to Wendell Berry, and his belief that if you don't know 17 where you are you don't know who you are. He is not talking about the kind of location that can be determined by looking at a map or a street sign. He is talking about the kind of knowing that involves the senses, the memory, the history of a family or a tribe. He is talking about the knowledge of place that comes from working in it in all weathers, making a living from it, suffering from its catastrophes, loving its mornings or evenings or hot noons, valuing it for the profound investment of labor and feeling that you, your parents and grandparents, your all-but-unknown ancestors have put into it. He is talking about the knowing that poets specialize in.

It is only a step from his pronouncement to another: that no 18 place is a place until it has had a poet. And that is about what Yeats was saying only a moment ago.

No place, not even a wild place, is a place until it has had that 19 human attention that at its highest reach we call poetry. What Frost did for New Hampshire and Vermont, what Faulkner did for Mississippi and Steinbeck for the Salinas Valley, Wendell Berry is doing for his family corner of Kentucky, and hundreds of other place-loving people, gifted or not, are doing for places they were born in, or reared in, or have adopted and made their own.

I doubt that we will ever get the motion out of the American, for 20 everything in his culture of opportunity and abundance has, up to now, urged motion on him as a form of virtue. Our tradition of restlessness will not be outgrown in a generation or two, even if the motives for restlessness are withdrawn. But after all, in a few months it will be half a millennium since Europeans first laid eyes on this continent. At least in geographical terms, the frontiers have been explored and crossed. It is probably time we settled down. It is probably time we looked around us instead of looking ahead. We have no business, any longer, in being impatient with history. We need to know our history in much greater depth, even back into the geology, which, as Henry Adams said, is only history projected a little way back from Mr. Jefferson.

21   History was part of the baggage we threw overboard when we launched ourselves into the New World. We threw it away because it recalled old tyrannies, old limitations, galling obligations, bloody memories. Plunging into the future through a landscape that had no history, we did both the country and ourselves some harm along with some good. Neither the country nor the society we built out of it can be healthy until we stop raiding and running, and learn to be quiet part of the time, and acquire the sense not of ownership but of belonging.

22   "The land was ours before we were the land's," says Robert Frost's poem. Only in the act of submission is the sense of place realized and a sustainable relationship between people and earth established.

____ CONSIDERATIONS _____

1. Describing Wendell Berry—see Berry's essay, "A Native Hill," (page 47)—Stegner says, "after some circling," Berry has settled "where he grew up and where his family has lived for many generations." Stegner might well have been describing the circling and settling done by another writer in this text, Donald Hall. Read his "Keeping Things," (page 237) and comment on the similarities and differences between the two "placed" persons, Berry and Hall.

2. In paragraph 2, Stegner refers to Henry David Thoreau as a "traveler in Concord" in contrast to a "displaced person" like Daniel Boone. The writer is referring to an often quoted line in Thoreau's book, *Walden.* How would you go about tracking down that line?

3. There are three terms in paragraph 4 that may not mean much to you: "atavist," "Natty Bumppo," and "sasquatch." What can you do about them?

4. Stegner closes with a line from a poem by Robert Frost, "The Gift Outright," printed on page 212 of this book. Read it with care to see whether it supports Stegner's idea.

5. "Neither place nor I had a chance of being anything unless we could live together for a while," writes Stegner in paragraph 6. "I spent my youth envying people who had lived all their lives in the houses they were born in, and had attics full of proof that they *had* lived." Which of the following essayists would come the closest to matching the people Stegner envied as a youth? E.

B. White (page 609), Wendell Berry (page 47), James D. Houston (page 280), or Donald Hall (page 237).

6. Stegner writes disapprovingly that "we have made a culture out of the open road, out of movement without place," and he blames "freedom, especially free land" for that state of affairs. Can you make a counter argument and attribute to "freedom, especially free land" the credit for generations escaping the deadly prejudices that imprisoned their elders?

Igor Stravinsky (1882–1971), usually considered the best modern composer, burst on the musical scene with The Firebird *in 1910 and* The Rites of Spring *in 1913—the latter an occasion for rioting in the auditorium. Born in Russia, he moved to Switzerland during the Great War and became an American citizen in 1945. In the United States he collaborated with Robert Craft to make three books of thought and reminiscence. These paragraphs are Stravinsky's answer to a question posed by Craft.*

79

IGOR STRAVINSKY
The Dearest City

1   The sounds of St. Petersburg are still close to the surface of my memory. Whereas visual images are recalled, in my case, mainly by unexpected shifts and combinations of pressures, sounds, once registered, appear to remain in a state of immediacy; and while my accounts of things seen are subject to exaggeration, to mistaken observation, and to the creations and distortions of memory itself (a memory being a whole cartel of invested interests), my recollections of sound must be faithful: I am proving as much, after all, every time I compose.

2   St. Petersburg street noises are especially vivid to me, perhaps for the reason that to my confining indoor life any sound of the outside world was memorable and attractive. The first such sounds to record themselves on my awareness were those of droshkies on cobblestone, or block-wood parquetry pavements. Only a few of these horse carriages had rubber tyres, and these few were doubly expensive; the whole city crackled with the iron-hooped wheels of the others. I also remember the sound of horse-drawn streetcars and, in particular, the rail-scraping noise they made as they turned the corner near our house and whipped up speed to cross the Krukov Canal Bridge. (Steeper

From *Expositions and Developments* by Igor Stravinsky and Robert Craft, pages 28–35. Copyright © 1959, 1960, 1962 by Igor Stravinsky. Reprinted by permission of the University of California Press.

bridges sometimes required the use of extra horses, and those were found at hitching posts throughout the city.) The noises of wheels and horses and the shouts and whipcracks of coachmen must have penetrated my earliest dreams; they are, at any rate, my first memory of the streets of childhood. (The clatter of automobiles and electric trolley cars, two decades later, was much less memorable, and I can hardly recall the city's mechanized aspect, such as it was when I last saw it in 1911. I remember my first automobile ride, though. The year was 1907, and the vehicle was an American-made taxi. I gave the driver a five-rouble gold piece and told him to motor me about for as long as the money allowed—a half-hour, as it happened.)

The cries of vendors are vivid in my memory, too, especially those of the Tartars—though, in truth, they did not so much cry as cluck. "Halaat, halaat," they used to say, "halaat" being their word for a kind of dressing-gown. Only rarely did they speak Russian, and the low, froglike noises of their own language were an irresistible invitation to mockery. (The Tartars, with their glabrous skins, in that heavily-bewhiskered epoch, and their rigid Mohammedan *mores*—they never drank alcohol—were always objects of mystery and fascination to me.) In contrast to them, the Russians would bawl every syllable too distinctly and with annoying deliberation. Their wares were carried on head-trays, and this required them to wobble their shoulders and caracole their bodies in perfect balance; they were more interesting to watch than to hear. They also sold *prianiki* (cookies of the kind the Germans call *Pfefferkuchen*) and *marozhennoyeh* (ice cream) in the streets. "Nye pozhelayet'l marozhennoyeh" ("Would you like some ice cream?") was a familiar fair-weather cry in our street. (It is still a cry, or rather, and alas, a "musical" jingle, in my street in Hollywood; my last act on earth might well turn out to be "The Death of the Good Humour Man.") Other edibles bruited this way were cranberries, or *klyookva*, the chief produce of the tundra (I still remember the old peasant *baba* who sold them); apples; pears; peaches; and even oranges. (Grapefruits and bananas were unknown in St. Petersburg then, however, and I did not taste them until many years later, in Paris.) But the most memorable street cry of all was the knife-grinder's: 3

The loudest diurnal noises of the city were the cannonade of bells from the Nikolsky Cathedral, near our house, and the noon sig- 4

nal from the Peter and Paul Fortress—a timepiece for the whole populace—but I recall with more nostalgia the sound of an accordion in a suburban street on a lonely Sunday afternoon, or the trilling wires of a balalaika orchestra in a restaurant or café. A final, *ad absurdum*, example of memorable *musique concrète* was the St. Petersburg telephone. It produced an even ruder tintinnabulation than the one we suffer today. (In fact, it sounded exactly like the opening bars of Act II of *The Nightingale*.) The first telephone call I ever made was to Rimsky-Korsakov, incidentally, and the Stravinsky and Rimsky households were among the first in the city to install the nuisance.

5   A city is also remembered by its odours. In the case of St. Petersburg, these were associated chiefly with droshkies. They smelled agreeably of tar, of leather, and of their horses. Usually, however, the strongest odour emanated from the driver himself. ("Que hombre," we would say of a particularly redolent coachman when savours of unwash had penetrated layers of clothing as thick as a mummy's, and as infrequently changed.) My own olfactory bearings were conditioned by the felt *bashlyk,* or hood, I was obliged to wear during the winter months, and my palate still retains a strong residual reek of wet felt. The general odour of the city returned only in the spring, however, with the liquefaction of the rivers and canals, and that odour I cannot describe. (In the case of something as personal as an odour, description, which depends upon comparison, is impossible.) One other aroma that permeated the city and, indeed, all Russia, was of the tobacco called Mahorka (from "mejor," "the best"); it was originally imported (probably from Spain, through Holland) by Peter the Great. I loved the smell of it, and I continued to smoke it in Switzerland during the war and for as long thereafter as I could buy it; when I moved to France, in 1920, a large stock of it went with me. (Perhaps this is the place to mention the tastes of the city—its typical degustations— the crayfish, the sterlets, the *zakooski* that were never quite the same anywhere else. Incidentally, my favourite St. Petersburg restaurant was the Dominique, and it was there that Diaghilev first met with me for a serious talk about my "future.")

6   While I do not claim reliability for my memory of colour, I remember St. Petersburg as an ochre city (in spite of such prominent red buildings as the Winter Palace and Anichkov Palace), and though I am equally unable to describe colours, I can say that I am often reminded of the tint of my native city, in Rome. But the architecture, as well as the colour, of St. Petersburg, was Italian, and Italian not merely by imitation but by the direct work of such architects as Quarenghi and Rastrelli. (I have often considered that the fact of my birth and upbringing in a Neo-Italian—rather than in a purely Slavic, or Oriental— city must be partly, and profoundly, responsible for the cultural direction of my later life.) Italian stylization and craftsmanship could be found in any work of the Catherine the Great period, whether in a

building, a statue, or an *objet d'art*. And the principal palaces were Italian not only in design but in material (marble). Even in the case of the ordinary St. Petersburg building stone, which was a local granite or an equally local brick, the outer surfaces were plastered, and painted Italian colours. My favourite buildings were the Bourse; the Smolny Cloister by Rastrelli (this was Lenin's headquarters during the Revolution); the Alexandrinsky Drama Theatre (now called the Pushkin Theatre); the Winter Palace; the Admiralty, with its handsome spire; and above all, the Mariinsky Theatre. The latter was a delight to me, no matter how often I saw it, and to walk from our house through the Offitserskaya to the Ulitsa Glinka, where I could see its dome, was to be consumed with Petersburger pride. To enter the blue-and-gold interior of that heavily-perfumed hall was, for me, like entering the most sacred of temples.

St. Petersburg was a city of islands and rivers. The latter were   7
called Neva, mostly—Great Neva, Small Neva, Great Small Neva, Middle Neva, and so on—but the other names escape my memory. The movements of boats and the life of the harbour are less significant in my recollections than one might expect, however, because of the long, icebound winters. I do remember the reappearance of boats in the canals in our sudden Russian spring, but the picture of them is less vivid than that of the waterways used as thoroughfares for sleighs. These radical equinoctial changes affected the aspect of the city in other ways, too, and not only the aspect, but the health, for an influenza epidemic followed each deceptive sign of spring, and plagues of mosquitoes appeared at the least hint of warm weather. The most striking change of décor came at Easter. In Russia, the week before Holy Week was known as Willow Week, and the willow replaced the palm on Palm Sunday. Brightly beribboned bunches of willows were seen and sold all over the city for as long as a fortnight.

St. Petersburg was also a city of large, open piazzas. One of these,   8
the Champs de Mars, might have been the scene of *Petroushka*. The Mardi Gras festivities were centered there, and as puppet shows were part of the carnival entertainment, it was there that I saw my first "Petroushka." "Russian Mountains"—roller-coasters for sleighs— were fixtures in the Champs de Mars, and the whole populace came there to sleigh, but a more beautiful spectacle was that of sleighs drawn by elks. These elegant creatures were brought to the city in carnival season by Finnish peasants, who used them to sell rides. They were part of a realistic fairy-tale world whose lost beauty I have tried to rediscover later in life, especially in Hans Christian Andersen (*The Nightingale, Le Baiser de la fée*). (I might also mention that I learned to bicycle in the Champs de Mars, though, of course, that was in a warmer season.)

Another attractive piazza was the Haymarket, where hundreds of   9
wains were stored to supply the city's huge horse population; to walk

there was to be reminded of the countryside. But my most animated promenades in St. Petersburg were on the Nevsky Prospect, a wide avenue, three miles long, and full of life and movement all the way. Here were the beautiful Stroganov Palace (by Rastrelli); the Lutheran Church (which Balakirev, a devout Orthodoxist, used to call the upside-down trousers); the Kazansky Cathedral, with its semicircle of

columns in imitation of St. Peter's in Rome; the Duma (City Hall); the Gastinny Dvor (Merchants' Court), a block of arcades with hundreds of shops; the Public Library; the Drama Theatre; and the Anichkov Palace, Tsar Alexander III's residence. The Nevsky Prospect was sometimes used for military parades and other Imperial convocations, and I remember being taken there in my early childhood to see the Tsar, or the visiting rulers of foreign powers. (I saw Sadi Carnot of France in one such procession, he who became popular later because of his assassination.) It was also the principal arena for amorous assignations, and at night it was full of "grues," and the officers and students who were their chief customers. (A letter of Leon Bakst's to me in Morges in 1915: "... you remember how in the Nevsky Prospect, on a beautiful, white, Russian night, the purple-painted whores yell after you, 'men, give us cigarettes'." The brothels themselves were maintained by "Puffmutters" from Riga.)

10   When I attempt to recall St. Petersburg, two different cities come to mind, the one gas-lit, the other electric; the smell of gas and kerosene lamps pervades all memories of my first eight years. (But I shall have to talk again about my memories of St. Petersburg interiors, for life there, more than in any other city of my experience, was indoors. I remember, for example, how I used to blow on a five-kopeck piece and hold it to the frost-covered window of my room, where it would melt through to a view of the world.) Electric lights—or, rather, oscillating carbon arcs—first appeared in the Nevsky Prospect. They were pale in colour and not very powerful, but St. Petersburg was too far north to require much lighting: the winters glared with snow, and the springs were bright with the aurora borealis. I remember that one May night, while preparing for my University examinations, I was able to work until 4 A.M. with no other illumination than these northern lights.

St. Petersburg is so much a part of my life that I am almost afraid 11
to look further into myself, lest I discover how much of me is still
joined to it. But even these few reminiscences must show that it is
dearer to my heart than any other city in the world.

_____ CONSIDERATIONS _____

1. In paragraph 1, Stravinsky calls memory "a whole cartel of invested
interests." What does he mean?

2. Stravinsky's vocabulary is noticeably larger than that of most native
speakers of English. His language thus provides many opportunities to try out
various methods of attacking unfamiliar words. In paragraph 9, for example,
he uses the word _grues._ What word-attack method would give you the approx-
imate meaning of the word?

3. Stravinsky comments, in paragraph 5, on the difficulty of describing
odors. Which of the five traditional senses—sight, smell, hearing, touch,
taste—is the most difficult to describe? Examine a few of the more descriptive
writers in your text, such as Henry Adams, Wendell Berry, Carol Bly, Annie
Dillard, Robert Finch, M. F. K. Fisher, Jane Kenyon, John McPhee, Gary Soto,
John Updike, and E. B. White, to see how they handle the senses. Write an essay on your conclusions.

4. Surprisingly, little details often make an author's work more memorable than any great truths it may have to offer. Find such a detail in paragraph
10 and discuss its use there.

5. Where would you find information about _musique concrète,_ mentioned by Stravinsky in paragraph 4?

6. Stravinsky's favorite city has undergone more than one name change.
It was founded as St. Petersburg by Peter the Great in 1703, called Petrograd
from 1914 to 1924, then changed to Leningrad. In 1991, the city resumed its
original name, St. Petersburg. At least some of the motivation for these name
changes was political. Similarly, the name "Indian" has given way to "native
American," "Negro" to "black," to "African American," "girl" to "young
woman," and so on. Despite Shakespeare's line, in _Romeo and Juliet,_ "a rose
by any other name would smell as sweet," we continue to be careful about
naming anything we care about. Discuss.

Jonathan Swift (1667–1745), the author of Gulliver's
Travels, *was a priest, a poet, and a master of English prose.
Some of his strongest satire took the form of reasonable
defense of the unthinkable, like his argument in favor of
abolishing Christianity in the British Isles. Born in Dublin,
he was angry all his life at England's misuse and
mistreatment of the subject Irish people. In 1729, he made
this modest proposal for solving the Irish problem.*

80

JONATHAN SWIFT
A Modest Proposal

FOR PREVENTING THE CHILDREN OF POOR PEOPLE IN IRELAND FROM
BEING A BURDEN TO THEIR PARENTS OR COUNTRY, AND FOR MAKING
THEM BENEFICIAL TO THE PUBLIC

1   It is a melancholy object to those who walk through this great
town or travel in the country, when they see the streets, the roads, and
cabin doors, crowded with beggars of the female sex, followed by
three, four, or six children, all in rags and importuning every passenger
for an alms. These mothers, instead of being able to work for their
honest livelihood, are forced to employ all their time in strolling to
beg sustenance for their helpless infants, who, as they grow up, either
turn thieves for want of work, or leave their dear native country to
fight for the Pretender in Spain, or sell themselves to the Barbadoes.

2   I think it is agreed by all parties that this prodigious number of
children in the arms, or on the backs, or at the heels of their mothers
and frequently of their fathers, is in the present deplorable state of the
kingdom a very great additional grievance; and therefore whoever
could find out a fair, cheap, and easy method of making these children
sound useful members of the commonwealth would deserve so well of
the public as to have his statue set up for a preserver of the nation.

3   But my intention is very far from being confined to provide only
for the children of professed beggars; it is of a much greater extent, and
shall take in the whole number of infants at a certain age who are born

of parents in effect as little able to support them as those who demand our charity in the streets.

As to my own part, having turned my thoughts for many years upon this important subject, and maturely weighed the several schemes of other projectors, I have always found them grossly mistaken in their computation. It is true, a child just dropped from its dam may be supported by her milk for a solar year, with little other nourishment; at most not above the value of two shillings, which the mother may certainly get, or the value in scraps, by her lawful occupation of begging; and it is exactly at one year old that I propose to provide for them in such a manner as instead of being a charge upon their parents or the parish, or wanting food and raiment for the rest of their lives, they shall on the contrary contribute to the feeding, and partly to the clothing, of many thousands.

There is likewise another great advantage in my scheme, that it will prevent those voluntary abortions, and that horrid practice of women murdering their bastard children, alas, too frequent among us, sacrificing the poor innocent babes, I doubt, more to avoid the expense than the shame, which would move tears and pity in the most savage and inhuman breast.

The number of souls in this kingdom being usually reckoned one million and a half, of these I calculate there may be about two hundred thousand couples whose wives are breeders; from which number I subtract thirty thousand couples who are able to maintain their own children, although I apprehend there cannot be so many under the present distress of the kingdom; but this being granted, there will remain an hundred and seventy thousand breeders. I again subtract fifty thousand for those women who miscarry, or whose children die by accident or disease within the year. There only remain an hundred and twenty thousand children of poor parents actually born. The question therefore is, how this number shall be reared and provided for, which, as I have already aid, under the present situation of affairs, is utterly impossible by all the methods hitherto proposed. For we can neither employ them in handicraft or agriculture; we neither build houses (I mean in the country) nor cultivate land. They can very seldom pick up a livelihood by stealing till they arrive at six years old, except where they are of towardly parts; although I confess they learn the rudiments much earlier, during which time they can however be looked upon only as probationers, as I have been informed by a principal gentleman in the country of Cavan, who protested to me that he never knew above one or two instances under the age of six, even in a part of the kingdom so renowned for the quickest proficiency in that art.

I am assured by our merchants that a boy or a girl before twelve years old is no salable commodity; and even when they come to this age they will not yield above three pounds, or three pounds and half a crown at most on the Exchange; which cannot turn to account either to the parents or the kingdom, the charge of nutriment and rags having been at least four times that value.

8   I shall now therefore humbly propose my own thoughts, which I hope will not be liable to the least objection.

9   I have been assured by a very knowing American of my acquaintance in London, that a young healthy child well nursed is at a year old a most delicious, nourishing, and wholesome food, whether stewed, roasted, baked, or boiled; and I make no doubt that it will equally serve in a fricassee or a ragout.

10   I do therefore humbly offer it to public consideration that of the hundred and twenty thousand children, already computed, twenty thousand may be reserved for breed, whereof only one fourth part to be males, which is more than we allow to sheep, black cattle, or swine; and my reason is that these children are seldom the fruits of marriage, a circumstance not much regarded by our savages, therefore one male will be sufficient to serve four females. That the remaining hundred thousand may at a year old be offered in sale to the persons of quality and fortune through the kingdom, always advising the mother to let them suck plentifully in the last month, so as to render them plump and fat for a good table. A child will make two dishes at an entertainment for friends; and when the family dines alone, the fore or hind quarter will make a reasonable dish, and seasoned with a little pepper or salt will be very good boiled on the fourth day, especially in the winter.

11   I have reckoned upon a medium that a child just born will weigh twelve pounds, and in a solar year if tolerably nursed increaseth to twenty-eight pounds.

12   I grant this food will be somewhat dear, and therefore very proper for landlords, who, as they have already devoured most of the parents, seem to have the best title to the children.

13   Infant's flesh will be in season throughout the year, but more plentiful in March, and a little before and after. For we are told by a grave author, an eminent French physician, that fish being a prolific diet, there are more children born in Roman Catholic countries about nine months after Lent than at any other season; therefore, reckoning a year after Lent, the markets will be more glutted than usual, because the number of popish infants is at least three to one in this kingdom; and therefore it will have one other collateral advantage, by lessening the number of Papists among us.

14   I have already computed the charge of nursing a beggar's child (in which list I reckon all cottagers, laborers, and four fifths of the farmers) to be about two shillings per annum, rags included; and I believe no gentleman would repine to give ten shillings for the carcass of a good fat child, which, as I have said, will make four dishes of excellent nutritive meat, when he hath only some particular friend or his own

family to dine with him. Thus the squire will learn to be a good land-lord, and grow popular among the tenants; the mother will have eight shillings net profit, and be fit for work till she produces another child.

Those who are more thrifty (as I must confess the times require) 15 may flay the carcass; the skin of which artificially dressed will make admirable gloves for ladies, and summer boots for fine gentlemen.

As to our city of Dublin, shambles may be appointed for this pur- 16 pose in the most convenient parts of it, and butchers we may be assured will not be wanting; although I rather recommend buying the children alive, and dressing them hot from the knife as we do roasting pigs.

A very worthy person, a true lover of his country, and whose 17 virtues I highly esteem, was lately pleased in discoursing on this matter to offer a refinement upon my scheme. He said that many gentlemen of his kingdom, having of late destroyed their deer, he conceived that the want of venison might be well supplied by the bodies of young lads and maidens, not exceeding fourteen years of age nor under twelve, so great a number of both sexes in every country being now ready to starve for want of work and service; and these to be disposed of by their parents, if alive, or otherwise by their nearest relations. But with due deference to so excellent a friend and so deserving a patriot, I cannot be altogether in his sentiments, for as to the males, my American acquaintance assured me from frequent experience that their flesh was generally tough and lean, like that of our schoolboys, by continual exercise, and their taste disagreeable; and to fatten them would not answer the charge. Then as to the females, it would, I think with humble submission, be a loss to the public, because they soon would become breeders themselves: and besides, it is not improbable that some scrupulous people might be apt to censure such a practice (although indeed very unjustly) as a little bordering upon cruelty; which, I confess, hath always been with me the strongest objection against any project, how well soever intended.

But in order to justify my friend, he confessed that this expedient 18 was put into his head by the famous Psalmanazar, a native of the island Formosa, who came from thence to London above twenty years ago, and in conversation told my friend that in his country when any young person happened to be put to death, the executioner sold the carcass to persons of quality as a prime dainty; and that in his time the body of a plump girl of fifteen, who was crucified for an attempt to poison the emperor, was sold to his Imperial Majesty's prime minister of state, and other great mandarins of the court, in joints from the gibbet, at four hundred crowns. Neither indeed can I deny that if the same use were made of several plump young girls in this town, who without one single groat to their fortunes cannot stir abroad without a chair, and appear at the playhouse and assemblies in foreign fineries which they never will pay for, the kingdom would not be the worse.

19   Some persons of a desponding spirit are in great concern about that vast number of poor people who are aged, diseased, or maimed, and I have been desired to employ my thoughts what course may be taken to ease the nation of so grievous an encumbrance. But I am not in the least pain upon that matter, because it is very well known that they are every day dying and rotting by cold and famine, and filth and vermin, as fast as can be reasonably expected. And as to the younger laborers, they are now in almost as hopeful a condition. They cannot get work, and consequently pine away for want of nourishment to a degree that if at any time they are accidentally hired to common labor, they have not strength to perform it; and thus the country and themselves are happily delivered from the evils to come.

20   I have too long digressed, and therefore shall return to my subject. I think the advantages by the proposal which I have made are obvious and many, as well as of the highest importance.

21   For first, as I have already observed, it would greatly lessen the number of Papists, with whom we are yearly overrun, being the principal breeders of the nation as well as our most dangerous enemies; and who stay at home on purpose to deliver the kingdom to the Pretender, hoping to take their advantage by the absence of so many good Protestants, who have chosen rather to leave their country than to stay at home and pay tithes against their conscience to an Episcopal curate.

22   Secondly, the poorer tenants will have something valuable of their own, which by law may be made liable to distress, and help to pay their landlord's rent, their corn and cattle being already seized and money a thing unknown.

23   Thirdly, whereas the maintenance of an hundred thousand children, from two years old and upwards, cannot be computed at less than ten shillings a piece per annum, the nation's stock will be thereby increased fifty thousand pounds per annum, besides the profit of a new dish introduced to the tables of all gentlemen of fortune in the kingdom who have any refinement in taste. And the money will circulate among ourselves, the goods being entirely of our own growth and manufacture.

24   Fourthly, the constant breeders, besides the gain of eight shillings sterling per annum by the sale of their children, will be rid of the charge of maintaining them after the first year.

25   Fifthly, this food would likewise bring great custom to taverns, where the vintners will certainly be so prudent as to procure the best recipes for dressing it to perfection, and consequently have their houses frequented by all the fine gentlemen, who justly value themselves upon their knowledge in good eating; and a skillful cook, who understands how to oblige his guests, will contrive to make it as expensive as they please.

Sixthly, this would be a great inducement to marriage, which all 26
wise nations have either encouraged by rewards or enforced by laws
and penalties. It would increase the care and tenderness of mothers toward their children, when they were sure of a settlement for life to the
poor babes, provided in some sort by the public, to their annual profit
instead of expense. We should see an honest emulation among the
married women, which of them could bring the fattest child to the
market. Men would become as fond of their wives during the time of
their pregnancy as they are now of their mares in foal, their cows in
calf, or sows when they are ready to farrow; nor offer to beat or kick
them (as is too frequent a practice) for fear of a miscarriage.

Many other advantages might be enumerated. For instance, the 27
addition of some thousand carcasses in our exportation of barreled
beef, the propagation of swine's flesh, and improvements in the art of
making good bacon, so much wanted among us by the great destruction of pigs, too frequent at our tables, which are no way comparable
in taste or magnificence to a well-grown, fat, yearling child, which
roasted whole will make a considerable figure at a lord mayor's feast
or any other public entertainment. But this and many others I omit,
being studious of brevity.

Supposing that one thousand families in this city would be con- 28
stant customers for infants' flesh, besides others who might have it at
merry meetings, particularly weddings and christenings, I compute
that Dublin would take off annually about twenty thousand carcasses,
and the rest of the kingdom (where probably they will be sold somewhat cheaper) the remaining eighty thousand.

I can think of no one objection that will possibly be raised 29
against this proposal, unless it should be urged that the number of
people will be thereby much lessened in the kingdom. This I freely
own, and it was indeed one principal design in offering it to the world.
I desire the reader will observe, that I calculate my remedy for this one
individual kingdom of Ireland and for no other that ever was, is, or I
think ever can be upon earth. Therefore let no man talk to me of other
expedients: of taxing our absentees at five shillings a pound; of using
neither clothes nor household furniture except what is of our own
growth and manufacture; of utterly rejecting the materials and instruments that promote foreign luxury; of curing the expensiveness of
pride, vanity, idleness, and gaming in our women; of introducing a
vein of parsimony, prudence, and temperance; of learning to love our
country, in the want of which we differ even from Laplanders and the
inhabitants of Topinamboo; of quitting our animosities and factions,
nor acting any longer like the Jews, who were murdering one another
at the very moment their city was taken; of being a little cautious not
to sell our country and conscience for nothing; of teaching landlords
to have at least one degree of mercy toward their tenants; lastly, of

putting a spirit of honesty, industry, and skill into our shopkeepers; who, if a resolution could now be taken to buy only our native goods, would immediately unite to cheat and exact upon us in the price, the measure, and the goodness, nor could ever yet be brought to make one fair proposal of just dealing, though often and earnestly invited to it.

30   Therefore, I repeat, let no man talk to me of these and the like expedients, till he hath at least some glimpse of hope that there will ever be some hearty and sincere attempt to put them in practice.

31   But as to myself, having been wearied out for many years with offering vain, idle, visionary thoughts, and at length utterly despairing of success, I fortunately fell upon this proposal, which, as it is wholly new, so it hath something solid and real, of no expense and little trouble, full in our own power, and whereby we can incur no danger in disobliging England. For this kind of commodity will not bear exportation, the flesh being of too tender a consistence to admit a long continuance in salt, although perhaps I could name a country which would be glad to eat up our whole nation without it.

32   After all, I am not so violently bent upon my own opinions as to reject any offer proposed by wise men, which shall be found equally innocent, cheap, easy, and effectual. But before something of that kind shall be advanced in contradiction to my scheme, and offering a better, I desire the author or authors will be pleased maturely to consider two points. First, as things now stand, how they will be able to find food and raiment for an hundred thousand useless mouths and backs. And secondly, there being a round million of creatures in human figure throughout this kingdom, whose sole subsistence put into a common stock would leave them in debt two millions of pounds sterling, adding those who are beggars by profession to the bulk of farmers, cottagers, and laborers, with their wives and children who are beggars in effect; I desire those politicians who dislike my overture, and may perhaps be so bold to attempt an answer, that they will first ask the parents of these mortals whether they would not at this day think it a great happiness to have been sold for food at a year old in this manner I prescribe, and thereby have avoided such a perpetual scene of misfortunes as they have since gone through by the oppression of landlords, the impossibility of paying rent without money or trade, the want of common sustenance, with neither house nor clothes to cover them from the inclemencies of the weather, and the most inevitable prospect of entailing the like or greater miseries upon their breed forever.

33   I profess, in the sincerity of my heart, that I have not the least personal interest in endeavoring to promote this necessary work, having no other motive than the public good of my country, by advancing our trade, providing for infants, relieving the poor, and giving some pleasure to the rich. I have no children by which I can propose to get a

single penny; the youngest being nine years old, and my wife past childbearing.

—— **CONSIDERATIONS** ————————————————

1. The biggest risk a satirist runs is that the reader will be too literal-minded to understand that a work is meant as satire. Can you imagine a reader missing the satiric nature of Swift's "A Modest Proposal"? It has happened many times. What might such a reader think of the author? Consider the same problem with regard to Ambrose Bierce, Nora Ephron, Molly Ivins, or Mark Twain.

2. One clue to the satire is Swift's diction in certain passages. In paragraph 4, for example, note the phrase, "just dropped from its dam," in reference to a newborn child. How do these words make a sign to the reader? Look for other such words.

3. What words and phrases does Swift use to give the impression of straightforward seriousness?

4. How does Swift turn his satirical talent against religious intolerance?

5. What is the chief target of his satire toward the end of the essay?

6. How, if at all, is Swift's satire relevant today? Explain, using specifics from the essay and from what you observe in the world around you.

*Studs Terkel (b. 1912) has been an actor on stage and
television, and has conducted a successful radio interview
show in Chicago.* His best-known books, collections of
interviews, are Division Street America *(1966),* Hard
Times *(1970),* Working *(1974)—from which we take this
example of American speech—and* The Good War *(1984).
In 1977 he published* Talking to Myself, *his
autobiography, and in 1980* American Dreams Lost and
Found. Race: How Blacks and Whites Think and Feel
About the American Obsession *appeared in 1992 and*
Coming of Age *in 1995.*

81

STUDS TERKEL

Phil Stallings, Spot Welder

1   *He is a spot welder at the Ford assembly plant on the far South
Side of Chicago. He is twenty-seven years old; recently married. He
works the third shift: 3:30 P.M. to midnight.*

2   I start the automobile, the first welds. From there it goes to another line, where the floor's put on, the roof, the trunk hood, the
doors. Then it's put on a frame. There is hundreds of lines.

3   The welding gun's got a square handle, with a button on the top
for high voltage and a button on the bottom for low. The first is to
clamp the metal together. The second is to fuse it.

4   The gun hangs from a ceiling, over tables that ride on a track. It
travels in a circle, oblong, like an egg. You stand on a cement platform, maybe six inches from the ground.

5   I stand in one spot, about two- or three-feet area, all night. The
only time a person stops is when the line stops. We do about thirty-
two jobs per car, per unit. Forty-eight units an hour, eight hours a day.
Thirty-two times forty-eight times eight. Figure it out. That's how
may times I push that button.

The noise, oh it's tremendous. You open your mouth and you're 6
liable to get a mouthful of sparks. (Shows his arms.) That's a burn,
these are burns. You don't compete against the noise. You got to yell
and at the same time you're straining to maneuver the gun to where
you have to weld.

You got some guys that are uptight, and they're not sociable. It's 7
too rough. You pretty much stay to yourself. You get involved with
yourself. You dream, you think of things you've done. I drift back continuously to when I was a kid and what me and my brothers did. The
things you love most are the things you drift back into.

Lots of times I worked from the time I started to the time of the 8
break and I never realized I had even worked. When you dream, you
reduce the chances of friction with the foreman or with the next guy.

It don't stop. It just goes and goes and goes. I bet there's men who 9
have lived and died out there, never seen the end of that line. And they
never will—because it's endless. It's like a serpent. It's just all body,
no tail. It can do things to you . . . (Laughs.)

Repetition is such that if you were to think about the job itself, 10
you'd slowly go out of your mind. You'd let your problems build up,
you'd get to a point where you'd be at the fellow next to you—his
throat. Every time the foreman came by and looked at you, you'd have
something to say. You just strike out at anything you can. So if you involve yourself by yourself, you overcome this.

I don't like the pressure, the intimidation. How would you like 11
to go up to someone and say, "I would like to go to the bathroom?" If
the foreman doesn't like you, he'll make you hold it, just ignore you.
Should I leave this job to go to the bathroom I risk being fired. The
line moves all the time.

I work next to Jim Grayson and he's preoccupied. The guy on my 12
left, he's a Mexican, speaking Spanish, so it's pretty hard to understand him. You just avoid him. Brophy, he's a young fella, he's going
to college. He works catty-corner from me. Him and I talk from time
to time. If he ain't in the mood, I don't talk. If I ain't in the mood, he
knows it.

Oh sure, there's tension here. It's not always obvious, but the 13
whites stay with the whites and the coloreds stay with the coloreds.
When you go into Ford, Ford says, "Can you work with other men?"
This stops a lot of trouble, 'cause when you're working side by side
with a guy, they can't afford to have guys fighting. When two men
don't socialize, that means two guys are gonna do more work, know
what I mean?

I don't understand how come more guys don't flip. Because 14
you're nothing more than a machine when you hit this type of thing.
They give better care to that machine than they will to you. They'll
have more respect, give more attention to that machine. And you

know this. Somehow you get the feeling that the machine is better than you are. (Laughs.)

15   You really begin to wonder. What price do they put on me? Look at the price they put on the machine. If that machine breaks down, there's somebody out there to fix it right away. If I break down, I'm just pushed over to the other side till another man takes my place. The only thing they have on their mind is to keep that line running.

16   I'll do the best I can. I believe in an eight-hour pay for an eight-hour day. But I will not try to outreach my limits. If I can't cut it, I just don't do it. I've been there three years and I keep my nose pretty clean. I never cussed anybody or anything like that. But I've had some real brushes with foremen.

17   What happened was my job was overloaded. I got cut and it got infected. I got blood poisoning. The drill broke. I took it to the foreman's desk. I says, "Change this as soon as you can." We were running specials for XL hoods. I told him I wasn't a repair man. That's how the conflict began. I says, "If you want, take me to the Green House." Which is a superintendent's office—disciplinary station. This is when he says, "Guys like you I'd like to see in the parking lot."

18   One foreman I now, he's about the youngest out here, he has this idea: I'm it and if you don't like it, you know what you can do. Anything this other foreman says, he usually overrides. Even in some cases, the foremen don't get along. They're pretty hard to live with, even with each other.

19   Oh yeah, the foreman's got somebody knuckling down on him, putting the screws to him. But a foreman is still free to go to the bathroom, go get a cup of coffee. He doesn't face the penalties. When I first went in there, I kind of envied foremen. Now, I wouldn't have a foreman's job. I wouldn't give 'em the time of the day.

20   When a man becomes a foreman, he has to forget about even being human, as far as feelings are concerned. You see a guy there bleeding to death. So what, buddy? That line's gotta keep goin'. I can't live like that. To me, if a man gets hurt, first thing you do is get him some attention.

21   About the blood poisoning. It came from the inside of a hood rubbin' against me. It caused quite a bit of pain. I went down to the medics. They said it was a boil. Got to my doctor that night. He said blood poisoning. Running fever and all this. Now I've smartened up.

22   They have a department of medics. It's basically first aid. There's no doctor on our shift, just two or three nurses, that's it. They've got a door with a sign on it that says Lab. Another door with a sign on it: Major Surgery. But my own personal opinion, I'm afraid of 'em. I'm afraid if I were to get hurt, I'd get nothin' but back talk. I got hit square in the chest one day with a bar from a rack and it cut me down this side. They didn't take x-rays or nothing. Sent me back on the job. I

missed three and a half days two weeks ago. I had bronchitis. They told me I was all right. I didn't have a fever. I went home and my doctor told me I couldn't go back to work for two weeks. I really needed the money, so I had to go back the next day. I woke up still sick, so I took off the rest of the week.

I pulled a muscle on my neck, straining. This gun, when you grab 23 this thing from the ceiling, cable, weight, I mean you're pulling everything. Your neck, your shoulders, and your back. I'm very surprised more accidents don't happen. You have to lean over, at the same time holding down the gun. This whole edge here is sharp. I go through a shirt every two weeks, it just goes right through. My coveralls catch on fire. I've had gloves catch on fire. (Indicates arm.) See them little holes? That's what sparks do. I've got burns across here from last night.

I know I could find better places to work. But where could I get 24 the money I'm making? Let's face it, $4.32 an hour. That's real good money now. Funny thing is, I don't mind working at body construction. To a great degree, I enjoy it. I love using my hands—more than I do my mind. I love to be able to put things together and see something in the long run. I'll be the first to admit I've got the easiest job on the line. But I'm against this thing where I'm being held back. I'll work like a dog until I get what I want. The job I really want is utility.

It's where I can stand and say I can do any job in this department, 25 and nobody has to worry about me. As it is now, out of say, sixty jobs, I can do almost half of 'em. I want to get away from standing in one spot. Utility can do a different job every day. Instead of working right there for eight hours I could work over there for eight, I could work the other place for eight. Every day it would change. I would be around more people. I go out on my lunch break and work on the fork truck for a half-hour—to get the experience. As soon as I got it down pretty good, the foreman in charge says he'll take me. I don't want the other guys to see me. When I hit that fork lift, you just stop your thinking and you concentrate. Something right there in front of you, not in the past, not in the future. This is real healthy.

I don't eat lunch at work. I may grab a candy bar, that's enough. I 26 wouldn't be able to hold it down. The tension your body is put under by the speed of the line. . . . When you hit them brakes, you just can't stop. There's a certain momentum that carries you forward. I could hold the food, but it wouldn't set right.

Proud of my work? How can I feel pride in a job where I call a 27 foreman's attention to a mistake, a bad piece of equipment, and he'll ignore it. Pretty soon you get the idea they don't care. You keep doing this and finally you're titled a troublemaker. So you just go about your work. You *have* to have pride. So you throw it off to something else. And that's my stamp collection.

28   I'd break both my legs to get into social work. I see all over so many kids really gettin' a raw deal. I think I'd go into juvenile. I tell kids on the line, "Man, go out there and get that college." Because it's too late for me now.

29   When you go into Ford, first thing they try to do is break your spirit. I seen them bring a tall guy where they needed a short guy. I seen them bring a short guy where you have to stand on two guys' backs to do something. Last night, they brought a fifty-eight-year-old man to do the job I was on. That man's my father's age. I know damn well my father couldn't do it. To me, this is humanely wrong. A job should be a job, not a death sentence.

30   The younger worker, when he gets uptight, he talks back. But you take an old fellow, he's got a year, two years, maybe three years to go. If it was me, I wouldn't say a word, I wouldn't care what they did. 'Cause, baby, for another two years I can stick it out. I can't blame it man. I respect him because he had enough will power to stick it out for thirty years.

31   It's gonna change. There's a trend. We're getting younger and younger men. We got this new Thirty and Out. Thirty years seniority and out. The whole idea is to give a man more time, more time to slow down and live. While he's still in his fifties, he can settle down in a camper and go out and fish. I've sat down and thought about it. I've got twenty-seven years to go. (Laughs.) That's why I don't go around causin' trouble or lookin' for a cause.

32   The only time I get involved is when it affects me or it affects a man on the line in a condition that could be me. I don't believe in lost causes, but when it all happened. . . . (He pauses, appears bewildered.)

33   The foreman was riding the guy. The guy either told him to go away or pushed him, grabbed him. . . . You can't blame the guy—Jim Grayson. I don't want nobody stickin' their finger in my face. I'd've probably hit him beside the head. The whole thing was: Damn it, it's about time we took a stand. Let's stick up for the guy. We stopped the line. (He pauses, grins.) Ford lost about twenty units. I'd figure about five grand a unit—whattaya got? (Laughs.)

34   I said, "Let's all go home." When the line's down like that, you can go up to one man and say, "You gonna work?" If he says no, they can fire him. See what I mean? But if nobody was there, who the hell were they gonna walk up to and say, "Are you gonna work?" Man, there woulda been nobody there! If it were up to me, we'd gone home.

35   Jim Grayson, the guy I work next to, he's colored. Absolutely. That's the first time I've seen unity on that line. Now it's happened once, it'll happen again. Because everybody just sat down. Believe you me. (Laughs.) It stopped at eight and it didn't start till twenty after eight. Everybody and his brother were down there. It was really nice to see, it really was.

____ CONSIDERATIONS _____

1. Terkel is famous for his ability to catch the voice of the people he interviews. Study the language of Phil Stallings and list some of the features of his voice.

2. In addition to diction, what removes this selection from the category of "essay"?

3. How does Stallings indicate his opinion that the company puts a higher value on its machines than on its men?

4. Does Stallings agree with what Caroline Bird says in her essay on the value of college?

5. What occurrence on the line, described toward the end of the interview, reveals Stallings's social consciousness?

6. Interview someone you find interesting. Try to shape the material from the interview into something with a point.

Paul Theroux (b. 1941) is a traveler. He was born in Massachusetts, and returns to Cape Cod every summer; the rest of the year he lives in England when he is not taking trains across China for Riding the Iron Rooster *(1988) or anyplace else.* The Old Patagonian Express: By Train Through the Americas *(1979);* The Great Railway Bazaar: By Train Through Asia *(1985). Most of the time he writes novels, including* The Family Arsenal *(1976),* The Mosquito Coast *(1982), and, most recently,* Millroy the Magician *(1994). Because he has supported himself for decades as a freelance writer, he has written many articles for many magazines. He collected his best essays in* Sunrise with Seamonsters *(1985), from which we take "Burning Grass."*

82

PAUL THEROUX
Burning Grass

1   In July, it was very cold in Malawi. On the day that Malawi gained her independence the wind swept down from Soche Hill into the Central stadium bringing with it cold mists. The Africans call this wind *chiperoni* and dread it because they don't have enough clothes to withstand its penetration. They also know that it lasts only a few weeks and that once this difficult period is gotten through they can go out again into the fields and dig furrows for planting.

2   Independence Day was very dark, yet despite the cold winds the people came to see their newly designed flag raised. The Prime Minister told everyone that Malawi is a black man's country. The cold seemed to turn everything, everyone, to wood; even the slogans were frozen, the gladness caged in trembling bodies.

3   Through August it became warmer. The violent flames of the jacaranda, the deep red of the bougainvillaea, the hibiscus, each bloom

a delicate shell—all suddenly appeared out of the cold of the African winter.

In September, two months had passed since that winter, two   4
months since that freezing Independence Day. And now, in this dry season, the people have begun to burn the grass.

September 8 was the first day of school. On this same day three   5
members of the cabinet were asked to resign. Shortly afterward all the ministers but two resigned in protest. The Prime Minister, "the Lion of Malawi," was left with only two of his former ministers. Two months after independence the government smoldered in the heat of argument.

The custom of burning grass dates back to prehistoric times   6
when there was a great deal of land and only few farmers; much of the land could lie fallow while the rest was burned. It was thought that the burning was necessary for a good crop the following year. The scientists say this is not true, but there are only a handful of scientists in this country of four million farmers. So each year, in the dry season, the grass is burned. A few weeks ago I saw thin trails of blue smoke winding out of valleys and off the hills to disappear in the clouds. And at night I saw the flicker of fires out at a great distance. A short time ago the fires were not great; I could still see the huge Mlanje plateau, a crouching animal, streaked with green, disappearing into Mozambique.

Last night I walked outside and saw the fires again. It can be ter-   7
rifying to see things burning at night, wild bush fires creeping up a mountain like flaming snakes edging sideways to the summit. Even behind the mountains I could see fires, and off into the darkness that is the edge of Malawi I saw the glowing dots of fires just begun. They could burn all night, light the whole sky and make the shadows of trees leap in the flames. During the day the flames would drive the pigs and hyenas out of their thickets; the heat and smoke would turn the fleeing ravens into frightened asterisks of feathers.

Today the portent was real. Early this morning the radio said   8
there would be heavy smoke haze. I looked off and Mlanje, Mozambique, even the small hills that had always lain so patiently in the sun, were obscured by the smoke of the bush fires. The horizon has crept close to my house. The horizon is still blue, not the cold blue of the air at a distance, but the heavy pigment of smoke and fresh ashes lingering low over the landscape, close to me.

In this season the ministers who have broken from the govern-   9
ment are making speeches against the Prime Minister. They are angry. They say that this government is worse than the one it replaced. They say that in two months the Prime Minister has kept none of his

promises; the ministers have spread to all the provinces where, before great numbers of people, they repeat their accusations. The air is heavy with threats and indignation; the people are gathering in groups to talk of this split in the government. They take time off from burning the grass to speak of the government now, after two green months, in flames.

10   Fire in Africa can go out of control, out of reach of any human being, without disturbing much. It can sweep across the long plains and up the mountains and then, after the fire has burned its length, will flicker and go out. Later the burned ground will be replaced by the woven green of new grass. For a while very little will clear; the smoke will hang in the air and people will either dash about in its arms blindly or will be restless before it, anxiously waiting for it to disperse.

11   We all know that the horizon will soon move back and back, and another season will come in Malawi. The prolonged fires will delay planting but planting will certainly begin; perhaps the harvest will be later than usual.

12   Yet now we have the flames and we must somehow live with the heat, the smoke, the urgency of fires on mountains, the terror of fires at night, the burning grass, the dry fields waiting to be lighted, and all the creatures that live in the forest scattering this way and that, away from the charred and smoky ground.

___ CONSIDERATIONS _____

1. Where and what is Malawi?

2. How does Theroux use two very different subjects: the annual burning of the grasslands and the fate of the new government of Malawi?

3. How does Theroux's short report illustrate the universal conflict between tradition and science?

4. Why are the following vivid images useful: "the violent flames of the jacaranda," "the gladness caged in trembling bodies," "the huge Mlanje plateau, a crouching animal, streaked with green," "turn the fleeing ravens into frightened asterisks of feathers"?

Lewis Thomas (1913–1993) was a medical doctor, teacher, and writer, born in New York where he became president of Memorial Sloan-Kettering Cancer Center. Earlier, he taught medicine at the University of Minnesota, was department chairman, and dean at New York University-Bellevue, and was a dean at Yale Medical School. The Lives of a Cell *won a National Book Award in 1975, and he wrote many subsequent books, including* The Fragile Species *(1992).* The New England Journal of Medicine *originally printed the articles collected in that volume, articles that at the same time make contributions to medicine and literature. His scientific mind, like the best minds in whatever field, extended itself by language to investigate everything human, and to speculate beyond the human. This essay comes from* The Lives of a Cell.

83

LEWIS THOMAS
Ceti

Tau Ceti is a relatively nearby star that sufficiently resembles   1
our sun to make its solar system a plausible candidate for the existence of life. We are, it appears, ready to begin getting in touch with
Ceti, and with any other interested celestial body in more remote
places, out to the edge. CETI is also, by intention, the acronym of the
First International Conference on Communication with Extraterrestrial Intelligence, held in 1972 in Soviet Armenia under the joint sponsorship of the National Academy of Sciences of the United States and
the Soviet Academy, which involved eminent physicists and as-
tronomers from various countries, most of whom are convinced that
the odds for the existence of life elsewhere are very high, with a reasonable probability that there are civilizations, one place or another,
with technologic mastery matching or exceeding ours.

2   On this assumption, the conferees thought it likely that radio-astronomy would be the generally accepted mode of interstellar communication, on grounds of speed and economy. They made a formal recommendation that we organize an international cooperative program, with new and immense radio telescopes, to probe the reaches of deep space for electromagnetic signals making sense. Eventually, we would plan to send out messages on our own and receive answers, but at the outset it seems more practical to begin by catching snatches of conversation between others.

3   So, the highest of all our complex technologies in the hardest of our sciences will soon be engaged, full scale, in what is essentially biologic research—and with some aspects of social science, at that.

4   The earth has become, just in the last decade, too small a place. We have the feeling of being confined—shut in; it is something like outgrowing a small town in a small county. The views of the dark, pocked surface of Mars, still lifeless to judge from the latest photographs, do not seem to have extended our reach; instead, they bring closer, too close, another unsatisfactory feature of our local environment. The blue noonday sky, cloudless, has lost its old look of immensity. The word is out that the sky is not limitless; it is finite. It is, in truth, only a kind of local roof, a membrane under which we live, luminous but confusingly refractile when suffused with sunlight; we can sense its concave surface a few miles over our heads. We know that it is tough and thick enough so that when hard objects strike it from the outside they burst into flames. The color photographs of the earth are more amazing than anything outside: we live inside a blue chamber, a bubble of air blown by ourselves. The other sky beyond, absolutely black and appalling, is wide-open country, irresistible for exploration.

5   Here we go, then. An extraterrestrial embryologist, having a close look at us from time to time, would probably conclude that the morphogenesis of the earth is coming along well, with the beginnings of a nervous system and fair-sized ganglions in the form of cities, and now with specialized, dish-shaped sensory organs, miles across, ready to receive stimuli. He may well wonder, however, how we will go about responding. We are evolving into the situation of a Skinner pigeon in a Skinner box, peering about in all directions, trying to make connections, probing.

6   When the first word comes in from outer space, finally, we will probably be used to the idea. We can already provide a quite good explanation for the origin of life, here or elsewhere. Given a moist planet with methane, formaldehyde, ammonia, and some usable minerals, all of which abound, exposed to lightning or ultraviolet irradiation at the right temperature, life might start off almost anywhere. The tricky, unsolved thing is how to get the polymers to arrange in membranes and invent replication. The rest is clear going. If they follow our proto-

col, it will be anaerobic life at first, then photosynthesis and the first exhalation of oxygen, then respiring life and the great burst of variation, then speciation, and, finally, some kind of consciousness. It is easy, in the telling.

I suspect that when we have recovered from the first easy acceptance of signs of life from elsewhere, and finished nodding at each other, and finished smiling, we will be in shock. We have had it our way, relatively speaking, being unique all these years, and it will be hard to deal with the thought that the whole, infinitely huge, spinning, clocklike apparatus around us is itself animate, and can sprout life whenever the conditions are right. We will respond, beyond doubt, by making connections after the fashion of established life, floating out our filaments, extending pili, but we will end up feeling smaller than ever, as small as a single cell, with a quite new sense of continuity. It will take some getting used to. 7

The immediate problem, however, is a much more practical, down-to-earth matter, and must be giving insomnia to the CETI participants. Let us assume that there is, indeed, sentient life in one or another part of remote space, and that we will be successful in getting in touch with it. What on earth are we going to talk about? If, as seems likely, it is a hundred or more light years away, there are going to be some very long pauses. The barest amenities, on which we rely for opening conversations—Hello, are you there?, from us, followed by Yes, hello, from them—will take two hundred years at least. By the time we have our party we may have forgotten what we had in mind. 8

We could begin by gambling on the rightness of our technology and just send out news of ourselves, like a mimeographed Christmas letter, but we would have to choose our items carefully, with durability of meaning in mind. Whatever information we provide must still make sense to us two centuries later, and must still seem important, or the conversation will be an embarrassment to all concerned. In two hundred years it is, as we have found, easy to lose the thread. 9

Perhaps the safest thing to do at the outset, if technology permits, is to send music. This language may be the best we have for explaining what we are like to others in space, with least ambiguity. I would vote for Bach, all of Bach, streamed out into space, over and over again. We would be bragging, of course, but it is surely excusable for us to put the best possible face on at the beginning of such an acquaintance. We can tell the harder truths later. And, to do ourselves justice, music would give a fairer picture of what we are really like than some of the other things we might be sending, like *Time*, say, or a history of the U.N. or Presidential speeches. We could send out our science, of course, but just think of the wincing at this end when the polite comments arrive two hundred years from now. Whatever we offer as today's items of liveliest interest are bound to be out of date and irrelevant, maybe even ridiculous. I think we should stick to music. 10

11   Perhaps, if the technology can be adapted to it, we should send some paintings. Nothing would better describe what this place is like, to an outsider, than the Cézanne demonstrations that an apple is really part fruit, part earth.

12   What kinds of questions should we ask? The choices will be hard, and everyone will want his special question first. What are your smallest particles? Did you think yourselves unique? Do you have colds? Have you anything quicker than light? Do you always tell the truth? Do you cry? There is no end to the list.

13   Perhaps we should wait a while, until we are sure we know what we want to know, before we get down to detailed questions. After all, the main question will be the opener: Hello, are you there? If the reply should turn out to be Yes, hello, we might want to stop there and think about that, for quite a long time.

____ CONSIDERATIONS _____

1. If you were to decide on our first communication with life in outer space, what message would you send? Why?

2. Why must people working on interplanetary communication keep time in mind?

3. Thomas skillfully uses figurative language to help us see what he is talking about. Consider, for example, his description of our sky in paragraph 4.

4. Point out some stylistic features in Thomas's essay that account for the highly informal, even jaunty tone.

5. Thomas touches on the shock we will feel when we have proof that mankind is not, after all, unique. What does he mean by saying "we will end up feeling smaller than ever, as small as a single cell, with quite a new sense of continuity"?

6. Why Bach rather than The Beatles or Bob Dylan or The Grateful Dead?

7. Discuss the role played by assumptions in an attempted communication. You might use as a starting point one of the following innocent-sounding questions:

> Will you be home tonight?
> How much is that doggy in the window?
> Did you ever see such a gorgeous day?
> Why did you vote for Senator Blowhard?
> Was this paper turned in late?

Henry David Thoreau (1817–1862) is one of the greatest American writers, and Walden *one of the great American books. Thoreau attended Concord Academy, in the Massachusetts town where he was born and lived. Then he went to Harvard and completed his formal education, which was extensive in mathematics, literature, Greek, Latin, and French—and included smatterings of Spanish and Italian and some of the literature of India and China. He and his brother founded a school that lasted four years, and then he was a private tutor to a family. He also worked for his father, manufacturing pencils. But mostly Thoreau walked, meditated, observed nature, and wrote.*

*A friend of Ralph Waldo Emerson's, Thoreau was influenced by the older man, and by Transcendentalism— a doctrine that recognized the unity of man and nature. For Thoreau, an idea required testing by life itself; it never remained merely mental. In his daily work on his journals, and in the books he carved from them—*A Week on the Concord and Merrimack Rivers *(1849) as well as* Walden *(1854)—he observed the detail of daily life, human and natural, and he speculated on the universal laws he could derive from this observation.*

"To know it by experience, and be able to give a true account of it"—these words could be carved on Thoreau's gravestone. "To give a true account" he became a great writer, a master of observation.

"Civil Disobedience" began as a lecture; it has become one of the most influential essays ever written, promulgating ideas of nonviolent resistance to injustice. Leo Tolstoy and Mahatma Ghandi cited Thoreau as a mentor. Thoreau went to prison when he refused to pay a poll tax because of his opposition to the Mexican War.

84

HENRY DAVID THOREAU
Civil Disobedience

1   I heartily accept the motto, "That government is best which governs least"; and I should like to see it acted up to more rapidly and systematically. Carried out, it finally amounts to this, which also I believe—"That government is best which governs not at all"; and when men are prepared for it, that will be the kind of government which they will have. Government is at best but an expedient; but most governments are usually, and all governments are sometimes, inexpedient. The objections which have been brought against a standing army, and they are many and weighty, and deserve to prevail, may also at last be brought against a standing government. The standing army is only an arm of the standing government. The government itself, which is only the mode which the people have chosen to execute their will, is equally liable to be abused and perverted before the people can act through it. Witness the present Mexican war, the work of comparatively a few individuals using the standing government as their tool; for, in the outset, the people would not have consented to this measure.

2   This American government—what is it but a tradition, though a recent one, endeavoring to transmit itself unimpaired to posterity, but each instant losing some of its integrity? It has not the vitality and force of a single living man; for a single man can bend it to his will. It is a sort of wooden gun to the people themselves. But it is not the less necessary for this; for the people must have some complicated machinery or other, and hear its din, to satisfy that idea of government which they have. Governments show thus how successfully men can be imposed on, even impose on themselves, for their own advantage. It is excellent, we must all allow. Yet this government never of itself furthered any enterprise, but by the alacrity with which it got out of its way. *It* does not keep the country free. *It* does not settle the West. *It* does not educate. The character inherent in the American people has done all that has been accomplished; and it would have done somewhat more, if the government had not sometimes got in its way. For government is an expedient by which men would fain succeed in letting one another alone; and, as has been said, when it is most expedient, the governed are most let alone by it. Trade and commerce, if

they were not made of india-rubber, would never manage to bounce over the obstacles which legislators are continually putting in their way; and, if one were to judge these men wholly by the effects of their actions and not partly by their intentions, they would deserve to be classed and punished with those mischievous persons who put obstructions on the railroads.

But, to speak practically and as a citizen, unlike those who call 3 themselves no-government men, I ask for, not at once no government, but *at once* a better government. Let every man make known what kind of government would command his respect, and that will be one step toward obtaining it.

After all, the practical reason why, when the power is once in the 4 hands of the people, a majority are permitted, and for a long period continue, to rule is not because they are most likely to be in the right, nor because this seems fairest to the minority, but because they are physically the strongest. But a government in which the majority rule in all cases cannot be based on justice, even as far as men understand it. Can there not be a government in which majorities do not virtually decide right and wrong, but conscience?—in which majorities decide only those questions to which the rule of expediency is applicable? Must the citizen ever for a moment, or in the least degree, resign his conscience to the legislator? Why has every man a conscience, then? I think that we should be men first, and subjects afterward. It is not desirable to cultivate a respect for the law, so much as for the right. The only obligation which I have a right to assume is to do at any time what I think right. It is truly enough said that a corporation has no conscience; but a corporation of conscientious men is a corporation *with* a conscience. Law never made men a whit more just; and, by means of their respect for it, even the well-disposed are daily made the agents of injustice. A common and natural result of an undue respect for law is, that you may see a file of soldiers, colonel, captain, corporal, privates, powder-monkeys, and all, marching in admirable order over hill and dale to the wars, against their wills, ay, against their common sense and consciences, which makes it very steep marching indeed, and produces a palpitation of the heart. They have no doubt that it is a damnable business in which they are all concerned; they are all peaceably inclined. Now, what are they? Men at all? or small movable forts and magazines, at the service of some unscrupulous man in power? Visit the Navy Yard, and behold a marine, such a man as an American government can make, or such as it can make a man with its black arts—a mere shadow and reminiscence of humanity, a man laid out alive and standing, and already, as one may say, buried, under arms with funeral accompaniments, though it may be,

"Not a drum was heard, not a funeral note,

> As his corse to the rampart we hurried;
> Not a soldier discharged his farewell shot
> O'er the grave where our hero we buried."*

5   The mass of men serve the state thus, not as men mainly, but as machines, with their bodies. They are the standing army, and the militia, jailers, constables, *posse comitatus*, etc. In most cases there is no free exercise whatever of the judgment or of the moral sense; but they put themselves on a level with wood and earth and stones; and wooden men can perhaps be manufactured that will serve the purpose as well. Such command no more respect than men of straw or a lump of dirt. They have the same sort of worth only as horses and dogs. Yet such as these even are commonly esteemed good citizens. Others—as most legislators, politicians, lawyers, ministers, and office-holders— serve the state chiefly with their heads; and, as they rarely make any moral distinctions, they are as likely to serve the devil, without *in-tending* it, as God. A very few—as heroes, patriots, martyrs, reformers in the great sense, and *men*—serve the state with their consciences also, and so necessarily resist it for the most part; and they are commonly treated as enemies by it. A wise man will only be useful as a man, and will not submit to be "clay," and "stop a hole to keep the wind away,"† but leave that office to his dust at least:

> "I am too high-born to be propertied,
> To be a secondary at control,
> Or useful serving-man and instrument
> To any sovereign state throughout the world."‡

6   He who gives himself entirely to his fellow men appears to them useless and selfish; but he who gives himself partially to them is pronounced a benefactor and philanthropist.

7   How does it become a man to behave toward this American government today? I answer, that he cannot without disgrace be associated with it. I cannot for an instant recognize that political organization as *my* government which is the *slave's* government also.

8   All men recognize the right of revolution; that is, the right to refuse allegiance to, and to resist, the government, when its tyranny or its inefficiency are great and unendurable. But almost all say that such is not the case now. But such was the case, they think, in the Revolution of '75. If one were to tell me that this was a bad government because it taxed certain foreign commodities brought to its ports, it is most probable that I should not make an ado about it, for I can do

---

*"Not . . . buried": the opening lines of "Burial of Sir John Moore at Corunna," by the Irish clergyman-poet Charles Wolfe (1791–1823).

†A . . . away: Cf. Shakespeare, *Hamlet*, V.i.236–37.

‡"I . . . world": Cf. Shakespeare, *King John*, V.ii.79–82.

without them. All machines have their friction; and possibly this does enough good to counterbalance the evil. At any rate, it is a great evil to make a stir about it. But when the friction comes to have its machine, and oppression and robbery are organized, I say, let us not have such a machine any longer. In other words, when a sixth of the population of a nation which has undertaken to be the refuge of liberty are slaves, and a whole country is unjustly overrun and conquered by a foreign army, and subjected to military law, I think that it is not too soon for honest men to rebel and revolutionize. What makes this duty the more urgent is the fact that the country so overrun is not our own, but ours is the invading army.

Paley,* a common authority with many on moral questions, in his chapter on the "Duty of Submission to Civil Government," resolves all civil obligation into expediency; and he proceeds to say that "so long as the interest of the whole society requires it, that is, so long as the established government cannot be resisted or changed without public inconveniency, it is the will of God ... that the established government be obeyed—and no longer. This principle being admitted, the justice of every particular case of resistance is reduced to a computation of the quantity of the danger and grievance on the one side, and of the probability and expense of redressing it on the other." Of this, he says, every man shall judge for himself. But Paley appears never to have contemplated those cases to which the rule of expediency does not apply, in which a people as well as an individual, must do justice, cost what it may. If I have unjustly wrested a plank from a drowning man, I must restore it to him though I drown myself. This, according to Paley, would be inconvenient. But he that would save his life, in such a case, shall lose it. This people must cease to hold slaves, and to make war on Mexico, though it cost them their existence as a people. 9

In their practice, nations agree with Paley; but does anyone think that Massachusetts does exactly what is right at the present crisis? 10

"A drab of state, a cloth-o'-silver slut,
To have her train borne up, and her soul train in the dirt."

Practically speaking, the opponents to a reform in Massachusetts are not a hundred thousand politicians at the South, but a hundred thousand merchants and farmers here, who are more interested in commerce and agriculture than they are in humanity, and are not prepared to do justice to the slave and to Mexico, *cost what it may.* I quarrel not with far-off foes, but with those who, near at home, co-operate with, and do the bidding of, those far away, and without whom

---

*Paley: William Paley (1743–1805), British philosopher, whose moral utilitarianism is exemplified by this quotation from his *Principles of Moral and Political Philosophy* (1785).

the latter would be harmless. We are accustomed to say, that the mass of men are unprepared; but improvement is slow, because the few are not materially wiser or better than the many. It is not so important that many should be as good as you, as that there be some absolute goodness somewhere; for that will leaven the whole lump. There are thousands who are *in opinion* opposed to slavery and to the war, who yet in effect do nothing to put an end to them; who, esteeming themselves children of Washington and Franklin, sit down with their hands in their pockets, and say that they know not what to do, and do nothing; who even postpone the question of freedom to the question of free trade, and quietly read the prices-current along with the latest advices from Mexico, after dinner, and, it may be, fall asleep over them both. What is the price-current of an honest man and patriot today? They hesitate, and they regret, and sometimes they petition; but they do nothing in earnest and with effect. They will wait, well disposed, for others to remedy the evil, that they may no longer have it to regret. At most, they give only a cheap vote, and a feeble countenance and God-speed, to the right, as it goes by them. There are nine hundred and ninety-nine patrons of virtue to one virtuous man. But it is easier to deal with the real possessor of a thing than with the temporary guardian of it.

11   All voting is a sort of gaming, like checkers or backgammon, with a slight moral tinge to it, a playing with right and wrong, with moral questions; and betting naturally accompanies it. The character of the voters is not staked. I cast my vote, perchance, as I think right; but I am not vitally concerned that that right should prevail. I am willing to leave it to the majority. Its obligation, therefore, never exceeds that of expediency. Even voting *for the right* is *doing* nothing for it. It is only expressing to men feebly your desire that it should prevail. A wise man will not leave the right to the mercy of chance, nor wish it to prevail through the power of the majority. There is but little virtue in the action of masses of men. When the majority shall at length vote for the abolition of slavery, it will be because they are indifferent to slavery, or because there is but little slavery left to be abolished by their vote. *They* will then be the only slaves. Only *his* voice can hasten the abolition of slavery who asserts his own freedom by his vote.

12   I hear of a convention to be held at Baltimore, or elsewhere, for the selection of a candidate for the Presidency, made up chiefly of editors, and men who are politicians by profession; but I think, what is it to any independent, intelligent, and respectable man what decision they may come to? Shall we not have the advantage of his wisdom and honesty, nevertheless? Can we not count upon some independent votes? Are there not many individuals in the country who do not attend conventions? But no: I find that the respectable man, so called, has immediately drifted from his position, and despairs of his country, when his country has more reason to despair of him. He forthwith

adopts one of the candidates thus selected as the only *available* one, thus proving that he is himself *available* for any purposes of the demagogue. His vote is of no more worth than that of any unprincipled foreigner or hireling native, who may have been bought. O for a man who is a *man*, and, as my neighbor says, has a bone in his back which you cannot pass your hand through! Our statistics are at fault: the population has been returned too large. How many *men* are there to a square thousand miles in this country? Hardly one. Does not America offer any inducement for men to settle here? The American has dwindled into an Odd Fellow—one who may be known by the development of his organ of gregariousness, and a manifest lack of intellect and cheerful self-reliance; whose first and chief concern, on coming into the world, is to see that the almshouses are in good repair; and, before yet he has lawfully donned the virile garb, to collect a fund for the support of the widows and orphans that may be; who, in short, ventures to live only by the aid of the Mutual Insurance company, which has promised to bury him decently.

It is not a man's duty, as a matter of course, to devote himself to   13
the eradication of any, even the most enormous, wrong; he may still properly have other concerns to engage him; but it is his duty, at least, to wash his hands of it, and, if he gives it no thought longer, not to give it practically his support. If I devote myself to other pursuits and contemplations, I must first see, at least, that I do not pursue them sitting upon another man's shoulders. I must get off him first, that he may pursue his contemplations too. See what gross inconsistency is tolerated. I have heard some of my townsmen say, "I should like to have them order me out to help put down an insurrection of the slaves, or to march to Mexico—see if I would go"; and yet these very men have each, directly by their allegiance, and so indirectly, at least, by their money, furnished a substitute. The soldier is applauded who refuses to serve in an unjust war by those who do not refuse to sustain the unjust government which makes the war; is applauded by those whose own act and authority he disregards and sets at naught; as if the state were penitent to that degree that it hired one to scourge it while it sinned, but not to that degree that it left off sinning for a moment. Thus, under the name of Order and Civil Government, we are all made at last to pay homage to and support our own meanness. After the first blush of sin comes its indifference; and from immoral it becomes, as it were, *un*moral, and not quite unnecessary to that life which we have made.

The broadest and most prevalent error requires the most disinter-   14
ested virtue to sustain it. The slight reproach to which the virtue of patriotism is commonly liable, the noble are most likely to incur. Those who, while they disapprove of the character and measures of a government, yield to it their allegiance and support are undoubtedly its most conscientious supporters, and so frequently the most serious

obstacles to reform. Some are petitioning the State to dissolve the Union, to disregard the requisitions of the President. Why do they not dissolve it to themselves—the union between themselves and the State—and refuse to pay their quota into its treasury? Do not they stand in the same relation to the State that the State does to the Union? And have not the same reasons prevented the State from resisting the Union which have prevented them from resisting the State?

15 How can a man be satisfied to entertain an opinion merely, and enjoy *it*? Is there any enjoyment in it, if his opinion is that he is aggrieved? If you are cheated out of a single dollar by your neighbor, you do not rest satisfied with knowing that you are cheated, or with saying that you are cheated, or even with petitioning him to pay you your due; but you take effectual steps at once to obtain the full amount, and see that you are never cheated again. Action from principle, the perception and the performance of right, changes things and relations; it is essentially revolutionary, and does not consist wholly with anything which was. It not only divides States and churches, it divides families; ay, it divides the *individual,* separating the diabolical in him from the divine.

16 Unjust laws exist: shall we be content to obey them, or shall we endeavor to amend them, and obey them until we have succeeded, or shall we transgress them at once? Men generally, under such a government as this, think that they ought to wait until they have persuaded the majority to alter them. They think that, if they should resist, the remedy would be worse than the evil. But it is the fault of the government itself that the remedy *is* worse than the evil. *It* makes it worse. Why is it not more apt to anticipate and provide for reform? Why does it not cherish its wise minority? Why does it cry and resist before it is hurt? Why does it not encourage its citizens to be on the alert to point out its faults, and *do* better than it would have them? Why does it always crucify Christ, and excommunicate Copernicus and Luther, and pronounce Washington and Franklin rebels?

17 One would think, that a deliberate and practical denial of its authority was the only offence never contemplated by government: else, why has it not assigned its definite, its suitable and proportionate, penalty? If a man who has no property refuses but once to earn nine shillings for the State, he is put in prison for a period unlimited by any law that I know, and determined only by the discretion of those who placed him there; but if he should steal ninety times nine shillings from the State, he is soon permitted to go at large again.

18 If the injustice is part of the necessary friction of the machine of government, let it go, let it go: perchance it will wear smooth—certainly the machine will wear out. If the injustice has a spring, or a pulley, or a rope, or a crank, exclusively for itself, then perhaps you may consider whether the remedy will not be worse than the evil; but if it

is of such a nature that it requires you to be the agent of injustice to another, then, I say, break the law. Let your life be a counter-friction to stop the machine. What I have to do is to see, at any rate, that I do not lend myself to the wrong which I condemn.

As for adopting the ways which the State has provided for reme- 19 dying the evil, I know not of such ways. They take too much time, and a man's life will be gone. I have other affairs to attend to. I came into this world, not chiefly to make this a good place to live in, but to live in it, be it good or bad. A man has not everything to do, but something; and because he cannot do *everything*, it is not necessary that he should do *something* wrong. It is not my business to be petitioning the Governor or the Legislature any more than it is theirs to petition me; and if they should not hear my petition, what should I do then? But in this case the State has provided no way: its very Constitution is the evil. This may seem to be harsh and stubborn and unconciliatory; but it is to treat with the utmost kindness and consideration the only spirit that can appreciate or deserves it. So is all change for the better, like birth and death, which convulse the body.

I do not hesitate to say, that those who call themselves Aboli- 20 tionists should at once effectually withdraw their support, both in person and property, from the government of Massachusetts, and not wait till they constitute a majority of one, before they suffer the right to prevail through them. I think that it is enough if they have God on their side, without waiting for that other one. Moreover, any man more right than his neighbors constitutes a majority of one already.

I meet this American government, or its representative, the State 21 government, directly, and face to face, once a year—no more—in the person of its tax-gatherer; this is the only mode in which a man situated as I am necessarily meets it; and it then says distinctly, Recognize me; and the simplest, the most effectual, and, in the present posture of affairs, the indispensablest mode of treating with it on this head, of expressing your little satisfaction with and love for it, is to deny it then. My civil neighbor, the tax-gatherer, is the very man I have to deal with—for it is, after all, with men and not with parchment that I quarrel—and he has voluntarily chosen to be an agent of the government. How shall he ever know well what he is and does as an officer of the government, or as a man, until he is obliged to consider whether he shall treat me, his neighbor, for whom he has respect, as a neighbor and well-disposed man, or as a maniac and disturber of the peace, and see if he can get over this obstruction to his neighborliness without a ruder and more impetuous thought or speech corresponding with his action. I know this well, that if one thousand, if one hundred, if ten men whom I could name—if ten *honest* men only—ay, if *one* HONEST man, in this State of Massachusetts, *ceasing to hold slaves*, were actually to withdraw from this copartnership, and be locked up in the county jail therefor, it would be the abolition of slavery in America. For it matters now how small the beginning may seem to be: what is once well done is done forever. But we love better to talk about it: that we say is our mission. Reform keeps many scores of newspapers in its service, but not one man. If my esteemed neighbor, the State's ambassador,* who will devote his days to the settlement of the question of human rights in the Council Chamber, instead of being threatened with the prisons of Carolina, were to sit down the prisoner of Massachusetts, that Sate which is so anxious to foist the sin of slavery upon her sister—though at present she can discover only an act of inhospitality to be the ground of a quarrel with her—the Legislature would not wholly waive the subject the following winter.

22   Under a government which imprisons any unjustly, the true place for a just man is also a prison. The proper place today, the only place which Massachusetts has provided for her freer and less desponding spirits, is in her prisons, to be put out and locked out of the State by her own act, as they have already put themselves out by their principles. It is there that the fugitive slave, and the Mexican prisoner on parole, and the Indian come to plead the wrongs of his race should find them; on that separate, but more free and honorable, ground, where the State places those who are not *with* her, but *against* her— the only house in a slave State in which a free man can abide with honor. If any think that their influence would be lost there, and their voices no longer afflict the ear of the State, that they would not be as an enemy within its walls, they do not know by how much truth is stronger than error, nor how much more eloquently and effectively he can combat injustice who has experienced a little in his own person. Cast your whole vote, not a strip of paper merely, but your whole influence. A minority is powerless while it conforms to the majority; it is not even a minority then; but it is irresistible when it clogs by its whole weight. If the alternative is to keep all just men in prison, or give up war and slavery, the State will not hesitate which to choose. If a thousand men were not to pay their tax-bills this year, that would not be a violent and bloody measure, as it would be to pay them, and enable the State to commit violence and shed innocent blood. This is, in fact, the definition of a peaceable revolution, if any such is possible. If the tax-gatherer, or any other public officer, asks me, as one has done, "But what shall I do?" my answer is, "If you really wish to do anything, resign your office." When the subject has refused allegiance, and the officer has resigned his office, then the revolution is accomplished. But even suppose blood should flow. Is there not a sort of blood shed when the conscience is wounded? Through this wound a

---

*The State's ambassador: Samuel Hoar (1778–1856), Concord lawyer and congressman, was sent to Charleston, S.C., to represent black seamen from Massachusetts threatened with arrest and enslavement. Hoar was forcibly expelled from the port.

man's real manhood and immortality flow out, and he bleeds to an everlasting death. I see this blood flowing now.

I have contemplated the imprisonment of the offender, rather 23
than the seizure of his goods—though both will serve the same purpose—because they who assert the purest right, and consequently are most dangerous to a corrupt State, commonly have not spent much time in accumulating property. To such the State renders comparatively small service, and a slight tax is wont to appear exorbitant, particularly if they are obliged to earn it by special labor with their hands. If there were one who lived wholly without the use of money, the State itself would hesitate to demand it of him. But the rich man—not to make any invidious comparison—is always sold to the institution which makes him rich. Absolutely speaking, the more money, the less virtue; for money comes between a man and his objects, and obtains them for him; and it was certainly no great virtue to obtain it. It puts to rest many questions which he would otherwise be taxed to answer; while the only new question which it puts is the hard but superfluous one, how to spend it. Thus his moral ground is taken from under his feet. The opportunities of living are diminished in proportion as what are called the "means" are increased. The best thing a man can do for his culture when he is rich is to endeavor to carry out those schemes which he entertained when he was poor. Christ answered the Herodians according to their condition. "Show me the tribute-money," said he—and one took a penny out of his pocket—if you use money which has the image of Caesar on it, and which he has made current and valuable, that is, *if you are men of the State,* and gladly enjoy the advantages of Caesar's government, then pay him back some of his own when he demands it. "Render therefore to Caesar that which is Caesar's, and to God those things which are God's"*—leaving them no wiser than before as to which was which; for they did no wish to know.

When I converse with the freest of my neighbors, I perceive that, 24
whatever they may say about the magnitude and seriousness of the question, and their regard for the public tranquility, the long and the short of the matter is, that they cannot spare the protection of the existing government, and they dread the consequences to their property and families of disobedience to it. For my own part, I should not like to think that I ever rely on the protection of the State. But, if I deny the authority of the State when it presents its tax bill, it will soon take and waste all my property, and so harass me and my children without end. This is hard. This makes it impossible for a man to live honestly, and at the same time comfortably, in outward respects. It will not be worth the while to accumulate property; that would be sure to go

---

*Matthew 22:21.

again. You must hire or squat somewhere, and raise but a small crop, and eat that soon. You must live within yourself, and depend upon yourself always tucked up and ready for a start, and not have many affairs. A man may grow rich in Turkey even, if he will be in all respects a good subject of the Turkish government. Confucius said: "If a state is governed by the principles of reason, poverty and misery are subjects of shame; if a state is not governed by the principles of reason, riches and honors are the subjects of shame." No: until I want the protection of Massachusetts to be extended to me in some distant Southern port, where my liberty is endangered, or until I am bent solely on building up an estate at home by peaceful enterprise, I can afford to refuse allegiance to Massachusetts, and her right to my property and life. It costs me less in every sense to incur the penalty of disobedience to the State than it would to obey. I should feel as if I were worth less in that case.

25   Some years ago, the State met me in behalf of the Church, and commanded me to pay a certain sum toward the support of a clergyman whose preaching my father attended, but never I myself. "Pay," it said, "or be locked up in the jail." I declined to pay.* But, unfortunately, another man saw fit to pay it. I did not see why the schoolmaster should be taxed to support the priest, and not the priest the schoolmaster; for I was not the State's schoolmaster, but I supported myself by voluntary subscription. I did not see why the lyceum should not present its tax bill, and have the State to back its demand, as well as the Church. However, at the request of the selectmen, I condescended to make some such statement as this in writing: "Know all men by these presents, that I, Henry Thoreau, do not wish to be regarded as a member of any incorporated society which I have not joined." This I gave to the town clerk; and he has it. The State, having thus learned that I did not wish to be regarded as a member of that church, has never made a like demand on me since; though it said that it must adhere to its original presumption that time. If I had known how to name them, I should then have signed off in detail from all the societies which I never signed on to; but I did not know where to find a complete list.

26   I have paid no poll-tax for six years. I was put into a jail once on this account, for one night; and, as I stood considering the walls of solid stone, two or three feet thick, the door of wood and iron, a foot thick, and the iron grating which strained the light, I could not help being struck with the foolishness of that institution which treated me as if I were mere flesh and blood and bones, to be locked up. I wondered that it should have concluded at length that this was the best

---

*"I . . . pay": Thoreau signed off from church taxes in 1838 and went to jail in July 1846, for refusing to pay his poll tax.

use it could put me to, and had never thought to avail itself of my services in some way. I saw that, if there was a wall of stone between me and my townsmen, there was a still more difficult one to climb or break through before they could get to be as free as I was. I did not for a moment feel confined, and the walls seemed a great waste of stone and mortar. I felt as if I alone of all my townsmen had paid my tax. They plainly did not know how to treat me, but behaved like persons who are underbred. In every threat and in every compliment there was a blunder; for they thought that my chief desire was to stand the other side of that stone wall. I could not but smile to see how industriously they locked the door on my meditations, which followed them out again without let or hindrance, and *they* were really all that was dangerous. As they could not reach me, they had resolved to punish my body; just as boys, if they cannot come at some person against whom they have a spite, will abuse his dog. I saw that the State was half-witted, that it was timid as a lone woman with her silver spoons, and that it did not know its friends from its foes, and I lost all my remaining respect for it, and pitied it.

Thus the State never intentionally confronts a man's sense, intellectual or moral, but only his body, his senses. It is not armed with superior wit or honesty, but with superior physical strength. I was not born to be forced. I will breathe after my own fashion. Let us see who is the strongest. What force has a multitude? They only can force me who obey a higher law than I. They force me to become like themselves. I do not hear of *men* being *forced* to live this way or that by masses of men. What sort of life were that to live? When I meet a government which says to me, "Your money or your life," why should I be in haste to give it my money? It may be in a great strait, and not know what to do: I cannot help that. It must help itself; do as I do. It is not worth the while to snivel about it. I am not responsible for the successful working of the machinery of society. I am not the son of the engineer. I perceive that, when an acorn and a chestnut fall side by side, the one does not remain inert to make way for the other, but both obey their own laws, and spring and grow and flourish as best they can, till one, perchance, overshadows and destroys the other. If a plant cannot live according to its nature, it dies; and so a man. 27

The night in prison was novel and interesting enough. The prisoners in their shirtsleeves were enjoying a chat and the evening air in the doorway, when I entered. But the jailer said, "Come, boys, it is time to lock up"; and so they dispersed, and I heard the sound of their steps returning into the hollow apartments. My room-mate was introduced to me by the jailer as "a first-rate fellow and a clever man." When the door was locked, he showed me where to hang my hat, and how he managed matters there. The rooms were white-washed once a month; and this one, at least, was the whitest, most simply furnished, and probably the neatest apartment in the town. He naturally wanted 28 to know where I came from, and what brought me there; and, when I had told him, I asked him in my turn how he came there, presuming him to be an honest man, of course; and, as the world goes, I believe he was. "Why," said he, "they accuse me of burning a barn; but I never did it." As near as I could discover, he had probably gone to bed in a barn when drunk, and smoked his pipe there; and so a barn was burnt. He had the reputation of being a clever man, had been there some three months waiting for his trial to come on, and would have to wait as much longer; but he was quite domesticated and contented, since he got his board for nothing, and thought that he was well treated.

29   He occupied one window, and I the other; and I saw that if one stayed there long, his principal business would be to look out the window. I had soon read all the tracts that were left there, and examined where former prisoners had broken out, and where a grate had been sawed off, and heard the history of the various occupants of that room; for I found that even here there was a history and a gossip which never circulated beyond the walls of the jail. Probably this is the only house in the town where verses are composed, which are afterward printed in a circular form, but not published. I was shown quite a long list of verses which were composed by some young men who had been detected in an attempt to escape, who avenged themselves by singing them.

30   I pumped my fellow-prisoner as dry as I could, for fear I should never see him again; but at length he showed me which was my bed, and left me to blow out the lamp.

31   It was like traveling into a far country, such as I had never expected to behold, to lie there for one night. It seemed to me that I never had heard the town clock strike before, nor the evening sounds of the village; for we slept with the windows open, which were inside the grating. It was to see my native village in the light of the Middle Ages, and our Concord was turned into a Rhine stream, and visions of knights and castles passed before me. They were the voices of old burghers that I heard in the streets. I was an involuntary spectator and auditor of whatever was done and said in the kitchen of the adjacent village inn—a wholly new and rare experience to me. It was a closer view of my native town. I was fairly inside of it. I never had seen its institutions before. This is one of its peculiar institutions; for it is a shire town. I began to comprehend what its inhabitants were about.

32   In the morning, our breakfasts were put through the hole in the door, in small oblong-square tin pans, made to fit, and holding a pint of chocolate, with brown bread, and an iron spoon. When they called for the vessels again, I was green enough to return what bread I had left; but my comrade seized it, and said that I should lay that up for lunch or dinner. Soon after he was let out to work at haying in a neighboring field, whither he went every day, and would not be back till

noon; so he bade me good-day, saying that he doubted if he should see me again.

When I came out of prison—for some one interfered, and paid 33 that tax—I did not perceive that great changes had taken place on the common, such as he observed who went in a youth and emerged a tottering and gray-headed man; and yet a change had to my eyes come over the scene—the town, and State, and country—greater than any that mere time could effect. I saw yet more distinctly the State in which I lived. I saw to what extent the people among whom I lived could be trusted as good neighbors and friends; that their friendship was for summer weather only; that they did not greatly propose to do right; that they were a distinct race from me by their prejudices and superstitions, as the Chinamen and Malays are; that in their sacrifices to humanity they ran no risks, not even to their property; that after all they were no so noble but they treated the thief as he had treated them, and hoped, by a certain outward observance and a few prayers, and by walking in a particular straight though useless path from time to time, to save their souls. This may be to judge my neighbors harshly; for I believe that many of them are not aware that they have such an institution as the jail in their village.

It was formerly the custom in our village, when a poor debtor 34 came out of jail, for his acquaintances to salute him, looking through their fingers, which were crossed to represent the grating of a jail window, "How do ye do?" My neighbors did not thus salute me, but first looked at me, and then at one another, as if I had returned from a long journey. I was put into jail as I was going to the shoemaker's to get a shoe which was mended. When I was let out the next morning, I proceeded to finish my errand, and, having put on my mended shoe, joined a huckleberry party, who were impatient to put themselves under my conduct; and in half an hour—for the horse was soon tackled—was in the midst of a huckleberry field, on one of our highest hills, two miles off, and then the State was nowhere to be seen.

This is the whole history of "My Prisons."* 35

I have never declined paying the highway tax, because I am as de- 36 sirous of being a good neighbor as I am of being a bad subject; and as for supporting schools, I am doing my part to educate my fellow-countrymen now. It is for no particular item in the tax bill that I refuse to pay it. I simply wish to refuse allegiance to the State, to withdraw and stand aloof from it effectually. I do not care to trace the course of my dollar, if I could, till it buys a man or a musket to shoot one with—the dollar is innocent—but I am concerned to trace the effects of my allegiance. In fact, I quietly declare war with the State, after my fashion,

---

*"My Prisons": English translation of the title *Le Mie Prigioni*, a record of his Austrian incarceration by the Italian patriot and poet Silvio Pellico (1789–1854).

though I will still make what use and get what advantage of her I can, as is usual in such cases.

37   If others pay the tax which is demanded of me, from a sympathy with the State, they do but what they have already done in their own case, or rather they abet injustice to a greater extent than the State requires. If they pay the tax from a mistaken interest in the individual taxed, to save his property, or prevent his going to jail, it is because they have not considered wisely how far they let their private feelings interfere with the public good.

38   This, then, is my position at present. But one cannot be too much on his guard in such a case, lest his action be biased by obstinacy or an undue regard for the opinions of men. Let him see that he does only what belongs to himself and to the hour.

39   I think sometimes, Why, this people mean well, they are only ignorant; they would do better if they knew how: why give your neighbors his pain to treat you as they are not inclined to? But I think again, This is no reason why I should do as they do, or permit others to suffer much greater pain of a different kind. Again, I sometimes say to myself, When many millions of men, without heat, without ill will, without personal feeling of any kind, demand of you a few shillings only, without the possibility, such is their constitution, of retracting or altering their present demand, and without the possibility, on your side, of appeal to any other millions, why expose yourself to this overwhelming brute force? You do not resist cold and hunger, the winds and the waves, thus obstinately; you quietly submit to a thousand similar necessities. You do not put your head into the fire. But just in proportion as I regard this as not wholly a brute force, but partly a human force, and consider that I have relations to those millions as to so many millions of men, and not of mere brute or inanimate things, I see that appeal is possible, first and instantaneously, from them to the Maker of them, and, secondly, from them to themselves. But if I put my head deliberately into the fire, there is no appeal to fire or to the Maker of fire, and I have only myself to blame. If I could convince myself that I have any right to be satisfied with men as they are, and to treat them accordingly, and not according, in some respects, to my requisitions and expectations of what they and I ought to be, then, like a good Mussulman and fatalist, I should endeavor to be satisfied with things as they are, and say it is the will of God. And, above all, there is this difference between resisting this and a purely brute or natural force, that I can resist this with some effect; but I cannot expect, like Orpheus, to change the nature of the rocks and trees and beasts.

40   I do not wish to quarrel with any man or nation. I do not wish to split hairs, to make fine distinctions, or set myself up as better than my neighbors. I seek rather, I may say, even an excuse for conforming to the laws of the land. I am but too ready to conform to them. Indeed,

I have reason to suspect myself on this head; and each year, as the tax-gatherer comes round, I find myself disposed to review the acts and position of the general and State governments, and the spirit of the people, to discover a pretext for conformity.

> "We must affect our country as our parents,
> And if at any time we alienate
> Our love or industry from doing it honor,
> We must respect effects and teach the soul
> Matter of conscience and religion,
> And not desire of rule or benefit."

I believe that the State will soon be able to take all my work of this sort out of my hands, and then I shall be no better a patriot than my fellow-countrymen. Seen from a lower point of view, the Constitution, with all its faults, is very good; the law and the courts are very respectable; even this State and this American government are, in many respects, very admirable, and rare things, to be thankful for, such as a great many have described them; but seen from a point of view a little higher, they are what I have described them; seen from a higher still, and the highest, who shall say what they are, or that they are worth looking at or thinking of at all?

However, the government does not concern me much, and I shall   41
bestow the fewest possible thoughts on it. It is not many moments that I live under a government, even in this world. If a man is thought-free, fancy-free, imagination-free, that which *is not* never for a long time appearing *to be* to him, unwise rulers or reformers cannot fatally interrupt him.

I know that most men think differently from myself; but those   42
whose lives are by profession devoted to the study of these or kindred subjects content me as little as any. Statesmen and legislators, standing so completely within the institution, never distinctly and nakedly behold it. They speak of moving society, but have no resting-place without it. They may be men of a certain experience and discrimination, and have no doubt invented ingenious and even useful systems, for which we sincerely thank them; but all their wit and usefulness lie within certain not very wide limits. They are wont to forget that the world is not governed by policy and expediency. Webster never goes behind government, and so cannot speak with authority about it. His words are wisdom to those legislators who contemplate no essential reform in the existing government; but for thinkers, and those who legislate for all time, he never once glances at the subject. I know of those whose serene and wise speculations on this theme would soon reveal the limits of his mind's range and hospitality. Yet, compared with the cheap professions of most reformers, and the still cheaper wisdom and eloquence of politicians in general, his are almost the

only sensible and valuable words, and we thank Heaven for him. Comparatively, he is always strong, original, and above all, practical. Still, his quality is not wisdom, but prudence. The lawyer's truth is not Truth, but consistency or a consistent expediency. Truth is always in harmony with herself, and is not concerned chiefly to reveal the justice that may consist with wrong-doing. He well deserves to be called, as he has been called, the Defender of the Constitution. There are really no blows to be given by him but defensive ones. He is not a leader, but a follower. His leaders are the men of '87. "I have never made an effort," he says, "and never propose to make an effort; I have never countenanced an effort, and never mean to countenance an effort, to disturb the arrangement as originally made, by which the various States came into the Union." Still thinking of the sanction which the Constitution gives to slavery, he says, "Because it was a part of the original compact—let it stand." Notwithstanding his special acuteness and ability, he is unable to take a fact out of its merely political relations, and behold it as it lies absolutely to be disposed of by the intellect—what, for instance, it behooves a man to do here in America today with regard to slavery—but ventures, or is drive, to make some such desperate answer as the following, while professing to speak absolutely, and as a private man—from which what new and singular code of social duties might be inferred? "The manner," says he, "in which the governments of those states where slavery exists are to regulate it is for their own consideration, under their responsibility to their constituents, to the general laws of propriety, humanity, and justice, and to God. Associations formed elsewhere, springing from a feeling of humanity, or any other cause, have nothing whatever to do with it. They have never received any encouragement from me, and they never will."

43   They who know of no purer sources of truth, who have traced up its stream no higher, stand, and wisely stand, by the Bible and the Constitution, and drink at it there with reverence and humility; but they who behold where it comes trickling into his lake or that pool, gird up their loins once more, and continue their pilgrimage toward its fountainhead.

44   No man with a genius for legislation has appeared in America. They are rare in the history of the world. There are orators, politicians, and eloquent men, by the thousand; but the speaker has not yet opened his mouth to speak who is capable of settling the much-vexed questions of the day. We love eloquence for its own sake, and not for any truth which it may utter, or any heroism it may inspire. Our legislators have not yet learned the comparative value of free trade and of freedom, of union, and of rectitude, to a nation. They have no genius or talent for comparatively humble questions of taxation and finance, commerce and manufactures and agriculture. If we were left solely to

the wordy wit of legislators in Congress for our guidance, uncorrected by the seasonable experience and the effectual complaints of the people, America would not long retain her rank among the nations. For eighteen hundred years, though perchance I have no right to say it, the New Testament has been written; yet where is the legislator who has wisdom and practical talent enough to avail himself of the light which it sheds on the science of legislation?

The authority of government, even such as I am willing to submit to—for I will cheerfully obey those who know and can do better than I, and in many things even those who neither know nor can do so well—is still an impure one: to be strictly just, it must have the sanction and consent of the governed. It can have no pure right over my person and property but what I concede to it. The progress from an absolute to a limited monarchy, from a limited monarchy to a democracy, is a progress toward a true respect for the individual. Even the Chinese philosopher was wise enough to regard the individual as the basis of the empire. Is a democracy, such as we know it, the last improvement possible in government? Is it not possible to take a step further towards recognizing and organizing the rights of man? There will never be a really free and enlightened State until the State comes to recognize the individual as a higher and independent power, from which all its own power and authority are derived, and treats him accordingly. I please myself with imagining a State at last which can afford to be just to all men, and to treat the individual with respect as a neighbor; which even would not think it inconsistent with its own repose if a few were to live aloof from it, not meddling with it, nor embraced by it, who fulfilled all the duties of neighbors and fellow men. A State which bore this kind of fruit, and suffered it to drop off as fast as it ripened, would prepare the way for a still more perfect and glorious State, which also I have imagined, but not yet anywhere seen.

45

_____ CONSIDERATIONS _____

1. "But to be *liked,* you must never disagree. And if you never disagree, it's like breathing in and never breathing out!" This is a line from *The Night Thoreau Spent in Jail,* a widely produced play by Jerome Lawrence and Robert E. Lee (1971). Can you find lines in "Civil Disobedience" that sound a little like this Thoreau character in the play?

2. Thoreau, sometimes depicted as a grimly serious man, had his own dry sense of humor, as seen in paragraph 25, especially the last few sentences. What are the strengths and risks of using humor in a serious essay like "Civil Disobedience"?

3. Specifically, what paradoxical discovery did Thoreau make during his night in jail that made him lose all his remaining respect for the state?

4. To illustrate his dissatisfaction with politicians (paragraph 42), Thoreau comments at length on a particular man who had become for many the image of a wise statement. Who is that man, and what are some of the faults Thoreau finds in him?

5. Is Thoreau a liberal or a conservative? Find evidence for your opinion in "Civil Disobedience."

6. Thoreau makes emphatic use of the word "expedient." Study his uses of the word and consider some alternatives.

7. Why does Thoreau say voting is more like a game than anything else?

Thoreau was disgusted with fellow Northerners who accepted enforcement of the Fugitive Slave Act. Two entries from his journal, on two successive days, respond to one dreadful occasion involving the case of Anthony Burns. When a mob tried to free the fugitive slave, the government called out the militia to ensure that the trial was held. Burns was returned to the South, although his identity as an escaped slave was doubtful. Never again was the Fugitive Slave Act enforced in Massachusetts. Here is the first of those two entries.

85

HENRY DAVID THOREAU
From The Journals: June 16, 1854 *and* November 30, 1858

June 16, 1854

The effect of a good government is to make life more valuable,— of a bad government, to make it less valuable. We can afford that railroad and all merely material stock should depreciate, for that only compels us to live more simply and economically; but suppose the value of life itself should be depreciated. Every man in New England capable of the sentiment of patriotism must have lived the last three weeks with the sense of having suffered a vast, indefinite loss. I had never respected this government, but I had foolishly thought that I might manage to live here, attending to my private affairs, and forget it. For my part, my old and and worthiest pursuits have lost I cannot say how much of their attraction, and I feel that my investment in life here is worth many per cent, less since Massachusetts last deliberately and forcibly restored an innocent man, Anthony Burns, to slavery. I dwelt before in the illusion that my life passed somewhere only between heaven and hell, but now I cannot persuade myself that I do not dwell wholly within hell. The sight of that political organization

1

called Massachusetts is to me morally covered with scoriæ and volcanic cinders, such as Milton imagined. If there is any hell more unprincipled than our rulers and our people, I feel curious to visit it. Life itself being worthless, all things with it, that feed it, are worthless. Suppose you have a small library, with pictures to adorn the walls,—a garden laid out around—and contemplate scientific and literary pursuits, etc., etc., and discover suddenly that your villa, with all its contents, is located in hell, and that the justice of the peace is one of the devil's angels, has a cloven foot and forked tail,—do not these things suddenly lose their value in your eyes? Are you not disposed to sell at a great sacrifice?

2   I feel that, to some extent, the State has fatally interfered with my just and proper business. It has not merely interrupted me in my passage through Court Street on errands of trade, but it has, to some extent, interrupted me and every man on his onward and upward path, on which he had trusted soon to leave Court Street far behind. I have found that hollow which I had relied on for solid.

3   I am surprised to see men going about their business as if nothing had happened, and say to myself, "Unfortunates! they have not heard the news"; that the man whom I just met on horseback should be so earnest to overtake his newly bought cows running away,—since all property is insecure, and if they do not run away again, they may be taken away from him when he gets them. Fool! does he not know that his seed-corn is worth less this year,—that all beneficent harvests fail as he approaches the empire of hell? No prudent man will build a stone house under these circumstances, or engage in any peaceful enterprise which it requires a long time to accomplish. Art is as long as ever, but life is more interrupted and less available for a man's proper pursuits. It is time we had done referring to our ancestors. We have used up all our inherited freedom, like the young bird the albumen in the egg. It is not an era of repose. If we would save our lives, we must fight for them.

4   The discovery is what matter of men your countrymen are. They steadily worship mammon—and on the seventh day curse God with a tintamarre from one end of the *Union* to the other. I heard the other day of a meek and sleek devil of a Bishop Somebody, who commended the law and order with which Burns was given up. I would like before I sit down to a table to inquire if there is one in the company who styles himself or is styled Bishop, and he or I should go out of it. I would have such a man wear his bishop's hat and his clerical bib and tucker, that we may know him.

5   Why will men be such fools as [to] trust to lawyers for a *moral* reform? I do not believe that there is a judge in this country prepared to decide by the principle that a law is immoral and therefore of no force. They put themselves, or rather are by character, exactly on a level

with the marine who discharges his musket in any direction in which he is ordered. They are just as much tools, and as little men.

> *These passages come from his journal, the disciplined daily writing from which Thoreau shaped his finished books. Here he writes about the bream—a small, silvery, flattish freshwater fish—not so much by describing it as by recounting his reaction to it and by ruminating on the relationship between people and the natural world.*

November 30, 1858

I cannot but see still in my mind's eye those little striped breams   1 poised in Walden's glaucous water. They balance all the rest of the world in my estimation at present, for this is the bream that I have just found, and for the time I neglect all its brethren and am ready to kill the fatted calf on its account. For more than two centuries have men fished here and have not distinguished this permanent settler of the township. It is not like a new bird, a transient visitor that may not be seen again for years, but there it dwells and has dwelt permanently, who can tell how long? When my eyes first rested on Walden the striped bream was poised on it, though I did not see it, and when Tahatawan paddled his canoe there. How wild it makes the pond and the township to find a new fish in it! America renews her youth here. But in my account of this bream I cannot go a hair's breadth beyond the mere statement that it exists,—the miracle of its existence, my contemporary and neighbor, yet so different from me! I can only poise my thought there by its side and try to think like a bream for a moment. I can only think of precious jewels, of music, poetry, beauty, and the mystery of life. I only see the bream in its orbit, as I see a star, but I care not to measure its distance or weight. The bream, appreciated, floats in the pond as the centre of the system, another image of God. Its life no man can explain more than he can his own. I want you to perceive the mystery of the bream. I have a contemporary in Walden. It has fins where I have legs and arms. I have a friend among the fishes, at least a new acquaintance. Its character will interest me, I trust, not its clothes and anatomy. I do not want it to eat. Acquaintance with it is to make my life more rich and eventful. It is as if a poet or an anchorite had moved into the town, whom I can see from time to time and think of yet oftener. Perhaps there are a thousand of these striped bream which no one had thought of in that pond—not their mere impressions in stone, but in the full tide of the bream life.

Though science may sometimes compare herself to a child pick-   2 ing up pebbles on the seashore, that is a rare mood with her; ordinarily her practical belief is that it is only a few pebbles which are *not* known, weighed and measured. A new species of fish signifies hardly more than a new name. See what is contributed in the scientific reports. One counts the fin-rays, another measures the intestines, a third daguerreotypes a scale, etc., etc.; otherwise there's nothing to be said. As if all but this were done, and these were very rich and generous contributions to science. Her votaries may be seen wandering along the shore of the ocean of truth, with their backs to that ocean, ready to seize on the shells which are cast up. You would say that the scientific bodies were terribly put to it for objects and subjects. A dead specimen of an animal, if it is only preserved in alcohol, is just as good for science as a living one preserved in its native element.

3   What is the amount of my discovery to me? It is not that I have got one in a bottle, that it has got a name in a book, but that I have a little fishy friend in the pond. How was it when the youth first discovered fishes? Was it the number of their fin-rays or their arrangement, or the place of the fish in some system that made the boy dream of them? Is it these things that interest mankind in the fish, the inhabitant of the water? No, but a faint recognition of a living contemporary, a provoking mystery. One boy thinks of fishes and goes a-fishing from the same motive that his brother searches the poets for rare lines. It is the poetry of fishes which is their chief use; their flesh is their lowest use. The beauty of the fish, that is what it is best worth the while to measure. Its place in our systems is of comparatively little importance. Generally the boy loses some of his perception and his interest in the fish; he degenerates into a fisherman or an ichthyologist.

____ CONSIDERATIONS _____

June 16, 1854

   1. In expressing disgust over the Fugitive Slave Act at work in his own state of Massachusetts, Thoreau distinguishes between a high material standard of living and a high valuing of life itself. Thus, he would be willing to dispense with railroads and other creature comforts if the value of life could be preserved. Do you hold similar feelings? Are you willing to trade civil liberties for comforts and conveniences? Is such a trade necessary?
   2. To show how the court decisions about Anthony Burns have changed his life, Thoreau makes use of allusion—a literary device—when he refers to Milton's description of hell. If that allusion does not elicit the dramatic effect Thoreau intends, turn to "Book 1" of Milton's *Paradise Lost*. In your next essay, try to employ an allusion—not necessarily to Milton—to strength a point.
   3. How does Thoreau use his knowledge of natural history to make credible his statement that "We have used up all our inherited freedom"?
   4. Can you connect Thoreau's thinking with any of the arguments over present unrest in our cities?

November 30, 1858

1. Thoreau's excitement in describing the bream was generated by his discovery of a species living unnoticed in Walden Pond. But why, according to him, can he do no more than say that it exists? Why is that statement sufficient?

2. What kind of truth—scientific, philosophic, economic, aesthetic—can you find in Thoreau's statement that the bream "is the center of the system, another image of God"? Look carefully at his sentence in paragraph 1. Why pay particular attention to the word "appreciated," which is set off by commas?

3. What does Thoreau's excitement over discovering the bream have in common with Wendell Berry's "A Native Hill," Robert Finch's "Very Like a Whale," or E. B. White's "Once More to the Lake"?

4. Why, in his closing statement, does Thoreau consider both the fisherman and the ichthyologist pitiable?

5. "Mystery" is an important word in Thoreau's essay. What is there about the way scientists work that limits their appreciation of the mystery of creation? Perhaps Nancy Mairs' "The Unmaking of a Scientist," page 347, and Richard Feynman's "It's as Simple as One, Two, Three," page 195, would be of help on this question.

James Thurber (1894–1961) was born in Columbus, Ohio, the scene of many of his funniest stories. He graduated from Ohio State University, and after a period as a newspaperman in Paris, began to work for the New Yorker. *For years his comic writing and his cartoons— drawings of sausage-shaped dogs and of men and women forever at battle—were fixtures of that magazine. His collections of essays, short stories, and cartoons include* The Owl in the Attic and Other Perplexities *(1931),* The Seal in the Bedroom and Other Predicaments *(1932),* My Life and Hard Times *(1933),* Men, Women, and Dogs *(1943), and* Alarms and Diversions *(1957). He also wrote an account of life on the* New Yorker *staff,* The Years with Ross *(1959).* Selected Letters of James Thurber *appeared in 1981.*

An elegant stylist, Thurber was always fussy about language. "Which" is an example not only of his fascination with language—which became obsessive at times—but also of his humor.

86

JAMES THURBER

Which

1   The relative pronoun "which" can cause more trouble than any other word, if recklessly used. Foolhardy persons sometimes get lost in which-clauses and are never heard of again. My distinguished contemporary, Fowler, cites several tragic cases, of which the following is one: "It was rumoured that Beaconsfield intended opening the Conference with a speech in French, his pronunciation of which language leaving everything to be desired . . ." That's as much as Mr. Fowler quotes because, at his age, he was afraid to go any farther.* The young

---

    *Thurber refers to H. W. Fowler (1858–1933), whose *A Dictionary of Modern English Usage* has been a source of amusement and useful information since its first edition in 1926.

man who originally got into that sentence was never found. His fate, however, was not as terrible as that of another adventurer who became involved in a remarkable which-mire. Fowler has followed his devious course as far as he safely could on foot: "Surely what applies to games should also apply to racing, the leaders of which being the very people from whom an example might well be looked for . . ." Not even Henry James could have successfully emerged from a sentence with "which," "whom," and "being" in it. The safest way to avoid such things is to follow in the path of the American author, Ernest Hemingway. In his youth he was trapped in a which-clause one time and barely escaped with his mind. He was going along on solid ground until he got into this: "It was the one thing of which, being very much afraid—for whom has not been warned to fear such things—he . . ." Being a young and powerfully built man, Hemingway was able to fight his way back to where he had started, and begin again. This time he skirted the treacherous morass in this way: "He was afraid of one thing. This was the one thing. He had been warned to fear such things. Everybody has been warned to fear such things." Today Hemingway is alive and well, and many happy writers are following along the trail he blazed.

What most people don't realize is that one "which" leads to another. Trying to cross a paragraph by leaping from "which" to "which" is like Eliza crossing the ice. The danger is in missing a "which" and falling in. A case in point is this: "He went up to a pew which was in the gallery, which brought him under a colored window which he loved and always quieted his spirit." The writer, worn out, missed the last "which"—the one that should come just before "always" in that sentence. But supposing he had got it in! We would have: "He went up to a pew which was in the gallery, which brought him under a colored window which he loved and which always quieted his spirit." Your inveterate whicher in this way gives the effect of tweeting like a bird or walking with a crutch, and is not welcome in the best company.

It is well to remember that one "which" leads to two and that two "whiches" multiply like rabbits. You should never start out with the idea that you can get by with one "which." Suddenly they are all around you. Take a sentence like this: "It imposes a problem which we either solve, or perish." On a hot night, or after a hard day's work, a man often lets himself get by with a monstrosity like that, but suppose he dictates that sentence bright and early in the morning. It comes to him typed out by his stenographer and he instantly senses that something is the matter with it. He tries to reconstruct the sentence, still clinging to the "which," and gets something like this: "It imposes a problem which we either solve, or which, failing to solve, we must perish on account of." He goes to the water-cooler, gets a drink, sharpens his pencil, and grimly tries again. "It imposes a problem which we either solve or which we don't solve . . ." He begins once more: "It imposes a problem which we either solve, or which we do not solve, and from which . . ." The more times he does it the more "whiches" he gets. The way out is simple. "We must either solve this problem, or perish." Never monkey with "which." Nothing except getting tangled up in a typewriter ribbon is worse.

_____ CONSIDERATIONS _____

1. James Thurber concentrates on one word from an important class of function words. These relative pronouns often complicate life for the writer wishing to write clear sentences more complex than "I see Spot. Spot is a dog. Spot sees me." What other words belong to this class? Do you find any of them tripping you up in your sentences?

2. A grammar lesson may seem a peculiar place to find humor, but humor is Thurber's habit, whatever his subject. How does he make his treatment of the relative pronoun "which" entertaining?

3. Compare Fowler's book with an American version such as Wilson Follett's *Modern American Usage.* Think about usage as the ultimate authority in establishing conventions of grammar, spelling, definition, and punctuation.

4. "One 'which' leads to another" is a play on the old saying "One drink leads to another." Consider how changing one word can revive a thought that otherwise would be hackneyed phrase. See how it is done by substituting a key word in several familiar sayings.

5. The two writers Thurber mentions, Henry James and Ernest Hemingway, are not idly chosen. Why not?

6. In addition to many books of humorous and satirical stories and essays, Thurber wrote several fairy tales for children, including *The Wonderful O* (1957), an account of what would happen if the letter "O" were banned from the language. Said one character: "We shall have mantels but no clocks, shelves without crocks, keys without locks, walls without doors, rugs without floors." Select some peculiarity of the language that tickles your imagination and try your hand, Thurber style, at developing it into a mock report.

Barbara Tuchman (1912–1989) was born in New York, graduated from Radcliffe, and began her career as an editor and writer for the Nation. *But her interests led her away from the politics of the moment to the politics of the past, which is to say, history.* The Guns of August, *which won the Pulitzer Prize in 1963, recounted the first weeks of the great war of 1914–1918.* Stilwell and the American Experience in China *won the Pulitzer Prize in 1972. Her major work,* A Distant Mirror: The Calamitous 14th Century *(1973), from which the following essay was adapted, brought her into the forefront of American historians. Although she appeared to have deserted modern history for medieval, she did no such thing. This "six-hundred-year-old mirror" reflects ourselves. Her last book was* The First Salute *(1988), an unusual approach to the story of the American Revolution. Barbara Tuchman wrote clean exposition, laying out for us clearly what she meant us to understand, supplying detail adequate to her argument and fascinating in itself. She loved the feel and shape of an odd and illuminating detail; she collected it with gusto, and she used it with skill.*

87

BARBARA TUCHMAN
History as Mirror

At a time when everyone's mind is on the explosions of the moment, it might seem obtuse of me to discuss the fourteenth century. But I think a backward look at that disordered, violent, bewildered, disintegrating, and calamity-prone age can be consoling and possibly instructive in a time of similar disarray. Reflected in a six-hundred-year-old mirror, a more revealing image of ourselves and our species might be seen than is visible in the clutter of circumstances under our noses. The value of historical comparison was made keenly apparent to the French medievalist, Edouard Perroy, when he was writing his book on the Hundred Years' War while dodging the Gestapo in World War II. "Certain ways of behaving," he wrote, "certain reactions against fate, throw mutual light upon each other."

2   Besides, if one suspects that the twentieth century's record of inhumanity and folly represents a phase of mankind at its worst, and that our last decade of collapsing assumptions has been one of unprecedented discomfort, it is reassuring to discover that the human race has been in this box before—and emerged. The historian has the comfort of knowing that man (meaning, here and hereafter, the species, not the sex) is always capable of his worst; has indulged in it, painfully struggled up from it, slid back, and gone on again.

3   In what follows, the parallels are not always in physical events but rather in the effect on society, and sometimes in both.

4   The afflictions of the fourteenth century were the classic riders of the Apocalypse—famine, plague, war, and death, this time on a black horse. These combined to produce an epidemic of violence, depopulation, bad government, oppressive taxes, an accelerated breakdown of feudal bonds, working class insurrection, monetary crisis, decline of morals and rise in crime, decay of chivalry, the governing idea of the governing class, and above all, corruption of society's central institution, the Church, whose loss of authority and prestige deprived man of his accustomed guide in a darkening world.

5   Yet amidst the disintegration were sprouting, invisible to contemporaries, the green shoots of the Renaissance to come. In human affairs as in nature, decay is compost for new growth.

6   Some medievalists reject the title of decline for the fourteenth century, asserting instead that it was the dawn of a new age. Since the processes obviously overlap, I am not sure that the question is worth arguing, but it becomes poignantly interesting when applied to ourselves. Do *we* walk amidst trends of a new world without knowing it? How far ahead is the dividing line? Or are we on it? What designation will our age earn from historians six hundred years hence? One wishes one could make a pact with the devil like Enoch Soames, the neglected poet in Max Beerbohm's story, allowing us to return and look ourselves up in the library catalogue. In that future history book, shall we find the chapter title for the twentieth century reading Decline and Fall, or Eve of Revival?

7   The fourteenth century opened with a series of famines brought on when population growth outstripped the techniques of food production. The precarious balance was tipped by a series of heavy rains and floods and by a chilling of the climate in what has been called the Little Ice Age. Upon a people thus weakened fell the century's central disaster, the Black Death, an eruption of bubonic plague which swept the known world in the years 1347–1349 and carried off an estimated

one-third of the population in two and a half years. This makes it the most lethal episode known to history, which is of some interest to an age equipped with the tools of overkill.

The plague raged at terrifying speed, increasing the impression of 8
horror. In a given locality it accomplished its kill within four to six months, except in the larger cities, where it struck again in spring after lying dormant in winter. The death rate in Avignon was said to have claimed half the population, of whom ten thousand were buried in the first six weeks in a single mass grave. The mortality was in fact erratic. Some communities whose last survivors fled in despair were simply wiped out and disappeared from the map forever, leaving only a grassed-over hump as their mortal trace.

Whole families died, leaving empty houses and property a prey to 9
looters. Wolves came down from the mountains to attack plague-stricken villages, crops went unharvested, dikes crumbled, salt water reinvaded and soured the lowlands, the forest crept back, and second growth, with the awful energy of nature unchecked, reconverted cleared land to waste. For lack of hands to cultivate, it was thought impossible that the world could ever regain its former prosperity.

Once the dark bubonic swellings appeared in armpit and groin, 10
death followed rapidly within one to three days, often overnight. For lack of gravediggers, corpses piled up in the streets or were buried so hastily that dogs dug them up and ate them. Doctors were helpless, and priests lacking to administer that final sacrament so that people died believing they must go to hell. No bells tolled, the dead were buried without prayers or funeral rites or tears; families did not weep for the loss of loved ones, for everyone expected death. Matteo Villani, taking up the chronicle of Florence from the hands of his dead brother, believed he was recording the "extermination of mankind."

People reacted variously, as they always do: some prayed, some 11
robbed, some tried to help, most fled if they could, others abandoned themselves to debauchery on the theory that there would be no tomorrow. On balance, the dominant reaction was fear and a desire to save one's own skin regardless of the closest ties. "A father did not visit his son, nor the son his father; charity was dead," wrote one physician, and that was not an isolated observation. Boccaccio in his famous account reports that "kinsfolk held aloof, brother was forsaken by brother ... often times husband by wife; nay what is more, and scarcely to be believed, fathers and mothers were found to abandon their own children to their fate, untended, unvisited as if they had been strangers."

"Men grew bold," wrote another chronicler, "in their indulgence 12
in pleasure.... No fear of God or law of man deterred a criminal. Seeing that all perished alike, they reflected that offenses against human or Divine law would bring no punishment for no one would live long

enough to be held to account." This is an accurate summary, but it was written by Thucydides about the Plague of Athens in the fifth century B.C.—which indicates a certain permanence of human behavior.

13   The nightmare of the plague was compounded for the fourteenth century by the awful mystery of its cause. The idea of disease carried by insect bite was undreamed of. Fleas and rats, which were in fact the carriers, are not mentioned in the plague writings. Contagion could be observed but not explained and thus seemed doubly sinister. The medical faculty of the University of Paris favored a theory of poisonous air spread by a conjunction of the planets, but the general and fundamental belief, made official by a papal bull, was that the pestilence was divine punishment for man's sins. Such horror could only be caused by the wrath of God. "In the year of our Lord, 1348," sadly wrote a professor of law at the University of Pisa, "the hostility of God was greater than the hostility of men."

14   That belief enhanced the sense of guilt, or rather the consciousness of sin (guilt, I suspect, is modern; sin is medieval), which was always so close to the surface throughout the Middle Ages. Out of the effort to appease divine wrath came the flagellants, a morbid frenzy of self-punishment that almost at once found a better object in the Jews.

15   A storm of pogroms followed in the track of the Black Death, widely stimulated by the flagellants, who often rushed straight for the Jewish quarter, even in towns which had not yet suffered the plague. As outsiders within the unity of Christendom the Jews were natural persons to suspect of evil design on the Christian world. They were accused of poisoning the wells. Although the Pope condemned the attacks as inspired by "that liar the devil," pointing out that Jews died of plague like everyone else, the populace wanted victims, and fell upon them in three hundred communities throughout Europe. Slaughtered and burned alive, the entire colonies of Frankfurt, Cologne, Manz, and other towns of Germany and the Lowlands were exterminated, despite the restraining efforts of town authorities. Elsewhere the Jews were expelled by judicial process after confession of well-poisoning was extracted by torture. In every case their goods and property, whether looted or confiscated, ended in the hands of the persecutors. The process was lucrative, as it was to be again in our time under the Nazis, although the fourteenth century had no gold teeth to rob from the corpses. Where survivors slowly returned and the communities revived, it was on worse terms than before and in walled isolation. This was the beginning of the ghetto.

16   Men of the fourteenth century were particularly vulnerable because of the loss of credibility by the Church, which alone could absolve sin and offer salvation from hell. When the papal schism dating from 1378 divided the Church under two popes, it brought the highest authority in society into disrepute, a situation with which we are fa-

miliar. The schism was the second great calamity of the time, displaying before all the world the unedifying spectacle of twin vicars of God, each trying to bump the other off the chair of St. Peter, each appointing his own college of cardinals, each collecting tithes and revenues and excommunicating the partisans of his rival. No conflict of ideology was involved; the split arose from a simple squabble for the office of the papacy and remained no more than that for the fifty years the schism lasted. Plunged in this scandal, the Church lost moral authority, the more so as its two halves scrambled in the political arena for support. Kingdoms, principalities, even towns, took sides, finding new cause for the endless wars that scourged the times.

The Church's corruption by worldliness long antedated the 17 schism. By the fourteenth century the papal court at Avignon was called Babylon and rivaled temporal courts in luxury and magnificence. Its bureaucracy was enormous and its upkeep mired in a commercial traffic in spiritual things. Pardons, indulgences, prayers, every benefice and bishopric, everything the Church had or was, from cardinal's hat to pilgrim's relic, everything that represented man's relation to God, was for sale. Today it is the processes of government that are for sale, especially the electoral process, which is as vital to our political security as salvation was to the emotional security of the fourteenth century.

Men still craved God and spun off from the Church in sects and 18 heresies, seeking to purify the realm of the spirit. They too yearned for a greening of the system. The yearning, and disgust with the Establishment, produced freak orders of mystics who lived in coeducational communes, rejected marriage, and glorified sexual indulgence. Passionate reformers ranged from St. Catherine of Siena, who scolded everyone in the hierarchy from the popes down, to John Wycliffe, who plowed the soil of Protestant revolt. Both strove to renew the Church, which for so long had been the only institution to give order and meaning to the untidy business of living on earth. When in the last quarter of the century the schism brought the Church into scorn and ridicule and fratricidal war, serious men took alarm. The University of Paris made strenuous and ceaseless efforts to find a remedy, finally demanding submission of the conflict to a supreme Council of the Church whose object should be not only reunification but reform.

Without reform, said the University's theologians in their letter 19 to the popes, the damaging effect of the current scandal could be irreversible. In words that could have been addressed to our own secular potentate although he is—happily—not double, they wrote, "The Church will suffer for your overconfidence if you repent too late of having neglected reform. If you postpone it longer the harm will be incurable. Do you think people will suffer forever from your bad government? Who do you think can endure, amid so many other abuses . . .

your elevation of men without literacy or virtue to the most eminent positions?" The echo sounds over the gulf of six hundred years with a timeliness almost supernatural.

20   When the twin popes failed to respond, pressure at last brought about a series of Church councils which endeavored to limit and constitutionalize the powers of the papacy. After a thirty-year struggle, the councils succeeded in ending the schism but the papacy resisted reform. The decades of debate only served to prove that the institution could not be reformed from within. Eighty years of mounting protest were to pass before pressure produced Luther and the great crack.

21   Despite the parallel with the present struggle between Congress and the presidency, there is no historical law that says the outcome must necessarily be the same. The American presidency at age two hundred is not a massive rock of ages embedded in a thousand years of acceptance as was the medieval Church, and should be easier to reform. One can wish for Congress a better result than the councils had in the effort to curb the executive—or at least one can hope.

22   The more important parallel lies in the decay of public confidence in our governing institutions, as the fourteenth-century public lost confidence in the Church. Who believes today in the integrity of government?—or of business, or of law or justice or labor unions or the military or the police? Even physicians, the last of the admired, are now in disfavor. I have a theory that the credibility vacuum owes something to our nurture in that conspiracy of fables called advertising, which we daily absorb without believing. Since public affairs and ideas and candidates are now presented to us as a form of advertising, we automatically suspend belief or suspect fraud as soon as we recognize the familiar slickness. I realize, of course, that the roots of disbelief go down to deeper ground. Meanwhile the effect is a loss of trust in all authority which leaves us guideless and dismayed and cynical—even as in the fourteenth century.

23   Over that whole century hung the smoke of war—dominated by the Anglo-French conflict known to us, though fortunately not to them, as the Hundred Years' War. (With the clock still ticking in Indochina, one wonders how many years there are still to go in that conflict.) Fought on French soil and extending into Flanders and Spain, the Hundred Years' War actually lasted for more than a century, from 1337 to 1453. In addition, the English fought the Scots; the French fought incessant civil wars against Gascons, Bretons, Normans, and Navarrese; the Italian republics fought each other—Florence against Pisa, Venice against Genoa, Milan against everybody; the kingdom of Naples and Sicily was fought over by claimants from Hungary to Aragon; the papacy fought a war that included unbridled massacre to reconquer the Papal States; the Savoyards fought the Lombards; the

Swiss fought the Austrians; the tangled wars of Bohemia, Poland, and the German Empire defy listing; crusades were launched against the Saracens, and to fill up any pauses the Teutonic Knights conducted annual campaigns against pagan Lithuania which other knights could join for extra practice. Fighting was the function of the Second Estate, that is, of the landed nobles and knights. A knight without a war or tournament to go to felt as restless as a man who cannot go to the office.

Every one of these conflicts threw off Free Companies of merce- 24
naries, organized for brigandage under a professional captain, which became an evil of the period as malignant as the plague. In the money economy of the fourteenth century, armed forces were no longer feudal levies serving under a vassal's obligation who went home after forty days, but were recruited bodies who served for pay. Since this was at great cost to the sovereign, he cut off the payroll as soon as he safely could during halts of truce or negotiation. Thrown on their own resources and having acquired a taste for plunder, the men-at-arms banded together in the Free Companies, whose savage success swelled their ranks with landless knights and squires and roving adventurers.

The companies contracted their services to whatever ruler was in 25
need of troops, and between contracts held up towns for huge ransom, ravaged the countryside, and burned, pillaged, raped, and slaughtered their way back and forth across Europe. No one was safe, no town or village knew when it might be attacked. The leaders, prototypes of the *condottieri* in Italy, became powers and made fortunes and even became respectable like Sir John Hawkwood, commander of the famous White Company. Smaller bands, called in France the *tards-venus* (late-comers), scavenged like jackals, living off the land, plundering, killing, carrying off women, torturing peasants for their small horde of grain or townsmen for their hidden goods, and burning, always burning. They set fire to whatever they left behind, farmhouses, vineyards, abbeys, in a kind of madness to destroy the very sources off which they lived, or would live tomorrow. Destruction and cruelty became self-engendering, not merely for loot but almost one might say for sport. The phenomenon is not peculiar to any one time or people, as we know from the experience of our own century, but in the fourteenth century it seems to have reached a degree an extent beyond explanation.

It must be added that in practice and often personnel the Free 26
Companies were hardly distinguishable from the troops of organized official wars. About 80 percent of the activity of a declared war consisted of raids of plunder and burning through enemy territory. That paragon of chivalry, the Black Prince, could well have earned his name from the blackened ruins he left across France. His baggage train and

men-at-arms were often so heavily laden with loot that they moved as slowly as a woman's litter.

27   The saddest aspect of the Hundred Years' War was the persistent but vain efforts of the belligerents themselves to stop it. As in our case, it spread political damage at home, and the cost was appalling. Moreover it harmed the relations of all the powers at a time when they were anxious to unite to repel the infidel at the gates. For Christendom was now on the defensive against the encroaching Turks. For that reason the Church, too, tried to end the war that was keeping Europe at odds. On the very morning of the fatal battle of Poitiers, two cardinals hurried with offers and counter-offers between the two armed camps, trying in vain to prevent the clash. During periods of truce the parties held long parleys lasting months and sometimes years in the effort to negotiate a definitive peace. It always eluded them, failing over questions of prestige, or put off by the feeling of whichever side held a slight advantage that one more push would bring the desired gains.

28   All this took place under a code of chivalry whose creed was honor, loyalty, and courtesy and whose purpose, like that of every social code evolved by man in his long search for order, was to civilize and supply a pattern of rules. A knight's task under the code was to uphold the Church, defend his land and vassals, maintain the peace of his province, protect the weak and guard the poor from injustice, shed his blood for his comrade, and lay down his life if needs must. For the land-owning warrior class, chivalry was their ideology, their politics, their system—what democracy is to us or Marxism to the Communists.

29   Originating out of feudal needs, it was already slipping into anachronism by the fourteenth century because the development of monarchy and a royal bureaucracy was taking away the knight's functions, economic facts were forcing him to commute labor dues for money, and a rival element was appearing in the urban magnates. Even his military prowess was being nullified by trained bodies of English longbowmen and Swiss pikemen, nonmembers of the warrior class who in feudal theory had no business in battle at all.

30   Yet in decadence chivalry threw its brightest light; never were its ceremonies more brilliant, its jousts and tournaments so brave, its apparel so splendid, its manners so gay and amorous, its entertainments so festive, its self-glorification more eloquent. The gentry elaborated the forms of chivalry just *because* institutions around them were crumbling. They clung to what gave their status meaning in a desperate embrace of the past. This is the time when the Order of the Garter was founded by the King of England, the Order of the Star by the King of France, the Golden Fleece by the Duke of Burgundy—in deliberate imitation of King Arthur's Knights of the Round Table.

The rules still worked well enough among themselves, with oc- 31
casional notorious exceptions such as Charles of Navarre, a bad man
appropriately known as Charles the Bad. Whenever necessity required
him to swear loyal reconciliation and fealty to the King of France, his
mortal enemy, he promptly engaged in treacherous intrigues with the
King of England, leaving his knightly oaths to become, in the White
House word, inoperative. On the whole, however, the nobility laid
great stress on high standards of honor. It was vis-à-vis the Third Estate that chivalry fell so far short of the theory. Yet it remained an
ideal of human relations, as Christianity remained an ideal of faith,
that kept men reaching for the unattainable. The effort of society is always toward order, away from anarchy. Sometimes it moves forward,
sometimes it slips back. Which is the direction of one's own time may
be obscure.

The fourteenth century was further afflicted by a series of con- 32
vulsions and upheavals in the working class, both urban and rural.
Causes were various: the cost of constant war was thrown upon the
people in hearth taxes, salt taxes, sales taxes, and debasement of
coinage. In France the failure of the knights to protect the populace
from incessant ravaging was a factor. It exacerbated the peasants' misery, giving it the energy of anger which erupted in the ferocious mid-
century rising called the *Jacquerie*. Shortage of labor caused by the
plague had temporarily brought higher wages and rising expectations.
When these were met, especially in England, by statutes clamping
wages at pre-plague levels, the result was the historic Peasants' Revolt
of 1381. In the towns, capitalism was widening the gap between masters and artisans, producing the sustained weavers' revolts in the cloth
towns of Flanders and major outbreaks in Florence and Paris. In Paris,
too, the merchant class rose against the royal councillors, whom they
despised as both corrupt and incompetent. To frighten the regent into
submission, they murdered his two chief councillors in his presence.

All these struggles had one thing in common: they were doomed. 33
United against a common threat, the ruling class could summon
greater strength than its antagonists and acted to suppress insurrection with savagery equal to the fury from below. Yet discontent had
found its voice; dissent and rejection of authority for the first time in
the Middle Ages became a social force. Demagogues and determined
leaders, reformers and agitators came to the surface. Though all were
killed, several by mobs of their own followers, the uprisings they led
were the beginning of modern, conscious, class war.

Meanwhile, over the second half-century, the plague returned 34
with lesser virulence at intervals of every twelve to fifteen years. It is
hardly to be wondered that people of the time saw man's fate as an
endless succession of evils. He must indeed be wicked and his enemy

Satan finally triumphant. According to a popular belief at the end of the century, no one since the beginning of the schism had entered Paradise.

35 Pessimism was a mark of the age and the *Danse Macabre* or Dance of Death its most vivid expression. Performed at occasions of popular drama and public sermons, it was an actual dance or pantomime in which a figure from every walk of life—king, clerk, lawyer, friar, goldsmith, bailiff, and so on—confronts the loathsome corpse he must become. In the accompanying verses and illustrations which have survived, the theme repeats itself over and over: the end of all life is putrefaction and the grave; no one escapes; no matter what beauty or kingly power or poor man's misery has been the lot in life, all end alike as food for worms. Death is not treated poetically as the soul's flight to reunion with God; it is a skeleton grinning at the vanity of life.

36 Life as well as death was viewed with disgust. The vices and corruptions of the age, a low opinion of one's fellowmen, and nostalgia for the well-ordered past were the favorite themes of literary men. Even Boccaccio in his later works became ill-tempered. "All good customs fail," laments Christine di Pisan of France, "and virtues are held at little worth." Eustache Deschamps complains that "the child of today has become a ruffian. . . . People are gluttons and drunkards, haughty of heart, caring for nought, not honor nor goodness nor kindness . . ." and he ends each verse with the refrain, "Time past had virtue and righteousness but today reigns only vice." In England John Gower denounces Rome for simony, Lollards for heresy, clergy and monks for idleness and lust, kings, nobles, and knights for self-indulgence and rapine, the law for bribery, merchants for usury and fraud, the commons for ignorance, and in general the sins of perjury, lechery, avarice, and pride as displayed in extravagant fashions.

37 These last did indeed, as in all distracted times, reflect a reaching for the absurd, especially in the long pointed shoes which kept getting longer until the points had to be tied up around the knee, and the young men's doublets which kept getting shorter until they revealed the buttocks, to the censure of moralists and snickers of the crowd. Leaving miniskirts to the males, the ladies inexplicably adopted a fashion of gowns and posture designed to make them look pregnant.

38 Self-disgust, it seems to me, has reappeared in our time, not without cause. The succession of events since 1914 has disqualified belief in moral progress, and pollution of the physical world is our bubonic plague. Like the fourteenth century, we have lost confidence in man's capacity to control his fate and even in his capacity to be good. So we have a literature of the anti-hero aimlessly wandering among the perverse, absurd, and depraved; we have porn and pop and blank canvases and anti-music designed to deafen. I am not sure

whether in all this the artists are expressing contempt for their fellow-man or the loud laugh that bespeaks emptiness of feeling, but whatever the message, it has a faint ring of the *Danse Macabre.*

Historians until recently have hurried over the fourteenth century because like most people they prefer not to deal with failure. But it would be a mistake to imply that it was solid gloom. Seen from inside, especially from a position of privilege, it had beauties and wonders, and the ferment itself was exciting. "In these fifty years," said the renowned Comte de Foix to the chronicler Froissart in the year 1389, "there have been more feats of arms and more marvels in the world than in the three hundred years before." The Count himself, a famous huntsman, was known as Phoebus for his personal beauty and splendid court.

The streets of cities were bright with colored clothes; crimson fur-lined gowns of merchants, parti-colored velvets and silks of a nobleman's retinue, in sky blue and fawn or two shades of scarlet or it might be the all-emerald liveries of the Green Count of Savoy. Street sounds were those of human voices: criers of news and official announcements, shopkeepers in their doorways and itinerant vendors crying fresh eggs, charcoal at a penny a sack, candlewicks "brighter than the stars," cakes and waffles, mushrooms, hot baths. Mountebanks entertained the public in the town square or village green with tricks and magic and trained animals. Jongleurs sang ballads of adventure in Saracen lands. After church on Sundays, laborers gathered in cookshops and taverns; burghers promenaded in their gardens or visited their vineyards outside the city walls. Church bells marked the eight times of day from Matins through Vespers, when shops closed, work ceased, silence succeeded bustle, and the darkness of unlit night descended.

The gaudy extravagance of noble life was awesome. Now and then its patronage brought forth works of eternal beauty like the exquisite illuminated Books of Hours commissioned by the Duc de Berry. More often it was pure ostentation and conspicuous consumption. Charles V of France owned forty-seven jeweled and golden crowns and sixty-three complete sets of chapel furnishings, including vestments, gold crucifixes, altarpieces, reliquaries, and prayer books. Jewels and cloth of gold marked every occasion and every occasion was pretext for a spectacle—a grand procession, or ceremonial welcome to a visiting prince, a tournament of entertainment with music, and dancing by the light of great torches. When Gian Galeazzo Visconti, ruler of Milan, gave a wedding banquet for his daughter, eighteen double courses were served, each of fish and meat, including trout, quail, herons, eels, sturgeon, and suckling pig spouting fire. The gifts presented after *each* course to several hundred guests included greyhounds in gem-studded velvet collars, hawks in tinkling silver bells, suits of armor, rolls of silk and brocade, garments trimmed with pearls and ermine, fully caparisoned warhorses, and twelve fat oxen. For the entry into Paris of the new Queen, Isabel of Bavaria, the entire length of the Rue St. Denis was hung with a canopy representing the firmament twinkling with stars from which sweetly singing angels descended bearing a crown, and fountains ran with wine, distributed to the people in golden cups by lovely maidens wearing caps of solid gold.

42   One wonders where all the money came from for such luxury and festivity in a time of devastation. What taxes could burned-out and destitute people pay? This is a puzzle until one remembers that the Aga Khan got to be the richest man in the world on the backs of the poorest people, and that disaster is never as pervasive as it seems from recorded accounts. It is one of the pitfalls for historians that the very fact of being on the record makes a happening appear to have been continuous and all-inclusive, whereas in reality it is more likely to have been sporadic both in time and place. Besides, persistence of the normal is usually greater than the effect of disturbance, as we know from our own times. After absorbing the daily paper and weekly magazine, one expects to face a world consisting entirely of strikes, crimes, power shortages, broken water mains, stalled trains, school shutdowns, Black Panthers, addicts, transvestites, rapists, and militant lesbians. The fact is that one can come home in the evening—on a lucky day—without having encountered more than two or three of these phenomena. This has led me to formulate Tuchman's Law, as follows: "The fact of being reported increases the *apparent* extent of a deplorable development by a factor of ten." (I snatch the figure from the air and will leave it to the quantifiers to justify.)

43   The astonishing fact is that except for Boccaccio, to whom we owe the most vivid account, the Black Death was virtually ignored by the great writers of the time. Petrarch, who was forty-four when it happened, mentions it only as the occasion for the death of Laura; Chaucer, from what I have read, passes it over in silence; Jean Froissart, the Herodotus of his time, gives it no more than one casual paragraph, and even that second Isaiah, the author of *Piers Plowman*, who might have been expected to make it central to his theme of woe, uses it only incidentally. One could argue that in 1348 Chaucer was only eight or nine years old and Froissart ten or eleven and the unknown Langland probably of the same vintage, but that is old enough to absorb and remember a great catastrophe, especially when they lived through several returns of the plague as grown men.

44   Perhaps this tells us that disaster, once survived, leaves less track than one supposed, or that man's instinct for living pushes it down below the surface, or simply that his recuperative powers are remark-

able. Or was it just an accident of personality? Is it significant or just chance that Chaucer, the greatest writer of his age, was so uncharacteristic of it in sanguine temperament and good-humored view of his fellow creatures?

As for Froissart, never was a man more in love with his age. To him it appeared as a marvelous pageant of glittering armor and the beauty of emblazoned banners fluttering in the breeze and the clear shrill call of the trumpet. Still believing, still enraptured by the chivalric ideal, he reports savagery, treachery, limitless greed, and the pitiless slaughter of the poor when driven to revolt as minor stumbles in the grand adventure of valor and honor. Yet near the end, even Froissart could not hide from himself the decay made plain by a dissolute court, venality in high places, and a knighthood that kept losing battles. In 1397, the year he turned sixty, the defeat and massacre of the flower of chivalry at the hands of the Turks in the battle of Nicopolis set the seal on the incompetence of his heroes. Lastly, the murder of a King in England shocked him deeply, not for any love of Richard II but because the act was subversive of the whole order that sustained his world. As in Watergate, the underside had rolled to the surface all too visibly. Froissart had not the heart to continue and brought his chronicle to an end. 45

The sad century closed with a meeting between King Charles VI of France and the Emperor Wenceslaus, the one intermittently mad and the other regularly drunk. They met at Reims in 1397 to consult on means of ending the papal schism, but whenever Charles had a lucid interval, Wenceslaus was in a stupor and so the conference, proving fruitless, was called off. 46

It makes an artistic ending. Yet in the same year Johann Gutenberg, who was to change the world, was born. In the next century appeared Joan of Arc, embodying the new spirit of nationalism, still pure like mountain water before it runs downhill; and Columbus, who opened a new hemisphere; and Copernicus, who revolutionized the concept of the earth's relation to the universe; and Michelangelo, whose sculptured visions gave man a new status; in those proud, superb, unconquered figures, the human being, not God, was captain. 47

As our century enters its final quarter, I am not persuaded, despite the signs, that the end is necessarily doom. The doomsayers work by extrapolation; they take a trend and extend it, forgetting that the doom factor sooner or later generates a coping mechanism. I have a rule for this situation too, which is absolute: you cannot extrapolate any series in which the human element intrudes; history, that is, the human narrative, never follows, and will always fool, the scientific curve. I cannot tell you what twists it will take, but I expect, that like our ancestors, we, too, will muddle through. 48

_____ CONSIDERATIONS _____

1. Barbara Tuchman's essay is built on a useful and classic plan—comparisons and contrasts support and illustrate a main idea or thesis. Find three or four uses of comparison in this essay. Then see whether they do, in fact, undergird the author's major idea. Notice how contrasts are used in Henry Adams's short essay, "Winter and Summer," page 19.

2. As a professional historian, Tuchman verifies her facts in many kinds of research materials, although in this relatively informal essay she does not footnote her sources. Notice how she manages to acknowledge those sources and smoothly work the material into her discussion.

3. "Guilt, I suspect," writes Tuchman in paragraph 14, "is modern; sin is medieval." This highly compressed, neatly balanced statement is a good example of aphorism, and, more important, shows us, if we stop to think, a truly economical use of language. What is the point of the distinction?

4. What do you make of "Tuchman's Law," as the author mischievously puts it in paragraph 42? Is she just having fun, or can Tuchman's Law be demonstrated today as the mass media manage our awareness of trends?

5. Tuchman claims that much of the decaying public confidence in governing institutions comes from "our nurture in that conspiracy of fables called advertising." In what specific ways would Daniel Boorstin (see "The Pseudo-Event") agree or disagree with her?

6. History makes sense, students say, when it is clearly related to present life. Is Tuchman successful in bringing the two together? Explain.

Mark Twain is the pseudonym of Samuel Clemens (1835–1910), who wrote Tom Sawyer *(1876),* Huckleberry Finn *(1884), and other novels, as well as short stories, essays, and an autobiography. Born in Missouri, he settled with his wife in Hartford, Connecticut; at his best he wrote out of his midwestern past. Twain's humor disguised his gloom and the misanthropy that grew in his later years. The lightness of this essay's tone only thinly covers Twain's rage and contempt. His sense of human littleness puts Twain's vision in the modern tradition.*

88

MARK TWAIN
Was the World Made for Man?

Alfred Russel Wallace's revival of the theory that this earth is at the centre of the stellar universe, and is the only habitable globe, has aroused great interest in the world.

Literary Digest

For ourselves we do thoroughly believe that man, as he lives just here on this tiny earth, is in essence and possibilities the most sublime existence in all the range of non-divine being—the chief love and delight of God.

Chicago "Interior" (Presb.)

I seem to be the only scientist and theologian still remaining to be heard from on this important matter of whether the world was made for man or not. I feel that it is time for me to speak. 1

I stand almost with the others. They believe the world was made for man, I believe it likely that it was made for man; they think there is proof, astronomical mainly, that it was made for man. I think there is evidence only, not proof, that it was made for him. It is too early, yet, to arrange the verdict, the returns are not all in. When they are all in, I think they will show that the world was made for man; but we must not hurry, we must patiently wait till they are all in. 2

Now as far as we have got, astronomy is on our side. Mr. Wallace has clearly shown this. He has clearly shown two things: that the 3 world was made for man, and that the universe was made for the world—to stiddy it, you know. The astronomy part is settled, and cannot be challenged.

4   We come now to the geological part. This is the one where the evidence is not all in, yet. It is coming in, hourly, daily, coming in all the time, but naturally it comes with geological carefulness and deliberation, and we must not be impatient, we must not get excited, we must be calm, and wait. To lose our tranquility will not hurry geology; nothing hurries geology.

5   It takes a long time to prepare a world for man; such a thing is not done in a day. Some of the great scientists, carefully ciphering the evidences furnished by geology, have arrived at the conviction that our world is prodigiously old, and they may be right, but Lord Kelvin is not of their opinion. He takes a cautious, conservative view, in order to be on the safe side, and feels sure it is not so old as they think. As Lord Kelvin is the highest authority in science now living, I think we must yield to him and accept his view. He does not concede that the world is more than a hundred million years old. He believes it is that old, but not older. Lyell believed that our race was introduced into the world 31,000 years ago, Herbert Spencer makes it 32,000. Lord Kelvin agrees with Spencer.

6   Very well. According to these figures it took 99,968,000 years to prepare the world for man, impatient as the Creator doubtless was to see him and admire him. But a large enterprise like this has to be conducted warily, painstakingly, logically. It was foreseen that man would have to have the oyster. Therefore the first preparation was made for the oyster. Very well, you cannot make an oyster out of whole cloth, you must make the oyster's ancestor first. This is not done in a day. You must make a vast variety of invertebrates, to start with—belemnites, trilobites, Jebusites, Amalekites, and that sort of fry; and put them to soak in a primary sea, and wait and see what will happen. Some will be a disappointment—the belemnites, the Ammonites and such; they will be failures, they will die out and become extinct, in the course of the nineteen million years covered by the experiment, but all is not lost, for the Amalekites will fetch the homestake; they will develop gradually into encrinites, and stalactites, and blatherskites, and one thing and another as the mighty ages creep on and the Archaean and the Cambrian Periods pile their lofty crags in the primordial seas, and at last the first grand stage in the preparation of the world for man stands completed, the oyster is done. An oyster has hardly any more reasoning power than a scientist has; and so it is reasonably certain that this one jumped to the conclusion that the nineteen million years was a preparation for *him*; but that would be just like an oyster, which is the most conceited animal there is, except

man. And anyway, this one could not know, at that early date, that he was only an incident in a scheme, and that there was some more to the scheme, yet.

The oyster being achieved, the next thing to be arranged for in   7
the preparation of the world for man was fish. Fish and coal—to fry it with. So the Old Silurian seas were opened up to breed the fish in, and at the same time the great work of building Old Red Sandstone mountains eighty thousand feet high to cold-storage their fossils in was begun. This latter was quite indispensable, for there would be no end of failures again, no end of extinctions—millions of them—and it would be cheaper and less trouble to can them in the rocks than keep tally of them in a book. One does not build the coal beds and eighty thousand feet of perpendicular Old Red Sandstone in a brief time—no, it took twenty million years. In the first place, a coal bed is a slow and troublesome and tiresome thing to construct. You have to grow prodigious forests of tree-ferns and reeds and calamites and such things in a marshy region; then you have to sink them under out of sight and let them rot; then you have to turn the streams on them, so as to bury them under several feet of sediment, and the sediment must have time to harden and turn to rock; next you must grow another forest on top, then sink it and put on another layer of sediment and harden it; then more forest and more rock, layer upon layer, three miles deep— ah, indeed it is a sickening slow job to build a coal-measure and do it right!

So the millions of years drag on; and meantime the fish culture is   8
lazying along and frazzling out in a way to make a person tired. You have developed ten thousand kinds of fishes from the oyster; and come to look, you have raised nothing but fossils, nothing but extinctions. There is nothing left alive and progressive but a ganoid or two and perhaps half a dozen asteroids. Even the cat wouldn't each such.

Still, it is no great matter; there is plenty of time, yet, and they   9
will develop into something tasty before man is ready for them. Even a ganoid can be depended on for that, when he is not going to be called on for sixty million years.

The Paleozoic time limit having now been reached, it was neces-   10
sary to begin the next stage in the preparation of the world for man, by opening up the Mesozoic Age and instituting some reptiles. For man would need reptiles. Not to eat, but to develop himself from. This being the most important detail of the scheme, a spacious liberality of time was set apart for it—thirty million years. What wonders followed! From the remaining ganoids and asteroids and alkaloids were developed by slow and steady and painstaking culture those stupendous saurians that used to prowl about the steamy world in those remote ages, with their snaky heads reared forty feet in the air and sixty

feet of body and tail racing and thrashing after. All gone, now, alas—all extinct, except the little handful of Arkansawrians left stranded and lonely with us here upon this far-flung verge and fringe of time.

11   Yes, it took thirty million years and twenty million reptiles to get one that would stick long enough to develop into something else and let the scheme proceed to the next step.

12   Then the pterodactyl burst upon the world in all his impressive solemnity and grandeur, and all Nature recognized that the Cenozoic threshold was crossed and a new Period open for business, a new stage begun in the preparation of the globe for man. It may be that the pterodactyl thought the thirty million years had been intended as a preparation for himself, for there was nothing too foolish for a pterodactyl to imagine, but he was in error, the preparation was for man. Without doubt the pterodactyl attracted great attention, for even the least observant could see that there was the making of a bird in him. And so it turned out. Also the makings of a mammal, in time. One thing we have to say to his credit, that in the matter of picturesqueness he was the triumph of his Period; he wore wings and had teeth, and was a starchy and wonderful mixture altogether, a kind of long-distance premonitory symptom of Kipling's marine:

'E isn't one o' the reg'lar Line, nor 'e isn't one of the crew,
'E's a kind of giddy harumfrodite—soldier an' sailor too!

13   From this time onward for nearly another thirty million years the preparation moved briskly. From the pterodactyl was developed the bird; from the bird the kangaroo, from the kangaroo the other marsupials; from these the mastodon, the megatherium, the giant sloth, the Irish elk, and all that crowd that you make useful and instructive fossils out of—then came the first great Ice Sheet, and they all retreated before it and crossed over the bridge at Bering Strait and wandered around over Europe and Asia and died. All except a few, to carry on the preparation with. Six Glacial Periods with two million years between Periods chased these poor orphans up and down and about the earth, from weather to weather—from tropic swelter at the poles to Arctic frost at the equator and back again and to and fro, they never knowing what kind of weather was going to turn up next; and if ever they settled down anywhere the whole continent suddenly sank under them without the least notice and they had to trade places with the fishes and scramble off to where the seas had been, and scarcely a dry rag on them; and when there was nothing else doing a volcano would let go and fire them out from wherever they had located. They led this unsettled and irritating life for twenty-five million years, half the time afloat, half the time aground, and always wondering what it was all for, they never suspecting, of course, that it was a preparation for man

and had to be done just so or it wouldn't be any proper and harmonious place for him when he arrived.

And at last came the monkey, and anybody could see that man 14 wasn't far off, now. And in truth that was so. The monkey went on developing for close upon five million years, and then turned into a man—to all appearances.

Such is the history of it. Man has been here 32,000 years. That it 15 took a hundred million years to prepare the world for him is proof that that is what it was done for. I suppose it is. I dunno. If the Eiffel Tower were now representing the world's age, the skin of paint on the pinnacle-knob at its summit would represent man's share of that age; and anybody would perceive that that skin was what the tower was built for. I reckon they would, I dunno.

___ CONSIDERATIONS _____

1. How and when does Twain let us know what he is up to in this essay?

2. Twain urges us, as we study the history of man and the world, to be patient, to be calm, to jump to no conclusions. Note how he uses the oyster (paragraph 6) and the pterodactyl (paragraph 12) to strengthen his point.

3. "Was the World Made for Man?" begins with two epigraphs: quotations selected by the author and used to state or hint at the central theme or image of the piece. To learn the uses and limitations of this literary device, select epigraphs for one or two essays in this book. Consult Bartlett's *Familiar Quotations* for a little assistance.

4. One characteristic of satire is the use of gross exaggeration (see Jonathan Swift's "A Modest Proposal," page 516). Is exaggeration a feature of Twain's essay?

5. Twin uses the Eiffel Tower to help us get some idea of the length of time and the complexity of human history. Setting aside his satirical motives for a moment, observe that Twain is doing what every good writer tries to do: he presents abstractions in concrete terms. Try the technique yourself by inventing a concrete way of making comprehensible the distance from here to the sun.

John Updike (b. 1932) grew up in Pennsylvania and went to Harvard, where he edited the humor magazine, the Lampoon. *On a fellowship year at Oxford, Updike sold a poem to the* New Yorker *and began his long relationship with that magazine. First he worked on the staff of the* New Yorker, *contributing to "The Talk of the Town." When he quit to freelance, he continued to write stories, poems, reviews, and articles for the magazine.* The Poorhouse Fair *(1959), his first novel, appeared in the same year as his first collection of stories,* The Same Door.

Updike has published stories, novels, poems, and miscellaneous collections. Assorted Prose *(1965),* Picked-up Pieces *(1975), and* Hugging the Shore *(1983). Among his best novels are* The Centaur *(1963) and* Rabbit at Rest *(1990). He recently published a collection of short stories,* The Afterlife *(1994).*

This essay comes from an issue of the Michigan Quarterly Review *devoted to the male body. On page 38 is Margaret Atwood's contribution to the same issue.*

89

JOHN UPDIKE

The Disposable Rocket

1   Inhabiting a male body is much like having a bank account; as long as it's healthy, you don't think much about it. Compared to the female body, it is a low-maintenance proposition: a shower now and then, trim the fingernails every ten days, a haircut once a month. Oh yes, shaving—scraping or buzzing away at your face every morning. Byron, in *Don Juan*, thought the repeated nuisance of shaving balanced out the periodic agony, for females, of childbirth. Women are, his lines tell us,

> Condemn'd to child-bed, as men for their sins
> Have shaving too entail'd upon their chins,—

A daily plague, which in the aggregate
 May average on the whole with parturition.

From the standpoint of reproduction, the male body is a delivery system, as the female is a mazy device for retention. Once the delivery is
made, men feel a faint but distinct falling-off of interest. Yet against
the enduring female heroics of birth and nurture should be set the
male's superhuman frenzy to deliver his goods: he vaults walls, skips
sleep, risks wallet, health, and his political future all to ram home his
seed into the gut of the chosen woman. The sense of the chase lives in
him as the key to life. His body is, like a delivery rocket that falls
away in space, a disposable means. Men put their bodies at risk to experience the release from gravity.

When my tenancy of a male body was fairly new—of six or so   2
years' duration—I used to jump and fall just for the joy of it. Falling—
backwards, downstairs—became a specialty of mine, an attention-get-
ting stunt I was practicing into my thirties, at suburban parties.
Falling is, after all, a kind of flying, though of briefer duration than
would be ideal. My impulse to hurl myself from high windows and the
edges of cliffs belongs to my body, not my mind, which resists the
siren call of the chasm with all its might; the interior struggle knocks
the wind from my lungs and tightens my scrotum and gives any trip to
Europe, with its Alps, castle parapets, and gargoyled cathedral look-
outs, a flavor of nightmare. Falling, strangely, no longer figures in my
dreams, as it often did when I was a boy and my subconscious was
more honest with me. An airplane, that necessary evil, turns the earth
into a map so quickly the brain turns aloof and calm; still, I marvel
that there is no end of young men willing to become jet pilots.

Any accounting of male-female differences must include the   3
male's superior recklessness, a drive not, I think, toward death, as the
darker feminist cosmogonies would have it, but to test the limits, to
see what the traffic will bear—a kind of mechanic's curiosity. The
number of men who do lasting damage to their young bodies is striking; war and car accidents aside, secondary-school sports, with the approval of parents and the encouragement of brutish coaches, take a
fearful toll of skulls and knees. We were made for combat, back in the
post-simian, East African days, and the bumping, the whacking, the
breathlessness, the pain-smothering adrenaline rush, form a cumber-
some and unfashionable bliss, but bliss nevertheless. Take your body
to the edge, and see if it flies.

The male sense of space must differ from that of the female, who   4
has such interesting, active, and significant inner space. The space
that interests men is outer. The fly ball high against the sky, the long
pass spiraling overhead, the jet fighter like a scarcely visible pinpoint

nozzle laying down its vapor trail at forty thousand feet, the gazelle haunch flickering just beyond arrow-reach, the uncountable stars sprinkled on their great black wheel, the horizon, the mountaintop, the quasar—these bring portents with them, and awaken a sense of relation with the invisible, with the empty. The ideal male body is taut with lines of potential force, a diagram extending outward; the ideal female body curves around centers of repose. Of course, no one is ideal, and the sexes are somewhat androgynous subdivisions of a species: Diana the huntress is a more trendy body-type nowadays than languid, overweight Venus, and polymorphous Dionysus poses for more underwear ads than Mars. Relatively, though, men's bodies, however elegant, are designed for covering territory, for moving on.

5   An erection, too, defies gravity, flirts with it precariously. It extends the diagram of outward direction into downright detachability—objective in the case of the sperm, subjective in the case of the testicles and penis. Men's bodies, at this juncture, feel only partly theirs; a demon of sorts has been attached to their lower torsos, whose performance is erratic and whose errands seem, at times, ridiculous. It is like having a (much) smaller brother toward whom you feel both fond and impatient; if he is you, it is you in curiously simplified and ignoble form. This sense, of the male body being two of them, is acknowledged in verbal love play and erotic writing, where the penis is playfully given its own name, an individuation not even the rarest rapture grants a vagina. Here, where maleness gathers to a quintessence of itself, there can be no insincerity, there can be no hiding; for sheer nakedness, there is nothing like a hopeful phallus; its aggressive shape is indivisible from its tender-skinned vulnerability. The act of intercourse, from the point of view of a consenting female, has an element of mothering, of enwrapment, of merciful concealment, even. The male body, for this interval, is tucked out of harm's way.

6   To inhabit a male body, then, is to feel somewhat detached from it. It is not an enemy, but not entirely a friend. Our essence seems to lie not in cells and muscles but in the traces our thoughts and actions inscribe on the air. The male body skims the surface of nature's deep, wherein the blood and pain and mysterious cravings of women perpetuate the species. Participating less in nature's processes than the female body, the male body gives the impression—false—of being exempt from time. Its powers of strength and reach descend in early adolescence, along with acne and sweaty feet, and depart, in imperceptible increments, after thirty or so. It surprises me to discover, when I remove my shoes and socks, the same paper-white hairless ankles that struck me as pathetic when I observed them on my father. I felt betrayed when, in some tumble of touch football twenty years ago, I heard my tibia snap; and when, between two reading engagements in Cleveland, my appendix tried to burst; and when, the other day, not

for the first time, there arose to my nostrils out of my own body the musty attic smell my grandfather's body had.

A man's body does not betray its tenant as rapidly as a woman's.   7 Never as fine and lovely, it has less distance to fall; what rugged beauty it has is wrinkle-proof. It keeps its capability of procreation indecently long. Unless intense athletic demands are made on it, the thing serves well enough to sixty, which is my age now. From here on, it's chancy. There are no breasts or ovaries to admit cancer to the male body, but the prostate, that awkwardly located little source of seminal fluid, shows the strain of sexual function with fits of hysterical cell replication, and all that beer and potato chips add up in the coronary arteries. A writer, whose physical equipment can be minimal, as long as it gets him to the desk, the lectern, and New York City once in a while, cannot but be grateful to his body, especially to his eyes, those tender and intricate sites where the brain extrudes from the skull, and to his hands, which hold the pen or tap the keyboard. His body has been, not himself exactly, but a close pal, pot-bellied and balding like most of his other pals now. A man and his body are like a boy and the buddy who has a driver's license and the use of his father's car for the evening; he goes along, gratefully, for the ride.

___ CONSIDERATIONS _____

1. "... enduring female heroics ... male's superhuman frenzy ..." What do phrases like these tell you about Updike's attitude toward the subject of male-female relations?

2. In addition to the paired terms in No. 1 above, what other paired differences seem to interest Updike in his essay? What might be learned from his use of them?

3. In paragraph 5, Updike writes explicitly, if imaginatively, about male and female sexual organs. How does he avoid slipping into pornography? Or does he? See Margaret Atwood's "Pornography," Page 31, for help in explaining your answer.

4. Think about Updike's closing sentence of paragraph 7. Then explain it in terms of the first two sentences of paragraph 6.

5. One strength of Updike's style is his ability to provide not one, but a series of concrete examples to give body to his abstract statements. Experiment with his technique in your next essay.

6. Imagine Updike sitting down for a coffee with the following women, all represented by essays in this text: Virginia Woolf, Gretel Ehrlich, Michelle Cliff, and Margaret Atwood. What would the five find they had in common? Select one of the women and imagine her interviewing Updike. Write up the interview as though it were to appear in your college newspaper.

Gore Vidal (b. 1925) entered the army after graduating from Philips Exeter Academy and never attended college. He published his first novel the year he turned twenty-one. Since then, he has run for Congress and lived in Europe. Vidal's writing includes plays, essays, and chiefly, novels, including Julian *(1964),* Myra Breckinridge *(1968),* Burr *(1973),* Kalki *(1979),* Lincoln *(1984),* Empire *(1987), and* Live from Golgotha *(1992). In 1993 he published an immense volume of his collected essays:* United States: Essays 1952–1992.

90

GORE VIDAL

Drugs

1   It is possible to stop most drug addiction in the United States within a very short time. Simply make all drugs available and sell them at cost. Label each drug with a precise description of what effect—good and bad—the drug will have on the taker. This will require heroic honesty. Don't say that marijuana is addictive or dangerous when it is neither, as millions of people know—unlike "speed," which kills most unpleasantly, or heroin, which is addictive and difficult to kick.

2   For the record, I have tried—once—almost every drug and liked none, disproving the popular Fu Manchu theory that a single whiff of opium will enslave the mind. Nevertheless many drugs are bad for certain people to take and they should be told why in a sensible way.

3   Along with exhortation and warning, it might be good for our citizens to recall (or learn for the first time) that the United States was the creation of men who believed that each man has the right to do what he wants with his own life as long as he does not interfere with his neighbor's pursuit of happiness (that his neighbor's idea of happiness is persecuting others does confuse matters a bit).

This is a startling notion to the current generation of Americans.   4
They reflect a system of public education which has made the Bill of
Rights, literally, unacceptable to a majority of high school graduates
(see the annual Purdue reports) who now form the "silent majority"—
a phrase which that underestimated wit Richard Nixon took from
Homer who used it to describe the dead.

Now one can hear the warning rumble begin: if everyone is al-   5
lowed to take drugs everyone will and the GNP will decrease, the
Commies will stop us from making everyone free, and we shall end up
a race of Zombies, passively murmuring "groovie" to one another.
Alarming thought. Yet it seems most unlikely that any reasonably
sane person will become a drug addict if he knows in advance what addiction is going to be like.

Is everyone reasonably sane? No. Some people will always be-   6
come drug addicts just as some people will always become alcoholics,
and it is just too bad. Every man, however, has the power (and should
have the legal right) to kill himself if he chooses. But since most men
don't, they won't be mainliners either. Nevertheless, forbidding people things they like or think they might enjoy only makes them want
those things all the more. This psychological insight is, for some mysterious reason, perennially denied our governors.

It is a lucky thing for the American moralist that our country has   7
always existed in a kind of time-vacuum: we have no public memory
of anything that happened before last Tuesday. No one in Washington
today recalls what happened during the years alcohol was forbidden to
the people by a Congress that thought it had a divine mission to stamp
out Demon Rum—launching, in the process, the greatest crime wave
in the country's history, causing thousands of deaths from bad alcohol, and creating a general (and persisting) contempt among the citi-
zenry for the laws of the United States.

The same thing is happening today. But the government has   8
learned nothing from past attempts at prohibition, not to mention repression.

Last year when the supply of Mexican marijuana was slightly   9
curtailed by the Feds, the pushers got the kids hooked on heroin and
deaths increased dramatically, particularly in New York. Whose fault?
Evil men like the Mafiosi? Permissive Dr. Spock? Wild-eyed Dr.
Leary? No.

The Government of the United States was responsible for those   10
deaths. The bureaucratic machine has a vested interest in playing cops
and robbers. Both the Bureau of Narcotics and the Mafia want strong
laws against the sale and use of drugs because if drugs are sold at cost
there would be no money in it for anyone.

If there was no money in it for the Mafia, there would be no   11
friendly playground pushers, and addicts would not commit crimes to

pay for the next fix. Finally, if there was no money in it, the Bureau of Narcotics would wither away, something they are not about to do without a struggle.

12   Will anything sensible be done? Of course not. The American people are as devoted to the idea of sin and its punishment as they are to making money—and fighting drugs is nearly as big a business as pushing them. Since the combination of sin and money is irresistible (particularly to the professional politician), the situation will only grow worse.

_____ CONSIDERATIONS _____

1. One mark of the experienced arguer is the ability to anticipate and thus neutralize his opponent's rebuttal. Where does Vidal do this? How effective is his attempt?

2. Vidal's argument (paragraphs 10, 11, and 12) that "the bureaucratic machine has a vested interest in playing cops and robbers" rests on his implication that law enforcers are at least as interested in preserving their jobs as they are in preserving law and order. Does he present any evidence to support this argument? What kind of evidence could he offer? How could you support a counterargument?

3. Vidal contends that "every man . . . should have the legal right to kill himself." How far would he (or you) extend that "right"? To all varieties of suicide, for instance?

4. Refresh your memory of the Bill of Rights—where do you find it?—and explain why Vidal says it has become "unacceptable to a majority of high school graduates."

5. Is the slang term "groovie"—usually spelled "groovy"—still current? Linguists often study slang because it changes faster than standard language. For the same reason, geneticists study fruit flies because the quick turnover of generations allows them to investigate principles of genetics within a brief period of time. In what way(s) do changes in slang parallel changes in English in general?

6. Given Vidal's belief in freedom of the individual, how do you think he would approach the question of gun control?

7. Write a rebuttal to Vidal's argument, using current statistics and trends in drug abuse.

*Alice Walker (b. 1944) grew up in Georgia and went to
Sarah Lawrence College in New York City. She first
published as a poet, with* Once *and* Revolutionary
Petunias, *and has added collections of short stories, a
biography of Langston Hughes, and novels—notably* The
Color Purple *(1982), and more recently* The Temple of My
Familiar *(1989). In 1993 she published* Her Blue Body
Everything We Know: Earthling Poems, 1965–1990
Complete.

She collected her essays as In Search of Our Mothers'
Gardens, *from which we take this article originally
published in 1970. Elsewhere in* A Writer's Reader *you will
find the white Southern writers William Faulkner and
Flannery O'Connor, whom Alice Walker mentions in this
essay.*

91

ALICE WALKER
The Black Writer and the Southern Experience

My mother tells of an incident that happened to her in the thir- 1
ties during the Depression. She and my father lived in a small Georgia
town and had half a dozen children. They were sharecroppers, and
food, especially flour, was almost impossible to obtain. To get flour,
which was distributed by the Red Cross, one had to submit vouchers
signed by a local official. On the day my mother was to go into town
for flour she received a large box of clothes from one of my aunts who
was living in the North. The clothes were in good condition, though
well worn, and my mother needed a dress, so she immediately put on
one of those from the box and wore it into town. When she reached
the distribution center and presented her voucher she was confronted

by a white woman who looked her up and down with marked anger and envy.

2   "What'd you come up here for?" the woman asked.

3   "For some flour," said my mother, presenting her voucher.

4   "Humph," said the woman, looking at her more closely and with unconcealed fury. "Anybody dressed up as good as you don't need to come here *begging* for food."

5   "I ain't begging," said my mother, "the government is giving away flour to those that need it, and I need it. I wouldn't be here if I didn't. And these clothes I'm wearing was given to me." But the woman had already turned to the next person in line, saying over her shoulder to the white man who was behind the counter with her, "The *gall* of niggers coming in here dressed better than me!" This thought seemed to make her angrier still, and my mother, pulling three of her small children behind her and crying from humiliation, walked sadly back into the street.

6   "What did you and Daddy do for flour that winter?" I asked my mother.

7   "Well," she said, "Aunt Mandy Aikens lived down the road from us and she got plenty of flour. We had a good stand of corn so we had plenty of meal. Aunt Mandy would swap me a bucket of flour for a bucket of meal. We got by all right."

8   Then she added thoughtfully, "And that old woman that turned me off so short got down so bad in the end that she was walking on *two* sticks." And I knew she was thinking, though she never said it: Here I am today, my eight children healthy and grown and three of them in college and me with hardly a sick day for years. Ain't Jesus wonderful?

9   In this small story is revealed the condition and strength of a people. Outcasts to be used and humiliated by the larger society, the Southern black sharecropper and poor farmer clung to his own kind and to a religion that had been given to pacify him as a slave but which he soon transformed into an antidote against bitterness. Depending on one another, because they had nothing and no one else, the sharecroppers often managed to come through "all right." And when I listen to my mother tell and retell this story I find that the white woman's vindictiveness is less important than Aunt Mandy's resourceful generosity or my mother's ready stand of corn. For their lives were not about that pitiful example of Southern womanhood, but about themselves.

10   What the black Southern writer inherits as a natural right is a sense of *community.* Something simple but surprisingly hard, especially these days, to come by. My mother, who is a walking history of our community, tells me that when each of her children was born the midwife accepted as payment such home-grown or homemade items

as a pig, a quilt, jars of canned fruits and vegetables. But there was never any question that the midwife would come when she was needed, whatever the eventual payment for her services. I consider this each time I hear of a hospital that refuses to admit a woman in labor unless she can hand over a substantial sum of money, cash.

Nor am I nostalgic, as a French philosopher once wrote, for lost poverty. I am nostalgic for the solidarity and sharing a modest existence can sometimes bring. We knew, I suppose, that we were poor. Somebody knew; perhaps the landowner who grudgingly paid my father three hundred dollars a year for twelve months' labor. But we never considered ourselves to be poor, unless, of course, we were deliberately humiliated. And because we never believed we were poor, and therefore worthless, we could depend on one another without shame. And always there were the Burial Societies, the Sick-and-Shut-in Societies, that sprang up out of spontaneous need. And no one seemed terribly upset that black sharecroppers were ignored by white insurance companies. It went without saying, in my mother's day, that birth and death required assistance from the community, and that the magnitude of these events was lost on outsiders.   11

As a college student I came to reject the Christianity of my parents, and it took me years to realize that though they had been force-fed a white man's palliative, in the form of religion, they had made it into something at once simple and noble. True, even today, they can never successfully picture a God who is not white, and that is a major cruelty, but their lives testify to a greater comprehension of the teachings of Jesus than the lives of people who sincerely believe a God *must* have a color and that there can be such a phenomenon as a "white" church.   12

The richness of the black writer's experience in the South can be remarkable, though some people might not think so. Once, while in college, I told a white middle-aged Northerner that I hoped to be a poet. In the nicest possible language, which still made me as mad as I've ever been, he suggested that a "farmer's daughter" might not be the stuff of which poets are made. On one level, of course, he had a point. A shack with only a dozen or so books is an unlikely place to discover a young Keats. But it is narrow thinking, indeed, to believe that a Keats is the only kind of poet one would want to grow up to be. One wants to write poetry that is understood by one's people, not by the Queen of England. Of course, should she be able to profit by it too, so much the better, but since that is not likely, catering to her tastes would be a waste of time.   13

For the black Southern writer, coming straight out of the country, as Wright did—Natchez and Jackson are still not as citified as they like to think they are—there is the world of comparisons; between town and country, between the ugly crowding and griminess of the   14 cities and the spacious cleanliness (which actually seems impossible to dirty) of the country. A country person finds the city confining, like a too tight dress. And always, in one's memory, there remain all the rituals of one's growing up: the warmth and vividness of Sunday worship (never mind that you never quite believed) in a little church hidden from the road, and houses set so far back into the woods that at night it is impossible for strangers to find them. The daily dramas that evolve in such a private world are pure gold. But this view of a strictly private and hidden existence, with its triumphs, failures, grotesqueries, is not nearly as valuable to the socially conscious black Southern writer as his double vision is. For not only is he in a position to see his own world, and its close community ("Homecomings" on First Sundays, barbecues to raise money to send to Africa—one of the smaller ironies—the simplicity and eerie calm of a black funeral, where the beloved one is buried way in the middle of a wood with nothing to mark the spot but perhaps a wooden cross already coming apart), but also he is capable of knowing, with remarkably silent accuracy, the people who make up the larger world that surrounds and suppresses his own.

15   It is a credit to a writer like Ernest J. Gaines, a black writer who writes mainly about the people he grew up with in rural Louisiana, that he can write about whites and blacks exactly as he sees them and *knows* them, instead of writing of one group as a vast malignant lump and of the others as a conglomerate of perfect virtues.

16   In large measure, black Southern writers owe their clarity of vision to parents who refused to diminish themselves as human beings by succumbing to racism. Our parents seemed to know that an extreme negative emotion held against other human beings for reasons they do not control can be blinding. Blindness about other human beings, especially for a writer, is equivalent to death. Because of this blindness, which is, above all, racial, the works of many southern writers have died. Much that we read today is fast expiring.

17   My own slight attachment to William Faulkner was rudely broken by realizing, after reading statements he made in *Faulkner in the University*, that he believed whites superior morally to blacks; that whites had a duty (which at their convenience they would assume) to "bring blacks along" politically, since blacks, in Faulkner's opinion, were "not ready" yet to function properly in a democratic society. He also thought that a black man's intelligence is directly related to the amount of white blood he has.

18   For the black person coming of age in the sixties, where Martin Luther King stands against the murderers of Goodman, Chaney, and Schwerner, there appears no basis for such assumptions. Nor was there any in Garvey's day, or in Du Bois's or in Douglass's or in Nat Turner's. Nor at any other period in our history, from the very found-

ing of the country; for it was hardly incumbent upon slaves to be slaves and saints too. Unlike Tolstoy, Faulkner was not prepared to struggle to change the structure of the society he was born in. One might concede that in his fiction he did seek to examine the reasons for its decay, but unfortunately, as I have learned while trying to teach Faulkner to black students, it is not possible, from so short a range, to separate the man from his works.

One reads Faulkner knowing that his "colored" people had to 19 come through "Mr. William's" back door, and one feels uneasy, and finally enraged that Faulkner did not burn the whole house down. When the provincial mind starts out *and continues* on a narrow and unprotesting course, "genius" itself must run on a track.

Flannery O'Connor at least had the conviction that "reality" is at 20 best superficial and that the puzzle of humanity is less easy to solve than that of race. But Miss O'Connor was not so much of Georgia, as in it. The majority of Southern writers have been too confined by prevailing social customs to probe deeply into mysteries that the Citizens Councils insist must never be revealed.

Perhaps my Northern brothers will not believe me when I say 21 there is a great deal of positive material I can draw from my "underprivileged" background. But they have never lived, as I have, at the end of a long road in a house that was faced by the edge of the world on one side and nobody for miles on the other. They have never experienced the magnificent quiet of a summer day when the heat is intense and one is so very thirsty, as one moves across the dusty cotton fields, that one learns forever that water is the essence of all life. In the cities it cannot be so clear to one that he is a creature of the earth, feeling the soil between the toes, smelling the dust thrown up by the rain, loving the earth so much that one longs to taste it and sometimes does.

Nor do I intend to romanticize the Southern black country life. I 22 can recall that I hated it, generally. The hard work in the fields, the shabby houses, the evil greedy men who worked my father to death and almost broke the courage of that strong woman, my mother. No, I am simply saying that Southern black writers, like most writers, have a heritage of love and hate, but that they also have enormous richness and beauty to draw from. And, having been placed, as Camus says, "halfway between misery and the sun," they, too, know that "though all is not well under the sun, history is not everything."

No one could wish for a more advantageous heritage than that 23 bequeathed to the black writer in the South: a compassion for the earth, a trust in humanity beyond our knowledge of evil, and an abiding love of justice. We inherit a great responsibility as well, for we must give voice to centuries not only of silent bitterness and hate but also of neighborly kindness and sustaining love.

_____ **CONSIDERATIONS** _____

1. In paragraph 15, Alice Walker pays tribute to another black novelist, Ernest J. Gaines, for refusing to make his characters into stereotypes of the white villain and the black martyr. She has trouble acknowledging the achievements of another, more famous Southern novelist, William Faulkner. Why? Carefully read paragraph 18 for the answer.

2. Read Eudora Welty's short story, "A Worn Path," and speculate on what Walker might say about Welty's understanding of the black Southern experience.

3. Is Walker sentimental in expressing the values of her poverty-stricken childhood? Find specific statements or phrases to support your answer. Compare her tone with Louise Bogan's in "Miss Cooper and Me," Frank O'Connor's in "Christmas," E. B. White's in "Once More to the Lake," or Alexander Woollcott's in "Obituary."

4. "But Miss O'Connor was not so much of Georgia, as in it," writes Walker, in expressing her reservations about Flannery O'Connor's contribution. Why does she distinguish between "of Georgia" and "in it"?

5. Walker mentions several ironies in connection with the black experience in the American South. Isolate a few of these and try to explain the nature and appeal of irony in a writer's work.

6. How does the story in paragraphs 1 through 8 help make Walker's conclusions in paragraph 23 credible?

7. Compare Walker's comments with those of two other black writers: Ralph Ellison (see "On Becoming a Writer") and Shelby Steele (see "I'm Black, You're White, Who's Innocent?").

Eudora Welty (b. 1909) lives in her native Jackson,
Mississippi, where she continues to write, deliberately and
slowly, her perfect stories and novel. A Curtain of Green
(1941) was her first volume of collected stories. Her novels
include Losing Battles *(1970) and* The Optimist's Daughter
(1972), which won her a Pulitzer Prize. In 1980 The
Collected Stories of Eudora Welty *was published, and in*
1984, a reminiscence, One Writer's Beginnings. *She has*
also published volumes of her photographs.

92

EUDORA WELTY
A Worn Path

It was December—a bright frozen day in the early morning. Far 1
out in the country there was an old Negro woman with her head tied
in a red rag, coming along a path through the pinewoods. Her name
was Phoenix Jackson. She was very old and small and she walked
slowly in the dark pine shadows, moving a little from side to side in
her steps, with the balanced heaviness and lightness of a pendulum in
a grandfather clock. She carried a thin, small cane made from an umbrella, and with this she kept tapping the frozen earth in front of her.
This made a grave and persistent noise in the still air, that seemed
meditative, like the chirping of a solitary little bird.

She wore a dark striped dress reaching down to her shoetops, and 2
an equally long apron of bleached sugar sacks, with a full pocket; all
neat and tidy, but every time she took a step she might have fallen
over her shoelaces, which dragged from her unlaced shoes. She looked
straight ahead. Her eyes were blue with age. Her skin had a pattern all
its own of numberless branching wrinkles and as though a whole little
tree stood in the middle of her forehead, but a golden color ran underneath, and the two knobs of her cheeks were illuminated by a yellow
burning under the dark. Under the red rag her hair came down on her

neck in the frailest of ringlets, still black, and with an odor like copper.

3   Now and then there was a quivering in the thicket. Old Phoenix said, "Out of my way, all you foxes, owls, beetles, jack rabbits, coons, and wild animals! . . . Keep out from under these feet, little bob-whites. . . . Keep the big wild hogs out of my path. Don't let none of those come running in my direction. I got a long way." Under her small black-freckled hand her cane, limber as a buggy whip, would switch at the brush as if to rouse up any hiding things.

4   On she went. The woods were deep and still. The sun made the pine needles almost too bright to look at, up where the wind rocked. The cones dropped as light as feathers. Down in the hollow was the mourning dove—it was not too late for him.

5   The path ran up a hill. "Seem like there is chains about my feet, time I get this far," she said, in the voice of argument old people keep to use with themselves. "Something always take a hold on this hill— pleads I should stay."

6   After she got to the top she turned and gave a full, severe look behind her where she had come. "Up through pines," she said at length. "Now down through oaks."

7   Her eyes opened their widest and she started down gently. But before she got to the bottom of the hill a bush caught her dress.

8   Her fingers were busy and intent, but her skirts were full and long, so that before she could pull them free in one place they were caught in another. It was not possible to allow the dress to tear. "I in the thorny bush," she said. "Thorns, you doing your appointed work. Never want to let folks past—no sir. Old eyes thought you was a pretty little *green* bush."

9   Finally, trembling all over, she stood free, and after a moment dared to stoop for her cane.

10   "Sun so high!" she cried, leaning back and looking, while the thick tears went over her eyes. "The time getting all gone here."

11   At the foot of this hill was a place where a log was laid across the creek.

12   "Now comes the trial," said Phoenix.

13   Putting her right foot out, she mounted the log and shut her eyes. Lifting her skirt, leveling her cane fiercely before her, like a festival figure in some parade, she began to march across. Then she opened her eyes and she was safe on the other side.

14   "I wasn't as old as I thought," she said.

15   But she sat down to rest. She spread her skirts on the bank around her and folded her hands over her knees. Up above her was a tree in a pearly cloud of mistletoe. She did not dare to close her eyes, and when a little boy brought her a little plate with a slice of marble-

cake on it she spoke to him. "That would be acceptable," she said. But when she went to take it there was just her own hand in the air.

So she left that tree, and had to go through a barbed-wire fence. 16 There she had to creep and crawl, spreading her knees and stretching her fingers like a baby trying to climb the steps. but she talked loudly to herself: she could not let her dress be torn now, so late in the day, and she could not pay for having her arm or leg sawed off if she got caught fast where she was.

At last she was safe through the fence and risen up out in the 17 clearing. Big dead trees, like black men with one arm, were standing in the purple stalks of the withered cotton field. There sat a buzzard.

"Who you watching?" 18

In the furrow she made her way along 19

"Glad this not the season for bulls," she said, looking sideways, 20 "and the good Lord made his snakes to curl up and sleep in the winter. A pleasure I don't see no two-headed snake coming around that tree, where it come once. It took a while to get by him, back in the summer."

She passed through the old cotton and went into a field of dead 21 corn. It whispered and shook, and was taller than her head. "Through the maze now," she said, for there was no path.

Then there was something tall, black, and skinny there, moving 22 before her.

At first she took it for a man. It could have been a man dancing 23 in the field. But she stood still and listened, and it did not make a sound. It was as silent as a ghost.

"Ghost," she said sharply, "who be you the ghost of? For I have 24 heard of nary death close by."

But there was no answer, only the ragged dancing in the wind. 25

She shut her eyes, reached out her hand, and touched a sleeve. 26 She found a coat and inside that an emptiness, cold as ice.

"You scarecrow," she said. Her face lighted. "I ought to be shut 27 up for good," she said with laughter. "My senses is gone. I too old. I the oldest people I ever know. Dance, old scarecrow," she said, "while I dancing with you."

She kicked her foot over the furrow, and with mouth drawn 28 down shook her head once or twice in a little strutting way. Some husks blew down and whirled in streamers about her skirts.

Then she went on, parting her way from side to side with the 29 cane, through the whispering field. At last she came to the end, to a wagon track, where the silver grass blew between the red ruts. The quail were walking around like pullets, seeming all dainty and unseen.

"Walk pretty," she said. "This the easy place. This the easy 30 going."

31   She followed the track, swaying through the quiet bare fields, through the little strings of trees silver in their dead leaves, past cabins silver from weather, with the doors and windows boarded shut, all like old women under a spell sitting there. "I walking in their sleep," she said, nodding her head vigorously.

32   In a ravine she went where a spring was silently flowing through a hollow log. Old Phoenix bent and drank. "Sweetgum makes the water sweet," she said, and drank more. "Nobody knows who made this well, for it was here when I was born."

33   The track crossed a swampy part where the moss hung as white as lace from every limb. "Sleep on, alligators, and blow your bubbles." Then the track went into the road.

34   Deep, deep the road went down between the high green-colored banks. Overhead the live-oaks met, and it was as dark as a cave.

35   A black dog with a lolling tongue came up out of the weeds by the ditch. She was meditating, and not ready, and when he came at her she only hit him a little with her cane. Over she went in the ditch, like a little puff of milk-weed.

36   Down there, her senses drifted away. A dream visited her, and she reached her hand up, but nothing reached down and gave her a pull. So she lay there and presently went to talking. "Old woman," she said to herself, "that black dog come up out of the weeds to stall you off, and now there he sitting on his fine tail, smiling at you."

37   A white man finally came along and found her—a hunter, a young man, with his dog on a chain.

38   "Well, Granny!" he laughed. "What are you doing there?"

39   "Lying on my back like a June-bug waiting to be turned over, mister," she said, reaching up her hand.

40   He lifted her up, gave her a swing in the air, and set her down. "Anything broken, Granny?"

41   "No, sir, them old dead weeds is springy enough," said Phoenix, when she had got her breath. "I thank you for your trouble."

42   "Where do you live, Granny?" he asked, while the two dogs were growling at each other.

43   "Away back yonder, sir, behind that ridge. You can't even see it from here."

44   "On your way home?"

45   "No, sir, I going to town."

46   "Why that's too far! That's as far as I walk when I come out myself, and I get something for my trouble." He patted the stuffed bag he carried, and there hung down a little closed claw. It as one of the bobwhites, with its beak hooked bitterly to show it was dead. "Now you go on home, Granny!"

47   "I bound to go to town, mister," said Phoenix. "The time come around."

He gave another laugh, filling the whole landscape. "I know you 48
colored people! Wouldn't miss going to town to see Santa Claus!"

But something held Old Phoenix very still. The deep lines in her 49
face went into a fierce and different radiation. Without warning she
had seen with her own eyes a flashing nickel fall out of the man's
pocket on to the ground.

"How old are you, Granny?" he was saying. 50

"There is no telling, mister," she said, "no telling." 51

Then she gave a little cry and clapped her hands, and said, "Git 52
on away from here, dog! Look! Look at that dog!" She laughed as if in
admiration. "He ain't scared of nobody. He a big black dog." She whispered, "Sick him!"

"Watch me get rid of that cur," said the man. "Sick him, Pete! 53
Sick him!"

Phoenix heard the dogs fighting and heard the man running and 54
throwing sticks. She even heard a gunshot. But she was slowly bending forward by that time, further and further forward, the lids
stretched down over her eyes, as if she were doing this in her sleep.
Her chin was lowered almost to her knees. The yellow palm of her
hand came out from the fold of her apron. Her fingers slid down and
along the ground under the piece of money with the grace and care
they would have in lifting an egg from under a sitting hen. Then she
slowly straightened up, she stood erect, and the nickel was in her
apron pocket. A bird flew by. Her lips moved. "God watching me the
whole time. I come to stealing."

The man came back, and his own dog panted about them. "Well, 55
I scared him off that time," he said, and then he laughed and lifted his
gun and pointed it at Phoenix.

She stood straight and faced him. 56

"Doesn't the gun scare you?" he said, still pointing it. 57

"No, sir, I seen plenty go off closer by, in my day, and for less 58
what I done," she said, holding utterly still.

He smiled, and shouldered the gun. "Well, Granny," he said, 59
"you must be a hundred years old, and scared of nothing. I'd give you a
dime if I had any money with me. But you take my advice and stay
home, and nothing will happen to you."

"I bound to go on my way, mister," said Phoenix. She inclined 60
her head in the red rag. Then they went in different directions, but she
could hear the gun shooting again and again over the hill.

She walked on. The shadows hung from the oak trees to the road 61
like curtains. Then she smelled wood-smoke, and smelled the river,
and she saw a steeple and the cabins on their steep steps. Dozens of
little black children whirled around her. There ahead was Natchez
shining. Bells were ringing. She walked on.

62   In the paved city it was Christmas time. There were red and green electric lights strung and crisscrossed everywhere, and all turned on in the daytime. Old Phoenix would have been lost if she had not distrusted her eyesight and depended on her feet to know where to take her.

63   She paused quietly on the sidewalk, where people were passing by. A lady came along in the crowd, carrying an armful of red-, green-, and silver-wrapped presents; she gave off perfume like the red roses in hot summer, and Phoenix stopped her.

64   "Please, missy, will you lace up my shoe?" She held up her foot.

65   "What do you want, Grandma?"

66   "See my shoe," said Phoenix. "Do all right for out in the country, but wouldn't look right to go in a big building."

67   "Stand still then, Grandma," said the lady. She put her packages down carefully on the sidewalk beside her and laced and tied both shoes tightly.

68   "Can't lace 'em with a cane," said Phoenix. "Thank you, missy. I doesn't mind asking a nice lady to tie up my shoe when I gets out on the street."

69   Moving slowly and from side to side, she went into the stone building and into a tower of steps, where she walked up and around and around until her feet knew to stop.

70   She entered a door, and there she saw nailed up on the wall the document that had been stamped with the gold seal and framed in the gold frame which matched the dream that was hung up in her head.

71   "Here I be," she said. There was a fixed and ceremonial stiffness over her body.

72   "A charity case, I suppose," said an attendant who sat at the desk before her.

73   But Phoenix only looked above her head. There was sweat on her face; the wrinkles shone like a bright net.

74   "Speak up, Grandma" the woman said. "What's your name? We must have your history, you know. Have you been here before? What seems to be the trouble with you?"

75   Old Phoenix only gave a twitch to her face as if a fly were bothering her.

76   "Are you deaf?" cried the attendant.

77   But then the nurse came in.

78   "Oh, that's just old Aunt Phoenix," she said. "She doesn't come for herself—she has a little grandson. She makes these trips just as regular as clockwork. She lives away back off the Old Natchez Trace." She bent down. "Well, Aunt Phoenix, why don't you just take a seat? We won't keep you standing after your long trip." She pointed.

79   The old woman sat down, bolt upright in the chair.

80   "Now, how is the boy?" asked the nurse.

Old Phoenix did not speak. 81

"I said, how is the boy?" 82

But Phoenix only waited and stared straight ahead, her face very 83
solemn and withdrawn into rigidity.

"Is his throat any better?" asked the nurse. "Aunt Phoenix, don't 84
you hear me? Is your grandson's throat any better since the last time
you came for the medicine?"

With her hand on her knees, the old woman waited, silent, erect, 85
and motionless, just as if she were in armor.

"You mustn't take up our time this way, Aunt Phoenix," the 86
nurse said. "Tell us quickly about your grandson, and get it over. He
isn't dead, is he?"

At last there came a flicker and then a flame of comprehension 87
across her face, and she spoke.

"My grandson. It was my memory had left me. There I sat and 88
forgot why I made my long trip."

"Forgot?" The nurse frowned. "After you came so far?" 89

Then Phoenix was like an old woman begging a dignified forgive- 90
ness for waking up frightened in the night. "I never did go to school—I
was too old at the Surrender," she said in a soft voice. "I'm an old
woman without an education. It was my memory fail me. My little
grandson, he is just the same, and I forgot it in the coming."

"Throat never heals, does it?" said the nurse, speaking in a loud, 91
sure voice to Old Phoenix. By now she had a card with something
written on it, a little list. "Yes, Swallowed lye. When was it—January—two—three years ago—"

Phoenix spoke unasked now. "No, missy, he not dead, he just 92
the same. Every little while his throat begin to close up again, and he
not able to swallow. He not get his breath. He not able to help himself. So the time come around, and I go on another trip for soothing
medicine."

"All right. The doctor said as long as you came to get it you could 93
have it," said the nurse. "But it's an obstinate case."

"My little grandson, he sit up there in the house all wrapped up, 94
waiting by himself," Phoenix went on. "We is the only two left in the
world. He suffer and it don't seem to put him back at all. He got a
sweet look. He going to last. He wear a little patch quilt and peep out,
holding his mouth open like a little bird. I remembers so plain now. I
not going to forget him again, no, the whole enduring time. I could tell
him from all the others in creation."

"All right." The nurse was trying to hush her now. She brought 95
her a bottle of medicine. "Charity," she said, making a check mark in
a book.

Old Phoenix held the bottle close to her eyes and then carefully 96
put it into her pocket.

97   "I thank you," she said.

98   "It's Christmas time, Grandma," said the attendant. "Could I give you a few pennies out of my purse?"

99   "Five pennies is a nickel," said Phoenix stiffly.

100   "Here's a nickel," said the attendant.

101   Phoenix rose carefully and held out her hand. She received the nickel and then fished the other nickel out of her pocket and laid it beside the new one. She stared at her palm closely, with her head on one side.

102   Then she gave a tap with her cane on the floor.

103   "This is what come to me to do," she said. "I going to the store and buy my child a little windmill they sells, make out of paper. He going to find it hard to believe there such a thing in the world. I'll march myself back where he waiting, holding it straight up in this hand."

104   She lifted her free hand, gave a little nod, turned round, and walked out of the doctor's office. Then her slow step began on the stairs, going down.

CONSIDERATIONS

1. Some features of Old Phoenix's long journey might bring to mind Everyman's difficult travel through life. Do specific passages suggest that Old Phoenix's journey is symbolic or archetypal?

2. Would you say that Old Phoenix is senile, or is she in excellent control of her thoughts? What evidence can you find for your answer?

3. Is the grandson alive or dead? After you answer this question, read Welty's own comments on the story in the next selection.

4. Who was the little boy with the slice of marble-cake? Why does he appear and disappear so abruptly?

5. Eudora Welty makes no comment in the story on Old Phoenix's encounter with the white man. Do the details of that encounter reveal anything about relations between whites and blacks?

6. What do you learn of Old Phoenix's sense of morality, sense of humor, and feeling of personal worth?

7. Read William Faulkner's short story, "A Rose for Emily," and write an essay comparing Emily Grierson and Old Phoenix.

Here is a useful essay Welty wrote about her story "A Worn Path."

93

EUDORA WELTY
The Point of the Story

A story writer is more than happy to be read by students; the fact   1
that these serious readers think and feel something in response to his
work he finds life-giving. At the same time he may not always be able
to reply to their specific questions in kind. I wondered if it might clarify something, for both the questioners and myself, if I set down a general reply to the question that comes to me most often in the mail,
from both students and their teachers, after some classroom discussion. The unrivaled favorite is this: "Is Phoenix Jackson's grandson really *dead*?" It refers to a short story I wrote years ago called "A Worn
Path," which tells of a day's journey an old woman makes on foot
from deep in the country into town and into a doctor's office on behalf
of her little grandson; he is at home, periodically ill, and periodically
she comes for his medicine; they give it to her as usual, she receives it
and starts the journey back.

I had not meant to mystify readers by withholding any fact; it is   2
not a writer's business to tease. The story is told through Phoenix's
mind as she undertakes her errand. As the author at one with the character as I tell it, I must assume that the boy is alive. As the reader, you
are free to think as you like, of course: the story invites you to believe
that no matter what happens, Phoenix for as long as she is able to
walk and can hold to her purpose will make her journey. The *possibility* that she would keep on even if he were dead is there in her devo-
tion and its single-minded, single-track errand. Certainly the *artistic*
truth, which should be good enough for the fact, lies in Phoenix's own
answer to that question. When the nurse asks, "He isn't dead, is he?"
she speaks for herself: "He still the same. He going to last."

From the *New York Times Book Review*, March 5, 1978. Copyright © 1978 by
The New York Times Company. Reprinted by permission.

3   The grandchild is the incentive. But it is the journey, the going of the errand, that is the story, and the question is not whether the grandchild is in reality alive or dead. It doesn't affect the outcome of the story or its meaning from start to finish. But it is not the question itself that has struck me as much as the idea, almost without exception implied in the asking, that for Phoenix's grandson to be dead would somehow make the story "better."

4   It's *all right*, I want to say to the students who write to me, for things to be what they appear to be, and for words to mean what they say. It's all right, too, for words and appearances to mean more than one thing—ambiguity is a fact of life. A fiction writer's responsibility covers not only what he presents as the facts of a given story but what he chooses to stir up as their implications; in the end, these implications, too, become facts, in the larger, fictional sense. But it is not all right, not in good faith, for things not to mean what they say.

5   The grandson's plight was real and it made the truth of the story, which is the story of an errand of love carried out. If the child no longer lived, the truth would persist in the "wornness" of the path. But his being dead can't increase the truth of the story, can't affect it one way or the other. I think I signal this, because the end of the story has been reached before old Phoenix gets home again: she simply starts back. To the question "Is the grandson really dead?" I could reply that it doesn't make any difference. I could also say that I did not make him up in order to let him play a trick on Phoenix. But my best answer would be: "Phoenix is alive."

6   The origin of a story is sometimes a trustworthy clue to the author—or can provide him with the clue—to its key image; maybe in this case it will do the same for the reader. One day I saw a solitary old woman like Phoenix. She was walking; I saw her, at middle distance, in a winter country landscape, and watched her slowly make her way across my line of vision. That sight of her made me write the story. I invented an errand for her, but that only seemed a living part of the figure she was herself; what errand other than for someone else could be making her go? And her going was the first thing, her persisting in her landscape was the real thing, and the first and real were what I wanted and worked to keep. I brought her up close enough, by imagination, to describe her face, make her present to the eyes, but the full-length figure moving across the winter fields was the indelible one and the image to keep, and the perspective extending into the vanishing distance the true one to hold in mind.

7   I invented for my character as I wrote, some passing adventures—some dreams and harassments and a small triumph or two, some jolts to her pride, some flights of fancy to console her, one or two encounters to scare her, a moment that gave her cause to feel

ashamed, a moment to dance and preen—for it had to be a journey, and all these things belonged to that, parts of life's uncertainty.

A narrative line is in its deeper sense, of course, the tracing out of 8 a meaning, and the real continuity of a story lies in this probing forward. The real dramatic force of a story depends on the strength of the emotion that has set it going. The emotional value is the measure of the reach of the story. What gives any such content to "A Worn Path" is not its circumstances but its subject: the deep-grained habit of love.

What I hoped would come clear was that in the whole surround 9 of this story, the world it threads through, the only certain thing at all is the worn path. The habit of love cuts through confusion and stumbles or contrives its way out of difficulty, it remembers the way even when it forgets, for a dumbfounded moment, its reason for being. The path is the thing that matters.

Her victory—old Phoenix's—is when she sees the diploma in the 10 doctor's office, when she finds "nailed up on the wall the document that had been stamped with the gold seal and framed in the gold frame, which matched the dream that was hung up in her head." The return with the medicine is just a matter of retracing her own footsteps. It is the part of the journey, and of the story, that can now go without saying.

In the matter of function, old Phoenix's way might even do as a 11 sort of parallel to your way of work if you are a writer of stories. The way to get there is the all-important, all-absorbing problem, and this problem is your reason for undertaking this story. Your only guide, too, is your sureness about your subject, about what this subject is. Like Phoenix, you work all your life to find your way, through all the obstructions and the false appearances and the upsets you may have brought on yourself, to reach a meaning—using inventions of your imagination, perhaps helped out by your dreams and bits of good luck. And finally, too, like Phoenix, you have to assume that what you are working in aid of is life, not death.

But you would make the trip anyway—wouldn't you?—just on 12 hope.

_____ **CONSIDERATIONS** _____

1. Welty says that old Phoenix's return trip is "the part of the journey, and of the story, that can now go without saying." If you were writing this story would you choose a different place to end it? Would you follow Old Phoenix all the way back into the hills? Would you show the grandson? Why?

2. How does Welty feel about writers who intentionally mystify their readers?

3. Does "A Worn Path" illustrate what Welty means when she says, "A narrative line is in its deeper sense . . . the tracing out of a meaning"?

4. In paragraph 4, Welty touches on the "factuality" of a work of fiction. This introduces a fascinating (if maddening) question: what is the difference between fiction and nonfiction?

5. Another Southern writer, William Faulkner, wrote a short novel, *As I Lay Dying,* that can be read as a fuller version of "A Worn Path." It too is based on "an errand of love," as Welty puts it. Read the novel and discuss its parallels with Welty's story.

6. What do you think of Welty's response to the question about her story? Does it help you understand and appreciate the story? Does it avoid the initial question? See paragraph 39 in Richard Wright's "The Library Card," page 624.

E. B. White (1899–1985) was born in Mount Vernon, New York, graduated from Cornell in 1921, and joined the staff of the New Yorker *in 1926. For many years, he wrote the brief essay that led off that magazine's "Talk of the Town" and edited other "Talk" segments. In 1929, White collaborated with James Thurber on a book called* Is Sex Necessary? *and from time to time he published collections of essays and poems, most of them taken from the* New Yorker *and* Harper's. *Some of his best known collections are* One Man's Meat *(1942),* The Second Tree from the Corner *(1953), and* The Points of My Compass *(1962). He is also the author of children's books, most notably* Stuart Little *(1945) and* Charlotte's Web *(1952), and the celebrated book on prose,* The Elements of Style *(with William Strunk, Jr., 1959).*

In 1937, White retired from the New Yorker *and moved to a farm in Maine, where he continued to write those minimal, devastating comments attached to the proofhacks and other errors printed at the ends of the* New Yorker's *columns. There he continued his slow, consistent writing of superb prose. The collected* Letters of E. B. White *(1976),* Essays of E. B. White *(1977), and* Poems and Sketches of E. B. White *(1981) have reconfirmed this country's infatuation with the versatile author. A special citation from the Pulitzer Prize Committee in 1978 celebrated the publication of White's letters.*

94

E. B. WHITE
Once More to the Lake

One summer, along about 1904, my father rented a camp on a lake in Maine and took us all there for the month of August. We all got ringworm from some kittens and had to rub Pond's Extract on our

1

arms and legs night and morning, and my father rolled over in a canoe with all his clothes on; but outside of that the vacation was a success and from then on none of us ever thought there was any place in the world like that lake in Maine. We returned summer after summer—always on August 1st for one month. I have since become a salt-water man, but sometimes in summer there are days when the restlessness of the tides and the fearful cold of the sea water and the incessant wind that blows across the afternoon and into the evening make me wish for the placidity of a lake in the woods. A few weeks ago this feeling got so strong I bought myself a couple of bass hooks and a spinner and returned to the lake where we used to go, for a week's fishing and to revisit old haunts.

2   I took along my son, who had never had any fresh water up his nose and who had seen lily pads only from train windows. On the journey over to the lake I began to wonder what it would be like. I wondered how time would have marred this unique, this holy spot— the coves and streams, the hills that the sun set behind, the camps and the paths behind the camps. I was sure that the tarred road would have found it out and I wondered in what other ways it would be desolated. It is strange how much you can remember about places like that once you allow your mind to return into the grooves that lead back. You remember one thing, and that suddenly reminds you of another thing. I guess I remembered clearest of all the early mornings, when the lake was cool and motionless, remembered how the bedroom smelled of the lumber it was made of and of the wet woods whose scent entered through the screen. The partitions in the camp were thin and did not extend clear to the top of the rooms, and as I was always the first up I would dress softly so as not to wake the others, and sneak out into the sweet outdoors and start out in the canoe, keeping close along the shore in the long shadows of the pines. I remembered being very careful never to rub my paddle against the gunwale for fear of disturbing the stillness of the cathedral.

3   The lake had never been what you would call a wild lake. There were cottages sprinkled around the shores, and it was in farming country although the shores of the lake were quite heavily wooded. Some of the cottages were owned by nearby farmers, and you would live at the shore and eat your meals at the farmhouse. That's what our family did. But although it wasn't wild, it was a fairly large and undisturbed lake and there were places in it which, to a child at least, seemed infinitely remote and primeval.

4   I was right about the tar: it led to within half a mile of the shore. But when I got back there, with my boy, and we settled into a camp near a farmhouse and into the kind of summertime I had known, I could tell that it was going to be pretty much the same as it had been before—I knew it, lying in bed the first morning, smelling the bedroom, and hearing the boy sneak quietly out and go off along the shore

in a boat. I began to sustain the illusion that he was I, and therefore, by simple transposition, that I was my father. This sensation persisted, kept cropping up all the time we were there. It was not an entirely new feeling, but in this setting it grew much stronger. I seemed to be living a dual existence. I would be in the middle of some simple act, I would be picking up a bait box or laying down a table fork, or I would be saying something, and suddenly it would be not I but my father who was saying the words or making the gesture. It gave me a creepy sensation.

We went fishing the first morning. I felt the same damp moss 5 covering the worms in the bait can, and saw the dragonfly alight on the tip of my rod as it hovered a few inches from the surface of the water. It was the arrival of this fly that convinced me beyond any doubt that everything was as it always had been, that the years were a mirage and there had been no years. The small waves were the same, chucking the rowboat under the chin as we fished at anchor, and the boat was the same boat, the same color green and the ribs broken in the same places, and under the floor-boards the same fresh-water leavings and débris—the dead hellgrammite, the wisps of moss, the rusty discarded fishhook, the dried blood from yesterday's catch. We stared silently at the tips of our rods, at the dragonflies that came and went. I lowered the tip of mine into the water, tentatively, pensively dislodging the fly, which darted two feet away, poised, darted two feet back, and came to rest again a little farther up the rod. There had been no years between the ducking of this dragonfly and the other one—the one that was part of memory. I looked at the boy, who was silently watching his fly, and it was my hands that held his rod, my eyes watching. I felt dizzy and didn't know which rod I was at the end of.

We caught two bass, hauling them in briskly as though they were 6 mackerel, pulling them over the side of the boat in a businesslike manner without any landing net, and stunning them with a blow on the back of the head. When we got back for a swim before lunch, the lake was exactly where we had left it, the same number of inches from the dock, and there was only the merest suggestion of a breeze. This seemed an utterly enchanted sea, this lake you could leave to its own devices for a few hours and come back to, and find that it had not stirred, this constant and trustworthy body of water. In the shallows, the dark, water-soaked sticks and twigs, smooth and old, were undulating in clusters on the bottom against the clean ribbed sand, and the track of the mussel was plain. A school of minnows swam by, each minnow with its small individual shadow, doubling the attendance, so clear and sharp in the sunlight. Some of the other campers were in swimming, along the shore, one of them with a cake of soap, and the water felt thin and clear and unsubstantial. Over the years there had been this person with the cake of soap, this cultist, and here he was. There had been no years.

7   Up to the farmhouse to dinner through the teeming, dusty field, the road under our sneakers was only a two-track road. The middle track was missing, the one with the marks of the hooves and splotches of dried, flaky manure. There had always been three tracks to choose from in choosing which track to walk in; now the choice was narrowed down to two. For a moment I missed terribly the middle alternative. But the way led past the tennis court, and something about the way it lay there in the sun reassured me; the tape had loosened along the backline, the alleys were green with plantains and other weeds, and the net (installed in June and removed in September) sagged in the dry noon, and the whole place steamed with midday heat and hunger and emptiness. There was a choice of pie for dessert, and one was blueberry and one was apple, and the waitresses were the same country girls, there having been no passage of time, only the illusion of it as in a dropped curtain—the waitresses were still fifteen; their hair had been washed, that was the only difference—they had been to the movies and seen the pretty girls with the clean hair.

8   Summertime, oh summertime, pattern of life indelible, the fade-proof lake, the woods unshatterable, the pasture with the sweetfern and the juniper forever and ever, summer without end; this was the background, and the life along the shore was the design, the cottages with their innocent and tranquil design, their tiny docks with the flag-pole and the American flag floating against the white clouds in the blue sky, the little paths over the roots of the trees leading from camp to camp and the paths leading back to the outhouses and the can of lime for sprinkling, and at the souvenir counters at the store the miniature birch-bark canoes and the post cards that showed things looking a little better than they looked. This was the American family at play, escaping the city heat, wondering whether the newcomers in the camp at the head of the cove were "common" or "nice," wondering whether it was true that the people who drove up for Sunday dinner at the farmhouse were turned away because there wasn't enough chicken.

9   It seemed to me, as I kept remembering all this, that those times and those summers had been infinitely precious and worth saving. There had been jollity and peace and goodness. The arriving (at the beginning of August) had been so big a business in itself, at the railway station the farm wagon drawn up, the first smell of the pine-laden air, the first glimpse of the smiling farmer, and the great importance of the trunks and your father's enormous authority in such matters, and the feel of the wagon under you for the long ten-mile haul, and at the top of the last long hill catching the first view of the lake after eleven months of not seeing this cherished body of water. The shouts and cries of the other campers when they saw you, and the trunks to be unpacked, to give up their rich burden. (Arriving was less exciting

nowadays, when you sneaked up in your car and parked it under a tree near the camp and took out the bags and in five minutes it was all over, no fuss, no loud wonderful fuss about trunks.)

Peace and goodness and jollity. The only thing that was wrong 10 now, really, was the sound of the place, an unfamiliar nervous sound of the outboard motors. This was the note that jarred, the one thing that would sometimes break the illusion and set the years moving. In those other summertimes all motors were inboard; and when they were at a little distance, the noise they made was a sedative, an ingredient of summer sleep. They were one-cylinder and two-cylinder engines, and some were make-and-break and some were jump-spark, but they all made a sleepy sound across the lake. The one-lungers throbbed and fluttered, and the twin-cylinder ones purred and purred and that was a quiet sound too. But now the campers all had outboards. In the daytime, in the hot mornings, these motors made a petulant, irritable sound; at night, in the still evening when the afterglow lit the water, they whined about one's ears like mosquitoes. My boy loved our rented outboard, and his great desire was to achieve singlehanded mastery over it, and authority, and he soon learned the trick of choking it a little (but not too much), and the adjustment of the needle valve. Watching him I would remember the things you could do with the old one-cylinder engine with the heavy flywheel, how you could have it eating out of your hand if you got really close to it spiritually. Motor boats in those days didn't have clutches, and you would make a landing by shutting off the motor at the proper time and coasting in with a dead rudder. But there was a way of reversing them, if you learned the trick, by cutting the switch and putting it on again exactly on the final dying revolution of the flywheel, so that it would kick back against compression and begin reversing. Approaching a dock in a strong following breeze, it was difficult to slow up sufficiently by the ordinary coasting method, and if a boy felt he had complete mastery over his motor, he was tempted to keep it running beyond its time and then reverse it a few feet from the dock. It took a cool nerve, because if you threw the switch a twentieth of a second too soon you could catch the flywheel when it still had speed enough to go up past center, and the boat would leap ahead, charging bull-fashion at the dock.

We had a good week at the camp. The bass were biting well and 11 the sun shone endlessly, day after day. We would be tired at night and lie down in the accumulated heat of the little bedrooms after the long hot day and the breeze would stir almost imperceptibly outside and the smell of the swamp drift in through the rusty screens. Sleep would come easily and in the morning the red squirrel would be on the roof, tapping out his gay routine. I kept remembering everything, lying in bed in the mornings—the small steamboat that had a long rounded stern like the lip of a Ubangi, and how quietly she ran on the moonlight sails, when the older boys played their mandolins and the girls sang and we ate doughnuts dipped in sugar, and how sweet the music was on the water in the shining light, and what it had felt like to think about girls then. After breakfast we would go up to the store and the things were in the same place—the minnows in a bottle, the plugs and spinners disarranged and pawed over by the youngsters from the boys' camp, the fig newtons and the Beeman's gum. Outside, the road was tarred and cars stood in front of the store. Inside, all was just as it had always been, except there was more Coca-Cola and not so much Moxie and root beer and birch beer and sarsaparilla. We would walk out with a bottle of pop apiece and sometimes the pop would backfire up our noses and hurt. We explored the streams, quietly, where the turtles slid off the sunny logs and dug their way into the soft bottom; and we lay on the town wharf and fed worms to the tame bass. Everywhere we went I had trouble making out which was I, the one walking at my side, the one walking in my pants.

12   One afternoon while we were there at that lake a thunderstorm came up. It was like the revival of an old melodrama that I had seen long ago with childish awe. The second-act climax of the drama of the electrical disturbance over a lake in America had not changed in any important respect. This was the big scene, still the big scene. The whole thing was so familiar, the first feeling of oppression and heat and a general air around camp of not wanting to go very far away. In midafternoon (it was all the same) a curious darkening of the sky, and a lull in everything that had made life tick; and then the way the boats suddenly swung the other way at their moorings with the coming of a breeze out of the new quarter, and the premonitory rumble. Then the kettle drum, then the snare, then the bass drum and cymbals, then crackling light against the dark, and the gods grinning and licking their chops in the hills. Afterward the calm, the rain steadily rustling in the calm lake, the return of light and hope and spirits, and the campers running out in joy and relief to go swimming in the rain, their bright cries perpetuating the deathless joke about how they were getting simply drenched, and the children screaming with delight at the new sensation of bathing in the rain, and the joke about getting drenched linking the generations in a strong indestructible chain. And the comedian who waded in carrying an umbrella.

13   When the others went swimming my son said he was going in too. He pulled his dripping trunks from the line where they had hung all through the shower, and wrung them out. Languidly, and with no thought of going in, I watched him, his hard little body, skinny and bare, saw him wince slightly as he pulled up around his vitals the small, soggy, icy garment. As he buckled the swollen belt suddenly my groin felt the chill of death.

_____ CONSIDERATIONS _____

1. A master of the personal essay, E. B. White transforms an exercise in memory into something universal, timeless, and profound. Study paragraph 4 to see how.

2. White rejuvenates bits and pieces of language that have become worn and lackluster through repetition. Can you find an example of this technique in paragraph 2?

3. White notes many changes at the old summer place, but he is more moved by the sameness. Locate examples of his feeling of sameness and consider how these examples contribute to his themes.

4. The author expresses a predictable dislike of outboard motors on the otherwise quiet lake. Does he avoid stereotype when he writes about motors elsewhere in this essay?

5. What device does White use in his description of the thunderstorm in paragraph 12.

6. How is the last sentence of the essay a surprise? How has White prepared us for it?

Virginia Woolf (1882–1941) is best known as a novelist.
The Voyage Out *appeared in 1915, followed by* Night and
Day *(1919),* Jacob's Room *(1922),* Mrs. Dalloway *(1925),* To
the Lighthouse *(1927),* Orlando *(1928),* The Waves *(1931),*
The Years *(1937), and* Between the Acts, *published shortly
after her death. Daughter of Sir Leslie Stephen, Victorian
critic and essayist who edited the* Dictionary of National
Biography, *she was educated at home and began her
literary career as a critic for the* Times Literary
Supplement. *She wrote essays regularly until her death;
four volumes of her* Collected Essays *appeared in the
United States in 1967. More recently, her publishers have
issued six volumes of her collected letters, and her diary is
being published.*

*With her sister Vanessa, a painter, her husband Leonard
Woolf, an editor and writer, and Vanessa's husband Clive
Bell, an art critic, Woolf lived at the center of the
Bloomsbury group—artists and intellectuals who gathered
informally to talk and to amuse each other, and whose
unconventional ideas and habits, when they were known,
shocked the stolid British public. John Maynard Keynes,
the economist, was a member of the varied group, which
also included the biographer Lytton Strachey, the novelist
E. M. Forster, and eventually the expatriate American poet
T. S. Eliot. With her husband, Virginia Woolf founded The
Hogarth Press, a small firm dedicated to publishing
superior works. Among its authors were Eliot and Woolf
herself.*

Virginia Woolf, *a biography by her nephew, Quentin
Bell, gives an intimate picture of the whole group. Of all
the Bloomsbury people, Woolf was perhaps the most
talented. Through most of her life, she struggled against
recurring mental illness, which brought intense depression
and suicidal impulses. When she was fifty-nine she
drowned herself in the River Ouse. The following famous
passage from* A Room of One's Own *(1929) presents a
feminist argument by means of a memorable supposition.*

95

VIRGINIA WOOLF
If Shakespeare Had Had a Sister

It is a perennial puzzle why no woman wrote a word of that ex- 1
traordinary (Elizabethan) literature when every other man, it seemed
was capable of song or sonnet. What were the conditions in which
women lived, I asked myself; for fiction, imaginative work that is, is
not dropped like a pebble upon the ground, as science may be; fiction
is like a spider's web, attached ever so lightly perhaps, but still attached to life at all four corners. Often the attachment is scarcely perceptible; Shakespeare's plays, for instance, seem to hang there complete by themselves. But when the web is pulled askew, hooked up at
the edge, torn in the middle, one remembers that these webs are not
spun in midair by incorporeal creatures, but are the work of suffering
human beings, and are attached to grossly material things, like health
and money and the house we live in. . . .

But what I find . . . is that nothing is known about women before 2
the eighteenth century. I have no model in my mind to turn about this
way and that. Here am I asking why women did not write poetry in
the Elizabethan age, and I am not sure how they were educated;
whether they were taught to write; whether they had sitting-rooms to
themselves; how many women had children before they were twenty-
one; what, in short, they did from eight in the morning till eight at
night. They had no money, evidently; according to Professor
Trevelyan they were married whether they liked it or not before they
were out of the nursery, at fifteen or sixteen very likely. It would have
been extremely odd, even upon this showing, had one of them suddenly written the plays of Shakespeare, I concluded, and I thought of
that old gentleman, who is dead now, but was a bishop, I think, who
declared that it was impossible for any woman, past, present, or to
come, to have the genius of Shakespeare. He wrote to the papers about
it. He also told a lady who applied to him for information that cats do

not as a matter of fact go to heaven, though they have, he added, souls of a sort. How much thinking those old gentlemen used to save one! How the borders of ignorance shrank back at their approach! Cats do not go to heaven. Women cannot write the plays of Shakespeare.

3   Be that as it may, I could not help thinking, as I looked at the works of Shakespeare on the shelf, that the bishop was right at least in this; it would have been impossible, completely and entirely, for any woman to have written the plays of Shakespeare in the age of Shakespeare. Let me imagine, since facts are so hard to come by, what would have happened had Shakespeare had a wonderfully gifted sister, called Judith, let us say. Shakespeare himself went, very probably—his mother was an heiress—to the grammar school, where he may have learned Latin—Ovid, Virgil and Horace—and the elements of grammar and logic. He was, it is well known, a wild boy who poached rabbits, perhaps shot a deer, and had, rather sooner than he should have done, to marry a woman in the neighbourhood, who bore him a child rather quicker than was right. That escapade sent him to seek his fortune in London. He had, it seemed, a taste for the theater; he began by holding horses at the stage door. Very soon he got work in the theatre, became a successful actor, and lived at the hub of the universe, meeting everybody, knowing everybody, practising his art on the boards, exercising his wits in the streets, and even getting access to the palace of the queen. Meanwhile his extraordinarily gifted sister, let us suppose, remained at home. She was as adventurous, as imaginative, as agog to see the world as he was. But she was not sent to school. She had no chance of learning grammar and logic, let alone of reading Horace and Virgil. She picked up a book now and then, one of her brother's perhaps, and read a few pages. But then her parents came in and told her to mend the stockings or mind the stew and not moon about with books and papers. They would have spoken sharply but kindly, for they were substantial people who knew the conditions of life for a woman and loved their daughter—indeed, more likely than not she was the apple of her father's eye. Perhaps she scribbled some pages up in an apple loft on the sly, but was careful to hide them or set fire to them. Soon, however, before she was out of her teens, she was to be betrothed to the son of a neighbouring wool-stapler. She cried out that marriage was hateful to her, and for that she was severely beaten by her father. Then he ceased to scold her. He begged her instead not to hurt him, not to shame him in this matter of her marriage. He would give her a chain of beads or a fine petticoat, he said; and there were tears in his eyes. How could she disobey him? How could she break his heart? The force of her own gift alone drove her to it. She made up a small parcel of her belongings, let herself down by a rope one summer's night and took the road to London. She was not seventeen. The birds that sang in the hedge were not more musical than she was. She

had the quickest fancy, a gift like her brother's, for the tune of words. Like him, she had a taste for the theatre. She stood at the stage door; she wanted to act, she said. Men laughed in her face. The manager—a fat, loose-lipped man—guffawed. He bellowed something about poodles dancing and women acting—no woman, he said, could possibly be an actress. He hinted—you can imagine what. She could get no training in her craft. Could she even seek her dinner in a tavern or roam the streets at midnight? Yet her genius was for fiction and lusted to feed abundantly upon the lives of men and women and the study of their ways. At last—for she was very young, oddly like Shakespeare the poet in her face, with the same grey eyes and rounded brows—at last Nick Greene the actor-manager took pity on her; she found herself with child by that gentleman and so—who shall measure the heat and violence of the poet's heart when caught and tangled in a woman's body?—killed herself one winter's night and lies buried at some crossroads where the omnibuses now stop outside the Elephant and Castle.

That, more or less, is how the story would run, I think, if a woman in Shakespeare's day had had Shakespeare's genius. But for my part, I agree with the deceased bishop, if such he was—it is unthinkable that any woman in Shakespeare's day should have had Shakespeare's genius. For genius like Shakespeare's is not born among labouring, uneducated, servile people. It was not born in England among the Saxons and the Britons. It is not born today among the working classes. How, then, could it have been born among women whose work began, according to Professor Trevelyan, almost before they were out of the nursery, who were forced to it by their parents and held to it by all the power of law and custom? 4

_____ CONSIDERATIONS _____

1. In paragraph 3, Woolf develops at length an imaginary sister of Shakespeare. Why does the writer call that sister Judith rather than Priscilla or Elizabeth or Megan? A quick look at Shakespeare's biography will give you the answer and alert you to a mischievous side of Woolf.

2. At the end of paragraph 2, Woolf says, "How the borders of ignorance shrank back at their approach!" Is this a straight statement, or does she mean something other than what the words say? Study the differences among the following terms, which often are used mistakenly as synonyms: sarcasm, satire, irony, wit, humor, cynicism, invective, the sardonic.

3. Woolf's essay consists of four paragraphs, one of which accounts for more than half of the composition. Can you find a justification for this disproportionately long paragraph?

4. Concoct an imaginary biography, with a purpose, like Woolf's account of Judith: for example, Mozart's daughter, Napoleon's father, the brother of Jesus Christ, the Queen of Luxembourg, Tolstoy's nephew or niece.

5. "... for fiction ... is not dropped like a pebble upon the ground, as science may be ... " (paragraph 1). In what sense is science dropped like a pebble upon the ground? What is the point of this odd comparison?

6. If you were to invite three authors from this book to an informal discussion of Woolf's essay, whom would you select? Why? Make your selections on the basis of some relationship between their ideas and hers. What sort of outcome would you expect from such a conversation? Write a page of this dialogue.

7. Woolf wrote in the informal idiom of an educated Englishwoman of the 1920s; there are a number of differences between her language and ours. Circle a half dozen such differences and contrast British English with American English.

Alexander Woollcott (1887–1943) was a drama critic, centered in New York, whose work is gossipy, waspish, and fanciful. A member of the Algonquin Round Table—a literary circle that included Dorothy Parker, Harpo Marx, and Robert Benchley—he was more famous for his personality than for his published work. (If he had lived, we would have known him on television talk shows.) Moss Hart and George Kaufman's play The Man Who Came to Dinner *is based on the character of Alexander Woollcott.*

96

ALEXANDER WOOLLCOTT
Obituary

A SHORT *history of the magician's daughter who was the managing mother of the Four Marx Brothers.*

October 1929

Last week the Marx Brothers buried their mother. On the preceding Friday night, more from gregariousness than from appetite, she had eaten two dinners instead of the conventional one, and, after finishing off with a brief, hilarious game of ping-pong, was homeward bound across the Queensboro Bridge when paralysis seized her. Within an hour she was dead in her Harpo's arms. Of the people I have met, I would name her as among the few of whom it could be said that they had greatness. 1

Minnie Marx was in this world sixty-five years and *lived* all sixty-five of them. None knew better than her sons that she had not only borne them, brought them up, and (with a bit of coaxing here and a *schlag* there) turned them into successful play-actors. She had done much more than that. She had *invented* them. They were just comics she imagined for her own amusement. They amused no one more, and their reward was her ravishing smile. 2

3　　　It was her idea that they should go into the theater at all. She herself was doing sweat-shop lace-work when she married a tailor named Sam Marx. But for fifty years her father was a roving magician in Hanover, and as a child she had known the excitement of their barnstorming cart-rides from one German town to another. Now here she was, sidetracked in a Third Avenue tenement, with a swarm of children on her hands. But hadn't her brother deserted his career as a pants-presser to go into vaudeville? You remember the song about Mr. Gallagher and Mr. Shean? Well, that was her brother—Mr. Shean. His first success only strengthened her conviction that she came of show-folks, and she was determined that her sons should enter into that inheritance. She had six, in all. One died as a baby. After the war, she lost another to the silk-dress business. This defection from her now notable quartet did not baffle her long. Reaching for Zeppo, her youngest, she yanked him out of high school and flung him into the breach.

4　　　At first she had an undisputed monopoly of the idea that her boys would do well in the theater. Even they did not share it with her. To be sure, Chico, her eldest, was a piano player. Fortunately for her peace of mind, she didn't know where. But she knew he was a piano player, for she herself had amassed the weekly quarter which paid for his lessons. Then her Julius—that's Groucho—had a promising soprano voice. After cleaning up the breakfast things, she used to tether the youngest to the kitchen table and sit all day in agents' offices, until finally she got her Julius a job. Then, when she had incredibly launched her vaudeville act—it consisted of a son or so, pieced out with a pretty girl and a tenor—she couldn't bear the thought of setting forth on tour while her Harpo stayed behind, a bellhop at the Seville, with no one to see that he ate properly. It was a woman of magnificent decision who therefore called a cab, drove to the Seville, snatched Harpo from his employment and, en route to Henderson's at Coney Island, transformed him with a white duck suit, so that, just as the curtain was rising, she could catapult him into the act. Really, one cannot say that the Marxes ever *went* on the stage. They were pushed on.

5　　　The uphill stretch was a long one, humble, worrisome, yet somehow rollicking. The Third Avenue flat, with the rent money never once on time in ten years, gave way to a Chicago house, with an equally oppressive mortgage. And when in their trouping through that territory they would grow so harumscarum that there was real danger of a fine by the management, she would have to subdue them by a magic word whispered piercingly from the wings. The word was "Greenbaum." You see, Mr. Greenbaum held the mortgage aforesaid.

6　　　It was eighteen years after her first homespun efforts as an impresario that her great night came. That was when, for the first time, the words "Marx Brothers" were written in lamps over the door of a Broadway theater. For the première of *I'll Say She Is*, she felt entitled to a new gown, with which she proposed to sweep to her seat in the proscenium box. But while she was standing on a chair to have it fitted, the incompetent chair gave way, and she broke her ankle. So she couldn't exactly sweep to her seat on the first night. They had to carry her. But she got there.

Her trouble was that her boys had got there too. They had arrived. Thereafter, I think she took less interest in their professional lives. When someone paid them a king's ransom to make their first talkie, she only yawned. What she sighed for was the best of beginnings. Why, I hear that last year she was caught hauling her embarrassed chauffeur off to a dancing-school, with the idea of putting *him* on the stage. In her boredom she took to poker, her game being marked by so incurable a weakness for inside straights that, as often as not, her rings were missing and her bureau drawer littered with sheepish pawntickets. On the night *Animal Crackers* opened she was so absorbed that she almost forgot to go at all. But at the last moment she sent her husband for her best wig, dispatched her chauffeur to fetch her new teeth, and, assembling herself on the way downtown, reached the theater in time to greet the audience. Pretty as a picture she was, as she met us in the aisle. "We have a big success," she said.

Minnie Marx was a wise, tolerant, generous, gallant matriarch. In the passing of such a one, a woman full of years, with her work done, and children and grandchildren to hug her memory all their days, you have no more of a sense of death than you have when the Hudson—sunlit, steady, all-conquering—leaves you behind on the shore on its way to the fathomless sea.

She died during rehearsals, in the one week of the year when all her boys would be around her—back from their summer roamings, that is, but not yet gone forth on tour. Had she foreseen this—I'm not sure she didn't—she would have chuckled, and, combining a sly wink with her beautiful smile, she would have said, "How's that for perfect timing?"

_____ **CONSIDERATIONS** _____

1. Woollcott says that Minnie Marx brought up her sons "with a bit of coaxing here and a *schlag* there." What, precisely, is a schlag, and why is it appropriate in this context?

2. What theater experience had Minnie Marx before deciding on an acting career for her sons?

3. Why does Woollcott deny (with italics) that the Marxes ever *went* on the stage?

4. In what sense is the second sentence of paragraph 8 a surprise?

5. American history quiz question: Aside from the death of Minnie Marx, what happened in October of 1929?

Richard Wright (1908–1960) was born on a plantation in Natchez, Mississippi. A restless and unruly child, he left home at fifteen and supported himself doing unskilled work, gradually improving his employment until he became a clerk in a post office. In this essay from his autobiography Black Boy *(1944) he writes about an occasion that transformed his life. By chance he became obsessed with the notion of reading H. L. Mencken, the iconoclastic editor and essayist. He schemed and plotted to borrow Mencken's books from the library, and when he succeeded, his career as a writer began.*

Determined to be a successful writer, Richard Wright worked on the Federal Writers' Project, wrote for the New Masses, *and finally won a prize from Story magazine for a short novel called* Uncle Tom's Children. *The following year, he was awarded a Guggenheim Fellowship, and in 1940 he published his novel* Native Son, *which has become an American classic. In 1946 he emigrated to Paris, where he lived until his death. His later novels include* The Outsider *(1953) and* The Long Dream *(1958). In 1991 the Library of America issued Richard Wright's* Works *in two volumes.*

97

RICHARD WRIGHT

The Library Card

1   One morning I arrived early at work and went into the bank lobby where the Negro porter was mopping. I stood at a counter and picked up the Memphis *Commercial Appeal* and began my free reading of the press. I came finally to the editorial page and saw an article dealing with one H. L. Mencken. I knew by hearsay that he was the editor of the *American Mercury*, but aside from that I knew nothing

about him. The article was a furious denunciation of Mencken, concluding with one, hot, short sentence: Mencken is a fool.

I wondered what on earth this Mencken had done to call down 2
upon him the scorn of the South. The only people I had ever heard denounced in the South were Negroes, and this man was not a Negro. Then what ideas did Mencken hold that made a newspaper like the *Commercial Appeal* castigate him publicly? Undoubtedly he must be advocating ideas that the South did not like. Were there, then, people other than Negroes who criticized the South? I knew that during the Civil War the South had hated northern whites, but I had not encountered such hate during my life. Knowing no more of Mencken than I did at that moment, I felt a vague sympathy for him. Had not the South, which had assigned me the role of a non-man, cast at him its hardest words?

Now, how could I find out about this Mencken? There was a 3
huge library near the riverfront, but I knew that Negroes were not allowed to patronize its shelves any more than they were the parks and playgrounds of the city. I had gone into the library several times to get books for the white men on the job. Which of them would now help me to get books? And how could I read them without causing concern to the white men with whom I worked? I had so far been successful in hiding my thoughts and feelings from them, but I knew that I would create hostility if I went about the business of reading in a clumsy way.

I weighed the personalities of the men on the job. There was 4
Don, a Jew; but I distrusted him. His position was not much better than mine and I knew that he was uneasy and insecure; he had always treated me in an offhand, bantering way that barely concealed his contempt. I was afraid to ask him to help me get books; his frantic desire to demonstrate a racial solidarity with the whites against Negroes might make him betray me.

Then how about the boss? No, he was a Baptist and I had the sus- 5
picion that he would not be quite able to comprehend why a black boy would want to read Mencken. There were other white men on the job whose attitudes showed clearly that they were Kluxers or sympathizers, and they were out of the question.

There remained only one man whose attitude did not fit into an 6
anti-Negro category, for I had heard the white men refer to him as a "Pope lover." He was an Irish Catholic and was hated by the white Southerners. I knew that he read books, because I had got him volumes from the library several times. Since he, too, was an object of hatred, I felt that he might refuse me but would hardly betray me. I hesitated, weighing and balancing the imponderable realities.

One morning I paused before the Catholic fellow's desk. 7

"I want to ask you a favor," I whispered to him. 8

9   "What is it?"

10   "I want to read. I can't get books from the library. I wonder if you'd let me use your card?"

11   He looked at me suspiciously.

12   "My card is full most of the time," he said.

13   "I see," I said and waited, posing my question silently.

14   "You're not trying to get me into trouble, are you, boy?" he asked, staring at me.

15   "Oh, no, sir."

16   "What book do you want?"

17   "A book by H. L. Mencken."

18   "Which one?"

19   "I don't know. Has he written more than one?"

20   "He has written several."

21   "I didn't know that."

22   "What makes you want to read Mencken?"

23   "Oh, I just saw his name in the newspaper," I said.

24   "It's good of you to want to read," he said. "But you ought to read the right things."

25   I said nothing. Would he want to supervise my reading?

26   "Let me think," he said. "I'll figure out something."

27   I turned from him and he called me back. He stared at me quizzically.

28   "Richard, don't mention this to the other white men," he said.

29   "I understand," I said. "I won't say a word."

30   A few days later he called me to him.

31   "I've got a card in my wife's name," he said. "Here's mine."

32   "Thank you, sir."

33   "Do you think you can manage it?"

34   "I'll manage fine," I said.

35   "If they suspect you, you'll get in trouble," he said.

36   "I'll write the same kind of notes to the library that you wrote when you sent me for books," I told him. "I'll sign your name."

37   He laughed.

38   "Go ahead. Let me see what you get," he said.

39   That afternoon I addressed myself to forging a note. Now, what were the names of books written by H. L. Mencken? I did not know any of them. I finally wrote what I thought would be a foolproof note: *Dear Madam: Will you please let this nigger boy*—I used the word "nigger" to make the librarian feel that I could not possibly be the author of the note—*have some books by H. L. Mencken?* I forged the white man's name.

40   I entered the library as I had always done when on errands for whites, but I felt that I would somehow slip up and betray myself. I doffed my hat, stood a respectful distance from the desk, looked as unbookish as possible, and waited for the white patrons to be taken care

of. When the desk was clear of people, I still waited. The white librarian looked at me.

"What do you want, boy?"   41

As though I did not possess the power of speech, I stepped for- 42
ward and simply handed her the forged note, not parting my lips.

"What books by Mencken does he want?" she asked.   43

"I don't know, ma'am," I said, avoiding her eyes.   44

"Who gave you this card?"   45

"Mr. Falk," I said.   46

"Where is he?"   47

"He's at work, at the M—— Optical Company," I said. "I've been 48
in here for him before."

"I remember," the woman said. "But he never wrote notes like 49
this."

Oh, God, she's suspicious. Perhaps she would not let me have 50
the books? If she had turned her back at that moment, I would have
ducked out the door and never gone back. Then I thought of a bold
idea.

"You can call him up, ma'am," I said, my heart pounding.   51

"You're not using these books, are you?" she asked pointedly.   52

"Oh, no, ma'am. I can't read."   53

"I don't know what he wants by Mencken," she said under her 54
breath.

I knew now that I had won; she was thinking of other things and 55
the race question had gone out of her mind. She went to the shelves.
Once or twice she looked over her shoulder at me, as though she was
still doubtful. Finally she came forward with two books in her hand.

"I'm sending him two books," she said. "But tell Mr. Falk to 56
come in next time, or send me the names of the books he wants. I
don't know what he wants to read."

I said nothing. She stamped the card and handed me the books. 57
Not daring to glance at them, I went out of the library, fearing that the
woman would call me back for further questioning. A block away
from the library I opened one of the books and read a title: *A Book of
Prefaces.* I was nearing my nineteenth birthday and I did not know
how to pronounce the word "preface." I thumbed the pages and saw
strange words and strange names. I shook my head, disappointed. I
looked at the other book; it was called *Prejudices.* I knew what that
word meant; I had heard it all my life. And right off I was on guard
against Mencken's books. Why would a man want to call a book Prejudices? The word was so stained with all my memories of racial hate
that I could not conceive of anybody using it for a title. Perhaps I had
made a mistake about Mencken? A man who had prejudices must be
wrong.

When I showed the books to Mr. Falk, he looked at me and 58
frowned.

59   "That librarian might telephone you," I warned him.

60   "That's all right," he said. "But when you're through reading those books, I want you to tell me what you get out of them."

61   That night in my rented room, while letting the hot water run over my can of pork and beans in the sink, I opened *A Book of Prefaces* and began to read. I was jarred and shocked by the style, the clear, clean sweeping sentences. Why did he write like that? And how did one write like that? I pictured the man as a raging demon, slashing with his pen, consumed with hate, denouncing everything American, extolling everything European or German, laughing at the weaknesses of people, mocking God, authority. What was this? I stood up, trying to realize what reality lay behind the meaning of the words. . . . Yes, this man was fighting, fighting with words. He was using words as a weapon, using them as one would use a club. Could words be weapons? Well, yes, for here they were. Then, maybe, perhaps, I could use them as a weapon? No. It frightened me. I read on and what amazed me was not what he said, but how on earth anybody had the courage to say it.

62   Occasionally I glanced up to reassure myself that I was alone in the room. Who were these men about whom Mencken was talking so passionately? Who was Anatole France? Joseph Conrad? Sinclair Lewis, Sherwood Anderson, Dostoevski, George Moore, Gustave Flaubert, Maupassant, Tolstoy, Frank Harris, Mark Twain, Thomas Hardy, Arnold Bennett, Stephen Crane, Zola, Norris, Gorky, Bergson, Ibsen, Balzac, Bernard Shaw, Dumas, Poe, Thomas Mann, O. Henry, Dreiser, H. G. Wells, Gogol, T. S. Eliot, Gide, Baudelaire, Edgar Lee Masters, Stendhal, Turgenev, Huneker, Nietzsche, and scores of others? Were these men real? Did they exist or had they existed? And how did one pronounce their names?

63   I ran across many words whose meanings I did not know, and I either looked them up in a dictionary or, before I had a chance to do that, encountered the word in a context that made its meaning clear. But what strange world was this? I concluded the book with the conviction that I had somehow overlooked something terribly important in life. I had once tried to write, had once reveled in feeling, had let my crude imagination roam, but the impulse to dream had been slowly beaten out of me by experience. Now it surged up again and I hungered for books, new ways of looking and seeing. It was not a matter of believing or disbelieving what I read, but of feeling something new, of being affected by something that made the look of the world different.

64   As dawn broke I ate my pork and beans, feeling dopey, sleepy. I went to work, but the mood of the book would not die; it lingered, coloring everything I saw, heard, did. I now felt that I knew what the white men were feeling. Merely because I had read a book that had spoken of how they lived and thought, I identified myself with that

book. I felt vaguely guilty. Would I, filled with bookish notions, act in a manner that would make the whites dislike me?

I forged more notes and my trips to the library became frequent. 65 Reading grew into a passion. My first serious novel was Sinclair Lewis's *Main Street*. It made me see my boss, Mr. Gerald, and identify him as an American type. I would smile when I saw him lugging his golf bags into the office. I had always felt a vast distance separating me from the boss, and now I felt closer to him, though still distant. I felt now that I knew him, that I could feel the very limits of his narrow life. And this had happened because I had read a novel about a mythical man called George F. Babbitt.

The plots and stories in the novels did not interest me so much 66 as the point of view revealed. I gave myself over to each novel without reserve, without trying to criticize it; it was enough for me to see and feel something different. And for me, everything was something different. Reading was like a drug, a dope. The novels created moods in which I lived for days. But I could not conquer my sense of guilt, my feeling that the white men around me knew that I was changing, that I had begun to regard them differently.

Whenever I brought a book to the job, I wrapped it in newspa- 67 per—a habit that was to persist for years in other cities and under other circumstances. But some of the white men pried into my packages when I was absent and they questioned me.

"Boy, what are you reading those books for?"   68

"Oh, I don't know, sir."   69

"That's deep stuff you're reading, boy."   70

"I'm just killing time, sir."   71

"You'll addle your brains if you don't watch out."   72

I read Dreiser's *Jennie Gerhardt* and *Sister Carrie* and they re- 73 vived in me a vivid sense of my mother's suffering; I was overwhelmed. I grew silent, wondering about the life around me. It would have been impossible for me to have told anyone what I derived from these novels, for it was nothing less than a sense of life itself. All my life had shaped me for the realism, the naturalism of the modern novel, and I could not read enough of them.

Steeped in new moods and ideas, I bought a ream of paper and 74 tried to write; but nothing would come, or what did come was flat beyond telling. I discovered that more than desire and feeling were necessary to write and I dropped the idea. Yet I still wondered how it was possible to know people sufficiently to write about them? Could I ever learn about life and people? To me, with my vast ignorance, my Jim Crow station in life, it seemed a task impossible of achievement. I now knew what being a Negro meant. I could endure the hunger. I had learned to live with hate. But to feel that there were feelings denied me, that the very breadth of life itself was beyond my reach, that more than anything else hurt, wounded me. I had a new hunger.

75   In buoying me up, reading also cast me down, made me see what was possible, what I had missed. My tension returned, new, terrible, bitter, surging, almost too great to be contained. I no longer *felt* that the world about me was hostile, killing; I *knew* it. A million times I asked myself what I could do to save myself, and there were no answers. I seemed forever condemned, ringed by walls.

76   I did not discuss my reading with Mr. Falk, who had lent me his library card; it would have meant talking about myself and that would have been too painful. I smiled each day, fighting desperately to maintain my old behavior, to keep my disposition seemingly sunny. But some of the white men discerned that I had begun to brood.

77   "Wake up there, boy!" Mr. Olin said one day.

78   "Sir!" I answered for the lack of a better word.

79   "You act like you've stolen something," he said.

80   I laughed in the way I knew he expected me to laugh, but I resolved to be more conscious of myself, to watch my every act, to guard and hide the new knowledge that was dawning within me.

81   If I went north, would it be possible for me to build a new life then? But how could a man build a life upon vague, unformed yearnings? I wanted to write and I did not even know the English language. I bought English grammars and found them dull. I felt that I was getting a better sense of the language from novels than from grammars. I read hard, discarding a writer as soon as I felt that I had grasped his point of view. At night the printed page stood before my eyes in sleep.

82   Mrs. Moss, my landlady, asked me one Sunday morning:

83   "Son, what is this you keep on reading?"

84   "Oh, nothing. Just novels."

85   "What you get out of 'em?"

86   "I'm just killing time," I said.

87   "I hope you know your own mind," she said in a tone which implied that she doubted if I had a mind.

88   I knew of no Negroes who read the books I liked and I wondered if any Negroes ever thought of them. I knew that there were Negro doctors, lawyers, newspapermen, but I never saw any of them. When I read a Negro newspaper I never caught the faintest echo of my preoccupation in its pages. I felt trapped and occasionally, for a few days, I would stop reading. But a vague hunger would come over me for books, books that opened up new avenues of feeling and seeing, and again I would forge another note to the white librarian. Again I would read an wonder as only the naïve and unlettered can read and wonder, feeling that I carried a secret, criminal burden about with me each day.

89   That winter my mother and brother came and we set up housekeeping, buying furniture on the installment plan, being cheated and yet knowing no way to avoid it. I began to eat warm food and to my surprise found that regular meals enabled me to read faster. I may have lived through many illnesses and survived them, never suspecting

that I was ill. My brother obtained a job and we began to save toward the trip north, plotting our time, setting tentative dates for departure. I told none of the white men on the job that I was planning to go north; I knew that the moment they felt I was thinking of the North they would change toward me. It would have made them feel that I did not like the life I was living, and because my life was completely conditioned by what they said or did, it would have been tantamount to challenging them.

I could calculate my chances for life in the South as a Negro   90 fairly clearly now.

I could fight the Southern whites by organizing with other Ne-   91 groes, as my grandfather had done. But I knew that I could never win that way; there were many whites and there were but few blacks. They were strong and we were weak. Outright black rebellion could never win. If I fought openly I would die and I did not want to die. News of lynchings were frequent.

I could submit and live the life of a genial slave, but that was im-   92 possible. All my life had shaped me to live by my own feelings, and thoughts. I could make up to Bess and marry her and inherit the house. But that, too, would be the life of a slave; if I did that, I would crush to death something within me, and I would hate myself as much as I knew the whites already hated those who had submitted. Neither could I ever willingly present myself to be kicked, as Shorty had done. I would rather have died than do that.

I could drain off my restlessness by fighting with Shorty and Har-   93 rison. I had seen many Negroes solve the problem of being black by transferring their hatred of themselves to others with a black skin and fighting them. I would have to be cold to do that, and I was not cold and I could never be.

I could, of course, forget what I had read, thrust the whites out of   94 my mind, forget them; and find release from anxiety and longing in sex and alcohol. But the memory of how my father had conducted himself made that course repugnant. If I did not want others to violate my life, how could I voluntarily violate it myself?

I had no hope whatever of being a professional man. Not only had   95 I been so conditioned that I did not desire it, but the fulfillment of such an ambition was beyond my capabilities. Well-to-do Negroes lived in a world that was almost as alien to me as the world inhabited by whites.

What, then, was there? I held my life in my mind, in my con-   96 sciousness each day, feeling at times that I would stumble and drop it, spill it forever. My reading had created a vast sense of distance between me and the world in which I lived and tried to make a living, and that sense of distance was increasing each day. My days and nights were one long, quiet, continuously contained dream of terror, tension, and anxiety. I wondered how long I could bear it.

_____ CONSIDERATIONS _____

1. How do you heat a can of beans if you don't have a hot plate or a stove? How is Wright's answer to this question an autobiographical fact that might affect your appreciation of his essay?

2. In paragraph 65, Wright says of himself, "Reading grew into a passion." You don't have to look too far in the lives of other writers to find similar statements about reading. Reread the first paragraph of the preface to this book, and think about the importance of reading to your prospects of improving as a writer. See also Ralph Ellison's "On Becoming a Writer."

3. Compare what Wright had to endure to use the public library with your own introduction to the same institution. How do you account for the motivation Wright needed to break the barriers between him and freedom to read?

4. The word Wright uses throughout to refer to his own race is no longer widely accepted? Why? What other words have been used at other times in American history? What difference does a name make?

5. Notice how Wright uses dialogue in this essay. How do you decide when to use dialogue? What are its purposes?

6. The authors mentioned by Wright in his essay would make a formidable reading program for anyone. If you were to lay out such a program for yourself, what titles would you include? Why?

A Rhetorical Index

The various writing patterns—argument and persuasion, description, exposition, and narration—are amply illustrated in the many essays, stories, journal entries, and poems in *A Writer's Reader*. If any classification of writing according to type is suspect—because good writers inevitably merge the types—this index offers one plausible arrangement. Anyone looking for models or examples for study and imitation may well begin here.

A word about subcategories: We index two sorts of argument—formal and implicit—because some selections are obvious attempts to defend a stated proposition, often in high style, whereas others argue indirectly, informally, or diffusely, but persuasively nonetheless. Under "Description" we index selections that primarily describe persons, places, or miscellaneous phenomena. Under "Exposition" are those selections that clearly show the various rhetorical patterns of development: cause and effect; classification; comparison, contrast, and analogy; definition; example; and process analysis. "Narration" categorizes memoirs, essays, stories, and nonfiction nonautobiographical narratives.

At the end, we list the nonessay materials in the *Reader*—journal entries, short stories, poems, and drama.

Informal, Subdued, Oblique, Elliptical, Implied

DESCRIPTION

EXPOSITION

A Thematic Index

EDUCATION, THE ACQUISITION OF WISDOM

EPIPHANY, IMAGINATION, VISION

FAMILIES, PARENTS, OFFSPRING

FREEDOM AND RESTRAINT, OPPRESSORS AND OPPRESSED

HEROES, LEADERS, PERFORMERS

HISTORY, THE POWER OF THE PAST

HUMOR, WIT, SATIRE

THE IMPORTANCE OF PLACE, ROOTS

INDIVIDUALITY, PRIVACY, SOLITUDE

MEN AND WOMEN, LOVE, SEXUALITY

MUTABILITY, AGING, DEATH

NATURE, ENVIRONMENT, WONDERS OF CREATION

WORKING

WRITING, LANGUAGE, RHETORIC, AND STYLE

THE ARTS AND THE MEDIA